Learn Microsoft Office 2000

Covers:

Word
Excel
Access
PowerPoint
Outlook
Publisher
FrontPage

Michael Busby and Russell A. Stultz

Wordware Publishing, Inc.

Library of Congress Cataloging-in-Publication Data

Busby, Michael.
    Learn Microsoft Office 2000 / by Michael Busby and Russell A. Stultz.
       p.   cm.
    Includes index.
    ISBN 1-55622-716-7 (pbk.)
    1. Microsoft Office. 2. Microsoft Word. 3. Microsoft Excel for Windows. 4. Microsoft
Access. 5. Microsoft PowerPoint (Computer file). 6. Microsoft Outlook. 7. Microsoft
Publisher. 8. Microsoft FrontPage. 9. Business--Computer programs. I. Stultz, Russell
Allen. II. Title.
    HF5548.4.M525 B874   2000
    005.369--dc21   00-028961
                                                CIP

ISBN 1-55622-716-7
10 9 8 7 6 5 4 3 2 1
0003

All inquiries for volume purchases of this book should be addressed to Wordware Publishing, Inc., at the above
address. Telephone inquiries may be made by calling:

(972) 423-0090

Contents

Part 1—Microsoft Office 2000 Overview

Section I—About This Book **3**
Introduction 3
Organization 3
The Companion CD 4
Hardware and Software Requirements 4
What You Should Know 5
Before You Begin 5
Conventions Used in This Book 5
What's Next? 6

Section 2—The Office 2000 Toolset and General Utilities **7**
Introduction 7
Office Assistant 7
Launching the Office Shortcut Toolbar 9
Customizing the Shortcut Bar 10
Browsing the Shortcut Bar Buttons 12
Adding an MS-DOS Button 16
Hands-on Activity 17
Summary 18

Part 2—Microsoft Word 2000

Section 3—About This Part **21**
Introduction 21
What is Word? 21
Companion Files 22
What's Next? 22

Section 4—Starting (or "Launching") Word **23**
Microsoft Word 2000 Controls 24
Menus 25
Horizontal Ruler 28
Vertical Ruler 29
Scroll Bars 29
Status Bar 29

Adjusting (Turning Off and On) Displayed Elements   29
Enhancements to Word 2000   31
Summary   31

Section 5—Creating, Saving, Importing, Exporting, and Inserting Files. 32
Introduction   32
Creating a New File   32
Saving a New File   33
Saving a File Under a New Name   33
Saving a File for Use with Another Word Processing Program 36
Opening an Existing File   36
Importing a File Created by Another Word Processing Program 37
Inserting an Existing File Into the Body of the Current Document 37
Save Version   38
Hands-on Activities   38
    Creating and Saving a New File   38
    Opening an Existing File   39
    Saving a File Using a New Name   40
    Saving a File for Use with Another Word Processing Program 41
    Importing a File Created by Another Word Processing Program 41
    Inserting an Existing File into the Body of the Current Document 41
    Saving Versions   42
Summary   43

Section 6—Formatting Pages, Paragraphs, and Sections 44
Introduction   44
Pages   44
Paragraphs   44
Sections   44
Hands-on Activity   45
Summary   47

Section 7—Indents and Outdents 48
Introduction   48
Indenting Paragraphs   48
Hanging Indents   49
Outdenting (Printing in the Margins)   49
Indenting Rows in a Table   49
Summary   49

Section 8—Creating Lists and Numbering Headings 50
Introduction   50
Hands-on Activity   51
    Heading Numbering   53
Summary   53

Section 9—Styles, Fonts, and Font Sizes 54
Introduction   54
Styles   54
    The Importance of Styles   54
    Creating and Modifying Styles   55
    Style Creations Shortcut   56

Deleting a Style   56
Copying Styles to Other Documents   56
Fonts   57
Font Sizes   57
Type Styles (or "Attributes")   58
Changing Case   58
Hands-on Activity   58
Summary   59

Section 10—Editing Text **60**
Introduction   60
Insert and Overstrike   60
Cutting, Copying, and Pasting   60
Delete   61
Selecting Text   61
Shortcut Menu   61
Hands-on Activity   62
Summary   63

Section 11—Positioning and Viewing Text **64**
Introduction   64
Hands-on Activity   65
Summary   68

Section 12—Using Tabs **69**
Introduction   69
Setting Tabs   69
Using the Mouse   70
Using the Format|Tabs Menu Selection   70
Hands-on Activity   70
Summary   72

Section 13—Tabs and Tables **73**
Introduction   73
Creating Tables   73
Using the Insert Table Button   73
Using the Insert Table Dialog Box   73
Using the Tables and Borders Dialog and the Table Draw Tool   74
Using the Convert Text to Table Dialog Box   75
The Table Menu   76
Changing Row Heights and Column Widths   77
Hands-on Activity   77
Summary   80

Section 14—Tabs and Dot Leaders **81**
Introduction   81
Setting Up Dot Leaders   81
Hands-on Activity   82
Summary   83

Section 15—Finding and Replacing Text **84**
Introduction   84

The Edit|Find Menu Selection   84
The Edit|Find and Edit|Replace Menu Selections   85
Finding Special Characters (Advanced Search Criteria)   86
Hands-on Activity   87
Summary   89

Section 16—Inserting Page Breaks, Page Numbers, Bookmarks, Symbols, and Dates **90**
Introduction   90
The Insert Menu   90
Bookmarks   91
Hands-on Activity   92
Summary   93

Section 17—Headers, Footers, Footnotes, Endnotes, and Comments. **94**
Introduction   94
Headers and Footers   95
Hands-on Activity   96
Summary   97

Section 18—Working with Text Boxes and Frames **98**
Introduction   98
Hands-on Activity   100
Summary   102

Section 19—Working with Columns **103**
Introduction   103
Hands-on Activity   104
Summary   105

Section 20—Working with Pictures **106**
Introduction   106
The Drawing Toolbar   106
Hands-on Activity   107
Summary   109

Section 21—Working with Charts and Graphs **110**
Introduction   110
Exploring Microsoft Graph   110
Hands-on Activity   112
Summary   114

Section 22—Working with Forms. **115**
Introduction   115
Hands-on Activity   116
Summary   119

Section 23—Working with Tools **120**
Introduction   120
Spell Check and AutoCorrect   120
   Spell Check   120
   AutoCorrect   121
AutoFormat   122
AutoText   122

To use a stored AutoText item: 123
To remove an AutoText item: 123
Grammar Check 123
Thesaurus 123
Hyphenation 124
Hands-on Activity 125
Summary 126

Section 24—Working with Objects—WordArt, Equations, and Worksheets . . 127
Introduction 127
WordArt 127
Microsoft Equation 3.0 (the Equation Editor) 129
Equation Editor Menus 129
The Equation Toolbar 131
Excel Worksheets 132
Working with Other Objects 132
Hands-on Activities 133
Insert Microsoft WordArt 3.2 Object 133
Insert Microsoft Equation 3.0 Object 134
Insert Microsoft Excel Object 135
Insert Microsoft Paintbrush Object 135
Exiting Word 136
Summary 136

Section 25—Automating Your Work with Macros. 137
Introduction 137
The Macro Recorder 137
Editing Macros 138
Hands-on Activity 139
Summary 140

Section 26—Printing. 141
Introduction 141
Some Ways to Print 141
Print Preview 142
Printing Multiple Documents 143
Printing Envelopes 143
Mail Merge 144
Mail Merge Toolbar 145
Hands-on Activity 149
Summary 150

Section 27—Master Document 151
Introduction 151
The Outlining and Master Document Toolbars 151
Outlining Toolbar 152
Master Document Toolbar 152
Using Master Document 153
Document Creation 153
Starting Each Section on a New Page 154
Adding Headers and Footers 155

Creating a Table of Contents or Figures 155
Creating an Alphabetical Index 156
Hands-on Activities 156
Inserting Subdocuments 156
Starting Each Section (or Subdocument) on an Odd-Numbered,
Right-Hand Page 157
Inserting Headers and Footers; Putting Page Numbers in the Footers 157
Construct a Table of Contents 159
Construct an Alphabetical Index: 159
Examine the Paginated Document Using Print Preview or By Printing It ... 161
Finishing Up 161
Summary 162

Section 28—Macros and Security Issues **163**
Introduction 163
Understanding Macro Viruses 163
Supplied Macros 164
Security Levels 164
Digital Signatures 165
Passwords 166
Message Encryption 166
Additional Security Considerations 166
Loss Prevention 167
Hands-on Activities 168
Supplied Macros 168
Creating a Password 170
Changing or Removing a Password 171
Protecting Form Fields 171
Saving Documents Automatically 172
Automatically Recovering Files 173
Saving Backup Copies 173
Opening a Backup Copy of a Document 174
Recovering Text From Damaged Documents 174
Using Versioning to Save Current State 175
Automatically Saving a Version When Closing 175
Saving Document Version as Separate File 175
Summary 175

Part 3—Microsoft Excel 2000

Section 29—About This Part **179**
Introduction 179
What is Excel? 179
Companion Files 179
What's Next? 180
Section 30—Starting (or "Launching") Excel **181**
Microsoft Excel 2000 Controls 182

Contents

Terminology   182

Section 31—Creating Worksheets and Workbooks. **183**
    Introduction   183
    Notation Used in This Part   183
    Starting and Exiting the Program   184
    Getting Help   184
    Toolbars   185
    The Cancel and Undo Keys   185
    Setting Up (Tools|Options)   186
    Hands-on Activities   188
       Travel Expense Worksheet   188
       Regional Sales and Expense Worksheet   194
    Summary   198

Section 32—Opening and Saving Workbooks and Exiting Excel **199**
    Introduction   199
    The File Menu   199
    Opening Workbooks   200
       Opening Files From Other Directories and Disk Drives   201
       Opening Two or More Workbooks   201
       Open Dialog Box   202
    Saving Workbooks   204
       Save   204
       Save As   204
    Hands-on Activity   205
       Exiting Excel   205
    Summary   205

Section 33—Formatting Numbers and Text **206**
    Introduction   206
    The Format Menu   206
    Format Cells Dialog   207
    Other Selections   208
    The Formatting Toolbar   209
    Hands-on Activity   210
    Summary   212

Section 34—Using Labels, Names, and Protection. **213**
    Introduction   213
    Using Labels and Names in Formulas   213
       Naming Data   213
       Naming Cells, Formulas, and Constants   214
       Using Dates as Labels   215
    General Naming Procedures   216
       Naming a Cell or a Range of Cells   216
       Naming Cells by Using Existing Row and Column Labels   216
       Naming Cells on More Than One Worksheet Using a 3-D Reference.   216
       Defining a Name to Represent a Formula or a Constant Value   217
       Defining a Name That Refers to Cells in Another Workbook   217
       Changing Cell References in Formulas to Names   217

Hands-on Activities	217
Naming a Range of Cells	217
Protecting Cells	219
Protecting Workbooks	219
Summary	220
Section 35—Producing Charts	**221**
Introduction	221
Hands-on Activity	221
Summary	224
Section 36—Printing Operations	**225**
Introduction	225
Summary	227
Section 37—Window	**228**
Introduction	228
The Window Menu	228
Hands-on Activity	231
Summary	232
Section 38—Linking Workbooks	**233**
Introduction	233
Establishing Workbook Links	234
Consolidation	234
Hands-on Activity	235
Summary	238
Section 39—Macros	**239**
Introduction	239
Uses for Macros	239
Creating and Storing Macros	239
Running Macros	240
Summary	241
Section 40—Database	**242**
Introduction	242
The Data Menu	242
Extracting Information	244
Hands-on Activities	245
Ad Hoc Filtering	245
Advanced Filter	247
Pivot Table	248
Summary	251
Section 41—Using Tables	**252**
Introduction	252
Data Table Types	252
Hands-on Activities	253
One-Variable Table	253
Two-Variable Table	255
Summary	257

Section 42—Using Files with Other Programs **258**
    Introduction 258
    Benefits 258
    Automatic File Conversion 259
    Microsoft Query 259
    Exporting and Importing Files 259
        ASCII Text Files 260
        Using Data|Text to Columns 260
    Comma-Separated Values 260
    Using Worksheets with Word Processors 261
    Using Excel with Database Programs 261
        Using Excel with Microsoft Access 261
        Using Excel with dBase or FoxPro 261
    Hands-on Activities 262
        Parse 262
        Microsoft Query 263
    Summary 267

Section 43—Putting Excel Data on the Web. **268**
    Introduction 268
    Requirements for Saving or Publishing a Web Page 268
    Limitations 268
        Spreadsheet Limitations 269
        PivotTable Limitations 270
        Chart Limitations 271
    Preparing Excel Data for Web Publication 272
    Publishing Excel Data on the Web 272
    Hands-on Activity 272
    Summary 275

Part 4—Microsoft Access 2000

Section 44—About This Part **279**
    Introduction 279
    What is Access? 279
    Companion Files 280
    What's New? 280
    What's Next? 280

Section 45—Starting (or "Launching") Access **281**
    Microsoft Access 2000 Controls 281

Section 46—Understanding Databases **283**
    Introduction 283
    Terms and Definitions 283
        Databases and Tables 283
        Forms 285
        Queries 286
        Reports 286

Summary   286
Section 47—Creating Tables **287**
  Introduction   287
  Hands-on Activity: Creating Your First Database and Table   287
  Hands-on Activity: Creating More Tables   296
    Billing Table   297
    Fees Table   299
    Rating Table   301
  Changing Table Contents and Table Design   302
    Toolbars   303
    Adding and Editing Records   303
    Changing Column Widths, Hiding Columns, and Freezing Columns   303
    Changing Table Properties   304
  Hands-on Activity: Creating Relationships Between Tables   304
  Adding OLE Object Fields to a Table   306
  Importing and Exporting Data Between Other Programs   308
  Shortcut Menus   309
  Summary   309
Section 48—Creating Queries **310**
  Introduction   310
  Using the Query Window   310
  Using Criteria and Saving Queries   314
    Criteria Expressions and Operators   315
    Entry Conventions   316
  Changing a Query and Totaling   316
  Printing a Dynaset   318
  Hands-on Activity   320
    Creating a Query to Find Tennis Ratings   320
  Summary   322
Section 49—Getting Started with Forms. **323**
  Introduction   323
  Hands-on Activity: Using the Form Wizards   323
  Form Design Without Form Wizards   324
    Form Design Toolbar   325
    Toolbox Toolbar   326
  Hands-on Activity: Creating Forms Without Wizards   327
  Controlling the Appearance of Text   330
  Adding a Picture Object   332
  Hands-on Activity: Working with Subforms   334
  Summary   336
Section 50—More About Forms **337**
  Introduction   337
  Hands-on Activity: Putting a List Box on Your Form   337
  Selecting and Resizing Labels and Data   339
  Hands-on Activities   340
    Formatting Labels   340
    Moving Labels and Data   341

Adding and Editing Labels 342
Using Data Validation 345
Default Values 346
Hands-on Activity: Using the Rectangle and Line Tools 346
Summary 347

Section 51—Finding Information in a Database **348**
Introduction 348
Finding Values 348
Creating Filters 349
Hands-on Activity 349
Saving a Frequently Used Filter for Future Use 351
Summary 352

Section 52—Creating Reports **353**
Introduction 353
Hands-on Activities 353
Creating a Single-Column Report 353
Creating a Grouped Data Report 356
Summary 359

Section 53—Adding Charts to Your Reports **360**
Introduction 360
Working with Microsoft Graph 360
Hands-on Activities 360
Adding a Chart to a Report 360
Putting a Chart on a Form 364
Summary 367

Section 54—Creating Mailing Labels **368**
Introduction 368
Hands-on Activity 368
Summary 371

Section 55—Automating Your Work with Macros **372**
Introduction 372
Hands-on Activity: Macro Creation 372
Macro Command Buttons 376
Hands-on Activity: Creating a Macro Command Button 376
Synchronizing Records 377
Hands-on Activity: Synchronizing Records 377
Summary 379

Part 5—Microsoft PowerPoint 2000

Section 56—About This Part **383**
Introduction 383
What is PowerPoint? 383
Companion Files 384
What's Next? 384

Section 57—Starting (or "Launching") PowerPoint **385**
  Introduction   385
  Microsoft PowerPoint 2000 Controls   386
  The Main Screen   387
    Create/Open Presentation Dialog   387
    The Main Screen   388
  Summary   388
Section 58—PowerPoint Views **389**
  Introduction   389
  The View Buttons   389
  Summary   391
Section 59—Creating Your First Presentation **392**
  Introduction   392
  Hands-on Activity (Putting PowerPoint to Work)   392
  Summary   396
Section 60—More About Files **397**
  Introduction   397
  File Menu Overview   397
  Available Shortcut Keys   398
  Hands-on Activity   398
  Summary   399
Section 61—Built-in Wizards **400**
  Introduction   400
  Hands-on Activity: AutoContent Wizard   402
  Summary   404
Section 62—Working with Text and Lists **405**
  Introduction   405
  Controlling Text and Lists   405
  Text Control   405
  Color Control   406
  Hands-on Activity   407
  Summary   408
Section 63—Working with Colors and Transitions **409**
  Introduction   409
  Background Color Control   409
  Transition Control   411
  Applying a Slide Transition   412
  Hands-on Activity   412
  Summary   414
Section 64—Adding Headers and Footers **415**
  Introduction   415
  The Header and Footer Dialogs   415
    The Slide Dialog   415
    The Notes and Handouts Dialog   416
  Hands-on Activity   416
  Summary   417

Section 65—Drawing Tools **418**
   Introduction   418
   Drawing Tricks and Techniques   419
   Hands-on Activity   422
   Summary   424

Section 66—Animation and Sound. **425**
   Introduction   425
   Preset Animation   425
   Custom Animation   426
      Order and Timing   427
      Effects   427
      Chart Effects   428
      Multimedia Settings   428
      Action Settings   429
      Animation Preview   430
      Determining What to Animate   430
   Hands-on Activity   430
   Summary   431

Section 67—Importing Objects from Other Applications **432**
   Introduction   432
   The Tool Set   432
   Clip Art   432
   Excel Worksheets   434
      Direct Method: 434
      Cut and Paste Method: 434
   Word Tables   435
      Direct Method: 435
      Cut and Paste Method: 435
   Microsoft Graph   436
   Inserting Movies and Sound   437
   Hands-on Activities   438
      Creating Slides   438
      Using Cut and Paste to Create Slides   440
   Summary   441

Section 68—Automating Your Presentations **442**
   Introduction   442
   Setting Times   442
   Setting Sounds   443
   More Slide Show Dialogs   444
   Running the Show   446
   Hands-on Activity   447
   Summary   448

Section 69—Hyperlinks to External Resources. **449**
   Introduction   449
   The Action Settings Dialog   449
      Go to Another Slide   450
      Play a Sound   450

Run a Program   450
Run Macro   451
Hands-on Activity   451
Summary   453

Section 70—Printing Your Presentations **454**
Introduction   454
Printing Slides   454
Speaker Notes   455
Meeting Minder   455
Hands-on Activity   456
Summary   457

Section 71—Modifying and Integrating Presentations **458**
Introduction   458
Inserting a New Slide   458
Deleting a Slide   459
Repositioning Slides   459
Integrating Slides from Other Presentations   459
Hands-on Activity   459
Summary   461

Section 72—Distributing Presentations with the PowerPoint Viewer. **462**
Introduction   462
Packaging a Presentation   462
Retrieving the Presentation and PowerPoint Viewer   464
Running the PowerPoint Viewer   465
Hands-on Activities   466
Pack and Go   466
Viewer Setup   466
Using the PowerPoint Viewer   466
Summary   467

Part 6—Microsoft Outlook 2000

Section 73—About This Part **471**
Introduction   471
What is Outlook?   471
Mail   472
Calendar   472
Tasks   472
Contacts   472
Journal   473
Notes   473
What's Next?   473

Section 74—Starting (or "Launching") Outlook **474**
Microsoft Outlook 2000 Controls   474
Controlling How Outlook Starts   475
Outlook Tools   476

Access to Applications 477
Accessing Outlook's Features 478
Examining Outlook Today 478
Examining Mail's Inbox 479
Examining Calendar 480
Examining Contacts 481
Examining Tasks 482
Examining Notes 484
Examining Deleted Items 484
Examining My Shortcuts 484
Examining Drafts 484
Examining Outbox 484
Examining Sent Items 485
Examining Journal 485
Examining Outlook Update 485
Examining Other Shortcuts 485
Summary 486
Section 75—Using Mail **487**
Introduction 487
Connecting to a Mail Server 487
Additional Directory Services 492
E-mail Editors 495
E-mail Message Formats 496
Create New Message (Outbox) 496
Signatures 497
Multiple Signatures 498
vCards 498
General Signature and vCard Procedures 505
Select the Default Signature 505
Insert a Signature in a Message 505
Change a Signature 506
Stop Using an Automatic Signature or Stationery 506
Create a Signature When Using Word as The E-mail Editor 506
Include a vCard with Your Autosignature 506
Import a vCard into Outlook 507
Send a vCard to Someone in E-mail 507
File Attachments 507
Reading Your Messages (Inbox) 507
Auto Format Reply 508
Message Options and Tracking 508
Large Messages 511
Junk E-mail 511
Sent Items 511
Deleted Items 511
Hands-on Activities 511
Start a New Message 511
Create a Signature for Messages 513
Summary 514

Section 76—Using Calendar **515**
   Introduction   515
   Menus and Toolbars   516
      View Menu   516
      Actions Menu   516
   General Calendar Procedures   517
      Entering Appointments   517
      Editing Appointments   518
      Moving Appointments   518
      Deleting an Appointment   518
      Printing Appointments   518
      Schedule a Recurring Appointment   519
      Schedule a Meeting   520
      Schedule a Recurring Meeting   522
   Hands-on Activity   527
   Summary   535
Section 77—Using Tasks **536**
   Introduction   536
   Toolbars and Menus   538
      Menu Bar   538
      Views   538
      Advanced Toolbar   541
   Sorting   541
      Displaying Project Information   545
      Printing Your Information   545
   Hands-on Activity   546
   Summary   549
Section 78—Using Contacts **550**
   Introduction   550
   Menus and Toolbars   551
      Actions Menu Selections   551
      Advanced Toolbar   552
      Contact Dialog Tabs   552
      Finding a Contact   554
      Dialing a Telephone Number   554
      Printing Your Contacts List   554
      Putting an Address into a Word Document   554
   Hands-on Activity   556
   Summary   557
Section 79—Using Journal **558**
   Introduction   558
   How Journal Works   558
   Recording Journal Activities   560
      Automatically Recording Contacts in Journal   560
      Automatically Recording Documents in Journal   561
      Manually Recording an Item or Document in Journal   561
      Manually Recording any Activity in Journal   561

Recording in My Journal the Items Published in a Net Folder I Own 561
Turning Off Automatic Recording of Journal Entries for a Contact 561
Managing Journal Entries 561
Open a Journal Entry 561
Modify a Journal Entry 562
Move a Journal Entry 562
View Journal Entries for a Contact 562
Delete a Journal Entry 562
Open the Contact that a Journal Entry Refers To 562
Archiving Items 562
Turn on AutoArchive 562
Set AutoArchive Properties for a Particular Folder 563
Archive Items Manually 563
Deleting Items 564
Delete Old Items Automatically 564
Delete Expired E-mail Messages When Archiving 564
Hands-on Activity 564
Summary 564

Section 80—Using Notes **565**
Introduction 565
Menus and Toolbars 565
Reading, Deleting, and Creating Notes 566
Hands-on Activity 567
Summary 568

Section 81—Security **569**
Inroduction 569
Simple Security 569
HTML Settings Options 570
Plain Text Setting Options 570
Advanced Security 570
Setting Up Security 571
Using Digital Signatures 574
Summary 575

Section 82—Filters. **576**
Introduction 576
Filters 576
Filtering E-mail 577
Summary 583

Section 83—Miscellaneous Outlook Topics **584**
Introduction 584
Stationery 584
Forms 586
Designing Forms 586
NetMeeting Whiteboard 589
General Whiteboard Procedures 589
Timelines 591
Categories 591

Groups   592
Address Book   594
Tables and Cards   595
Summary   597

Part 7—Microsoft Publisher 2000

Section 84—About This Part **601**
Introduction   601
What is Publisher?   601
What's Next?   601
Section 85—Starting (or "Launching") Publisher. **602**
Microsoft Publisher 2000 Controls   603
Section 86—Publisher Fundamentals **604**
Introduction   604
Measurements   605
Hands-on Activity   607
Summary   615

Part 8—Microsoft FrontPage 2000

Section 87—About This Part **619**
Introduction   619
What is FrontPage?   619
What's Next?   619
Section 88—Starting (or "Launching") FrontPage **620**
Microsoft FrontPage 2000 Controls   620
Section 89—FrontPage Fundamentals. **622**
Introduction   622
The Web and Web Pages   623
FrontPage Server Extensions   623
Hands-on Activity   624
Summary   632

Index **633**

Part 1

Microsoft Office 2000 Overview

1 **About This Book**—Introduction, description of book and organization, hardware and software requirements, what you should know, text conventions, and use of the companion CD.

2 **The Office 2000 Toolset and General Utilities**—Introduction, customizing and adding buttons to the shortcut bar, and using the Office Assistant.

About This Book

Introduction

If you own and want to learn how to use one or all of the application programs included with Microsoft Office 2000, then this is the right book for you. Microsoft Office 2000 includes a rich collection of the most popular applications in use today. The Microsoft Office 2000 Professional Edition, or simply *Office* as it is referred to in the remainder of this book, includes the following programs:

- Microsoft Word 2000   Word processor application
- Microsoft Excel 2000   Spreadsheet application
- Microsoft Access 2000   Database application
- Microsoft PowerPoint 2000   Business presentation application
- Microsoft Outlook   Scheduler, planner, information application
- Microsoft Publisher 2000   Desktop publishing application
- Microsoft FrontPage 2000   Web page authoring application

Stand-alone versions of these programs are also sold separately, so if you are only using one or two of the programs listed above, the parts of this book dedicated to those programs will satisfy your needs. Unlike the simple programs offered by integrated programs like Microsoft Works, every program within Office is a full-featured, stand-alone application. For example, Word and Excel are both as rich in features as any other stand-alone word processing or spreadsheet programs available today. Their ability to interact with each other in addition to the other programs within Office make them even more attractive. Object linking and embedding (OLE) and the ability to drag and drop graphic and text objects between program documents give you the ability to create virtually any kind of integrated document. The result lets you share your ideas to others without the constraints imposed by earlier technologies.

Organization

This book is organized into eight "parts." Each part is dedicated to a Microsoft Office program, except for Part 1, which provides some background information about some of the features that are common to all Office programs. Within each of the parts are "sections." Sections present information about closely related features, in a simple to more advanced sequence. For example, you begin by learning how to create and edit simple documents and then advance to more involved file and formatting operations. Each section typically includes both descriptive and tutorial information.

Descriptions explain the purpose of each feature and present typical ways to use them. Where helpful, descriptions include illustrations that familiarize you with the appearance and use of toolbars, menus, and dialogs that correspond to the task at hand.

Many of the tutorial passages simplify complex processes by outlining the steps used to accomplish a task.

Hands-on learning activities comprise the heart of the tutorials, where you "learn by doing." This is the way most of us master common tasks, because it paves the road to learning with practical experience. Once learned, it's an easy matter to review the hands-on activities to refresh your memory relative to the sequence of steps necessary to successfully complete a common task. Furthermore, the hands-on activities include screen illustrations that let you compare your progress with expected outcomes.

The Companion CD

Wait for the instructions that tell you when and how to use the companion CD! The CD supplied with this book has a number of document and graphic files that are used with the hands-on activities. There are no Office 2000 "executable" programs, so don't try to run anything!

Each of the Office applications is supported by files that are used for either practice, reference, or both. As you move to each new part of the book, you are told when to open the appropriate file. Instructions for copying the activity files to your hard drive are given in Part 2.

Detailed descriptions of all the Office 2000 toolbars, menus, and buttons are listed as reference material on the CD. Due to size limitations, this information could not be included in the book.

Hardware and Software Requirements

You must have Windows 95/98 or Windows NT installed and running on a compatible computer. Your computer should be equipped with a CD-ROM drive, and a hard drive with a minimum of 121 megabytes of free space for the Office programs. Minimum to maximum disk space requirements depend on which features you decide to install. The companion files require an additional 3 megabytes of free space. These files can be removed after the hands-on activities to recover the disk space used.

Memory—Although most Office 2000 applications only require 16 megabytes of random access memory (RAM), at least 32 or more is highly recommended. This is particularly true if you wish to run multiple applications.

Printer—A properly installed Windows printer is also recommended, although it is not absolutely necessary, as you can most often use Print Preview to determine what your printed output will look like.

Operating System—This book assumes that you are running Windows 95/98 or NT; references to operating system utilities should be translated to the equivalent paint and file management utilities on your system if you choose to use others.

What You Should Know

You should know how to turn your computer on and off, and how to use your keyboard and mouse. You should also master the art of selecting and dragging objects with your mouse, as well as knowing how to double-click. Practicing these techniques makes you a more productive Windows user. You should also be familiar with the installed operating system, i.e., Windows 95/98 or Windows NT. You should know how to run (or *launch)* programs using the Taskbar; how to copy, move, rename, and delete files using the Windows Explorer; and how to use system tools, such as ScanDisk and Disk Defragmenter, to keep your hard disk tuned for optimum performance.

Before You Begin

Before moving to Section 2 of this book, be sure that you have run the Office 2000 Setup program and installed all Office programs. These are listed on page 3 of this section. You should also verify that the following add-ins have been installed if you wish to become familiar with their operation:

- Microsoft ClipArt
- Equation Editor 3.0
- Microsoft Graph 2000 Chart
- Microsoft WordArt 3.0
- Microsoft Query

If any of the programs or add-ins are not available, use the Add/Remove Programs utility in the Windows Control Panel in conjunction with the Office 2000 CD-ROM (or diskettes) to add them.

Conventions Used in This Book

There are a number of standard conventions used in this book. These are of particular significance in hands-on tutorial procedures. Following is a list of these conventions and some of the standard terms used within the book.

- Boldface type in procedures designates a keypress, typed text, or a clicked button.

Example	*Meaning*
Type **ABC** and press **<Enter>**.	Type the text "ABC" and press the Enter key.
Press **<Esc>**.	Press the Esc key.
Click **OK**.	Select and click the OK button.

■ Combination key sequences are connected with a + symbol. A series of keypresses is connected with commas.

Example	Meaning
Press **<Alt+F>**.	Press and hold Alt while typing the letter F.
Press **<Alt+IS>**.	Press and hold Alt while typing the letters I and S.
Press **<Alt, F, P>**.	Press and release Alt, then type F and P.

■ Select words, passages of text, menu items, option buttons, and check boxes.

Example	Meaning
Select the first sentence.	Drag the first sentence so that it is highlighted.
Use the **File|Save As** menu selection.	Pick Save As in the File menu.
Select the **AutoSave** option button.	Click the AutoSave option button so it is black.
Check the Standard toolbar check box.	Put a check in the Standard toolbar check box.

■ Here are some more examples that make use of your mouse.

Example	Meaning
Click **Cancel**.	Click the Cancel button (using the left mouse button).
Select the first sentence.	Drag the first sentence so that it is highlighted. You can also select a word or sentence by pressing the Shift key and then a cursor key.
Right-click your mouse.	Click the right mouse button; this usually displays a shortcut menu.
Drag a rectangle around the drawn circle.	Pick a point above and left of a drawn circle object. Press and hold the left mouse button and drag to a point below and right of the circle so that the circle is inside a rectangle (or square).
Double-click the ruler to display the Page Setup dialog.	Double-clicking the left mouse button in quick succession is a shortcut method of accessing various dialog boxes that correspond to what is currently selected with the mouse pointer.

What's Next?

At this point you should have the Office 2000 programs and recommended add-ins installed on your computer. You should also understand the simple conventions used in the tutorial procedures found in this book. It's time to move on to Section 2, where you learn about Office 2000 tools: the Shortcut Bar, Binders, and Web access through Internet Explorer. Although it is not necessary to use these features, they are designed to increase your productivity, and therefore, you should know about them as well as how to use them.

The Office 2000 Toolset and General Utilities

Introduction

This section introduces you to some of the productivity features included with Office 2000—the Shortcut Bar and Office Assistant. The Office 2000 Shortcut Bar gives you fast access to a variety of documents and tasks with the single click of a button. For example, you can go directly to a document, send an e-mail message or fax, look up an address, or display a reference book contained on the CD that accompanies your Office 2000 software. You can also customize your Shortcut Bar by changing the displayed buttons or even adding new buttons or toolbars that give you fast access to your programs. For example, if you want to click buttons to display the MS-DOS prompt, the Windows Explorer, the Windows Control Panel, and Windows Paint, just add a button for each to your Shortcut Bar. It only takes a few clicks of your mouse. You can also hide unwanted buttons by right-clicking on the unwanted button and then picking Hide Button from the displayed menu.

Office Assistant

Use Help menu options to review information about Word operations. Click the Help button on the Menu toolbar, then click the Microsoft Word Help button on the drop-down menu to display the default Office Assistant, Clipit.

Word 2000 includes seven other Office Assistants that will keep you amused and entertained as you go about searching for help. To use the Office Assistant, enter a keyword or a text string in Clipit's text box and click on Search. Note that Clipit is *context sensitive*. The use of context-sensitive help results in the display of information that is related to the current task.

What would you like to do?

- Troubleshoot importing graphics
- Add a button to a toolbar
- Troubleshoot saving and closing documents
- File format converters supplied with Microsoft Word
- Troubleshoot file conversions
- ▼ See more...

Type your question here, and then click Search.

[Options] [Search]

To display any of the other Office Assistants, click on Clipit's Options button. The Gallery and Options tabs will be displayed. Bring the Gallery tab forward by clicking on the Gallery tab. Clipit is the first Office Assistant shown. You can see and choose any of the other assistants by clicking on the Next button at the bottom of the folder. When you see the assistant you want to use, click on OK to close the dialog box. Voilà. Your new assistant is ready to go to work for you. The help is the same regardless of the assistant used. Try each one out. They can be amusing.

The gallery of assistants are:

 Clipit keeps you amused while getting your answers together.

 F1 is an answer-finding robot of the first class.

 Dot bounces all over the place while finding your answer.

 The Genius can find all the answers even if we don't know what the questions are.

 Office Logo spins and whirls to keep you entertained as you seek help.

 Links chases answers for you all day long

 Mother Nature assumes various flora and fauna images to "gently" help you.

 Rocky can sniff out any answer no matter the hiding place.

Click the Help button to display the Office Assistant. Notice how the Office Assistant is available to deliver help information about virtually any subject. Using Clipit's Search button is similar to using the Contents and Index tabs and manually searching for topics of interest.

The Contents, Answer Wizard, and Index folders are not displayed by default. You can either set them to display by default or access them through Clipit. To access the folders through Clipit, type any subject in Clipit's text box and click on Search. Clipit will return a selection of topics more or less related to the search subject. Click on one of the available selections and the Microsoft Help dialog will appear with specific information

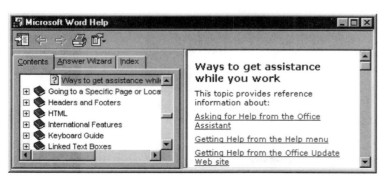

concerning the selected topic. Notice at the top of the dialog box several buttons. Click on 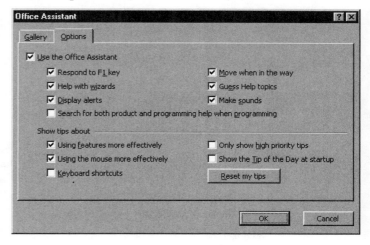 to view the Contents, Answer Wizard, and Index folders. Click on ⬛ to get back to the Help dialog box.

To set the Contents, Answer Wizard, and Index folders to be the default help program, display Clipit, then click on Options. The Office Assistant dialog includes a Gallery tab and an Options tab. Click on the Options tab, then uncheck the Use the Office

Assistant check box. Immediately, all the selections in the folder will become ghosted. Close the dialog box. Now when you press F1 for help or use the help menu button, you will get the old, familiar Contents and Index folders as the default help tools.

To return Clipit to work, just go to the Help button on the menu bar and click on Show the Office Assistant. Now, Clipit will be the default help tool. The Answer Wizard folder performs the same function as Clipit.

Launching the Office Shortcut Toolbar

If the Office shortcut icon was not placed on your desktop when you installed Office 2000, you may follow this procedure for getting the icon on your desktop for convenient launching of Office programs. The icon for the Office Shortcut toolbar is located in the C:\Windows\Start Menu\Programs\Office Tools directory. Go to this directory and right-click on the icon shown highlighted in the following screen shot.

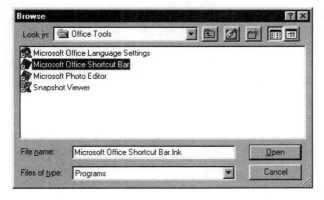

When you right-click on the Microsoft Office Shortcut Bar icon in the Office Tools directory, you will see the following drop-down menu. Click on Send To, then on Desktop (create shortcut).

The drop-down menus will close and you will now have the Office 2000 shortcut icon somewhere on your desktop. To launch the Shortcut toolbar, click on the Shortcut toolbar icon.

Customizing the Shortcut Bar

Like other Microsoft program toolbars, you can drag the Shortcut Bar to a more convenient location on your screen. For instance, you may want to drag and dock it against the right edge or the top edge of your screen. You can also place it on the middle of your desktop and then resize the Shortcut Bar window to modify the way buttons are arranged. Following is a view of the Shortcut Bar as it looks when placed in the middle of your desktop.

If you want to customize the Shortcut Bar, click the Office icon at the upper left of the Shortcut Bar and select **Customize** from the drop-down menu. Alternately, you

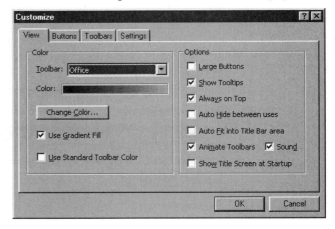

can double-click anywhere in the black area of the Office 2000 Shortcut Bar. This displays the Customize dialog.

Each tab in the Customize dialog gives you access to different controls. The Buttons tab allows you to hide or display any of the listed buttons by simply clicking the desired check box.

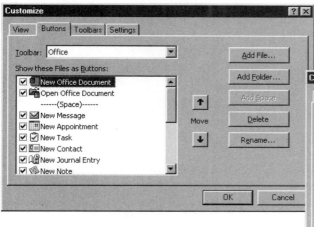

Use the Toolbars tab to display additional sets of shortcut buttons for quick access to other applications.

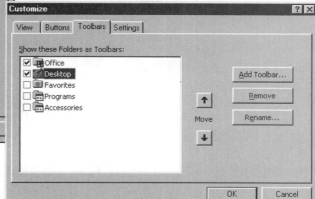

When two or more toolbars are active, they are accessible in the Toolbar list found at the top of the Buttons tab.

The following Office 2000 shortcut bar is now displaying my desktop toolbar.

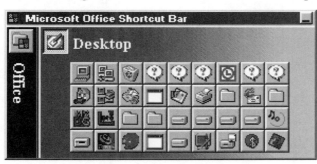

The Office 2000 toolbar can be displayed now by clicking the vertically aligned Office text on the toolbar.

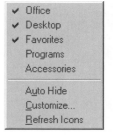

You can add other toolbars to the Office toolbar display by right-clicking anywhere in the dark area of the toolbar and selecting the toolbars you wish to have available. The following menu shows the Office, Desktop, and Favorites toolbars enabled. Programs and Accessories are additional choices.

After adding additional toolbars to the display, they are made available by clicking on the vertical text name (Office, Desktop, Favorites, etc.) of the toolbar on the shortcut toolbar.

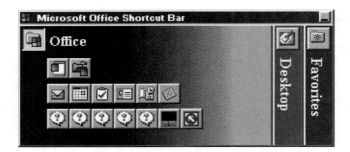

The Settings tab of the Customize dialog is used to specify alternate paths for user and workgroup template files. You will probably want to retain the default file paths that contain those templates that you installed during setup.

Browsing the Shortcut Bar Buttons

You can see each button's name by pointing to the button with your mouse and reading the fly-out label. A few of the standard buttons that are worthy of mention follow.

Shortcut Bar Control—This is the leftmost button, which displays the following drop-down menu when it is right-clicked:

Selecting Open displays a dialog that allows you to click on any Office 2000 icon to open or launch the program. The other selections are pretty much self-explanatory.

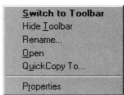

New Office Document—Click this button to open a variety of document types. Just click the appropriate tab in the New Office Document dialog and then click a template to launch the selected document type and controlling program.

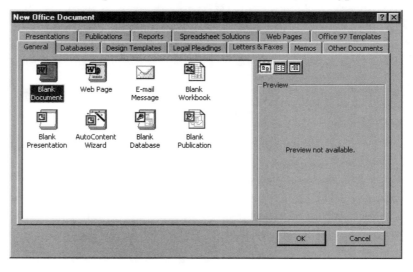

Open a Document—Clicking this button launches the Open dialog. Use it to locate an existing document you wish to open.

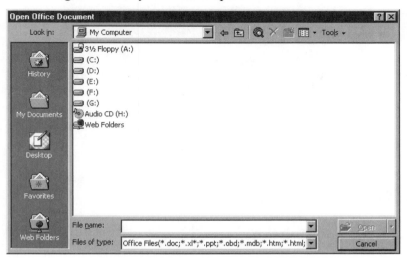

 New Message—This button launches Microsoft Exchange and the Sending message via Office 2000 Shortcut Bar dialog. From here, you can send a message as e-mail. Of course, you must have a modem and be configured for access to a message service, such as the Microsoft Network (MSN), America Online, CompuServe, or an independent Internet service provider. You may also be connected to a network through a network adapter.

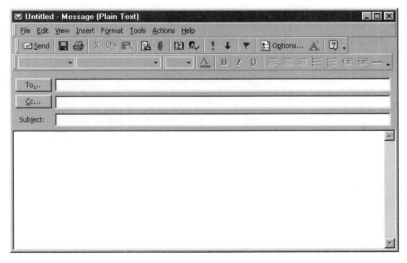

New Appointment—Click here to launch Outlook to make an appointment. Then use the Appointment dialog to enter your appointment. (See Part 6, Outlook 2000, of this book for details.)

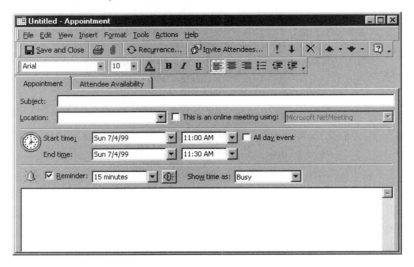

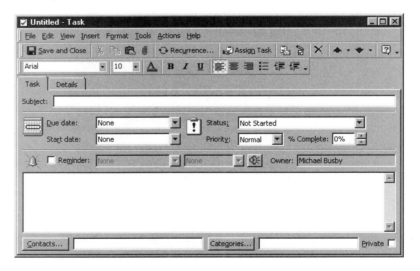 **New Task**—Like the preceding and next selection, this button also launches Outlook, where you can enter a task. (See Part 6, Outlook 2000, of this book for details.)

New Contact—This selection launches the Outlook Contacts dialog. This dialog is used to enter a new contact in your address book. (See Part 6, Outlook 2000, of this book for details.)

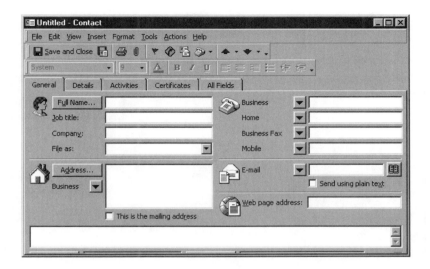

 New Journal Entry—This selection launches the Journal Entry dialog. The Journal Entry dialog allows you to keep track of daily events.

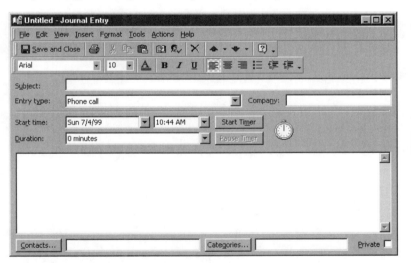

New Note—Like many of the preceding Shortcut Bar buttons, this button corresponds to a Microsoft Outlook 2000 application called Notes. Click New Note to display a "sticky note"-like window in which you can type your ideas, reminders, or questions for later reference. Once typed, save the note by clicking the Close button at the upper right-hand corner of the note. Review your notes by running Microsoft Outlook 2000. Click the Notes icon in the left-hand pane to

display your notes. Double-click the note of interest to open it (or select it and press <Ctrl+O> for File|Open).

The bottom row of buttons on the shortcut toolbar are buttons for launching applications. Click on the appropriate button to launch the application. The application name is visible when you move the mouse cursor over the button.

Adding an MS-DOS Button

Advanced topic

Following is a typical procedure for adding a button to your Shortcut Bar. You may want to perform the operation if you want to access MS-DOS from the Shortcut Bar. This is a general procedure you can use to add any available button to the toolbar you desire.

1. Double-click anywhere in the open, colored area of the toolbar to display the Customize dialog.

2. Click the **Buttons** tab. Display the Programs icons by clicking the Toolbar down arrow and select **Programs**. Scroll down the Show these files as buttons list until the MS-DOS Prompt check box is visible.

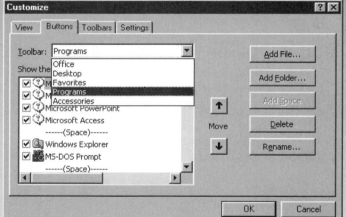

3. Check the MS-DOS Prompt check box and click **OK** to close the Customize dialog. Notice that the MS-DOS button is now displayed on the Shortcut Bar in the Programs toolbar and that there is an MS-DOS prompt in the upper right portion of the toolbar. (Also note that your toolbar will not look like mine as the programs installed on your computer are most likely different from mine.)

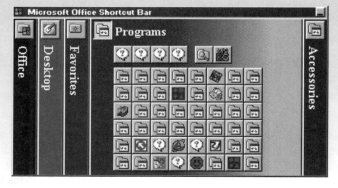

Hands-on Activity

In this activity you move the Shortcut Bar to different locations, customize it, and then use some of the buttons.

Note: To perform the following activity the Shortcut Bar must have been installed and must be displayed and ready for use. This occurs if it was included when you ran the Microsoft Office 2000 setup program. If you disabled the Shortcut Bar, then it will not be available. You can run setup to install it now or follow the procedure given above for placing it on your desktop. If you do not want to take advantage of the fast access features offered by the Shortcut Bar, then move on to the next section of this book. Otherwise, perform the following hands-on activity to familiarize yourself with the handy tools offered by the Shortcut Bar.

1. Click on the background of the Shortcut Bar (anywhere except on a button) and drag the Shortcut Bar down to the center of your screen.

2. Click on the top of the Shortcut Bar window, drag it to the right-hand edge of your screen, and release the mouse button. The operation is called *docking* the toolbar. Now click on a background area of the Shortcut Bar (not on a button) and dock it back at the top of the screen.

3. Double-click on the background. Select **Customize** and select the **Buttons** tab.

4. Examine the Show these Files as Buttons check boxes to see what is checked. Scroll down to see other selections.

5. Notice that the buttons that correspond to each of the check boxes are displayed in the Shortcut Bar.

6. Now hide the Word button using the following steps:
   a. Put the mouse on the Microsoft Word button.
   b. Right-click to display the menu.
   c. Click **Hide Button** to remove the underlying button from the Shortcut Bar.
   d. Click the **Control** button, select the **Buttons** tab, check the **Word** check box to redisplay the button, and click **OK**.

7. Click **New Document** and examine each of the tabs associated with each application.

8. Click **Cancel**. Then click **Open Office Document** and notice the displayed Open dialog. Here, you move to the folder containing your Office documents to open it in the governing application.

9. Continue examining the shortcut buttons to determine which ones you will want to use on a regular basis.

This completes the hands-on activity. Many activities are provided in this book that are designed to introduce you to the features of the Office 2000 programs. If you are a person who likes to learn by doing, then you should enjoy the activities included in this book.

Summary

Although the Shortcut Bar features are not essential parts of the programs supplied with Office 2000, you should find them useful. The more you use them, the more you will increase your productivity. In the following sections, you use all of the programs included in Office 2000. These are the most feature-filled applications of their kind. Therefore, when you complete all of the activities found in this book, you will be ready to tackle any job found around the office or home. Have fun!

Part 2

Word 2000

3 About This Part—Part organization, hardware and software requirements, and user prerequisites.

4 Starting (or "Launching") Word—Key Word controls.

5 Creating, Saving, Importing, Exporting, and Inserting Files—Creating new files, opening existing files, saving files, and importing and exporting files.

6 Formatting Pages, Paragraphs, and Sections—Setting page margins and paragraphs and using sections within a document.

7 Indents and Outdents—Indents, hanging indents, and outdents.

8 Creating Lists and Numbering Headings—Bulleted and numbered lists.

9 Styles, Fonts, and Font Sizes—Using and establishing styles; changing type fonts and type sizes.

10 Editing Text—Inserting, deleting, moving, and copying passages of text.

11 Positioning and Viewing Text—Viewing the page and its contents in different ways.

12 Using Tabs—Setting tab stops and selecting different types of tabs.

13 Tabs and Tables—Creating and editing tabular information.

14 Tabs and Dot Leaders—Setting tabs and dot leaders.

15 Finding and Replacing Text—Finding specified text and replacing one text string with another.

16 Inserting Page Breaks, Page Numbers, Bookmarks, Symbols, and Dates—Inserting page breaks, page numbers, reference points (or *bookmarks*), special symbols, and the date and time in a document.

17 Headers, Footers, Footnotes, Endnotes, and Comments—Adding headers, footers, footnotes, endnotes, and annotations to your document.

18 Working with Text Boxes and Frames—Using frames for sidebars, runarounds, and other special effects.

19 Working with Columns—Creating and editing columnar information.

20 Working with Pictures—Creating and inserting pictures using the Drawing Toolbar.

21 Working with Charts and Graphs—Creating charts and graphs using Microsoft Graph.

22 Working with Forms—Creating and using forms with the Forms Toolbar.

23 Working with Tools—Spell check, thesaurus, grammar check, sorting text, and hyphenation.

24 Working with Objects—WordArt, Equations, and Worksheets—Editing equations and inserting charts, pictures, worksheets, and display fonts.

25 Automating Your Work with Macros—Automating your work by recording and playing macros.

26 Printing—Printing documents and envelopes.

27 Master Document—The toolbars; creating and adding headers and footers, tables of content, and indexes.

28 Macros and Security Issues—Protecting files from computer viruses and protecting documents from unauthorized access.

About This Part

Introduction

Part 2 of this book guides you through Microsoft Word 2000. From this point forward, the name "Word" is used. When you complete the sections within this part of the book, you should be able to create, save, and print any kind of text document needed in your work or for personal correspondence. Before moving into the descriptive and tutorial sections of this part of the book, be sure to read the balance of this section, as important information about your companion CD is presented.

What is Word?

Word 2000 is the most full-featured word processing program in use today. Word makes use of all of the features available to programs designed specifically to run under a 32-bit operating system such as Windows 95/98/NT. This means that your version of Word runs faster and more reliably than the older 16-bit technology programs. When acquired as part of Microsoft Office 2000, Word uses the shared resources available to all Office programs. This includes fonts, clip art, drawing and charting tools, spelling and thesaurus resources, AutoCorrect, powerful Internet access features, and much more.

A real Office bonus is the ability to integrate documents and information created by other Office and Windows programs. For example, you can insert Excel worksheets and Access tables (Access is supplied with Office 2000 Professional) directly into your documents. The ease and flexibility of doing this is nothing short of a marvel. For example, you can cut a portion of a document created by another program and then paste it into your Word document. Or, you may prefer to "drag and drop" part of one document into another using your mouse. Finally, you may simply import one kind of document into another. This flexibility gives you the ability to work in ways that best suit your personal tastes.

Companion Files

The companion files used with the Word hands-on activities are on your companion CD. It is recommended that you copy the files to your hard drive. Additionally, some activities require you to save files in a directory structure you must create. The following instructions create the directory structure required and copy the companion files to hard drive C.

Note: In the following steps, you are instructed to use disk drive C for the hard drive. If your computer uses a different drive, simply substitute the correct drive letter used by your system.

1. Open My Computer by clicking on the icon on the desktop.
2. Click on the drive C icon.
3. Click on **File|New|Folder**.
4. Delete New Folder and rename the folder **MSOffice**.
5. Click on the MSOffice folder, then click on **File|New|Folder** and create a folder named **Files**.
6. Click on the Files folder.
7. Open the CD-ROM, select the companion files, and copy them to C:\MSOffice\Files folder. (The companion files are located on the CD-ROM in the Files folder.)
8. Select all the files you just copied (highlight them). Right-click with your mouse to display the pop-up menu and click on **Properties**. In the Properties dialog box that appears next, click on the **Read-only** box to deselect it. This turns off the Read-only property attribute.
9. Close all open folders.
10. Remove your companion CD and put it in a safe place when it is not in use.

What's Next?

Now that you have installed the companion files on your hard drive, you're ready to begin learning all about Word. In the next section you learn about Word's screen layout, menus, and common dialogs.

Starting (or "Launching") Word

If you installed the Office toolbar, the easiest way to launch Word is to click on the Word button. Otherwise, go to the Programs group (or the group in which you installed Word); start Word by clicking the Microsoft Word line. When Word starts the default Document1 loads.

Note: Occasionally when you start Word the program will display the following dialog. Do not be alarmed. This is Office 2000's way of getting to know you better. After Office configures itself Word will start normally.

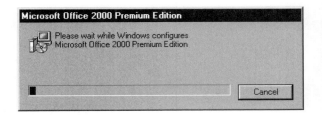

The first time you start Word you are invited to review "What's New," and the Office Assistant offers help. If you are familiar with Word 6.0, 7.0, or Word 97 you may want to close the Office Assistant for now. Go to the Menu bar and click on Help, then click on "Hide the Office Assistant." The default Document1 makes use of the Normal style sheet. Compare your display to the following illustration, which labels the various parts of the Word screen.

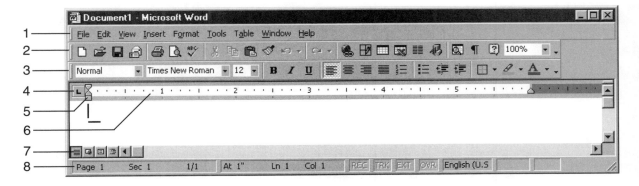

The above screen illustrates the Normal page view. The vertical ruler is not displayed in the Normal view, which is the default setting. If you wish, you can use the View menu to change the document view. With the document open, you can now type your text and use the menus and toolbars to change the page setup, font, text size, and more. Each Word screen control is summarized in the following list and then briefly described in the remaining paragraphs of this section. Detailed descriptions are found in the following sections of this book where you are guided through hands-on learning activities.

Note: The previous screen shot does not include program buttons on the Standard toolbar. Application program buttons may or may not be on your standard toolbar. If the programs are installed on your computer at the time you install Word 2000 or if the programs are installed at a later date, you will be prompted to add the buttons.

Microsoft Word 2000 Controls

The keyed screen illustration shows each of the various controls which are summarized below.

Key	Item	Description
1	Menu Bar	Used to access the Word menus and the Office Assistant (Help).
2	Standard toolbar	Includes buttons to perform the most frequently used file, editing, web and hyperlink, borders, column, drawing, document map, zoom, and Office Assistant (Help) operations.
3	Formatting toolbar	Includes buttons to change document styles, fonts, font sizes, type styles, paragraph alignment, list formats and indent levels, borders, and highlight and font color.
4	Tab Style button	Click to change the tab style from align left, align center, align right, or decimal tab. Once set, click on ruler to insert tabs; select and drag tabs from the ruler to remove.
5	Left Margin tools	Drag pointers right or left to control the indent of one or more selected paragraphs, the indent of the first line, or the indent of second and subsequent lines (hanging indent).
6	Horizontal Ruler	Use to see how text and graphics are arranged horizontally on the final page. A vertical ruler may also be displayed in the Print Layout view; use to see how text and graphics are arranged vertically on the final page.
7	View buttons	Click the Normal, Page Layout, or Outline View button to change the way your document is displayed.
8	Status line	Displays messages, page and section numbers, cursor position, and other information.

Menus

Word's menus are pulled down from the menu bar, located across the top of the screen. Menus are accessed by picking a menu name with the mouse or by pressing Alt+*xx*'s online Help provides information for almost all Word operations. Go ahead and pull down the menus and examine their contents by performing the following steps.

Note: Some of the following menus include "ghosted" entries. The ghosted entries become solid when the features they support are accessible. For example, the Edit menu's Cut, Copy, and Paste entries are active when a passage of text is marked and available on the Windows clipboard. The Table menu entries are available when a table is available and selected.

Menu and submenu items may be hidden and can be displayed by clicking on either a side arrow or down arrow if either are present. If a submenu item is hidden by a down arrow, the submenu item may also appear if the menu item is selected for several seconds.

1. Pull down the File menu by pressing **<Alt+F>**.

   The File menu is used to perform a variety of file and printing operations in addition to page setup (size, margins, and orientation). The Versions selection displays information about your documents. The Send To selection permits you to e-mail or fax your document, send it to a recipient via Microsoft Exchange, or send it to PowerPoint for use as part of a presentation. The Properties selection displays information about the current document. Note that the Exit selection quits the program. Word also displays recently saved files at the bottom of the File menu. You can open a recently used file by clicking it with your mouse or by typing the corresponding number.

Note: An ellipsis (...) following a menu item indicates a dialog box appears after the item is selected; an arrowhead signifies additional choices are available.

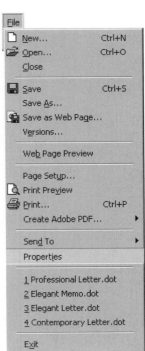

2. Pull down the Edit menu by pressing the **<Right Arrow>**.

The Edit menu is used to delete, copy, and move blocks of text. It also includes Undo and Repeat selections as well as Find and Replace functions. Go To invites you to go directly to a page, section, bookmark, or other object within the current document. The Paste Special selection is used to link pasted objects from other applications. The Paste as Hyperlink selection is used when creating a web site document. Select the text or other object is and then click **Paste Hyperlink**. A dialog invites you to enter the URL (uniform resource locator) name for a web site. *Hyperlinks* are used to access web sites. When clicked, the stored URL is issued.

3. Move to the View menu by pressing the **<Right Arrow>**.

The View menu lets you display your document in a number of ways including Normal, Web Layout, Print Layout, Outline, Document Map (the document's underlying structure showing heading styles), and Full Screen. You can try each to determine which you prefer. View is also used to turn off and on the display of toolbars, rulers, footnotes, and comments (previously called *annotations*), and to zoom the page size. Headers and footers are also created and edited using the View menu.

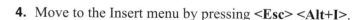

4. Move to the Insert menu by pressing **<Esc> <Alt+I>**.

Insert selections give you the ability to insert a variety of things into your document. Use this menu to insert page and section breaks; page numbers; the current date and/or time; symbols; comments; footnotes; captions for figures, tables, or equations; files; pictures; objects (including equation and WordArt objects); indexes and tables of contents; text boxes; and bookmarks. You can also identify text for an alphabetical index or table of contents.

5. Move to the Format menu: **<Esc> <Alt+O>**

The Format menu lists options for setting and modifying fonts, paragraph formats, borders, columns, bulleted and numbered lists, text styles, and background colors. In addition, you can insert drop caps, change text case, rotate text (within a selected text box), and use AutoFormat (automatically format an entire document based on a stored format control).

6. Move to the Tools menu: **<Esc> <Alt+T>**

Here you can use the built-in spelling and grammar checkers and thesaurus; perform word counts; display a statistical summary of the document; set special characters corresponding to different languages; adjust hyphenation settings and Word's AutoCorrect feature; prepare envelopes, labels, and mail merge documents; track document changes; create and run macros; customize toolbars, menus, and shortcut keys; and set Word options (page guidelines, autosave, etc.) to suit your personal preferences.

7. Move to the Table menu: **<Esc> <Alt+A>**

Use this menu to create and edit tables, sort data, insert formulas, and turn gridlines on and off.

8. Move to the Window menu: **\<Esc\> \<Alt+W\>**

The Window menu is used to create, arrange, and select document windows when more than one document is open.

9. Move to the Help menu: **\<Esc\> \<Alt+H\>**

Use Help menu options to review information about Word operations. Click the Help button on the Menu toolbar, then click the Microsoft Word Help button on the drop-down menu to display the default Office Assistant, Clipit. See Section 2 for detailed information.

Horizontal Ruler

The length of the ruler and margin locations are established by the current page setup. This is controlled using the File|Page Setup menu selection, where page size, margins, and page orientation are set. You can make adjustments to the ruler that affect the behavior of the current paragraph or a selected section of text. Be sure to make ruler adjustments only after you've selected all the text you want changed. Then use the ruler to make quick changes to indents, margins, and tab settings. Use the mouse pointer and Tab button, located at the beginning of the ruler, to insert tabs. You can also use the Format|Tabs menu selection to set several tabs at the same time, create dot leaders, and change the spacing of default tabs.

The default ruler contains a tab every one-half inch. These are represented by a small vertical line beneath each half-inch mark on the ruler. Clicking on the ruler inserts a tab at the mouse pointer location. The tab style is controlled by the tab type currently displayed on the Tab button at the left-hand end of the horizontal ruler. You can change the tab style by clicking it until you display the desired tab style. Default tabs to the left of an inserted tab are automatically removed. They are reinstated when you remove the inserted tab from the ruler.

You can also drag the margin and hanging indent buttons (the top and bottom triangles at the left-hand end of the ruler) to change text indentation. Dragging the rectangle below the indent triangles moves both triangles and hence the entire left margin.

Finally, the right margin is adjusted using the triangle at the right-hand end of the ruler. Many users prefer to learn and use keyboard shortcuts to control indents and margins. The following control key combinations are useful for indenting:

Shortcut Key	Description
Ctrl+M	Indent margin to next tab
Ctrl+Shift+M	Move margin indent back to previous tab
Ctrl+T	Hanging indent
Ctrl+Shift+T	Cancel hanging indent
Ctrl+1	Set single space
Ctrl+2	Set double space
Ctrl+5	Set space and one-half
Ctrl+0 (number 0)	Insert/remove a line space before the current paragraph
Ctrl+Q	Remove paragraph formatting (line spacing) from selected paragraph

Vertical Ruler

The vertical ruler is displayed in the Print Layout view. It is used to see how text and graphics are arranged vertically on the page.

Scroll Bars

The scroll bars are used to move your display horizontally and vertically. Horizontal scrolling is sometimes required when displaying text in the Page Layout view. This is particularly true when text is zoomed greater than 100 percent.

Status Bar

The status bar is located at the bottom of the screen. Here, you can view the page and section number and the horizontal and vertical cursor position. Notice REC, TRK, EXT, and OVR. When active, these labels tell you:

REC	Indicates the macro recorder is active.
TRK	Revision tracking is active.
EXT	Extend Selection (key F8) is active.
OVR	Overtype mode is active (rather than insert mode).

Adjusting (Turning Off and On) Displayed Elements

The scroll bars and status bar can be turned off with the Tools|Options menu selection. You can also use the Tools|Options menu selection to set a number of controls that change the Word interface. Notice that the Options dialog box has folder-like tabs which are used to access additional options.

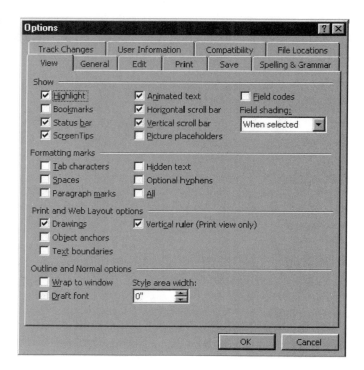

The categories of options are summarized below:

Dialog Box	Control for
View	Page layout, window elements, the display of field codes and non-printing characters, and shading.
General	Options for controlling ruler measurements, help and navigation keys for WordPerfect users, error beeps, 3D dialog and display effects, and more.
Edit	Typing replaces selection, drag and drop editing, automatic word selection, use of Insert key for paste, overtype/insert mode, smart cut and paste, and accented uppercase characters.
Print	Pagination order, printing of field codes and hidden text, background printing, printing annotations, summary info, and more.
Save	Backup copy creation, fast saves, prompt for summary info, automatically saving every n minutes, where n is a set number of minutes, and password protection.
Spelling & Grammar	Spelling and grammer checking and editing of the custom dictionary.
Track Changes	Marking of inserted, deleted, and changed text.

Dialog Box	Control for
User Information	Inserting your name, initials, and mailing address in such items as summary info and the return address for envelopes.
Compatibility	Setting the way Word 2000 treats document elements for compatibility with other word processors such as earlier versions of Word for Windows or WordPerfect.
File Locations	Setting the directories used for document, ClipArt, templates, and other support files.

Enhancements to Word 2000

Although most of the Word features are either the same or quite similar to those found in Word 6.0, Word 7.0 for Windows, and Word 97, a number of new features have been added. In particular, new Office Assistants, web authoring tools, and new document sharing features are just a few of the enhancements introduced by Word 2000. One way to see what's new is to click the Help button to launch the Office Assistant, then select Options. A dialog box with two folders is activated. Click on the Options folder, then disable the Office Assistant by clearing the Use the Office Assistant check box. Now press F1 (or click on Help|Microsoft Word Help on the Menu bar). A Help dialog box is now activated. Click on the Index tab. In the text box under "1. Type Keywords" type the word "help." On the right side of the dialog box you will see "Finding out what's new in Word 2000." Click on the text string and you will see various topics. Click on any topic of interest for a short discussion of new Word 2000 features related to the topic chosen.

Summary

As you can see, Word offers a huge number of features and controls for your document creation tasks. The remainder of this part guides you through the use of most of these. Once you are familiar with the features offered by Word, you will be able to create virtually any type of document, as you are able to produce documents containing pictures, charts, forms, databases, worksheets, and much more in a variety of document formats including native HTML.

Creating, Saving, Importing, Exporting, and Inserting Files

Introduction

This section describes file handling processes. The file handling processes discussed are:

- Creating and saving a new file
- Opening an existing file
- Saving a file under a new name
- Saving a file for use with another word processing program
- Importing a file created by another word processing program
- Inserting an existing file into the body of the current document

Creating a New File

Creating a new file is a necessary first step in working with a new document. A new file may be created by clicking on File|New or the New Blank Document button ⬜ on the Standard toolbar, then choosing an appropriate template. The New dialog gives you a choice of many different document templates to choose from. Besides the templates provided with Office 2000, you may find additional templates at a Microsoft web site. Choose a template that is most consistent with the ultimate objective of your document. A Blank Document template has no specific format, although it does have default settings for such document attributes as font type and font size, which you can change to suit your needs.

Also, from the New dialog, you may create a new template. This is a powerful tool that gives you the ability to capture and easily recall document formats used on a regular basis.

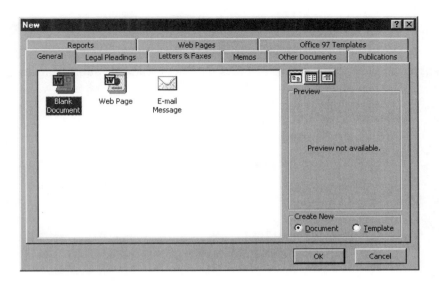

Saving a New File

To save a file (or template), select File|Save or press the Save button 💾.

The File|Save menu selection and Save button save the file with its current name and file type. The default name is DocumentX, where X is an integer whose value depends upon the number of new files already opened in the current work session. The default file type is the Word 2000 .doc type.

Saving a File Under a New Name

The File|Save As choice allows you to save your document under a new name and/or document type. You can save the file with a new name by changing the filename in the File name text box. Also, you can change the file type by choosing a different type from the Save as type text box.

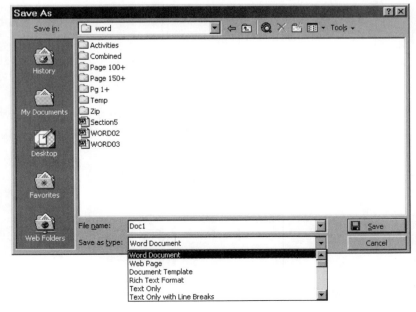

The Save As dialog includes the following elements:

Subdirectory icons that jump immediately to the specified subdirectory.

The History icon displays the documents and subdirectories of recently saved documents. Selecting a subdirectory from here will save the document in that subdirectory.

The My Documents icon saves the document in the C:\My Documents directory.

The Desktop icon saves the document to the Desktop directory.

The Favorites icon saves the document in whichever Favorites subdirectory you choose. A favorite subdirectory may be added to Favorites by selecting Tools located near the top right of the Save As dialog and choosing Add to Favorites.

The Web Folders icon saves the document in the My Computer\Web Folders directory.

The Save in: drop-down box allows you to choose the directory/subdirectory other than the current working directory where the file can be saved. Click on the down arrow to choose another location.

Office2000

Also, clicking on the up arrow just to the right of the Save in: box will take you up one place in the subdirectory hierarchy.

If you want to save the document as a web document, you can click on the Search the Web button which will start Internet Explorer and connect you to the Internet.

The Delete button will delete the subdirectory or file that is highlighted when the button is clicked.

The Create New Folder button allows the user to place the saved document into a new directory (folder).

The List button allows the user to select what file/directory information is displayed in the main dialog box.

The Tools button has a drop-down menu list that includes several file management processes and usage options. Delete deletes a file or directory. Rename allows a file or directory name to be changed. Add to Favorites will add the highlighted file or directory to the Favorites icon. Map Network Drive allows the user to save files on a remote network drive. Properties displays file or directory information.

Tools ▾

X Delete   Del
Rename
Add to Favorites
Map Network Drive...

Properties

Web Options...
General Options...
Save Version...

Web Options allows the selection of certain settings including the use of long filenames and the default encoding or language for the file.

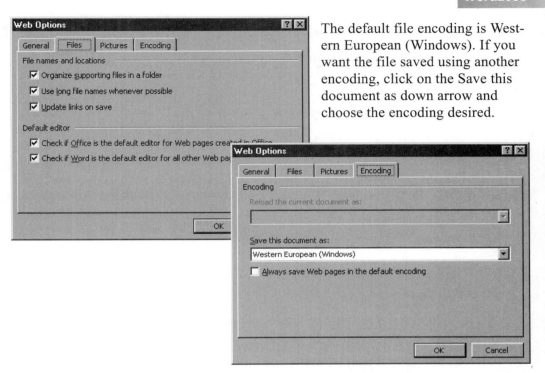

The default file encoding is Western European (Windows). If you want the file saved using another encoding, click on the Save this document as down arrow and choose the encoding desired.

The General Options|Save selection allows you to set the autorecovery timer. The Save AutoRecover info every setting should be adjusted to a value dependent upon the speed of the computer, the reliability of the power source, and the amount of risk acceptable to the user. For most situations, the default time of 10 minutes is acceptable.

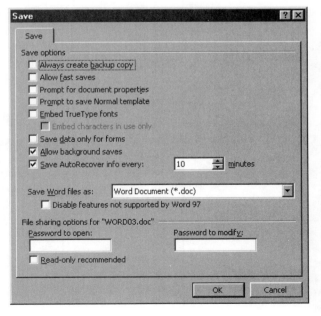

Note: Enabling Embed TrueType fonts will result in a greatly increased document size as the font information now becomes part of the document. For most uses, enabling Embed is a waste of disk space.

Saving a File for Use with Another Word Processing Program

The Save as type: drop-down text box includes many different file types that the document can be saved as. Just click on the box's down arrow and choose the document type desired.

Documents can be saved as file types:

Word document (*.doc)
web page (*.htm;*.html)
rich text format (*.rtf)
text (various types) (*.txt)
Windows Write—various versions (*.wri)
Word for Windows—various versions (*.doc)
Word for Macintosh—various versions (*.mcw)
Word for MS-DOS (*.doc)
WordPerfect—various versions (*.doc)
Works for Windows—various versions (*.wps)

When you are ready to finally save the file, click on the Save button located on the bottom right side of the Save dialog. Or, if you change your mind, click on Cancel.

Opening an Existing File

To open an existing file, select the File|Open menu selection or press the Open button . Notice the shortcut icons on the left side of the Open dialog. At the top of the dialog, there is a directory drop-down box allowing you to choose files from directories/subdirectories other than where you are currently located. To go to another file location, just click on the down arrow and choose the next option.

The Favorites icon opens another dialog allowing you to select documents from directories/subdirectories far removed from where your current working directory may be.

Of course, you must place your favorites in the Favorites location by going to the directory of interest, then clicking on Tools.

Importing a File Created by Another Word Processing Program

Word 2000 comes with filters that convert documents derived from other sources into the Word 2000 format, allowing you to import documents from a wide variety of sources and change them in Word 2000.

Begin by clicking File|Open. At the bottom of the Open dialog, there is a Files of type: drop-down text box. Click on the text box down arrow and see the different file formats that Word accommodates. When the format of interest is selected, all files with that type extension become visible in the Open dialog. Other document formats are converted when the file desired is highlighted in the Open dialog box, then opened by clicking on Open at the bottom right side of the dialog. Word converts the file to the Word 2000 format, then presents the document to the user in the familiar Word program ready for use.

Hint: Rich text files can take a long time to convert and save when working with them in Word. Convert already existing .rtf files to Word (.doc) and work with new documents in Word format. Only convert to rich text format as a final step.

Inserting an Existing File Into the Body of the Current Document

Word can insert a whole file inside a current working document. The document is inserted wherever the cursor is currently at. Begin by clicking on Insert|File to open the Insert File dialog. Choose the file of interest and press the Insert button on the bottom right of the dialog box. If you change your mind, click on Cancel.

Save Version

You can save multiple versions of the same document with comments describing the differences using the Save Version button. This is useful when you have two or more variations of the same document. Clicking the Save Version button 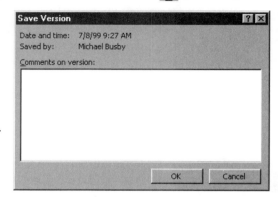 (found by clicking View|Toolbars|Reviewing) displays the Save Version dialog where you can enter comments about the current version.

Use the File|Versions menu selection to view different versions of the document. The date, time, and your comments are saved with each version so you can distinguish one from another.

Hands-on Activities

This activity demonstrates the file handling procedures.

Creating and Saving a New File

In this activity you create a small document file and save it with a name of your choice. Begin by starting Windows.

1. Start Word by clicking on Microsoft Word in the Start|Programs group (or click the Word button on the Office Shortcut bar).

2. Notice that Document1 is the default document name. The default style is Normal and the current font is Times New Roman 10 point.

3. Click the **Show/Hide** button ¶ (on the top toolbar) to display control characters including spaces, carriage returns, and tabs.

4. Change the size to 12-point and delete the 10-point carriage return: **<Ctrl+]>** **<Ctrl+]>** **<Enter>** **<Del>**.

5. Set the top, bottom, left, and right margins to 1 inch: Pick **File|Page Setup** (or double-click the horizontal strip above the ruler), type **1"** in the Top, Bottom, Left, and Right margin text boxes **<Enter>**.

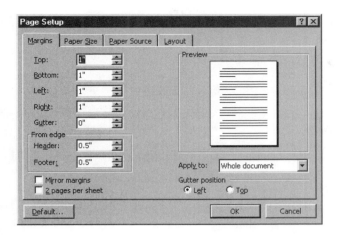

6. Type the following paragraph and press **<Enter>** at the end:

   This document is being typed using the Normal style. The font is Times New Roman. The point size is set to 12 points, where there are 72 points per vertical inch. All margins (top, bottom, left, and right) have been set to 1". Finally, nonprintable characters are displayed by clicking the Show/Hide button on the Standard toolbar.

7. Save the document with the name myfirst: Click **File|Save**, type **myfirst <Enter>**. Notice that the assigned name of your document is now displayed on the Microsoft Word title bar at the top of the screen. The file extension .doc is automatically assigned by Word. Windows lets you type descriptive names that can be as long as 254 characters and include spaces.

   You may use the Properties selection of the File menu, i.e., **File|Properties**, to view information about the document. You may also add descriptive information here, which can later be viewed using the **File|Properties** menu selection. Descriptive information can help you determine what's in the document at some future date.

8. Type **This is my first document** in the Comments box. Then click **OK** to save the properties information.

Opening an Existing File

In this activity you leave myfirst.doc open and displayed while opening a second file located on the C:\MSOffice\Files folder.

Note: When using the companion files, you will want to turn off the Autosave option to avoid writing over the files you have copied to your hard drive from the companion CD. Use the Tools|Options menu, select the Save tab, and click on the box next to Automatic Save Every to remove the X and toggle off the option.

1. Open the file Sample1: Click on the **Open** (folder) button on the toolbar to display the Open dialog box.

2. Locate the Sample1.doc file in the MSOffice\Files folder.

3. Double-click the filename **Sample1.doc** to open the file.

4. Pick the **Window** menu; notice that two document names are displayed and the active one has a check mark by it.

5. Press **<Esc>** to release the Window menu and return to the Sample1 document.

Saving a File Using a New Name

You can save a file using a new name at any time by using the File|Save As menu selection. Just pick the desired disk and file path, type the new filename, and click Save.

1. Click on **Window** on the menu toolbar. Select myfirst.doc to make it the active or currently displayed window.

2. Click **File|Save As**.

3. Select the C:\MSOffice\Files folder in the Save in: box.

4. Change the filename to **mysecond.doc**.

5. Ensure the file type is .doc in the Save as type: box. Note that you can choose other file types to save the document as.

6. Click on the **Save** button. You have now saved myfirst.doc as mysecond.doc.

Saving a File for Use with Another Word Processing Program

Word lets you save a variety of file types that can be used with other commonly used programs. This is a simple process, as it is controlled by a dialog box with a pick list of file types. In this activity you export the Sample1 document as a WordPerfect 5.1 document.

1. Click on the **File|Save As** menu selection; now click the Save as type down arrow to display a list of file types.

2. Use the scroll bar to see additional file types; click on the **Wordperfect 5.1 for MS-DOS** file type.

3. To prevent writing over the original Sample1.doc, type **Samplewp.wpg** as the File name and click **Save**. Word converts the file, including the embedded graphic, with the new name. Close the document with **<Alt+F, C>**.

Importing a File Created by Another Word Processing Program

Word also lets you import a variety of file types created by other popular programs. The import process is nearly identical to the export process, except that the File|Open menu selection is used. When Word detects a non-Word file format, you are automatically prompted for the file type. In this activity you import the Samplewp.doc file created in the preceding activity.

1. Click on the file **Open** button at the left end of the toolbar; type **Samplewp.wpg** as the filename and click **Open**.

2. Notice that Word detects a non-Word file type and automatically converts the WordPerfect 5.1 format file for use by Word.

3. The fonts and type sizes usually vary with the source document.

4. Close the file using the **File|Close** menu selection; click **No** in response to the Save File prompt.

Inserting an Existing File into the Body of the Current Document

Advanced topic

This activity inserts a file into the body of an open document. Begin with Sample1.doc as the currently open document. (Find it in the \MSOffice\Files folder and open it.)

1. Press **<Ctrl+End>** to move the cursor to the bottom of the document.

2. Click **Insert|File**, pick **Clubltr.doc** from the list, and click **OK**. Notice that Clubltr.doc is inserted at the cursor position.

3. Pick **File|Close** and respond with **No** to the Save Changes prompt.

Saving Versions

This activity shows you how to save different versions of a document.

1. Click on the **Window** menu selection, then choose **myfirst.doc** to make it the default, or displayed, document.

2. Click **View|Toolbars|Reviewing** to display the Reviewing toolbar.

3. Click on the **Save Version** button 🖳.

4. Enter the appropriate information concerning the document version in the Comments on version: text box. The text box is shown with author's comments.

5. Click on **OK**.

6. Repeat steps 2, 3, and 4 and enter **Newest myfirst.doc version.** in the Comments on version: text box.

7. Now click on **File|Versions**. See the different versions of myfirst.doc in the dialog.

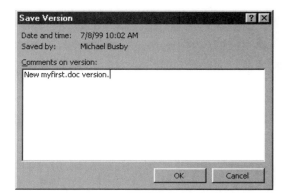

Note: You may have to click on the down arrow ≽ at the bottom of the File menu to see additional menu choices that include Versions.

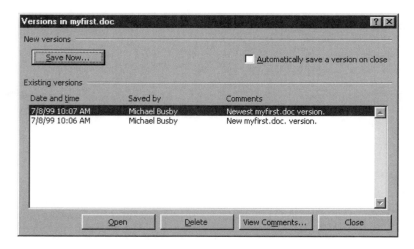

Note: You can view any saved version by clicking on the Open button. Also, you can view any additional comments (entered using the View|Toolbars|Reviewing|Insert Comments button   ) concerning the version by clicking on the View Comments button. In addition, you can choose to automatically save a new version when you close a document. But beware—if you have limited disk space and you choose to automatically save large documents, you may soon find disk space in short supply.

   8. Click on the **Delete** button to delete the highlighted version.

   9. Click on the remaining version by repeating Step 8.

   10. Click on the **Close** button.

   11. Pick **File|Close** and respond with **No** to the Save Changes prompt until all documents are closed.

   12. Press **<Alt+F4>** to exit Word; notice that the Windows desktop is redisplayed.

Summary

The activities in this section point out how easy it is to open, close, import, export, and insert files. As a Word user, you must perform file handling operations on a regular basis, so be sure that you are comfortable with the procedures presented in this section.

Note: In the remaining activities, your files will be in the \MSOffice\Files folder. Make this the default directory by changing the location of the document to C:\MSOffice\Files using the File Locations tab of the Options dialog. This is accessed using the Tools|Options menu. You can change this later to another convenient file location.

Formatting Pages, Paragraphs, and Sections

Introduction

In Section 5 you briefly used the File|Page Setup menu selection when you adjusted all page margins to one inch. Using the Format menu is another way to control the appearance of your document. Review the following information and then perform the hands-on activity.

Pages

Pages are formatted using the File|Page Setup manu selection to open the Page Setup dialog. The Page Setup dialog includes the Margins, Paper Size, Paper Source, and Layout tabs from which you may adjust the appropriate page features.

Paragraphs

The Format|Paragraph menu option brings up the Paragraphs dialog box, which provides independent control over indents, spacing, and text flow. Indents and spacing options control the indentation from the left and right margins, line spacing, the indent level of the first line (paragraph indent), and the indent level of the second and subsequent lines (hanging indent). Text flow options control the way a selected paragraph interacts with adjacent text elements and page breaks. For example, you can change the right and left margins of an individual paragraph, keep the paragraph together (prevent it from being split by a page break), change the line spacing, and set different spacing before and after the paragraph. A typical use of a uniquely formatted paragraph might be an embedded note. For emphasis, notes are often indented from the left and right margins and sometimes receive additional spacing before and/or after the text of the note.

Sections

General format settings, such as the normal margins and tab settings, are applied to the whole document, from the current point forward, or to a section where the document is subdivided into two or more sections. The Insert|Break menu option is used to insert both page and section breaks. Using the Break dialog box, you can begin a new section on the same page (click the Continuous button) or on a new page (click the Next page button). The Break dialog box is shown in the following illustration.

Note that you can delete both page and section breaks using the Del key. Once you establish two or more sections within a document, you can vary the margins, line spacing, and even the number of columns within each section independent of the others. Therefore, when using multiple formats within a document, be sure to insert a section for each unique format.

If you insert multiple-column text within a single-column document, the column operation automatically creates a new section for the selected text. This eliminates the need to insert a section break before selecting and converting a passage to columnar text.

Hands-on Activity

The following activity uses the Sample2.doc located in the \MSOffice\Files folder. This is a simple, single-column document. You use the File|Page Setup, Format|Paragraph, and Insert|Break menu selections to modify the appearance of the document.

1. Start the Word program and display the blank DocumentX page.

2. Use **File|Open** to load the Sample2.doc file.

3. Use **PgUp** and **PgDn** or the vertical scroll bar to examine this two-page document.

4. Use **File|Page Setup** and set all four margins to 1 inch.

Note: In the following step you use two new commands: Edit|Select All selects the entire document (use the shortcut Ctrl+A). Then use Ctrl+] to increase the type size of the selected passage by one point. (Ctrl+[reduces the type size.)

5. Select the entire document and change the point size to 12: **<Ctrl+A> <Ctrl+]>** **<Ctrl+]>**. Press **<Down Arrow>** to deselect the document.

6. Place the cursor at the beginning of the word NOTE; center the word by pressing **<Ctrl+E>**.

7. Indent the note text 1 inch from the left and right margins using the Format|Paragraph menu selection as follows:

   a. Select the note text (drag it with your mouse).

   b. **<Alt+O> P 1 <Tab> 1 <Enter>**.

8. Select and then use the Columns button on the top toolbar to make the terms and definitions portion of the document two-column as follows:

   a. Highlight all text beginning with the word "Point" through the last line of the "Font" definition text by placing the cursor in front of the P in Point, pressing **<Shift>** and dragging down until the above referenced selection is highlighted.

   b. Click on the **Columns** button and select two columns (click on the second column in the pop-down illustration). This creates two additional sections within your document.

9. Compare your document to the following illustration to see how sections are used for multiple formats within the same document. (Click **View|Print Layout** menu selection, then click **File|Print Preview**. Then use the Multiple Pages button and drag 1 x 2 Pages.)

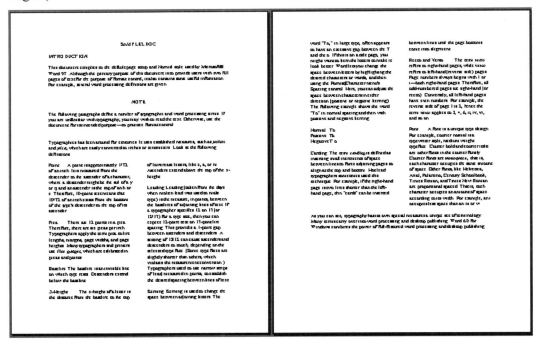

10. Exit Word and return to Windows without saving the changes made to the Sample2.doc file: click **<Alt+F4>** and the **No** button to prevent saving changes.

Summary

In this section you learned more about File|Page Setup and then saw how easy it is to mix document formats using the Format|Paragraph and Insert|Break menu selections. In the next section you learn how to create indents and outdents, which are both powerful and valuable Word features.

Note: If the Help for WordPerfect Users option was selected during installation, a Help for WordPerfect Users tip box may appear when you attempt to close a file using Alt+F4. To turn off Help for WordPerfect Users, select Help|WordPerfect Help, click on Options, and click on the check boxes next to Help for WordPerfect Users and Navigation Keys for WordPerfect Users to remove the X's in those boxes. Click OK, then click Close.

Indents and Outdents

Introduction

This section guides you through the process of indenting text including paragraph indents, hanging indents, and extending text to the left of the left margin (referred to as an outdent). Finally, the procedure used to indent rows within columns is described.

Indenting Paragraphs

You can indent paragraphs from either the left or right margin using the Format|Paragraph menu selection as described in the previous section. You can also indent the

first line or apply a hanging indent to a selected paragraph using the Indents and Spacing section of the Paragraph dialog box. In particular, you can choose (none), First Line, or Hanging in the Special box and put an indent value in the corresponding By box.

Check the Paragraph dialog box to see how the Indent selections control the indent distances from the left and right margins. Also check the Special box, which is used for both paragraph (first line) and hanging indents. You can create indents by dragging the margin buttons at the beginning of the ruler with your mouse. You can also use the shortcut keys:

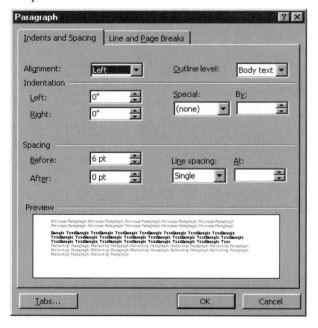

Ctrl+T	Hanging indent
Ctrl+Shift+T	Cancel hanging indent
Ctrl+M	Indent left margin
Ctrl+Shift+M	Cancel left margin indent
Ctrl+M, Ctrl+Shift+T	Paragraph indent

You can also use the Increase Indent and Decrease Indent buttons on the Format toolbar to change the indentation of a paragraph. Finally, notice that this dialog also lets you set line spacing and alignment.

Hanging Indents

A conventional hanging indent leaves the first line even with the established left margin and indents following lines, normally to the first tab stop. The first line of a hanging indent may also be indented from the left margin, say to the first tab stop; following lines are always indented more.

Following are two examples of a hanging indent.

In this example the first line of a hanging indent is even with the left margin; following lines are indented to the first tab stop. A series of hanging indents is used to separate elements in a list. (Use Ctrl+T for a conventional hanging indent.)

This is another example of a hanging indent. Notice that the first line is indented to a tab stop. (Ctrl+M or the Increase Indent button on the toolbar is used to indent the left margin. Then Ctrl+T is used to indent following lines to the second tab stop.)

Outdenting (Printing in the Margins)

Outdents are achieved using the Format|Paragraph menu selection's Indentation controls. Placing negative values in the Left and Right boxes moves the margins beyond the normal left and right margins.

Indenting Rows in a Table

You learn about tables in Section 13. Indenting text within a row and column of a table is the same method used for running text. Simply position the cursor in the desired row or column and use the Ctrl key sequences listed under Indenting Paragraphs in this section.

Summary

In this section you learned how to indent, outdent, and create hanging indents using menus, buttons, and control keys. In the next section you learn how to create bulleted and numbered lists, and you practice indenting and outdenting in the hands-on activities.

Creating Lists and Numbering Headings

Introduction

In Section 7 you learned how to format individual paragraphs, how to indent, and how to position text beyond the left margin, or outdent. This section guides you through another text formatting feature—the creation of lists. It also describes the **Format|Bullets and Numbering|Outline Numbered** selection, used to automatically apply numbers to paragraph headings and outlines.

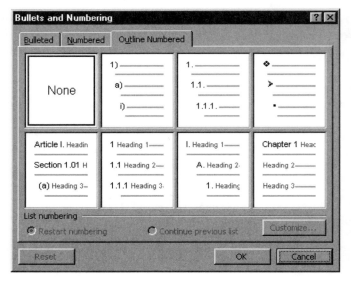

Word makes list creation and conversion simple. You can convert lines of text into numbered lists or procedural steps. Word automatically assigns the proper numeric sequence to a series of selected passages. Similarly, Word lets you select one or more paragraphs (or lines) of text and then convert the selected passage into a bulleted list. The **Format|Bullets and Numbering** menu selection lets you modify the bullet style or the numbering sequence.

The fastest way to create a numbered or bulleted list is to use the Numbering ⬛ or Bullets ⬛ buttons on the Format toolbar. Once text is selected, simply click the appropriate button to automatically convert your list to the desired form.

Hands-on Activity

The following activity guides you through the creation of numbered and bulleted lists. It also shows you how to change the number sequence and bullet style, and how to exchange numbers for bullets and bullets for numbers.

1. Start Word and open the Sample2.doc file.

2. Select the text associated with the terms "Point" through "X-Height."

3. Click the **Numbering** button ⣿; notice how numbers 1 through 4 are automatically inserted to the left of the text.

> 1. Point   A point is approximately 1/72 of an inch. It is measured from the descender to the ascender of a character, where a descender might be the tail of a y or q and an ascender is the top of an h or t. Therefore, 10-point text means that 10/72 of an inch exists from the bottom of the type's descender to the top of its ascender.
>
> 2. Pica   There are 12 points in a pica. Therefore, there are six picas per inch. Typographers apply the term pica to line lengths, margins, page widths, and page heights. Many typographers and printers use *line guages*, which are calibrated in picas and points.
>
> 3. Baseline The baseline is an invisible line on which type rests. Descenders extend below the baseline.
>
> 4. X-Height   The x-height of a letter is the distance from the baseline to the top of lowercase letters, like x, a, or m. Ascenders extend above the top of the x-height.

4. Select the **Format|Bullets and Numbering** menu selection's **Numbered** tab and select the **a., b., c.** format. Click **OK** and see how the numbers are changed to letters.

Tip: The Customize button of the Numbered tab is used to select additional numbering formats as well as the spacing.

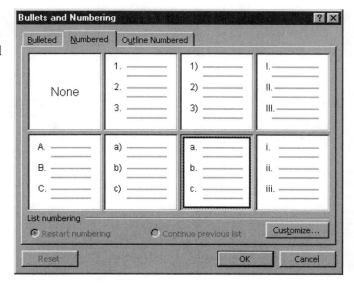

a. Point   A point is approximately 1/72 of an inch. It is measured from the descender to the ascender of a character, where a descender might be the tail of a y or q and an ascender is the top of an h or t. Therefore, 10-point text means that 10/72 of an inch exists from the bottom of the type's descender to the top of its ascender.

b. Pica   There are 12 points in a pica. Therefore, there are six picas per inch. Typographers apply the term pica to line lengths, margins, page widths, and page heights. Many typographers and printers use *line guages*, which are calibrated in picas and points.

c. Baseline The baseline is an invisible line on which type rests. Descenders extend below the baseline.

d. X-Height   The x-height of a letter is the distance from the baseline to the top of lowercase letters, like x, a, or m. Ascenders extend above the top of the x-height.

5. With the original passage still selected, click the **Bullets** button . Notice how the letters are replaced with bullets.

- Point   A point is approximately 1/72 of an inch. It is measured from the descender to the ascender of a character, where a descender might be the tail of a y or q and an ascender is the top of an h or t. Therefore, 10-point text means that 10/72 of an inch exists from the bottom of the type's descender to the top of its ascender.

- Pica   There are 12 points in a pica. Therefore, there are six picas per inch. Typographers apply the term pica to line lengths, margins, page widths, and page heights. Many typographers and printers use *line guages*, which are calibrated in picas and points.

- Baseline The baseline is an invisible line on which type rests. Descenders extend below the baseline.

- X-Height   The x-height of a letter is the distance from the baseline to the top of lowercase letters, like x, a, or m. Ascenders extend above the top of the x-height.

6. Use the Bulleted section of the Bullets and Numbering dialog box to change the bullet to a filled rectangle (the upper right selection box).

7. Click **OK** and notice the new bullet character.

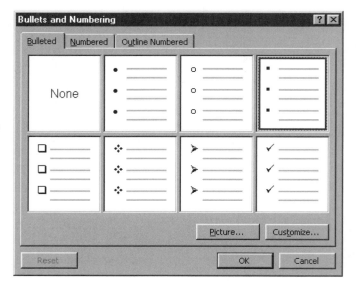

Heading Numbering

When you use different heading styles from the style box, i.e., Heading 1, Heading 2, etc., you can apply heading numbers using the Outline Numbered tab of the Bullets and Numbering dialog. Here, multilevel outlines and indentations are automatically applied. Just pick the style you want to use and click OK.

Tip: Styles are created, changed, and applied from the Style box on the Formatting toolbar. Just click on the text element and then choose the desired style.

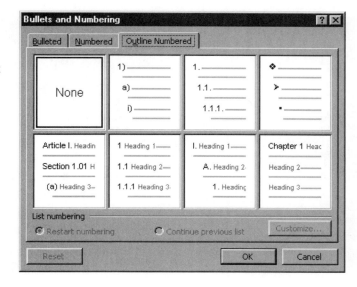

8. Press **<Alt+F4>** and click **No** to exit Word without saving your changes to the Sample2.doc file.

Summary

In this section you learned how to create numbered and bulleted lists. In the next section you learn how to control document styles, type fonts, and font sizes.

Styles, Fonts, and Font Sizes

Introduction

This section guides you through the use and creation of document styles and the selection of type fonts and font sizes. First, styles, fonts, and font sizes are introduced. Then a hands-on activity is provided to give you experience with the management of styles and to see how fonts and font sizes are controlled.

Styles

Word comes with a number of built-in styles that are applied to both document headings and normal text. Styles are accessed in the Style box at the left edge of the Formatting toolbar. Look at the Style box illustration at right.

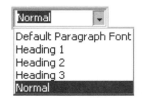

Most large documents make use of many different heading levels, just as a Roman-style outline has levels such as:

    I

        A

           1

              a

The levels are typically used to subordinate information under different subject headings. As you can see, Word accommodates this need by providing users with built-in heading styles named Heading 1, Heading 2, and so on.

The Importance of Styles

Styles are applied by placing the cursor on a heading or passage of text and then selecting the desired style name from the Formatting toolbar's Style dialog.

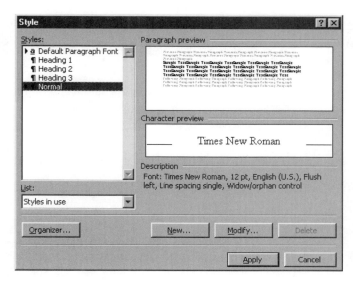

You can create styles of your own and add them. Just format a selection, highlight it, click on the style box, and type a descriptive style name. This can be saved to the global Normal.dot template using the Format|Style menu selection and corresponding dialogs. It's just as easy to change existing styles. For example, many users find the default 10-point font size is too small and change it to 12 points. You can also change the heading styles to suit your personal taste.

Applying heading styles is extremely important if you plan to use the Master Document and Outline views (see the View menu). The use of heading styles is also required when generating an automatic table of contents or table of figures (see Insert|Index and Tables), as Word relies on the style levels for format control.

You can also use the Style Gallery selection of the Format menu to select a supplied style for the creation of memos, fax sheets, letters, and more. Use Format|Style to add, delete, and change existing style templates.

Creating and Modifying Styles

Advanced topic

To create a style, simply format a paragraph using the desired margins, alignment, font, and font size selections. Then:

1. Select the paragraph by highlighting it with the mouse.

2. Use the **Format|Style** menu selection and click the **New** button to display the New Style dialog.

3. Type a meaningful name in the Name box and click **OK** in the first dialog. Click **Apply** to save the style, then click **Cancel** to discard it.

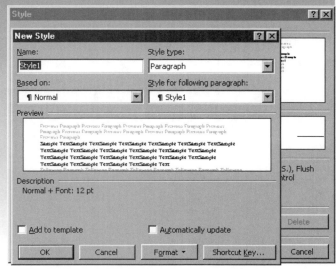

4. Change styles using the Style dialog's **Modify** button, which displays the following choices. (Notice that the **Format** button pick list is active.)

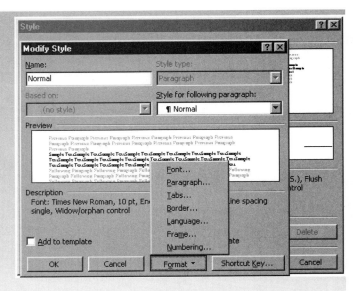

Use the Format button to modify the font, size, paragraph settings, borders, and more using corresponding dialogs. If you wish, you can use the Shortcut Key button to assign a shortcut key sequence to your new style. You can also use the Modify button to assign a shortcut key sequence to existing styles. This is intended as a time saver and is optional.

5. Once the format is set to your liking, click **OK** and check the format information in the Description area.

6. When finished, click the **Apply** button to save the style with the current document or click **Close** to avoid saving the style.

Style Creations Shortcut

You can also create a new style by selecting a paragraph containing the style parameters you want. Then:

1. Pick the Style box (left edge of the Format toolbar) with your mouse.

2. Type a meaningful style name.

3. Press <Enter> to finish adding the new style to your list.

Deleting a Style

Delete an unwanted style using the Format|Style selection. Just pick the style name in the Style dialog Styles list and click the Delete button. Finally, click Close to exit the dialog.

Copying Styles to Other Documents

You can use the Style dialog box to copy a new style to a template file. For example, you may want to put a Note title style in the Normal.dot template. Begin by opening the document in which the new style is available. Then open the Style dialog. Note that you can change the List setting to pick styles from different sources. When set, click the Organizer button to display the Organizer dialog box.

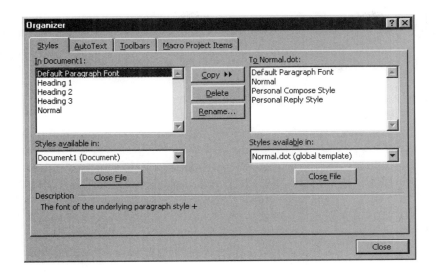

Pick the desired style name and click Copy to copy the style from the selected source document to the template. As you can see from the preceding dialog box illustration, you can also delete and rename styles here as well. Rename is often used to make a style name more descriptive or to eliminate conflicting names.

Fonts

Available fonts depend on the installed printer and Windows applications. If you are using Windows 95/98 with Microsoft TrueType fonts, you have a nice starter set. You can also install additional fonts by purchasing available font packs. Some applications, such as Microsoft Publisher and CorelDRAW!®, add many new fonts to Windows. If you have a PostScript printer, you may have several built-in printer fonts. Regardless of the installed printer, a type style usually requires several fonts to round out an entire font family. For example, you may have a normal, bold, and italic font. Therefore, Times New Roman normal, bold, and italic count as three fonts.

Fonts are changed by picking the font box and then pressing the Down Arrow to view a list of font names. Then pick the desired font name. You can type the first letter of a font, such as C, to move to the beginning of those fonts that start with the letter C. To change the font in an existing passage, simply highlight it and pick a new font name.

Font Sizes

Font sizes are increased or decreased using the Font Size box on the Formatting toolbar. The down arrow displays different numbers that correspond to point sizes (a point is 1/72 of an inch). You can pick a new size from the displayed list. You can also:

■ Increase the font size of a selected passage one point at a time with <Ctrl+]>.

■ Decrease the font size of a selected passage one point at a time with <Ctrl+[>.

Type Styles (or "Attributes")

Type attributes include normal, bold, italic, and underline. The default attribute setting is normal. You can change the attribute of existing text by selecting it (so that it is highlighted) and then clicking the B, I, or U button on the Formatting toolbar. If you are a keyboard person, you can also use one of the following key sequences to achieve the same result:

Ctrl+B	Boldface
Ctrl+I	Italic
Ctrl+U	Underline

To enter new text in the desired attribute, select the attribute button or key sequence and type the text. Click the button again or press the key sequence to turn off the attribute.

Changing Case

Word offers you a quick way to change uppercase to lowercase and initial capitals (first letter capitalized). To change case, select a passage of text and use the Format|Change Case menu selection to use the Change Case dialog. Or press <Shift+F3>. The first keypress changes the passage from all lowercase to an initial capital followed by lowercase. The second keypress changes it to all capitals. Pressing <Shift+F3> again changes the selection back to all lowercase.

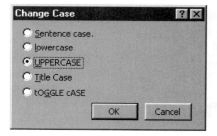

Hands-on Activity

In this activity you use the Sample2.doc file with the Font Style, Font, and Font Size commands described above.

1. Start Word and open the Sample2.doc file.

2. Use the **File|Page Setup** menu selection to set all margins to **1"** and click **OK**.

3. Press <**Ctrl+A**> to select all. Then click the **Font Size** down arrow on the Formatting toolbar and pick **12** points.

4. Put the cursor on the first paragraph. Pick the **Style** box, type **Norm12**, and press **Enter**.

5. Notice that Norm12 is displayed in the Style box at the left end of the Format toolbar.

Note: The Norm12 style is now attached to the Sample2.doc. If saved, it can be copied to the global Normal.dot template using the Format|Style menu selection's Organizer dialog.

6. Highlight the entire first paragraph of the document.

7. Click the **Arial** font (or another available font) on the Formatting toolbar. Notice how the paragraph changes.

8. With the passage still selected, pick **8** from the Font Size list. Notice how the font size of the selected passage changes.

9. Select the centered Sample2.doc title at the top of the first page, and press **<Shift+F3>** to change the case from uppercase to lowercase to initial capitals and then to uppercase again.

10. Exit Word with **<Alt+F4>** and pick the **No** button to avoid saving the changes.

Summary

This section introduced you to the style, font, and font size operations. It also showed you how to quickly change the case of a selected passage. In the next section you learn how Word is used to edit text, including copying and moving passages within a document or between documents.

Editing Text

Introduction

This section introduces you to basic editing features, including the commands used to insert, delete, move, and copy text. First, insert and delete are described. Then move and copy (or cut and paste) are presented. Following the descriptions, a hands-on activity guides you through actual use of these commands.

Insert and Overstrike

Word is normally in the insert mode. As text is typed, following text is pushed to the right and down. You can put Word into the overstrike mode by pressing the <Ins> or <Insert> key on the keyboard. OVR is displayed on the status bar at the bottom of the screen when in overstrike. Press <Ins> or <Insert> again to put Word back into the insert mode.

Cutting, Copying, and Pasting

Text is cut by selecting it and either using Edit|Cut or pressing <Ctrl+X>. This removes the selected passage from the screen and puts it on the Windows clipboard, from which it can be pasted. Similarly, text is copied to the clipboard by selecting it and either using Edit|Copy or pressing <Ctrl+C>. Copied text remains in the original position, while cut text is removed.

The clipboard is a designated portion of memory where cut or copied text or graphics are stored. Paste is used to insert the contents of the clipboard into a document or another Windows application. Text or a graphic image that resides on the clipboard is inserted into a document at the cursor position by using Edit|Paste or pressing <Ctrl+V>.

Text or a graphic image is moved or copied with these simple key sequences:

Ctrl+X	Cut
Ctrl+C	Copy
Ctrl+V	Paste

Delete

Delete a passage of text by selecting it and pressing <Del> or <Delete>. Delete one character at a time by putting the cursor on the character and pressing <Del>. You can delete words using the following sequences:

Ctrl+Del	Delete next word
Ctrl+Backspace	Delete previous word

Selecting Text

Select text by dragging it with the mouse. You can also select a word by double-clicking it. Paragraphs are selected by triple-clicking. You can select multiple words, lines, or paragraphs by holding <Shift> while moving the cursor with an arrow key or picking the different passages with your mouse. Marking text is accomplished by dragging it with the mouse or by holding the <Shift> key while pressing any key that moves the cursor including:

Home	left margin
End	right margin
PgUp	one screen up
PgDn	one screen down
Ctrl+PgUp	top of screen
Ctrl+PgDn	bottom of screen
Arrow key	up, down, left, or right
Ctrl+Home	top of file
Ctrl+End	bottom of file
Ctrl+Right Arrow	next word
Ctrl+Left Arrow	previous word
Ctrl+A	entire document

Shortcut Menu

You can display a shortcut editing menu by pressing the right mouse button. You can then pick the desired operation.

The shortcut menu is intended to save time, as it puts commonly used editing operations at your fingertips. It eliminates the need to move the mouse to the top of the document to pull down a menu.

Hands-on Activity

In this activity you use the insert, overstrike, cut, copy, and paste commands with the Sample2.doc file.

1. Start Word and open the Sample2.doc file.

2. Position the cursor at the beginning of the first line and type your name; notice how the following text is pushed ahead of the inserted text.

3. Press **<Home>** to move to the beginning of the line, then press **<Ins>** or **<Insert>** on the keyboard to put Word into the overstrike mode.

4. Retype your name and notice that the typed characters overstrike the existing ones.

5. Select the first paragraph (drag it with the mouse or use **<Shift+Down Arrow>**).

SAMPLE2.DOC

INTRODUCTION

This document complies to the default page setup and Normal style used by Microsoft® Word 2000. Although the primary purpose of this document is to provide users with two full pages of text for the purpose of format control, it also contains some useful information. For example, several word processing definitions are given.

NOTE

The following paragraphs define a number of typographic and word processing terms. If you are unfamiliar with typography, you may wish to read the text. Otherwise, use the document for its intended purpose—to practice format control.

6. Cut the selected passage with **<Ctrl+X>**; notice that it disappears.

SAMPLE2.DOC

INTRODUCTION

NOTE

The following paragraphs define a number of typographic and word processing terms. If you are unfamiliar with typography, you may wish to read the text. Otherwise, use the document for its intended purpose—to practice format control.

7. Move to the end of the document using **<Ctrl+End>**.

8. Paste the cut text from the clipboard with **<Ctrl+V>**; notice that it is inserted at the cursor position. (You have achieved a move operation.)

9. Select the paragraph immediately preceding the moved passage.

Tip: You can select lines and paragraphs by putting the mouse cursor outside the left margin until it turns into an arrow. Then click to select the line to the right. Drag to select multiple lines or double-click to select the paragraph.

10. Copy the selected passage as follows:

   a. Press **<Ctrl+C>** to copy the selected passage to the clipboard.

   b. Press **<Ctrl+Home>** to move to the beginning of the document.

   c. Press **<Ctrl+V>** to paste the copied passage from the clipboard.

11. Press **<Alt+F4>** and click **No** to exit Word without saving.

Summary

Word makes basic editing a breeze with the insert, delete, cut, copy, and paste functions. You will use these basic editing commands almost every time you create a new document. Practice their use until you are completely familiar with them.

Section 11 introduces you to those commands used to position and view text in different ways. The different views are important to those users who must stare at their screen for extended periods of time. You may find that you prefer one view over another. For example, if the toolbars and rulers are distracting, you may wish to work in the full-screen view, which hides the main menu, toolbars, and status bar so you can see more of the document.

Positioning and Viewing Text

Introduction

Word provides a number of document views. You can change the way a page is displayed using the View menu or the View buttons at the bottom left edge of the screen. In addition, toolbar buttons are available to change the view and size. When Word is started, it is usually in the Normal view. If you wish to look at the information in a different way, you can change the presentation by picking one of the following views from the View menu.

Note: View buttons are located on the View button toolbar at the bottom left side of the main view window.

 Normal—A WYSIWYG (what you see is what you get) presentation. Font styles and sizes, and line spacing are shown. This is a simple view and is used for most word processing tasks.

 Web Layout—Shows you the document layout (or a "map") in a pane at the left as well as the contents of the document at the right. This view is ideal for examining your document's organization including main topics.

Print Layout—A WYSIWYG view that allows you to see a replica of what the page will look like when printed. You can use View|Zoom (or the Zoom button) to change the size of the view.

Outline—An outline presentation showing different paragraph levels. This view displays the Outline toolbar used to select and change (expand or collapse) those levels displayed. To be most useful, the current documents should make use of styles. The Outline view is ideal for examining the structure of a document to ensure proper subordination. It is also useful for dragging and dropping one or more selected headings and/or paragraphs from one location to another.

Master Document—This view, available from the outline selection, is used for combining two or more subdocuments into a larger, multichapter master document. You can either view a skeleton of each of the subdocuments or the contents of the document by clicking a + or − button to expand or collapse the display. Master documents are presented in Section 27.

Toolbars—Turn toolbar displays off or back on with this selection. You can drag toolbars to the bottom, top, or a side using your mouse.

Ruler—Turn the ruler display off or back on with this selection.

Document Map—This view displays a pane at the left showing a map of your document. It retains the formatting of the current document view, unlike the Outline View, which wraps text to fit the right document pane.

Header and Footer—Used to create or edit headers and footers. These special features are presented in Section 17 of this book.

Footnotes—Display the document with footnotes (presented in Section 17). Footnotes are added using Insert|Footnotes.

Comments—Displays the document with user annotations (presented in Section 17). Comments are added using Insert|Comments.

Full Screen—This view removes menus, toolbars, and scroll bars from the screen, leaving only the document and a Full Screen button in the lower left-hand corner of the screen. Although the menus are hidden, you can still access them using the shortcut keys. Click the Full Screen button or press <Esc> to cancel the full screen view.

Zoom—Zooming changes the size of the page display. It is normally displayed at 100%; changing it to 75% displays more information, but it is smaller. You can manually set a zoom factor to one that suits your situation. Notice that you can also view multiple pages.

View Buttons—The four buttons at the left-hand edge of the horizontal scroll bar let you select the Normal, Web Layout, Print Layout, or Outline view.

Print Preview Button—This button, located on the Standard toolbar, displays the document as it would print.

Hands-on Activity

In this activity you display the Sample2.doc using a number of different views. You also insert a field using the **Insert|Field** menu selection.

1. Start Word and open the Sample2.doc file.

2. Click on the **View|Zoom** menu selection to display the document in various screen sizes.

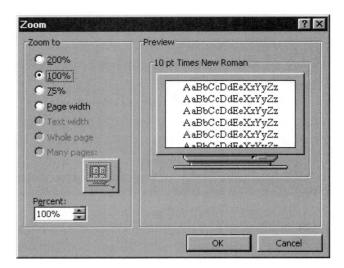

3. Click the **Show/Hide** button (¶) on the Standard toolbar to display hidden characters.

4. Pick the **View|Outline** menu selection and check the effect on the displayed document.

5. Pick the **View|Web Layout** menu selection and notice the changed display.

6. Click the **View|Print Layout** menu selection, then click the **View|Zoom** menu selection. Select the **Many Pages** button, pick **1 x 2**, and click **OK**.

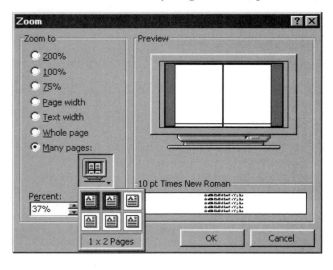

7. Notice how two pages are displayed side by side.

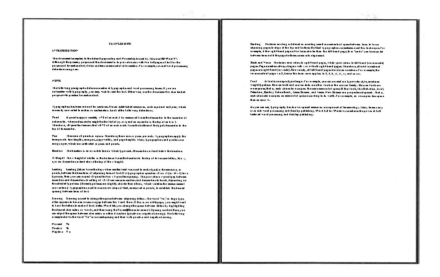

8. Now use **View|Zoom** and zoom to 100%.

   Click the **File|Print Preview** button on the toolbar then select the **Multiple Pages** button, drag **1 x 2 Pages**, and release the mouse button. Notice that both pages are displayed as with the **Many Pages** zoom.

9. Click the **Close** button to return to the Print Layout view.

Note: The **File|Print Preview** menu selection is enabled only when in the **View|Print Layout** view.

10. Return to normal view by selecting **View|Normal**.

11. Press **<Ctrl+End>** to move to the bottom of the document and proceed as follows to insert a derived calculation field:

   a. Click the **Insert|Field** menu selection to display the Field dialog box.

   b. Configure the Field dialog box to match the following selections and value in the Categories, Field Names, and Field Codes boxes.

   c. Click **OK**. Notice that the result of the equation and format code is displayed at the cursor position.

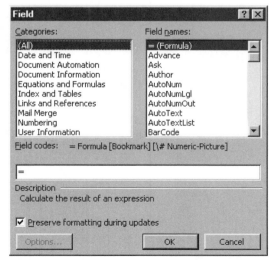

12. Select **View|Toolbars** and examine the available selections.

13. Select **View|Ruler** and notice how the ruler is hidden. Select it again to redisplay the ruler.

14. Press **<Alt+F4>** and click **No** to exit Word without saving the changes to the Sample2.doc file.

Summary

Word offers a huge repertoire of views. This capability lets you select a view that suits your personal taste. Or, you can change the views to put variety into your word processing tasks. If you didn't notice, the Insert|Field menu selection provides a powerful mathematical capability. You can type a wide range of mathematical expressions, giving you a built-in command line calculator. You can also use the Table|Formula menu selection to calculate the values within rows and columns of tables.

In the next section you learn about Word's tab types and how to set them. It is important to understand tabs and tab-related features, as they are key to the creation of tables, columnar editing, and formulas.

Using Tabs

Introduction

Tab stops, or simply "tabs," are used to control the alignment of text within a document. Word provides seven kinds of tabs. They are:

Standard (flush left) tab—Aligns text flush left at the tab stop.

Center tab—Centers text beneath the tab stop.

Flush right tab—Aligns text flush right at the tab stop.

Decimal tab—Aligns text on an embedded decimal point or period; typically used with financial tables.

Bar tab—Places a vertical bar at the tab position.

First Line Indent tab—Indents the first line of a paragraph.

Hanging Indent tab—Indents each line of text; commonly used for glossary terms, bibliographical entries, and bulleted and numbered lists.

The left edge of the ruler displays a Tab button, which is changed by clicking it. Each click displays one of these seven tab types in the order listed:

> Standard (Align Left) tab
> Align Center tab
> Align Right tab
> Decimal tab
> Bar tab
> First Line Indent tab
> Hanging Indent tab

Setting Tabs

Notice how the ruler displays a preset tab stop every one-half inch. These are represented by a vertical line as shown in the following illustration. You can change the preset (or default) tab stops using the Format|Tabs menu selection or by double-clicking on the ruler to access the Tabs dialog box.

Using the Mouse

You can click the Tab button to display the desired tab type. Then use the mouse pointer and click on the ruler where you want the tab to appear. When this is done, all preceding tab stops are removed and the selected tab becomes the first one on the ruler. Look at the following ruler, which illustrates the insertion of a single flush left tab at the 2-inch position on the ruler.

If you change your mind, you can drag unwanted tabs below the ruler to remove them. You can drag tabs right or left to change a position.

Using the Format/Tabs Menu Selection

The Format|Tabs menu selection lets you put tabs on the ruler using precise dimensions rather than picking points with the mouse. For example, you may wish to set a decimal tab every 1.5 inches. The Tabs dialog box shown here illustrates this.

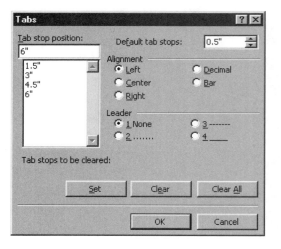

Notice the Tab stop position box. Here, you can set different tab stops at specific locations. Simply pick the tab type button and type a position. The above example shows the dialog box with a different type of tab set at 1.5, 3, 4.5, and 6 inches. Note that as you set each tab, you can pick the tab type and position and click the Set button. When all tabs are set, click OK to complete the job.

If you wish to return to the default settings, use the Clear All button on the Tabs dialog box. To clear individual tabs, select the tab in the Tab stop position box and click the Clear button.

Hands-on Activity

In this activity you use different techniques for setting and removing tab stops. You also use different tab types to determine their effect.

1. Start Word and display a blank document (Document1).

2. Check the tab settings on the ruler and notice that a tab is set at every one-half inch. Also notice that the flush left tab type is automatically selected.

3. Use your mouse to place a flush left tab at the 1.75-inch mark on the ruler.

4. Click the **Tab** button twice to display the flush right tab type and place a tab at the 3.25-inch mark.

5. Select the decimal tab type; then place a tab at the 5-inch mark. Your ruler should resemble the following illustration.

6. **Tab** to each tab stop and type the indicated text as shown in the following illustration. (Press **<Enter>** at the end of each line following the number.)

Note: The tab arrows are made visible by clicking the Show/Hide button ¶.

7. Pick the **Format|Tabs** menu selection to display the Tabs dialog box. Check to see if yours matches the following illustration.

	Row·1 → Flush·right·1		1234.56¶
	Row·2 → Flush·right·2		2345.67¶
	Row·3 → Flush·right·3		456.78¶

8. Press the **<Down Arrow>** and notice how the Alignment buttons change to match the tab type. Now press **<Esc>** and use **<Ctrl+A>** to select all text.

9. Use the **Format|Tabs** menu selection to redisplay the Tabs dialog box. Click the **Clear All** button to clear all tab stops. Then reset the tab stops by typing new values in the Tab stop position box, clicking the corresponding **Alignment** button, and then clicking the **Set** button for each, using the following table as a guide.

Tab Stop Position	Alignment
1.5"	Left
3.0"	Right
4.5"	Decimal

10. Compare your Tabs dialog box to the following illustration. You can click on the different tab stop position values to determine the alignment type.

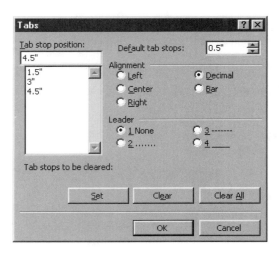

11. Click **OK** to apply the new tab settings to the selected text.

12. Press **<Alt+F4>** and click **No** to exit Word without saving the document.

Summary

Word gives you a variety of tab types and makes it easy to set and modify them. You can use the mouse and tab buttons, or if you prefer, you can use the Tabs dialog box to establish precise tab positions. In either case, the ruler shows you exactly where each tab is located; the different tab symbols designate the type of tab.

Tabs are vital in the creation and adjustment of tables. In the next section, you learn more about how tabs are applied to the design of sophisticated tables.

Section 13

Tabs and Tables

Introduction

In the previous section you learned how to set tab stops. You also learned about the types of tabs available within Word. In this section you learn the relationship of tabs to table creation and editing.

Creating Tables

A table is simply information arranged in rows and columns. Word creates tables in four ways:

- Insert Table button
- Insert Table dialog box (Table|Insert Table menu selection)
- Tables and Borders button
- Table|Convert Text to Table menu selection

Using the Insert Table Button

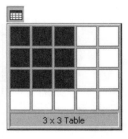

To use the Insert Table button, drag the desired number of rows and columns, and release the button. A blank table is inserted at the cursor position.

Using the Insert Table Dialog Box

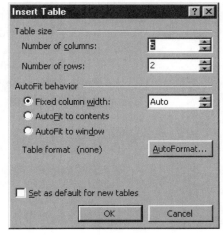

This dialog box lets you tell Word how many columns and rows you want. You can set the width of each column by entering the desired value. You can also use the default (Auto), which divides the table into columns of equal width between the established page margins.

You can use the AutoFormat button if you want to use a stored format. You can also use the Table menu's Table AutoFormat selection to apply one of the stored formats to an existing table. The Table AutoFormat dialog is shown on the following page.

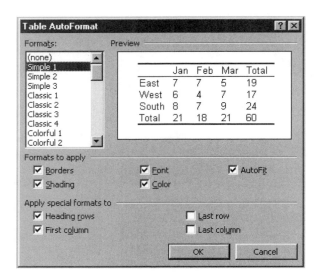

Using the Tables and Borders Dialog and the Table Draw Tool

Click the Tables and Borders button  to display the Tables and Borders dialog.

The Draw Table (pencil) tool is used to draw the outside border of a table as well as interior row and column lines. Use the Eraser tool to remove unwanted rows or columns. Other tools are available to split or merge cells, redistribute rows and columns, align text, apply a stored format (AutoFormat), fill one or more cells with a background color, sort the data, enter a formula, and rotate the table text.

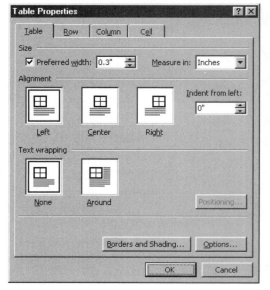

The best way to appreciate the power of this tool is to experiment with it on a scratch document. Just open a blank document and draw a table on the page. Then experiment with the buttons to determine their use. The Table tab of the Table Properties dialog contains useful controls for aligning and wrapping text in table cells. Also, the Row, Column, and Cell tabs contain controls for setting row height, column width, and cell text vertical alignment.

Clicking on the Borders and Shading button on the Table tab will open the following dialog box. Play around with the various shading and border options to determine which combination of borders and shading yields a pleasing appearance. If you want to only include a portion of a border, enable or disable sections by clicking on the border line controls on the left side of the dialog box.

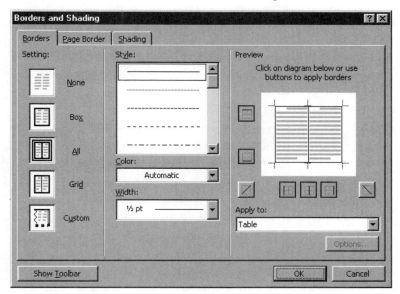

After you are finished playing on the scratch document, you can close it without saving it, if desired.

Using the Convert Text to Table Dialog Box

If you have tabular text or numbers in which columns are separated by tabs, you can select the tabular text and then use the Table|Convert Text to Table menu selection to bring up the Convert Text to Table dialog.

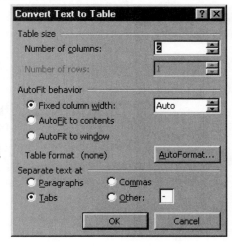

After checking the setup, click OK to convert the tabular text to a table. Gridlines are displayed to show the boundaries between rows and columns. You can drag the column widths with the mouse to readjust the column widths visually. The Auto selection divides the column widths evenly between the margins.

Note that the column separator (or delimiter) is a tab. You must be consistent in the way that you use tabs. Try to have the same number of column entries in each row and separate each column using a tab. Variances in the number of tabs used yield unexpected results. Convert Text to Table changes to Convert Table to Text so you can restore the original text.

The Table Menu

Now that you know about table creation, it is appropriate to examine the Table menu a little more closely. Each menu selection is briefly described. Note that menu entries vary to correspond with what is currently selected in your document. Therefore, the menu illustration here may be slightly different from what you see on your screen. Also, several menu choices are ghosted until a table exists and is selected.

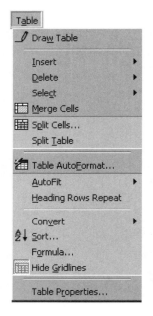

Draw Table—This menu item displays the Tables and Borders dialog with the Draw Table tool selected. Use it to sketch the table borders and interior rows and columns on the page.

Insert Table—This menu line is hidden and is displayed by highlighting the Table|Insert menu item. When displayed, it is used to create a table from the Insert Table dialog. Simply specify the rows, columns, and column width.

Insert Rows/Columns/Cells—This menu item is hidden and is displayed by highlighting the Table|Insert menu item. Note that Cells is visible when the down arrow of the submenu is highlighted. This menu item changes to correspond to what is selected, i.e., a row, column, or cell. A cell is a single row-column intersection. This entry is used to insert a new row, column, or cell. You can also add new rows or columns by selecting a row or column and clicking the Table button. New rows and columns are also added when copied and pasted. Finally, new rows are added to the bottom of a table by moving to the rightmost column in the last row and pressing Tab.

Delete Table—This menu line is hidden and is displayed by highlighting the Table|Delete menu item, then by clicking the down arrow at the bottom of the menu. It is used to delete a table.

Delete Rows/Columns/Cells—This menu item is hidden and is displayed by highlighting the Table|Delete menu item. As with Insert, this menu item also changes to correspond to what is selected. It is used to delete a selected row, column, or cell. You can also select and cut a row or column to remove it from a table.

Select Row—Select the entire row in which the cursor is located.

Select Column—Select the entire column in which the cursor is located.

Select Table—Select the entire table (or press Alt+Num Pad 5).

Merge Cells—Use this selection to combine the contents of two or more selected cells into a single cell.

Split Cells—Use this selection to separate a merged cell.

Split Table—Separate the table in two at the current row position. A return is inserted to split the table.

Table AutoFormat—Display the AutoFormat dialog box for stored table format selection.

Distribute Rows Evenly—Distribute selected rows evenly.

Distribute Columns Evenly—Distribute selected columns evenly; if the entire table is selected, distributes all columns evenly from border to border.

Cell Height and Width—Adjust the height and/or width of rows and columns and set the alignment and indentation of interior text. The resulting dialog box is also used to allow or prevent rows from breaking across pages.

Headings—Turn the table heading attribute on or off. This automatically repeats the table heading at the top of subsequent pages.

Convert Text to Table—This selection converts a selected passage of tabular text into a table. When a table is selected, this selection changes to Convert Table to Text.

Sort—Performs an alphanumeric sort which is ideal for directories and indexes. You can sort in either ascending or descending order. The sort is based on the text in the selected column.

Formula—Insert a formula, such as =SUM(ABOVE) or =AVG(LEFT), to perform mathematical calculations. Also lets you pick a format for the calculated result.

Hide/Show Gridlines—Turn the gridlines on or off. Gridlines are used to visually separate rows and columns.

Changing Row Heights and Column Widths

Row heights and column widths are adjusted in several ways. First, you can change the dimensions of a row or column using the Table|Table Properties| Row and Column dialog boxes. The height and/or width is adjusted using the Row and Column dialog boxes by activating the appropriate dialog box and changing the row height or column width values.

You can also change the row height or column width using the mouse to drag a column's right-hand boundary or a row's bottom boundary. When you move the mouse to the vertical division point of a table, the cursor changes to a double arrowhead.

Hands-on Activity

In this activity you create a table in two different ways: by using the Insert Table button and by preparing a block of tabular text and converting it to a table. Then, you use the Border button to add a border and interior rules.

1. Start Word and display a blank document (Document1).

2. Use **File|Page Setup** to set all margins to **1"**.

3. Press **<Enter>** twice. Then click the **Table** button 🏢 to create a 3 x 3 table.

4. Use **Table|Table Properties** to bring up the Table Properties tab. Click on the Column tab and set the column widths to **1.5"** as shown in the illustration at right. Use the **Width of Column** and the **Next Column** button to adjust the width of all three columns.

5. Click **OK** and notice how the column widths adjust to 1.5 inches.

6. Type the text shown below, using **<Tab>** to move to the next cell. (The special characters are displayed by clicking the Show/Hide button on the toolbar.)

8	1 x 4 x 8	Yellow Pine
2	2 x 2 x 8	Yellow Pine
4	3-0 x 6-8	Hollow Core Door

7. Position the cursor within the table and use the **Table|Select Table** menu selection to select the entire table.

8. With the table highlighted, click the **Tables and Borders** button 🔲 on the Standard toolbar to display the Tables and Borders toolbar.

9. Use the **Line Style** and **Outside Border** buttons to put ¾-point outside dotted line borders in place of the existing outside solid line borders. Close the Tables and Borders toolbar.

Tip: You can also use the **Format|Borders and Shading** dialog box to accomplish this task.

10. Insert a row above the first one as follows:
    a. Put the cursor in the first column of the first row.
    b. Select the **TableInsert|Rows Above** menu selection.
    c. Move to the first column of row 1. Then insert column headings as follows: **<Ctrl+I>** type **Quantity <Tab> <Ctrl+I>** type **Description <Tab><Ctrl+I>** type **Material**.

Quantity	Description	Material
8	1 x 4 x 8	Yellow Pine
2	2 x 2 x 8	Yellow Pine
4	3-0 x 6-8	Hollow Core Door

11. Use the mouse and drag the right edge of the first column until it is at the .75-inch mark on the ruler. (You can also do this by dragging the column pad on the ruler.)

12. With the cursor in the first row, use the **Table|Delete|Cells** menu selection, click the **Delete Entire Row** button, and click **OK** to delete the first row.

13. Press **<Ctrl+End>** to move to the end of the document and press **<Enter>** twice.

14. Set a left tab at 1 inch and a decimal tab at 3 inches on the ruler.

15. Create the following table by pressing **<Tab>** between each column and **<Enter>** at the end of each line:

Date	Description	Amount
10/21/99	Airfare	266.00
10/21/99	Taxi	22.00
10/21/99	Dinner	16.55
10/21/99	Hotel	108.68

16. Select the table (drag the mouse down the left margin until all rows are highlighted).

17. Use **Table|Convert|Text to Table** to create a table from the tabular text. The Convert Text to Table dialog box is displayed.

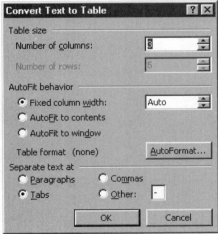

18. Select **Table|Table AutoFormat**, pick **Classic 2**, and then click **OK** twice.

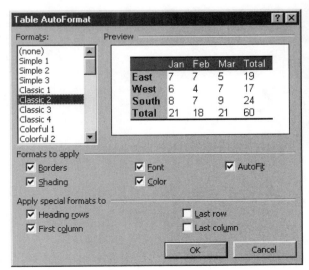

19. Observe the resulting table.

Date	Description	Amount
10/21/99	Airfare	266.00
10/21/99	Taxi	22.00
10/21/99	Dinner	16.55
10/21/99	Hotel	108.68

20. Press **<Alt+F4>** and click **No** to close the document without saving.

Summary

In this section you learned how easily tables are created and modified. You also experienced the power of the Tables and Borders dialog. You can experiment with the other Table menu features by creating a sample table and testing the effect of the other buttons in this dialog. In the next section you continue your encounter with tabs by learning how they are used to create dot leaders.

Section 14

Tabs and Dot Leaders

Introduction

This section continues your encounter with tabs by showing you how they are used in conjunction with leaders, especially dot leaders. A dot leader is a row of dots or dashes that is inserted between two text elements. For example, a table of contents page often uses a dot leader between a chapter name and the corresponding page number. It "leads" the eye across the page to ensure that you visually connect corresponding elements. Look at the following contents excerpt.

Section	Description	Page
1	About This Book	1
2	A Guided Tour	3
3	Creating, Loading, and Saving Files	9
4	Formatting Pages, Paragraphs, and Sections	15

Setting Up Dot Leaders

Dot leaders are set up with the Tabs dialog box, which is called from the Format|Tabs menu selection or by double-clicking on the ruler. In addition to assigning the tab

type, you can use this dialog box to attach one of four leader attributes to a selected tab. The Tabs dialog box setup for the preceding example is shown at right.

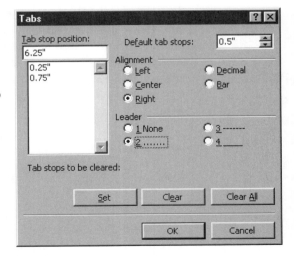

Notice that the third tab, which is set up for right alignment, is also set for a dot-style leader (the second leader type). You can establish or change the alignment and leader attribute of any selected tab using this dialog box, then click OK (or press <Enter>) to accept the settings. If you need to change the position or attribute of a tab, simply re-enter the dialog box and make your changes.

Hands-on Activity

Use this hands-on activity to see just how easy it is to create and modify dot leaders.

1. Start Word and display a blank document (Document1).

Note: You can look at the finished table shown after step 8 to better understand the purpose of each of the following steps.

2. Use the **File|Page Setup|Margins** menu selection and set all margins to **1"**.

3. Center the word "Contents" in boldface on the first line: **<Ctrl+B> <Ctrl+E> Contents <Ctrl+B> <Enter> <Ctrl+L> <Enter>**.

4. Open the Tabs dialog box using the **Format|Tabs** menu selection and set the tabs as follows, clicking **OK** when done:

Position	Alignment	Leader
.25"	Center	1 None
1.5"	Left	1 None
3.25"	Center	1 None
6.25"	Center	1 None

Note: The tabs you are about to set are valid at the current cursor position and any additional lines following the current cursor position if the line was created by pressing Enter on the keyboard after creating the tabs. In other words, if you create the tabs at some cursor position, then skip down to some other line previously created, you will not find the tabs as they will not exist for that line. Create the tabs at the cursor position you intend to use them.

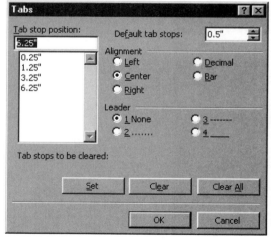

5. Enter column headings as follows: **<Tab> <Ctrl+I> Section <Tab> <Tab> Description <Tab> Page <Ctrl+I> <Enter>**.

6. Use your mouse to drag the tab located at 3.25" down and off the ruler.

7. Use the **Format|Tabs** menu selection to reopen the Tabs dialog box. Then pick the 6.25" tab, click the **2** (dots) Leader button, and click **OK**.

8. Type the information shown in the body of the following table of contents example, pressing **<Tab>** before each typed entry. Notice how the dot leader is automatically inserted when you tab to the last tab stop (located at 6.25").

Contents

Section	Description	Page
1	Description 1
2	Unpacking and Installation 3
3	Operating Instructions 4
4	Theory of Operation 11
5	Maintenance Instructions 28
6	Parts List 34
7	Index. 37

9. Press **<Alt+F4>** and click **No** to exit Word without saving the document.

Summary

With this section behind you, you should have a good background in the use of tab stops and tables. In the next section you learn how to find and replace selected passages of text. This is an invaluable Word capability that every serious user should understand and use.

Finding and Replacing Text

Introduction

This section introduces you to a powerful and frequently used word processing feature—that of searching for a specified word, text passage, number, symbol, paragraph style, etc. The search (or find) text is often referred to as the *find string*. You can also specify a replacement string. In addition to finding conventional characters and numbers, you can also find special characters and symbols, such as tabs and paragraph symbols. You can even use *wildcards,* or substitution characters (such as ? and *), in your search strings.

The Edit|Find Menu Selection

The **Edit|Find** menu selection displays the Find and Replace dialog.

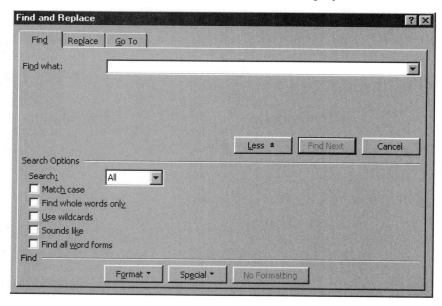

This dialog box is also displayed using <Ctrl+F>, <Ctrl+H> for Replace, or <Ctrl+G> for Go To. Notice the Replace and Go To tabs. Also notice that you can click a More or Less button to display or hide the search options. Each of the Search options within the Find and Replace dialog box is explained on the following page.

Find what:—Accepts the characters or word you want to find.

Search: (Up/Down/All)—Search forward (from cursor position down) or backward (from cursor position up), or search entire document.

Match case—Find only those words that match the upper- and lowercase of the Find What value exactly as typed.

Find whole words only—Eliminate interior strings, such as *the* in the word *their*, from the search specification.

Use wildcards—Check this box if you intend to use question marks or asterisks (? and *) as wildcards. This lets you search variations of the same text string. For example, th??e finds three, those, and there. St. * finds all words like St. Paul, St. Petersburg, St. Croix, and St. Augustine. In addition to being able to use conventional wildcards, other pattern matching symbols are also available. See Finding Special Characters later in this section.

Sounds like—This check box helps you find words that sound like the search string. For example, you can find merchandise and merchandize, color and colour, and Ann and Anne.

Find all word forms—Replace different word forms such as "walk" with "run" and "walking" with "running."

Find Next button—Click to find the next occurrence of the find string.

Cancel button—Click (or press <Esc>) to cancel the find operation and return to the document.

More/Less button—Click to display or hide search options and the No Formatting, Format, and Special buttons.

No Formatting button—This button is active when the Find what string is formatted as bold, italic, and/or underline. (You can apply standard character formats to your search strings.) When clicked, it removes all formatting from the search string.

Format button—Pick a font, paragraph setup (alignment, indentation, etc.), language attribute, or style (normal, Heading 1, etc.). This isolates the Find what string to more specific parameters, eliminating unwanted finds from the operation.

Special button—Pick special symbols (such as tabs and paragraph marks), annotations, graphics, and much more from a displayed list.

The Edit|Find and Edit|Replace Menu Selections

The Edit|Find menu selection (or the Find folder of the Find and Replace dialog) is used to display the Find options. Find Next lets you find the next occurrence from the cursor of the "Find what:" value. The More button allows you to choose search criteria such as case and wildcards.

The Edit|Replace menu selection (or the Replace folder of the Find and Replace dialog) is used to display the Replace options. Replace lets you replace the "Find what:" value with a "Replace with:" value. The Replace dialog is shown here.

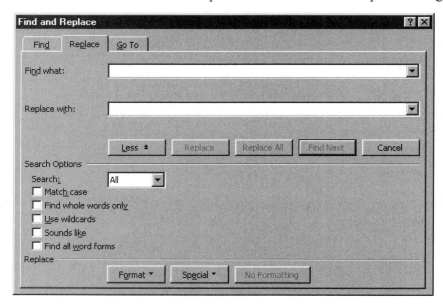

Pressing <Ctrl+H> also displays this dialog box. Notice that this dialog adds three additional features to the Find dialog box:

Replace with:—Enter the replacement string here.

Replace button—Click to replace the current find.

Replace All button—Click to replace every occurrence of the search string without user intervention.

Finding Special Characters (Advanced Search Criteria)

You can find special characters and use wildcards with Word's Find and Replace operations using the Special button to display special characters. In addition to these, Word features advanced search criteria used for what is often referred to as *pattern matching.* Check Use wildcards to take advantage of the pattern matching feature.

Character	Description
?	Wildcard for a single character; **ca?** finds the words cab, cad, cat, etc.; not available in Replace.
*	Find a string; **t*e** finds the, these, those, tease, tee, etc.
[ ]	Find one of the specified characters; **sh[ou]t** finds shot or shut.
[-]	Find a single character within a range; **[b-e]at** finds bat, cat, dat, and eat.
{n}	Find exactly *n* occurrences of the preceding character string; **re{2}?** finds reed and reel but not red.
{n,}	Find at least *n* occurrences of the preceding character string; **re{1,}?** finds reed, reel, and red.
{n,m}	Find from *n* to *m* occurrences of the character or string; **3{1,4}** finds 30, 300, 3000, and 30000.

@	Find one or more occurrences of the previous character or string; **ho@t** finds hot and hoot.
<(beg)	Find the beginning of a word; **<(pre)** finds words like prefix, prepare, and previous.
(end)>	Find the end of a word; **(ing)>** finds words like dining, thing, sing, sting, etc.
*	Find the asterisk character; to find an asterisk, precede it with the backslash character to prevent it from being interpreted as a wildcard.
\2\1	Used in the Replace with box; to transpose the expression **also ran** to **ran also**, type **(also)(ran)** in the Find what box and **\2\1** in the Replace with box.

Hands-on Activity

In this activity you use Find and Replace operations to familiarize yourself with how they work.

1. Start Word; use **File|Open** to open the Sample2.doc file.

2. Press **<Ctrl+F>** to open the Find and Replace dialog and type **the** in the Find what area.

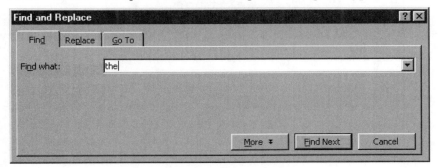

   Click the **Find Next** button several times until the words *Otherwise* and *Therefore* are found. Then click the **Cancel** button.

3. Press **<Ctrl+Home>** to return to the top of the file. Repeat step 2, only this time click on the **More** button, then put a check mark in the **Find whole words only** check box. Notice how *Otherwise* and *Therefore* are skipped. Click **Cancel**.

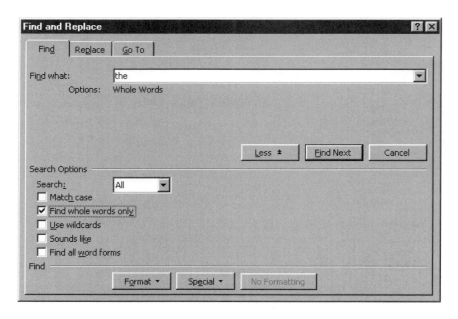

4. Press **<Ctrl+F>** and locate a paragraph mark (created by pressing <Enter>). Click **More|Special** and select **Paragraph Mark** from the pick list to put ^p in the **Find what** box. Click the **Find Next** button. Notice how the found paragraph mark is highlighted. Click the **Cancel** button and then press **<Ctrl+Home>** to return to the top of the document.

The paragraph mark (¶) appears as the control code ^p in the Find what: text box of the Find and Replace dialog.

Paragraph Mark
Tab Character
Comment Mark
Any Character
Any Digit
Any Letter
Caret Character
Column Break
Em Dash
En Dash
Endnote Mark
Field
Footnote Mark
Graphic
Manual Line Break
Manual Page Break
Nonbreaking Hyphen
Nonbreaking Space
Optional Hyphen
Section Break
White Space

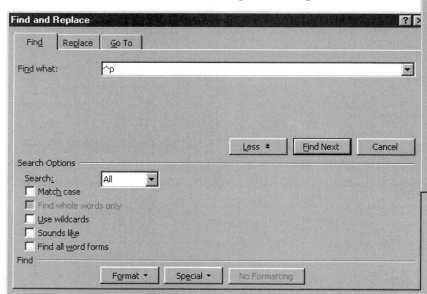

5. Use **Edit|Replace** (or press **<Ctrl+H>**) to replace *the* with *thx*: Type **the** in the **Find what** box and type **thx** in the **Replace with** box.

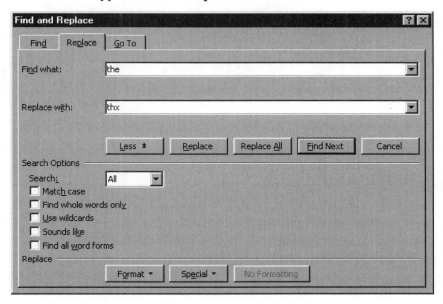

Then click the **Replace All** button. Word replaces the words and displays a message box saying Word has finished searching the document and 64 replacements were made. Click **OK** and then click the **Close** button. Notice how occurrences of *the* are replaced with *thx*. (You can press **<Ctrl+Z>** to undo the replace operation.)

6. Press **<Alt+F4>** and click **No** to exit Word without saving any changes.

Summary

In this section you experimented with a powerful set of tools—the Find and Replace operations. These tools are ideal for making changes that affect the entire document, particularly if it is large.

In the next section you learn how to insert a variety of elements into your documents including page breaks, page numbers, special symbols, and dates and times.

Inserting Page Breaks, Page Numbers, Bookmarks, Symbols, and Dates

Introduction

This section guides you through some uses of the Insert menu. In particular, you learn how to insert page breaks, page numbers, special symbols, and dates and times into your documents.

The Insert Menu

The Insert menu, shown here, includes a number of selections. Once you know its uses, a substantial amount of power is placed at your fingertips.

This section deals with a few of the Insert menu's capabilities. Following sections address the remainder of the menu items. Below is a list of what each of the menu selections does. Then a hands-on activity guides you through the use of several of these.

Break—Inserts a page break, column break, or section break at the current cursor position.

Page Numbers—Inserts a page number and controls the format, position, and value.

Date and Time—Inserts the current date and/or time. Pick the format from a list.

AutoText—Inserts frequently used words, names, or titles or displays the AutoCorrect dialog. AutoCorrect automatically corrects common typographical errors, automatically numbers lists, replaces certain strings with equivalent symbols, such as (r) with ®, and much more.

Field—Inserts selected information (from a pick list) at the current document location. Used to merge an equation, table of contents, index, selected data in another file, etc., into the current document.

Symbol—Inserts a selected symbol from a displayed list of fonts and a corresponding symbol table.

Comment—Inserts a comment and activates the *comment pane*, in which a comment can be recorded about a selected passage. Double-clicking a comment symbol displays the corresponding comment. Word automatically assigns sequential comment numbers as each is added.

Footnote—Inserts a footnote reference at the current cursor position.

Caption—Inserts a figure or table caption above or below a selected object.

Cross-reference—Cross references headings, bookmarks, footnotes, endnotes, equations, figures, and tables to corresponding items such as page numbers, paragraph numbers, heading numbers, captions, footnote and endnote numbers, etc.

Index and Tables—Used to create and edit an index, table of contents, table of figures, or table of authorities (bibliography-style references).

Picture—Inserts a picture (graphic file) into the displayed document.

Text Box—Inserts a text box (framed text) within a document. Ideal for sidebars in newsletters and brochures.

File—Inserts a named file at the current cursor position; displays a pick list of filenames.

Object—Inserts a picture, equation, drawing, chart, worksheet, or another object from other applications.

Bookmark—Inserts a reference point in a document. Once inserted, use Edit|Go To to jump to a selected bookmark.

Hyperlink—Applies a hyperlink to a selected passage of text within the current document. Hyperlinks provide direct access to web sites on the Internet.

Bookmarks

You can insert one or more invisible bookmarks into your documents using the Insert|Bookmark menu. A bookmark can be a letter, number, or passage of your choice. The Bookmark dialog box lets you add or delete bookmarks as needed. Once a bookmark is established, use Edit|Go To (or press <Ctrl+G>) to select and "jump" directly to the designated bookmark. You create and use a bookmark in the following hands-on activity.

Hands-on Activity

In this activity you load the Sample2.doc file and insert a number of elements into the document.

1. Start Word and open Sample2.doc.

SAMPLE2.DOC

INTRODUCTION

This document complies to the default page setup and Normal style used by Microsoft® Word 2000. Although the primary purpose of this document is to provide users with two full pages of text for the purpose of format control, it also contains some useful information. For example, several word processing definitions are given.

2. Move to the blank line following the centered title "Sample2.doc" and insert the current date as follows:

   a. Click **Insert|Date and Time** to display a pick list.

   b. Pick a date format you like, such as Month, Day, Year (or Day, Month, Year if you're outside the U.S.), and click **OK**.

   c. Notice how the system date is inserted at the current cursor position.

3. Use **Insert|Page Numbers** to place page numbers at the bottom right of each page; your Page Numbers dialog box should look like the following one before clicking **OK**.

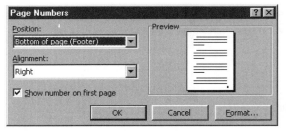

4. Press **<Ctrl+End>** to move to the bottom of page 2; then press **<PgDn>** until the page number (page 2) comes into view to verify that page numbers have been inserted.

Note: The Format button within the Page Numbers dialog box displays a Page Number Format dialog box. Use this box to change the page number style, i.e., 1, 2, 3; A, B, C; i, ii, iii; etc., and to start the page number sequence at a value greater than 1.

5. Move to the beginning of the word "Kerning" near the bottom of the first page. Press **<Ctrl+Enter>** and notice that you have inserted a manual page break. (You can also use **Insert|Break** to display the Break dialog box as an alternate method.)

6. Select the text of the NOTE near the beginning of the document.

7. Use the **Insert|Bookmark** menu selection and enter **note** in the Bookmark name text box. Click **Add**; this establishes a bookmark named "note."

8. Press **<Ctrl+End>** to move to the bottom of the document. Now jump back to the bookmark named "note" by pressing **<Ctrl+G>** (for Go To), pick **Bookmark** from the list, check that "note" is displayed, and click **Go To**.

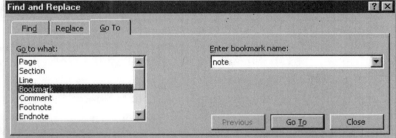

9. Click **Close** to exit the Find and Replace dialog.

10. Press **<Ctrl+End>** to jump to the bottom of the document. Press **<Enter>** twice. Now insert the pound sterling symbol as follows:

    a. Use **Insert|Symbol**, select "(normal text)" in the Font text box, and choose the £ symbol (on my screen it is the fourth row, fourteenth column). Click **Insert** and press **<Esc>** to close the dialog box.

    b. Notice how the £ symbol is inserted at the cursor position.

11. Press **<Alt+F4>** and click **No** to exit Word without saving the changes to your document.

Summary

In this section you learned some important capabilities of the Insert menu in addition to a bit about bookmarks. The next section continues the explanation about this menu by showing you how to use footnotes, endnotes, and comments. You also learn the use of headers and footers, which are accessed from the View menu.

Headers, Footers, Footnotes, Endnotes, and Comments

Introduction

A footnote or endnote is normally a reference to a supporting item, such as a book or magazine article. A superscript number is inserted following a footnoted or endnoted word or phrase. A corresponding number and descriptive information are typed in the footnote or endnote box. Footnotes are placed at the bottom of a page, while endnotes are placed at the end of the document.

A comment (formerly called *annotation*) is a note to yourself; your initials and a sequential number are assigned to each comment and are displayed in brackets within the document. The comment text is displayed when it is created or when you double-click on the comment reference. However, because comments are for your personal use, the text is displayed but not printed.

Footnotes, endnotes, and comments are numbered sequentially and provide a box in which you can type or edit the corresponding text. Footnotes, endnotes, and comments are created using the Insert menu. Insert|Footnote places a superscript (elevated) footnote/endnote number at the current cursor position and displays the dialog box shown here.

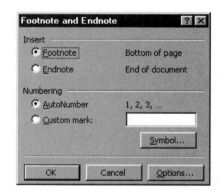

Notice that you can designate the entry as either a footnote or endnote. You can also customize the numbering sequence and use special symbols with the radio buttons on the Footnote and Endnote dialog box. Once you click OK, you are placed at the footnote/endnote text entry position.

Similarly, Insert|Comment places a comment reference such as [MB1], which is my initials with the comment number, at the current cursor position. To display or edit a footnote, endnote, or comment, simply double-click on the footnote/endnote/comment reference within the body of your document.

When a comment is inserted, a text entry window is displayed at the bottom of the screen. You can type the text of the comment here. A comment box, with the user initials and a sequential number, is inserted in the text. You can double-click the comment box to display the comments text window at the bottom of the screen. Within this window you can edit existing comments. If you delete a footnote or comment, highlight the comment or footnote reference and press the <Del> key. The sequence numbers are automatically adjusted as necessary.

Notice the yellow speaker in the comment text box. The speaker signifies there is an audio comment included with the text comment. By clicking on the cassette button located just left of the Close button, you may insert audio comments. Also, note the text where the comment is inserted is now highlighted in yellow.

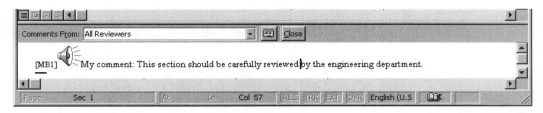

Headers and Footers

Headers and footers are used to put such information as document or chapter titles or page numbers at the top or bottom of each page. The *running head* at the top of this page is an example of a header.

The View|Header and Footer menu selection is used to create headers and footers. A header is displayed and printed at the top of your page, while a footer is positioned at the bottom. Both headers and footers are in the margin area and do not reduce the text area of your document.

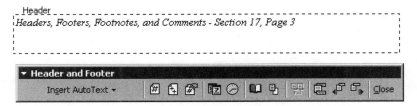

Headers can be the same on all pages, can vary between left- and right-hand pages, or between sections within a document, or can be omitted from the first page of a document. Controls for these variations are available in the Layout section of the Page Setup dialog box. There is a Page Setup button in the Header and Footer toolbar, or you can use the File|Page Setup menu selection to display the same dialog box.

Tip: If your header or footer information does not print, go to File|Page Setup and change the top and bottom margins, as required, to at least .7".

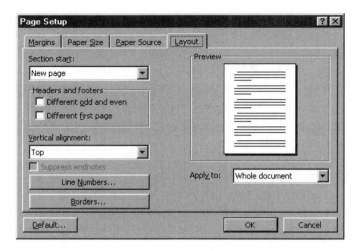

When a document is viewed in the Normal mode, the header/footer text is not displayed. In the Page Layout mode, header and footer text is displayed in light gray. You can double-click on header or footer text to activate and edit it; This will make the body text of your document grayed. Click Close to return to the document.

Hands-on Activity

In this activity you create a header and a footnote. Footers and comments use similar procedures, so you can adapt what you learn here to footers and comments. The activity makes use of the Sample2.doc file.

1. Start Word and open the Sample2.doc file.

2. Use **View| Page Layout** to display the document in the Page Layout view.

3. Use **View|Header and Footer**; notice the Header entry window.

4. Enter **Sample2.doc, Page**, press **Spacebar**, and pick the Page Numbers (#) button; compare your display to the following illustration.

5. Pick the **Close** button to return to the document. Notice that the header is dimmed.

6. Select **View|Normal** and notice that the header display disappears.

Tip: When you are in the Page Layout view, you can reopen a header or footer box by double-clicking on the header or footer text. You can also insert a page number using the Insert|Page Numbers menu selection.

7. Place the cursor immediately following the word *terms* on the first line of the note at the top of page 1. Use **View| Print Layout** to display the page in the Page Layout view.

8. Use **Insert|Footnote** then press **<Enter>** (or click **OK**) to accept the dialog box settings.

   Type the footnote text shown in the following illustration.

> [1] Many of today's PC-based word processors have adopted standard desktop publishing features and terms.

9. Notice the superscript footnote number "1" is inserted. The Footnote and Endnote dialog allows you to auto-number footnotes and endnotes or you may custom number them.

10. Press **<Alt+F4>** and click **No** to exit Word without saving the changes.

Summary

Word makes the insertion of footnotes, comments, headers, and footers a breeze. It automatically numbers footers and endnotes and even adjusts the numbers when one is deleted or new ones are added.

In the next section you learn about text boxes and frames, which are used to box text, graphics, and even tables. Text boxes and frames provide a number of document creation capabilities that are typically achieved with sophisticated desktop publishing systems.

Working with Text Boxes and Frames

Introduction

A text box is an open rectangle that is placed within a document using the Insert|Text Box menu selection. You can type text within the text box. The text can be rotated 90 degrees for special effects. One text box can be linked to a following, empty text box so that text that overflows the boundaries of the first text box continues into another designated text box. Text boxes can contain pictures as well as text, and therefore can be used like a frame. Text box border lines and colors are changed or removed using the Colors and Lines tab of the Format Text Box dialog (accessed from the Format menu).

Previous versions of Word made use of frames. Readers who are familiar with frames should know that a text box can be quickly converted to a frame. This is done by selecting a text box and clicking Format|Text Box to access the Format Text Box dialog. Then select the Text Box tab and click the Convert to Frame button. Word's menu selections and dialog boxes often vary with the current selection. For example, when you select a frame, Format|Frame replaces Format|Text Box. Word 2000 frames are similar, but not identical, to earlier Word frames. For example, precise scaling of a graphic object is no longer possible using the percentage readout on the status bar.

Both text boxes and frames can be clicked and dragged, resized, and even copied and deleted just like any other object within a Word document. You can also select a passage of text and use Insert|Text Box to put the selected text inside a text box. Finally, the Drawing toolbar includes a Text Box button, making it easy to put a drawing inside a text box. Once a text box is inserted into your document, you can select it and use the Format Text Box dialog box, which is displayed using the Format|Text Box menu selection, to set a number of controls including text wrapping, position, and the distance to adjacent elements.

There are a number of available cursors associated with frames and other inserted objects.

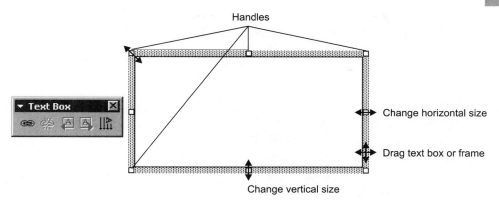

Note: After clicking Insert|Text Box, you will see the cursor at the place you chose to place the text box. The mouse pointer will change to crosshairs, which is your prompt to left-click and drag the crosshairs to dimension the size of the text box. The Text Box dialog shown becomes visible when you select the text box by clicking on it.

A *cross hair cursor* is used to insert and size a frame.

Handles are filled squares located in the corners and on the center of each side. This tells you that the text box or frame is selected and ready for modification. When active, it can be resized, repositioned, deleted, cut, or copied.

A *double-headed arrow* is used to stretch the text box or frame horizontally, vertically, or diagonally. Placing the cursor near a handle changes it into a double-headed arrow. You can *crop* out unwanted white space or images by pressing the <Shift> key while dragging a handle in or out. Cropping is a technique used to take out unwanted background areas. Press the <Ctrl> key to adjust opposite sides by the same amount.

The *crossed double-headed arrow cursor* is used to move the text box or frame. When the cursor changes to a crossed double-headed arrow symbol, you can pick a text box or frame with a mouse click and drag it to a new location within your document. You can also cut and paste a frame to move it to another location in your document or, for that matter, to another document using drag and drop.

An *anchor* symbol indicates the paragraph to which a text box or frame is tied. If the line moves when preceding text is inserted or deleted, the text box or frame moves with the paragraph to which it is anchored.

Charts and pictures, which are typical *objects*, are automatically loaded into resizable frames of their own. You can also put an object within a text box or frame to achieve text *runarounds*, in which the text of your document wraps around an object, such as a picture or chart. There are a number of runaround settings to choose from. The hands-on activity shows you the effect of runarounds.

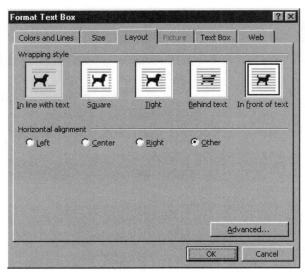

The text box borders are controlled by the Colors and Lines tab of the Format Text Box dialog. You can also use the Format|Borders and Shading menu to adjust the appearance of borders. The combination of the Format Text Box and Borders and Shading dialogs gives you a large number of options for borders, colors, interior fills, and shading.

The following hands-on activity guides you through the creation and editing of text boxes and borders. It also introduces you to text box links.

Hands-on Activity

In this activity you use the TextBox.doc supplied on the companion CD and insert text boxes and borders into text.

1. Start Word and open the **TextBox.doc** file.

2. Notice that the TextBox.doc has two embedded illustrations—a sun and a map.

3. Pick the sun picture so that handles are displayed. Then use **Insert|Text Box** (you are inserting a text box into a text box) and see how the text wraps around the text box. This is an example of a text *runaround*.

4. With the handles still displayed, drag the lower right-hand handle up so that the text box border outlines the border of the picture.

5. Move the mouse so that the crossed double arrow cursor is displayed. Drag the picture horizontally to the right margin. Notice how the text readjusts.

The Daily Blatt

Volume 3, Number 6   March 14, 1999

Today's Weather:
Mostly sunny with some clouds and a chance of evening thunder showers.

ROADWORK BAFFLES CITIZENS

Road building continues in Centerville as drivers and pedestrians alike are inconvenienced by the barricades, rubble, and heavy equipment. Mayor Johnson and the city council appear to be reaping the

6. Select the volume-date line near the top of the document by clicking to the left of it so that it is highlighted. Use the **Outside Border** button on the Formatting toolbar to draw a border around the volume-date line. Then use the **Format|Borders and Shading** menu selection to display the following dialog. Pick the **Shading** tab, and make the background light gray (15%). Note that light gray 15% is in the seventh row and eighth column.

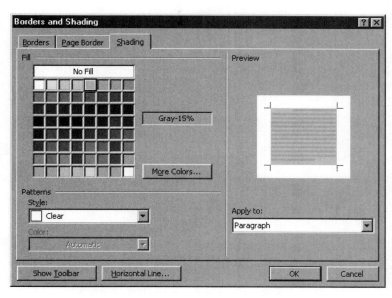

7. Click **OK** to return to the document. The volume-date line should now have a gray background.

The Daily Blatt

Volume 3, Number 6   March 14, 1999

Today's Weather:
Mostly sunny with some clouds and a chance of evening thunder showers.

ROADWORK BAFFLES CITIZENS

Road building continues in Centerville as drivers and pedestrians alike are inconvenienced by the barricades, rubble, and heavy equipment. Mayor Johnson and the city council appear to be reaping the

8. Select the map of Centerville to display handles. Then pick **Insert|Text Box**. Use the bottom right-hand handle and drag the corner down and to the right so that the map is square. Notice that "Yard" is cropped out of the picture. Click so that the text box frame is displayed; drag the map so that the right edge of the border aligns to the right-hand margin. Your result should resemble the following illustration.

Tip: It's easier to maintain the scale of a text box, picture, or frame by dragging from a corner. Dragging a horizontal or vertical handle distorts the image by elongating or shortening a side. Dragging from a border rather than from a handle moves the box.

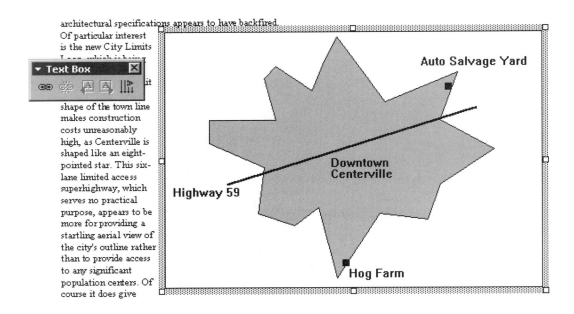

9. Use **File|Save As** and save the document with the name TextBox2.doc.

10. Press **<Ctrl+N>** to open a new blank document.

11. Use **Insert|Text Box** and drag a small text box (about 1-inch square) onto the blank page. Type several lines of text until the text box is completely full and overflows.

12. Create a second small text box to the right of the first one. Then select the first text box and click the **Link** button on the Text Box toolbar. Notice that the cursor changes to a pitcher.

13. Place the pitcher cursor over the second, empty text box and click. Notice how the overflow text from the first text box flows into the linked text box.

14. Press **<Alt+F4>** to exit Word; click **No** in response to the Save dialog.

Summary

In this section you learned how to use text boxes and borders. You saw how text boxes control the way text flows, or "runs around," inserted objects. You were also told how to convert a text box to a frame. Finally, you learned how to flow text from one text box to another. You may wish to experiment further with this option and the Format|Text Box dialog box to determine other effects.

In the next section you begin working with columns. There, you use the TextBox2.doc as a basis for your work with columns. You saved the TextBox2.doc file in the preceding hands-on activity. Therefore, do not modify this document, as your next hands-on activity assumes that you saved the TextBox2.doc as modified here.

Working with Columns

Introduction

Word makes working with columnar text a breeze. You can use the Format|Columns menu selection to specify the number of columns, the space between columns, and whether or not the column setting should apply to the entire document, from the current point forward, or the current section.

You can also insert a line between columns by picking the Line Between check box. Once a columnar format is established, you can use the Column button on the toolbar to change the column setup. The Column button is also used to create and apply a columnar format to the current section in the document. See Section 6 of this part for a description of sections.

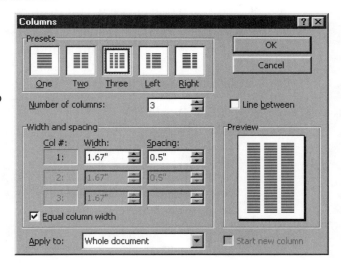

The Columns dialog box provides a series of "presets" that can be clicked to give you instant column construction. It also lets you create a column layout of your own. Columns dialog box selections include:

Number of Columns—The number of columns you want to use.

Width and Spacing—Sets individual column widths and the space between columns, sometimes referred to as a gutter.

Line Between—Inserts a vertical line between columns when checked.

Equal Column Width—Automatically creates equal-width columns when checked.

Apply To—Apply columnar format to either the whole document, the current section, or from the current cursor position forward.

Start New Column—Begin a new section of columnar text at the current cursor position.

Hands-on Activity

In this activity you use the TextBox2.doc you saved in the previous section and convert it to a columnar format. The activity shows you how easy it is to convert a document from single column to multiple column.

1. Start Word and open the TextBox2.doc file.

2. Be sure the Show/Hide (**¶**) button on the Standard toolbar is active (you should see carriage returns, tabs, and space dots).

3. Position the cursor on the first carriage return (¶) following the Number and Date box.

4. Highlight all the text below the Volume 3, Number 6 and date line to the end of the document. Select **Format|Columns**, set the dialog box to **3** columns, **0.25"** (place cursor in the spacing text box, delete the text, and enter .25) spacing, and select **Selected Text** in the **Apply To** text box.

5. Drag the sun picture to the left edge of the document and delete the extra carriage return. Drag the map text box up the page. Resize the map text box if necessary. Your document should resemble the illustration at right.

6. Press <Ctrl+S> to save the document. Then press <Alt+F4> to exit Word. Saving is important as the document is used again with the hands-on activity in Section 23. Also, you can review your handiwork and even show colleagues what can be done with Word with just a few clicks of the mouse.

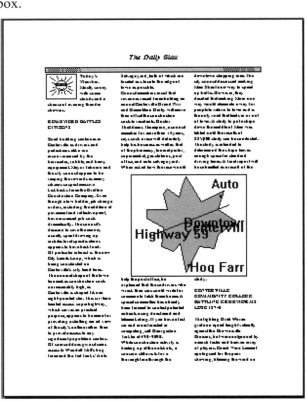

Summary

In this activity you learned how to convert a single-column document to three-column. You could have used other column and spacing values. If you want to apply columnar text to parts of a document, you can create a section using the Insert|Break menu selection. Then move to the new section and apply the Format| Columns menu selection to the selected area.

You have already worked with pictures in this and the previous section. In the next section, you create a picture and then insert it into a document.

Working with Pictures

Introduction

Word includes a set of drawing tools when you display the Drawing toolbar. This is done using either the View|Toolbars menu selection or by clicking the Drawing button ![] on the Standard toolbar.

The Drawing Toolbar

Once you click the Drawing button, the Drawing toolbar is displayed along the bottom of your screen. Here, you can select tools that allow you to draw lines, boxes, and circles. Other tools let you draw such things as maps or "Mr. Sun." Following is an illustration of the Drawing toolbar and a brief description of each tool.

Draw—Select a control from a drop-down box to group/ungroup, arrange the order, nudge, align, rotate, apply a grid, etc., to one or more selected objects.

Select Objects—Select one or more objects by either clicking or dragging a box around them.

Free Rotate—Click a drawing object and then click this button. Drag a corner to rotate the selected drawing object.

AutoShapes—Select one of many shapes including lines, arrows, flowchart symbols, stars and banners, and callouts.

Line—Drag a line by picking the starting point and dragging to the endpoint.

Arrow—Click and then drag an arrow onto the page.

Rectangle—Drag a rectangle or square with this tool. Pick one corner and drag to the opposite corner, then press <Shift> and drag to draw a perfect square. Use Line Style and Line Color tools to change the line weights and colors. Use Fill Color to change the interior (fill) color.

Oval—Draw a circle or an oval by selecting the tool, placing the cursor at a desired point, and dragging the circle or ellipse. Press <Shift> while dragging the circumference to create a perfect circle. Use Line Style and Line Color tools to change line weights and colors.

Text Box—Drag a text box onto the page into which you can type and rotate text.

Insert WordArt—Start the WordArt add-in to create a WordArt text object. Use the drop-down box to select a style. Type the text in a displayed WordArt window and click OK. You can also highlight text before clicking the WordArt button.

Insert Clip Art—Open the Insert ClipArt dialog to insert clip art at the current cursor position.

Fill Color—Change the interior color of a drawing object such as a rectangle, circle, freeform shape, or callout box.

Line Color—Change the color of a line, rectangle, circle, arc, callout box, etc.

Font Color—Change the font color using a drop-down palette box.

Line Style—Change the line style including such characteristics as thickness, double lines, etc.

Dash Line—Change or apply a dashed line to one or more selected lines by choosing one from a drop-down box.

Arrow Style—Change or apply an arrow style to a selected line or arrow by choosing one from a drop-down box.

Shadow—Apply a shadow effect to the selected object from a drop-down box of shadowed objects that correspond to the selected object.

3-D—Apply a 3-D effect to the selected object from a drop-down box of 3-D shapes that correspond to the selected object.

Hands-on Activity

In this activity you open a blank document (Document1.doc) and create and edit a drawing.

1. Start Word and display a blank document.

2. Use the **File|Page Setup|Margins** menu selection to set all margins to **1"**. Close the Margins dialog.

3. Click the **Show/Hide** (¶) button as necessary to hide paragraph marks and other special symbols.

4. Click the **Drawing** button to display the Drawing toolbar.

5. Use the **Line** and **Text Box** tools to draw and annotate the simple map shown in the following Word-produced illustration. Be sure to adjust the sizes of the text boxes by dragging them so that interior text fits properly.

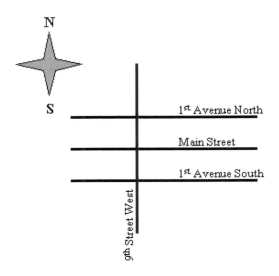

Tips: Use the following tools to draw the map. Set all text to Times New
Roman. Thicken the lines to 2-1/4 pt using the Line Style tool. Insert the
four-point star using **AutoShapes|Stars and Banners**. Make the star
gray using the Fill Color tool on the Drawing toolbar. Remove the lines
from around the text boxes using **Format|Text Box|Colors and Lines**,
and selecting **No Line** in the **Line Color** text box. (The cursor must be
inside the text box before the Format menu selection will enable the Text
Box option.) Use **Format|Text Direction** to rotate the 9th Street text 90
degrees. Select each text box and use the Draw button's **Order|Send to
Back** options. Use the Ctrl+Arrow keys to nudge the text into place next
to the streets.

6. Click the **Select Objects** (the leftmost arrow on the Drawing tool bar) tool and drag a
   selection box around the four-pointed star and the N and S text boxes.

7. With handles visible on all three objects, use **Draw|Group** to combine the three
   selected objects into a single group.

8. Click the **Select Objects** tool again and drag a selection box around the entire drawing
   so that all items are selected.

9. Use **Draw|Group** to combine all items into a single group. This allows you to move the
   entire drawing in unison when it is placed with text on the page.

10. Press <**Alt+F4**> and click **No** to exit Word without saving your drawing document.

Summary

In this section you used the Drawing toolbar and several of its tools to create and edit a simple map. The map was embedded in a document. You should now know how to create drawings in your documents. You can also import an existing array of documents using the Insert|Picture menu selection. These "canned" pictures are supplied with Office 2000 and are found in the ClipArt directory.

In the next section you learn how to create and edit charts. There, you see how easy it is to embed charts into your documents.

Working with Charts and Graphs

Introduction

This section introduces you to the use of Microsoft Graph 2000 Chart, or simply "Graph," which is an easy-to-use Office 2000 add-in that gives you the ability to create and insert charts into your documents. The Graph add-in is activated by picking Microsoft Graph 2000 Chart from the Insert|Object pick list.

The Graph program displays a datasheet table and graph when first launched. The Word menu selections are also changed to correspond to Graph's features. The datasheet contains row and column values and headings. You can modify the values and type your own heading to produce a chart that reflects the typed information. Once you enter data (numbers and label names) in the datasheet, you can select the kind of chart you want from a gallery of graph types, add grids and titles, and change colors and patterns. Then click away from the graph to return to the normal Word display with the graph in place. If you wish to edit your graph, double-click it to redisplay the Graph datasheet and menus. Make your changes and then move back to the document, where your changes take effect.

Exploring Microsoft Graph

Start Graph by first placing the cursor at the point in your document where you want to insert a chart. Then select Insert|Object, pick Microsoft Graph 2000 Chart from the list, and click OK. Your display should resemble the illustration on the following page.

The datasheet and chart and the Graph menu set plus a Graph toolbar are displayed. The datasheet is turned on and off by clicking the View Datasheet button on the Graph toolbar or you can use the View|Datasheet menu selection. As mentioned previously, you can adjust your graph by changing the values in the datasheet. As changes to datasheet values are made, they are reflected in the companion chart. You can change chart types, headings, and the other elements using the toolbar buttons and/or the available menu selections. You may wish to explore the menu selections by pulling each down and comparing them to the normal Word menu set. You'll notice that the Graph menus are shorter, as most deal only with graph operations. Also notice that Word's Table menu is replaced by Graph's Data and Chart menus, which control column and row orientation, chart types, and other options.

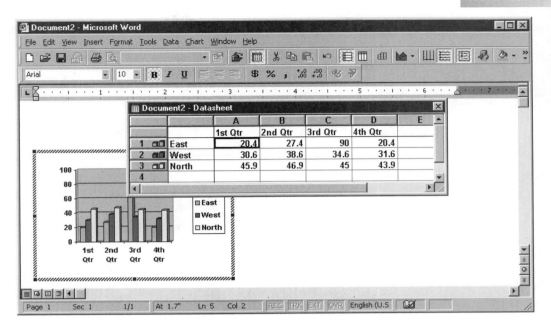

The Graph toolbar buttons provide shortcuts to some of the more frequently used menu items. Following is a brief description of each toolbar button. The buttons are described as they appear from left to right. Put your cursor on each toolbar button to see the button's name in the "tool tip" box.

 **New Blank Document, Open, Save, Print, Print Preview**—Usual file management tools.

 **Chart Objects**—Select a specific object on the chart, such as the chart area, legend, or a specific series.

 Format Chart Area—Display a dialog that corresponds to the selected Graph object.

Import File—Used to import a worksheet from Excel or another spreadsheet program, which provides an alternate source of data for your charts.

 View Datasheet—Click this button to view or hide the datasheet, where you can edit data values and labels.

 Cut, Copy, Paste, Undo—These buttons operate identically to the Cut, Copy, Paste, and Undo buttons found in Word. They cut or copy selected elements to the clipboard, paste them from the clipboard, and undo previous operations.

By Row and By Column—Click these buttons to set the orientation of your graph. By Row plots the datasheet values from top to bottom (beginning at row 1, then row 2, and so on), while By Column plots the datasheet values from left to right by column.

Data Table—Integrate a data table into the chart display. Click once to display the data table, and click again to hide it.

Chart Type—Use the button to display a gallery of chart types. Simply click the one you like and see if the resulting display communicates the information the way you want it to.

Category Axis Gridlines, Value Axis Gridlines—Use these buttons to add or remove vertical or horizontal gridlines to or from your chart.

Legend—Click to display/hide a chart legend.

Drawing—Click to display the Drawing toolbar.

Fill Color—Use this button to fill the selected graph object with a color.

Help—Click to display the Office Assistant for help information about a selected item.

Zoom—Enlarge or reduce the size of the active graph.

The following hands-on activity touches on chart creation and some of the available features. You should experiment with the gallery of available charts to satisfy your curiosity about how a chart looks in different formats.

Hands-on Activity

In this activity you open a blank document, type a line of text, and then create and insert a simple chart. Then you return to the chart, make modifications, and view the results.

1. Start Word and display the default blank document (Document1.doc).

2. Type **MY FIRST GRAPH** and press **<Enter>** four times.

3. Move the cursor in front of the second to last carriage return (be sure that the hidden characters such as carriage returns and spaces are displayed).

4. Use the **Insert|Object** menu selection and launch Microsoft Graph 2000 Chart. Notice that the default datasheet and graph are displayed.

5. Click in the open area (away from the displayed datasheet and chart) to redisplay Document1. Notice how the graph is inserted at the cursor position.

MY·FIRST·GRAPH¶
¶
¶

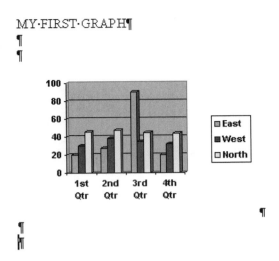

¶

¶
H

6. Double-click on the chart to launch Graph again. Click the **Datasheet** button as necessary to display the datasheet.

7. Modify the datasheet values as shown in the following illustration.

		A	B	C	D	E
		1st Qtr	2nd Qtr	3rd Qtr	4th Qtr	
1	East	10.1	15.2	16.9	17.5	
2	West	9.8	7.6	9.9	12.2	
3	North	12.6	18.2	16.1	22.5	
4						

8. Click on the chart window. Then use the **Chart|Chart Options** menu selection. In the Titles tab enter **My Chart** as the Chart title and click **OK**.

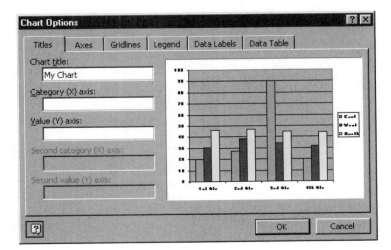

9. Click the **Chart Type** button's down arrow to display the gallery; pick the **Area Chart** (the upper left chart type) and see how the graph changes. Now click on the underlying page to return to the document view. Select and drag the chart to the center of the page. Now compare your screen to the following illustration.

MY FIRST GRAPH

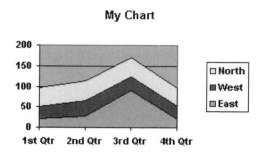

10. With the handles displayed, use the **Format|Borders and Shading** menu selection to place a black 0.75-point border around the graph. Also notice the dialog tabs.

Tip: You can adjust the size, position, and the way text wraps around your chart using this dialog.

11. This completes the activity. Press **<Alt+F4>** and click **No** to exit without saving.

Summary

As this activity shows you, it's easy to create charts and graphs using Word. You can now add both pictures and graphs to your documents, giving them the ability to communicate virtually any kind of information. In the next section you learn how to create and modify fill-in style forms that are displayed and used on your computer's screen.

Working with Forms

Introduction

Word 2000 gives you the ability to create and edit on-screen forms that can be used to enter information or respond to questionnaires. Forms are created and modified using the Forms toolbar, which is displayed using the View|Toolbars menu selection. All toolbars can be dragged to the sides, top, or bottom of your screen to move them out of the way of your work. Dragging them to a side is called *docking* the toolbar. Although the Forms toolbar is first displayed at the upper right-hand corner of your page, you may wish to move it to the top or one side of your screen to view more of your form document.

The Forms toolbar buttons (or *tools*) are briefly described in the following list. You can place your cursor on each button to display the button name in the tool tip box. Note that each of these fields is created and modified by selecting the field and using the Form Field Options button to display a corresponding dialog box. For the form entities to operate properly, the form must first be protected using the Protect Form button. To return to the editing mode, unprotect the form by clicking the Protect Form button again.

From left to right, the buttons are:

Text Form Field—Inserts a field in which a user types text.

Check Box Form Field—Inserts a check box field; clicking a check box inserts or removes an "X."

Drop-Down Form Field—Creates a drop-down pick list from which one entry is picked.

Form Field Options—Displays a dialog box used with each of the field types.

Draw Table—Draws a table on the form; identical to the Draw Table button on the Standard toolbar.

Insert Table—Inserts a new table; identical to the Insert Table button on Word's Standard toolbar.

Insert Frame—Inserts a new, empty frame or puts a frame around a selected object.

Form Field Shading—Controls the shading of one or more selected form fields.

Protect Form—Protects the form for use. Click again to enable form editing.

115

Hands-on Activity

In this activity you create and use a form to enroll students in a learning center. Begin by starting Word and displaying a blank screen.

1. Create the document shown in the following illustration. Use the exact number of carriage returns indicated. Note that the heading is 16-point, bold, and centered. All other typed headings are 12-point bold.

Enrollment·Questionnaire¶

To day's·Date¶
¶
Student·Information¶
¶
Education·(check·highest·level·attained)¶
¶
Subject·(pick·one)¶
¶

2. Use **View|Toolbars**, check the Forms check box, and click **OK** to display the Forms toolbar.

Note: In the following step, you can check the status bar for "Ln 6."

3. Put the cursor on the sixth line (following Student Information:). Then click the **Insert Table** button and drag a three-row by six-column table.

4. Type the information in the cells as shown. Align each entry to the right (use the **Align Right** button or press <**Ctrl+R**>).

Enrollment·Questionnaire¶

To day's·Date¶
¶
Student·Information¶

Name▫	▫	Age▫	▫	Telephone▫	▫	▫
Address▫	▫	▫	▫	▫	▫	▫
City▫	▫	County▫	▫	Postal·Code▫	▫	▫

¶
Education·(check·highest·level·attained)¶
¶
Subject·(pick·one)¶
¶

5. Insert text form fields in each of the indicated fields (see the next illustration) as follows:

a. Position the cursor in the desired location (in this case, a table cell).

b. Click the **Text Form Field** button, and then click the **Form Field Options** button.

c. Type the field text shown and click **OK**.

Tip: If you goof, just double-click on any form field to re-enter the dialog box. Make your changes and click **OK** to save your corrections.

6. Notice that the text fields wrap in some cells. Drag as necessary to put all text on a single line. Then select the second through sixth cells on the Address row and use **Table|Merge Cells** to combine them. (You may have to do this by selecting the second cell, pressing the **<Shift>** key, and then moving to the sixth column with the right arrow.)

⊞ **Student Information:**

Name	First, MI, Last		Age	Years & Mo's		Telephone	Home
Address	Home Address						
City	City or Town		County	Home County		Postal Code	Zip Code

7. Put the cursor to the right of "Today's Date:", press the **Spacebar**, click the **Text Form Field** button, then click the **Form Field Options** button. Pick **Current Date** from the Type pick list and click **OK**. The current system date should be displayed in your new text field.

8. Put the cursor on line 11 following "Education (check highest level attained):" Then use the **Insert** button to drag a one-row by three-column table by placing the cursor in the bottom left-hand block and dragging to the right and up until the appropriate number of row and columns are shaded.

9. Type the text shown in the following illustration, then put a check box form field after each text entry by positioning the cursor and clicking the **Check Box Form Field** button.

Enrollment Questionnaire

Today's Date: 5/12/99

⅂ **Student Information:**

Name	First, MI, Last		Age	Years & Mo's		Telephone	Home
Address	Home Address						
City	City or Town		County	Home County		Postal Code	Zip Code

Education (check highest level attained):

Elementary ☒	Middle School ☒	High School ☒

Subject (pick one):

10. Put the cursor on the last line of your document. Then click the **Drop-Down Form Field** button and the **Form Field Options** button. Add the entries shown below by typing the words in the Drop-Down Item text box and clicking the **Add** button. Use the Add and Remove buttons as necessary. You can rearrange the order of entries by highlighting them with the mouse and clicking one of the Move arrows.

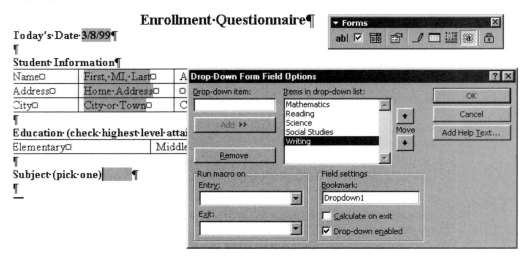

11. Click **OK** after adding Writing. Now your form is complete. Click the **Protect Form** button. Then use the **<Tab>** keys to move from field to field to see how the fill-in form operates.

Enrollment Questionnaire

Today's Date: 5/12/99

Student Information:

Name	First, MI, Last	Age	Years & Mo's	Telephone	Home
Address	Home Address				
City	City or Town	County	Home County	Postal Code	Zip Code

Education (check highest level attained):

Elementary ☒	Middle School ☒	High School ☒

Subject (pick one):
Mathematics ▾

12. Click the check boxes to see how they work. Then click the drop-down field arrow to display the selections and pick **Reading**.

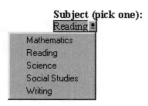

13. Use **File|Save As**, type **Myform1,** and press **<Enter>**. Then press **<Alt+F4>** to exit Word.

Summary

Forms are used to capture information from the keyboard. Once a form is filled in, it can be saved for future use or printed and then cleared for the next use. When a form is used, be sure to turn off the Forms toolbar to prevent unwanted meddling. You can access the View|Toolbar menu selection by double-clicking an open area of any displayed toolbar. You can also create a macro to automatically control your forms.

You may also wish to display your forms using View|Full Screen to eliminate unwanted distractions from toolbars, scroll bars, the status bar, and rulers. Remove previous text from displayed text fields by selecting each and pressing <Del>. Finally, users can add or remove an X within a check box by clicking with the mouse or pressing the Spacebar.

Now that you know how to create and modify forms, you're ready to move on. In the next section you learn how to use a variety of powerful word processing tools supplied with Word. Here, you learn how to run spelling checks and use the thesaurus, hyphenation, AutoText, and more.

Section 23

Working with Tools

Introduction

In this section you learn how to use several of Word's popular tools, including:

- Spell check
- Thesaurus
- Grammar check
- AutoCorrect
- AutoText
- AutoFormat
- Hyphenation

Although extremely helpful and powerful, Word makes using these tools a breeze with buttons and descriptive dialog boxes.

Spell Check and AutoCorrect

Both the spell checker and AutoCorrect are used to help you produce error-free documents. In addition, when Tools|Options|Spelling & Grammar—"Check spelling as you type" is active (the default setting), misspelled words are marked with a red wavy underline. You can move your cursor to the challenged word and click the right mouse button. A pop-up menu is displayed; if a suggestion exists, it is displayed. Click AutoCorrect to replace the misspelled word. Otherwise, you can pick Ignore All, Add, or Spelling (which launches the Spelling and Grammar dialog). While spell check is run to find misspelled words and typos, AutoCorrect is aimed at fixing typos as you go, eliminating many common keyboard entry errors.

Spell Check

Spell check is run by selecting Tools|Spelling, by clicking the Spelling & Grammar button ![button], or by right-clicking on an underlined word. You can check an entire document or a selected word or passage. Before running a spell check, you should know

120

that it checks either from the current cursor position down or from the beginning of the document to the end. Of course you can interrupt the spelling check anytime by clicking the Cancel button or pressing <Esc>.

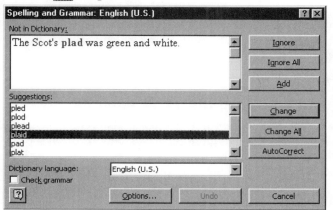

Note that you can click Ignore to bypass a misspelled word or click Ignore All to skip all following occurrences of the challenged word. Click Change to replace the challenged word displayed in the Not in Dictionary box with the word shown in the Suggestions box. You can also type a correction in the Not in Dictionary box. For example, if you omitted a space between two words, type them correctly and then click Change. The Change All button tells Word to change every occurrence of the challenged word to the one displayed in the Suggestions box or as corrected in the Not in Dictionary box. The Add button puts the Not in Dictionary word into the dictionary. This could be a last name or the name of a city that you commonly use but is not in the main dictionary. Undo is used to reverse the last change in case you goof. Words that are close in meaning to the challenged word are displayed in the Suggestions text box. Cancel ends the spell check. Clicking the Options button displays the Spelling and Grammar dialog in which you can set the way you want the spelling and grammar checks to operate.

AutoCorrect

AutoCorrect stores a list of common typographical errors and their correct spellings. When you make a typo, Word detects it and inserts the correctly spelled version of the word. You can add words to the AutoCorrect list based on the mistakes you make. Look at the AutoCorrect dialog box, accessed from the Tools|AutoCorrect menu selection.

Note that (tm) is automatically replaced with the trademark symbol. This is just one example of many symbol substitutions. The list also includes hundreds of common typographical errors that are automatically corrected when

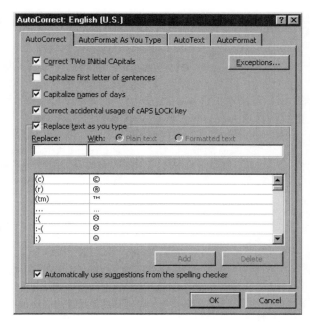

encountered. You can add and delete words and symbols to and from your AutoCorrect list as desired.

AutoFormat

Use AutoFormat to reformat an entire document using a selected document style as a basis for the format changes. Templates are supplied with Word, or you can create your own templates based on a document in which styles are applied to text, headings, lists, and other text and graphic elements within the document. You can use Format|AutoFormat to view and apply available format styles to your document. AutoFormat applies a style to every paragraph and heading. It typically replaces indentations created with spaces or tabs with paragraph indents. It also replaces asterisks at the beginning of items in a list with bullets, double dashes with em dashes (—), and so on.

AutoText

The AutoText feature lets you store and recall commonly used passages, such as addresses, contract clauses, and even letterhead graphics. To create an AutoText entry:

1. Select a graphic or text block such as your name and address in your document.

2. Pick the Insert|AutoText|AutoText menu selection; then click the AutoText tab to display the AutoText dialog.

3. Type a short name in the Enter AutoText entries here box; click Add.

Tip: You can also select a text passage or graphic and then press <Alt+F3> to display a Create AutoText dialog. Type an AutoText name and click OK. You can also display an AutoText toolbar for direct access to the AutoText or Create AutoText dialogs.

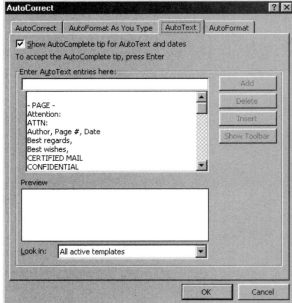

To use a stored AutoText item:

1. Place the cursor where you want to insert the text.

2. Pick Insert|AutoText|AutoText.

3. Check that the correct AutoText item is selected and click Insert.

To remove an AutoText item:

1. Pick Insert|AutoText|AutoText to display the AutoText dialog.

2. Pick an AutoText name and click Delete and then Close.

Grammar Check

The Tools|Spelling and Grammar menu selection is used to check the grammar within your documents. (You can access Grammar Check directly by pressing F7.)

You can check the entire document or select an isolated passage before running the grammar check. During a grammar check, spelling errors and readability statistics are also

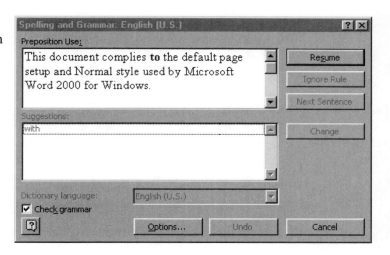

checked. You can disable spell check and readability statistics by picking the Options button and clearing the corresponding check boxes. You can also enable or disable grammar check criteria by clicking the Settings button and then checking the desired grammar and style options. Once set, click OK twice to resume the grammar check. You can make corrections in the dialog box or move to the document by clicking on it to make your corrections directly in the text. If you move out and back into the dialog box, resume the grammar check by clicking the Resume button. Document statistics are displayed using the Tools|Word Count and File|Properties menu selections.

Thesaurus

The Tools|Language|Thesaurus menu selection gives you possible meanings and synonyms for selected words in your documents. This helps you be more precise in your writing. To use the thesaurus, position the cursor in front of a word or highlight it. Use the Tools|Language|Thesaurus menu selection or press <Shift+F7>.

Lists of possible meanings and synonyms are displayed. Pick a desired word so that it is in the Replace with Synonym box and click the Replace button to use it. Use the Look Up button to find alternate meanings of a selected word. Click Cancel to exit the Thesaurus dialog without accepting any of the suggested changes.

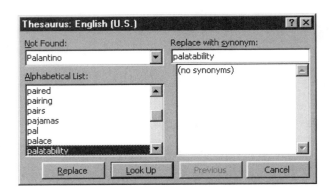

Hyphenation

End-of-line hyphenation is activated using the Tools|Language|Hyphenation menu selection, which displays the following dialog.

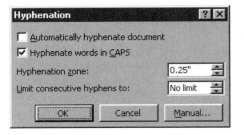

You can hyphenate a selected passage of text; if no text is selected, Word hyphenates the entire document. Hyphenation prevents your right margin from being overly ragged. If you are using justified text, it reduces excessive space between interior words. Use hyphenation when you produce documents having narrow widths, such as in two- or three-column newsletters.

The hyphenation zone is a distance from the right margin in which words are hyphenated. If a word cannot be properly broken in this zone, Word tries to hyphenate the first word on the following line. The smaller the hyphenation zone, the smoother the right margin. The Limit consecutive hyphens to value tells Word how many lines can be hyphenated consecutively. As a rule of thumb, you should not exceed two consecutive hyphens to improve a document's readability.

Be sure the Hyphenate words in CAPS check box is checked if you wish to break capitalized words. Click the Manual button if you wish to confirm each hyphenation break before it occurs. This displays the Manual Hyphenation dialog box.

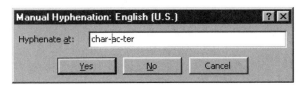

Otherwise, Word will hyphenate words automatically, eliminating your intervention. When manual hyphenation is used, you can change the suggested hyphenation point within a word using the left and right arrow keys. Click OK to accept the hyphenation setup; click No to avoid hyphenating the current word. Click Cancel to stop the hyphenation process.

When editing changes are made to a hyphenated document, only the hyphens at the
end of lines print. Those that are moved to the interior of lines do not print.

Hands-on Activity

In this activity you load the TextBox2.doc last saved in Section 19. Then you run a
spelling check and grammar check, change words using the thesaurus, and finally
smooth the right margin using hyphenation.

1. Start Word and open the TextBox2.doc saved in Section 19.

2. With the cursor at the beginning of the document, click the **Spelling** button on the
   toolbar. Notice that *Blatt* is challenged. A list of possible alternatives is displayed. If
   this were a real word used frequently, you could add it to your personal dictionary with
   the Add button. However, click **Ignore** to continue the spell check.

3. Notice that the grammar
   checker challenges a
   passage containing
   passive voice.

4. Click the **help** button
   (the button with the
   question mark) in the
   lower left-hand corner
   of the dialog to display
   an explanation. Notice
   that the Office Assistant
   provides a description
   of passive voice. Then
   click **Options** to see

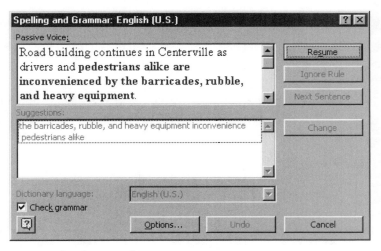

   how you can modify the grammar check operation.

5. Click the **Cancel** button to close the Options dialog without making any changes. Then
   click **Cancel** again to close the grammar check dialog. Finally, close the Office
   Assistant box.

6. Press **<Ctrl+Home>** to move back to the top of the document. Then move the cursor to
   the beginning of the word Daily.

7. Use the **Tools|Language|Thesaurus** menu selection (or press **<Shift+F7>**) to display
   meanings and synonyms for the word Daily. Compare your dialog box to the following
   one.

8. Click the **Cancel** button to stop the thesaurus operation. Press the **<Left Arrow>** to deselect Daily.

9. Use **Tools|Language| Hyphenation** to display the Hyphenation dialog. Put **2** in the Limit consecutive hyphens to box. Then click **Manual** to start the hyphenation process. Accept the first three suggestions by clicking **Yes**.

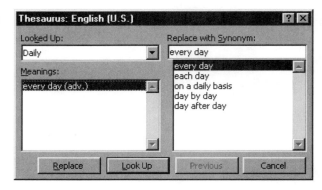

10. Click **Cancel** and then restart hyphenation, only this time check **Automatically hyphenate document** and click **OK** to let Word hyphenate the remainder of the document for you.

11. Press **<Ctrl+End>** to move to the bottom of your document. Type your name and address and select the new passage by dragging it with your mouse.

12. Press **<Alt+F3>** to display the Create AutoText dialog. Click **OK** to accept the default name.

13. Press **<Del>** to delete the selected name and address. Then use the **Insert|AutoText|AutoText** menu selection. Pick your name from the list and click **Insert** to put your name and address into the document.

14. Press **<Alt+F4>** to exit the document. Click **No** to avoid saving the changes. You may wish to hyphenate the document again later and add additional AutoText passages once all activities are completed.

Summary

In this section you familiarized yourself with several significant word processing tools. You should run a spelling and grammar check on every document. You should also hyphenate all of your documents that make use of narrow columns.

In the next section you are introduced to Word's Equation Editor. You also become familiar with the insertion of objects, such as graphs, pictures, and worksheets, into your documents.

Working with Objects—WordArt, Equations, and Worksheets

Introduction

Objects are pictures, charts, worksheets, and other elements typically created by other applications. Word is supplied with several add-in applications, two of which are described here—WordArt and the Equation Editor. In addition, this section shows you how to access Microsoft Excel worksheets from within Word, as well as Paintbrush pictures.

To use WordArt and Equation Editor, they must have been selected when you first ran Word (or Microsoft Office 2000) Setup. Otherwise, run Setup and add them now if you want to learn how to use them. Once installed, they are accessed by using the Insert|Object menu selection. (You can also access WordArt from the WordArt and Drawing toolbars.) If you did not install these applications and have no interest in learning about them, move on to Section 25 where you learn how to automate repetitive tasks with macros.

WordArt

The WordArt program is used to create, insert, and edit fancy type in your documents. WordArt adds additional display-style type fonts that are ideal for brochures, fliers, and even presentations. With WordArt, you can create vertical, slanted, and curved text for eye-catching headings and banners.

WordArt is started from an open Word document using Insert|Object and then picking Microsoft WordArt 3.2 from a displayed list of objects. You'll see other types of objects that are created and saved by other programs. These include drawings, charts, graphs, worksheets, macrosheets, documents, and even Paintbrush pictures. Word has the ability to convert these objects and use them in your Word documents.

Tip: You can also cut or copy information in other programs and then use Edit|Paste Special to insert and dynamically link them. The dynamic link automatically updates your document when the source file is changed by the originating program.

When Microsoft WordArt 3.2 is selected, the full WordArt editing screen is displayed.

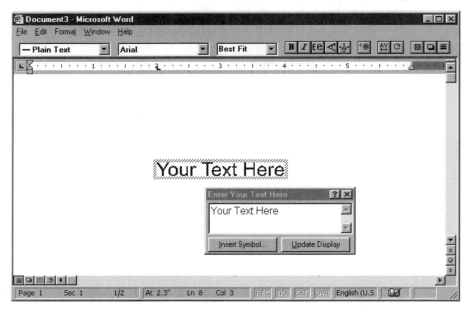

Here, you enter or edit text in the Enter Your Text Here dialog box. Use the WordArt toolbar to achieve a number of special effects.

The operation of each toolbar button is described in the following list in left to right order.

Shape—Pick the shape of the text, such as Plain Text, Slant Up, or Circle.

Font—Choose a font from a drop-down pick list.

Size—Choose a font size; Best Fit automatically adjusts text to fit the available area.

Bold—Bold the displayed type.

Italic—Italicize the displayed type.

Even Height—Make all letters the same height regardless of capitalization.

Flip—Turn WordArt text on its side.

Stretch—Spread the text horizontally and/or vertically to fit the available space.

Align—Align text centered, left, or right.

Spacing Between Characters—Spread and shrink the space between characters.

Special Effects—Rotate the text by entering the degrees of rotation or use the slider control to change the shape.

Shading—Pick a fill pattern for the WordArt text.

Shadow—Display a list of special effects with shadows for the WordArt text.

Border—Display a list of border selections for the WordArt text.

As you can see, WordArt offers many powerful features for emphasizing your written communications with special sizing, stretching, rotation, font selection, shading, and more. If you wish to insert a special symbol, such as a trademark or Wingding symbol, click the Insert Symbol button at the bottom of the Enter Your Text Here dialog. The displayed symbols use the current font. Use the Update Display button to change the displayed WordArt text in your document. Once the WordArt text suits you, click on the underlying document (away from the Enter Your Text Here dialog box and WordArt toolbar) to return to the normal document screen. Just like other inserted objects, WordArt objects are inserted at the cursor position. You can double-click on the WordArt text to restart WordArt for further modifications. The hands-on activity at the end of this section guides you through the use of WordArt.

Microsoft Equation 3.0 (the Equation Editor)

Like Microsoft WordArt 3.2, the built-in Equation Editor is also accessed using the Insert|Object menu selection. Pick Microsoft Equation 3.0 from the displayed list of application objects. Either double-click Microsoft Equation 3.0 or click OK to start the Equation Editor. When the Equation Editor is active, you see a screen similar to the following illustration.

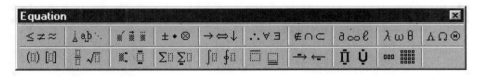

At this point you are ready to create an equation. Notice the Equation toolbar and the new menu items. The toolbar buttons are used to pick Greek and math symbols, equation fences (or boundaries), and a number of other items typically used in equations. The name of each button is listed on the following page for your information. Following the button list is a brief description of each menu.

Equation Editor Menus

The Equation Editor menus are used to select fonts, sizes, boldface, italics, and much more. Following is a brief overview of the purpose of each menu.

File—This menu performs the same basic file operations as the Word File menu.

Edit—Choices are typical of Edit menus, including Undo, Cut, Copy, Paste, Clear, and Select All.

View—This menu provides different zoom selections. It also lets you Show All and Redraw the current equation. Redraw is helpful if you delete an element and a residual image remains.

Format—Here, you can align equation elements left, center, right, or on an equal or percent sign. You can also control the spacing between lines for superscripts and subscripts and between matrix elements. A matrix selection lets you control the format of a mathematical matrix consisting of rows and columns of values.

Style—This menu is used to apply a specific style to a selected group of elements or to elements typed following the style selection. Styles include:

> **Math**—Choose function or variable font automatically based on selection.
>
> **Text**—Use to apply standard text fonts and character styles.
>
> **Function**—Use to apply function fonts and character styles to one or more characters or symbols.
>
> **Variable**—Use to apply variable fonts and character styles to one or more characters or symbols.
>
> **Greek**—Use to apply Greek fonts and character styles. Also accessed with <Ctrl+Shift+G>. You can use <Ctrl+Shift+G> to enter the next characters typed as Greek, or to convert a selection from normal text to Greek text.
>
> **Matrix-Vector**—Also accessed with <Ctrl+Shift+B>, this selection is used to apply vector fonts and styles to selected characters.
>
> **Other**—Use to apply another font and to designate it as bold or italic.
>
> **Define**—Use the displayed dialog box to define the fonts to be used with each of the style selections. You can also use a Bold and Italic check box to designate the use of normal, bold, or italic.

Size—Apply an appropriate size to one or more selected elements including Full, Subscript, Sub-Subscript, Symbol, and Sub-Symbol. Other lets you choose a point size, while Define lets you modify the sizes of equation elements.

Window—This menu item is identical to Word's document Window menu in which you can move between documents, arrange (or tile) the open Word documents in separate windows, or split the active document into two working panes.

Help—This menu item is like other Help selections, as it provides helpful information about Equation Editor features and operation.

In the hands-on activity at the end of this section you use the Equation Editor to prepare an equation in a practice document. This experience should be sufficient to encourage your continued use of this powerful Word utility program.

The Equation Toolbar

Look at the Equation toolbar illustration.

When you click one of the buttons on the Equation toolbar, an addi-

tional series of buttons is displayed. Select your templates, symbols, and special characters by holding down the left mouse button until your choice is highlighted; then release the button and the selection is displayed in the outlined equation object area. You can control the placement of equation elements by highlighting them and then using <Ctrl+Arrow Key> to move them up, down, left, or right. Use the Size|Subscript menu selection to create a subscript/superscript-size character. Then nudge the character into position. Space between equation elements is added using the Spaces and Ellipses button. The Equation Editor does not accept normal Spacebar entries unless you select Text from the Format menu. Once an equation is set, click on the document to insert it in your document. To return to the Equation Editor, just double-click on the equation object.

Note: When you place the cursor over a toolbar button, the button function becomes visible in a small text box. Also, the button function is displayed in the information bar at the bottom of the page on the left side. After you click on a toolbar button, then place the cursor over a symbol and hold the left mouse button down, the symbol description is visible on the information bar at the bottom of the page on the left side.

The following math symbol templates are available in Word 2000. Explore the various buttons to see what symbols are available.

≤≠≈	Relational Symbols	(::) [::]	Fence Templates
⅃ɑḃ˙·	Spaces and Ellipses	╫ √☐	Fractions and Radical Templates
x̌ x̌ x̌	Embellishments	☒ ☐	Subscript and Superscript Templates
± • ⊗	Operator Symbols	Σ☐ Σ☐	Summation Templates
→ ⇔ ↓	Arrow Symbols	∫☐ ∮☐	Integral Templates
∴∀∃	Logical Symbols	☐ ☐	Underbar and Overbar Templates
∉∩⊂	Set Theory Symbols	→ ←	Labeled Arrow Templates
∂∞ℓ	Miscellaneous Symbols	Ọ Ụ	Products and Set Theory Templates
λ ω θ	Greek Characters (lowercase)	░░░ ▦	Matrix Templates
Δ Ω ⊗	Greek Characters (uppercase)		

Excel Worksheets

If Excel is installed on your system, either independently or as part of Microsoft Office 2000, Word gives you direct access to the power of Excel worksheets. This is done by first positioning the text cursor at the desired insertion point within your document. Then click the Insert Microsoft Excel Worksheet button 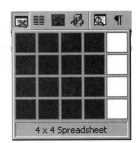 on the Standard toolbar. Drag the number of rows and columns and release the mouse button. The example here shows a 4 x 4 cell worksheet.

After a brief period (depending on your processor speed and the amount of available memory), a blank Excel worksheet appears in your document. In addition, the Excel menu and toolbar are displayed.

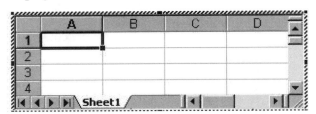

At this point you can create or load a stored worksheet file. Although the use of Excel 2000 is not the focus of this part of the book, the following hands-on activity guides you through the use of Excel. For an in-depth Excel tutorial, see Part 3 of this book.

Working with Other Objects

Advanced topic

In addition to accessing WordArt, Equation, and Excel Worksheet objects, you can also use the Insert|Objects menu selection to create new files or use existing files produced by other Windows-based programst. When you import an existing file, it can be updated using the originating program. For example, if you use the Create from File section of the Object dialog box to insert a Paintbrush picture, you can later use Paintbrush to edit the picture and automatically update the picture in your Word document. This is an example of *object linking*.

When you use the Create New tab of the Object dialog box, you can create a new object within the current document. Once active, you can create a new worksheet, picture, graph, etc. This lets you run the application directly from Word without having to move out of Word to start the application.

You can also use the Create from File tab to import existing files. Once inserted in your document, the inserted material becomes an integral part of your document. Just double-click it to launch the application for editing.

The hands-on activity guides you through the insertion of a Paintbrush picture. This activity is typical of how files created by other programs can be used in your documents.

Hands-on Activities

In the following activities you create and embed WordArt, equation, and Excel objects into a document. Then you create and insert a Paintbrush picture object. If you have not installed WordArt, the Equation Editor, or Excel, skip the activities relating to the missing program(s) and move to the next one. Be sure to end your activity by performing the Paintbrush Object activity.

1. Start Word and display the blank Document1 screen.

2. Type **Object Document;** press **<Ctrl+E> <Enter> <Ctrl+L><Enter> <Enter><Enter>**; then press **<Up Arrow>** once.

3. Perform the following activities that make use of the programs installed on your computer, i.e., WordArt, Equation 3.0, or Excel.

Insert Microsoft WordArt 3.2 Object

1. Use **Insert|Object**, pick **Microsoft WordArt 3.2**, and click **OK**.

2. Backspace to delete the text in the Enter Your Text Here box. Type **Microsoft <Enter> WordArt <Enter> Object**. Then click the **Shape** down arrow and select the **Button (Pour)** shape (third row, fourth column).

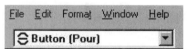

3. Pick the **Font** down arrow and pick a script font such as **Brush Script MT**.

4. Pick the **Border** button (rightmost button on the toolbar), pick **Normal**, and click **OK**.

5. Click on the underlying document. Then drag the WordArt object to the center of the page.

6. Press **<Ctrl+End>** to move to the end of the document. Now press **<Enter>** four times and then press **<Up Arrow>** once in preparation for the next activity.

Insert Microsoft Equation 3.0 Object

1. Use **Insert|Object**, pick **Microsoft Equation 3.0**, and click the **OK** button to start the Equation Editor.

2. Type the equation shown here using the indicated steps.

   a. Type **XC=**.

   b. Pick the **Fraction and Radical Templates** button on the bottom row of the Equation toolbar, select the fraction template (the first template), and release the mouse button.

   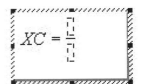

   c. Type **1**, press **<Tab>**, then type **2**.

   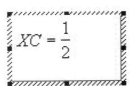

   d. Pick the pi character (use the Greek lowercase button—rightmost character on the fourth row).

   e. Pick the **Fraction and Radical Templates** button again, select the square root symbol (the one with the interior dashed box fourth row, first column), and release the mouse button.

   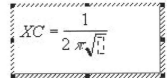

   f. Type **FC** to complete the equation entry.

   $$XC = \frac{1}{2\,\pi\sqrt{FC}}$$

   g. Select (highlight) the C in XC. Then pick **Size|Subscript** from the menu bar.

   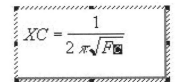

   h. "Nudge" the subscript C by pressing **<Ctrl+Down Arrow>** six times; then press **<Ctrl+Left Arrow>** twice.

   i. Pick **View|Redraw** to clean up the displayed equation.

3. Click on the underlying document to leave the Equation Editor and return to the document; notice that the equation is inserted.

4. Drag the equation to center it. Your equation should resemble the one shown here.

$$XC = \frac{1}{2\pi\sqrt{F_c}}$$

5. Press **<Ctrl+End>** to move to the end of the document. Now press **<Enter>** four times and then press **<Up Arrow>** once in preparation for the next activity.

Insert Microsoft Excel Object

1. Pick the **Insert Microsoft Excel Worksheet** button on the Standard toolbar. Drag a 4 x 4 cell area and release the mouse button.

2. Use your mouse or an arrow key to select each cell, type the information as shown below, and press **<Enter>** after each entry.

	A	B	C	D
1	Item	1st Half	2nd Half	Year
2	Income	448	534	=SUM(B2:C2)
3	Expense	467	472	=SUM(B3:C3)
4	Profit/Loss	=B2-B3	=C2-C3	=SUM(B4:C4)

Note: To view the formulas in the cells, click on **Tools|Protection** and then on **Protect Sheet**; check all check boxes. Close the Protection dialog box. Now, click on **Tools|Options|View|Window Options** and click on **Formulas**.

3. Drag cells A1 through D4 so they are highlighted. Then use **Table|AutoFit|AutoFit to Contents** to automatically adjust all column widths.

4. Compare your Excel display to the following illustration.

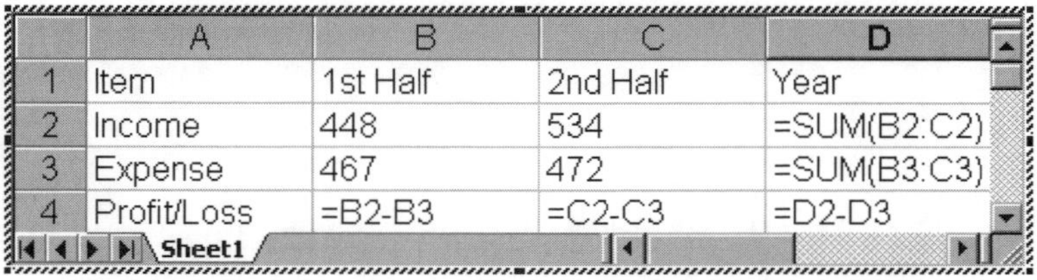

	A	B	C	D
1	Item	1st Half	2nd Half	Year
2	Income	448	534	=SUM(B2:C2)
3	Expense	467	472	=SUM(B3:C3)
4	Profit/Loss	=B2-B3	=C2-C3	=D2-D3

Sheet1

5. Click away from the worksheet and toolbar to move back to your document.

6. Press **<Ctrl+End>** to move to the end of the document. Now press **<Enter>** four times and then press **<Up Arrow>** once in preparation for the next activity.

Insert Microsoft Paintbrush Object

1. Use the **Insert|Object** selection, pick **Paintbrush Picture**, and click **OK**. Notice how Windows Paintbrush runs inside Word.

2. Draw an overlapping rectangle and circle (look at the following example).

| **Tip:** | Select the Line tool and click the second line weight. When dragging the rectangle and circle, press \<Shift\> to ensure that a square box and round circle are drawn. Drag each from the upper left-hand corner so that they overlap as shown. |

a. Click the **Rectangle** tool, drag a rectangular shape, and release the mouse button.

b. Click the **Ellipse** tool. Starting at the upper left-hand corner, drag a circular shape over the rectangle and release the mouse button.

c. Click on the underlying document to return to Document1. Notice how the Paintbrush picture object is automatically inserted in the document.

d. Press the **Crop** button on the Picture toolbar and crop out (remove) the excess space around the drawing.

Notice how this activity demonstrates the "seamless" integration of several Windows 95/98 applications.

Exiting Word

1. Before exiting Word, you may wish to start one or more of the controlling programs for the embedded objects by double-clicking on the objects.

2. When you are finished experimenting with your document, press \<**Alt+F4**\> and click **No** to exit Document1 without saving the practice material.

Summary

You should now be familiar with how WordArt and the Equation Editor are used and how to embed an Excel worksheet in your documents. The Paintbrush picture insertion is an example of object linking and embedding (OLE). In the next section you learn how you can automate some of your word processing tasks by recording and playing back a series of keystrokes and mouse clicks. These recordings are called macros.

Automating Your Work with Macros

Introduction

A *macro* is a series of keystrokes and mouse clicks that can be called with the simple click of a mouse. Advanced users often create and use macros to automate frequently used operations. This provides time-saving shortcuts to speed up repetitive word processing tasks. In this section you learn how to record and then run macros to speed up such operations.

The Macro Recorder

Macros are created by recording a series of keystrokes using Word's Tools|Macro|Record New Macro menu selection. The Record Macro dialog lets you assign a name and a brief description to your macro.

Once a name and description are entered, click OK to record your keystrokes and menu selections. Prior to recording, you can add a toolbar button or shortcut key to run the macro. You can use the Tools|Macro|Macros menu selection or press <Alt+F8> to display the Macros dialog. Here, you can select a macro name, and click the Run button to start a macro if you decide against a button or shortcut key.

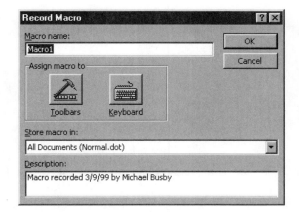

Begin recording your macro by performing normal word processing operations using keystrokes and mouse clicks. Be sure to enter your keystrokes carefully. If you accidentally press the wrong key, the macro records the erroneous entry. Stop and Pause buttons are automatically displayed in the document window for your use during a macro recording session. Click Stop to end macro recording; click Pause to temporarily stop recording in order to perform some other task. Then click Pause again to resume the recording process.

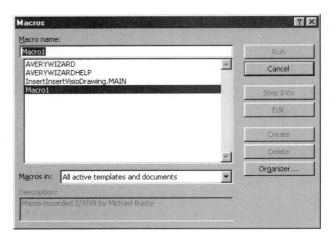

As mentioned previously, you can assign a toolbar button or shortcut key to your macros by clicking the Toolbars or Keyboard button in the Record Macro dialog. If you use a button, select an icon and then drag it to a toolbar. If you decide that a macro is used often enough to warrant assigning a shortcut key or button on a toolbar, you can also use Tools|Customize, pick Macro, and enter a button, menu selection, or shortcut key sequence, such as <Ctrl+Alt+M>. Once the macro is recorded, run it using the assigned button, shortcut key sequence, or by clicking the Run button in the Tools|Macro|Macros dialog.

Editing Macros

An Edit button is available within the Tools|Macros dialog box. To edit a macro, pick the macro name and click Edit. Review the macro code (which is in Visual Basic syntax) to determine what needs to be edited. If it is unclear, you may wish to make changes by recording the macro again. Also, you can rename and even delete selected macros using this dialog. Before a macro can be deleted, it must be closed.

If you choose to edit a macro, the contents of the macro are displayed in the Visual Basic language. A detailed treatment of the Visual Basic language is beyond the scope of this book. However, the following text shows the contents of a macro created in the following hands-on activity.

```
Sub NoteSet()
'
' NoteSet Macro
' Center NOTE; indent 1" from each margin
'
        Selection.ParagraphFormat.Alignment = wdAlignParagraphCenter
        Selection.Font.Bold = wdToggle
```

```
            Selection.TypeText Text:="NOTE"
            Selection.Font.Bold = wdToggle
            Selection.TypeParagraph
            Selection.ParagraphFormat.Alignment = wdAlignParagraphLeft
            Selection.TypeParagraph
            With Selection.ParagraphFormat
                    .LeftIndent = InchesToPoints(1)
                    .RightIndent = InchesToPoints(1)
                    .SpaceBefore = 0
                    .SpaceAfter = 0
                    .LineSpacingRule = wdLineSpaceSingle
                    .Alignment = wdAlignParagraphLeft
                    .WidowControl = True
                    .KeepWithNext = False
                    .KeepTogether = False
                    .PageBreakBefore = False
                    .NoLineNumber = False
                    .Hyphenation = True
                    .FirstLineIndent = InchesToPoints(0)
                    .OutlineLevel = wdOutlineLevelBodyText
            End With
    End Sub
```

If you create a macro while working with a document, Word normally saves the macro as a *global* macro. This gives you access to the macro when working on other documents. You can also use the Save changes in box of the Customize Keyboard or the Save in box of the Toolbars|Customize dialog to restrict use of the macro to the current document. Otherwise, the macro will be part of your universal NORMAL.DOT template.

Hands-on Activity

In this activity you use the Macro Recorder to create a macro named NoteSet. This macro centers the word NOTE in boldface and indents following text 1 inch from the left and right margins. You assign the shortcut sequence <Ctrl+Alt+M> to the macro. You can also create an optional macro that resets the indentation to 0.

1. Start the Word program and display a blank document screen.

2. Use **Tools|Macro|Record New Macro** to display the Record Macro dialog.

3. Type the Macro name as **NoteSet**; then move the cursor to the Description box and type **Center NOTE; indent 1" from each margin**.

4. Click the **Keyboard** button. When the Customize Keyboard dialog appears, move to the Press new shortcut key box, press **<Ctrl+Alt+A>**, put **Document1** in the Save changes in box, click **Assign**, and click **Close**.

5. Record the macro as follows:

   a. Press **<Ctrl+E> <Ctrl+B>**, type **NOTE**, and press **<Ctrl+B> <Enter> <Ctrl+L> <Enter>**.

   b. Pick **Format|Paragraph**, type **1** in the Indentation Left and Right boxes, and click **OK**.

   c. Click the **Macro Stop** button to end the recording.

6. Notice that your actions centered and boldfaced NOTE and indented the note body text 1 inch from each margin.

7. Pick **Format|Paragraph** and reset the left and right indentations to **0"**.

8. Press **<Ctrl+Alt+A>** to run the macro, which inserts a note.

9. If you wish, you can create a NoteEnd macro that automates resetting your margins to 0.

10. Press **<Alt+F4>** and click **No** to exit Word without saving.

Summary

As you can see, macros are easy to create. Word creates the Visual Basic macro code that corresponds to your keystrokes. If you examine the contents of a macro by using the Edit button in the Macros dialog, you should find yourself learning a good part of the macro language by simply comparing the entries to your keyboard and mouse operations to what is recorded. If you want to find out what code corresponds to a particular operation, turn on the recorder, perform the operation, and then examine the resulting code.

You can also gain fast access to your macros by assigning shortcut keys or buttons as you set up your recording session. Be sure to automate frequently used operations with macros. The more often you create and use macros, the more efficient your word processing tasks become.

Each of the Office 2000 applications make use of the Visual Basic programming language. Each application-specific rendition of Visual Basic includes special extensions that are useful for the host application.

In the next section you delve into printing operations. There, you see how easy it is to print the current document. You can also queue up a series of documents for printing. Finally, you examine the power of Word's mail merge feature, which merges database information into documents. This is intended for mass mailings, form letters, and directories.

Printing

Introduction

Word makes printing a breeze by offering you several ways to print your documents. As long as you have properly installed a Windows printer, Word's print operations quickly and efficiently put your documents on paper.

Some Ways to Print

If you want to print the current document in its entirety using the current printer settings, just click the Print button ⊟ on the Standard toolbar. If you want to print specific pages of a multipage document, use the File|Print menu selection (or press <Ctrl+P>). This selection presents a Print dialog box.

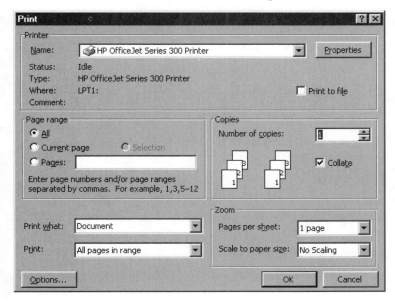

Here, you can specify the current page or the range of pages you want to print. In addition, you can change printers by clicking the down arrow of the Name text box of the Printer dialog. Note that you can select only from the list of printers that have been previously installed. Previous Office versions operating with Windows 95 made provision for installing new printers from either the Microsoft Word File menu or the Printer dialog. However, Windows 98 has an Add Printer manager found by clicking Start|Settings|Printers in the Windows 98 desktop toolbar. All printers must be added/installed using the desktop toolbar. See the Windows 98 Printers dialog below. Depending upon your installed software you may or may not see the same dialog as illustrated.

You can change print options by clicking the Options button in the Print dialog. This displays the Print page of the Options dialog box (also accessed with Tools|Options). You may wish to review the Help information about printing to determine what each printing parameter offers. You can also set different check boxes and then use Print Preview, described next, to determine the effect.

Print Preview

You can preview the pages of a document before they are printed to make sure they are arranged properly. Simply click the Print Preview button or use File|Print Preview to display the document. Print Preview gives you a thumbnail sketch of one or more pages at a time. You can also enlarge the document using the Magnifier button or Zoom Control 100% and perform editing right on the Print Preview screen. When you use Print Preview, several special preview buttons are displayed.

You may wish to view two pages to see if facing pages are balanced. You can also display a half-dozen pages to check the general layout and page breaks. From left to right, the toolbar buttons are:

Print—Print the displayed document.

Magnifier—Turn the zoom mode on or off; enlarge and reduce the document size by clicking the left and right mouse buttons.

One Page—Display a single page.

Multiple Pages—Click and drag to display multiple pages at the same time. Here, you can select the display format by choosing the number of rows and columns you want to use.

Zoom—Zoom the page size by typing a value or picking one from a drop-down pick list.

View Ruler—Turn a vertical and horizontal ruler on or off with this button.

Shrink One Page—Shrink the type size of the displayed document to make it fit on one less page.

Full Screen—Hide the menu, scroll bars, and status bar to display the page full-screen; the toolbar is still displayed.

Close Preview—Close Print Preview; return to the previous document view.

Context Sensitive Help—Display help information about a selected item.

Print Preview is an excellent way to see how your document will look when it is printed, before you actually commit it to paper. This lets you shape the appearance of the printed document before you unnecessarily waste printing time and paper.

Printing Multiple Documents

You can queue up several documents at once and then print them. To do this:

1. Click **File|Open**.

2. Press and hold <**Ctrl**> and click on each document you want to print. (Note that all documents must be in the same folder.) Another useful method for printing multiple documents, if all the documents are in sequential order, is to highlight the first selection, press the Shift key, and use the down arrow to highlight the rest of the files.

3. Click on **Tools** in the Open dialog box and then click on **Print**.

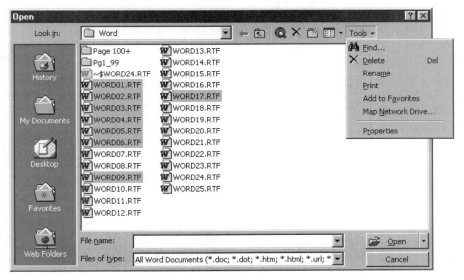

Printing Envelopes

You can print an envelope using the Tools|Envelopes and Labels menu selection. The displayed dialog box automatically displays the address typed at the beginning of a letter document in the Delivery Address text box. If the document does not have an address, you can type one. In addition, you can copy addresses from a document and paste them into the Delivery Address text box.

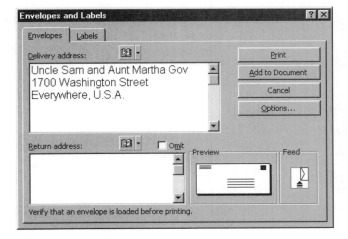

Use the Options button to change envelope sizes.

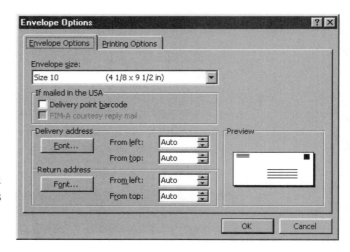

You can omit the return address by clicking the Omit check box on the Envelopes tab of the Envelopes and Labels dialog box. This is commonly done when using stationery that has a preprinted return address. You may change the return address for this envelope only by typing a different one in the Return Address text box of the Envelope tab. Use Tools|Options|User Information to change the default return address in the Return Address text box.

The Add to Document button of the Envelope dialog box is used to insert an envelope at the beginning of the current document. It is inserted as page 0 and prints as the first page when the document is printed. Once all is ready, click the Print button to print the envelope.

The Labels tab of the dialog box provides the ability to print a single label or a whole sheet of labels. Use the Options button to select various standard label sizes from a Product Number pick list in which common Avery label product numbers are listed.

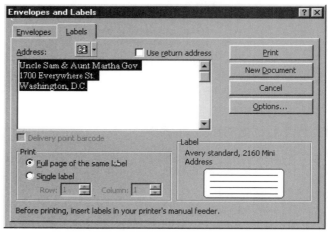

Mail Merge

The Tools|Mail Merge menu selection is used to merge a list of information, such as names, addresses, and phone numbers (called *data* or *data source*) into what is called a *main document*. The main document contains merge fields into which data is placed. The main document is created using the Mail Merge Helper dialog box. The data document can be a database file, a table with rows (records) and columns (fields), or a *comma-delimited* ASCII text file, in which each line represents a record and the commas are used to separate (or delimit) one field from another. You can also use the Address Book in Microsoft Outlook as a data resource.

Mail Merge Toolbar

The Mail Merge toolbar contains the tools necessary to perform mail merge functions. Each tool is explained in the following discussion.

Insert Merge Field—select data fields desired in merged heading.

Insert Word Field—insert various decision-making prompts for selecting specific merge records.

View Merged Data—displays the main document merged with information from the chosen data records.

First Record—displays the main document merged with information from the first data record selected for merging.

Previous Record—displays the main document merged with information from the selected record.

Go To Record—displays the main document merged with information from the selected record.

Next Record—displays the main document merged with information from the next data record selected for merging.

Last Record—displays the main document merged with information from the last data record selected for merging.

Mail Merge Helper—used to produce form letters, mailing labels, envelopes, catalogs, and other types of merged documents.

Check for Errors—reports errors in the main document or the data source that may prevent merging.

Merge to New Document—runs the mail merge and places the results in a single, new document.

Merge to Printer—runs the mail merge and prints the results.

Start Mail Merge—opens the Mail Merge dialog.

Find Record—searches for specific data records within a selected field.

Edit Data Source—opens the Data Form dialog where mail merge data can be viewed and edited one record at a time.

Here's how the general Mail Merge process works.

1. Open a new blank document.

2. Create your data by either typing it into a table or by importing it from a database, spreadsheet program, or ASCII text file. Look at the following example. Notice how column or field headings are placed in the first row; these are used to identify each data element in the main document.

Title	Fname	Lname	Address	City	State	Zip	Telephone
Mr.	John	Wilson	123 Main Street	Austin	TX	78757	512-234-5555
Ms.	Nancy	Spivey	4212 Vern Lane	Sattler	TX	77545	210-263-7111
Dr.	Bernard	Runyan	121 Medical Dr.	Dallas	TX	75075	512-238-9090

Note: Do not put any leading characters prior to "Title." That is, make sure there are no spaces or carriage returns, etc.

3. Save the data document (in the example, Mrgdata.doc is used as the filename).

4. Click the New button (or use File|New) to open another new document; then use Tools|Mail Merge to display the Mail Merge Helper dialog.

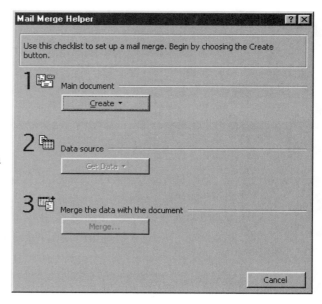

5. Click the Create button to display a list of Mail Merge choices.

6a. Pick Form Letters (or another appropriate choice).

6b. Pick the Active Window button to use the displayed blank document.

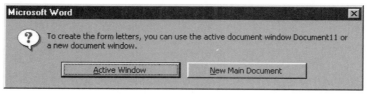

Note: You may open a new document in another active document by selecting New Main Document.

In this case, Document11 is shown in the illustration in Step 8; Document2 is more likely if you've only opened two new documents. In any case, the document number will be the number associated with the number of new documents you have opened in this session of Word, and is really immaterial. (You could also pick an existing form letter document here if one were prepared.)

7a. Use the Get Data button of the Mail Merge Helper dialog to specify the data resource you want to use. Click on Open Data Source....

7b. Select the appropriate data source file in the Open Data Source dialog (Mrgdata.doc in this example), then click the Open button.

7c. Select the proper field delimiter by clicking the Field delimeter down arrow and highlighting the appropriate delimiter (separator). If your data source uses tabs to delimit (separate) the data fields, then highlight Tab, click on OK, and click on Close.

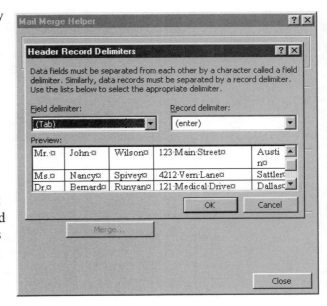

Note: If you previously attempted to perform a mail merge operation with the data source, you will not necessarily see the Header Record Delimiters dialog. It only appears the first time you use the file as a data source and then only if you are not using the default delimiters.

7d. Click on the Edit Main Document button.

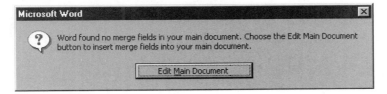

8. Now create a main document that resembles the following one, using the Insert Merge Field button to pick and insert the merge field names at the cursor position. Be sure to insert spaces and punctuation as needed.

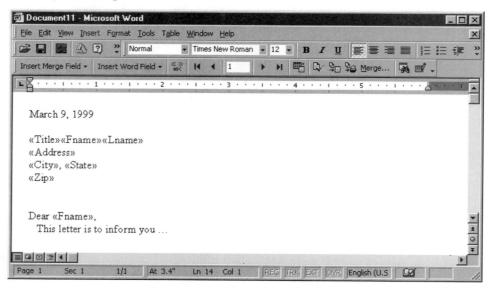

9. Use File|Save and give the new document a name, such as Mrgmain.doc. Then click the Mail Merge Helper button on the Mail Merge toolbar to check the names of the Main Document and Data Sources filenames. Click the Merge button if the filenames are correct.

10. Use the View Merged Data, Next Record, and Previous Record buttons to see how the data looks when merged.

11. If, after checking for errors, all is well, you are ready to print your document to your printer or to a file. The default name of the merged document is Form Letters1. Closing this document returns you to the main document where the Mail Merge toolbar is displayed. From here you can use the appropriate button on the Mail Merge toolbar to print or examine your data.

Merge documents can be used for a variety of purposes. In addition to form letters, you can also create telephone directories, customer lists, inventory reports, and much more, you can read information into Word from other programs including databases and spreadsheets. You can also read ASCII files into a data document. These file types all serve as data files that are frequently used by a main mail merge document.

Hands-on Activity

In this activity you print the TextBox2.doc file. Then you create and print a mail merge document.

1. Start the Word program; click the **Open** button on the toolbar and open the **TextBox2.doc** file from the companion CD.

2. Prepare your printer for printing; then click the **Print** button on the toolbar to print the document.

3. Use **File|Close** to close the TextBox2.doc file.

4. Click the **New** button on the Standard toolbar to open a blank Document2.

5. Type the following data fields in a 6 x 6 table. Then save it as **Clubdat.doc**. (Or use Insert|File and pick Clubdat.doc from the \MSOffice\Files folder to save time.)

Mrms	Fname	Lname	Address	CSZ	Phone
Mr.	John	Simmons	123 Jogging Dr.	Austin, TX 78058	(512) 345-0987
Ms.	Linda	Garcia	1412 Elk Road	Denver, CO 58675	(303) 569-0987
Mr.	Tom	Johnson	36 Polynesia	Naples, FL 39037	(813) 468-0980
Ms.	Denise	McEvoy	44 5th Avenue	New York, NY 01220	(212) 444-5555
Mr.	Hernando	Mendez	12 Boeing Dr.	El Paso, TX 76905	(915) 514-5432

6. Click the **New** button again to open a second document. Now use **Tools|Mail Merge** to display the Mail Merge Helper dialog.

7. Click the **Create** button, pick **Form Letters**, and then click the **Active Window** button to choose the open document as the main document.

8. Click **Get Data**, select **Open Data Source**, select **Clubdat**, and click **Open**. Then click the **Edit Main Document** button.

9. Type the following text. (Do not type bracketed items.) Position your cursor and then use the **Insert Merge Field** button to display and insert the indicated mail merge field names into your main document.

March 19, 2000

‹‹Mrms›› ‹‹Fname›› ‹‹Lname››
‹‹Address››
‹‹CSZ››

Dear ‹‹Fname››,
This letter is to inform you

10. Click the **Mail Merge Helper** button to verify the filenames.

11. Try several of the buttons on the Mail Merge toolbar including the View Merged Data, Next Record, Previous Record, Check for Errors, Edit Data, Mail Merge, Find Record, and Edit Data Source buttons to determine their effect.

12. If you wish, use the **Merge to Printer** or **Merge to New Document** buttons to see the finished results.

13. Click the **Save** button to save the Main Document as **Clubmain.doc**.

14. Press <**Alt+F4**> to exit Word. You may wish to save the documents for later referral.

Summary

As you can see, it is easy to print your Word documents. The Mail Merge operation is also easy once you explore its features. You should be ready to create virtually any kind of document using the power of Word 2000. In the next section, you learn about Word's powerful Master Document feature, which is designed for use with large, multichapter documents.

Master Document

Introduction

Word's master document feature, which is accessed using View|Outline, is used to combine two or more documents into a larger, fully paginated document. An ideal use for the master document feature is to integrate and control the pagination (page numbers, headers, footers, etc.) of several documents containing chapters of a book into a single, multichapter book. Master documents put the pages of each *subdocument* (such as a chapter) in the proper sequential order, i.e., 1 to *n*. You can also use Insert|Index and Tables to prepare a complete table of contents, table of figures, table of authorities, and an alphabetical index.

Changes to subdocuments within a book often move headings and words contained in your alphabetical index to different pages. The new page numbers associated with moved elements are automatically adjusted. Just delete the old table or index and rerun the table of contents and re-index to capture the changes. This eliminates the need to edit your book's *front matter* (list of tables) and indexes every time you make a change. If you create large, multichapter documents, becoming proficient with Word's master document feature will save you a lot of time.

Each new subdocument within a master document is put in a separate section. You can use the Layout tab of the Page Setup dialog to control the way your sections behave. For example, you may want each section to begin on an odd-numbered, right-hand page; have a running header on every left-hand page of the book and unique chapter headers on the right-hand pages; and use small Roman numerals in the front matter (title page, copyright page, and contents pages) and regular Arabic numerals in the balance of the book. It is easy to obtain these effects when you use the Master Document and Section features available in Word.

The Outlining and Master Document Toolbars

When you display a document in the Outline view, the Outlining and Master Document toolbars appear.

Use the Outlining toolbar to apply different heading levels or body text to selected headings, paragraphs, and lists. The Outlining toolbar begins with the Promote button ◄ and includes all the buttons to the right until the Master Document View button.

The Master Document toolbar begins with the Master Document View button 🔲 and includes all the toolbar buttons to the right. Use the Master Document toolbar to manage subdocuments that comprise the master document under construction.

You can display the button names in the usual manner. Just put your mouse pointer on a button to display a descriptive label. Look at the status bar at the bottom of your screen to see additional information about the button. Following is a description of each of the buttons on the Outlining and Master Document toolbars. These toolbars are displayed when you choose View|Master Document.

Outlining Toolbar

This toolbar promotes, demotes, and applies different heading styles to one or more selected list elements or paragraphs.

Promote—Increase the selected paragraph to the next higher heading level, i.e., promote a "Heading 3" to a "Heading 2."

Demote—Decrease the selected paragraph to the next lower heading level, i.e., demote a "Heading 1" to a "Heading 2."

Demote to Body Text—Change the selected heading to Normal (or body text).

Move Up—Move the selected heading or paragraphs ahead of the preceding heading or paragraph.

Move Down—Move the selected heading or paragraphs below the following heading or paragraph.

Expand—Display the next lower level headings and/or paragraphs by selecting a heading and clicking the Expand button.

Collapse—Hide the next lower level headings and/or paragraphs by selecting a heading and clicking the Collapse button.

Show Heading 1 through 7—Click the 1 through 7 button to display those headings at and higher than the selected level. For example, if you wish to display headings 1, 2, and 3, click 3.

All—Display all heading levels.

Show First Line Only—Show only the first line of text of each paragraph.

Show Formatting—Show or alternately hide heading formats; when hidden, headings are shown as normal text.

Master Document Toolbar

Master Document View—Display or hide the Master Document toolbar buttons.

Collapse or Expand Subdocuments—Collapse or expand the display of subdocuments within the master document.

Create Subdocument—Insert a new subdocument within the current master document.

Remove Subdocument—Remove the selected subdocument from the master document.

Insert Subdocument—Open a document and insert it as a subdocument.

Merge Subdocument—Merge two or more adjacent subdocuments as a single subdocument.

Split Subdocument—Divide a subdocument into two subdocument sections.

Lock Document—Lock the selected subdocument to prevent changes. Also, use this button to unlock the document when changes are required.

Using Master Document

Following is a step-by-step approach for creating a book (or similar multichapter document) that is created by using several smaller documents. The procedure also guides you through creating a table of contents and index.

Note: The following procedure makes use of existing documents. These are inserted into the master document as *subdocuments*. You can also create and edit new and revised documents directly into a master document. Hence, there are many ways to create and save master documents. You may wish to experiment with the Master Document toolbar until you find the method you like best.

Document Creation

1. Create and save each section or chapter of a book as an individual document. End each document with a carriage return. Be sure to assign a descriptive name, such as Chap01.doc, Chap02.doc, etc. Using sequential names sorts them within the active file folder, making each subdocument file easy to find.

2. Open a new document after all individual chapter documents have been created and saved.

3. Click View|Outline to display the Outlining and Master Document toolbars.

4. Click the Insert Subdocument button, pick the first document in sequence, and click OK.

5. Press <Ctrl+End> to go to the end of the first document. Backspace so that you delete the section break at the bottom of the inserted document.

6. With the cursor on a new line (at the end of the first section), click Insert Subdocument again.

7. Pick the second document to be inserted and click OK. The first two subdocuments are inserted.

8. Again, delete the last section break and put the cursor on a new line at the bottom of the last section. Then insert the third subdocument as above.

9. Continue inserting your subdocuments in the proper order until all are included within your master document.

Starting Each Section on a New Page

Now set the Layout tab of the Page Setup dialog as shown so that each section starts on a new page.

Tip: In this procedure you start each new subdocument on a new page. However, if you want to start each subdocument (or "chapter") on a right-hand page, as is the practice with many printed books, select Odd Page instead of New Page. Right-hand pages are always odd-numbered. Conversely, even-numbered pages are always on the left-hand side when the book is lying open. Check Different Odd and Even if you want to alternate the copy and/or placement of headers and footers. Check Different First Page if you want to omit a header and/or footer on the opening page of each subdocument (or chapter).

1. Move to each subsection and set the Layout tab of the File|Page Setup dialog as shown in the following illustration.

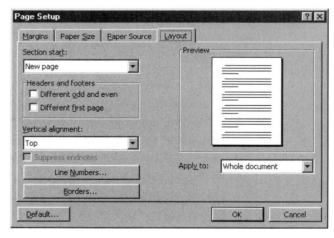

2. Be sure that every subdocument (or chapter) has been set up so that each of your sections start on a new page. Also check the Different Odd and Even and Different First Page check boxes. If you think you missed a section, it's easy to check. Simply put the cursor in the subdocument and display the Page Setup dialog to display your settings. Change as necessary.

3. Click the Print Preview button on the Standard toolbar to ensure that every subdocument starts on a new page.

Adding Headers and Footers

In the preceding section you provided for different odd and even pages and first pages using the check boxes. With these settings in place, you can add alternating headers and footers.

1. Use the View|Header and Footer menu selection to enter header and footer text.

2. Use Align Left for even-numbered headers and footers and Align Right for odd-numbered headers and footers.

3. Go to the first page of the first subdocument that uses Arabic page numbers. Then move to the footer (using View|Header and Footer).

4. Click the Page Numbers button on the Header and Footer toolbar to insert a page number.

5. Use the Insert|Page Number menu selection to set the first number to 1. Set the Alignment to Outside. Click the Format button and select the number style and starting value. Click OK twice to close both dialogs.

6. Set the page number font, point size, and weight (bold, italic, etc.) to your preferences.

7. Close the Header and Footer toolbar. Then use Page Preview to examine each page number and its placement. Make adjustments as necessary.

Tip: You can use the Page Setup button on the Header and Footer toolbar to make any necessary page layout adjustments. Pay particular attention to the Same As Previous button to ensure that unwanted header or footer information is not carried over from the previous section.

8. Once the headers and footers are properly adjusted and examined, you are ready to create a table of contents.

Creating a Table of Contents or Figures

If your section headings and titles use the styles on the Formatting toolbar, then creating an automatic table of contents is easy.

Once styles are applied to all headings (such as Heading 1, Heading 2, etc.), place the cursor at the position where the table of contents should begin.Then use the Insert|Index and Tables menu selection to display the Index and Tables dialog. Click on the Table of Contents tab, and select the format you like (check it in the Preview box). Use the Options and Modify buttons if you wish to change the order, add more heading levels, or insert a custom heading style. Click OK once all is set up to your liking.

To create a table of figures, use the Table of Figures tab is used in the Index and Tables dialog.

Creating an Alphabetical Index

It is an easy matter to mark various text entries for inclusion in an alphabetical index. Indexes are normally found at the end of a multichapter document.

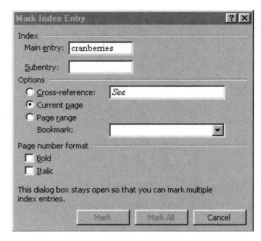

First, find and highlight (drag) the word or phrase you want to include. Then use the Insert|Index and Tables menu selection to display the Index and Tables dialog. Click the Index tab. Then click the Mark Entry button. The selected word or phrase is displayed as the Main Entry on the Mark Index Entry dialog as shown here.

Click Mark on the Mark Entry Index dialog (or Mark All to find every occurrence of a word or phrase). Then click Close and move to the next word to be indexed.

Tip: You can type alternate forms of the word or phrase to help your readers locate information. You can also use subentries that are printed below a main word, such as:

      Potato
            Baked
            Boiled
            Fried

Place the cursor at the index insertion point within your document, then use the Index tab of the Index and Tables dialog to pick the format you want to use. Click OK; the index is compiled and inserted in the specified format.

Hands-on Activities

The companion CD contains seven small files named Basics00.doc through Basics06.doc. These are provided to give you some hands-on experience in assembling a master document. Begin by launching Word and displaying a blank document.

Inserting Subdocuments

1. Use the **View|Outline Document** menu selection to display the Outlining and Master Document toolbars.

2. Click the **Insert Subdocument** button on the Master document toolbar, select the Basics00.doc companion file, and click **Open**.

3. Press **<Ctrl+End>** to move to the end of the document.

4. Put the cursor on a blank line at the extreme bottom of the document. Be sure that there is a carriage return on the line above the cursor. Then click **Insert Subdocument**, select Basics01.doc, and click **Open**.

5. Repeat steps 3 and 4 and insert the remaining files Basics02.doc through Basics06.doc. Respond by clicking **No to All** when the Title 1 Style already exists dialog is displayed.

Starting Each Section (or Subdocument) on an Odd-Numbered, Right-Hand Page

6. Go to each subdocument and set the **Layout** tab of the **Page Setup** dialog as shown here:

   Each subdocument should start on a new page.

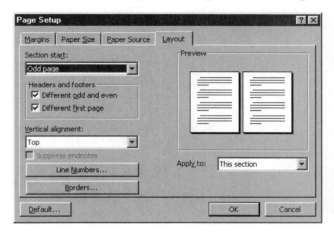

Inserting Headers and Footers; Putting Page Numbers in the Footers

7. Go to the beginning of the first subdocument. Use the **View|Print Layout** menu selection.

   a. Use the **View|Header and Footer** menu selection to display the Header and Footer toolbar.

   b. Click the **Switch Between Header and Footer** button to move to the footer of the title page (first page of the first subdocument).

   c. Click the **Insert Page Numbers** button on the Header and Footer toolbar.

   d. Click **Format Page Number** and set the page number value to small Roman letter **i**. (This is the convention normally used for the *front matter* of a book.) Click **Start at** and verify that it is **i**.

   e. Click **OK**. Then click **Close** to close the Header and Footer toolbar.

f. Use **Insert|Page Numbers** and set the Alignment to **Outside**. Make sure **Show number on first page** is not checked.

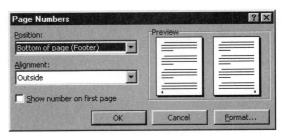

8. Go to the beginning of the second subdocument (named "Section 1"). Repeat 7a through 7f above, setting the **Page Numbers** dialog as shown in the two illustrations shown here.

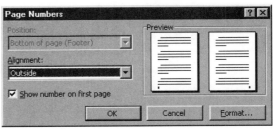

(This starts the first section with page number 1 on an odd-numbered, right-hand page.)

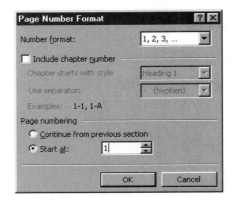

9. Go to the beginning of each of the remaining subdocuments. Repeat 7a through 7f above, setting the **Page Number Format** dialog as shown in the illustration at right. (Note that these continue the page numbering scheme from the previous sections. Also, each new section starts with an odd number.)

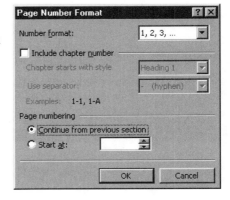

Tip: When even-numbered pages are blank (called a *blank back*), they are skipped. For example, if page 7 has a blank back, blank page 8 is skipped. Page 9 starts the next section on an odd-numbered, right-hand page.

Construct a Table of Contents

10. Go to the second page. Move the cursor to the blank line following the word "Contents."

11. Use the **Insert|Index and Tables** menu selection and click the **Table of Contents** tab.

12. Click the **Options** button. Set the TOC Level numbers opposite the Available Styles as listed below. Scroll down to the Heading 1 heading and put 1 in the TOC Level box. Be sure that all unused headings are blank except for those shown in the following list.

Available Styles	TOC Level	Available Styles	TOC Level
Title 1	1	Heading1	2
Heading2	3	Heading3	4

13. Click **OK**. Your dialog should resemble this one:

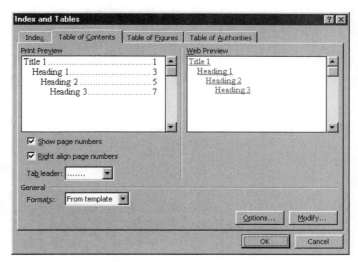

14. Click **OK** again to compile the table of contents. When completed, you have a full table of contents with heading names, dot leaders, and page numbers.

Tip: If you make changes and want to recompile the table of contents, click on the table of contents with your mouse to select it. Delete it (with Del). Then repeat steps 11 through 14 as necessary to recompile the table of contents to the current document configuration.

Construct an Alphabetical Index:

15. Select ten or twelve headings, words, and phrases for inclusion in an alphabetical index as follows:

a. Drag the first selection so that it is highlighted (such as "Seeing what's on your computer").

b. Using the **Insert|Index and Tables** menu selection, click the **Index** tab and click **Mark Entry**. Your dialog should resemble the following one:

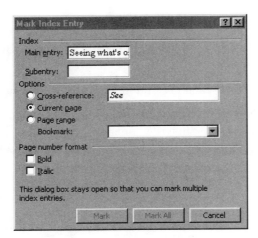

c. Click **Mark** to identify the entry for your index.

d. Close the dialog and continue selecting and marking entries until you have selected ten or twelve. Notice that "XE" field codes are inserted following each selection.

Section·1—The·Basics·(Getting·Your·Work·Done)¶

Seeing·what's·on·your·computer{·XE·"Seeing·what's·on· your·computer"·}{·XE·"Seeing·what's·on·your·computer" }¶

In·Windows,·you·store·your·work·in·folders{·XE·"folders".·}·just·like·you·would·in·your·office·or·at·home.· You·can·look·at·your·files·and·folders·by·using·My·Computer.·Inside·My·Computer,·you·can·see·a·list·of·all· of·the·disk·drives·attached·to·your·computer.·Just·double-click·on·any·icon·to·see·what's·inside.·When·you· open·a·disk·drive,·you·can·see·the·files·and·folders·that·it·contains.·Folders·can·contain·files,·programs,·and· even·other·folders.¶

Finding·a·file·or·folder·in·a·hurry{·XE·"Finding·a·file·or· folder·in·a·hurry"·}¶

It's·easy·to·locate·files·and·folders·on·your·computer.·You·can·always·browse·through·your·folders·in·My· Computer,·but·if·you·want·to·find·something·quickly,·you·can·use·the·Find·command·on·the·Start·menu·

Tip: You can also position your cursor, use the Insert|Field menu selection, and use the dialog as shown here to manually enter your index entries.

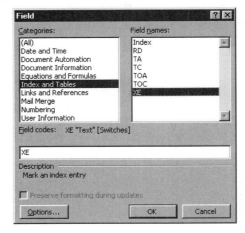

16. Place the cursor on the line following the word "Index" in the last subdocument.

17. Use the **Insert|Index and Tables** menu selection and click the **Index** tab.

18. Select the Classic format as shown in the following illustration and click **OK** to compile the index.

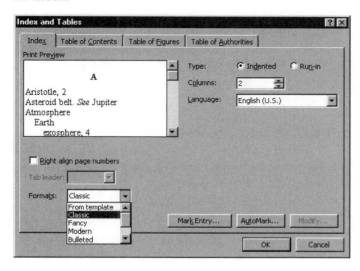

19. Notice that the index is inserted at the cursor position.

Examine the Paginated Document Using Print Preview or By Printing It

20. Press **<Ctrl+Home>** to go to the top of the document.

21. Click the **Page Preview** button on the Standard toolbar.

22. Display two to four pages at a time using the **Multiple Pages** button.

23. Page through the document checking the layout and page numbering. If you wish, you can click the **Print** button to see the actual output.

Finishing Up

This completes the master document activity. As you can see, master documents are ideal for creating large, multichapter documents. Now you can exit Word without saving or, if you prefer, save the document for additional experimentation. When saved, sections are automatically locked to protect the integrity of the document. Use the Lock Document button on the Master Document toolbar to unlock each subdocument when changes are required. If you have time for another practice activity, try adding alternating right- and left-hand headers. Here, add the book title to left-hand page headers and the section number to the right-hand page headers. Put the headers at the outside of each page. You should also omit headers from the first page of each section, which is a common publishing practice. You may also want to see how easy it is to promote and demote heading styles using the Outlining toolbar. Just put the cursor on a paragraph heading and click the buttons to see how they work.

Summary

As you can see, the master document view is ideal for assembling many small documents into a book or lengthy proposal. Of particular importance are the control of consecutive page numbers, tables of contents, and alphabetical indexes. If you regularly work with books and manuals, be sure to begin using the master document view on a regular basis. With a little practice, this feature will increase your productivity, saving you hours of valuable time.

Macros and Security Issues

Introduction

This section discusses security issues such as protecting your computer files from some types of malicious viruses and protecting your documents from unauthorized access. Passwords and macros are part of the discussion. Security issues are applicable to all of the Office 2000 applications, but the topic is more relevant to Word as most Office 2000 usage is perhaps done in Word. This section will focus on security issues as applicable to Word.

Melissa. A pretty name for a girl. An ugly name for a computer virus. Melissa took the world by storm in 1998 and we thought computer viruses would never be the same again. But what is Melissa and just what is a computer virus? A *computer virus* is a piece of software code that hitches a ride piggyback style into your computer and then destroys files and/or programs. There are many types of computer viruses and there are various ways they hitch the ride into your computer.

Melissa was a particularly effective virus. Melissa is a macro that comes to you via an e-mail Microsoft Word attachment. When you open the innocuous-looking Microsoft Word e-mail attachment, which comes to you courtesy of a known and trusted source such as a friend, the virus immediately resends itself to the first 50 addresses in your address book. So you innocently pass it on to another 50 people who think they are getting an e-mail from a known and trusted source. Assuming, of course, you have 50 addresses. Otherwise, it just e-mails itself to however many addresses there are.

Understanding Macro Viruses

A *macro virus* is a computer virus that uses macro code to manipulate your computer to perform some malicious operation that adversely impacts your system and maybe others as well. It is stored in a macro within a document, template, or add-in. When you open such a document or perform an action that triggers a macro containing viral code, the macro virus may be activated, or it may be put to sleep for a period of time or until a specific action is performed, or it may be stored in a file such as the Normal or global template. Once it is appended to a file, every open document could be automatically "infected" with the macro virus as it appends itself to the opened documents. If other users open the infected documents, the macro virus is transmitted to their computers. And on and on and on… The only way to guarantee 100% safe

163

operation is to never, ever have contact with the rest of the world. Never use any one else's data or programs, and never connect to the Internet. But, if you cannot live a computer-monk lifestyle, you must observe a few common sense precautions. One such precaution is using an up-to-date virus detection program.

Supplied Macros

Microsoft Word includes a template, called Support9.dot, containing two macros that may be useful in your daily work. You can load the template as a global template and then assign the macro to a toolbar button, menu item, or shortcut key. The Support9.dot sample macros were created by Microsoft Technical Support. You might be asked to use one of these macros if you contact Microsoft Technical Support Engineering for assistance when resolving a problem.

Support9.dot template is located in Program Files\Microsoft Office\Office\Macros directory. If it is not available, you may need to install it. The file is located in D:\PFiles\MSOffice\Office\Macros in the pre-production version of Office 2000. Copy the file from D:\PFiles\MSOffice\Office\Macros to C:\Program Files\Microsoft Office\Office\Macros if necessary. The table provides the details of the two macros.

Macro	Description	Modules and Forms
Edit Conversion Options	Customize unique settings for text converters and graphic filters.	Common EditOptCommon EditCnvOptionsForm
Registry Options	Modify Microsoft Word settings in the Windows registry file.	RegOptions RegOptionsForm

Security Levels

Word allows the user to set the following security levels to reduce the chances that macro viruses will infect documents, templates, or add-ins. The Security dialog is accessed via the Tools|Macro|Security menu selection.

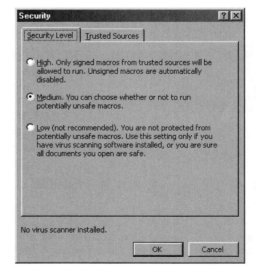

■ **High**—only runs macros that have been digitally signed and have been confirmed by the user to be from a trusted source. Before trusting a source, the user should confirm that the source uses a virus detector before signing macros. Unsigned macros are automatically disabled, and Word opens the document without any warning concerning the disabled micros.

- **Medium**—displays a warning whenever Word encounters a macro from a source that is not on your list of trusted sources. You can decide whether to enable or disable the macros when the document is opened. If it is possible the document might contain a virus, you should choose to disable macros.

- **Low**—should only be selected if you are certain all your documents and add-ins are safe. This option turns off macro virus protection in Word. At this security level, macros are always enabled when the documents are opened.

If the network administrator has not enforced a security level for your organization, you may change the security level any time you are working in Word. If the security level is set to Medium or High, a list of trusted macro sources can be maintained.

When you open a document or load an add-in that contains macros developed by any of these trusted sources, the macros are automatically enabled.

When you open a template or load an add-in that was already installed when you installed Word 2000, macros within the file are automatically enabled. Word can warn you about previously installed templates and add-ins according to the level of security you have chosen.

Note: Word will not scan floppy disks, hard disks, or network drives to find and remove macro viruses. If you want this kind of protection, you need to purchase and install specialized antivirus software.

Digital Signatures

One way to determine if a macro is safe to use is by its digital signature. A digital signature on a macro is similar to a wax seal on an envelope. The signature confirms that the macro originated from the macro developer who signed it and the macro has not been altered from the time the developer created it to the time you received it. You must have Internet Explorer version 4.0 or later installed on your computer to use digital signatures.

When a document is opened or an add-in is loaded that contains a digitally signed macro, the digital signature appears on your computer as a certificate. The certificate identifies the macro's source, and provides additional information about the identity and integrity of that source. A digital signature does not just by itself guarantee the safety of a macro, and the user must decide whether or not to trust a macro that has been digitally signed. You might trust macros signed by someone you know or by a well-established company with a reputation for providing clean documents. If you are unsure about a document or add-in that contains digitally signed macros, carefully examine the certificate before enabling macros; if you are not certain, disable the macros. If you know you can always trust macros from a particular source, you can add that macro developer to the list of trusted sources when you open the document or load the add-in.

Note that Excel does not consider Excel templates to be from trusted sources. Regardless of the Trust all installed add-ins and templates check box selection, if you have selected Medium or High security level, you will receive a macro virus warning every time you open an Excel template. Of course, setting the security level to Low will prevent the warning from appearing.

Passwords

There are good reasons for using passwords. You maintain a great degree of privacy and therefore can select who may, or may not, view your work. When you create a password to protect a document, write it down and keep it in a secure place. If you lose the password, you cannot open or gain access to the password-protected document.

A password can contain any combination of letters, numerals, spaces, and symbols. It can be up to 15 characters long. Passwords are case-sensitive, so if you vary the capitalization when you assign the password, users must type the same capitalization when they enter the password. To remove or change a password, you must know the password.

When you save a document as a Web page, it does not maintain password protection or enable you to create a password once you've created the Web page. To preserve a document with a password, save a copy of your file as a document before saving it as a Web page.

Message Encryption

Microsoft Exchange Server allows you to encrypt messages. Both you and your recipients must be using Microsoft Exchange Server. Your system administrator must also have set up Microsoft Exchange Server security features on the computers. Click **Options|Security|Encrypt message contents and attachments**.

Additional Security Considerations

Before passing on copies of your documents, make sure the document doesn't contain invisible information. There may be hidden information in your document such as revision marks for tracked changes, comments, and hidden text. It's a good idea to review this invisible information and decide whether or not it's appropriate to include before you pass a copy of the document on. You may want to omit the information in a printed version of the document, or remove the information completely before you distribute the document online.

You can save multiple versions of a document within the same document if you want a record of changes to a document. Word saves only the differences between one saved version of the document and the next version. After you've saved several versions of the document, you can go back and review, open, print, and delete earlier versions. If you specified for Word to save one or more versions of your document in the same file, those versions are saved as hidden information in the document, so that you can retrieve them later. The File|Versions menu selection allows you to save versions of a document in the same file.

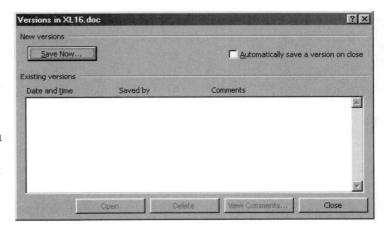

Individuals who review your documents may open previous versions of a document when you enable saving the previous versions. To prevent them from opening a previous version, save the current version as a separate document and distribute only the separate document or delete the versions from the document. Note that versions of a document do not remain hidden if the document is saved in another format.

Loss Prevention

Word can automatically recover unsaved changes to documents if the program stops responding or the computer power goes off. When AutoRecover is enabled (Tools|Options|Save menu selection), changes made to the document are saved at set intervals in a separate, temporary recovery file. Then, if you have to restart Word or your computer without having an opportunity to save the work, Word automatically opens the recovery file. The recovery file will contain your changes up until the last time AutoRecover saved the document. For example, if you set AutoRecover to save every ten minutes, you will not lose more than ten minutes of work. AutoRecover is not a good substitute for regularly saving documents.

If you lose power and restart your computer when the power returns, then open Word, you will be prompted to save the recovery file. If you choose not to save the recovery file, the file is deleted and your unsaved changes are lost. If you save the recovery file, it replaces the original document unless you specify a new filename.

Word can be set to automatically save a backup copy each time you save a document. The backup copy provides a previously saved copy, so you have the current saved information in the original document and the information saved prior to that in the backup copy. Each time you save the document, a new backup copy replaces the existing backup copy. Saving a backup copy can protect your work if you accidentally save changes you don't want to keep or you delete the original file. To save backup copies, use Tools|Options|Save menu selection and choose Always create backup copy.

Your document might be damaged if your computer stops responding when you try to open a document. The next time Word is started, the program automatically uses a special file recovery converter to recover the text from the damaged document. This file converter can be used at any time to open a document that has been damaged and recover the text. After you successfully open the damaged document, save it. Text in paragraphs, headers, footers, footnotes, endnotes, and fields are recovered as plain text. Document formats, graphics, fields, drawing objects, and any other information that is not text are not recovered

Hands-on Activities

Supplied Macros

To copy the supplied macros to the Normal.dot file, use the following procedure. Note the file Normal.dot is in the **C:\Windows\Application Data\Microsoft\Templates** subdirectory.

1. Click on the **Tools|Macro|Macros** menu selection.

2. Click on **Organizer**.

3. Open Support9.dot in the left pane and Normal.dot in the right pane. Choose the **Macro Project Items** tab. Use the **Copy** button to copy all the modules and forms (CConverterTable, Common, EditCnvOptionsForm, EditOptCommon, RegOptions, RegOptionsForm) from Support9 to the Normal.dot template.

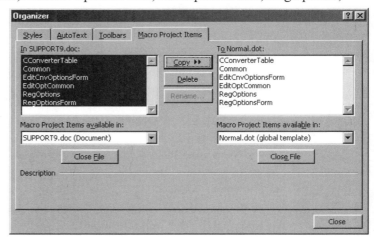

4. Click on **Close**. Now you are ready to run the macros.

5. Go to **C:\Windows\Application Data\Microsoft\Templates** and open Normal.dot.

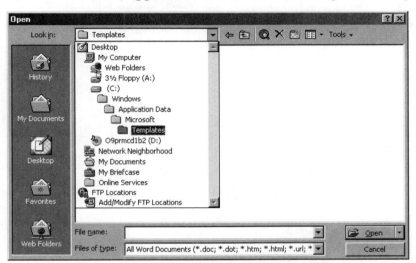

6. We will run the macro that allows you to change the registry settings for Word. Click the **Tools|Macro|Macros** menu selection and highlight Normal.RegOptions.RegOptions. Then click **Run**.

7. Notice there are several options available depending upon which elements of the registry you wish to change. We will not change any.

8. View the various registry elements. Notice the Setting text box where you change the current setting. Below the Setting text box is a text window that describes what the registry element is and what the valid

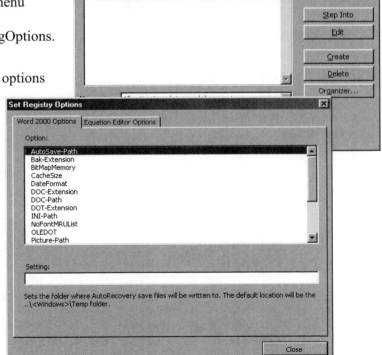

range of choices are for that
element. Click on **Close**.

9. To view the macro code, select
Tools|Macro|Macros. Choose
Support9.dot (template) from the
Macros In list box and select the
macro.

10. Click on **Edit**.

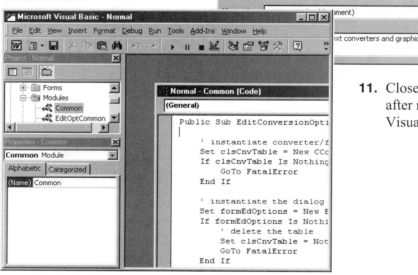

11. Close the window
after reviewing the
Visual Basic Editor.

Creating a Password

When you create a password, write it
down and keep it in a secure place. If
you lose the password, you cannot
open or gain access to the password-protected document.

1. Open a new document by clicking
File|New menu selection.

2. Click **File|Save As** menu selection

3. Click on the Tools menu on the left side
of the **Save As** dialog box, then click
General Options.

4. In the **Password to open** box, type a
password and then click **OK**. Note that

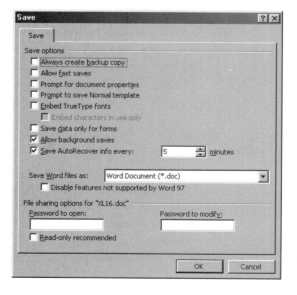

you can set a different password to allow
someone else to modify the document.

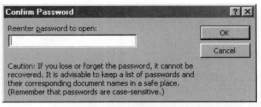

5. In the **Reenter password to open** box,
type the password again and click **OK**.

6. Enter a name for the file in the **File name**
text box. Click **Save**.

7. To verify the password, click on **File|Open** and
open the document you just saved. Observe the
following dialog is now active. Type in the
password you entered in the previous steps, then
click **OK**.

Changing or Removing a Password

1. Open the password-protected document by clicking on **File|Open**.

2. Enter the password in the Password dialog text box. Click on **OK**.

3. Click on **File|Save As** menu selection.
Click **Tools|General Options**.

4. In the **Password to open** box or the
Password to modify box, select the
placeholder symbols (usually asterisks)
that represent the existing password.

5. Do one of the following:

   a. To remove the password, press
   Delete, and then click **OK**.

   b. To change the password, type the
   new password, and then click **OK**.
   Reenter the new password, and
   then click **OK**.

6. Click **Save**.

7. Close Password.doc without saving.

Protecting Form Fields

After creating a form that users will view and complete in Word, you must protect it
so users will be able to enter information only in the designated areas, or *fields*.

1. Select **Tools|Protect Document**.

2. Select **Forms** on the Protect Document dialog.

3. To assign a password to the form so that users who know the password can remove the protection and change the form, type a password in the **Password** box. Users who don't know the password may still enter information in the form fields; they just cannot change the form itself.

4. Click **OK**. Now the entire form is protected. To protect only parts of a form, those parts must be in separate sections. The next steps show you how to protect specific sections of a document.

5. Open Password.doc. Place the cursor to the left and above each line. Select **Insert|Break**. Under Section break types, click **Next Page**.

6. Select **Tools|Protect Document**, and select **Forms**. Then click on the **Sections** button.

7. Clear the check boxes of the sections you don't want to protect. This example shows all the sections are selected for password protection. Click on **OK**.

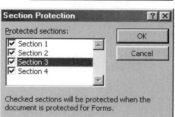

Tip: When designing or changing a form, you can quickly protect the form or remove protection from it by clicking the **Protect Form** button 🔒 on the Forms toolbar.

8. Close Password.doc without saving it.

Saving Documents Automatically

1. Open any Word file, and select **Tools|Options**.

2. Click the **Save** tab.

3. Select the **Save AutoRecover info every** check box. In the **Minutes** box, enter the interval for how often you want Word to save documents. The more frequently Word saves documents, the more information is recovered if there is a power failure or similar problem while a document is open in Word.

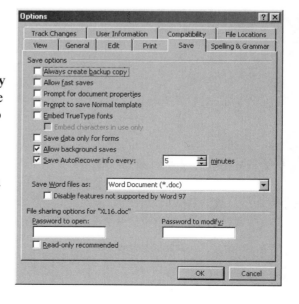

Note: AutoRecover is not a replacement for regularly saving documents. If you choose not to save the recovery file after Word opens it, the file is deleted and your unsaved changes are lost. If you save the recovery file, it replaces the original document unless a new filename is specified.

4. Close the Word file.

Automatically Recovering Files

1. Open any Word file.

2. Select **Tools|Options**, and then click the **File Locations** tab.

3. In the **File types** box, click **AutoRecover files**.

4. Click **Modify**.

   If you want to store automatically recovered files in a different folder, locate and open the folder.

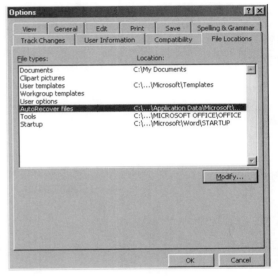

Note: If you use Word on a computer running Windows 95/98, automatically recovered files are by default stored in the Windows\Application Data\Microsoft\ Word folder. If you use Windows NT version 4.0 or later, or you use a computer on which there is more than one active user profile, automatically recovered files are stored in the Windows\Profiles*username*\ Application Data\Microsoft\Word folder.

5. Close the Word document.

Saving Backup Copies

1. Open any Word document.

2. Select **File|Save As**.

3. Click **Tools**, and then click **General Options**.

4. Select the **Always create backup copy** check box.

5. Click **OK**.

6. Click **Save** and close the document.

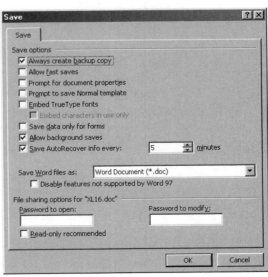

Opening a Backup Copy of a Document

To be able to recover the previous version of your document after a power failure or similar problem, you must have the Always create backup copy check box selected on the Save tab in the Options dialog box (Tools menu) before the problem occurs, and you must have saved the document more than once.

1. Start Word.

2. Select **File|Open**.

3. In the **Files of type** box, click **All Files**.

4. If you want to open a backup copy that was saved in a different folder, locate the folder and open it. Click the **Views** button ⊞, and then click **Details**. In the **Name** column, the backup copy name appears as "Backup of *document name*"; in the **Type** column, the file type for the backup copy appears as "Microsoft Word Backup Document."

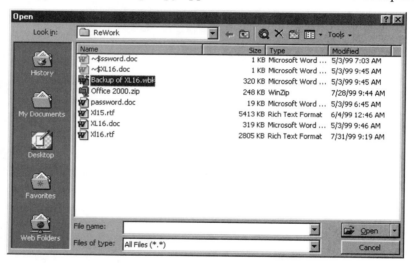

5. Locate the backup copy, then double-click it to open the file.

Recovering Text From Damaged Documents

1. Select **Tools|Options**, and then click the **General** tab.

2. Select the **Confirm conversion at Open** check box. Click **OK**.

3. Select **File|Open**.

4. In the **Files of type** box, click **Recover Text from Any File**.

5. Open the document as usual.

Note: If you don't see **Recover Text from Any File** in the **Files of type** box, you need to install the file converter.

Using Versioning to Save Current State

1. Open Word.

2. Select **File|Versions** menu selection.

3. Click **Save Now**. In the **Comments on version** box, type descriptive information about the version being saved.

Note: Because you are archiving document versions, you cannot go back and modify a saved version of a document. Before you can modify an earlier version, you must open that version and use the **Save As** command to save it as a separate file.

Automatically Saving a Version When Closing

1. Open Word.

2. Select **File|Versions**.

3. Select the **Automatically save a version on close** check box.

4. Click **Close**.

Saving Document Version as Separate File

1. Open Word.

2. Select **File|Versions**.

3. Click the version of the document you want to save as a separate file.

4. Click **Open**.

5. Click **File|Save As** menu selection.

6. In the **File name** box, enter a name, and then click **Save**.

Summary

This concludes the learning material about macros and security. You now have the tools to protect your computer and documents against malicious and prying folks and power interruptions. This also ends the material about Word. The next part guides you through the use of Microsoft Excel 2000, a full-featured spreadsheet program that can be used for business-related and personal finance matters.

Part 3

Microsoft Excel 2000

29 About This Part—Part organization and brief description of Excel.

30 Starting (or "Launching") Excel—Key Excel controls and terminology.

31 Creating Worksheets and Workbooks—Creation and use of two handy worksheets.

32 Opening and Saving Workbooks and Exiting Excel—Opening, saving, and exiting worksheets; common file operations.

33 Formatting Numbers and Text—Adjusting column widths, text placement, and numerical notation.

34 Using Labels, Names, and Protection—Referencing cells, protecting cells from accidentally typing over important information and unprotecting cells to allow changes.

35 Producing Charts—Presenting numerical information in graphical form.

36 Printing Operations—Printing worksheets and graphs on paper; special printing effects.

37 Window—Placing borders around worksheets; displaying and using multiple worksheets.

38 Linking Workbooks—Combining and/or consolidating information from two or more worksheets.

39 Macros—Automating common worksheet operations.

40 **Database**—Entering, manipulating, and reporting a mixture of text- and numeric-based information.

41 **Using Tables**—Creating and using lookup tables to find a series of incremental values.

42 **Using Files with Other Programs**—Exchanging and/or converting worksheet information for use with other programs.

43 **Putting Excel Data on the Web**—Placing Excel data on the web as an interactive file.

About This Part

Introduction

Part 3 of this book guides you through the use of Microsoft Excel 2000. From this point forward, the common name "Excel" is used. When you complete the sections within this part of the book, you should be able to create, save, and print many kinds of worksheets needed to support both business-related and personal finance matters. Before moving into the descriptive and tutorial sections of this part, be sure to read the remainder of this section.

What is Excel?

Excel is a full-featured spreadsheet program that is used by millions of people around the world. Excel 2000 makes use of all of the features available to programs designed specifically to run with a 32-bit operating system such as Windows 95/98/2000 and NT. This means your version of Excel runs faster and more reliably than the older 16-bit technology programs. When acquired as part of Office 2000, Excel uses a number of shared Office resources. These shared resources include fonts, ClipArt, spelling resources, AutoCorrect, AutoText, and more.

As with the other Office programs, Excel can also integrate documents and information created by other Office and Windows programs. For example, you can insert Word documents and Access tables directly into your Excel documents. In fact, you can put up to 32,000 bytes (or characters) in an Excel 2000 cell. The ease and flexibility of doing this is impressive. For example, you can cut a portion of a document created by another program and then paste it into your Excel worksheet. Or, you may prefer to "drag and drop" part of one document into another using your mouse. With Office 2000, you can now easily place your Excel data on the web as an interactive file for others to view or even change. Finally, you may simply import one kind of document into another. This flexibility gives you the ability to work in ways that best suit your personal tastes.

Companion Files

The Excel companion files are located on your *Learn Office 2000* companion CD-ROM in the Files folder.

What's Next?

You're ready to begin learning all about Excel. In the next section you examine the layout of an Excel worksheet. With this background in place, you then move to Section 31 where you actually begin creating and saving worksheets.

Section 30

Starting (or "Launching") Excel

If you installed the Office toolbar, the easiest way to launch Excel is to click on the Excel button. Otherwise, go to the Programs group (or the group in which you installed Excel); start Excel by clicking the Microsoft Excel line. When Excel starts, the default Book1 loads.

The first time you start Excel you are invited to review "What's New," and the Office Assistant offers help. If you are familiar with previous versions of Excel you may want to close the Office Assistant for now. Go to the Menu bar and click on Help, then click on Hide the Office Assistant. The default Book11 makes use of the Normal style sheet. Compare your display to the following illustration, which labels the various parts of the Excel screen.

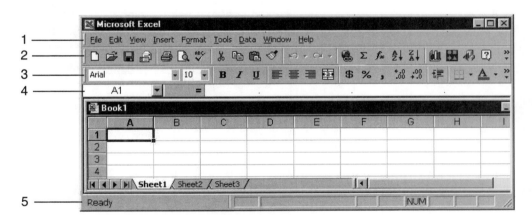

The above screen illustrates the Normal page view. If you wish, you can use the View menu to change the document view. With a spreadsheet open, you can now type your text, numbers, and formulas and use the menus and toolbars to change the page setup, font, text size, and more. Each Excel screen control is summarized in the appendices on the accompanying CD. Detailed descriptions are found in the following sections of this book where you are guided through hands-on learning activities.

181

Note that the Visio button [icon] may or may not be on your toolbar. Buttons of application programs designed to work with any of the Office 2000 suite of programs can be installed on the shortcut bar. When you install such a program, it will ask you if you want to place a button on the Office 2000 toolbar.

Microsoft Excel 2000 Controls

The keyed screen illustration shows each of the various controls which are summarized in the list that follows.

Key	Item	Description
1	Worksheet Menu Bar	Used to access the Excel menus and the Office Assistant (Help)
2	Standard Toolbar	Includes buttons to perform the most frequently used file, editing, web and hyperlink, charting, cell calculations, sorting, and Office Assistant (Help) operations.
3	Formatting Toolbar	Includes buttons to perform the most frequent file formatting operations such as specifying fonts and font size; specifying text, number, and formula characteristics such as bold, italic, underling; text, number, and formula positioning (left margin, center, right margin); merging cells; formatting currency, percents, and decimals; and formatting indentation operations.
4	Formula bar	Displays cell name box and formula/number box.
5	Status line	Displays messages.

Terminology

Worksheet—A worksheet, sometimes called a *spreadsheet*, is nothing more than a large planning form made up of columns and rows. Excel uses a workbook-style presentation which is made up of several worksheets, like pages in a notebook.

Rows and Columns—Notice that the rows are numbered from top to bottom along the left edge of the worksheet. The first row is numbered 1, the second 2, and so on. There are 65,536 rows. The columns are labeled from left to right with letters. The first column is A, the second is B, and so on until you reach Z. Then come columns AA through IV. The last (or rightmost) column of the worksheet, IV, is the 256th column.

Cells—A cell is the intersection of a row and column. For example, the uppermost cell is A1 (column A, row 1). Cell E6 is the intersection of column E, row 6.

Two or more adjacent cells are referred to as a *range* of cells. Ranges specify the first and last cell in a row, column, or rectangular area. Here are two examples of ranges.

E3:E12—All cells in column E from row 3 up to and including row 12.

C3:G20—All cells in the rectangular area bounded by C3 at the upper left and G20 at the lower right.

Creating Worksheets and Workbooks

Introduction

This section guides you through the creation of two useful worksheets. The first maintains travel expenses; the second maintains sales, expenses, and profit information. Follow each step carefully. Compare the progress of your worksheet to the worksheet illustrations in this part. A successful comparison verifies the accuracy of your work.

Notation Used in This Part

To make your data entry efficient and quick, the following notation is used. A series of special keystrokes is used to put Excel through its paces. In general, function keys F1 through F12, combination keys, such as pressing and holding Shift while typing Del (designated by <**Shift+Del**>), and pressing special keys such as Home, End, or Esc, are presented in a shorthand way to eliminate unnecessary text.

The passage "Press the Alt key and then type F" is reduced to "<Alt, F>." Following is a list of notations and meanings used throughout this part.

Notation	Meaning
<Key Name>	Press the named key.
[B2]	Move cell pointer to cell B2 (starting or ending cell position).
B2:B14	The range of cells from B2 through B14.

Tip: A fast and accurate way to move to a cell is to press F5 (the GoTo key), type the indicated cell coordinate, such as G3, and press <Enter>. GoTo is not available during formula entry, so use the cursor keys or mouse. The cell coordinate appears on the formula entry line at the top left portion of your screen.

Examples:

<Enter>	Press Enter.
Amount	Type the word *Amount* in the designated cell.
<Alt+F4>	Press and hold Alt, press F4, release Alt.

<**Right**><**Up**>	Press Right Arrow; then press Up Arrow.
<.>	Press the period key.
Select [**B2:B14**]	Select cell B2; then press and hold the left mouse button and drag down to cell B14, which highlights the range of cells from B2 to B14. Once the cells are highlighted, release the mouse button.
[B2] <**Alt, E, C**>	Move to cell B2, press Alt, type E, then type C.
[F5] <**Ctrl+Ins**> [F6] <**Shift+Ins**>	Select cell F5, press Ctrl and Ins together, select cell F6, and then press Shift and Ins together.
File|Save As	Use the **Save As** selection of the File menu.
Pick	Pick an item from a menu or pick list.
Click	Click a button, check box, or dialog tab with the left mouse button.
Right-click	Click the right mouse button.
Drag	Click on an item, such as a graphic element, press and hold the left mouse button, drag the element to a new location on the screen, and release the mouse button. You can also select multiple cells by dragging from one corner diagonally to the opposite corner.

Starting and Exiting the Program

1. Start Microsoft Windows 95/98/NT.

2. From the Programs group list or the Office 2000 toolbar, click Microsoft Excel.

3. Notice that a blank workbook named Book1 is displayed; the first worksheet tab, labeled Sheet1, is active and ready for your entries.

4. Press <Alt+F4> or use <Alt, F, X> to exit the worksheet program, returning to the Windows desktop.

In the following activities, you start and exit Excel from Windows several times. Therefore, avoid exiting Windows unless you are ready to turn off your computer and return later.

Getting Help

To display help information using the Office Assistant, click the Help button on the Standard toolbar or press F1 in the Ready mode, i.e., when "Ready" is displayed at the bottom left-hand corner of the worksheet. You can also use <Alt, H> (or pick Help on the menu bar with your mouse). If you use the Help menu, select Contents and Index to display a Help Topics dialog. Use the Index tab to access information by typing a word or phrase. Use the Contents tab to pick a subject from a list of help topics. Use

the What's This selection (or press <Shift+F1>) to access context-sensitive help. Just point to an object and Excel's context-sensitive Help feature describes the selected item. Press <Alt+F4> to close the Help dialog. When a menu item is highlighted, such as the Clear selection on the Edit menu (referred to as Edit|Clear), you can press F1 to display helpful information about the current process. When involved in some process, the Help feature senses the feature in use and displays information that corresponds to the current activity.

Toolbars

Excel displays one or more *toolbars* containing a row of related buttons across the top of your screen. When you first start Excel, the Standard and Formatting toolbars are displayed; the Formula bar, which is used to enter and edit cell values, is also displayed. Each button on a toolbar offers a shortcut method of performing commonly used file and workbook operations. For example, clicking the Open (file folder) button performs the File|Open menu operation.

You can open and close toolbars using the View|Toolbars menu selection. Display of the Formula Bar (where a formula, text, or value within a selected cell is displayed) is controlled by clicking the View|Formula Bar menu selection. Use the Toolbars list by clicking on the check boxes to display or hide toolbars.

Use Customize to display the Customize dialog. Here, you can modify existing toolbars and even create new toolbars of your own. Use the Toolbars tab to select the toolbar you want to modify. Use the Commands tab to drag buttons to the desired toolbar. The Customize feature gives you a way to add shortcuts to frequently used items.

The Cancel and Undo Keys

The Esc key is used to back out of a process and return to the worksheet. If you've opened a window, you may have to use Ctrl+F4 or Alt+F4 to close it. This lets you display menus and submenus and then gracefully back out of them without having to use unwanted features. If you make an error, Excel provides an Undo selection in the Edit menu. For example, if you accidentally delete something, use Edit|Undo (or press Ctrl+Z) to restore it. Excel maintains up to 16 undo levels.

Setting Up (Tools|Options)

The Tools|Options menu selection displays a dialog box that controls the way Excel looks and works. There are ten different Options dialog boxes that are accessed by clicking the tabs, each of which is briefly described here. You can examine Excel's built-in Help information about any dialog box by displaying it and then pressing F1.

View—Use the check boxes to control what is displayed and hidden. This dialog box is critical to both displayed and printed information.

Calculation—Change the way Excel performs its calculations.

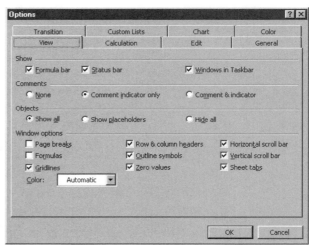

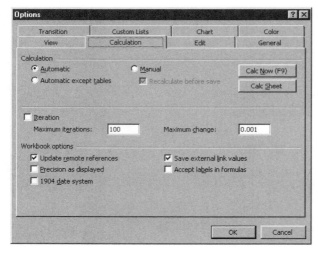

Edit—Use the check boxes to control the way

information is entered into cells and transferred between them.

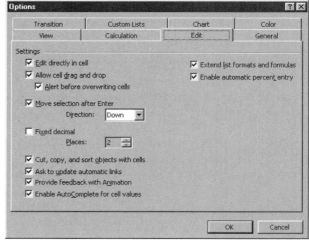

General—Use this tab to set cell reference style (A1=R1C1), number of workbook sheets, the standard font and size, the default file path for workbooks, and the user name.

Transition—Set the format of saved files, Excel menu and help keys, and the way formulas from imported files are evaluated.

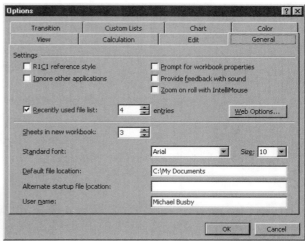

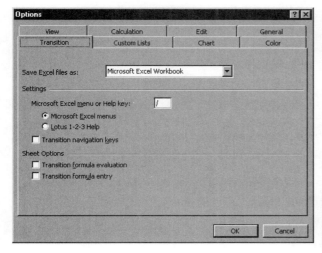

Custom Lists—Use these lists when using Edit|Fill|Series|AutoFill. You can add your own custom lists for use with AutoFill. Just type the first element in the series, highlight the target row or column, and click the Series dialog's OK button.

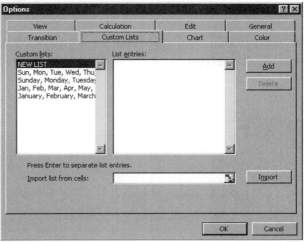

Chart—Use this dialog to set the way values within a chart are plotted. Also establishes what is displayed or ignored, such as zero values.

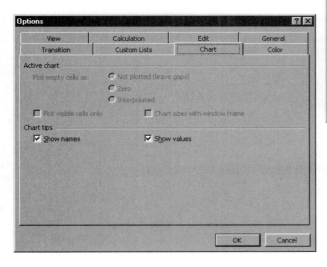

Color—Set the standard colors to use for your workbooks and charts.

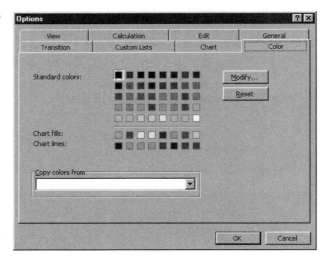

Hands-on Activities

Two worksheet creation activities are presented here. The first creates and saves a travel expense worksheet. The second is useful for sales and expense analysis. These worksheets are also available on the companion CD. Although you can load finished worksheets from the CD, you should create them from scratch in order to learn how they were created. This hands-on approach familiarizes you with the principles of creating, saving, and printing worksheets.

Travel Expense Worksheet

Create a travel expense worksheet. Begin by starting Excel and displaying a blank worksheet. Sheet1 of Book1 is displayed.

Tip: Move to cell coordinates within brackets, such as [A2], with the mouse or by typing A2 and pressing <Enter>. This is particularly helpful when moving to a distant cell. Use <Ctrl+Home> to move to A1.

Tip: You may edit a cell after you have made an entry by moving to the cell, then clicking in the cell reference area, just above the column heading. The mouse pointer will change to a text cursor. Now you can edit the cell information.

1. Type a worksheet title: [A1] type **Travel Expense Diary** <Enter>.

2. Type the column headings shown below by clicking on cell A3, holding the mouse button down, and dragging to cell E3. Then type the indicated text and press <**Enter**> after each column heading entry.

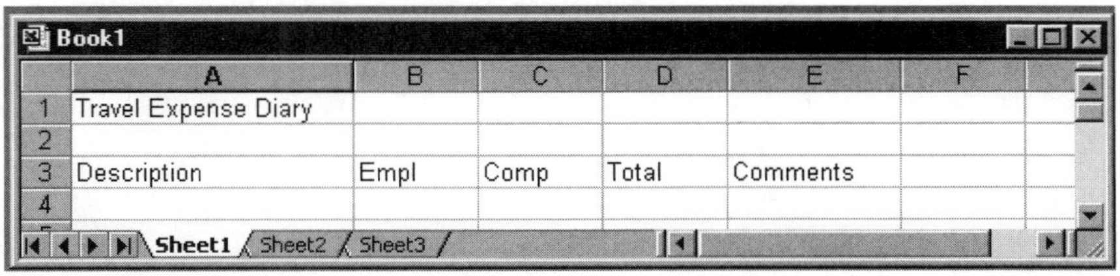

Book1						
	A	B	C	D	E	F
1	Travel Expense Diary					
2						
3	Description	Empl	Comp	Total	Comments	
4						

Sheet1 / Sheet2 / Sheet3 /

3. Increase the width of column A as follows: move to column A [A1], pick **Format|Column|Width**, type **20** for column A, and click **OK**. Repeat for column E and set it to **12**.

4. Move to A5 and type the row headings as shown in the following illustration, pressing **<Enter>** after each entry.

5. Enter the formula =B5+C5 in cell D5: [D5] <=> **<Left> <Left>** <+> **<Left> <Enter>**.

Note: In the following step, select cells D5 through D17 as follows: Pick cell D5, hold the mouse button down, drag down to D17, and then release the mouse button.

Tip: There are at least three ways to perform a copy operation. These are:

■ Select a source cell or range, press <Ctrl+C>, select the destination cell or range, and press Enter.

■ Select a source cell or range, click the right mouse button to display Edit selections, pick Copy, select the destination cell or range, and press Enter.

■ Select a source cell or range, type <Alt, E, C>, select the destination cell or range, and press Enter.

6. Copy the D5 formula to cells D6:D17: [D5] **<Alt, E, C>** drag down (or select the range) [D6:D17] **<Enter>**.

7. Enter formula =SUM(B5:B17) in cell B19: [B19] **=SUM(B5:B17) <Enter>**.

8. Copy the formula in B19 to C19:D19: [B19] **<Alt, E, C>** drag right to [D19] release the mouse button **<Enter>**.

9. Check your worksheet against the following illustration.

Note: To view the worksheet with the formulas you entered displayed in their cells, select Tools|Options, select the View tab, and click the Formulas check box in the Window Options area. To redisplay the cell values, select Tools|Options and click the Formulas check box again to remove the check mark.

```
┌─────────────────────────────────────────────────────────────────┐
│ 📊 Book1.xls                                          _ □ ×      │
├─────────────────────────────────────────────────────────────────┤
│        A              B           C          D           E        │
│  1  Travel Expense Diary                                          │
│  2                                                                │
│  3  Description     Empl        Comp       Total      Comments    │
│  4                                                                │
│  5  Ground Transit                        =B5+C5                  │
│  6  Tolls                                 =B6+C6                  │
│  7  Baggage Handling                      =B7+C7                  │
│  8  Airfare                               =B8+C8                  │
│  9  Breakfast                             =B9+C9                  │
│ 10  Lunch                                 =B10+C10                │
│ 11  Dinner                                =B11+C11                │
│ 12  Hotel                                 =B12+C12                │
│ 13  Telephone                             =B13+C13                │
│ 14  Car Rental/Taxi                       =B14+C14                │
│ 15  Parking                               =B15+C15                │
│ 16  Other 1 (Describe)                    =B16+C16                │
│ 17  Other 2                               =B17+C17                │
│ 18                                                                │
│ 19  Daily Total   =SUM(B5:B17) =SUM(C5:C17) =SUM(D5:D17)         │
│ 20                                                                │
│ |◄ ◄ ► ►|\ Sheet1 / Sheet2 / Sheet3 /        |◄|              ►|  │
└─────────────────────────────────────────────────────────────────┘
```

10. Format the block B5:D19 to two decimal places: [B5], select the range [B5:D19] **<Alt, O, E>** click the **Number** tab, pick **Number** from the Category text box, set Decimal places to **2**, and click **OK**.

Tip: As an alternate way to format cells, you can right-click your mouse to access the Format Cells dialog. Also, consider using the Increase Decimal or Decrease Decimal buttons on the Formatting toolbar to change the number of decimal places in a selected cell or range of cells.

11. Copy the range A1:E19 containing the daily diary information to the range A1:E19 of Sheet2 through Sheet4 as follows:

   a. Add Sheet4 by pressing **<Alt+I,W>**; drag Sheet4 to the right of Sheet3.

   b. Click the Sheet1 tab, select the range [A1:E19], press **<Ctrl+C>** (to copy the range to the Windows clipboard).

   c. Click the Sheet2 tab, move to [A1] of Sheet2, and press **<Ctrl+V>** to paste.

   d. Click the Sheet3 tab, move to [A1] of Sheet3, and press **<Ctrl+V>** to paste.

   e. Click the Sheet4 tab, move to [A1] of Sheet4, and press **<Ctrl+V>** to paste.

12. Double-click Sheet1 through Sheet4 tabs and change the names as follows:

   a. Change Sheet1 to **Tue 7-5**.

   b. Change Sheet2 to **Wed 7-6**.

   c. Change Sheet3 to **Thu 7-7**.

   d. Change Sheet4 to **Total**.

13. Move to A7 of each of the four sheets and use **Format|Column|AutoFit Selection** to adjust the width of column A.

14. Move to the Total sheet and enter the formulas for the grand totals. Notice how worksheet names are treated in formulas.

   a. [B5] ='**Tue 7-5'!B5+'Wed 7-6'!B5+'Thu 7-7'!B5 <Enter>**.

   b. [B5] **<Ctrl+C>** select range [C5:D5] **<Ctrl+V>**.

   c. Select the range [B5:D5] **<Ctrl+C>**.

   d. Select the range [B6:B17] **<Ctrl+V>**; then select [B19] **<Ctrl+V>**.

Note: Formulas are viewed and edited on the Formula Bar above the worksheet, which is normally displayed. If it is not, display the Formula Bar using the View|Formula Bar menu selection. Place a check mark to the left of Formula Bar.

   e. Type Grand Total in A19 and Travel Expense Totals in A1 of the Total worksheet: [A19] type **Grand Total <Enter>** [A1] type **Travel Expense Totals <Enter>**. Your finished Total worksheet should resemble this one:

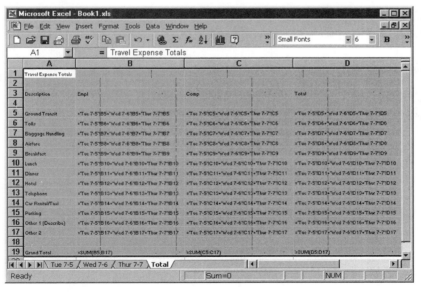

Pay particular attention to how the formulas were copied and automatically adjusted for you.

15. Use the Tools|Options menu selection, display the General dialog box, type **C:\MSOffice\Files** in the Default File Location box, and press **<Enter>**. Excel will save your workbooks to this folder until you designate another folder.

Note: The file folder \MSOffice\Files was created if you followed the instructions in Section 3 for copying the companion files to your hard disk. If you did not create it there, then use the Windows Explorer to create the folder. There, you save your practice files and copy the Excel files from the companion CD.

16. Save the workbook as Travbk: **<Alt, F, S>** type **Travbk** and click **Save**. This step saves a copy of your blank workbook which can be loaded and used many times. If a dialog box pops up saying a file with that name exists and asking if you want to replace that file, click **Yes**.

Note: Saving a file with the same name as another will overwrite the existing file. Don't worry; if you make a mistake in these examples, you can always get the original file from the CD.

17. Type the expense information in columns B, C, and E as shown in each worksheet illustration. Remember, you access each worksheet by clicking on the specified workbook tab.

   a. Type the Tue 7-5 expense information as shown:

Description	Empl	Comp
Ground Transit	8.40	
Tolls	0.50	
Baggage Handling	2.00	
Airfare		576.00
Breakfast		
Lunch		
Dinner		15.40
Hotel		124.42
Telephone		
Car Rental/Taxi	16.00	
Parking		
Other 1 (Describe)		
Other		

   b. Type the Wed 7-6 expense information as shown:

Description	Empl	Comp
Ground Transit		
Tolls		
Baggage Handling		
Airfare		
Breakfast	3.80	
Lunch	8.85	
Dinner	16.40	
Hotel		124.42
Telephone		3.80

Description	Empl	Comp
Car Rental/Taxi	4.40	
Parking		
Other 1 (Describe)		
Other		

c. Type the Thu 7-7 expense information as shown:

Description	Empl	Comp
Ground Transit	8.40	
Tolls		
Baggage Handling	2.00	
Airfare		
Breakfast		6.65
Lunch	6.00	
Dinner		
Hotel		
Telephone		
Car Rental/Taxi	18.00	
Parking	18.00	
Other 1 (Describe)		
Other		

18. Click the Total worksheet tab to view the total expense amounts.

19. Save the workbook as Travbk1: **<Alt, F, A>** type **Travbk1** and click **Save**.

By saving the workbook with a new name, such as Travbk1, you keep the original workbook Travbk intact for future use.

20. Exit the program using the x button in the upper right-hand corner of the screen. (If you prefer, you can use **<Alt+F4>** to close programs.)

	A	B	C	D
1	Travel Expense Totals			
2				
3	Description	Empl	Comp	Total
4				
5	Ground Transit	16.80	0.00	16.80
6	Tolls	0.50	0.00	0.50
7	Baggage Handling	4.00	0.00	4.00
8	Airfare	0.00	576.00	576.00
9	Breakfast	3.80	6.65	10.45
10	Lunch	14.85	0.00	14.85
11	Dinner	16.40	15.40	31.80
12	Hotel	0.00	248.84	248.84
13	Telephone	0.00	3.80	3.80
14	Car Rental/Taxi	38.40	0.00	38.40
15	Parking	18.00	0.00	18.00
16	Other 1 (Describe)	0.00	0.00	0.00
17	Other 2	0.00	0.00	0.00
18				
19	Grand Total	112.75	850.69	963.44
20				

Travbk1.xls — Tue 7-5 / Wed 7-6 / Thur 7-7

Regional Sales and Expense Worksheet

The following worksheet is used to track sales office revenues and expenses to determine profitability. It is typical of financial analysis worksheets. It is used later in Section 38 to show how several worksheets can be consolidated to provide an overall financial picture of multiple operating units, such as sales offices or manufacturing plants. Begin by starting the program and displaying a blank worksheet.

1. Type the title and row and column titles as shown in the following illustration; use the **Increase Indent** button ![increase indent button] to achieve the indents as shown.

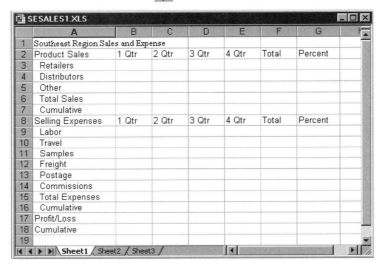

2. Widen column A to 16: Click column label **A**, right-click and select **Column Width**, type **16**, **<Enter>**. (You can also use the mouse to drag the right edge of the column border by picking the intersection line between column labels.)

3. Set the width of columns B through F to seven characters: Select column labels B through F, right-click and select **Column Width**, type **7**, **<Enter>**.

4. Copy the column headings in B2:G2 to B8:G8: Select [B2:G2] **<Ctrl+C>** pick [B8] **<Enter>**.

Tip: In steps 5 and 6, you can use the **B** and *I* buttons as a shortcut to boldface or italicize selected text.

5. Change the text in A1 to Times New Roman boldface (leave it at 10 point): [A1] pick **Times New Roman** from the font pick list (or type the font name in the text box). Then click the **Bold** **B** button on the Formatting toolbar.

6. Italicize and underline the text in A2:G2 and A8:G8: Select [A2:G2] click the **Italic** and **Underline** buttons on the Formatting toolbar. Select [A8:G8] click the **Italic** *I* and **Underline** **U** buttons on the Formatting toolbar.

7. Set the column headings in B2:G2 and B8:G8 flush right so that they align over the numbers: Select [A2:G2], press and hold **<Ctrl>**, select [A8:G8], release **<Ctrl>**, and click the **Align Right** ≡ button on the Formatting toolbar. Compare your display to the following screen illustration.

	A	B	C	D	E	F	G
1	Southeast Region Sales and Expense						
2	*Product Sales*	*1 Qtr*	*2 Qtr*	*3 Qtr*	*4 Qtr*	*Total*	*Percent*
3	Retailers						
4	Distributors						
5	Other						
6	Total Sales						
7	Cumulative						
8	*Selling Expenses*	*1 Qtr*	*2 Qtr*	*3 Qtr*	*4 Qtr*	*Total*	*Percent*
9	Labor						
10	Travel						
11	Samples						
12	Freight						
13	Postage						
14	Commissions						
15	Total Expenses						
16	Cumulative						
17	Profit/Loss						
18	Cumulative						

SESALES1.XLS — Sheet1 / Sheet2 / Sheet3

8. Enter a Total Sales formula in B6: [B6] click the AutoSum button, select [B3:B5] **<Enter>**. (Check for =SUM(B3:B5) on the Formula Bar.)

9. Copy the Total Sales formula to C6:F6: [B6] **<Ctrl+C>** select [C6:F6] **<Enter>**.

10. Enter the Cumulative formulas in B7:E7 in three steps:
   a. [B7] <=> **<Up>** **<Enter>**. (Check for =B6 in cell B7.)
   b. [C7] <=> **<Left>** <+> **<Up>** **<Enter>**. (Check for =B7+C6.)
   c. Copy the Cumulative formula in C7 to D7:E7: [C7] **<Ctrl+C>** select [D7:E7] **<Enter>**.

11. Enter the Total Expenses formula in B15: [B15] click the **AutoSum** button, select [B9:B14] **<Enter>**. (Check for =SUM(B9:B14) in cell B15.)

12. Copy the Total Expenses formula from B15 to C15:F15: [B15] **<Ctrl+C>** select [C15:F15] **<Enter>**.

13. Copy the cumulative sales formulas in B7:E7 to the cumulative expense line B16:E16: Select [B7:E7] **<Ctrl+C>** [B16] **<Enter>**.

14. Enter the Profit/Loss formula in B17:F17 in two steps:
   a. [B17] **=B6–B15** **<Enter>**.
   b. [B17] **<Ctrl+C>** select [C17:F17] **<Enter>**.

15. Enter the Cumulative profit/loss formulas in B18:E18 in two steps:
   a. [B18] **=B7–B16** **<Enter>**.

b. [B18] **<Ctrl+C>** select [C18:E18] **<Enter>**.

16. Enter the row Total formulas for F3:F5 in two steps:

a. [F3] click the **AutoSum** button, select [B3:E3] **<Enter>**.

b. [F3] **<Ctrl+C>** select [F4:F5] **<Enter>**.

17. Copy the formula in F3 to F9:F14: [F3] **<Ctrl+C>** select [F9:F14] **<Enter>**.

Note: In the following steps, an error message is displayed because the percentage formula attempts to divide by zero. The #DIV/0! disappears when you begin entering numbers into the worksheet later in this activity.

18. Enter the Percent formulas using the following four steps:

a. [G3] **<+>** [F3] **</>** [F6] **<F4>** **<Enter>**.

b. Copy G3 down three cells: [G3] **<Ctrl+C>** select [G4:G6] **<Enter>**.

c. Enter expense percent formulas: [G9] **<+>** [F9] **</>** [F15] **<F4>** **<Enter>**.

d. Copy G9 to G10:G15: [G9] **<Ctrl+C>** select [G10:G15] **<Enter>**.

19. Format the value area (B3:F18) to two decimal places: Select [B3:F18], right-click, pick **Format Cells**, click **Number** in the Category text box, put **2** in the Decimal places box, and click **OK**.

20. Format the Percent column to show percent: Select [G3:G15], right-click, pick **Format Cells**, click **Percentage** in the Category text box, put **2** in the Decimal places box, and click **OK**.

21. Compare your worksheet to the following illustration.

	A	B	C	D	E	F	G
1	**Southeast Region Sales and Expense**						
2	*Product Sales*	*1st Qtr*	*2nd Qtr*	*3rd Qtr*	*4th Qtr*	*Total*	*Percent*
3	Retailers					0.00	#DIV/0!
4	Distributors					0.00	#DIV/0!
5	Other					0.00	#DIV/0!
6	Total Sales	0.00	0.00	0.00	0.00	0.00	#DIV/0!
7	Cumulative	0.00	0.00	0.00	0.00		
8	*Selling Expenses*	*1st Qtr*	*2nd Qtr*	*3rd Qtr*	*4th Qtr*	*Total*	*Percent*
9	Labor					0.00	#DIV/0!
10	Travel					0.00	#DIV/0!
11	Samples					0.00	#DIV/0!
12	Freight					0.00	#DIV/0!
13	Postage					0.00	#DIV/0!
14	Commissions					0.00	#DIV/0!
15	Total Expenses	0.00	0.00	0.00	0.00	0.00	#DIV/0!
16	Cumulative	0.00	0.00	0.00	0.00		
17	Profit/Loss	0.00	0.00	0.00	0.00	0.00	
18	Cumulative	0.00	0.00	0.00	0.00		

Sesales1.xls

Sheet1 / Sheet2 / Sheet3 /

22. Use the following three steps to protect all formulas and titles from your accidentally typing over them:

    a. Select [B3:E5], press and hold down **<Ctrl>** and select [B9:E14]. Notice that both ranges are selected.

    b. Press **<Alt, O, E>**, pick the **Protection** tab, click on the **Locked** check box to remove the check mark, and click **OK**.

    c. Press **<Alt, T, P, P>** and **<Enter>** to protect the worksheet; do not enter a password.

23. Save the workbook as Sesales: [A1] click the **Save** button, type **Sesales** (if you have not previously saved the worksheet), and press **<Enter>**.

24. Type numbers in the data entry cells to see how the workbook operates. Begin with values of your own choosing. Then enter the values shown.

Sesales2.xls						
A	B	C	D	E	F	G
1 Southeast Region Sales and Expense						
2 Product Sales	1st Qtr	2nd Qtr	3rd Qtr	4th Qtr	Total	Percent
3 Retailers	56.30	60.20	58.40	65.40	240.30	51.81%
4 Distributors	59.40	38.70	44.50	41.20	183.80	39.63%
5 Other	4.50	9.50	11.20	14.50	39.70	8.56%
6 Total Sales	120.20	108.40	114.10	121.10	463.80	100.00%
7 Cumulative	120.20	228.60	342.70	463.80	463.80	
8 Selling Expenses	1st Qtr	2nd Qtr	3rd Qtr	4th Qtr	Total	Percent
9 Labor	4.50	4.50	4.80	4.80	18.60	24.97%
10 Travel	3.60	4.00	4.10	3.90	15.60	20.94%
11 Samples	0.50	0.60	1.10	0.80	3.00	4.03%
12 Freight	0.70	0.90	0.70	1.00	3.30	4.43%
13 Postage	0.30	0.40	0.30	0.50	1.50	2.01%
14 Commissions	8.40	7.60	8.00	8.50	32.50	43.62%
15 Total Expenses	18.00	18.00	19.00	19.50	74.50	100.00%
16 Cumulative	18.00	36.00	55.00	74.50	74.50	1.00
17 Profit/Loss	102.20	72.40	59.10	46.60	389.30	
18 Cumulative	102.20	192.60	287.70	389.30		
Sheet1 / Sheet2 / Sheet3						

Tip: If you've made any errors in your formulas, use **Tools|Protection| Unprotect Sheet**, make corrections to the formulas as necessary, and then use **Tools|Protection|Protect Sheet** again.

Tip: When a cell width is too small to display a number, it will contain number signs (####). Click on **Format|Column|Width** and increase the width sufficiently to display the number.

25. Produce a chart using the values in A2:E5 as a basis by performing the following steps.

    a. Unprotect the worksheet using the Tools|Protection menu selection: **<Alt, T, P>**.

    b. Select [A1:E5], click the **Chart Wizard** button 📊 on the Standard toolbar, examine the dialog, and click **Finish**.

c. Compare your chart to the following illustration:

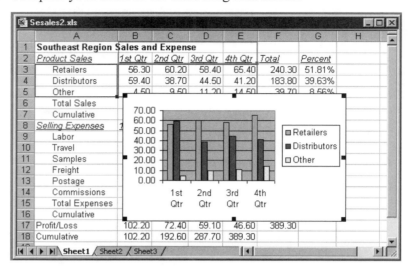

d. With the handles still displayed around the chart object, press **<Del>** to remove the chart from the worksheet.

26. Save the completed workbook as Sesales1.xls with the values shown in the illustration following step 24: [A1] **<Alt, F, A> Sesales1 <Enter>**.

27. Press **<Alt+F4>** to exit Excel.

Summary

This concludes the workbook creation activities. In these activities you learned a number of important workbook operations, including starting and exiting the Excel program, and entering text, formulas, and values. You also learned how to use different sheets of a workbook and how to save and retrieve workbooks. Formatting numbers and text styles, as well as changing the width of one or more columns was also covered. In addition, copying formulas to one or more cells, protecting and unprotecting titles and formulas, error handling, and graphing were discussed.

Opening and Saving Workbooks and Exiting Excel

Introduction

This section describes the procedures used to open and save workbooks in addition to appropriate ways to quit your workbook sessions. This section also includes several hands-on activities to familiarize you with the opening, saving, and quitting operations. Before getting into the hands-on activities, a brief description of each selection on the File menu is provided.

The File Menu

You may wish to review the purpose of each selection on the File menu. Each selection is briefly summarized in the following list.

New—Open a new blank workbook, chart, or macro sheet. Excel provides a New button (the page button) on the Standard toolbar.

Open—Open a new workbook. This selection lets you load multiple workbooks in different windows. You can use your mouse or the Window menu to move between open workbooks. You can also load files created by other programs, such as dBASE and Lotus 1-2-3. Excel analyzes foreign files and converts them as they are loaded. Excel also provides an Open button (the file folder) on the Standard toolbar.

Close—Close the current (or active) workbook.

Save—Save the current workbook. Unnamed workbooks are named. Existing workbooks are either replaced or a backup file can be produced. You can also specify different save formats. Excel provides a Save button (the diskette button) on the Standard toolbar.

Save As—Save the current worksheet under a new filename, or export a file in another file format such as a Lotus 1-2-3 or Multiplan worksheet or an Access or dBASE database file.

Save as Web Page—Save the current worksheet in HTML format.

Save Workspace—Save all currently active and open documents, window layouts, chart settings, etc. When a workspace is loaded at a later time, the previously saved environment, including all documents, charts, etc., is opened.

Web Page Preview—View the current worksheet as it would appear as a Web document. The worksheet is loaded into Internet Explorer and displayed on the screen.

Page Setup—Set the appearance of a printed workbook, macro sheet, chart, or info window, including such items as margins, headers and footers, sizing, centering, and more.

Print Area—Define the selected range of cells as the area to print; non-selected cells are omitted from what is printed. This selection is also used to clear (reset) a selected print area.

Print Preview—Display a graphic representation of the printed workbook.

Print—Print the open workbook to the selected Windows printer, or preview the worksheet on screen. (Excel includes the Page Setup dialog with this selection.) You may also use the Print button on the standard toolbar to print the current selection.

Send To—Send the workbook to other people using Microsoft Exchange, as regular e-mail, or to a recipient whose address is stored in Microsoft Outlook.

Properties—Display a Properties dialog showing information about the active file such as the title, author, content information, dates, size, etc.

Opening Workbooks

A blank workbook, titled Book1, is automatically opened and ready for you to begin workbook creation when you first start Excel. If you wish to retrieve an existing workbook, you can click the Open button or use the File|Open command <Alt, F, O> to display an Open dialog box. Here, a list of files is displayed. Excel workbooks have the file extension xls. Pick the file of your choice and click Open. The file is opened and ready to use. Once a workbook file is open, you can enter values, edit it, display charts, print it, or create and edit macros. (Charts, printing, and macros are discussed in detail in following sections of this book.)

Tip: Notice that the last four filenames used are displayed at the bottom of the File menu. You can pick one of these names or type the corresponding number, 1 through 4, to open the file. You can use Tools|Options to change the number of files displayed at the bottom of the File menu.

To open the Travbk workbook, perform the following steps.

1. Start Excel.

2. Load the Travbk workbook: Click the **Open** button, pick **Travbk <Enter>**.

3. Notice that the Travbk workbook is displayed, ready for use.

4. Quit the program: **<Alt+F4>** (or use the **File|Exit** menu selection).

Opening Files From Other Directories and Disk Drives

Files are selected from the dialog box that is displayed when you click the Open button, press <Ctrl+O>, or use the File|Open menu selection. You can double-click the desired filename or select it and click Open. If you want to load a workbook from another disk drive, such as drive A, or from another file folder, just type the drive designator, file path, and the filename in the File name box. For example, typing A:\WKS\TRAVEL loads the named workbook from the \WKS path on the diskette in drive A. Once typed, press Enter or click Open. You can also pick a drive and pathname from the Open dialog. Just click the Look in: box's down triangle to display a list of drives and pathnames from which to choose.

The Open dialog box includes a Files of type pick list from which you can import a variety of file types created by other programs. For example, you can import an Excel workbook produced by Microsoft Excel 4.0 or 5.0, Quattro, Lotus 1-2-3, or even dBASE database format. You may wish to experiment with the Open dialog buttons to determine their purpose. Of particular interest is the Look in Favorites button. This button gives you instant access to file folders that you select for saving and retrieving files.

If you pick a different disk drive and/or file path, Excel "remembers" your selection and uses it until you either exit the program or change to another drive and/or file path.

Opening Two or More Workbooks

You can open more than one workbook at a time. Each workbook remains in its own window and is accessed using the Window menu. Use <Alt, W, 1> to display the first workbook, <Alt, W, 2> to display the second, and so on. You can use the mouse to adjust window sizes so that they overlap. This technique lets you pick the desired window with your mouse. Finally, you can use Window|Arrange to tile or cascade workbook windows on the screen. Experiment with two open workbooks using the following steps.

1. Start Excel. Notice that a blank Book1 is displayed.

2. Open the Travbk1 workbook: **<Alt, F, O>** pick **Travbk1**, click **Open**.

(This assumes you have not changed directories and are still in the MSOffice\Files directory. If you are not, you may change to the directory by clicking Open and using the Look In box to move to the correct directory. But, if you must do this, go ahead and use the Open dialog to open the file.)

3. Open the Sesales1 workbook: **<Alt, F, O>** pick **Sesales1**, click **Open**.

   (This assumes you have not changed directories and are still in the MSOffice\Files directory. If you are not, you may change to the directory by clicking on Open and using the Look In box to move to the correct directory. But, if you must do this, go ahead and use the Open dialog to open the file.)

4. Display Travbk1 (the first window) again: **<Alt, W, 2>**.

5. Display both worksheets: **<Alt, W, A>** choose **Tiled <Enter>**.

6. The two worksheets should now be displayed side by side in the Excel workspace.

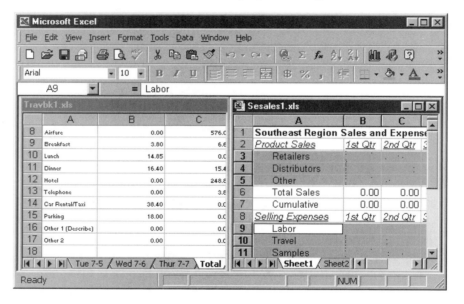

Open Dialog Box

The File|Open menu selection, Open button, or <Ctrl+O> displays the Open dialog box. This dialog is used to find, open, delete, and copy files in addition to accessing the Internet. As you pick workbook names, you can display information about each file using the List, Details, Properties, Preview, and Commands and Settings buttons. In the following illustration, the Commands and Settings button and the corresponding menu selections are shown. You can click each button to determine its effect. Following is a brief description of each.

Note: The Open dialog provides numerous search aids. For example, you can find files that match criteria that you supply. Use the Tools|Find menu selection to display another dialog that finds files that contain specified information. You can also save commonly used searches for later use.

These commands are located at the top of the Open dialog box:

Up One Level—Use to move up one file folder level.

Search the Web—Use to access the Internet by launching Microsoft Internet Explorer.

Delete—Remove the folder or file currently highlighted in the Open text box.

New Folder—Create a new folder in the directory or subdirectory currently displayed in the Open text box.

Views—Select one of several different file viewing options.

> **List**—Use to find files in different directories and/or on different disks. Also use to specify the file types to list by supplying different file extensions or wild cards. This selection also lets you name and save your search setups for future use.
>
> **Details**—Display detailed information for each file listed.
>
> **Properties**—Display summary information about the selected file including such things as author name, saved by, date created, date modified, company, etc.
>
> **Preview**—Use to display a thumbnail sketch of the selected workbook file.
>
> **Arrange Icons**—File folders are displayed in the Open dialog text box in the order selected. Files can be ordered by name, type, size, or date.

Tools▾ **Tools**—Select one of several file and folder processing options.

> **Find**—Use to find a file or folder by name.
>
> **Delete**—Use to delete a file or folder.
>
> **Rename**—Use to rename a file or folder.
>
> **Print**—Use to print one or more selected files; this choice displays the Print dialog box.
>
> **Add to Favorites**—Use to add the currently selected folder as a "favorite," which is then accessed using the Favorites button.
>
> **Map Network Drive**—Connects you to the selected (or "mapped") drive of a networked computer.
>
> **Properties**—Display detailed information about the selected workbook file.

The Open and Cancel buttons are located at the bottom of the Open dialog box:

 Open—Open a file for processing. Use the following Open commands to perform one of the following file operations:

> *Open*—Open file with no restrictions.
>
> *Open Read Only*—Open file; "read-only" prevents changes.
>
> *Open As Copy*—Open a copy of the selected file, leaving the original intact.
>
> *Open In Browser*—Open file and display it in a Web browser.

Cancel **Cancel**—Cancel the Open operation.

These commands are located on the left side of the dialog box:

History—Select the files and folders previously opened.

My Documents—Select the files and folders in the My Documents directory.

Desktop—Select the files and folders in the Desktop directory.

Favorites—Use to access those files or folders stored as "favorites."

Web Folders— Use to access those files or folders stored as Web documents.

Saving Workbooks

There are two general ways to save workbook files: File|Save and File|Save As. You can also click the Save button on the Standard toolbar or press <Ctrl+S>, which are both shortcuts for File|Save.

Save

You can save the current workbook using <Alt, F, S> (for File|Save) or by clicking the Save button. The current workbook is saved to disk. If the workbook is a new one and has not been saved previously, you are prompted for a filename. If the current workbook already exists, it simply writes over the previous version. If you wish to keep both the old version and new version of the current workbook, use File|Save As.

Save As

This file option, accessed with <Alt, F, A>, saves the current workbook with a new filename, creates a backup file, or saves the file in a different format.

The simplest Save As operation lets you type a new filename and click Save. Use the Save as type selection to save a file in a different file format. There are 29 file formats to choose from, depending on what was selected during setup. These formats include spreadsheet, text, and database formats.

An ideal use for Save As is when you load a standard workbook, enter data, and then save it with a new descriptive name. For example, you can load the Travbk workbook, enter expense data that corresponds to a specific trip, and then save as Travel 11-99, which might indicate travel for November 1999.

You can also use File|Save As to export workbooks for use in other programs including word processors, database programs, and other spreadsheet programs such as Lotus 1-2-3 or Multiplan. You can save the workbook as a CSV text file if you want to use it as a word processor mail merge file. For example, most word processing programs, such as Microsoft Word and Corel WordPerfect, make use of comma-delimited data files.

Hands-on Activity

The following activity uses File|Open and File|Save As to open and save the Sesales1 workbook as a text file. This workbook was created and saved in the previous section. Begin by starting Excel and displaying a blank workbook.

1. Open the Travbk1 workbook: **<Alt, F>** pick **Travbk1.xls** listed at the bottom of the File menu, **<Enter>**.

   (This assumes you have not opened and/or closed other files since the last hands-on activity and Travbk1.xls is still on the File menu. If the filename is not present on the File menu, open the file using the Open dialog of the File menu.)

2. Save the workbook as an ASCII text file: **<Alt, F, A>**, click the down arrow in the Save as type text box, pick **Text (Unicode or MS-DOS) (*.txt)**, **<Enter>**. Then click **OK** when the message box appears, telling you the selected file type will save only the active sheet.

3. Launch the Windows Explorer and locate the **Travbk1.txt** file (found in the MSOffice\Files directory).

4. Double-click the **Travbk1.txt** text file and notice that it is displayed in the Windows Notepad. This demonstrates that the file was exported in text format.

5. Close the Notepad and Explorer applications and return to Excel using the Microsoft Excel button on the Windows 95/98 Taskbar.

Exiting Excel

Exiting the program returns you to the Windows desktop. Exit by either pressing <Alt+F4>, using the File menu <Alt, F, X> sequence, or by clicking the Close [X] button in the upper right-hand corner of the application window. Be sure to save any workbook changes prior to exiting the Excel program. Otherwise, changes are lost.

Summary

Now that you know how to open and save workbooks, you're ready to move on to more workbook operations. In the next section, you learn how to format numbers and text.

Formatting Numbers and Text

Introduction

The Format menu, which is accessed using <Alt, O>, lets you change the way numbers and text are displayed. You can also use formatting buttons on the Format toolbar to display values as currency or percentages, with commas, or to increase or decrease the number of displayed decimal places. Both the Format menu and the Format toolbar provide an easy means for controlling number formats, fonts, size, colors, and much more. The use of both the Format menu, along with its dialog boxes, and the Format toolbar are presented in this section.

The Format Menu

The Format menu and its dialogs guide you through a variety of format choices. Notice that some selections are followed by a filled triangle, indicating a submenu. The choices followed by the ellipsis (...) display dialog boxes. The dialog boxes associated with Cells, AutoFormat, and Style are described and illustrated later in this section. A clarifying hands-on activity is also provided to give you the opportunity to experiment with a number of the format selections.

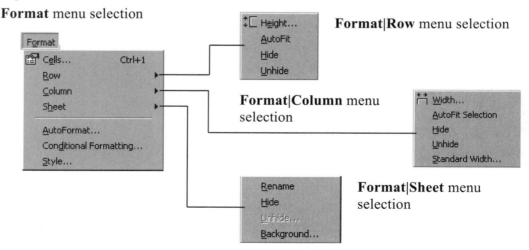

Format menu selection

Format|Row menu selection

Format|Column menu selection

Format|Sheet menu selection

Format|Cells menu selection. See the dialog box later in this section.

Format|AutoFormat menu selection. See the dialog box later in this section.

Format|Conditional Formatting menu selection. See the dialog box later in this section.

Format|Style menu selection. See the dialog box later in this section.

Format Cells Dialog

Notice that six different format selection folders are included in the Format Cells dialog. You can display a dialog folder by clicking the corresponding note-book-style tab.

Number—This dialog box is shown here. It is used to set the format of numbers, dates, or text within the currently selected cells. A sample box displays an example of the selected format.

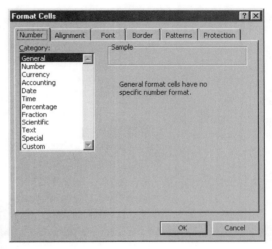

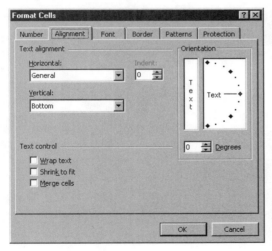

Alignment—Use to set the horizontal and vertical alignment of selected values. The Wrap Text check box is used to wrap text within the current cell(s).

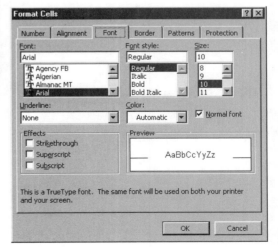

Font—Use to select a font name, style, size, color, and special effect.

Border—Use to put boxes and rules around one or more selected cells.

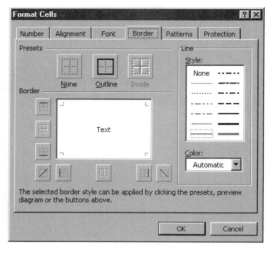

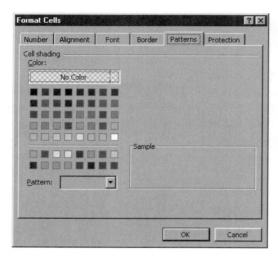

Patterns—Use to put a color or pattern within one or more selected cells.

Protection—Use to protect or hide formulas within selected cells. Protection has no effect unless you follow up by using Tools|Protection to protect a worksheet.

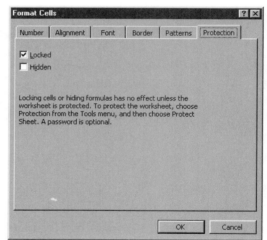

Other Selections

Format|Row—Use to adjust the height and to hide or unhide selected rows.

Format|Column—Use to adjust the width and to hide or unhide selected columns.

Format|AutoFormat—Use to change the look of your data by picking one of the preset formats. The AutoFormat dialog box is shown with the Options button activated.

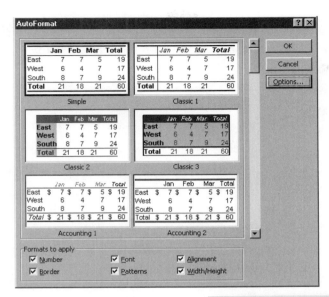

Format|Conditional Formatting—Use to change formatting depending upon cell contents.

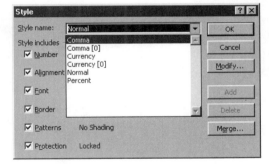

Format|Style—Use to set up format settings to selected styles. Preset styles are easily applied to the values in one or more selected cells.

The Formatting Toolbar

The Formatting toolbar is normally displayed when you start Excel. If it isn't, use View|Toolbars, click the Formatting check box, and click OK. Each of the buttons on the Formatting toolbar is illustrated and described for you. To use the formatting buttons, select the desired cells and click the appropriate formatting buttons.

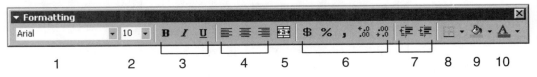

1—Set the font by picking a font name from the pick list.

2—Set the font size of the text or numbers within the selected cells.

3—Set text or numbers within selected cells as follows: **B**=Boldface, *I* = Italic, U = Underline.

4—Align selected cells left, center, or right.

5—Center text in one or more selected columns.

6—Format value as currency, percent, or comma style, or increase/decrease decimal places.

7—Increase/decrease indent of text within selected cells.

8—Apply borders or rules to selected cells.

9—Fill selected cells with a color or pattern.

10—Apply color or pattern to selected text.

Hands-on Activity

In this activity you use the Format workbook from the companion CD or create it using the following workbook illustration as your guide. Notice that column D contains the indicated formulas; once these formulas are entered, the derived values are displayed in their place.

Tip: You can use **Tools|Options**, pick the **View** tab, and then click the Formulas check box in the Window Options section to display formulas.

	A	B	C	D
1	Item	Quantity	Price	Totals
2	Table, 30x60	6	132	=B2*C2
3	Table, Conf	2	389	=B3*C3
4	Chair, Side	28	68	=B4*C4
5	Chair, Exec	4	158	=B5*C5
6	Chair, Steno	2	105	=B6*C6
7	Desk, 30x60	3	225	=B7*C7
8	Desk, Steno	2	286	=B8*C8
9	Desk, Exec	2	349	=B9*C9
10	Credenza	2	248	=B10*C10
11	Cabinet, File	8	78	=B11*C11
12	Cabinet, Storage	4	141	=B12*C12
13	Grand Total			=SUM(D2:D12)
14				

Format.xls — Sheet1 / Sheet2 / Sheet3

Begin this activity by starting Excel. A blank workbook is displayed.

1. Open the **Format** workbook from the \MSOffice\Files folder.

Note: If you create your own worksheet instead of using the provided Format workbook, select the range of cells containing text and numbers and use Format|Column|AutoFit Selection to adjust column widths. As changes are made, you can use this technique to ensure that all data is easily viewed.

	A	B	C	D	E
1	Item	Quantity	Price	Totals	
2	Table, 30x60	6	132	792	
3	Table, Conf	2	389	778	
4	Chair, Side	28	68	1904	
5	Chair, Exec	4	158	632	
6	Chair, Steno	2	105	210	
7	Desk, 30x60	3	225	675	
8	Desk, Steno	2	286	572	
9	Desk, Exec	2	349	698	
10	Credenza	2	248	496	
11	Cabinet, File	8	78	624	
12	Cabinet, Storage	4	141	564	
13	Grand Total			7945	
14					

Format.xls — Sheet1 / Sheet2 / Sheet3

2. Format B2:B12 to two decimal places: Select [B2:B12], click the **Increase Decimals** button on the Formatting toolbar twice. (You could also use Format|Cells|Number and pick Number in the Category list; then put 2 in the Decimal Places box.)

3. Format C2:D13 to currency: Select [C2:D13] and click the **Currency** button. Notice how the column widths automatically adjust to accommodate the increased width of the new values.

4. Format D13 to scientific: [D13] **<Alt, O, E>** pick **Scientific** from the Category list, put **2** in the Decimal Places box **<Enter>**.

5. Format D13 back to currency: [D13] click the **Currency** button. Compare your workbook to the illustration here.

6. Use the Formatting toolbar to format the labels in A1:D1 to Times New Roman 10 point bold: Click on the row 1 label to highlight row 1; pick **Times New Roman** from the Font pick list, pick **10** in the Font Size list, and click the **Bold** button.

	A	B	C	D	E
1	Item	Quantity	Price	Totals	
2	Table, 30x60	6.00	$132.00	$792.00	
3	Table, Conf	2.00	$389.00	$778.00	
4	Chair, Side	28.00	$68.00	$1,904.00	
5	Chair, Exec	4.00	$158.00	$632.00	
6	Chair, Steno	2.00	$105.00	$210.00	
7	Desk, 30x60	3.00	$225.00	$675.00	
8	Desk, Steno	2.00	$286.00	$572.00	
9	Desk, Exec	2.00	$349.00	$698.00	
10	Credenza	2.00	$248.00	$496.00	
11	Cabinet, File	8.00	$78.00	$624.00	
12	Cabinet, Storage	4.00	$141.00	$564.00	
13	Grand Total			$7,945.00	
14					

Format.xls — Sheet1 / Sheet2 / Sheet3

7. Draw a thick rule at the intersection of rows 1 and 2: Select [A1:D1] click the down arrow next to the Borders button and then pick the **Thick Bottom Border** box (second row, second column).

8. Format B2:B12 to integers: Select [B2:B12] and click the **Decrease Decimals** button twice.

9. With B2:B12 still selected, use the alignment buttons to adjust the column of numbers to center, flush left, and finally flush right: Select [B2:B12], click the **Center** button, the **Align Left** button, and finally the **Align Right** button.

10. Select A1:D13 and use Format|AutoFormat and the 3D Effects 2 selection: Select [A1:D13] <Alt, O, A> pick **Table Format 3D Effects 2 <Enter>**. Compare your workbook to the illustration here.

11. Enter the present date in E1: [E1] type =**TODAY( ) <Enter>**. Or, click on **Format|Cells|Number** and select **Date** in the Category text box.

	A	B	C	D	E
1	**Item**	**Quantity**	**Price**	**Totals**	
2	Table, 30x60	6.00	132.00	792.00	
3	Table, Conf	2.00	389.00	778.00	
4	Chair, Side	28.00	68.00	1904.00	
5	Chair, Exec	4.00	158.00	632.00	
6	Chair, Steno	2.00	105.00	210.00	
7	Desk, 30x60	3.00	225.00	675.00	
8	Desk, Steno	2.00	286.00	572.00	
9	Desk, Exec	2.00	349.00	698.00	
10	Credenza	2.00	248.00	496.00	
11	Cabinet, File	8.00	78.00	624.00	
12	Cabinet, Storage	4.00	141.00	564.00	
13	**Grand Total**			$7,945.00	
14					

Format1.xls — Sheet1 / Sheet2 / Sheet3

12. Hide the prices in column C: [C1] <**Alt, O, C, H**>.

13. Unhide the prices in column C: <**Alt, O, C, U**>.

14. Save the workbook as Format1.xls: <**Alt, F, A**> type **Format1 <Enter>**.

Summary

This concludes your introduction to formatting. With this background, you can use the various menus, dialog boxes, and buttons to control the way your workbooks look when they are displayed and printed.

Using Labels, Names, and Protection

Introduction

Referencing cells by their location or cell number, such as A1, may be meaningful (read that as memorable) if there are only two or three cells used. However, referencing Z23 by its cell number does not give the user a clue what Z23 is if there are 597 other cell numbers (A1..Z22). And who can remember what all 598 cells contain? Fortunately, Excel includes a useful tool for specifying in more memorable terms what a cell contains.

Using Labels and Names in Formulas

Typical worksheets contain labels at the top of each column and on the left of each row describing the data within the worksheet. These labels may be utilized within formulas when you want to refer to the related data. Also, descriptive names, such as MyOwnData, that you specify or create and are not either row or column labels on the worksheet may be created to represent cells, ranges of cells, formulas, or constants.

	A	B	C
1	Label A	Label D	Label E
2	Label B		
3	Label C		

Naming Data

When a formula is created that refers to a range of data in a worksheet, the column and row labels in the worksheet can be used to refer to the range of data. If the data does not have labels or if the information is stored on one worksheet and used on other sheets, a name can be assigned that describes the cell or range.

A descriptive name in a formula makes it easier to understand the purpose of the formula. For example, the formula "=SUM(FirstQuarterSales)" might be easier to understand than "=SUM(Sales!B10:B20)." In this example, the name FirstQuarterSales represents the range B10:B20 on the worksheet named Sales.

Names are available to all worksheets. If the name ProjectedSales refers to the range C15:C25 on the first worksheet in a workbook, the name ProjectedSales can be used on any other sheet in the same workbook to refer to range C15:C25 on the first worksheet. Names are also used to represent formulas or values, called constants, that do not change. The name SalesTax can be used to represent the sales tax amount (such as 8.125 percent) applied to sales transactions. Names utilize absolute cell references and not relative references. In other words, if you copy a cell with a name in it to another cell, the cell copied into will refer to the same exact original element in the named cell.

Note: You cannot use a space in the formula names; use an underscore (_) to designate a space in formulas. Better yet, use the Microsoft convention of no spaces or underscores anywhere and capitalizing the first letter of each word, such as "Product1" or "NoSpacesAllowedInLabels."

Naming Cells, Formulas, and Constants

The first character of a name must be a letter or the underscore character (_). The remaining characters in the name may be any combination of letters, numbers, periods, and underscore characters except names cannot be the same as a cell reference, such as X$100 or M1F1. More than one word may be used in a name but spaces are not allowed. Use underscore characters and periods as word separators—for example, Sales_Tax or Second.Quarter.

Windows 98 allows up to 255 characters for names. If a name defined for a range contains more than 253 characters, it cannot be selected from the Name box. Names may contain uppercase and lowercase letters. For example, if you have created the name Sales and then create another name called SALES in the same workbook, the second name will replace the first one.

Suppose you created numerous formulas in your workbook before you decided to create names. All is not lost. Excel provides a way to retroactively replace cell references in formulas with names. By using the Insert|Name|Apply menu selection, all cell references in formulas can be easily replaced with their name counterpart.

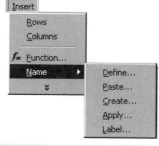

Excel uses the Insert|Name menu selection to manage the worksheet naming tools. Insert|Name has five tools available to assist the user with naming data. They are:

Define—Use Define to define a new name using a label reference in the same or another (external) workbook. If the name is referenced to a label in the same workbook, the result is the same as using the Create tool. However, any external reference must use Define.

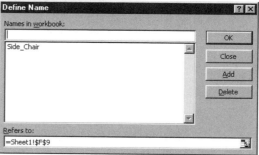

Paste—Use Paste to copy a name into a cell.

Create—Use Create to define a new name using a

label reference in the same workbook. Any external reference to a workbook must use Define to create or define the name.

Apply—The Apply Names box lists all the names defined in a work-

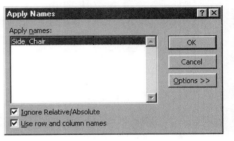

book that refer to an individual cell or a range of cells. When you want to use names in lieu of references, click the names you want to use in the Apply Names box.

Label—When you select cells in labeled ranges to create formulas, Excel can insert the labels in place of cell references in your formulas. Using labels can make it easier to see how a formula is constructed. Use the Insert|Name|Label menu selection to open the Label Ranges dialog box to specify the ranges that contain column and row labels on your worksheet. This dialog is used to associate a name (usually a column or row label) with a range of usually related data. Notice the Row labels and Column labels radio buttons in the Label Ranges dialog. The range selected must be associated with a row or column label using one of the two buttons.

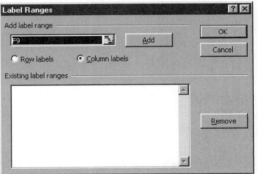

Using Dates as Labels

When you label a range using the Label Ranges dialog box and the range contains a year or date as a label, Excel defines the date as a label by placing single quotation marks around the label when you type it in a formula. For example, suppose your worksheet contains the label 1999 and you have specified these labels by using the Label Ranges dialog box. When you type the formula =SUM(1999), Excel automatically updates the formula to =SUM('1999').

Note: When you click on the question mark on the Label Ranges dialog (upper right corner), you will receive additional information about labeling ranges.

Note: If you label a list by using the Label command and then zoom the view of the worksheet to 39 percent or less, Excel adds a blue border around the labels you have specified with the Label Ranges command on the worksheet. The blue border does not print and is not displayed when you zoom the worksheet view above 39 percent.

General Naming Procedures

The following procedures are general procedures for implementing and using the naming conventions previously discussed.

Naming a Cell or a Range of Cells

1. Select the cell, range of cells, or nonadjacent cells you want to name.

2. Click on the Name box at the left end of the formula bar.

3. Type the name you want for the cells.

4. Press <Enter>.

Note: A cell cannot be named while you are changing the contents of the cell.

Naming Cells by Using Existing Row and Column Labels

1. Select the range you want to name, including the row or column labels.

2. On the Insert menu, point to Name, and then click Create.

3. In the Create names in box, designate the location that contains the labels by selecting the Top row, Left column, Bottom row, or Right column check box.

Note: A name created using this procedure refers only to the cells that contain values and does not include the existing row and column labels.

Naming Cells on More Than One Worksheet Using a 3-D Reference.

1. Choose Insert|Name|Define.

2. In the Names in workbook box, type the name.

3. If the Refers To box contains a reference, select the equal sign (=) and the reference and press Backspace.

4. In the Refers To box, type = (equal sign).

5. Click the tab for the first worksheet to be referenced.

6. Hold down <Shift> and click the tab for the last worksheet to be referenced.

7. Select the cell or range of cells to be referenced.

Defining a Name to Represent a Formula or a Constant Value

1. Choose Insert|Name|Define.

2. In the Names in workbook box, enter the name for the formula.

3. In the Refers To box, type = (equal sign), followed by the formula or constant value.

Defining a Name That Refers to Cells in Another Workbook

When you define a name that refers to a cell or range of cells in another workbook, you create a link known as an external reference. When you perform this procedure, make sure the workbook you want to refer to is open and that it has been saved.

1. In the workbook in which you want to create the external reference, click on Insert|Name|Define.

2. In the Names In Workbook box, enter the name for the external reference.

3. Click on the Refers To box.

4. Activate the workbook that contains the cell you want to refer to by clicking the name of the workbook on the Window menu.

5. Select the cell or range of cells you want to refer to.

6. In the Define Name dialog box, click Add.

Changing Cell References in Formulas to Names

1. Select the range containing formulas in which you want to change references to names.

Note: To change the references to names in all formulas on the worksheet, select a single cell.

2. Choose Insert|Name|Apply.

3. In the Apply Names box, highlight one or more names.

4. Click OK.

Hands-on Activities

Naming a Range of Cells

In this activity you practice using existing row and column labels and creating new names for a range of cells for use in formulas. Recall that your companion files are contained in the \MSOffice\Files folder. Start Excel and display a blank workbook.

1. Use existing row and column labels for creating cell names. A name created using this procedure refers only to the cells that contain values; it does not include the existing

row and column labels as part of the name. Open the Format1.xls workbook: **<Alt, F, O>** pick **Format1.xls <Enter>**.

2. Select **Quantity** and all the Quantity values (B1:B12).

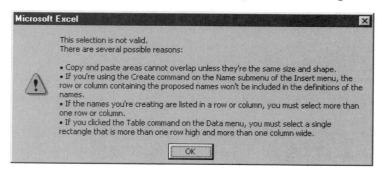

3. Click on **Insert|Name|Create**. In the Create Names dialog, designate the location that contains the label by selecting the Top row, Left column, Bottom row, or Right column check box as appropriate. In this example, click on **Top Row**.

Note: Excel uses the space character to identify the intersection of rows and columns. If a row or column label has a space in it, such as "Sales 1st Quarter" you cannot create a name. Change all spaces in labels to the underscore character (_) or delete the spaces.

Example: **Sales1stQuarter** or **Sales_1st_Quarter**

If your label contains spaces you will get the following error dialog:

Microsoft Excel

This selection is not valid.
There are several possible reasons:

• Copy and paste areas cannot overlap unless they're the same size and shape.
• If you're using the Create command on the Name submenu of the Insert menu, the row or column containing the proposed names won't be included in the definitions of the names.
• If the names you're creating are listed in a row or column, you must select more than one row or column.
• If you clicked the Table command on the Data menu, you must select a single rectangle that is more than one row high and more than one column wide.

OK

Protecting Cells

It is important to protect your row and column titles, formulas, and constant values to prevent them from being accidentally changed. While your cells are automatically protected when you use Tools|Protection|Protect Sheet, others can be unprotected to permit the entry of your variable values. To protect and unprotect certain cells, the following general procedure is used with the Protection dialog box of the Format|Cells menu selection and the Tools|Protection menu selection.

1. First, select one or more cells designated for the entry of variable information, such as numbers, dates, or text.

2. Use **Format|Cells|Protection** and click the **Locked** check box to remove the check mark.

3. Use **Tools|Protection|Protect Sheet**.

This simple process protects, or "locks," all cells on the worksheet not specifically designated as unlocked.

Protecting Workbooks

In this activity you use the Format1 workbook saved in Section 33. Recall that your companion files are contained in the \MSOffice\Files folder. Start Excel and display a blank workbook.

1. Open the Format1.xls workbook: **<Alt, F, O>** pick **Format1.xls <Enter>**.

2. Enable workbook protection: **<Alt, T, P, P>** (Do not enter a password; if you forget it you will not be able to change the workbook.) **<Enter>**.

3. Move to B3 and attempt to enter the number 5: [B3] **<5>**; notice the message. Press **<Enter>**.

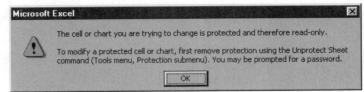

4. Disable worksheet protection: **<Alt, T, P, P>**.

5. Unlock B2:C12 (the variable cells) to enable typed entries: Select [B2:C12] **<Alt, O, E>**, click the **Protection** tab, click **Locked** to clear the check box, click **OK**.

6. Enable worksheet protection again: **<Alt, T, P, P> <Enter>**.

7. Change the value in B3 from 2 to 5: [B3] **<5>**. Notice that the cell is now unlocked.

8. Attempt to type Table in A3: [A3] **<T>**; notice the message; **<Enter>**.

9. This completes the protection activity. Exit without saving: **<Alt+F4>** pick **No** to avoid saving the changed file.

Summary

Names and labels are much more meaningful than cryptic references to cell identifiers. Isn't "Extended Value =Price * Quantity" much more informative than "B12=C3*E5"? Names and labels can add much to understanding worksheet formulas, especially after a prolonged absence from working with the worksheet and formulas. And remember to protect those cells that should remain intact. This typically applies to standard labels and formulas. Now move on to Section 35 where you learn to produce charts.

Producing Charts

Introduction

A chart provides a visual representation of the values contained on a worksheet. To create a chart, select a range of cells containing both labels and numeric values. Then either use Insert|Chart or the Chart Wizard button on the Standard toolbar. Either approach produces identical results. Note that the dimension of charts depends on selected data.

First, select the range of cells containing the labels and values that you want reflected in your chart. Then start the Chart Wizard and make the desired adjustments to the selected range of cells, chart type, legends, and title. Click the Finish button to display the chart on the underlying worksheet. You can also click on the chart to display handles. When the handles are displayed, you can resize the chart or drag it to a new location. Click on specific objects within your chart, such as the title or legend, to make changes.

Hands-on Activity

The best way to see how easy it is to create charts using Excel is to create one yourself. In this activity, you create a simple sales and expense table and then chart the information using Excel's Chart Wizard.

1. Start Excel and then type the information as shown in the illustration shown here.

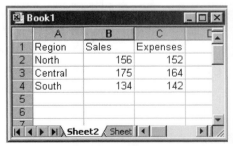

2. Select ranges A1:C1 and A2:A4 simultaneously and set them to boldface: Select [A1:C1], press and hold <Ctrl>, select [A2:A4], release <Ctrl>, click the **Bold** button.

Tip: <Ctrl+B>, <Ctrl+I>, and <Ctrl+U> are shortcut keys for boldface, italics, and underline.

3. Select the range A1:C4 and use **Format|Column|AutoFit Selection** to automatically adjust the column widths: [A1:C4] **<Alt, O, C, A>**.

4. With A1:C4 still selected, click the **Chart Wizard** button. Look at the following dialog.

Tip: If you click Finish now, Excel displays a chart using default values. Continue using Next> so you can see the available Chart Wizard dialog boxes.

5. Close the Office Assistant if it is open. Then click **Press and Hold to View Sample** to preview the chart.

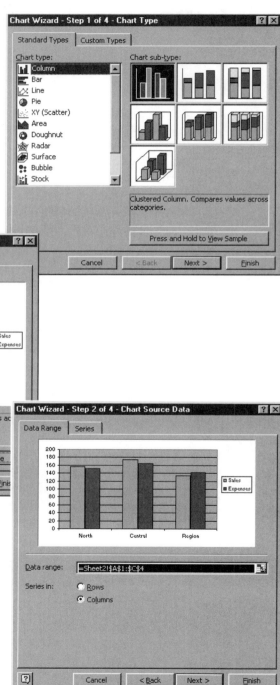

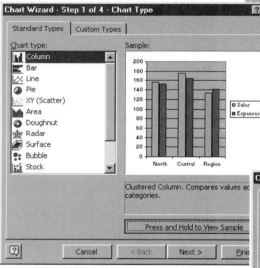

6. Click **Next>** to view dialog 2 of 4. Here you can change the data range and the series. Examine the two tabs to see how the series, labels, name, and values are established.

7. Click **Next>** to view dialog 3 of 4. Type the Chart title, Category (X) axis, and Value (Y) axis as shown in the following illustration.

8. Click **Next>** to view dialog 4 of 4. Here, you can place the chart in either a new sheet or on an existing sheet by picking the option button and corresponding name.

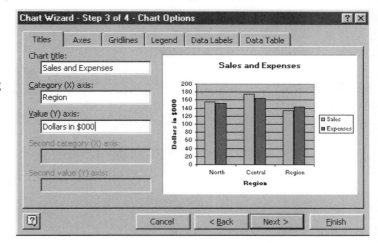

9. Click **Finish** to place the chart with your data on Sheet1.

10. Now compare your chart to the following illustration.

11. Save the workbook: **<Ctrl+S>** type **Charting <Enter>**.

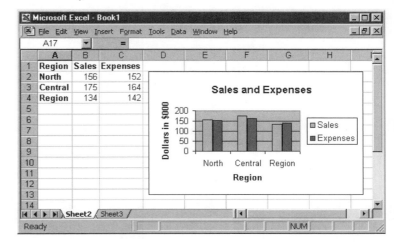

Note: You can change the chart using the Chart menu. This menu is available when you select the chart. Here, you can change the chart type as well as add gridlines, change colors, and much more.

12. Spend a few minutes experimenting with the Chart menu selections. In particular, check the folders of the Chart Options dialog.

13. Close the Chart Options dialog and double-click the chart to display the Format Chart Area dialog, which is used to change chart colors and patterns, text fonts, and other chart properties.

Tip: You can also double-click specific objects on your charts to display corresponding dialogs that are used to change different features.

14. This completes the charting activity. Close any open dialogs and press **<Alt+F4>** to exit Excel. Click **No** to exit without saving your experimental changes.

Summary

As you can see, Excel's Chart Wizard greatly simplifies the chart creation and editing processes. This is typical of many of Microsoft's applications that incorporate wizards. Now that you can translate your numerical information into stunning charts, you're ready to print and distribute your information in both numeric and graphical formats. The next section introduces you to Excel's printing features.

Printing Operations

Introduction

This section describes the printing process to familiarize you with the normal steps. The File menu has four selections that are used with printing. These are Page Setup, Print Area, Print Preview, and Print.

Page Setup—This selection displays a four-part dialog that is used to lay out your page. Click the appropriate tab to display the corresponding dialog.

Page—Use this dialog box to set page orientation, scaling, and paper size.

Margins—Use this dialog box to set the left, right, top, and bottom margins, the distance from the edge of the page to headers and/or footers, and page centering. Click Options to select paper, print quality, fonts, and device options.

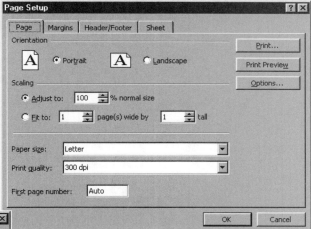

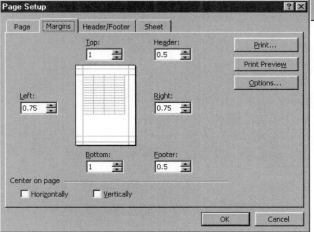

Header/Footer—If you wish to use headers and/or footers, use this dialog, illustrated on the following page, to create and position the text. The Custom buttons provide the ability to insert the page number, date, time, filename, or tab name. You can also arrange the header/footer information at the left, center, and/or right.

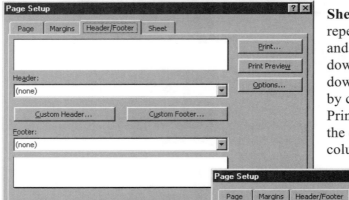

Sheet—Use to set the print area, repeating row and column titles, and page printing order, i.e., down, then over or over, then down. You can enter a print area by clicking the button in the Print area box and then dragging the desired cell range. Row and column titles can also be entered

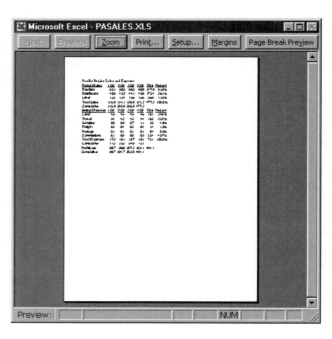

by picking the desired cells. You can also print gridlines, column and row headings, and comments, and set black and white and draft quality printing. Finally, you can create and place comments.

Print Area—Print Area is used to select or to clear the current range of selected (highlighted) cells.

Print Preview—Print Preview is used to display an image of the printed page before you send it to your printer.

Note the Print section of the Page Setup dialog has several options including Gridlines. Depending upon the complexity and purpose of the intended printout, gridlines may be useful or even necessary. Click on the Gridlines check box if you want gridlines.

Print Preview without gridlines:

Print Preview with gridlines:

Notice that Print Preview gives you direct access to the Print and Page Setup dialog boxes. The other buttons let you page through a large worksheet, zoom (enlarge or reduce the display), display and adjust margin guidelines, close the preview, and display Help.

Print—Use this dialog to specify the pages to print and the printer to use, and to print your work.

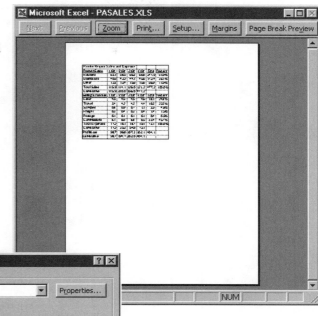

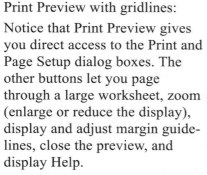

You can also access the Print Preview dialog box here. The Printer area at the top of the Print dialog is used to select a printer when more than one is installed. With some printers, you can pick the paper tray and either portrait (vertical) or landscape (horizontal) page orientation. Because you can access the Print Preview dialog box, you can start with this selection, perform all necessary preview and setup operations, and then print your workbook.

Summary

This concludes the section on printing with Excel. As you can see, the Excel dialogs give you all the controls you need to print your tables and graphs. In the next section you learn how to use the Window menu commands to display your information in a variety of ways.

Section 37

Window

Introduction

A *window* is a rectangular area or square frame in which a worksheet is displayed. Each worksheet is displayed in a single main window through which you view your data. If information is not visible, you can scroll the worksheet horizontally and vertically to bring the desired range of cells into view.

Worksheets are placed into windows using the File|Open menu selection or Open button. For example, if you wish to open the SESALES1 workbook, use <Alt, F, O>, pick the appropriate filename, in this case SESALES1, and <Enter>. The workbook is loaded and the SESALES1 worksheet is displayed in a window. To see all presently available windows, use <Alt, W> and look at the list of document names at the bottom of the Window menu. Each name is preceded by a number. To display a different worksheet window, pick the name or type the window number, such as 1 or 2. To change back, use <Alt, W, *n*>, where *n* is the original window number. You can also move to the next higher numbered window using <Ctrl+F6>. If you are presently in the highest numbered window, <Ctrl+F6> takes you to the first window.

The Window Menu

You can perform a number of helpful operations by using the Window menu selections. Each Window menu selection is briefly described, and then an activity guides you through the use of these selections.

New Window—A new window of the selected document is displayed. This lets you look at different areas of the same worksheet at the same time.

Arrange—Display all active worksheets in a tiled, horizontal, vertical, or cascade arrangement. A Windows of Active Workbook check box displays all worksheets in addition to all the panes of a split worksheet when checked.

Tiled Arrangement

Horizontal Arrangement

Vertical Arrangement

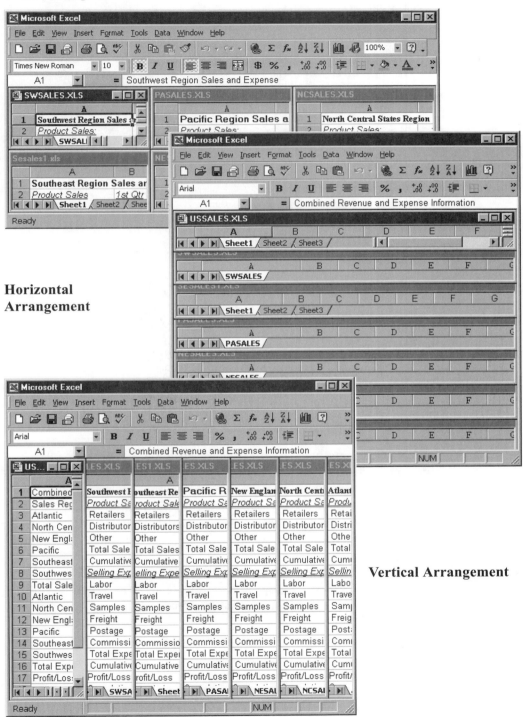

Cascade Arrangement

Clicking the Maximize button in the upper right-hand corner of any displayed window enlarges the selected window to full size; click the Window button to restore the previous window arrangement.

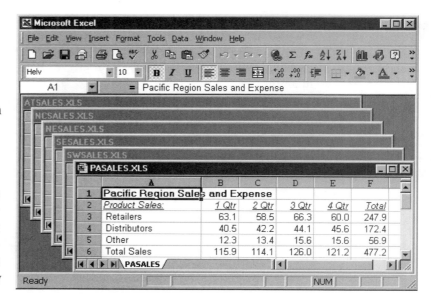

Hide—Suppresses the display of the selected worksheet; removes the hidden workbook name from the filename list at the bottom of the Window menu.

Unhide—Prompts you for the name of the hidden workbook. Once entered, the workbook is unhidden.

Split—Splits the displayed worksheet into four "panes." If the cell pointer is in A1, the split divides the worksheet into four equal panes. Otherwise, the split occurs at the upper left-hand corner of the selected cell. The panes are synchronized so that moving the cell pointer moves all adjacent cells in unison.

Freeze Panes—Use to freeze column and row titles in place while interior values are scrolled horizontally and vertically. For example, if months are displayed across row 1 and names down column A, put the cell pointer in B2 and press <Alt, W, F> to freeze the titles in place. Freezing panes is ideal for keeping information, such as titles or dependent values, in view while you scroll information within the body of the worksheet. Without the ability to split a worksheet, it's difficult to know what column you're in or the results of new value entries without continually moving back to check the headings.

Tip: If your worksheet is just a bit too big to view all of its contents, consider using View|Zoom to display a larger area.

Filename list—This lists all active, unhidden workbooks. Picking one of the filenames zooms the corresponding window to full screen.

Hands-on Activity

In this activity you load a series of sales region workbooks that are included on your companion CD. You created and saved one of the files, SESALES1, in Section 31. Begin by starting Excel and displaying a blank workbook.

1. Close Book1: **<Alt, F, C>**.

2. Open the following six workbooks by clicking the **Open** button, picking a filename in the order indicated, and clicking **Open** for each.

    ATSALES
    NCSALES
    NESALES
    PASALES
    SESALES1
    SWSALES

3. Tile the workbooks using the Window|Arrange selection: **<Alt, W, A, T>** click **OK**.

4. Compare your display to the following illustration.

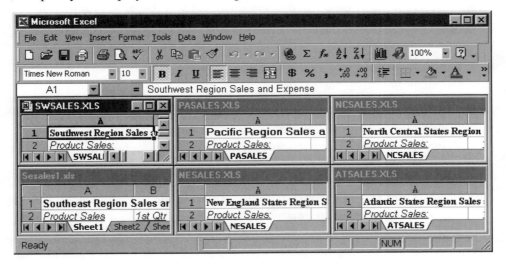

Note: In the following step, notice that a new Save Workspace selection is added to the File menu. This lets you save your setup when multiple workbooks are used.

5. Save the group of workbooks as a *workspace*: **<Alt, F, W>** type **SALES** **<Enter>**.

Tip: Workspaces automatically add the file extension XLW when saved.

6. Exit Excel: **<Alt+F4>**.

7. Restart Excel and close Book1. Then load the SALES workspace with: **<Alt, F, O>** pick **SALES**, click **Open**. Notice that all workbooks are automatically loaded in the original order.

8. Select and hide the PASALES worksheet; then arrange the remaining worksheets: Select the PASALES window, **<Alt, W, H> <Alt, W, A> <Enter>**.

9. Now unhide PASALES and use Windows|Arrange to tile all worksheets again: <Alt, W, U> check that PASALES is selected and click OK. **<Alt, W, A>** click **OK**.

10. Cascade the worksheets: **<Alt, W, A, C>** click **OK**. Check your display against the following illustration.

11. Click the Maximize button in the upper right-hand corner of the PASALES worksheet.

12. Put the cell pointer in B3 and use Window|Freeze Panes: [B3] **<Alt, W, F>**.

13. Go to J21 or some cell out of the view area and see how the row and column headings stay frozen in place: **<F5>** type **J21 <Enter>**.

14. Exit Excel without saving any changes: **<Alt+F4>** click **No**.

Note: Retain the SALES workspace as it is used in following activities.

Summary

This completes the window activity. As you can see, it is a simple matter to simultaneously view multiple workbooks. You can also view different sections and even different sheets of the same workbook at the same time. This is particularly helpful when you are working in large worksheets that require you to see two or more areas at the same time. Finally, when you frequently use two or more workbooks at the same time, you can save your setup as a workspace. This lets you open all of your workbooks with a single command rather than having to open them one at a time. The next section shows how to link workbooks.

Linking Workbooks

Introduction

Workbooks can be linked to permit consolidation of values from supporting workbooks to a master workbook. For example, you may maintain workbooks for different stores, operating divisions, or sales regions. Similarly, different worksheets within a single workbook can be used to accomplish the same result. The revenue and expense data computed in each of the divisional or regional worksheets can be combined to provide an overall view of how the top entity is performing. This section presents both approaches: the consolidation of workbooks and the consolidation of different worksheets within a single workbook.

Excel also lets you link worksheets to non-Excel documents. This feature makes use of the built-in dynamic data exchange (DDE) and object linking and embedding (OLE) capabilities that are part of most current Windows applications.

For example, Microsoft Word 2000 features an Excel button on its toolbar. Clicking this button lets users embed (or insert) a full-featured worksheet within the body of a document. You can also copy worksheet data or charts to the Windows clipboard and then paste the contents into a Word document. This same capability exists with other Microsoft Office 2000 programs such as Microsoft Access and PowerPoint.

One of the advantages to pasting a linked object, i.e., paragraph, table, or chart, is that changes to the source file are reflected in the pasted object. The dynamic linking eliminates the need for you to make a change in two places. To achieve the linkage, copy a selected passage to the Windows clipboard, position the cursor within your worksheet, then use Edit|Paste Special and pick Paste or Paste link to finish the job. Once the object is pasted, you can double-click it to edit the source.

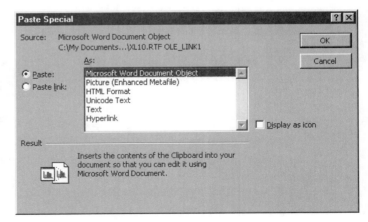

233

Establishing Workbook Links

You can point to values in supporting workbooks as if they were part of the current workbook. This is done by specifying a supporting workbook name and sheet and a cell or range of cells. For example, the expression

='C:\MSOFFICE\FILES\[ATSALES.XLS]SHEET1'!B3

points to the value in cell B3 of Sheet1 of the ATSALES workbook. Note that the disk drive and directory are also included. The drive and directory can be dropped if the workbook is in the same folder as the current one. In addition to using cell coordinates, you can use cell or range names. Names, such as GrandTotal, are assigned by selecting one or more cells and then using Insert|Name|Define.

Consolidation

Consolidating values from multiple workbooks is a fast way to derive the sum, product, standard deviation, or some other relationship between two or more identically structured worksheets. It combines, or *consolidates*, all numeric entries in a selected range. A detailed consolidation of each division's sales and expenses is a good example. Consolidation differs from linking. Linking extracts data from one or more supporting workbooks. Consolidation combines values using a function such as Sum, Count, Average, Max, Min, Product, etc. Perform the following consolidation activity to see how it works.

1. Open the Excel program with blank Book1 displayed.

2. Select B3 and display the Consolidate dialog box: [B3] <Alt, D, N>.

3. Use the following procedure for each of the six designated workbooks. Be sure that the Sum function is displayed in the Function box. The filenames and formula entries are listed below.

> ATSALES.XLS!B3:F18
> NCSALES.XLS!B3:F18
> NESALES.XLS!B3:F18
> PASALES.XLS!B3:F18
> SESALES2.XLS!B3:F18
> SWSALES.XLS!B3:F18

a. Use the Browse button and double-click on the specified workbook name.

b. Type the rest of each formula and click Add.

c. Repeat steps a and b for the rest of the workbooks.

d. Compare your dialog box to the following illustration.

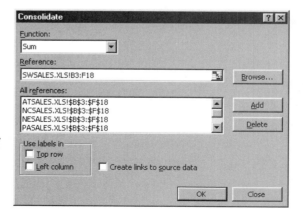

4. Click OK and compare the following example to yours.

5. Exit Excel without saving: <Alt+F4> and click No to exit without saving.

Tip: If you want to use other functions, such as Average, Min, or Max, you can easily return to the Consolidate dialog box, change the function setting, and click OK. The new results are calculated and displayed. You can also display the titles in the top row and leftmost column by including them in the cell range and clicking an X in the Top Row and Left Column check boxes.

Microsoft Excel - Book1					
A24	=				
	A	B	C	D	E	F
1						
2						
3		281.6	283.0	286.6	290.3	1141.5
4		184.4	187.4	192.0	209.6	773.4
5		77.1	66.4	68.0	72.4	283.9
6		543.1	536.8	546.6	572.3	2198.8
7		543.1	1079.9	1626.5	2198.8	
8						
9		20.3	20.4	21.1	21.5	83.3
10		17.0	18.3	19.3	18.7	73.3
11		4.7	5.3	4.1	5.4	19.5
12		1.5	1.9	1.9	2.1	7.4
13		0.7	0.5	0.6	0.6	2.4
14		38.0	37.6	38.3	40.1	154.0
15		82.2	84.0	85.3	88.4	339.9
16		82.2	166.2	251.5	339.9	
17		460.9	452.8	461.3	483.9	1858.9
18		460.9	913.7	1375.0	1858.9	

Sheet1 / Sheet2 / Sheet3 /

Ready — NUM

Hands-on Activity

In this activity you open a blank workbook, establish links, and then clear the links. These operations are accomplished in steps 1 through 5. In step 6 you open the SALES.XLW workspace created and saved in Section 37. Then you create a revenue and expense workbook by linking it to the six supporting regional sales workbooks. Begin by starting Excel and displaying a blank Book1 workbook.

1. Link B3 of NESALES.XLS to Book1: [B3] type **=NESALES.XLS!B3** <Enter>. Notice that the value is displayed.

Tip: Use <Ctrl+F10> as a shortcut for maximizing the displayed worksheet.

2. Open the SESALES2 workbook and maximize it: **<Alt, F, O>** pick **SESALES2** **<Enter> <Ctrl+F10>**.

3. Copy B4:E4 from SESALES2 to B4:E4 of Book1 Sheet1 using the following steps:
   a. Select SESALES2 [B4:E4].
   b. Press **<Ctrl+C>** which copies the selected cells to the clipboard.
   c. Select B4 of Book1: **<Ctrl+F6>** [B4].
   d. Press **<Ctrl+V>** to paste.
   e. Arrange the two workbooks in horizontal windows: **<Alt, W, A, O>** **<Enter>**.

f. Check your display.

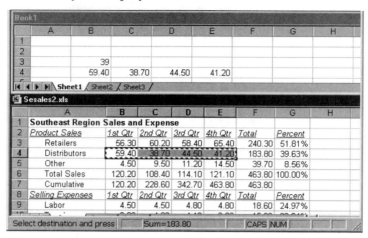

4. Select the SESALES2 workbook and close it: **<Ctrl+F6> <Alt, F, C>.**

5. Maximize Book1, select B3:E4, and clear the contents: **<Ctrl+F10>** [B3:E4] click the right mouse button to display editing operations, and pick **Clear Contents**.

6. Open the SALES workspace created and saved in Section 37: **<Ctrl+O>, put Workspaces (*.xlw)** in the Files of type box, pick **SALES.XLW <Enter>.**

7. Display the Book1 worksheet: **<Alt, W, 7>.**

8. Type the title and column and row headings as shown. (Set width of column A to 15.)

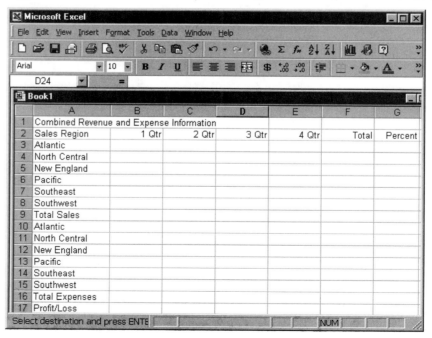

9. Align the column titles right: Select [B2:G2] click the **Align Right** button.

Tip: In the following step you can pick B9, click the AutoSum button, and drag cells B3:B8 as a shortcut to typing the Sum formula.

10. Insert the Total Sales formula in B9: [B9] **=SUM(B3:B8) <Enter>**.

11. Copy the formula in B9 to C9:E9: [B9] **<Ctrl+C>** pick [C9:E9] **<Enter>**.

12. Copy the Total Sales formulas in B9:E9 to B16: [B9:E9] **<Ctrl+C>** [B16] **<Enter>**.

13. Insert a row Total formula in F3: [F3] **=SUM(B3:E3) <Enter>**.

14. Copy the row Total formula from F3 down to F4:F16: [F3] **<Ctrl+C>** select [F4:F16] **<Enter>**.

15. Insert the revenue Percent formula in G3: [G3] **<=> <F3> </> [F9] <F4> <Enter>**. (Ignore #DIV/0!.)

16. Copy the Percent formula in G3 down to G4:G9: [G3] **<Ctrl+C>** select [G4:G9] **<Enter>**.

17. Insert the expense Percent formula in G10: [G10] **<=> <F10> </> [F16] <F4> <Enter>**. (Ignore #DIV/0!.)

18. Copy the Percent formula in G10 down to G11:G16: [G10] **<Ctrl+C>** select [G11:G16] **<Enter>**.

19. Enter a Profit/Loss formula in B17: [B17] **=B9–B16 <Enter>**.

20. Copy the Profit/Loss formula in B17 across to C17:F17: [B17] **<Ctrl+C>** select [C17:F17] **<Enter>**.

21. Format G3:G16 as percent: [G2:G16] click the **Percent** button.

22. Establish links between the Total Sales and Total Expenses rows of the six regional workbooks to Book1 as follows (working on Book1 and choosing Sheet1 when asked to select sheet).
    a. [B3] **=ATSALES.XLS!B6 <Enter>**.
    b. [B4] **=NCSALES.XLS!B6 <Enter>**.
    c. [B5] **=NESALES.XLS!B6 <Enter>**.
    d. [B6] **=PASALES.XLS!B6 <Enter>**.
    e. [B7] **=SESALES2.XLS!B6 <Enter>**.
    f. [B8] **=SWSALES.XLS!B6 <Enter>**.
    g. [B10] **=ATSALES.XLS!B15 <Enter>**.
    h. [B11] **=NCSALES.XLS!B15 <Enter>**.
    i. [B12] **=NESALES.XLS!B15 <Enter>**.
    j. [B13] **=PASALES.XLS!B15 <Enter>**.

    k. [B14] =SESALES22.XLS!B15 <Enter>.

    l. [B15] =SWSALES.XLS!B15 <Enter>.

23. Copy the links in B3:B8 to C3:E8: [B3:B8] **<Ctrl+C>** [C3:E3] **<Enter>**.

24. Copy the links in B10:B15 to C10:E15: [B10:B15] **<Ctrl+C>** [C10:E15] **<Enter>**.

25. Set the range B3:F17 to comma style: [B3:F17] click **Comma Style <Alt, O, C, A>**.

26. Compare your worksheet to the illustration.

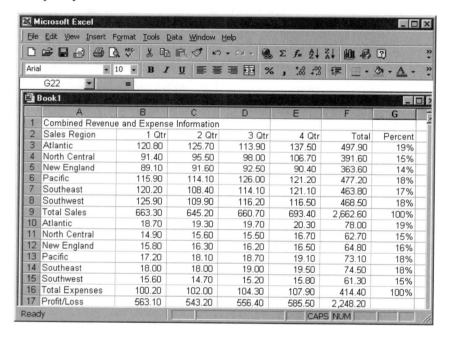

27. Save the workbook as USSALES: **<Ctrl+Home> <Ctrl+S>** type **USSALES <Enter>**.

28. Arrange all worksheets on the display: **<Alt, W, A, T> <Enter>**.

29. Save the workspace using the name USSALES, which now includes the USSALES workbook and exit the worksheet: **<Alt, F, W>** type **USSALES <Enter> <Alt+F4>**.

Now that links are established to supporting regional workbooks, changes to numbers in supporting workbooks are automatically reflected in the dependent workbook.

Summary

Linking and consolidating are important spreadsheet features, because both save time during workbook design. Be sure to consider these features whenever you design multisheet workbooks. In the next section you examine another time-saving device called *macros*.

Macros

Introduction

A *macro* is a collection of keystrokes that is created, saved, and later called by typing an assigned control key or selecting a menu item. A macro is like a DOS "batch file" because it contains a list of commands. As each command is encountered, it is executed and a resulting action takes place. Today, all full-featured programs provide macro creation and editing capabilities. You learned about Word macros in Part 2. Here, you learn about Excel macros, which are nearly identical in recording, running, and editing.

Like the other Office 2000 programs, Excel 2000 makes use of the Visual Basic language. Although you examine and make minor modifications to the Visual Basic code that is created by the Excel Macro Recorder, a complete presentation of Visual Basic is not possible here.

Uses for Macros

A macro automates frequently used operations by converting a few keypresses into a stored series of worksheet manipulations. You may wish to use a macro to guide the data entry process of an inexperienced user. Once a new set of values is typed into a worksheet, such as current sales or cost information, a macro could then print a standard report and a corresponding chart. Because macros are so flexible, your imagination is the only real limitation to their potential use.

Creating and Storing Macros

You can create a macro in one of two ways. The first is to enter the Record Macro mode using the Tools|Macro|Record New Macro menu selection.

A Record Macro dialog prompts you for a macro name. You can also assign a shortcut key or add a selection to the bottom of the Tools menu to run the macro. The shortcut key is stored with the current workbook. If the macro

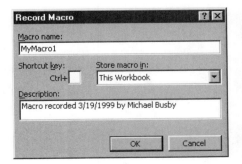

shortcut key is the same as a standard Excel shortcut key, it replaces the standard shortcut in the current workbook. Shortcut keys use either Ctrl+*x* or Ctrl+Shift+*x*, where *x* is any letter a through z.

When using the Record Macro dialog, each keystroke is recorded. The word "REC" is highlighted at the bottom of the screen to tell you that the macro recorder is on and a Stop button is also displayed in a small dialog. When you finish recording your keystrokes, either click the Stop button (which is easier) or use the Tools|Macro|Stop Recorder selection. You can view your macro code using the Tools|Macro|Macros menu selection and then click the Edit button.

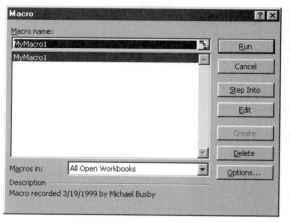

This puts you in the Visual Basic Integrated Development Environment (IDE). Once you view or edit your code, return to the worksheet by using File|Close and Return to Microsoft Excel (or press Alt+Q).

The other way to create a macro is to begin the Macro Recorder, type a few keystrokes, and then click Stop. Then enter the IDE using the Macro dialog's Edit button. At this point you can type your macro commands directly if you understand the Visual Basic language and know how to navigate the Visual Basic environment.

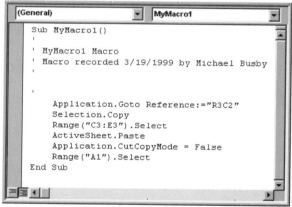

Running Macros

Just like the creation process, you can run a macro in a number of ways. First, display the worksheet for which the macro was designed. Then use Tools|Macro|Macros (also accessed with Alt+F8), pick the macro name, and click the Run button. You can also press the shortcut key assigned when the macro was created. Shortcut keys can be added later using the Macro dialog's Options button. If you are satisfied with the operation of your macro, you can save the workbook containing the macro in the normal way.

Summary

Now that you're familiar with how to record and run macros, you can record your own frequently used routines to simplify your tasks. You should also consider learning more about the Visual Basic programming language, which will help you perform complex tasks with workbooks.

The next section introduces databases.

Database

Introduction

A database is nothing more than a collection of organized information. A database might contain employee, customer, or inventory records, where a record pertains to a specific employee, customer, or inventory item. A record corresponds to a worksheet row. Each record contains a collection of data elements, or fields, that correspond to columns. For example, column A might contain a part number, column B a description, column C the unit cost, and so on.

The following chart shows a typical inventory database. Look at how each row, or record, pertains to a specific part. Each column, or field, contains a common element of information about the part.

PN	Description	QtyIn	Sold	OnOrd	Cost	Price	Measure
BGSAE75	Bolt, Hex	1050	324	0	0.115	0.2	Each
NGSAE75	Nut, Hex	975	392	500	0.065	0.12	Each
WSG75	Washer, Split	1000	586	500	0.03	0.07	Each
WFG75	Washer, Flat	1000	950	1000	0.03	0.07	Each
NB8P	Nail, Brt, 8P	200	85	300	0.32	0.55	Pound
NB6P	Nail, Brt, 6P	300	110	300	0.26	0.5	Pound

The Data Menu

Using the Data menu's assortment of commands, you can perform a number of powerful operations. These are briefly described in the following paragraphs of this section.

Sort—Sort one or more selected columns or rows in ascending or descending order. Ideal for sorting names or numbers either alphabetically or numerically within a list.

Filter—Filter selected information within the database to display and/or print only those records matching an established criteria.

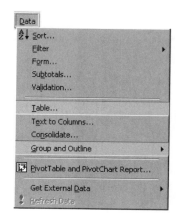

AutoFilter—Filter selected information automatically using list boxes. This gives you the ability to display or print only that information that matches a value or range of values.

AutoFilter
Show All
Advanced Filter...

Show All—Restore the display of all information upon completion of a filtering operation.

Advanced Filter—Use a dialog box to establish filtering criteria.

Form—Display the fields of each record and use buttons to find, change, or add information to the selected area.

Subtotals—Perform calculations on selected entries within the database using a dialog to make your selections.

Validation—Establish criteria to control the type of data permitted in selected cells.

Table—Create a table using the contents of the database.

Text to Columns—Convert text information to columnar format using a common separation character (or *delimiter*) such as a tab, comma, or series of spaces. This process is often called *parsing*.

Consolidate—Consolidate values from multiple worksheets into selected cells. This is ideal for finding sums or averages of multiple worksheets. Available functions include:

Sum	Min
Count	Standard Deviations
Average	Products
Max	Variances

Group and Outline—Hide and expand detailed information within a worksheet to provide for a summary view. For example, you may wish to show total amounts without showing all the intermediate subtotals.

Hide Detail
Show Detail
➡ Group...
⬅ Ungroup...

Auto Outline
Clear Outline
Settings...

Hide Detail—Hide preselected columns or rows.

Show Detail—Show preselected columns or rows.

Group—Combine two or more columns or rows which can be simultaneously hidden or shown.

Ungroup—Ungroup selected columns or rows.

Auto Outline—Automatically creates a summary view (outline) of a worksheet; computed totals are shown and detail values are grouped and hidden.

Clear Outline—Clear an outline view from a selected range of cells.

Settings—Controls placement of summary information and the use of styles.

Pivot Table and Pivot Chart Report—Creates or modifies a pivot table and chart (described later in this section), which is another way to select and summarize information within a worksheet. A Pivot Table Wizard guides you through the setup steps using a series of four dialogs.

Get External Data—Provides access to queries on the web, start Microsoft Query to import values from a selected external source, or create a new query. The selected query is loaded into the open workbook. Other choices permit you to edit a query, select a data range, and establish parameters to control the way data is processed and displayed.

Run Saved Query—Run a query that was previously saved to retrieve data from an intranet or Web site.

New Web Query—Format a new query to retrieve text or data from an intranet or Web site.

New Database Query—Format a new query for use with a database.

Import Text File—Import text files into the workspace. Tabular data delimited with commas or tabs or data with fixed width columns can be easily imported/converted to the workspace.

Edit Query—Use to make changes to existing queries.

Data Range Properties—Use to change the data property names of imported Web and text data files.

Parameters—Use to specify data that you wish to retrieve from an external data source. For example, if you are querying a national sales database, you can specify sales data from a particular region.

Refresh Data—Refresh values within the selected worksheet. The selected worksheet may be an open worksheet residing on the desktop or it may be a server-based or a web-based worksheet.

Tip: You can open files in common database formats and load them directly into an open workbook. Typical file formats that can be loaded directly include Microsoft Access, dBASE, and FoxPro.

Extracting Information

Excel's database feature lets you extract selected information from an Excel database for analysis and reporting purposes. To quickly extract information from a selected range of cells, perform the following general steps.

1. Identify and select the area (or range) of cells that contains the database content and column headings (or *field names*).

2. Use Data|Filter|AutoFilter; this places pull-down boxes at the right side of each column heading.

3. Pick one or more columns, pull down the pick list, and establish a criteria. For example, you may want to see all records having quantities greater than 500 and less than 1,000. This is a "custom" criteria. Click Custom to display and use the following dialog box.

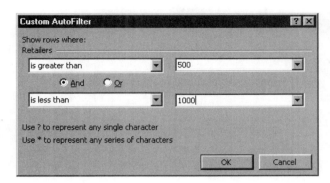

Another approach to filtering information is to use the Data|Filter|Advanced Filter selection. This method requires that you create a criteria range that contains field names across the top. If you plan to copy matching records from the database portion of an Excel worksheet to another location, you must prepare a "copy to" range in which field names are also entered across the top of the range.

The activities that follow show you how to use the first two approaches. Before beginning the activities, you should be familiar with a few simple mathematical operators and special codes.

Math operators include:

=	equal to	>=	greater than or equal to
>	greater than	<=	less than or equal to
<	less than	<>	not equal to

Codes include:

* This is a wild card that replaces all or a portion of a string. For example, * alone is a substitute for any text string. S* is a substitute for all strings that begin with S.

? This wild card replaces a literal character. The expression F??E is a substitute for such words as FILE, FARE, or FIRE.

~ The tilde character placed in front of a ? or * accepts these as characters rather than as codes. The expression ~? interprets the literal question mark.

Hands-on Activities

Ad Hoc Filtering

The following hands-on activity guides you through the use of the Data|Filter|AutoFilter method of making ad hoc database queries. It makes use of the Parts file supplied on your companion CD. Begin by starting Excel and displaying a blank workbook.

1. Open the Parts workbook.

2. Verify that the Parts workbook resembles the following illustration.

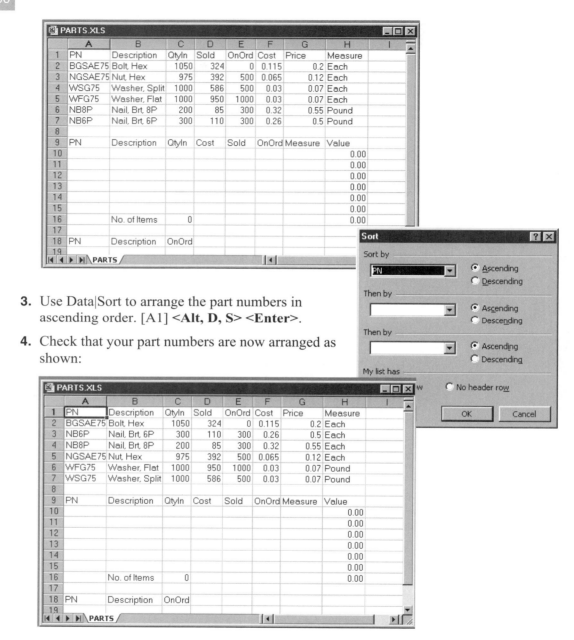

3. Use Data|Sort to arrange the part numbers in ascending order. [A1] **<Alt, D, S> <Enter>**.

4. Check that your part numbers are now arranged as shown:

5. Use Data|Filter|AutoFilter to prepare for ad hoc queries. Then display all records having a value greater than 0 in the OnOrd field (column E): **<Alt, D, F, F>**; click the **OnOrd** down arrow, pick **(Custom...)**, enter the values shown in the following dialog illustration, and click **OK**.

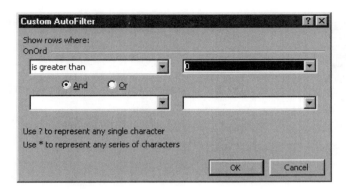

6. Click **OK**. Notice that the Bolt, Hex record containing 0 in the OnOrd column is hidden. Now redisplay all records using Data|Filter|Show All: **<Alt, D, F, S>**.

7. Remove the pull-down arrows using Data|Filter|AutoFilter: **<Alt, D, F, F>**.

Advanced Filter

With the Parts workbook still displayed, use Data|Filter|Advanced Filter to display all records having the part number N??P, any Description text, and OnOrd values greater than or equal to 0. Note that ?? are wild cards.

1. Enter the values as shown in A19:C19.

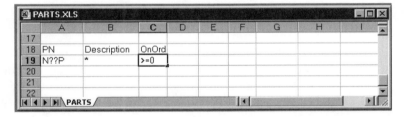

2. Set up the Advanced Filter dialog box as shown, including the Copy to Another Location button. You can enter each of the cell ranges by clicking the buttons within the text boxes, dragging the range, and pressing **<Enter>**.

3. Click **OK** to transfer the matching records to the Copy to range. Compare your results with the following screen illustration.

PARTS.XLS

	A	B	C	D	E	F	G	H	I
1	PN	Description	QtyIn	Sold	OnOrd	Cost	Price	Measure	
2	BGSAE75	Bolt, Hex	1050	324	0	0.115	0.2	Each	
3	NB6P	Nail, Brt, 6P	300	110	300	0.26	0.5	Each	
4	NB8P	Nail, Brt, 8P	200	85	300	0.32	0.55	Each	
5	NGSAE75	Nut, Hex	975	392	500	0.065	0.12	Each	
6	WFG75	Washer, Flat	1000	950	1000	0.03	0.07	Pound	
7	WSG75	Washer, Split	1000	586	500	0.03	0.07	Pound	
8									
9	PN	Description	QtyIn	Cost	Sold	OnOrd	Measure	Value	
10	NB6P	Nail, Brt, 6P	300	0.26	110	300	Each	710.26	
11	NB8P	Nail, Brt, 8P	200	0.32	85	300	Each	585.32	
12								0.00	
13								0.00	
14								0.00	
15								0.00	
16		No. of Items	2					2.00	
17									
18	PN	Description	OnOrd						
19	N??P	*	>=0						

PARTS

4. Close the workbook without saving your changes: **<Alt, F, C, N>**.

This completes the database filtering activities. As you can see, Excel provides some powerful tools for selecting and displaying records matching specified criteria. In the next part of this section, you learn still another way to view data using what is called a *pivot table*.

Pivot Table

A pivot table is used to summarize and view information in different ways. In the following activity, you open a workbook named Pivot from your companion CD. This is a tabulation of the number of sales calls made and resulting sales and sales amounts made by the members of the New York area sales team. Each team member has a geographical area in and around the New York City area. In the following activity, you create a pivot table so you can summarize the information by area.

1. Start Excel and open the Pivot file that was supplied on your companion CD. The table resembles the following screen illustration.

2. Position the cell pointer in A1 and use Data|PivotTable Report to summarize sales information by each area as follows:

PIVOT.XLS

	A	B	C	D	E	F
1	Area	Sales Rep	Calls	Sales	Amount	
2	Queens	A. Fleming	165	108	2698.92	
3	Queens	B. Moore	157	94	2349.06	
4	Bronx	B. Wilson	149	88	2199.12	
5	Brooklyn	F. Washin	144	86	2149.14	
6	Manhattan	G. Briggs	136	86	2149.14	
7	Bronx	H. Bishop	132	91	2274.09	
8	Long Islan	H. Rainey	189	123	3073.77	
9	Brooklyn	L. Johnson	122	78	1949.22	
10	Long Islan	S. Walters	177	132	3298.68	
11	Staten Isla	T. Shultz	119	73	1824.27	
12	Manhattan	W. Snyder	145	91	2274.09	
13	**Totals**		1635	1050	26239.5	
14						

Sheet1 / Sheet2 / Sheet3 /

a. [A1] **<Alt, D, P>**; examine the dialog box.

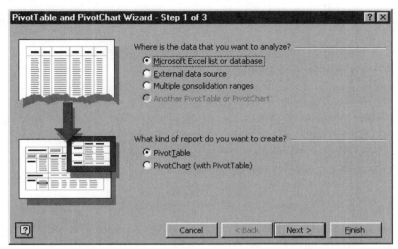

b. Click **Next>**. Notice that the area A1:E13 is selected.

Tip: Whenever you want to change the range, just click the text box button, drag the desired range of cells, and press <Enter>.

c. Click **Next>** and **Layout**. Now drag the displayed title buttons (Area, Calls, Sales, and Amount) located on the right side of the dialog box into the row (Area) and column (Calls, Sales, Amount) data areas as shown in the following illustration. Note that "Sum of" is added by Excel.

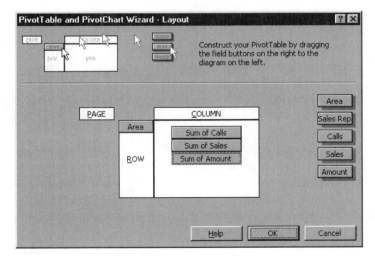

d. Click **OK** then click **Options**. Use the default options shown in the screen illustration. Notice the name of the pivot table is PivotTable1. You can have more than one pivot table in a worksheet.

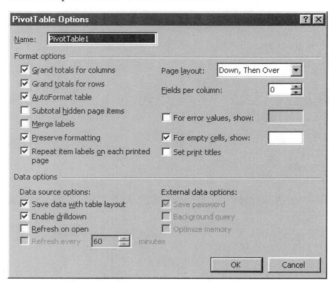

e. Click **OK**, then click **Next>**. Now examine the following dialog illustration. Leave it as is to place the pivot table on a new worksheet. This adds Sheet4 to the workbook that contains the pivot table.

f. Click **Finish**. Now examine the resulting pivot table to see how each area is summarized.

Tip: You can use the Pivot Table toolbar to select and group/ungroup two or more region areas. You can also display or hide individual items using the toolbar's Show Detail and Hide Detail buttons. And you can use the toolbar to select data to chart. These features provide a powerful analytical tool when you want to get the most information out of your data.

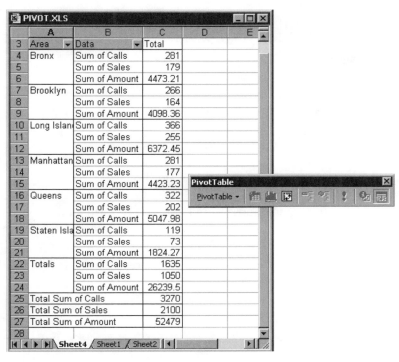

3. Exit Excel without saving: **<Alt+F4> <N>**.

Summary

As you can see, the Data menu has a number of tools that are used to view and print the contents of your workbooks in a variety of ways. In particular, you can summarize information using the database filters, pivot tables, and outlining tools. In the next section, you are introduced to one- and two-variable tables, which are frequently used by Excel users who work with financial records.

Using Tables

Introduction

Many kinds of tables are used in business and finance. Excel lets you create your own table that is based on a formula that contains either one or two variables. For example, you can create a financial amortization table from a formula used to calculate a periodic payment, an interest rate, or the balance due on a loan. Similarly, you can create a payroll table based on hours worked and different pay rates.

Before we create any tables, a few definitions are provided to be sure that you understand the basic terminology.

Tables—A table is a range of cells within a worksheet that contains input values, formulas, and the results of calculations.

Variables—A variable is part of a formula that is changed to get a different result.

Constants—A constant is an unchanging value. The formula =G5/12 contains the variable G5, which can be changed by typing a new number in cell G5, and the constant 12.

Input Cell—This is where you type a variable value that controls values generated in the resulting table. Each variable in a formula uses a different input cell.

Input Value—A table contains input values that are used in place of the variables contained in a corresponding formula.

Result Range—The result of a calculation is put in one or more cells in the result range, which makes up the body of a table.

Data Table Types

There are two general types of data tables: a one-variable and a two-variable table. The one-variable table operates with a formula having a single variable, while the two-variable table operates with a formula having two variables. Perform the following two activities to use both table types.

Hands-on Activities

One-Variable Table

In this activity you create a simple one-variable table. Begin by starting Excel and displaying a blank workbook.

1. Enter the information as shown in the following worksheet example, including the formulas.

Note: The formulas are displayed by placing a check mark in the Window options Formulas check box of the Tools|Options|View dialog box. Redisplay values after the information has been added.

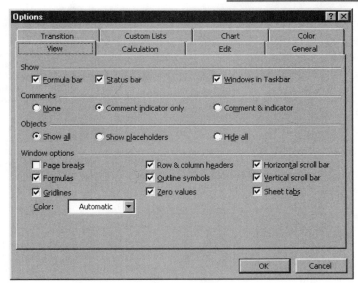

2. Select B5:F15 and then enter B1 as the input value: Select [B5:F15] **<Alt, D, T> <Tab>** to the Column input cell box, click the button, pick [B1] **<Enter>**, and click **OK**.

3. Format B1, B3, and the range B5:F15 as currency: Right-click, pick **Format Cells**, pick **Currency**, and click **OK**.

4. Format B2 as a percentage: Click the **Percent Style** button **%**; set to two decimal places using the **Increase Decimal** button.

5. Type 5.96 in B1 and look at the sales tax in B3 and C5: [B1] **5.96** **<Enter>**.

6. Compare your display to the following screen illustration.

7. Enter other values to see how the table operates. You can also change the percentage in B2 to correspond to the sales tax rate used in your area. Notice that the table displays sales tax amounts based on the dollar amount in column B.

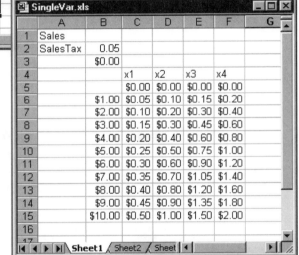

8. You may save the worksheet if desired by selecting File|SaveAs and save using an appropriate name or you may erase the worksheet. Erase the worksheet in preparation for the two-variable table activity: Select [A1:F15] **<Del>**.

Two-Variable Table

In this activity you create a simple two-variable table. Begin with a blank worksheet displayed.

1. Select A1:F15, set the number format category to General: [A1:F15], click the right mouse button, pick **Format|Cells**, pick the **Number** tab and the **General** category, and click **OK**. Enter the information as shown in the following worksheet example, including the formula in B5. This formula is used to derive the periodic payment based on the principal amount of a loan, the rate of interest, and the number of payments. (The formula in cell B5 is displayed by selecting the cell and pressing F2.)

	A	B	C	D	E	F	G	H	I
1	Principal	1000							
2	Interest	0.08							
3	Payments	12							
4			(Monthly Payment Amounts for Different Terms)						
5		=PMT(B2/12,B3,-B1)	12	24	36	48	60		
6		0.05							
7		0.055							
8		0.06							
9		0.065							
10		0.07							
11		0.075							
12		0.08							
13		0.085							
14		0.09							
15		0.095							
16		0.1							
17		0.105							
18		0.11							
19		0.115							
20		0.12							

AMORT.XLS — Sheet1 / Sheet2 / Sheet3

Tip: You can automatically fill the values in the cells B6:B20. Just type 0.05 in B6, 0.055 in B7, select B6 through B20, and use Edit|Fill|Series with Series in Columns and a Step value of .005.

2. Select B5:G20 and use Data|Table to designate B3 as the Row Input Cell and B2 as the Column Input Cell: Select [B5:G20] **<Alt, D, T>** pick [B3] **<Tab>** pick [B2] click **OK**.

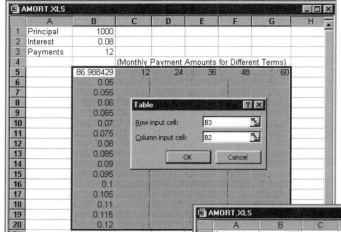

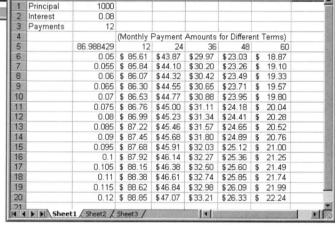

3. An amortization schedule fills the table area for interest rates from 5% to 12%.

4. Format B1 and C6:G20 as Currency ($1,234.00). Notice cells C6:G20 are filled with ####.

5. Format B2 and B6:B20 as Percentage; use two decimal places.

6. Highlight C6:G6. Click on **Format|Column|AutoFit Selection.** Notice cells C6:G20 are now filled with monetary values. Compare your display to the following screen illustration.

7. Change the principal amount to $2,000.00: [B1] **2000 <Enter>**. If necessary, increase the width of column C by dragging the right edge of the C label to the right. Now compare your display to the following illustration.

	A	B	C	D	E	F	G	H
	AMORT.XLS							
1	Principal	$2,000.00						
2	Interest	8.0%						
3	Payments	12						
4			(Monthly Payment Amounts for Different Terms)					
5		$173.98	12	24	36	48	60	
6		5.0%	$171.21	$87.74	$59.94	$46.06	$ 37.74	
7		5.5%	$171.67	$88.19	$60.39	$46.51	$ 38.20	
8		6.0%	$172.13	$88.64	$60.84	$46.97	$ 38.67	
9		6.5%	$172.59	$89.09	$61.30	$47.43	$ 39.13	
10		7.0%	$173.05	$89.55	$61.75	$47.89	$ 39.60	
11		7.5%	$173.51	$90.00	$62.21	$48.36	$ 40.08	
12		8.0%	$173.98	$90.45	$62.67	$48.83	$ 40.55	
13		8.5%	$174.44	$90.91	$63.14	$49.30	$ 41.03	
14		9.0%	$174.90	$91.37	$63.60	$49.77	$ 41.52	
15		9.5%	$175.37	$91.83	$64.07	$50.25	$ 42.00	
16		10.0%	$175.83	$92.29	$64.53	$50.73	$ 42.49	
17		10.5%	$176.30	$92.75	$65.00	$51.21	$ 42.99	
18		11.0%	$176.76	$93.22	$65.48	$51.69	$ 43.48	
19		11.5%	$177.23	$93.68	$65.95	$52.18	$ 43.99	
20		12.0%	$177.70	$94.15	$66.43	$52.67	$ 44.49	
21								

Sheet1 / Sheet2 / Sheet3 /

8. This concludes the table activities. Save the file as AMORT.XLS: **<File|SaveAs>** Exit Excel: **<Alt+F4> <N>**.

Summary

You may wish to experiment with one- and two-variable tables. There are hundreds of uses for data tables, and you may be able to apply them to a number of your own financial needs. In the next section you examine Excel's ability to exchange files with other programs.

Using Files with Other Programs

Introduction

This section describes some ways to use your workbooks and the files they create with other popular programs. It also tells you how you can import data into Excel from worksheets and databases created by other programs such as Lotus® 1-2-3® and dBase®.

Benefits

Being able to transfer files between Excel and your favorite word processor or database program gives you the power of all contributing programs. This is one of the benefits of a completely integrated program like Microsoft Office 2000. Office gives you the ability to run Word and/or Access at the same time. The Windows clipboard is available to "grab" Excel information and move it to other Office applications. Similarly, you can cut information from one application document and paste it into another. By now, you should know how to select and cut or copy (Ctrl+X or Ctrl+C) and paste (Ctrl+V) information from one document to another.

You can also read files produced by other spreadsheet and database programs as well as write files that can be used by other worksheet and database programs. This is done during the File|Save As process by simply specifying an available file type.

There was a time when integrated programs provided users with a way to transfer information between applications. Today, the Windows 95/98 environment, and in particular, Microsoft Office 2000, gives you the ability to access information from a variety of sources. For example, with the click of a few buttons you can access documents and graphic files located on other computers on a connected network as well as from web sites located around the world. All Office 2000 applications include web buttons. You can even view web pages in your applications by making use of the built-in HTML filters.

Therefore, knowing how to import and export document and graphic files between other applications on your computer and between other locations on either a network or the Internet is important to your productivity.

Another benefit of being able to import and export files is data sharing. You can work with colleagues who use other worksheet programs such as Lotus 1-2-3, Quattro Pro, or Multiplan. In this way, you can share business information without possessing identical computers and/or application programs.

Automatic File Conversion

Excel converts many files from other worksheet and database programs automatically as they are opened or saved. The File|Open command reads the file extension (or *file type*) and file header and then performs automatic conversion of files created by the programs. Similarly, Excel's File|Save and Save As dialog boxes give you file conversion choices. A list of available file conversion choices is contained in the Save As dialog box.

Microsoft Query

Advanced topic

If you installed Microsoft Query when you ran Setup, you can launch Query by choosing the Get External Data selection of the Excel Data menu. Query lets you create a new query, where you select a data source (or file type), such as Access, FoxPro, or dBase. Available selections depend on what you picked during setup. After picking a file type, add the file to your query. The Query dialogs let you establish criteria so that unwanted information is filtered and therefore not displayed. In addition, Query lets you open multiple databases, so that displayed information can be from several related files. Once the query is open and organized to your liking, the information is transferred to the current workbook, where it can be integrated with other information, graphed, and printed. A Query activity is included later in this section to familiarize you with opening a database file and transferring the contents into an Excel workbook.

If you had used criteria to filter out unwanted information, your workbook would only include the values you want. For example, you may only want to see snack and beverage items. MS Query is a powerful add-on feature that gives you control over the data you import from external databases and tables. You may wish to explore the MS Query menus and toolbar buttons to familiarize yourself with available features. In particular, you should examine the criteria (or data filtering) capabilities. These are similar to the criteria control offered by Microsoft Access and the Excel data criteria entries used in Section 41.

Exporting and Importing Files

Exporting files is achieved by picking the desired file type in either the Save or Save As dialog. You can import files created by various versions of dBase and Lotus 1-2-3 by picking the DBF or WKS filename using File|Open. Similarly, you can import ASCII and comma-delimited files, which are easily produced by most word processing programs.

ASCII Text Files

Excel opens plain ASCII text files automatically. You may wish to use the filename extension TXT as a standard for ASCII-type text files. If you are loading a comma-separated value (CSV) file, you can arrange your worksheet to match the column widths either before or after you load the file. When loading a plain text file, the text will often "bridge" worksheet columns. The information is also treated as long labels, rather than being arranged in Excel columns. When this happens, you can use the Data|Text to Columns menu selection to *parse* the incoming text. This separates the information into individual columns.

Using Data/Text to Columns

To separate (or parse) imported ASCII text into columns, you perform the following steps.

1. Open an ASCII text file.

2. View the data within the Text Import Wizard - Step 1 of 3 dialog box.

3. Click the **Next>** button and arrange the column break lines to accommodate the imported text.

4. Click the **Next>** button to select column data formats or to skip unwanted columns.

5. Click **Finish** to complete the import process. The resulting text is parsed according to the setup you established using the Text Import Wizard.

Comma-Separated Values

Comma-separated (or *delimited*) value files are imported using the List file of type text box of the File|Open dialog box. Simply pick the (csv) file type and Excel does the rest. A comma-separated value file is organized like a database. Records are normally separated by carriage returns at the end of each line, while fields within records are separated by commas. Look at the following two examples.

Mr.,John,Williams,1234 Main Street,Suite 100,Tampa,FL,34098
Mr.,Juan,Jimanez,432 Sycamore Blvd,Dime Box,Texas,76905

"Mr.","John","Williams","1234 Main Street","Suite 100","Tampa","FL","34098"
"Mr.","Juan","Jimanez","432 Sycamore Blvd","","Dime Box","Texas","76905"

The first example is comma delimited. The second is comma and quotation mark delimited. Excel operates with either type of file.

The quotation marks are used to embed commas. For example, having quotation marks around "Jones, Jr." interprets the embedded comma as a normal text character rather than as a field separator.

Using Worksheets with Word Processors

As you should already know, you can either create or import Excel worksheets directly into your Word documents. If you are using another word processor, you can import an ASCII text file. Therefore, you can output an Excel worksheet for use with a word processor by saving the file as a TXT file using Excel's File|Save or Save As menu selection. This gives the file a TXT file extension and puts it in ASCII format. Almost all word processors can read ASCII files. Although this was once necessary, today almost all modern word processors can import Excel files directly. This is because Excel is the most popular worksheet program in use today.

Using Excel with Database Programs

Excel's automatic file conversion makes reading and saving database files a breeze. This is true of Access, FoxPro, dBase, and Paradox database files (or table). Just use the File|Open menu selection and Excel does the rest.

Using Excel with Microsoft Access

As a user of both Microsoft Excel and Access, you can quickly transfer information between Excel workbooks and Access tables by simply cutting and pasting or by opening an Access file directly into Excel. The Edit|Paste Special menu selection is an excellent way to link an Access database into your Excel worksheet. As you should recall from the earlier treatment of Paste Special, you can modify the database file in Access; the changes automatically take effect in the Excel presentation.

Using Excel with dBase or FoxPro

Excel recognizes and reads most xBase files directly, without special handling. As discussed earlier in this section, you can create a query to filter the database contents using Microsoft Query. Of course you can convert database files into ASCII format for use by Excel. All dBase (or *xBase*) language-based programs including dBase III, III Plus, IV, FoxBASE, FoxPro, and Clipper have the ability to import and export both DBF and ASCII files. The format can be a plain ASCII text file or comma separated. To export a file from a dBase-compatible program for use in Excel, use the following syntax from either the dot prompt or as statements in a Clipper command file. Assume that the filename is CUSTOMER.DBF. Note that && is used for comments and is not part of the dBase syntax.

```
. USE CUSTOMER              && Opens the CUSTOMER.DBF file.
. COPY TO CUST1 SDF         && Copies the contents as an ASCII text file
                               to CUST1.TXT.
. COPY TO CUST2 DELIMITED   && Copies the contents as comma-quotation
                               mark delimited to CUST2.TXT.
```

You can also save worksheets in DBF format. Another way to export a worksheet from Excel to dBase is to save the Excel worksheet as a Lotus 1-2-3 WKS file. Then create a database file that has a compatible record structure. Finally, use the dBase command APPEND FROM *filename* TYPE WKS.

There are many ways to exchange files between Excel and other popular, non-Office 2000 programs. As you become more comfortable with Excel and your other applications, i.e., database managers, word processors, and accounting programs, you can experiment with file interchange until you find the approach that best suits the way you work.

Hands-on Activities

Parse

In this activity you use the steps outlined above to import the Parse.txt file supplied on the companion CD. Begin by starting the Excel program and displaying a blank workbook.

1. Open the Parse text file: **<Alt, F, O>** pick **Parse**, click **OK**.

2. Compare your display to the following screen illustration.

3. Move to the Text Import Wizard - 2 of 3 dialog box: Click **Next>**.

4. Notice that the Text Import Wizard "guesses" at how the data should be parsed.

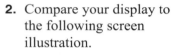

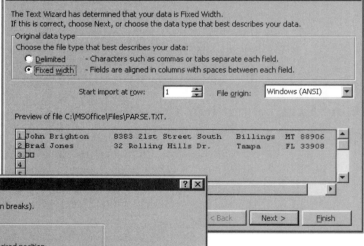

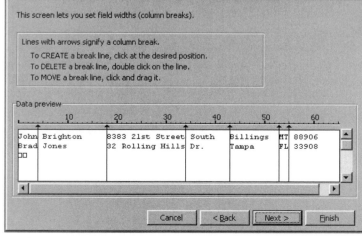

5. Double-click the vertical line located at 34 on the ruler to remove it. Then click **Next>** to display the Text Import Wizard - Step 3 of 3 dialog box.

6. Leave the Column Data Formats as shown. These could be changed if you wanted to remove columns or differentiate between dates and text. Click **Finish**.

7. Delete the end-of-file mark from A3. Then adjust the column widths: **<Ctrl+A> <Alt+O, C, A>**. Now compare your display to the following illustration.

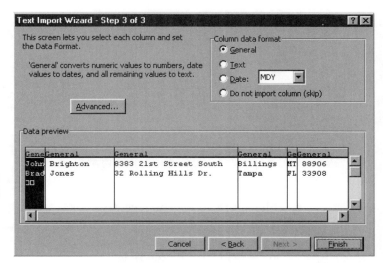

8. This completes the parse activity. Exit Excel without saving: **<Alt+F4> <N>**.

The preceding activity shows you how simple it is to parse text into columns. The parse feature can be invaluable when you must import information from a word processor to your worksheets.

Microsoft Query

If you did not install Microsoft Query during setup, skip this activity. Otherwise, use Microsoft Query to view the contents of a dBase file. The file Query.dbf is supplied on the companion CD. Begin by starting the Excel program and displaying a blank workbook.

1. Use **Data|Get External Data|New Database Query** to launch Microsoft Query.

2. Select **dBase Files** from the Databases list and click **OK**. The Choose Data Source dialog appears as shown here.

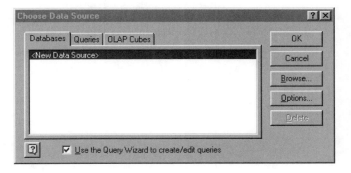

3. Click on **Options**.

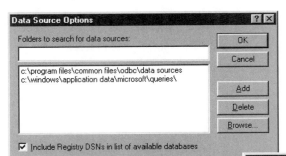

4. Click on **Browse**. The Select Directory dialog appears. Add **,*.dbf** to the text string in the File name text box. Change the directory to **MSOffice\Files**. Click on **OK**. The Data Source Options dialog reappears.

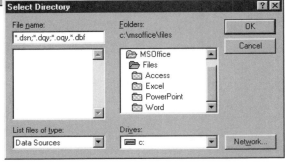

5. Click on **Add** and on **OK**.

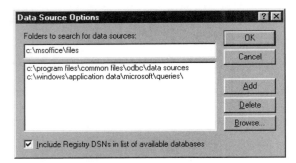

6. In the Create New Data Source dialog add a name for the data source in the first text box. Notice as soon as you type the first letter of the name, text box 2 becomes enabled. Next, click on the text box 2 down arrow and select **Microsoft dBase driver (*.dbf)**. Click on **Connect**.

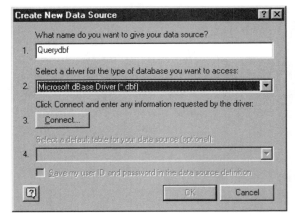

7. Click on **OK** in the ODBC dBASE Setup dialog.

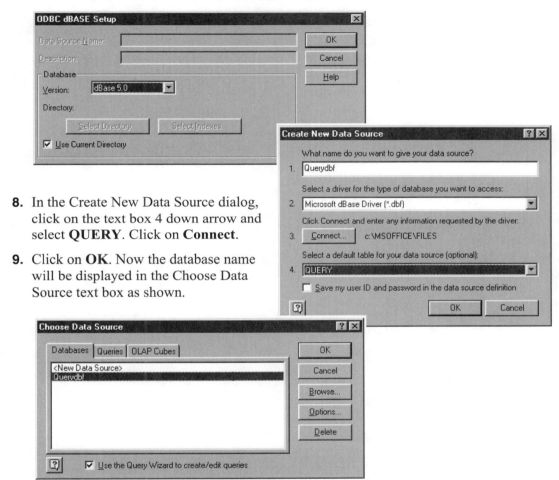

8. In the Create New Data Source dialog, click on the text box 4 down arrow and select **QUERY**. Click on **Connect**.

9. Click on **OK**. Now the database name will be displayed in the Choose Data Source text box as shown.

10. Click on **OK**. The Query Wizard dialog box is now displayed.

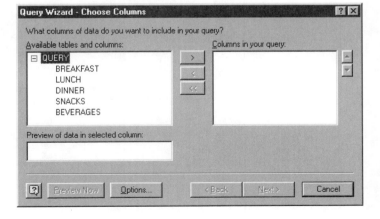

11. With QUERY highlighted in the Query Wizard dialog's Available Tables and Columns text box, click on the > between the two text boxes. After you click the >, your screen should look like the following:

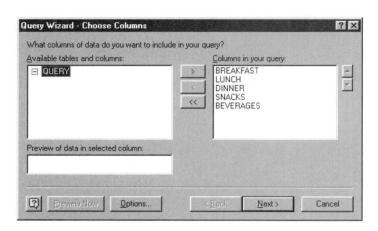

Tip: You can expand or contract listed database files by clicking on the + or – sign. When expanded, the field names are displayed.

12. Click **Next>** to display the next dialog; here, you can filter unwanted information.

13. Click **Next>** to set the sort order. Here, you pick one or more field names using the Sort by and Then by text boxes. Then set the Ascending or Descending option buttons as desired.

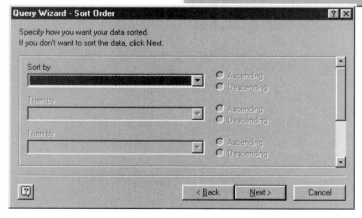

14. Click **Next>** to see the last dialog.

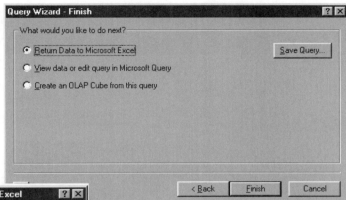

15. Click **Finish**.

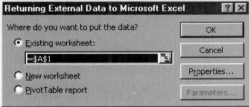

16. Click **OK** to return the data to Microsoft Excel (the open worksheet). Now compare your display to the following.

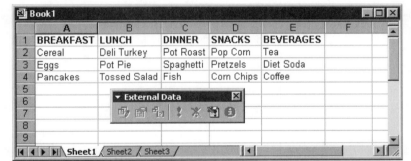

17. This completes the Query activity. Exit Excel without saving.

Summary

This concludes the file importing/exporting activity. Using the power of Office 2000 tools, you can easily import and export a wide array of files and data to and from your Excel workbooks. In the next section you learn how to use the menu commands to place your Excel data onto the web.

Putting Excel Data on the Web

Introduction

This section describes how to place your workbooks onto intranets and the World Wide Web. It also tells you how you can update your web-based data, and retrieve data from web sites. There is a useful purpose for using Office 2000 for web-based computing—users do not need a copy of Excel to look at, retrieve, and update your web-based data. This method of conducting business is very useful to such professions as marketing and sales.

Requirements for Saving or Publishing a Web Page

Before a Microsoft Excel workbook or worksheet is saved or published as a web page, there are several issues and limitations to be aware of. Several programs must be installed on the computer, including Office Web components. These components are used to put interactive (can change the data) spreadsheets, PivotTable lists, charts, and data access pages on the web. The programs required are:

- Microsoft Office 2000 Standard, Professional, or Premier Edition
- Microsoft Office Web Components
- Microsoft Internet Explorer 4.01 or later if the Property Toolbox is used or Microsoft Internet Explorer 4.0 if the Property Toolbox is not used (Microsoft Internet Explorer 5.0 is available with Microsoft Office 2000)
- A connection to an intranet or the Internet and an Internet service provider (ISP)

You must have the following items installed on your computer to post non-interactive (for viewing only, cannot change the information) Excel data as a web page:

- Microsoft Office 2000 Standard, Professional, or Premier edition or Microsoft Excel 2000
- Any Web browser

Limitations

The following tables provide information about limitations when publishing or saving data when the *Add interactivity with* setting is selected in the Publish as Web Page dialog. Some features and formatting may not work or may appear differently when data is saved or published as a web page. The limitation issues are not a deficiency of Excel, but are limitations imposed by the native HTML web language. The features and formatting limitations are dependent upon the type of data being saved as a web page and how the data is formatted.

Spreadsheet Limitations

Feature	Result as a Web Page
Custom views	Not retained. Custom views are visible only when the web page is first opened. The custom view cannot be used again after the view is changed.
Data consolidation	Consolidation information is not retained.
Scenarios	Not retained.
Shared workbook information	Not retained.
Nested functions	Not retained.
Rotated or vertical text	Text is converted to horizontal text.
Pattern fills	Not retained.
Dotted or broken borders	Not retained with non-interactive web pages. Changed to solid borders in interactive web pages.
Graphics	Not retained if the entire worksheet is saved or published.
Names of cells and ranges	Not retained. Formulas are automatically translated to use references instead of names.
Drawing object layers	Not retained.
Word wrap in cells	Not retained.
Multiple fonts in a single cell	Not retained. Default font is used.
Conditional formatting	Not retained. Default formatting is used.
Outlining	Not retained.
Password protection	Not retained.
Cell comments	Not retained.
Data validation restrictions and messages	Not retained.
Precision as displayed	Not supported.
Array formulas	Not retained.
Distributed alignment	Not retained, but will appear if the web page is re-opened in Excel.
Thai alignment	Not retained, but will appear if the web page is re-opened in Excel.
Indented text	Not retained, but will appear if the web page is re-opened in Excel.
English language formulas	Saved with references.
Rotated or vertical text	Converted to horizontal text.
Cell with no background color surrounded by cells with background color	In non-interactive web pages, the cell surrounded by colored cells takes on the background color of the surrounding colored cells. Format the cell background as white rather than with no color to avoid this problem.

Feature	Result as a Web Page
References to data on other worksheets	Formulas that reference data on other worksheets are converted to values.
Subtotals	Numbers and calculations appear correctly. Group and outline features are lost.

PivotTable Limitations

Feature	Result as a Web Page
Calculated fields	Change to total fields, using the default summary function for the field (Sum, Count, Min, or Max).
Calculated items	Not retained.
Summary functions	Only data fields summarized with Sum, Count, Min, or Max are retained. Data fields that use other summary functions are lost.
Custom calculations	The data fields using custom calculation are lost.
Character and cell formatting	Changes made to fonts, text size, text color, and cell backgrounds are lost.
Custom subtotals	If you change the summary function in Excel, the subtotal or grand total reverts to the summary function of the total field in a PivotTable list.
Number formats	If a custom number format or a number format not supported by Excel is used, the numbers appear with the same number format as the Excel PivotTable report. If the number format for the field in the PivotTable list is subsequently changed, the field cannot be returned to the custom number format.
Print settings	The Excel settings to repeat PivotTable row and column labels on each page, repeat item labels after page breaks, and set page breaks between sections are lost.
Grouped items in fields	Items are no longer grouped.
Custom sort order	Excel custom sort orders are not retained; instead the data will be in the order in which it is retrieved from the source database.
Indented formats	Fields are in the same positions, but the character and cell formatting are lost, not retained. Blank rows between item groups are lost.
Subtotals at top of group items	Subtotals appear at the bottom of each group.
Top/bottom items AutoShow	All items are displayed.
Customized errors and empty values	Displayed as blank cells.
Page fields in rows or columns	Page fields become filter fields, which are always displayed across the top.
Password settings	If the password is saved with the query in Excel, users in the browser must enter the password when they open the Web page.

Feature	Result as a Web Page
Background refresh, retrieving data for each item in a page field individually	The PivotTable list on the web is always refreshed in the foreground and all data for filter fields is retrieved in one operation.
Changes to Excel source data	Excel source data must be changed in Excel and republished.
Offline cube file data sources	Cannot reconnect to the original server database from the published PivotTable list, or make changes to the content of the offline cube file from the PivotTable list. If either of these operations must be performed, do so in Excel and then republish to the PivotTable list.

Chart Limitations

Charts must be saved or published separately from other data in the workbook for the charts to appear correctly on the web page. When a chart is published or saved without interactive functionality, the chart is saved as a .gif file. When a chart is saved or published with interactive functionality, some features will not appear as they do in Excel. Before placing interactive charts on the Web, make sure they are not using any features, such as 3-D charts, that appear different on the web than they do in Excel. See the following Chart Limitation table for functional limitations.

Feature	Result as a Web Page
3-D chart type	Changed to 2-D chart type.
Surface chart type	Changed to column chart.
Autoscale fonts	Changed to default font size.
Drawing objects, text boxes, or pictures on the chart	Not retained.
Semi-transparent fills	Not retained.
Time-scale axes	Change to default category axis with text labels.
Individual data label formatting	Changed to default data label formatting.
Custom positioning and sizing of chart items	Changed to default position and size.
Multi-column legend layout	Not retained.
Hi-low lines	Not retained.
Series lines	Not retained.
Shadows	Not retained.
Moving average trendlines	Not retained.
Error bars calculated using standard error	Error bars changed to use default calculation.
Error bars calculated using standard deviation	Error bars changed to use default calculation.
Secondary value axis	Cannot be modified by another design program.
Vary colors by point	Cannot be modified by another design program.
Some combination charts (i.e., column + pie)	Cannot be modified by another design program.

Preparing Excel Data for Web Publication

Save the original worksheet or item on the worksheet before it is published or saved as a web page. If an entire workbook is saved, it can be opened later in Excel without losing any features. When it is then published or saved, the .xls file remains on the hard disk, and Excel creates a new HTML-format (.htm) file in the location specified. The data can be placed on the web with or without interactive functionality.

Before data with interactive functionality is placed on the web, make sure that the correct data appears in Excel and it is complete and accurate. Because some formatting does not appear the same way in Excel as it does on the web, it's better to format the data using FrontPage 2000 or data access page Design view in Access 2000 after it is published or saved. If the actual data must be changed, use Excel.

Publishing Excel Data on the Web

Note that changes to external data ranges will not be reflected on the web page when the data is published without interactive functionality enabled. Interactivity must be added with PivotTable functionality to put a refreshable external data range on a web page.

Preview the data (File|Web Page Preview) in the browser before saving or publishing it. To preview the page in interactive form, select the Open published web page in browser check box before clicking the Publish button. If the data does not appear as desired, open the original workbook (.xls), modify the data, and preview the web page again. Remember that some formatting and features appear differently in web pages than they do in Excel due to the native language capabilities, or limitations, of the web programming language HTML. Preview the web page with every browser that may be available to the users.

The workbook (.xls) can be saved directly to an Internet address. If all of the potential users of the workbook have Excel installed on their computers, or if the data is wanted in Excel format rather than HTML format, keep the data as an .xls file.

Hands-on Activity

In this activity you view a previously saved file as a web page and save/publish it as an interactive web page.

1. Open Pivot.xls: Click on **File|Open**, go to **C:\MSOffice\Files,** and select the file.

2. After the file opens, click on **File|Web Page Preview**. Verify your view with the following illustration. Yes, you opened the file in C:\MSOffice\Files but the browser shows another directory. This is normal as the browser copies the file to the temp directory. The table looks okay in the web preview view.

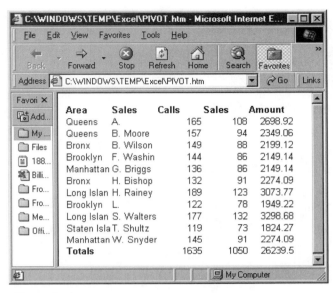

3. Close the browser.

4. Now we will save the file as a web page before looking at it in the browser. In Excel, click on **File|Save As**. In the **Save as type** box, select (***.htm; *.html**) **Web Page**. Notice the dialog changes and a Publish button appears on the lower right side of the dialog.

5. Click on **Publish**. Publish it to the MSOffice directory by typing **C:\MSOffice\Files\Page.htm** in the **File name** box. Enable **Add interactivity with** by clicking on the check box and selecting **Spreadsheet functionality** in the drop-down

box. If you do not want web users to change the data, do not enable Add interactivity with. Click on the **Open published web page in browser** check box.

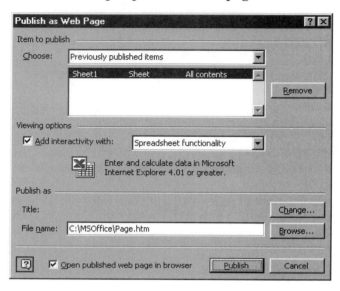

6. Click on **Publish**. Now the Pivot.xls is published as an interactive web page and can be viewed in the browser. Start your web browser and open Page.htm in the C:\MSOffice\Files directory.

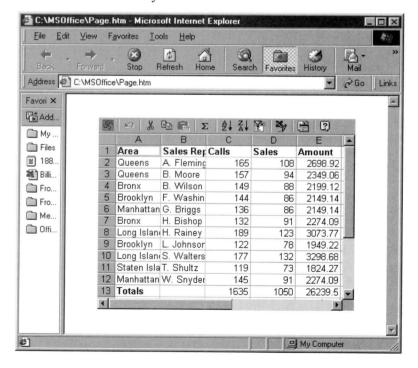

7. Page.htm was published interactively. Move the cursor to a cell, type in some value, then move the cursor to another location. Did the original location's value change? If so, we succeeded.

Summary

Excel worksheets and workbooks can be placed on the web both interactively and non-interactively. Due to HTML language limitations, not all Excel functionality is available in the web environment. The user must preview all potential Excel web postings to ensure the actual web page displayed to the world is adequate for its intended purpose.

This concludes the learning material about Microsoft Excel. At this point, you should be able to design and use a variety of useful Excel worksheets. To help you get started, review the workbooks found in this part, as there are many that can serve as models for ones that you need for managing budgets, inventory, financial schedules, and more.

Part 4

Microsoft Access 2000

44 About This Part—Part organization and brief description of Access.

45 Starting (or "Launching") Access—Key Access controls.

46 Understanding Databases—Introduction to database terminology, database structures, and an overview of the databases used in this part.

47 Creating Tables—Step-by-step instructions for creating a database with four tables. This includes the Member, Billing, Fees, and Rating tables.

48 Creating Queries—Information describing the creation and use of *queries* to find specific information. This section makes use of the built-in query wizards, which simplify the query construction process.

49 Getting Started with Forms—View, edit, and print information by creating and using Access forms. Here, you learn how to use form design tools and wizards to add form objects, such as graphics, and to arrange information in a useful format.

50 More About Forms—Add even more power to forms using the information in this section. Here, more tools are introduced in addition to showing readers how to modify forms to fulfill different requirements.

51 Finding Information in a Database—Find the exact information you need with Edit|Find and the corresponding dialogs. Build *filters* that isolate the displayed data to the precise information you want.

52 **Creating Reports**—Create fancy reports based on the information contained in your tables and queries. Like queries and forms, use the built-in wizards to design sophisticated reports in a matter of minutes.

53 **Adding Charts to Your Reports**—Add graphical pizzazz to your reports by learning how to use Microsoft Chart with Access. Here, you make use of the Chart Wizard, which is used to create and insert a Microsoft Chart object on your Access reports.

54 **Creating Mailing Labels**—No database application would be complete without the ability to create mailing labels. Access is no exception. Here you create mailing labels based on the Member table.

55 **Automating Your Work with Macros**—Automate frequently used tasks by learning to create Access macros. This section guides you through the creation and use of a simple Access macro to give you a foundation in macro development.

About This Part

Introduction

Part 4 of this book guides you through the use of Microsoft Access for Windows 2000. From this point forward, the common name "Access" is used. When you complete the sections within this part of the book, you should be able to create, save, and print many kinds of tables and reports needed in support of both business-related and personal records. Before moving into the descriptive and tutorial sections of this part, be sure to read the remainder of this section.

What is Access?

Access is a full-featured relational database management system (RDBMS) that is used by millions of people around the world. Database management programs are designed to store, manipulate, and report large volumes of information (or *data*). Typical examples of data include the information that comprises a telephone and address directory, large inventory databases (or parts lists), order records, contact lists, and much more. A common misuse of spreadsheet programs is that of data storage. However, once people realize what can be done with a database management program, they understand the folly of storing large volumes of data in spreadsheets. Like the other programs in the Office 2000 suite, Access makes use of all of the features available to programs designed specifically to run with a 32-bit operating system such as Windows 95/98 and Windows NT. As part of Office 2000, Access uses a number of shared Office resources as do the other applications. These include fonts, ClipArt, spelling resources, AutoCorrect, and more.

As with the other Office programs, Access can also integrate documents and information created by other Office and Windows programs. For example, you can insert Excel spreadsheet documents directly into an Access table. The ease and flexibility of doing this is impressive. For example, you can cut a portion of a document created by another program and then paste it into an Access table. Or, you may prefer to "drag and drop" part of one document into another using your mouse. Finally, you may simply import one kind of document into another. This flexibility gives you the ability to work in ways that best suit your personal tastes.

Companion Files

The companion files used with the Access hands-on activities were installed when you copied the *Learn Office 2000* files from the CD-ROM. The Files folder contains the tables, queries, forms, reports, and macros that you develop in this part of the book. You can check these by opening the supplied Club.mdb file and comparing them to the files that you create and save in the hands-on activities.

You can display the supplied Club.mdb file by using the Access File|Open Database menu option or by clicking the Open (file folder) button. Choose the C:\MSOffice\Files folder and click OK. When you are finished examining the companion files, use the Access File|Close Database menu selection to close the Club.mdb file.

What's New?

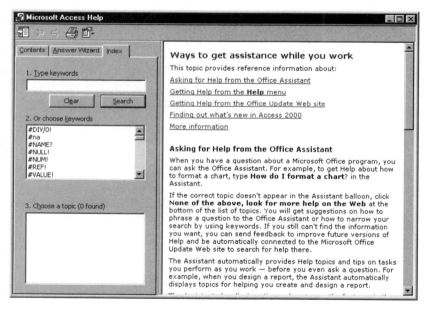

When Access help is started, the following dialog is displayed. By clicking on "Finding out what's new in Access 2000" you will be guided to another dialog that lists many of the new features not found in previous Access versions.

After clicking on "Finding out what's new…" in the dialog, Access help displays the "What's new…" dialog. Click on any topic of interest for a detailed explanation of the new feature and how it may improve your productivity.

What's Next?

Now you're ready to begin learning all about Access. In the next section you how to start Access. With this background in place, you then move to Section 46 where you find out about databases.

Starting (or "Launching") Access

If you installed the Office toolbar, the easiest way to launch Access is to click on the Access button. Otherwise, go to the Programs group (or the group in which you installed Access); start Access by clicking the Microsoft Access line. When Access starts the default Book1 loads.

The first time you start Access you are invited to review "What's New," and the Office Assistant offers help. If you are familiar with previous versions of Access you may want to close the Office Assistant for now. Go to the Menu bar and click on Help, then click on Hide the Office Assistant. The default Microsoft Access dialog will display. Click on Blank Access Database, then click on cancel on the File New Database dialog. Compare your display to the following illustration, which labels the various parts of the Access screen.

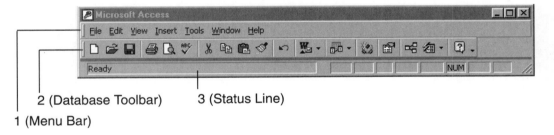

2 (Database Toolbar)   3 (Status Line)

1 (Menu Bar)

The above screen illustrates the view with no database selected. If you wish, you can use the View menu to change the document view if a database is selected. With a database open, you can now design and view the forms, tables, reports, queries, pages, and macros of the database. Each Access screen control is summarized in the appendices on the accompanying CD. Detailed descriptions are found in the following sections of this book where you are guided through hands-on learning activities.

Microsoft Access 2000 Controls

The keyed screen illustration shows each of the various controls which are summarized in the list that follows.

Key	Item	Description
1	Menu Bar	Used to access the Access menus and the Office Assistant (Help)
2	Database Toolbar	Includes buttons to perform the most frequently used database, file, and text management, editing, linking, coding, table designing, querying and Office Assistant (Help) operations.
3	Status Line	Displays messages.

Understanding Databases

Introduction

Microsoft Access is a powerful Windows 95/98 and NT-based relational database management system (RDBMS), which you can use to create and modify database tables, data entry forms, reports, and queries (customized requests for information from one or more tables). These concepts are explained in the following pages using a tennis and swim club membership system example. This example shows you how a relational database management system works. It also is used as the basis for the hands-on activities in the following sections of this part. In fact, when you are done with this part, you will have actually developed and used tables, queries, forms, reports, and macros designed around member and billing information.

Terms and Definitions

Database software comes with a lot of new terminology. Therefore, Appendix A on the companion CD provides a list of common terms and definitions that should be useful. This section clarifies some definitions that are specific to Access. Here, you'll see the actual structure of a few different database tables. You also see how they are created and how information is entered into tables and ultimately displayed. The creation and use of these tables clarifies many database concepts in a relatively short time.

Databases and Tables

In Access, a database is a collection of information. Examples of databases include private telephone directories, lists of customers and suppliers, parts in a warehouse or store, and even private tape, book, and compact disk collections. The information in an Access database is retained in tables. Tables consist of rows and columns. Each row is called a *record* and pertains to a specific person or supplier, inventory item, or event. Each column contains a discrete element of information, called a *field*. A field might be a name, telephone number, stock-keeping unit number, unit cost, or any other piece of information. The following table example helps to illustrate records, fields, and some RDBMS concepts.

A tennis and swim club must maintain a database for each of its members. Within the database, different tables are used to store:

■ Names, addresses, and telephone numbers (Member table)

■ Billing information (Billing table)

■ Detailed purchases and fees (Fees table)

■ Tennis proficiency ratings (Rating table)

The first database table (Member table) contains names, member numbers, addresses, telephone numbers, dates of birth, and membership dates. The number can include member name and privilege codes. For example, the first letter of the member number is the first letter of the member's last name. The last letter of the member number designates whether the member has a tennis (T) or swim (S) membership.

Number	FirstName	MiddleName	LastName	SpouseName	Address
S1465T	John	Gregory	Smith	Sheila	1234 Country Club Dr.
J1050S	Bill	T.	Johnson	Betty	1112 San Pedro Avenue
S1300T	Lisa	Anne	Stanley		985 Trenton Circle

(continued)

City	State	PostalCode	HomePhone	WorkPhone	Birthdate	Joindate
Houston	Texas	78905-3609	(713) 555-7890	(713) 232-2323	10/21/37	5/1/88
Cypress	Texas	78855-1005	(713) 555-6556	(713) 222-3333	1/24/63	6/1/95
Houston	Texas	78905-1015	(713) 555-1227	(713) 423-0908	3/29/50	11/1/96

The first line in the preceding table displays the name of each field. Then, three member records are shown. Notice how each field contains a different value.

Note: The field list could be expanded to contain other information such as children's names and ages, other affiliations, etc.

The Billing table contains billing information. Here, the total monthly charge accrued to each member's account is maintained. This is used as a basis for each member's monthly bill. It maintains the member number, total monthly charge, invoice date, and the date that the member's payment is received.

Number	Amount	Invoice Date	Payment Date	Amount Received	Past Due
J1050S	209.90	05/31/00	00/00/00	0.00	209.90
S1300T	210.00	05/31/00	06/08/00	210.00	0.00
S1465T	270.00	05/31/00	06/05/00	270.00	0.00

The billing information is derived from a third Fees table that itemizes membership charges for dues, food and beverages, league fees, tournament fees, pro shop merchandise, and other charges. These can be itemized on the member's monthly statement.

Number	Description	Date	Amount
J1050S	Dues for May	5/31/00	35.00
J1050S	Service, Massage	5/01/00	5.00
J1050S	Food & Beverage	5/05/00	16.40
S1300T	Pro Shop, Merchandise	5/31/00	148.50
S1300T	Dues for May	5/31/00	125.00

Finally, a Rating table is used to maintain tennis proficiency ratings for the tennis members. The ratings are used to place tennis members in the appropriate leagues.

Number	Date	Rating	Rated By	Comments
S1300T	01/30/97	3.5	L. Byers	Needs to improve backhand
S1465T	02/06/97	4.0	L. Byers	Move to next league level
J1200T	03/16/97	3.0	L. Byers	Schedule lessons
A1080T	04/12/97	4.0	L. Byers	Strong serve and volley
S1465T	02/06/97	4.5	L. Byers	Nominate for 5.0 team

A unique field is used to tie all four databases together. The Name field might be considered, but there could be two or more members with the same name. Therefore, the Number field is used, because no two members have the same number. Requests for information, or queries, can be made based on the member number. All four tables can be joined as if each member had one big record. However, since swim members don't have tennis proficiency ratings, there's no point in reserving space for empty fields. The same fact holds true for purchases. In addition to the member number, all that's needed is the date, purchase amount, and a brief item description. Adding fields for the member's address, phone number, or date of birth to each purchase record would be a duplication of information and a waste of disk space. This information already exists in the Member table. Therefore, the member number is used to tie charges in the Fees table to the Billing and Member tables.

Similarly, the Rating table contains member numbers, dates, ratings, the name of the person doing the rating, and comments. Tennis ratings are used to place players at the proper level for both tournament and league play.

Forms

Forms are designed to display certain fields and descriptive labels in a convenient format. For example, you can create a form that contains member names and telephone numbers. Here, you've omitted member number, address, and age information. A form lets you focus on the information you need without cluttering up the screen or printed output with unwanted text. Once a form is designed and saved, you can open and use it to add, edit, or delete information within the corresponding table.

Queries

Simply stated, a query is used to display information that resides in one or more tables. Queries are designed to organize and display information to answer certain questions. You can use queries to display information from multiple tables such as a member's number, name, amount due, and tennis rating. This query extracts information from three different tables. A query is also referred to as a dynaset. A dynaset is a dynamic set of information that changes with the contents of the supporting table. Queries extract and display information; they are not used to change information.

Reports

Reports are used to display and/or print information. With Access, you can produce spectacular reports by including graphics, charts, and a variety of type styles and fonts. These features give Access many advantages over the old, DOS-based flat file database programs. Like a query, a report is also a dynaset, as it is dependent on the current contents of supporting tables.

Summary

Armed with an understanding of a few terms and relational database management concepts, you're ready to move on to hands-on database development. In the next section you create the tables described in this section. Then, you begin developing forms, queries, and reports. Note that the companion files supplied with this book contains the tables, forms, reports, and queries. You can examine these by starting Access and opening them in the C:\MSOffice\Files directory. However, it is strongly recommended that you develop these files from scratch by following the steps outlined in the next sections. This assures a good understanding of the many tools available in Access. It also gives you the experience you need to develop your own applications from scratch.

Creating Tables

Introduction

In this section you learn how to create tables. Each table corresponds to those described in the previous section. First, you create the Member table. Instructions are provided to walk you through the creation process one step at a time. With the experience gained through creation of the first table, creation of the remaining tables is a breeze.

The companion CD contains the tables created in this section. If you encounter trouble or want to save a few minutes, you can always copy them from the CD to the working directory on your hard drive. However, there is a strong case for creating the tables yourself, as this experience is important for validating what you learned.

Before we go into greater detail, let us jump right into creating the tables we need for the remainder of this part of the book.

Hands-on Activity: Creating Your First Database and Table

Before you can create a table, a database must be established. In this section, you create a new database named Club. Then you create four tables having the names:

1. Member
2. Billing
3. Fees
4. Rating

Each table consists of rows and columns of information. As previously described, each row is a *record* about an item such as a customer, person, stock unit, or event. Each column is a *field* that contains a unique piece of information about the item.

Create the database as follows:

Note: Each activity in this part requires that you first start Windows 95/98/NT and then the Access program. Start (or *launch*) Access by clicking the Windows Start button. Display the Programs list and then click on Microsoft Access. (You can also start Access using the Office Toolbar if it is installed.) When the first Access screen appears, click Cancel (or press <Esc>) to close the first dialog. (This dialog is used to open an existing database or to create a new one. You use toolbar buttons and menus as an alternate way to accomplish these tasks.) Do each activity by carefully reading and performing each step in the procedure that follows.

1. At the Access opening screen, look at the toolbar across the top of the screen. Move your mouse pointer to a button and notice how a descriptive label is displayed. A brief description is also displayed on the status line at the bottom of the screen.

2. From the Access opening screen, click **File|New** (the New Database selection of the File menu). The New dialog is displayed.

Tip: You can also click the New Database button on the toolbar or press <Ctrl+N> to accomplish the same task. Access gives you alternate ways to do things to suit the way you like to work.

3. Click **OK** to use the default Database template. Select the MSOffice\Files path in the File New Database dialog.

4. In the Files folder, type **Club** in place of db1.mdb. Click **Create** to create a Club.mdb database file.

   The displayed Club: Database dialog is used to create tables, queries, forms, reports, macros, and modules. You can use the Insert menu to create any of these items. The remainder of this section guides you through the use of the Tables tab located under the Objects tab on the left side pane. Following sections in this part guide you through the use of the other tabs on the Database dialog.

5. Select **Tables** (the default) from the left pane and click the **New** button on the Database dialog to display the New Table dialog.

   Now select **Table Wizard** from the list and click **OK** to view the first Table Wizard dialog.

Tip: The Table Wizard includes a long list of sample table structures. These offer a variety of ready-made fields that can provide a starting point from which to build your own tables, such as, fields designed to accommodate a variety of data types including dates, telephone numbers, postal codes, and currency. Since these fields already exist in these tables, you should consider exploring the tables so you can use the type of fields you want to use in your new table. For example, you can take a currency field from one and a postal code from another. If you'd rather create a table from scratch, you can select Design View. This displays a blank table in which you type all of your own field names and optional descriptions and assign appropriate data types. This approach is used later in this section when you create the Billing, Fees, and Rating tables.

6. Select **Employees** from the **Sample Tables** box, as it is ideal for your membership roster. (You change the field names in a later step.) Now select each of the following fields by highlighting each one in the **Sample Fields** box and clicking the > button to move each field into the **Fields in my new table** box.

   EmployeeID
   FirstName
   MiddleName
   LastName
   SpouseName
   Address
   City
   StateorProvince
   PostalCode
   HomePhone
   WorkPhone
   Birthdate
   DateHired

7. Click **Next>** to display the next dialog box. Delete Employees from the What do you want to name your table text box and type **Member**; click **No, I'll set the primary key**.

8. Click **Next>** to see the next dialog box. Select **Employee ID** in the What field will hold data text box and be sure to click the **Numbers I enter when I add new records** option. (This lets you assign a unique number for each member in the club. Otherwise, Access automatically assigns a sequential number beginning with 1.)

9. Click **Next>** to display the next dialog. Select **Modify the table design** and click **Finish**.

10. In the Design View display that appears, change **EmployeeID** to **Number** and **DateHired** to **Joindate** by double-clicking each field name and typing the new name.

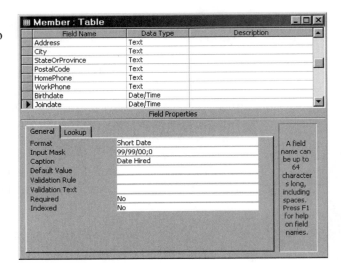

Original Field Name
EmployeeID
DateHired

Changed Field Name
Number
Joindate

Tip: Notice that the Number field has a key next to it.

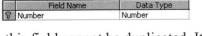

This indicates a key field, which means the value in this field cannot be duplicated. It is used to locate and combine information about each member using this and other tables.

11. Delete each caption in the Field Properties section (click on the **General** tab of the Field Properties area at the bottom of the dialog). When blank, the field name is automatically used as a label.

12. Select the **Data Type** field of the Number (formerly EmployeeID) field name. Pull down the Select list (click the down arrow) and select **Text**. Type **6** as the Field Size in the Field Properties section of the dialog box.

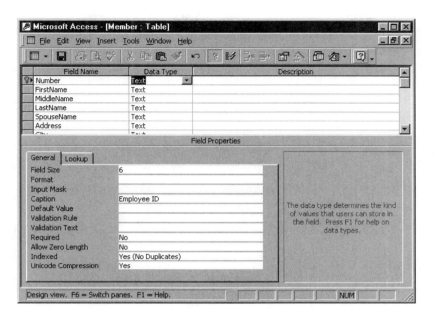

Tip:
Field names can be up to 64 characters in length including spaces. Data types can be selected from a pull-down select list as:

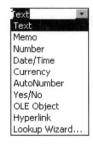

Text—Text and numbers

Memo—Passages of informative text or notes

Number—Integer or decimal numbers

Date/Time—A date or time value

Currency—Monetary values

AutoNumber—A unique record number, or counter, used when a unique field (or *key*) is unavailable.

Yes/No—A yes/no value; represents a *logical* true or false state.

OLE Object—Links a selected object, such as a picture or graph, to the record.

Hyperlink—A field in which a hyperlink address is stored. Ideal for e-mail and web page addresses.

Lookup Wizard—Creates a lookup column that displays a list of values from which you can choose.

Be sure to familiarize yourself with format control characters. You can review these using Access's online help information.

13. Use **File|Save** to save the current table structure. Once saved, you can use the Field Properties portion of the dialog box (at the bottom) to control the format of entered values for such things as telephone numbers and dates. Because the fields are already formatted by the supplied database templates, you won't have to make changes to the Input Mask line. However, look at a few so you know how to control field formats in

case the need should arise. Anytime you make changes to the structure, be sure to use **File|Save** to save the changes.

Tip: In addition to using **File|Save**, you can also save your work by either clicking the diskette button on the toolbar or pressing <Ctrl+S>, depending on how you like to work.

a. Click on the **HomePhone** line. Move the cursor to the **Input Mask** line. Look at the Input Mask line to see the format control codes for entering a phone number.

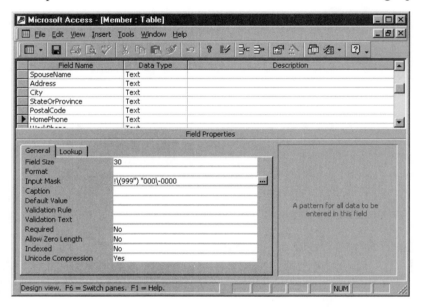

b. Click in the **Input Mask** line, then click the button (ellipsis) at the right side of the Input Mask line to display the Input Mask Wizard dialog. Select **Phone Number**, then click **Next>**.

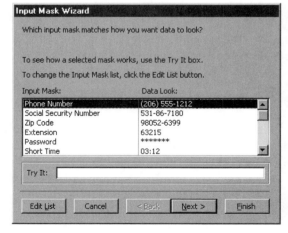

c. Click in the **Try It** text box to view the input mask (___) ___-____.

d. Click on **Next>**. The Input Mask Wizard now offers a choice how the phone number will be stored. The default is without symbols.

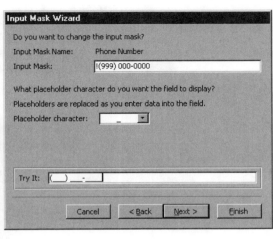

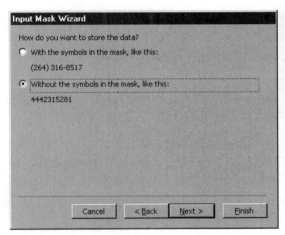

e. Click **Cancel** since the HomePhone is already formatted properly. Notice that the format control code !\(999") "000\-0000 is displayed on the Input Mask line.

14. Press <**Ctrl+S**> to save.

15. Select the **Birthdate** line. Click on the **Input Mask** line and click the ellipsis button. Verify that **Short Date** is selected; then click the **Try It** text box to view the input mask.

16. Click **Cancel** since the format control code is already set to 99/99/00.

17. Select the **Number** line. Type >@@@@@@ on the Format line of the General tab of the Field Properties. Press <**Ctrl+S**> to save this change.

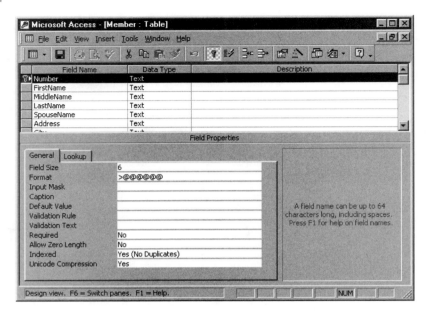

18. Enter the following descriptions in the Description column for each of the indicated field names.

Field Name	Description
Number	Member number
FirstName	Member's first name
MiddleName	Member's middle name
LastName	Member's last name
SpouseName	Name of member's spouse
Address	Member's address
City	Member's city
StateorProvince	Member's state
PostalCode	Member's zip code
HomePhone	Member's home phone number
WorkPhone	Member's business phone number
Birthdate	Member's date of birth
Joindate	Date member joined club

19. Compare the properties of each field to the following table and make changes as necessary. Be sure they match before saving.

Tip: When the Required property is set to "Yes," Access prompts the user for a required input. When "No," the field may be left blank.

Member Table Properties (Part 1 of 2)

Field Name	Number	FirstName	MiddleName	LastName	SpouseName	Address
Data Type	Text	Text	Text	Text	Text	Text
Description	Member number	Member's first name	Member's middle name	Member's last name	Name of member's spouse	Member's address
Field Size	6	50	30	50	50	255
Format	>@@@@@@					
Input Mask						
Required	Yes	Yes	No	Yes	No	Yes
Allow Zero Length	No	No	No	No	No	No
Indexed	Yes (No Duplicates)	No	No	Yes (Duplicates OK)	No	No
Unicode Compression	Yes	Yes	Yes	Yes	Yes	Yes

Member Table Properties (Part 2 of 2)

Field Name	City	State	PostalCode	HomePhone	WorkPhone	Birthdate	Joindate
Data Type	Text	Text	Text	Text	Text	Date/Time	Date/Time
Description	Member's city	Member's state	Member's zip code	Member's home phone number	Member's business phone number	Member's date of birth	Date member joined club
Field Size	50	50	20	30	30		
Format						Short Date	Short Date
Input Mask			00000\-9999	!\(999") "000\-0000	!\(999") "000\-0000	99/99/00	99/99/00
Required	Yes	Yes	Yes	No	No	No	Yes
Allow Zero Length	No	No	No	No	No		
Indexed	No	No	Yes (Duplicates OK)	No	No	No	No
Unicode Compression	Yes	Yes	Yes	Yes	Yes		

20. Press <Ctrl+S> to save; now click the **View|Datasheet View** button on the toolbar and enter the following information in the table.

Tip: Use the horizontal scroll bar to move left and right. Adjust the column widths to view all information by dragging on the intersection between column headings. Also notice how your input masks control the way phone numbers and dates are formatted.

Note: In the following entries, type the names and addresses in upper- and lowercase exactly as you would for a letter heading or envelope. The information in the table will be used to print mailing labels and customer statements.

Contents of Member Table

Number	FirstName	MiddleName	LastName	SpouseName	Address
S1465T	John	Gregory	Smith	Sheila	1234 Country Club Dr.
J1050S	Bill	T.	Johnson	Betty	1112 San Pedro Avenue
S1300T	Lisa	Anne	Stanley		985 Trenton Circle

Contents of Member Table (Continued)

City	State	PostalCode	HomePhone	WorkPhone	Birthdate	Joindate
Houston	Texas	78905-3609	(713) 555-7890	(713) 232-2323	10/21/37	05/01/78
Cypress	Texas	78855-1005	(713) 555-6556	(713) 222-3333	01/24/63	06/01/90
Houston	Texas	78905-1015	(713) 555-1227	(713) 423-0908	03/29/50	11/01/86

21. Click on **Datasheet View**.

22. Right-click on the leftmost column (Employee ID), then click on **Rename Column**.

23. Delete **Employee ID and key** in Number, click anywhere outside the cell, and close the Member: Table dialog.

24. Check your information for accuracy. Then press **<Ctrl+S>** to save the information and use **Close** to close the file.

You have successfully created the Member table using Access wizards and the Design View. Then you entered three records and saved them using the Table View.

Hands-on Activity: Creating More Tables

Now create the Billing, Fees, and Rating tables using the New Table button of the New Table dialog box and the information provided in this activity. After each table is created, you add several records and then save the completed table.

Tip: At least one key field must have a unique value, i.e., not duplicated in other records of the table. If no key field exists or is assigned, Access inserts an AutoNumber type field for you with the field name ID. Access prompts you when you save the table the first time. Responding with "Yes" automatically adds the ID field to the table. The ID field contains a number that corresponds to the record number within the table. You can also insert your own key field by selecting the field and then clicking the Primary Key button.

Billing Table

Create the Billing table as follows:

1. With the Club database still open, click **New** 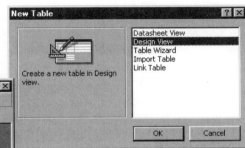.

Note: You may need to click on the Club: Database dialog icon 🔲 Club : Data... at the bottom of the screen (in the Taskbar) to bring the dialog forward.

2. Select **Design View** and click **OK** to bypass the Table wizards.

3. The Table Design View is displayed.

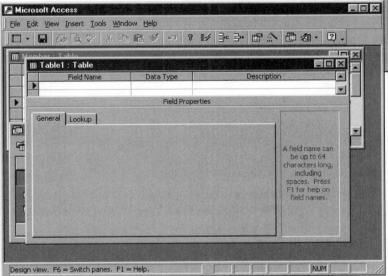

4. Type the field names, data types, and descriptions shown in the following Table Design View window illustration. Assign the property types given in the table that follows the illustration. Press **<Ctrl+S>** each time you use the Input Mask Wizard. The first time you save the table, enter the table name **Billing** and click **OK**. Access displays a "Create a primary key?" prompt. Respond by clicking the **Yes** button.

Note: Pull-down select lists are available to the data type and some property types. Clicking an ellipsis button displays a wizard dialog box. Format codes are described in Access Help. Be sure to use the format codes shown in this book until you familiarize yourself with the available codes by browsing the online Access Help information and Input Mask Wizard dialog boxes.

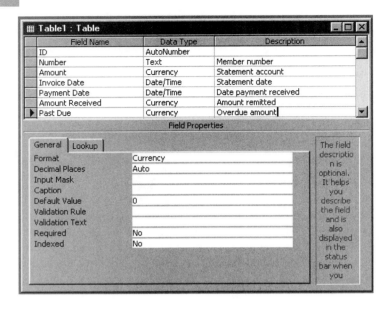

Billing Table Properties

Field Name	ID	Number	Amount	Invoice Date	Payment Date	Amount Received	Past Due
Data Type	Auto Number	Text	Currency	Date/Time	Date/Time	Currency	Currency
Description		Member number	Statement amount	Statement date	Date payment received	Amount remitted	Overdue amount
Field Size	Long Integer	6					
Format		>@@@@@@	Currency	Short Date	Short Date	Currency	Currency
Decimal Places			Auto			Auto	Auto
Input Mask				99/99/00	99/99/00		
Default Value			0			0	0
Required		Yes	Yes	Yes	No	No	No
Allow Zero Length		No					
Indexed	Yes (No Duplicates)	Yes (Duplicates OK)	No	No	No	No	No
New Values	Increment						

5. Be sure to designate the Indexed property of the Number field as "Yes (Duplicates OK)." This keeps all records having the same member number together.

6. Press **<Ctrl+S>** to save the table. Then click the **Datasheet View** button and enter the following information.

Contents of Billing Table

ID	Number	Amount	Invoice Date	Payment Date	Amount Received	Past Due
1	J1050S	65.90	5/31/99	Blank	0.00	65.90
2	S1300T	145.00	5/31/99	6/8/99	145.00	0.00
3	S1465T	170.00	5/31/99	6/5/99	170.00	0.00

7. Press **<Ctrl+S>** to save the table. Then use **File|Close** (or press **<Ctrl+W>**) to close the table.

Fees Table

Create the Fees table as follows:

1. With the Club database still open, click **New** on the **Club: Database** dialog.

Note: You may need to click on the Club: Database dialog icon at the bottom of the screen (in the Taskbar) to bring the dialog forward.

2. Select **Design View** and click **OK** to bypass the Table wizards.

3. The table Design View is displayed.

4. Type the field names, data types, and descriptions shown in the following Table Design View window illustration. Assign the property types given in the table that follows the illustration. Press **<Ctrl+S>** each time you use the Input Mask Wizard. The first time you save the table, enter the table name **Fees** and click **OK**. Access displays a "Create a primary key?" prompt. Respond by clicking the **Yes** button.

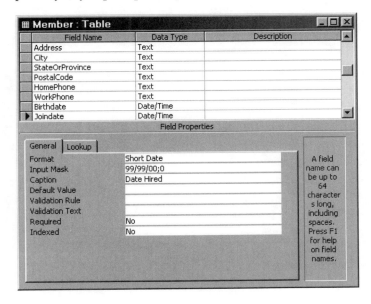

Fees Table Properties

Field Name	ID	Number	Description	Date	Amount
Data Type	AutoNumber	Text	Text	Date/Time	Currency
Description		Member number	Charge description	Transaction date	Transaction charge
Field Size	Long Integer	6	50		
Format		>@@@@@@		Short Date	Currency
Decimal Places					Auto
Input Mask				99/99/00	
Default Value					0
Required		Yes	Yes	Yes	Yes
Allow Zero Length		No	No		
Indexed	Yes (No Duplicates)	Yes (Duplicates OK)	No	No	No
New Values	Increment				

5. Be sure to designate the Indexed property of the Number field as "Yes (Duplicates OK)." This keeps all records having the same member number together.

6. Press <**Ctrl+S**> to save the table. Then click the **Datasheet View** button and enter the following information.

Tip: You can adjust the column width by dragging on the intersection between column headings as necessary.

Contents of Fees Table

ID	Number	Description	Date	Amount
1	J1050S	Dues for May	05/31/99	50.00
2	J1050S	Service-Massage	05/01/99	25.00
3	J1050S	Food & Beverage	05/05/99	16.40
4	S1300T	Pro Shop-Merchandise	05/31/99	78.50
5	S1300T	Dues for May	05/31/99	125.00
6	S1300T	League Fee	05/31/99	25.00
7	S1465T	Dues for May	05/31/99	125.00
8	S1465T	Guest Fee	05/22/99	5.00
9	S1465T	Pro Shop-Merchandise	05/22/99	22.50
10	S1465T	Pro Shop-Lesson	05/28/99	25.00

7. Press <**Ctrl+S**> to save the table. Then press <**Ctrl+W**> to close the table.

Rating Table

Create the tennis rating table as follows:

1. With the Club database still open, click **New** New.

Note: You may need to click on the Club: Database dialog icon Club : Data... at the bottom of the screen (in the Taskbar) to bring the dialog forward.

2. Select **Design View** and click **OK** to bypass the Table wizards.

3. The Table Design View is displayed.

4. Type the field names, data types, and descriptions shown in the following Table Design View window illustration. Assign the property types given in the table that follows the illustration. Press **<Ctrl+S>** each time you use the Input Mask Wizard. The first time you save the table, enter the table name **Rating** and click **OK**. Respond to the "Create a primary key?" prompt by clicking **Yes**.

Rating Table Properties

Field Name	ID	Number	Date	Rating	Rated By	Comments
Data Type	AutoNumber	Text	Date/Time	Number	Text	Memo
Description		Member number	Rating date	NTRP Rating	Certified by	Comments
Field Size	Long Integer	6		Double	50	
Format		>@@@@@@	Short Date	Fixed		
Decimal Places				1		
Input Mask			99/99/00			
Default Value				0		
Required		Yes	Yes	Yes	Yes	No
Allow Zero Length		No		No		No
Indexed	Yes (No Duplicates)	No	No	No	No	
New Values	Increment					

5. Press **<Ctrl+S>** to save the table. Then click the **Datasheet View** button and enter the following information.

Contents of Rating Table

ID	Number	Date	Rating	Rated By	Comments
1	S1300T	01/30/99	3.5	L. Byers	Needs to improve backhand
2	S1465T	02/06/99	4.0	L. Byers	Move to next league level
3	J1200T	03/16/99	3.0	L. Byers	Schedule lessons
4	A1080T	04/12/99	4.0	L. Byers	Strong serve and volley
5	S1470T	04/06/99	4.5	L. Byers	Nominate for 5.0 team

6. Select **File|Save** (or press **<Ctrl+S>**). Then use **Close** to close the table.

Changing Table Contents and Table Design

You may have noticed that the toolbars and menu selections change when you switch between the Table View and Design View. Access displays the toolbar and menu selections that correspond to the task being performed. A descriptive button label is displayed when you position the mouse cursor on a toolbar button. You can also use the View|Toolbars selection to display and hide toolbars at will. The View|Toolbars menu selection is shown here.

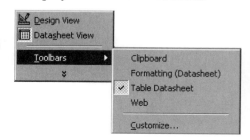

Toolbars

Use View|Toolbars to see the names of each of the available toolbars that correspond to the current operation. The Toolbars dialog box lets you hide or show any of the listed toolbars by clicking the toolbar name. You may want to display the toolbars and then display each button name using your mouse. Each toolbar button has a corresponding name label. Display button names by moving the mouse cursor on the desired button. You can also customize your toolbar buttons as with other Office applications by dragging and dropping the desired buttons to and from a selected toolbar.

Adding and Editing Records

Once a table has been designed and saved, it's a simple matter to add new information, delete unwanted information, or change existing information. Just select the table name and click the Open button (or double-click the table name). The table is displayed in the Table View.

Add, Cut, Copy, and Paste—You can add records by moving to the last row of a table and typing the new record information. You can also delete records or change the information within the table just as you would within a word processor. You can rearrange the way that information is displayed, insert new fields, delete unwanted ones, and much more. The Edit menu, which varies with the task at hand, gives you the ability to cut, copy, or paste information to and from the Windows clipboard, just as you would with any Windows-based word processor, spreadsheet, or graphics program. You can also position the cursor and use Insert Row to insert a new blank row ahead of the selected one. The Delete Row selection eliminates the current record.

Edit|Paste Special—The Paste Special selection is used to paste information from other applications via the Windows clipboard. When this is done the Windows Dynamic Data Linking (DDL) feature is used. When you use the original application, such as Excel or PowerPoint, to make changes to the source information, those changes are dynamically linked to the information (or graphic) used by Access. Hence, Access always uses the most recent information.

Changing Column Widths, Hiding Columns, and Freezing Columns

The width of a column is changed by placing the mouse cursor between column headings so that the cursor changes to a double-headed arrow. Press the left mouse button and drag the column margin left or right. Releasing the mouse button leaves the column in its new location. Use the Format|Hide Columns and Unhide Columns selection to suppress and return the display of selected columns.

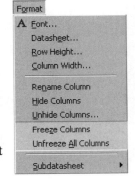

Use the Format|Freeze Columns and Unfreeze All Columns selection to keep one or more selected columns in place at the left edge of the screen as others are scrolled left and right. For example, you might want to keep the member names at the left edge of the screen while looking at information that is scrolled out of view. To return to normal scrolling, use Unfreeze All Columns.

Use the View menu to display the Table View or Design View, or to display or hide selected toolbars. Use the View|Options selection to set the way information is displayed.

Changing Table Properties

Access gives you a great deal of flexibility in the design and modification of tables, queries, forms, and reports. It's easy to change the design and properties of a table. This is done by selecting the table name and then clicking the Design button. Once the structure is displayed, you can change field lengths and formats, insert new fields, delete existing ones, and more. Once your changes are made, save the changed properties. If the data within the table doesn't adhere to the new properties, Access tells you and gives you the opportunity to make necessary changes to your contents. For example, if you change the Required property from No to Yes and a blank field exists, you can make the change before saving the table. Finally, use Edit|Set Primary Key (or the Set Primary Key button) to designate a field as a primary key field. A primary key field is unique and prevents you from having duplicate records. The Number field in the Member table and the ID AutoNumber-type fields are examples of primary key fields. You can have more than one primary key field in a table.

Hands-on Activity: Creating Relationships Between Tables

Advanced topic

You can establish relationships between two or more tables by associating common fields. In the Club database, the Number field is an indexed field in all tables. It is the primary field in the Member table. To establish a relationship between the Number fields in the Member, Fees, Billing, and Rating tables, proceed as follows.

1. Select the Club database to display the database window (if not already displayed).

2. Use the **Tools|Relationships** menu option to display the Show Table dialog box.

   Once displayed, select each of the four table names and click **Add** as follows:

   a. Select **Member** and click **Add**.

   b. Select **Billing** and click **Add**.

   c. Select **Fees** and click **Add**.

   d. Select **Rating** and click **Add**.

3. Close the **Show Table** dialog box by clicking **Close**. Now drag the table boxes so they are positioned approximately as shown in the following illustration. (The "join lines" are added in step 4.)

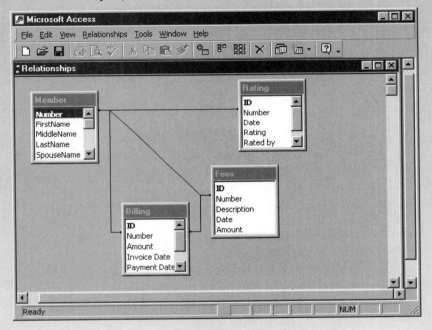

4. Establish the join lines (or *relationships*) as follows:

   a. Select **Number** in the Member box, drag to **Number** within the Billing box, and release the mouse button. Click **Create** in the Edit Relationships dialog box.

   b. Select **Number** in the Billing box, drag to **Number** within the Fees box, and release the mouse button. Click **Create**.

   c. Select **Number** in the Member box, drag to **Number** within the Fees box, and release the mouse button. Click **Create**.

   d. Select **Number** in the Member box, drag to **Number** within the Rating box, and release the mouse button. Click **Create**.

5. Verify that your join lines resemble those shown in the illustration. Then use **Close** and click **Yes** to save the relationships.

Adding OLE Object Fields to a Table

It is an easy matter to add an OLE object, such as a picture or chart created by another Windows application, to an Access table. Once the object is linked, it can be displayed in forms and reports. Access simply "fetches" the linked object and uses it as directed. Use the following procedure to add an OLE object field named Picture to the Member table. Note that the pictures are simple bitmap (bmp) graphic files. However, they could be scanned photographs, maps, and more.

1. Begin with the Club: Database window displayed.

   Proceed as follows to add pictures of your members.

2. Click the Tables tab, select Member, and click the Design button.

3. Add a new field to the bottom of the field list as follows: Type Picture in the Field Name column, click OLE Object as the Data Type, and type Member photo in the Description column. Press <Ctrl+S> to save the table. Use Close to close the Member: Table dialog.

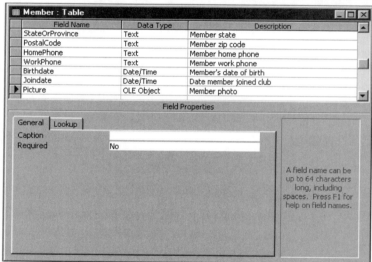

4. Click the Open button 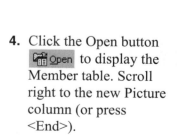 to display the Member table. Scroll right to the new Picture column (or press <End>).

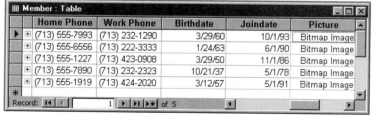

5. Insert picture objects as follows:

   a. Select the Picture field on the first row (Johnson's record).

   b. Use the Insert|Object menu selection to display the Insert Object dialog box, click the Create from File button, and put a check in the Link check box. Now click Browse to locate the C:\MSOffice\ Files\J1050S.bmp file as shown in the following illustration. Select the file and click Open and then OK.

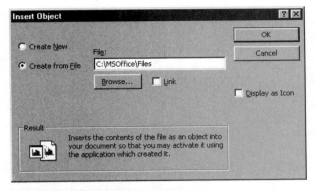

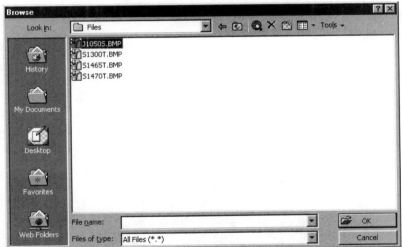

Note that linking the object causes source file changes to be reflected in the table. For example, if a drawing of a map or an Excel worksheet is linked to a table, you can use the originating program to change the map or worksheet source file. These changes take effect instantly when viewed within the linked Access table.

Tip: There are other ways to insert OLE objects into a table. For example, you could have used the Explorer to find a file, double-clicked on it to launch its parent application, or selected and copied it to the clipboard. Once an object is on the clipboard, you can use Access' Insert|Object menu selection to select a bitmap image. This launches Paint, where you can either draw a new picture or paste the contents of the clipboard into the Paint window. Then use the File menu to update the table and exit back to Access. Other object types (such as graphs and tables) and their controlling applications work in the same way.

   c. Select the Picture field on the second row and then the third row, performing step b for each. Use the S1300T.bmp graphic file for the second row and S1465T.bmp for the third row.

6. Double-click on Bitmap Image within the Picture column to display the pictures in Paint. Each should resemble the following illustration.

7. Press <Ctrl+S> to save your changes; then use File|Close to close the table.

8. Use File|Exit to exit the Access program.

Member pictures have now been linked to each record in your Member table. These are displayed again in Section 49, where you learn to create and edit forms.

Importing and Exporting Data Between Other Programs

Advanced topic

Another time-saving feature offered by Access is the ability to import information from other types of programs. For example, you can create a new table from an external database or worksheet file.

Here, you can import a file, such as an Excel worksheet, from which an entire table can be created. A number of other file formats can also be used. You can export a table to another application using the File|Save As/Export menu. The types of files you can import and export depends upon the converters that were installed when you ran the Access (or MS Office) setup program. Typically, you can import files from the following programs:

dBASE III, dBASE III Plus, dBASE IV, dBASE 5 files (*.dbf)
Text files (*.txt; *.csv;*.tab;*.asc)
Addins (*.mda)
Workgroup files (*.mdw)
MDE files (*.mde)
ADE files (*.ade)
Web pages (*.html;*.htm)
Exchange ()

HTML (*.html; *.htm)
Outlook ()
Microsoft FoxPro files ()
Microsoft Access databases (*.mdb)
Microsoft Access projects (*.)
Microsoft Excel spreadsheet files (*.xls)
ODBC databases ()
Paradox databases (*.db)
Lotus 1-2-3 spreadsheet files (*.wk*)

Similarly, you can export information from your Access tables. To see a list of export file types, open a table and click File|Export. Pull down the Save As Type list. Here, a number of format selections are displayed. Consider exporting your information in a text format so that any word processor can read and display the content of your Access database files.

Shortcut Menus

Finally, remember that you can right-click your mouse to access a list of menu selections that correspond to the task at hand. This feature is available in all Office 2000 applications.

Summary

This completes creation of the tables used in this book. These tables serve as a basis for the query, form, and report activities used in later sections. You've also entered data into the tables. In the next section, you learn how to create queries that give you instant access to specific information within your tables.

Creating Queries

Introduction

You can perform information inquiries (or *queries*) to display and edit specified information from one or more database tables. This section guides you through the creation of a few queries that should be useful to many kinds of database management systems. For example, you may wish to design a query that displays a member's billing activity. Because the Fees table doesn't contain the member's name (only the number), you may wish to use the name from the Member table and purchase transaction details from the Fees table. Another query might be to determine which members fall within a certain age bracket. Finally, you may want to see a tennis member's rating, or determine how many members have a specific rating to assist you in organizing leagues.

Using the Query Window

The following procedure guides you through the creation of a simple query. In this query you display the Number and Name fields from the Member table and the Date, Description, and Amount fields from the Fees table. This lets you review each member's number, name, and charges using the contents of two tables. Of course, you can also design simple queries that involve a single table or complex queries that involve many tables.

1. Begin with Access running and the Club.mdb database open. Click the Queries tab.

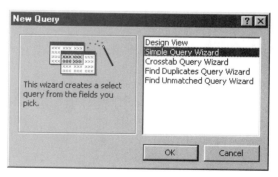

With the Queries tab selected, click New ; notice that the New Query dialog is displayed. Review the displayed choices.

Point of Interest: Query wizards are useful if you wish to create one of the following query types:

- *Design View* requires that you select tables and add each field to a blank desktop.
- *Simple Query Wizard* lets you select tables and fields from a simple set of dialogs.
- *Crosstab Query Wizard* totals both rows and columns.
- *Find Duplicates Query Wizard* finds all records within a table having a duplicate value.
- *Find Unmatched Query Wizard* finds all unique records within a table.

This procedure shows how to design a query using the Simple Query Wizard.

2. Pick Simple Query Wizard and click OK to display the Simple Query Wizard dialog.

3. Pick Table: Member from the Tables/Queries list and then put Number, FirstName, and LastName in the Selected Fields list using the > button.

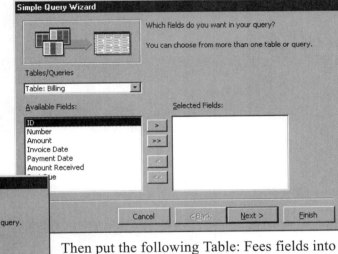

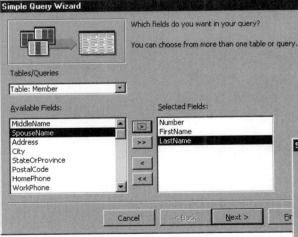

Then put the following Table: Fees fields into the Selected Fields list: Date, Description, and Amount. Compare your display to the following illustration.

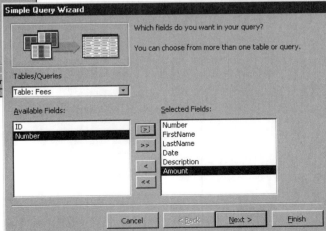

4. Click Next>. Check that the Detail item is selected.

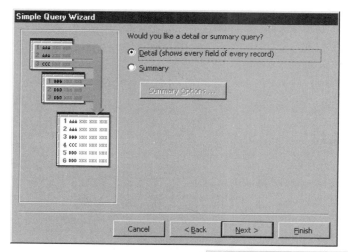

Click Next> to display the
next Simple Query Wizard
dialog.

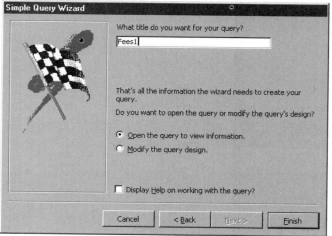

5. Type Fees1 as the query title.
    Leave the Open the query to
    view information button
    selected and click Finish to
    display your first query view.

6. Click the View button to
    display the Query Design view
    with field and table names.
    (You can also use the
    View|Query Design menu to
    switch views.)

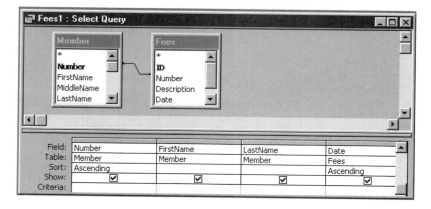

Point of Interest: If you had decided to create your query from scratch, you would have picked the involved table names and then the individual field names from each table box. The table and field names (in the form table.field) are put in each column one by one. You can also drag and drop field names from the table boxes to the desired columns of the query.

7. Notice that the query shows information from two tables, Member and Fees. Also, see how the member numbers are grouped together.

   Notice the check box in the Show row. A check mark in this box tells Access to show the field (or current column) in your query; an empty box tells Access to hide the field.

Point of Interest: In the last section you developed a relationship between the Member and Fees tables based on the Number field. This automatically establishes a *join line* between the Number fields of each table. (Notice the join line between the Member and Fees table boxes. Also notice how primary key fields are displayed in boldface type in each table box.) If you had failed to establish the relationship there, you could create a join line on the fly by picking the key field in the first table and then dragging to a matching field in the second table.

8. Move the cursor down to the Sort row of the first (Number) column. Pick the down arrow button and select Ascending to sort queried member numbers from A to Z.

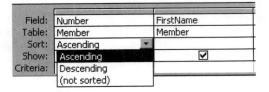

9. Click the Query View button 🔲 and examine the resulting display.

Fees1 : Select Query					
Number	**First Name**	**Last Name**	**Date**	**Description**	**Amount**
J1050S	Bill	Johnson	5/ 5/99	Food & Beverage	$16.40
J1050S	Bill	Johnson	5/ 1/99	Service-Massage	$25.00
J1050S	Bill	Johnson	5/31/99	Dues for May	$50.00
S1300T	Lisa	Stanley	5/31/99	League Fee	$25.00
S1300T	Lisa	Stanley	5/31/99	Dues for May	$125.00
S1300T	Lisa	Stanley	5/31/99	Pro Shop-Merchandise	$78.50
S1465T	John	Smith	5/28/99	Pro Shop-Lesson	$25.00
S1465T	John	Smith	5/22/99	Pro Shop-Merchandise	$22.50
S1465T	John	Smith	5/22/99	Guest Fee	$5.00
S1465T	John	Smith	5/31/99	Dues for May	$125.00

Record: 1 of 10

Adjust column widths as necessary. Notice that the Number field is sorted in ascending order. The resulting information is a simple form of what is referred to as a *dynaset*, i.e., a dynamic set of data that changes with the information contained in the supporting tables.

Using Criteria and Saving Queries

Now that you have designed the basis of a query, you can refine it by restricting what is displayed using the Criteria rows. For example, if you just want to see the charges for a single member, you can enter the member's number on the Criteria row of the Number column. Try this by performing the following steps:

1. Click the Design View button ![design view icon] (or pick View|Design View from the menu), then put the cursor on the Criteria row of the Number column.

Field:	Number	FirstName
Table:	Member	Member
Sort:	Ascending	
Show:	☑	☑
Criteria:			

2. Type "J1050S" (including the quotation marks).

Now click the View button ![view icon] to see the query and notice that only Bill Johnson's information is displayed.

Field:	Number	FirstName
Table:	Member	Member
Sort:	Ascending	
Show:	☑	☑
Criteria:	"J1050S"	

Fees1 : Select Query

Number	First Name	Last Name	Date	Description	Amount
J1050S	Bill	Johnson	5/ 5/99	Food & Beverage	$16.40
J1050S	Bill	Johnson	5/ 1/99	Service-Massage	$25.00
J1050S	Bill	Johnson	5/31/99	Dues for May	$50.00

Record: 1 of 3

3. Notice that the dates are in random order. Put them in ascending order by returning to the Design View and placing Ascending in the Date's Sort row. Then return to the query view to see the result.

Fees1 : Select Query

Number	First Name	Last Name	Date	Description	Amount
J1050S	Bill	Johnson	5/ 1/99	Service-Massage	$25.00
J1050S	Bill	Johnson	5/ 5/99	Food & Beverage	$16.40
J1050S	Bill	Johnson	5/31/99	Dues for May	$50.00

Record: 1 of 3

Points of Interest: You can also display two member numbers by putting a second number on the criteria row, such as "J1050S" or "S1300T." You can display all of the entries for the month of May by using an expression in the Criteria row of the Date column such as:

Between 5/1/99 And 5/31/99

Access converts this expression for you to the form:

Between #5/1/99# And #5/31/99#

To view and edit a lengthy expression, you can put the expression in a zoom window by positioning the cursor in the desired Criteria cell and then pressing <Shift+F2>.

4. Switch back to the Query Design view and delete the criteria from the Number column.

5. Press <Ctrl+S> to save the new Fees1 query. Then press <Ctrl+W> to close the query.

Criteria Expressions and Operators

Criteria expressions and operators used on the Field row include a combination of operators, identifiers, functions, literal values, and constants. These are briefly described in the following table. A list of operators and functions used in Access expressions is provided in Appendix C.

Element	Examples	Description
Operator	=, <, +, &, And, Or	Performs an operation on one or more elements within an expression.
Identifier	Forms![Charges]!Amount	References the value of a field, control, or property.
Function	Date, Sum, DCount	Returns a value corresponding to the result of a calculation or other operation. Functions can also be created using the Access Basic language.
Literal	24.95, #5/31/99#, "J1050S"	A number, date, or text entry (called string).
Constant	Null, True, False, Yes, No	A fixed value that doesn't change.

Example: [Date] Between #5/1/99# And #5/31/99#
         Operators: And
         Identifiers: [Date] (identifies a field name)
         Literal: #5/1/99#, #5/31/99#

Access2000

Entry Conventions

Access uses the following conventions for objects, such as field names, dates, and text strings.

- ■ Dates are entered within number signs (#).
- ■ Text strings are entered within quotation marks (").
- ■ Object names are typed within square brackets ([ ]).

If you omit the number signs, quotes, or brackets, Access often inserts them for you. Remember to see Appendix C for operators and functions that are used in criteria expressions.

Changing a Query and Totaling

It is easy to edit queries. In fact, you can open an existing query, make changes, and then use File|Save As to save the changed query under a new name. You can also create queries based on existing queries. In the previous query that you saved as Fees1, you could have established a Date criteria to display all transactions for the month of May 1999. If you wish to display a total of each member's charges for the month of May, you can quickly create a dependent query that is based on one or more fields of the Fees1 query. Dependent queries are often referred to as *nested* queries.

The following procedure shows how to develop a nested query to display the sum of each member's charges for the month of May.

Now perform the following steps.

1. Begin with the Club database still open, the Queries tab displayed and Create query in Design view highlighted.

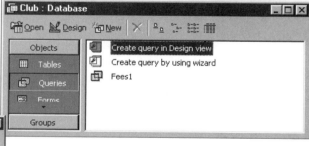

2. Click New [New] and pick Design View.

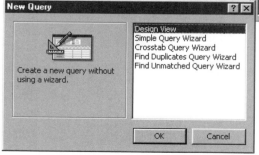

3. Then click OK. Pick the Queries tab of the Show Table dialog. Your screen should display the following Show Table dialog. Fees1 should be present in the text box and it should be highlighted.

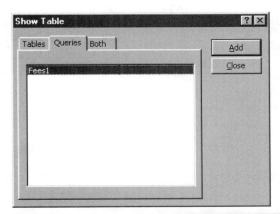

4. Click Add and then click Close. Notice that a Fees1 query box is displayed above the empty query design table.

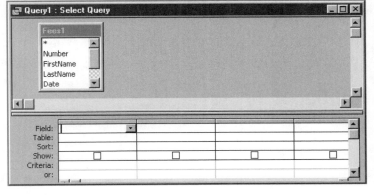

5. From left to right, insert the Number, LastName, Date, and Amount fields on the Field row. (Either drag the name from the Fees1 box to the appropriate column on the Field row, or double-click the field name in the Fees1 box. You can also click the down arrow button, and pick the appropriate field name from the pick list.)

6. Click the Totals button Σ on the Query Design toolbar to insert a Total row. Notice that each column has "Group By" on the Total row.

Field:	Number	LastName	Date	Amount
Table:	Fees1	Fees1	Fees1	Fees1
Total:	Group By	Group By	Group By	Group By

7. Move the cursor to the Total row in the Amount column. Click the down arrow button and pick Sum from the pick list.

8. Move the cursor to the Total row in the Date column. Click the down arrow button and pick Count from the pick list. Your query design should resemble the following illustration.

Field:	Number	LastName	Date	Amount
Table:	Fees1	Fees1	Fees1	Fees1
Total:	Group By	Group By	Count	Sum
Sort:				

9. Click the View button and compare the query to the following illustration.

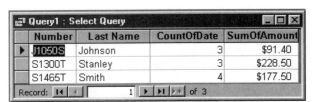

Notice how the CountOfDate column displays the number of dates, and hence transactions, for each member number. Also see how the SumOfAmount column contains the sum of each member's charges.

10. Click File|Save, type the name Fees1A in the query name box, and click OK.

11. Press <Ctrl+W> to close the new Fees1A query.

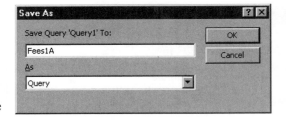

As you can see, building queries is a simple matter using the power of Access. The preceding activity also shows you how to use a nested query, i.e., one query that is based on another query.

Printing a Dynaset

A *dynaset*, which stands for dynamic set, is simply a query or form that is based on one or more database tables. The data is dynamic because it varies with changes to the contents of the supporting tables on which it depends.

Printing queries or forms based on one or more database tables is easy. To print the active table, query, or form, use the File|Print menu selection. You can display a simulation of the printout using the File|Print Preview menu selection. This lets you see the information and make adjustments before performing the final printing operation.

The procedure that follows explains how to print the Fees1A query.

1. With the Club database still open from the preceding activity, pick the Queries tab, pick Fees1A, and click Open.

2. Pick File|Print Preview and look at the displayed query. Maximize the Fees1A Select Query window to display the print preview full screen as shown here.

3. Click the Zoom button 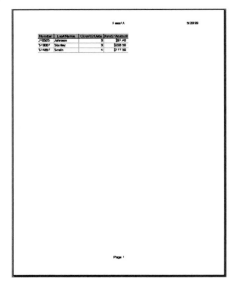 on the Print Preview toolbar to enlarge the image.

Fees1A   5/20/99

Number	Last Name	CountOfDate	SumOfAmount
J1050S	Johnson	3	$91.40
S1300T	Stanley	3	$228.50
S1465T	Smith	4	$177.50

Press the Zoom button  again to return to the usual print preview view. Also, you can click on the Zoom drop-down box on the Print Preview toolbar and select other zoom values.

Fit
200%
150%
100%
75%
50%
25%
10%
Fit

4. Notice the OfficeLinks button ▓ or ▓ or ▓ (the ▓ button is the default button but one of the other buttons may be displayed if a previous operation using that button was performed) on the Print Preview toolbar.

Clicking the down arrow on this button lets you publish the query as either a Word document or as mail merge data. You can also link the query to Excel for analysis in worksheet format.

5. Use the File|Page Setup selection to check the margin and page layout settings. Then click the Cancel button to close the Page Setup dialog box.

6. Use the File|Print menu selection to display the Print dialog. Notice that you can print one or more pages. You can also print to a file, which can then be imported into another program such as a word processor.

7. If your printer is ready, you can click OK. Otherwise, you can click Cancel to discontinue the printing process.

8. Use the File|Close menu selection to close the query and print preview.

9. Click the Minimize button ▬ to reduce the size of the Club: Database window.

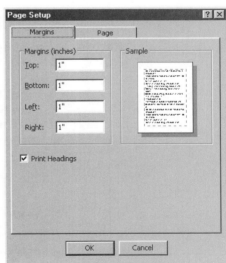

Hands-on Activity

Creating a Query to Find Tennis Ratings

Recall the Rating table described in Section 46 and created in Section 47. Here, you create a Ratings query to list member numbers, names, and rating information. Before constructing the query, open the Member table and add the following two new member records:

Number	First Name	Middle Name	Last Name	Spouse Name	Address	City
A1080T	Alan	G.	Aldridge	Rita	2112 San Pedro Dr.	Houston
S1470T	Glenda	Anne	Stevens	Harold	14 Main Place	Plantation

State/Province	Postal Code	Home Phone	Work Phone	Birthdate	Joindate
Texas	78905-3609	(713) 555-7993	(713) 232-1290	3/29/60	10/1/93
Texas	78925-3782	(713) 555-1919	(713) 424-2020	3/12/57	5/1/91

Save and close the Member table. Now create a Ratings query. Begin by clicking the **Queries** tab.

1. Click **New**, select **Simple Query Wizard** in the New Query dialog, and click **OK**.

Select the Member table by clicking on the down arrow of the Tables/Queries box.

Put the following Available Fields names in the Selected Fields box:

Table	Field
Member	Number
Member	FirstName
Member	LastName

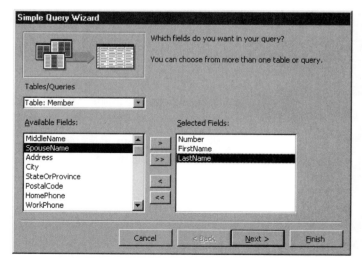

Select the Ratings table by clicking on the down arrow of the Tables/Queries box.

Table	Field
Rating	Date
Rating	Rating
Rating	Comments

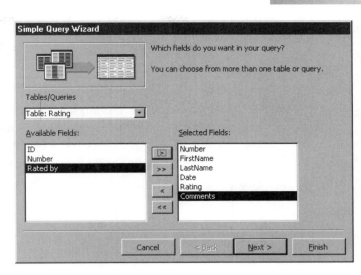

2. Click **Next>** and leave the Detail (shows every field of every record) item selected.

3. Click **Next>** and type **Ratings** as the query title. Leave Open the query to view information selected and click **Finish**.

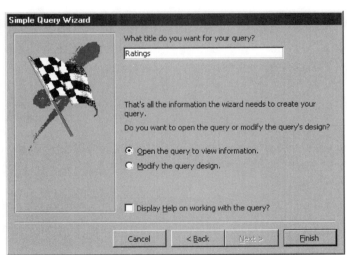

4. Compare your query to the following illustration.

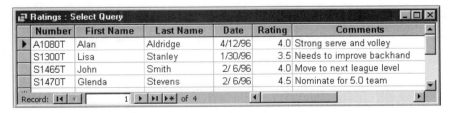

5. Click the **View** button to display the Design View. Put **Descending** on the Sort row of the Rating column.

Field:	FirstName	LastName	Date	Rating
Table:	Member	Member	Rating	Rating
Sort:				Descending
Show:	☑	☑	☑	☑

Then click the **View** button to look at the query again. Notice that the records are arranged from high to low in member rating order. Observe the sort routine utilizes the last name for a secondary sort key if the ratings are equal. In other words, Aldridge comes before Smith.

Ratings : Select Query

Number	First Name	Last Name	Date	Rating	Comments
S1470T	Glenda	Stevens	2/ 6/96	4.5	Nominate for 5.0 team
A1080T	Alan	Aldridge	4/12/96	4.0	Strong serve and volley
S1465T	John	Smith	2/ 6/96	4.0	Move to next league level
S1300T	Lisa	Stanley	1/30/96	3.5	Needs to improve backhand

6. Press **<Ctrl+S>** to save this query. Then press **<Ctrl+W>** to close it.

Summary

This completes the query creation activities in this section. With these completed, you should now be able to design a reasonable assortment of queries based on multiple tables. Don't forget to consider nested queries to isolate and summarize data. In the next section you learn about forms and how to design them.

Getting Started with Forms

Introduction

You can create forms to display, edit, or output your table or query information in almost any layout. Forms are based on the data contained in either tables or queries. Forms let you build your own unique views of your information rather than having to use the standard format presented by tables and queries. Form wizards are available to guide you through the creation of several standard form layouts. You can also build your forms from scratch using the form design toolbox. The activities in this section show you how to design forms using both methods.

Hands-on Activity: Using the Form Wizards

The following activity guides you through the design of a membership roster using a built-in Form Wizard. The form makes use of the Member table. The resulting form contains information about members in the club. Begin by starting Access and opening the Club database.

1. Click the **Forms** tab.

   Then click the **New** button. Notice the **New Form** dialog.

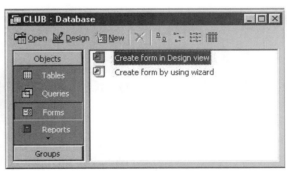

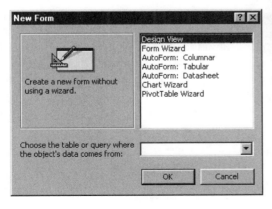

At this point you can *bind* the form to a table or query by putting a table or query name in the text box. Next, you must decide if you want to use a Form Wizard or begin with a blank form. In the next step you use the Form Wizards button. Later in this section you design a form using the Blank Form button.

2. Put **Member** in the Choose the table or query... box by picking it from the pick list (or by typing it directly). Then pick **AutoForm: Columnar** and click **OK**.

3. Examine the resulting form display.

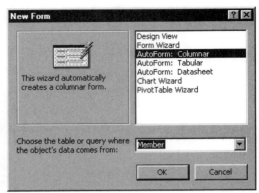

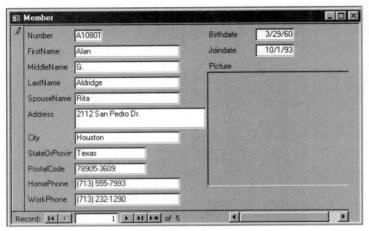

4. Click the Record arrows at the bottom left of the screen (or press **<PageDown>**/**<PageUp>**) to move between member records.

5. Press **<Ctrl+S>** to save; type **Roster** as the Form Name and click **OK**.

6. Press **<Ctrl+W>** to close the form.

As you can see, Access makes it extremely easy to create standard forms. You can modify the layout to your liking by using the design tools. Section 50 guides you through the modification process.

Form Design Without Form Wizards

You can design the same form from scratch using the Design View in the New Form dialog box. When you do this, you'll make use of the toolbox, the Forms List button, and the properties sheet. An alternative approach to forms design is to first use an AutoForm or Form Wizard to establish a basic structure. Then you can edit the form to reposition and add elements and use the Properties sheet to change labels, positioning, display attributes, and more.

Before beginning the design, a few definitions are in order. The term *control* refers to a field that is placed on the form. In addition to controls, there are objects. Both have *properties*, which are entered and listed in a corresponding properties sheet that is displayed when a control or object is selected and the Properties button on the toolbar is active.

Familiarize yourself with the location of key buttons on the Form Design toolbar by pointing to each with your mouse to display the descriptive label. Aside from the common print, cut, copy, and paste buttons, other useful buttons are summarized in the list following the button illustration:

Form Design Toolbar

Form View—Displays the Form view which inhibits adding to or making changes; if the desired view button is not visible, click the down arrow adjacent to the button and select from the choices available.

Design View—Displays the Design view which is used for adding to or changing the design; if the desired view button is not visible, click the down arrow adjacent to the button and select from the choices available.

Datasheet View—Displays the Datasheet view; if the desired view button is not visible, click the down arrow adjacent to the button and select from the choices available.

Save—Saves the layout of a datasheet, or the design of a table, query, stored procedure, SQL statement, form, data access page, report, view, structure, or macro content.

Print—Prints the selected report, form, datasheet, or data access page.

Print Preview—Displays a preview of the active object as it will appear when printed.

Spelling—Checks the spelling of text.

Cut—Removes the selected text or item and places it on the clipboard.

Copy—Copies the selected text to the clipboard (either Office or Windows).

Paste—Inserts an item or text from the clipboard into an active database object from the clipboard.

Format Painter—Copies formatting such as line styles, color, and font properties from one control to another.

Undo/Can't Undo—Reverses the most recent action if it can be reversed.

Hyperlink—Inserts or modifies a hyperlink address or Uniform Resource Locator (URL).

Field List—Displays a list of the fields contained in a form's or report's underlying record source; drag fields from the list to create controls that are automatically bound to the record source.

Toolbox—Opens or closes toolbox used to create form, report, or data access page controls.

AutoFormat—Applies predefined formats to a report or form.

Code—Opens the Visual Basic Editor and displays the code behind a selected form or report in the code window.

Properties—Displays the property sheet for the selected item such as a table field or form control. If nothing is selected, the active object's property sheet is displayed.

Build—Displays a builder for the selected item or property if a builder is available for the item/property.

Database Window—Displays the Database window listing all objects in the current Access database or Access project.

New Object Table—Creates a new database object based upon the type of database object previously selected from the Objects toolbar.

Help—Displays the Office Assistant or the Help dialog.

Toolbox Toolbar

The toolbox contains 20 buttons including the Select objects (Pointer) button at the left, or top, depending on where you want to drag it. These are summarized below.

Select Objects (Pointer)—Used to select a control, form, section, report, or data access page or to unlock a locked down toolbox button.

Control Wizards—Turns control wizards on and off.

Label—A control that displays descriptive text (title, caption, etc.) you enter.

Text Box—A box used to display, enter, or edit text, user input, or calculation results.

Option Group—Used (with check boxes, option buttons, or toggle buttons) to display a set of alternate values.

Toggle Button—An unbound control used to accept user input in a custom dialog box, or part of an option group.

Option Button—An unbound control used to accept user input in a custom dialog box, or part of an option group.

Check Box—An unbound control used to accept user input in a custom dialog box, or part of an option group.

Combo Box—Combines the functionality of a list box and a text box.

List Box—Displays a selectable and scrollable list of values.

Command Button—Used to perform actions such as finding or printing records, or applying a filter to a form.

Image—Displays a static picture on a form or report.

Unbound Object Frame—Displays an unbound OLE object such as an Excel spreadsheet.

Bound Object Frame—Displays OLE objects such as a series of images.

Page Break—Begins a new screen on a form, a new page on a printed form, or a new page on a report.

Tab Control—Creates a tabbed form or dialog.

Subform/Subreport—Displays data from more than one table on a report or form.

Line—Used to divide a form or page and to emphasize related or important information.

Rectangle—Used for attention-getting graphic effects.

More Controls (toolbox controls)—Lists available toolbars.

To see a description of each of the toolbox buttons, display the Office Assistant and type the button name in the Search box. A description and typical uses of each is displayed.

Hands-on Activity: Creating Forms Without Wizards

1. With the Club database open and the **Forms** tab selected, click **New** to display the New Form dialog.

Note: While **Fees1A** is shown out-lined (Fees1A) in the Club: Database dialog text window, it doesn't matter which form is highlighted or outlined as a new form is going to be created.

a. Select **Design View** and select **Fees1A** from the "Choose the table or query where the object's data comes from:" drop-down list.

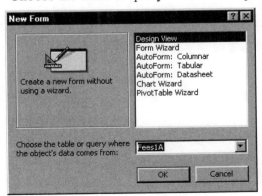

b. Click **OK**. The Form Design view is displayed.

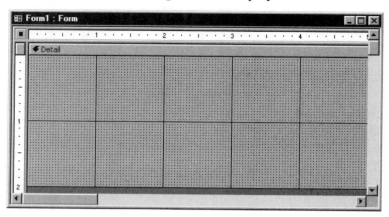

c. Click the **Toolbox** button 🛠 to display the Form Design toolbar.

d. Click the **Properties** button 🗒. Notice how the Form dialog (also known as a properties sheet) lists the Fees1A table as the Record Source.

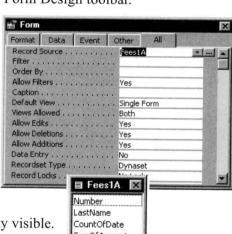

2. Use the left mouse button to drag the properties sheet so that it does not cover your work area (or you can hide and display it by clicking the **Properties** button).

3. Click the **Pointer** button ⤕ within the toolbox.

4. Click the **Field List** button 📋 on the Form Design (top) toolbar if the Field List is not already visible.

5. Using the mouse, drag the **Number**, **LastName**, and **SumOfAmount** fields into place as shown in the following screen illustration.

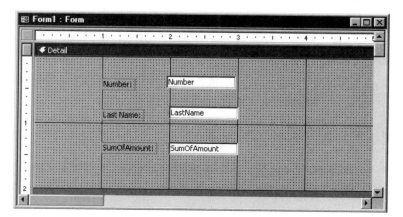

6. Click the **SumOfAmount** label (the lower left-hand label box).

Note: Do not confuse the left-handed label ⟨SumOfAmount⟩ with the right-handed text box ⟨SumOfAmount⟩.

With the **All** tab of the Label: Label dialog selected, put the cursor on the Properties sheet Caption row, type **Amount:** and press <**Enter**>. Compare your properties sheet to the one shown here.

7. Once you are satisfied with the layout of your form, click the **Form View** button to display the form.

Label: Label5	
Format	Data	Event	Other	All
Name	Label5
Caption	Amount
Visible	Yes
Display When	Always
Vertical	No
Left	1"
Top	1.1667"
Width	0.8542"
Height	0.1667"
Back Style	Transparent
Back Color	16777215
Special Effect	Flat
Border Style	Transparent

Form1 : Form

Number:	010505
Last Name:	Johnson
Amount	$91.40

Record: 1 of 3

8. Notice how the Amount value is flush right. Return to the Design view by clicking the **Design View** button. Select the **SumOfAmount** text box ⟨SumOfAmount⟩. Click on the **Properties** button on the toolbar. Alternately, you can right-click on the SumOfAmount text box, then click the Properties button at the bottom of the Properties dialog. Put **Left** in the Text Align property of the Property box by placing the cursor in the property text box, then clicking on the drop-down arrow that suddenly becomes visible. Now the SumOfAmount value aligns with the LastName and Number values. Note that the Text Align property is below the initially visible list of properties. You must use the vertical scroll bar on the right side of the dialog box to scroll down to the property.

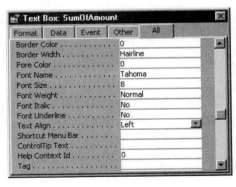

Text Box: SumOfAmount	
Format	Data	Event	Other	All
Border Color	0
Border Width	Hairline
Fore Color	0
Font Name	Tahoma
Font Size	8
Font Weight	Normal
Font Italic	No
Font Underline	No
Text Align	Left
Shortcut Menu Bar	
ControlTip Text	
Help Context Id	0
Tag	

9. Click the **Form View** button ▦ to display the form again. Now use the **File: Print Preview** button ◯ to display a print image of the form. Your form should resemble the following illustration.

10. Use **File|Save As**, type the form name **Fees1A**, and click **OK**.

11. Press **<Ctrl+W>** to close your form.

Number:	J10505
Last Name:	Johnson
Amount:	$91.40

Number:	S1300T
Last Name:	Stanley
Amount:	$228.50

Number:	S1465T
Last Name:	Smith
Amount:	$177.50

Controlling the Appearance of Text

When a label or control that contains text is selected (handles are displayed when selected), you can specify the typeface, size, style, and text alignment using either buttons on the Formatting toolbar or the Format menu. You can use the File/Back Color, Font/Fore Color, and Line/Border Color buttons on the Formatting toolbar to change the foreground, background, and border colors of the selected object. You can also use the other Formatting toolbar buttons and the Format menu for alignment, line and border widths, and special effects including raised, sunken, etched, and shadowed buttons. Format changes are displayed as you make them, so it's easy to see the effect. When you are satisfied with your changes, display the form to see the final result. To try out the color buttons, perform the next few steps with the Fees1A form displayed.

1. Select the Fees1A form and click the Design View button ▨.

2. Use Edit|Select All (or press <Ctrl+A>) to select all elements on the form (all elements should display handles).

3. Set the Fill/Back Color ◇▾ and Line/Border Color ✐▾ buttons to Transparent; set the Font/Fore Color **A** ▾ to Black. Select the Number text box and set the Fill/Back Color to White.

4. Click the Form View button ▦ and notice that the borders around the text controls are now cleared.

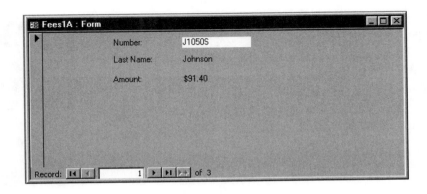

5. Click the Design View button again to return to the Design View.

Note: In the following steps, you use the Field List button to set a text box control. This is the easy way to assign a field control to an object on your forms.

6. Click the Field List button ▦ on the Form Design (top) toolbar to display the list of field names in the selected query, which is Fees1A in this case.

7. Pick the Amount and SumOfAmount boxes and drag them down. Adjust the spacing between each of the lines so that eight grid spaces separate these boxes from the Last Name boxes. (This makes room for an inserted object.)

8. Use the Pointer tool to drag the CountOfDate field to the form so that it fits in the gap between the LastName and SumOfAmount text boxes.

9. Pick the CountOfDate label so that a text cursor is displayed. Change the caption to Transactions: and press <Enter>. Now adjust the size of the CountOfDate text box so that it is 4 x 4 dots square.

10. Press <Ctrl+A> to select all. Then use Format|Align and pick Left. Use Format|Vertical Spacing and pick Make Equal.

11. Compare your design to the following illustration.

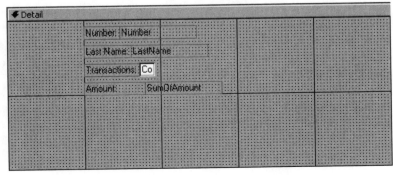

12. Click View and compare your form to the following screen illustration.

13. Press <Ctrl+S> and then <Ctrl+W> to save and close the form.

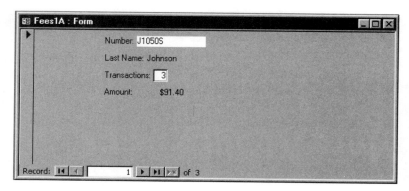

Adding a Picture Object

If you have scanned photos of your members (or any other object for that matter) and they are included as a field in your table or query, they can also be placed on your form. Recall from Section 47 that you linked three pictures to the Member table in the Picture field. In this activity you create a simple form using the Form Wizard. Your form displays the Member Number, LastName, and Picture fields. The pictures are actually bitmap drawings that were linked to the Member table in Section 47.

Begin this activity from the Club: Database window with the Forms tab selected.

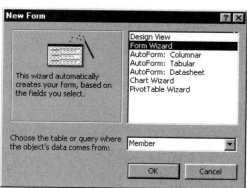

1. Click the New button to display the New Form dialog box. Then put the Member table in the Choose the table or query... box, pick Form Wizard, and click OK.

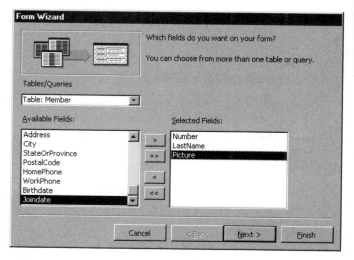

2. Select Table: Member in the Tables/Queries text box, then put Number, LastName, and Picture in the Selected Fields box and click Next>.

3. Click the Tabular option button, and click Next> again.

4. Select the International style and click Next>.

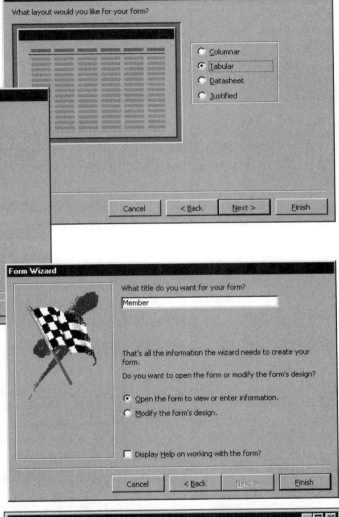

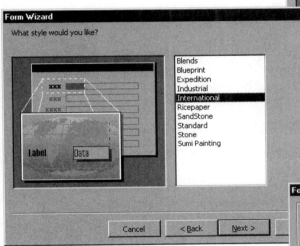

5. Leave the form title as Member in the Form Wizard. Leave Open the form to view... selected.

6. Click the Finish button to display your new form. Go to Records 2, 3, and 4 to see how the bitmap pictures are displayed. Use the Record buttons at the bottom of the Member form to scroll through the records.

7. Press <Ctrl+S> and then <Ctrl+W> to save and close the form.

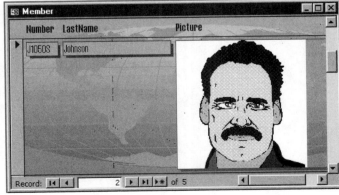

Now you have created a tabular form that displays a linked graphic object. Move to the next activity to learn how to design a form comprised of a main form that uses information from the Member table and a subform that uses information from the Fees table.

Hands-on Activity: Working with Subforms

Advanced topic

There are situations in which it is ideal to display multiple forms based on different tables or queries on the same page. In the following activity you combine the Member and Fees1A forms. These use data from the Member and Fees tables. Begin this activity from the Club: Database window with the Forms tab selected.

1. Select the **Roster** form and click **Design**.

   Note: The list of forms in your Club: Database pane will differ somewhat from the illustration. You have not yet created all the forms listed.

2. Drag the bottom of the design surface to 5 inches on the vertical ruler (left-click just above the form footer bar and drag the surface down).

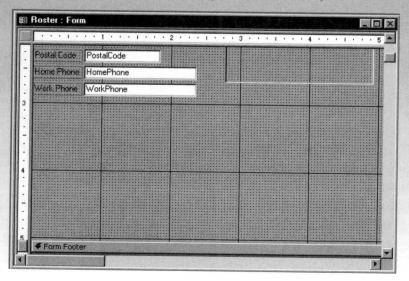

3. Click the **Subform/Subreport** tool 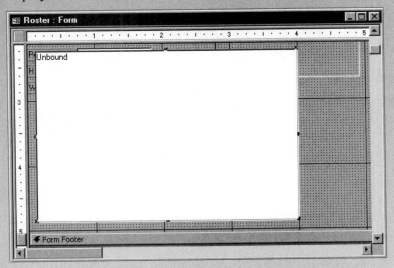 on the toolbox and drag an area below the displayed Roster fields as shown here. Click **Cancel** if a wizard displays.

4. Click on the Source Object row of the Properties box and click **Fees1A** as shown. Click on the **Properties** button if the Subform Properties dialog is not displayed.

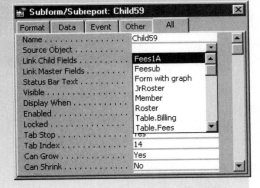

Note: Your Subform/Subreport title will differ from mine (Child59).

5. Click the Label box (the text in the box will be ChildX where X is some number) at the top left-hand side of the Fees1A subform area. Change the Caption row to **Billings**.

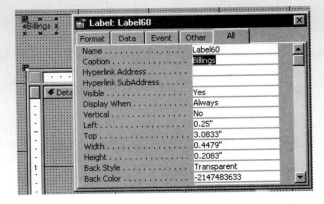

6. Click the **Form View** button 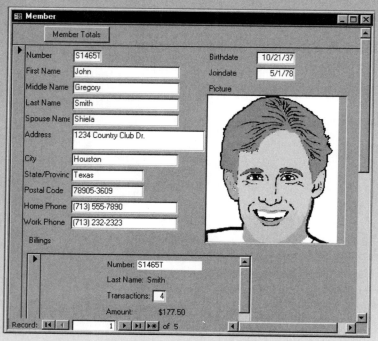 to see the resulting form. This demonstrates how a subform can show you information from different tables.

7. Use **File|Save As**, type **Feesub**, and click **OK**. Then press **<Ctrl+W>** to close the new form.

Note: If Amount is not shown, drag the bottom of the design surface lower (repeat steps 1 and 2).

Note: Recall that we have added transaction data for only three members. As a result, you may not see any billing information in the Billing subform area. If you do not see any billing information, click on the bottom Record button to advance the record shown until billing data is shown.

Summary

In this section you learned how to create three different types of forms. You used Form wizards and also learned how to create a form from scratch. You made use of an OLE object to display pictures. Finally, you learned how subforms let you integrate information from two different tables. In the next section you learn how to make your forms more attractive.

More About Forms

Introduction

In the last section you created several different forms. In this section you learn to use additional tools and properties that control the way your information is displayed and printed. The activities make use of the forms created in the last section in addition to guiding you through the creation of a few new forms that make use of more form design tools.

Hands-on Activity: Putting a List Box on Your Form

Advanced topic

The List Box tool in the forms toolbox lets you put a list of elements on your form. Perform the following activity to see how a list box is constructed. Begin with the Club: Database window displayed and the Forms tab selected.

1. Select **Roster** and click the **Design** button.

   Note: Drag and resize the Properties sheet as necessary to view your new list box.

2. Select the **List Box** button ⊞⊞ in the toolbox. Drag a rectangle as shown in the following illustration. (Click **Cancel** if a wizard displays.)

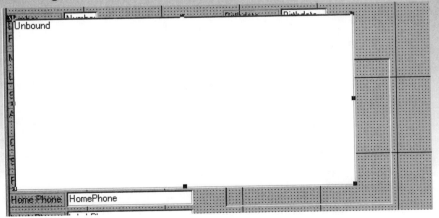

3. Click the **Properties** button 🖼️. Enter the information shown on the corresponding List Box properties sheet, then close the Properties dialog. The result is a two-column list.

Note: The name will not necessarily be "List59" as in this example. You will need to manually key in the information in the Source, Column Count, and Column Widths list boxes. See the following Point of Interest.

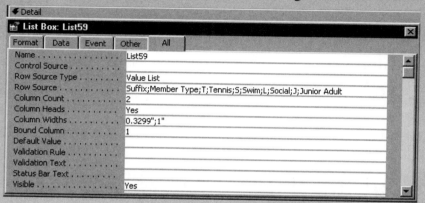

Note: In the Design View, shorten the Form Footer by placing the cursor near the bottom (cursor will change from an arrow pointer to a resize pointer) and dragging the edge up. Now you will be able to view a larger area of your form.

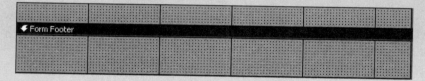

Point of Interest: When a list box is bound to a field within a table, whatever you select in the list box is put into the field of the selected record. This is an excellent way to enter repetitive values such as city names or part numbers.

■ When typing entries in a list box as done in this activity, separate each entry with a semicolon. To display column heads in the list box, type the column head text as the first element in the list. The Row Source line should read:

Suffix;Member Type;T;Tennis;S;Swim;L;Social;J;Junior Adult

■ Put the number of columns in the Column Count row and "Yes" in the Column Heads row.

■ Set and alter the width of each column by typing corresponding values on the Column Width row.

Set and alter the width of the list box by typing values in the Width and Height rows of the properties sheet.

4. Select the new Label box to the left of the new "Unbound" list box and press **<Del>** to remove the unneeded label. Otherwise, the label text will conflict with the Birthdate information when you display the form. Note: Your label box will probably contain text other than "List59."

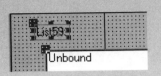

5. Click **View** and look at the new list box. Use the scroll bar to view all of the entries in the list. This is an example of a scrolling list box that can be used to display reference information.

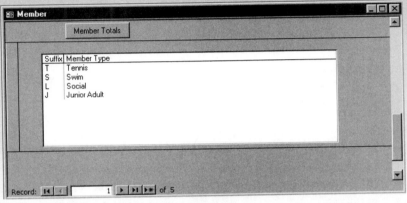

6. Click **View** to return to the form design. Leave this view displayed for the following activity.

Selecting and Resizing Labels and Data

It is easy to select and resize labels and data. When text-based objects are selected, you can change the font style, size, and color by selecting an alternate value on the Formatting toolbar. Select objects as follows:

- Select a single object by clicking it so that handles are displayed, or by selecting it from the list of object names in the Select Object select list (left-hand end of the Formatting toolbar).

- Select two or more objects by holding the Shift key down while selecting each (or use the Select Objects tool to drag a box around the desired objects).

- Select all objects on a form by pressing <Ctrl+A> (the shortcut for Edit|Select All).

- Select a column or row of objects by putting the mouse pointer above or at the left-hand edge of the form so that a thick black arrow appears. Then click to select the objects below or to the right.

The Select Object box at the left-hand end of the Formatting toolbar displays a name when you select an individual object. Once objects are selected, use the Font Name, Font Size, Bold, Italic, Underline, Align, and Color buttons as desired. Perform the following activity to see how these features work.

Hands-on Activities

Formatting Labels

1. Select the FirstName, MiddleName, and LastName text boxes. (Hold down the **Shift** key to select multiple objects.) Notice that handles are displayed on both the label and text box objects.

2. Select **Arial** (or a similar sans serif font) in the Font Name box, **10** in the Font Size box, and click the **Bold** and **Italic** buttons.

3. Click **View** to see the effect of your changes. Notice that the text boxes are changed, but the Label boxes are unchanged.

4. Click **View**; then select the FirstName, MiddleName, and LastName label boxes so that the handles are displayed on them, but not on the text boxes. Now select **Arial** in the Font Name box, **10** in the Font Size box, and click the **Bold** and **Italic** buttons.

5. Click **View** to see the effect of your changes on the form. Notice that the labels are now changed too. They may be too big to fit the allotted space. Disregard this, as these changes will not be saved. Now click **View** to display the Form Design for the next activity.

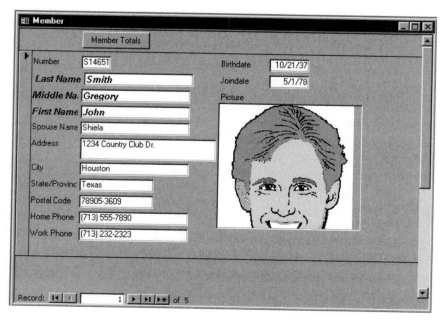

Point of Interest: Notice that the corresponding properties sheet reflects the font changes you make on the Font Name, Font Size, Font Weight, Font Italic, and Font Underline lines.

You could have entered these changes directly into the properties sheet as an alternate way to modify your form. The properties are maintained in the underlying code that is produced by Access to represent each object. The dialog box shown is titled "Multiple Selection" because all the label and text boxes were selected together by pressing the Shift key when clicking on each box. Then the Properties button ▣ was clicked.

Multiple selection	✕
Format | Data | Event | Other | **All**	
Border Width	Hairline
Fore Color	
Font Name	Arial
Font Size	10
Font Weight	Bold
Font Italic	Yes
Font Underline	No
Text Align	General
ControlTip Text	
Help Context Id	0
Tag	
Left Margin	0"
Top Margin	0"

Moving Labels and Data

It is a simple matter to move labels and data. Individual handles and the two-headed arrow cursor are used to resize objects. The hand cursor is used to drag a text box and its label to a new position. The pointing finger cursor is used to reposition either a label or a text box individually by dragging the large square handle at the upper left-hand corner of the box. Perform the following simple activity to see how this works.

1. Click on the **Joindate** text box on the right side of the form so that handles are displayed.

2. Use the hand cursor to drag the combined Joindate label and text box to the right of the Number text box as shown.

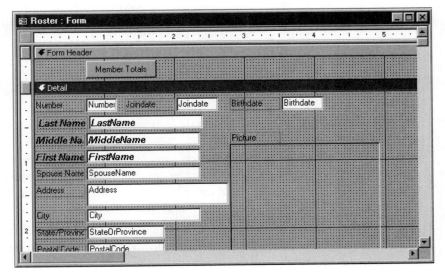

3. Select the **Joindate** label box and click the **Align Right** button ![align right button].

4. Click the **Form View** button ![form view button] to see the resulting form.

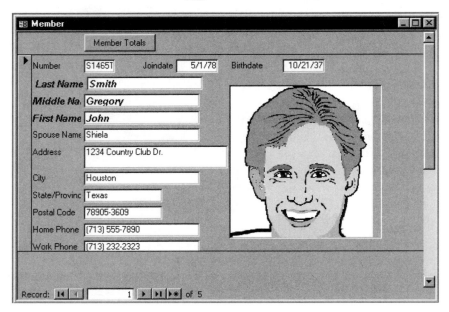

5. Now click the **Design View** button ![design view button] and leave the form design screen displayed in preparation for the next activity.

As you can see, it's easy to move your labels and text boxes by dragging them from one location to another. In the preceding example you could have moved your City, State, and PostalCode fields onto a single line. You could also put the phone numbers on one line. These changes would save space, making the form more compact and perhaps easier to read.

Adding and Editing Labels

Labels are easily added and edited using the techniques described for adding and editing other objects on your forms. Individual labels are added using the Label tool from the toolbox. You can edit a label by selecting it with the Select Object tool and then changing the properties on the corresponding properties sheet. You can change the Caption value by editing the current caption within the label box, itself. In the following activity, you add an unbound label and text box to the form header area to display the words "Roster as of:" and the current date. Proceed as follows:

1. In the Form Design view, drag the Detail bar down to display approximately 0.5 inch of Form Header area with which to work. Move the pointer cursor to the upper edge of the Detail bar and it will change to a resize pointer; then drag the bar down.

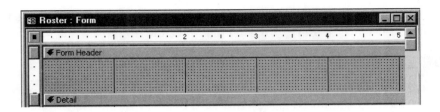

2. Select the **Text Box** tool from the toolbox. Then create a text box that resembles the one in the following illustration. Type **Roster as of:** in the label box and set it to a font size of 14 points and bold. Resize and drag both the label and text boxes as necessary.

3. In the Text Box properties sheet, click on the **Control Source** line. Then click the ellipsis button [...]. Now use the displayed Expression Builder dialog as follows:

   a. Double-click the **Functions** folder in the first column and select **Built-In Functions**.

   b. Select **Date/Time** in the center column and select **Now** in the right column.

   c. Click **Paste** to view the date function (which is Now()). Click **OK** to close the dialog.

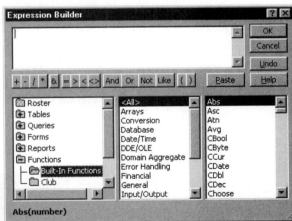

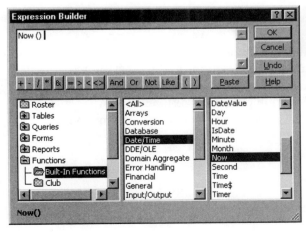

4. Notice that the expression =Now() has been pasted on the Control Source line. Close the dialog. Now click the **Form View** button to see the resulting header in the form view.

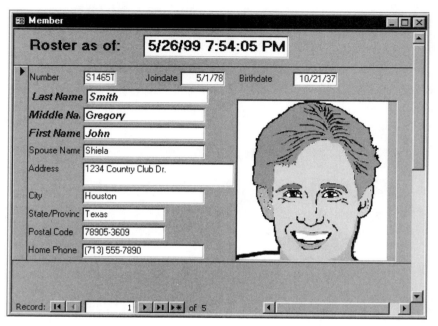

Note: Some functions may display the error #NAME? instead of a value. Some functions are provided through a separate dynamic link library (dll) file. If you see #NAME? instead of values, this file may be missing in the Microsoft Office\Office subdirectory. If the file msowcf.dll is missing, either reinstall Office 2000 or contact your network administrator.

5. Press **<Ctrl+W>** and click **No** to abandon the form without saving it.

Point of Interest: You can type functions directly into the properties sheet without using the Expression Builder dialog. For example, you can display the date and time by typing =Now() on the Control Source line. Of course, you have to be familiar with Access functions to do this. Use the Expression Builder to reveal expressions that are available within Access. Also, review the help information pertaining to functions. A good place to start is to ask the Office Assistant to search for information about "writing expressions."

Using Data Validation

Advanced
topic

If you wish to control the value of information typed into your fields, you can set a *validation rule* and type a corresponding *validation text*, which is displayed when an entry doesn't match the established validation rule. For example, you could enter a validation rule that says that the Birthdate field can only accept a value less than or equal to the current date less 21 years (21 years is about 7665 days). Since Access can calculate the number of days between dates, you can set a validation rule for the Birthdate field of <=Now()–7665.

The validation text might say, "Must be 21 or older."

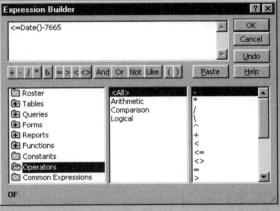

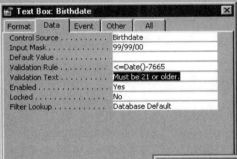

The message text is displayed in a message box like the one shown below when an attempt to add a value out of the validation range occurs.

This validation rule would prevent users from adding a member under 21 years of age.

An example of a date validation rule is >#12/31/98# AND <#1/1/00#. This rule accepts any valid 1999 date. Date values before or after 1999 are invalid and therefore excluded. Validation rules follow the schemes used in query criteria (see Section 48 and Appendix C).

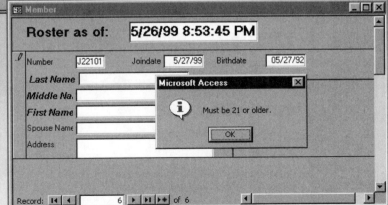

Note: The above discussion uses the function Now(). An equally useful function is Date(). However, if Date() returns an error, use Now().

Default Values

A default value is one that is automatically entered in a field. You can type the value on the Default Value line of the corresponding properties sheet. For example, you can enter a formula, number, or text string, depending on the data type of the field.

Hands-on Activity: Using the Rectangle and Line Tools

The Rectangle and Line tools are used to dress up the appearance of your forms. In the following activity, a simple form is created to demonstrate their use. Begin with the Club: Database window displayed and the Forms tab selected.

1. Select the **Fees1A** form and click **Design**.

2. Select the **Rectangle** tool ▭ from the toolbox and drag a large rectangle around the labels and text boxes.

3. With handles displayed on the rectangle, click the **Fill/Back Color** button ⬧ ▾ and select **light blue**. The filled rectangle hides the label and text objects.

4. Use the **Format|Send to Back** menu selection to bring the hidden label and text boxes to the front.

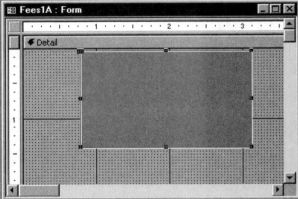

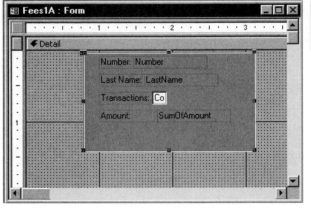

5. With the rectangle still selected, click the **Special Effect** button ▭ ▾ on the Formatting toolbar, and click the **Special Effect:Raised** button ▭ (top middle).

6. Now select each text box object and use the pointing finger cursor to move them right to insert space between the text boxes and label boxes as shown. Drag the rectangle object as necessary to fit it around the text and label objects. (This operation will serve as a good test of your ability to position objects on the work surface.)

More About Forms

347

Access2000

Tip: Click on the upper left corner handle of a text box or label box to see the pointing finger cursor. If you have trouble moving the text boxes, try changing the Left value in the Properties sheet manually.

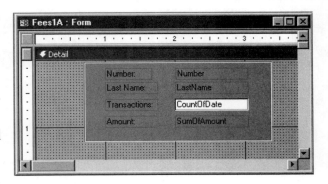

7. Press the **<Shift>** key and select all of the labels (not the text boxes). Use the **Format|Align|Right** button ≣ to align them flush right.

8. Select the **Line** tool ╲ and drag a vertical line as shown in the following illustration.

    With the vertical line still selected, click the **Line/Border Width** button ▔ and select **1 pt** ⊡ from the Border Width list.

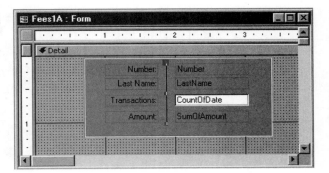

9. Select the four labels.

10. With all four label boxes selected, click the **Line/Border Color** tool ✎ and then click **Transparent**.

11. Click the **Form View** button ▦ to see the resulting form.

12. Press **<Ctrl+W>** and click **No** to abandon the form without saving it.

Summary

This completes additional form activities. In the next section you learn techniques used to find specific information within a table. Then, in Section 52, you begin working with reports. You'll notice that the toolbox and properties sheets are common elements to the design of both forms and reports.

Finding Information in a Database

Introduction

You can find information in a database table, query, or form by using Edit|Find, pressing <Ctrl+F>, or clicking the Find button 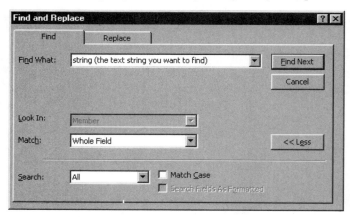. For example, if a table, query, or form is displayed, just select the field to be searched and press <Ctrl+F> to display the Find dialog. Then type the search *string* in the Find What box, such as a last name, and click Find Next. The Find dialog is shown here.

Finding Values

To find a value, use the following general procedure:

1. Display the table, query, or form.

2. Click the field to search and press <Ctrl+F> (or use Edit|Find).

3. Set the Search to All, Down, or Up. Click on >>More if the Search text box at the bottom of the Find dialog is not visible. Up and Down tells Access to search backward or forward in the table, query, or form.

4. Set Match to one of the following:

    a. Any Part of Field—This is a substring search, i.e., "ox" finds box and lox.

    b. Whole Field—Search string must match the entire value contained in the field.

    c. Start of Field—Search string must match the first part of the value, i.e., "Jo" finds Jones and Johnson.

5. Set the Match Case check box to constrain the search to match uppercase and lowercase within the search string.

6. Click the Close button to discontinue the find operation.

Creating Filters

You can also find information using *filters,* criteria used to control what is displayed or printed by a form. Filters operate with tables, queries, and forms. You can filter information based on a value selected within a field (*filter by selection*) or use an advanced filtering technique that can use multiple fields (*filter by form*) The Filter By Selection criteria is temporary in nature; it is used for a fast, interactive look at specified information. These filters disappear when the form is closed. On the other hand, the last Filter By Form criteria used is maintained. The other activity in this section steps you through the use of Filter By Form in which a filter is saved for reuse.

Hands-on Activity

Perform the steps in the following procedure to create and apply a filter using the Roster form created in the preceding section. Begin with the Club: Database window displayed and the Forms tab selected.

1. Pick the **Roster** form and click **Open** in the Club: Database dialog to display the form. Click on the **Form View** button ▦ if the Roster is opened in Design View. Notice the filter-related buttons on the Formatting toolbar:

   From left to right, these buttons are:

   ▼ **Filter By Selection**—Displays records containing values that match the current selection.

   ▼ **Filter By Form**—A form mask is displayed in which you can type your filter criteria. For example, you can type one or more city names in the City field, a range of ages in an Age field, a range of dates in a Date field, and so on.

   ▼ **Toggle (Apply/Remove) Filter**—Once a filter is applied, click this button to remove the filter restrictions. When using Filter By Form, click Apply Filter to apply the established criteria.

2. Select the **T** in the Number value. Then click the **Filter By Selection** button ▼. Notice that the four tennis member records are displayed because they end with "T." The swim member record (ending with "S") is filtered out.

3. Click the **Remove Filter** button ▼ to remove the filter.

4. Click the **Filter By Form** button ▼. Notice that a Filter menu selection is added to the menu bar; the dialog becomes "Filter by Form" and the values disappear.

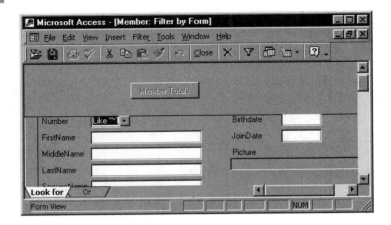

5. Delete **Like "*T"** from the Number field. Then click on the **City** field. Pick Cypress by clicking on the down arrow adjacent to the City field and selecting **Cypress**.

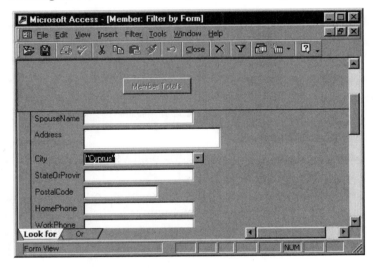

6. Click the **Or** tab at the bottom of the dialog, and click **Plantation** to set the filter to display all records with Cypress and Plantation in the City field.

7. Click the **Apply Filter** button. Notice that only two records contain Cypress or Plantation in the City field. All others are filtered out.

8. Click the **Remove Filter** button again to remove the current filter.

9. Click the **Filter By Form** button again. Use **Filter|Advanced Filter/Sort** to display an advanced Filter dialog.

10. Delete the City column by selecting it and pressing <**Del**>.

11. Drag **Birthdate** from the Fields list to the first column of the Field row, put **Ascending** on the Sort row, and **<=#2/1/62#** on the Criteria row.

(The criteria means "less than or equal to a date of 2/1/62.")

12. Click **Apply Filter** button. Now you can see who is eligible for the 35 and older tennis tournament based on the Birthdate field. The records are also sorted in ascending order according to birth date. Only three records pass the filter.

13. Click **Remove Filter** button again to remove the current filter.

14. Click **Filter By Form** button one more time. Remove the Birthdate criteria. Now type **?????S** in the Number field and click **Apply Filter button** to display swim member records. (You could use ?????T to display tennis member records.)

15. Press **<Ctrl+W>** to close the form. Now leave the Club database window open for the next activity.

Tip: You can use wild cards, i.e., the ? and * symbols, within your values. For example, Plan* could be used in place of Plantation. However, strings like Plano and Plant City would also be legitimate matches. Make your strings as precise as necessary.

Saving a Frequently Used Filter for Future Use

If you decide you want to keep the criteria of an established filter, you can save your filter setup under a new name so it can be used again. This is done by using **File|Save As** and entering a new, descriptive name. This procedure is illustrated below:

1. Open the Roster form. Then click the Filter By Form button 📇.

2. Use the Filter|Advanced Filter/Sort menu selection to display the RosterFilter1 : Filter window.

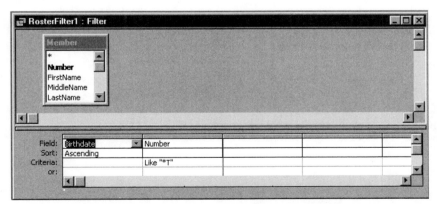

3. Delete columns containing fields. Then drag the * from the top row of the Member field list to the first column of the Field row (or pick Member.* from the Field pick list in the first column).

4. Drag Birthdate from the Member field list to the second column of the Field row. Then put Ascending on the Sort row and type >=#1/1/60# on the Criteria row of this column.

5. Compare your filter settings to the following one.

6. Click the Apply Filter button to see the result. Notice that only two records are shown for members having birth dates after January 1, 1960. Use File|Save As to save the form with the filter. Type JrRoster and click OK.

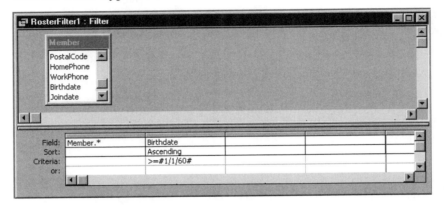

7. Press <Ctrl+W> to close the file. Now double-click on the JrRoster form to open it.

8. Click the Apply Filter button; notice that the filter displays the two records containing the two junior members.

Point of Interest: The original Roster form retains the last form filter used. However, since this is the base roster, you may wish to change filters to find different kinds of data. Therefore, if you create a complex filter that you plan to use on a regular basis, save the file with a new name to retain your filter. Otherwise, you will have to reconstruct it every time you want to view specific information.

9. Press <Ctrl+W> to close the JrRoster form.

10. Open the JrRoster form. Notice all five records are available. Click on the Apply Filter button. Now only two records are available.

11. Press <Ctrl+W> to close the JrRoster form.

Summary

You now know how to create tables, queries, forms, and how to apply filters. In the next section you learn how to prepare your data for printed output by preparing your first reports.

Creating Reports

Introduction

Reports are based on a table or query. Reports are used to print or display information in a prescribed format. You can use a report to group data and show subtotals and grand totals. Reports are always based on a single table or query. Unlike tables, queries, and forms, reports cannot be used to edit data. In fact, reports can only be displayed in the Print Preview or the Design View.

Reports are created using tools that are similar to those used to create forms. You can use a wizard to create a report, a chart, or mailing labels. You can also produce a fast tabular or columnar report using AutoReport selections. Once in the Design View, report design tools include the familiar toolbox and properties sheets. It's time to become familiar with the ease of report design by performing the following activities.

Hands-on Activities

To familiarize you with the report creation process, the activities contained in this section guide you through the creation and use of a few reports.

Creating a Single-Column Report

In this activity you use the AutoReport: Columnar selection to create a fast report based on the Fees1A query. Begin with the Club: Database window displayed.

1. Click the **Reports** tab; then click **New**.

2. Put **Fees1A** in the Choose the Table or Query... box. Then pick **AutoReport: Columnar**.

   Click **OK**. Notice that Access automatically creates a columnar report based on the selected query. Notice that only three records are displayed. The Fees1A query only displays information for members who have current billing records in the Fees table.

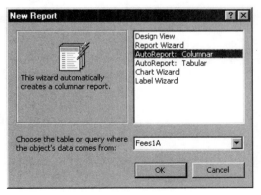

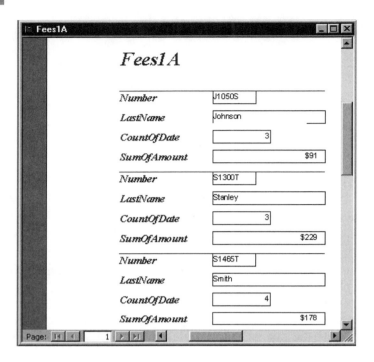

Point of Interest: If you had entered charges to the Fees table for the other two
members, you would see records for them, too. You should also recall
that the Fees1 query uses a criterion to restrict the display of queried
records to values that fall in the month of May 1996.

3. Click the **Design View** button 📐.

4. Select the **Fees1A** label in the header.
   Display the properties box by clicking the
   Properties button 📑 and type **Member
   Billings Report** on the Caption line of the
   properties sheet.

5. Close the properties sheet. Drag the right
   side of the label box so you can see the
   entire caption.

6. Select the **SumOfAmount** label. Type
   Subtotal: on the Caption line of the
   properties sheet.

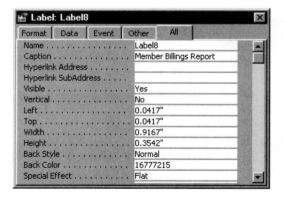

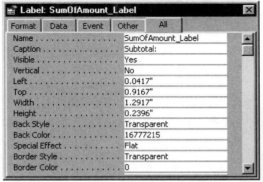

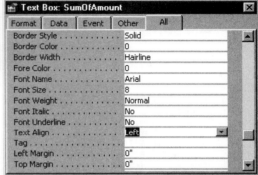

7. Select the **SumOfAmount** text box, and type **Left** on the Text Align row of the Properties dialog.

   Click the **Print Layout View** button. Notice the new Subtotal label and left alignment of the Subtotal value.

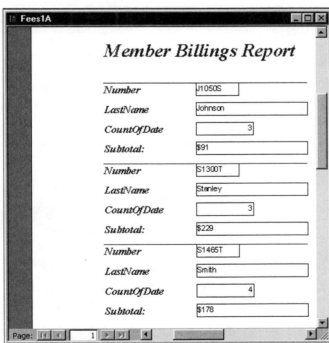

8. Click **Design View** and repeat steps 6 and 7 for the CountOfDate label and text box. Use the label caption **Transactions:** and left align the CountOfDate value. Click **View** to see the effect of your changes.

9. Press **<Ctrl+S>** to save the report. Type **Subtotals** as the report name and click **OK**.

10. Press **<Ctrl+W>** to close the new report. Leave the Club: Database window displayed for the next activity.

Creating a Grouped Data Report

Grouped data reports are ideal for automatically displaying detailed expense information with both subtotal and total values. In the following activity you create a Billing Detail Report to show both billing subtotals and a grand total. Begin with the Club: Database window displayed; be sure the Reports tab is still selected.

1. Click **New**; select **Fees1** in the Tables/ Queries pick list and then double-click **Report Wizard** (or highlight Report Wizard, then click OK).

2. Move the fields from the Available Fields box to the Selected Fields box in the order as shown.

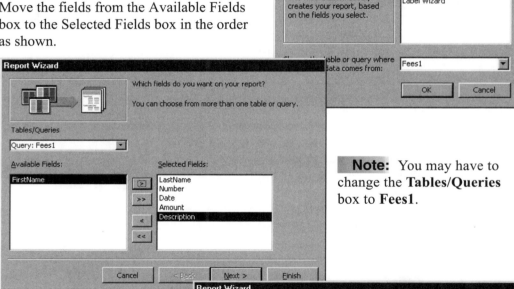

> **Note:** You may have to change the **Tables/Queries** box to **Fees1**.

3. Click **Next>**. Group by number by moving Number over to the right box.

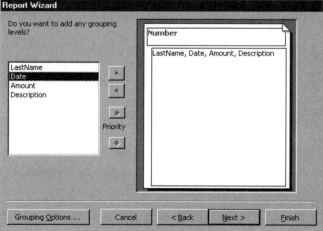

4. Click **Next>**. Put **Date** in sort box 1. Put **Amount** in sort box 2. Each member's information will be sorted in the order of the items in the numbered sort boxes. In other words, the records will be sorted and printed first by the Date, and then by the Amount. Leave the sort order boxes in descending, or A-Z, sort order.

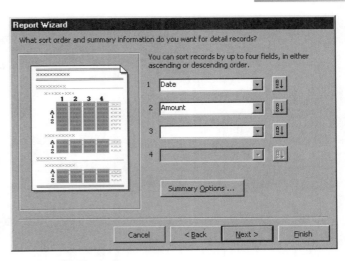

5. Click **Summary Options**. Click the **Sum** check box, then click **OK**.

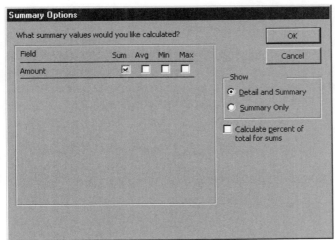

6. Leave the dialog that appears as is. Click **Next>** to bring up the following Report Wizard dialog.

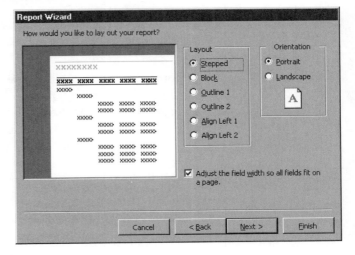

7. Click **Next>**. Leave the Corporate style selected and click **Next>** again.

Type **Billing Detail Report** for the title; check the Preview the report radio button, then click **Finish**.

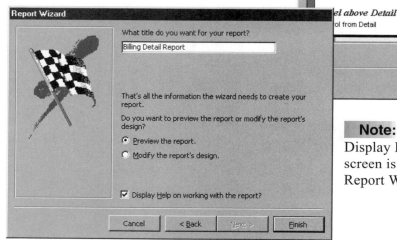

Note: If you click on the Display Help... box, a Help screen is displayed when the Report Wizard is finished.

9. Wait momentarily while the report is produced. Notice the Print Preview presentation.

Scroll the report and notice that detailed amounts, amount subtotals, and a report total are displayed. (Note that the illustration shown is reduced to display the report layout and all the features.)

10. Click **Close** to display the Report Design view.

Point of Interest: Notice that a section exists for each of the report elements, such as Report Header, Page Header, and so on. These sections are displayed as follows:

> Report Header—At the beginning of the report
> Page Header—At the top of each page
> Number Header—At the beginning of each new number (or group)
> Detail—Each record in the group
> Number Footer—At the end of each group's listing
> Page Footer—At the bottom of each page
> Report Footer—At the end of the report

You can type **No** on the Visible line of the corresponding properties sheet to suppress the display or printing of report sections, such as report headers and footers. (Click a section to display its properties sheet.) While in the Report Design view, use the View menu to turn the toolbox and properties sheets on and off so you can see your work and the results of your changes. You can also use View|Sorting and Grouping to modify the way your reports are sorted and/or grouped.

Billing Detail Report

Number	Date	Amount	LastName	Description
J1050S				
	5/1/96	$25	Johnson	Service-Massage
	5/5/96	$16	Johnson	Food & Beverage
	5/31/96	$50	Johnson	Dues for May
Summary for Number = J1050S (3 detail records)				
Sum		91.4		
S1300T				
	5/31/96	$25	Stanley	League Fee
	5/31/96	$79	Stanley	Pro Shop-Merchandise
	5/31/96	$125	Stanley	Dues for May
Summary for Number = S1300T (3 detail records)				
Sum		228.5		
S1465T				
	5/22/96	$5	Smith	Guest Fee
	5/22/96	$20	Smith	Pro Shop-Merchandise
	5/28/96	$25	Smith	Pro Shop-Lesson
	5/31/96	$125	Smith	Dues for May
Summary for Number = S1465T (4 detail records)				
Sum		177.5		
Grand Total		497.4		

Point of Interest: You can change the page orientation to portrait (vertical orientation) or landscape (horizontal orientation), and set margin widths and several other printing controls using the **File|Page Setup** dialog tabs. Once you make setup changes, use the Zoom button to see a thumbnail sketch of the overall results of your setup selections and then use the Zoom button and accompanying magnifying glass cursor to enlarge an area of interest.

11. Press **<Ctrl+W>** to return to the Club: Database window.

Summary

This completes the first report creation activity. As you can see, the built-in wizards are extremely powerful and practically intuitive. Now move to the next section to see how easy it is to add a graph to a report.

Adding Charts to Your Reports

Introduction

Microsoft Access features a powerful graphing program called Microsoft Graph. It is used to add and edit graphs, which can be placed on either reports or forms. You can treat a graph just like a label or text box relative to placement, format, and size. The labels and data points used by graphs are based on headings and numerical values found in the selected table or query. Access uses the values to plot the points on the graph. The Access Chart Wizard guides you through the creation of your graphs. You can also produce forms that only display graphs by opening a new blank form. Then use the Graph tool on the toolbox to open the Chart Wizard, which leads you through the selection of tables, queries, fields, and graph types.

In the previous section you created two reports. One used AutoReport: Columnar, while the second used the Report Wizard. In this section you create a report that integrates a graph using the Chart Wizard. Then you create a stand-alone graph on a form.

Working with Microsoft Graph

In Section 52 you created a simple single-column report that displays member names, numbers, and account balances. You can create a graph to see a pictorial representation of the account balances for each member. In this section, you add a graph to the Subtotals report. Display the Club: Database window, click the Reports tab, and proceed as follows to see how easy it is to add a graph to your report.

Hands-on Activities

Adding a Chart to a Report

1. Pick the **Subtotals** report and click the **Design** button. Notice that the Subtotals report is displayed in the Report Design view.

2. Pick the bottom of the Report Footer bar and drag it down two to three inches to make room for the addition of a chart at the end of the report.

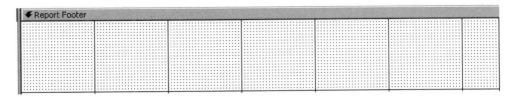

3. Use the **Insert|Chart** menu selection; drag a rectangular chart box that is approximately 2 inches high by 3.5 inches wide in the Report Footer area. Note that the Chart menu button may not be visible. Click on the double down arrow to display additional Insert menu selections.

Note: If a dialog box appears, click **Cancel** or **No** as appropriate.

4. Wait for the Chart Wizard dialog box to be displayed. Select the **Queries** option button; then pick **Fees1A**.

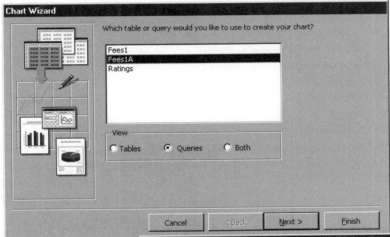

5. Click **Next>** and put **Number** and **SumOfAmount** in the Fields for Chart box.

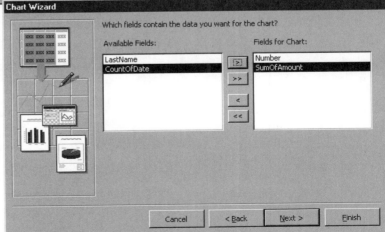

6. Click **Next>**. Leave the Column Chart selected.

7. Click **Next>** and compare your dialog to the following illustration. Be sure it matches.

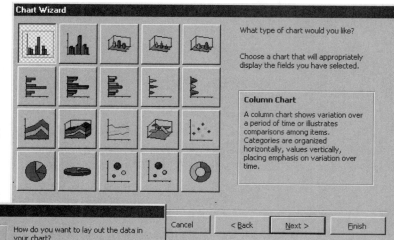

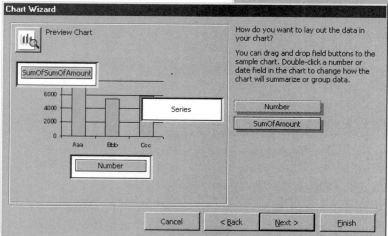

The SumOfAmount value controls the magnitude of the bars, while the member Number is used as the label.

8. Click **Next>**. You <u>do not</u> want the chart to be linked to individual records, which would show a chart for each member. Here, you want to display a billing summary. Therefore, delete Number from the Report Fields and Chart Fields boxes and click **Next>**.

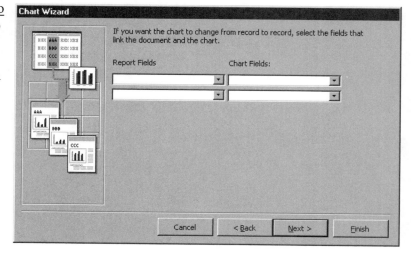

9. Type **Billing Summary** as the name, click the **No, don't display a legend** option button, and click **Finish**.

Chart Wizard

What title would you like for your chart?

Billing Summary

Do you want the chart to display a legend?

○ Yes, display a legend.

● No, don't display a legend.

☐ Display Help on working with my chart.

[Cancel] [< Back] [Next >] [Finish]

Tip: A legend for each of dozens of members (or graph elements) becomes confusing.

10. Drag the chart box to make it large enough to view all elements, including the member numbers and title. If necessary, drag the bottom of the Report Footer section. Your footer should resemble the following illustration.

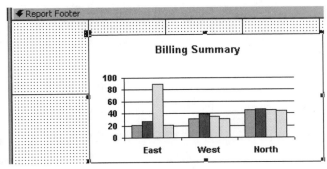

Point of Interest: Launch Microsoft Graph by double-clicking on the chart in the Report Design view. Then use Microsoft Graph to edit the way your graph is displayed. Label names, orientation, fonts, size, and much more are easily modified using the Microsoft Graph program menus and dialogs. For example, if you find that information does not fit within the area allotted, you can change the text fonts and point sizes. You can also change the label orientation, chart type, and much more. Legends are easily added using the **Insert|Legend** menu. At this point you may wish to launch and pull down the various menus to see available selections. Use **File|Exit** and Return to... to exit Microsoft Graphn. **File|Update** is used to save changes on the current report.

11. Click the **Print View** button 🔍 to display the report; scroll to the bottom of the page to view the resulting chart.

12. Use **File|Save As** to save your report. Give it the name **Subtotals with Chart** and click **OK**. Then press <Ctrl+W> to close the report.

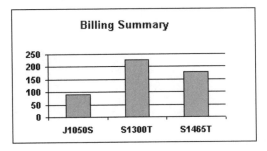

Putting a Chart on a Form

In this activity you create a stand-alone chart on a form. This chart uses data points from the Fees1A table. Begin at the Club: Database window.

1. Click the **Forms** tab. Then click **New**.

2. Put **Fees1A** in the table or query box and then click **Design View** and **OK** to display the Form Design view and a blank form.

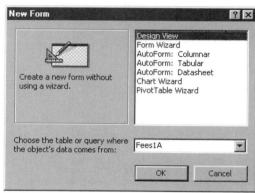

3. Now drag the bottom of the blank work surface down to 4 inches as measured on the vertical ruler. Drag it right to 6 inches on the horizontal ruler.

Note: Click **Cancel** or **No** on any dialogs that appear.

4. Use the **Insert|Chart** menu selection and drag a chart rectangle on the work surface beginning with the upper left-hand corner at 1.0 x 1.0 inches and drag the lower right-hand corner at 3.5 inches on the vertical ruler and 5 inches on the horizontal.

5. Access begins the chart creation process and then prompts you to select a data source for your chart. Click the **Queries** option button and pick **Fees1A** from the pick list.

6. Click **Next>**; and put **Number** and **SumOfAmount** to the Fields for Chart box.

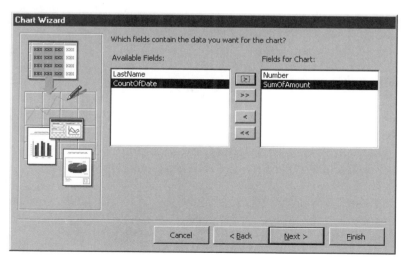

7. Click **Next>** to display the next dialog. Pick the Pie Chart (lower left-hand corner).

8. Click **Next>**. Leave Number and SumOfAmount as displayed.

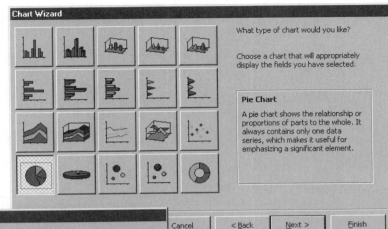

9. Click **Preview Chart** to see your chart, then click **Close** to close the preview.

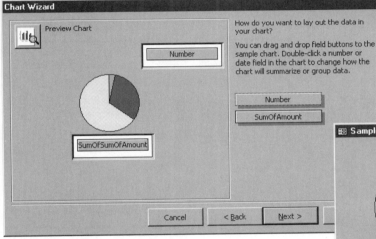

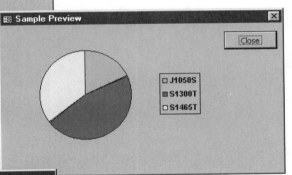

10. Click **Next>**. Delete the record links to the number field in both text boxes.

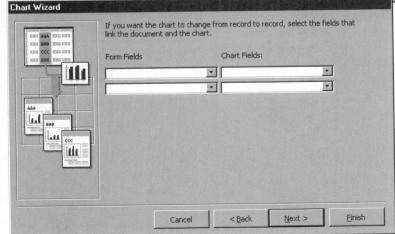

11. Click **Next>** and enter **une Revenues** as the chart title. Then click **Finish**.

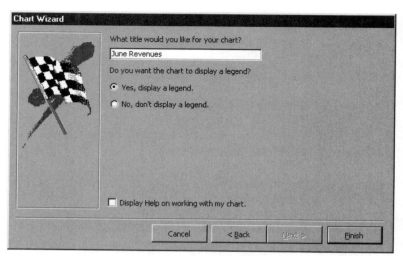

12. Double-click on the chart to start Microsoft Graph. xamine the display and then click anywhere outside the chart area to close Microsoft Chart.

13. Click the **Form View** button ▦ to see the chart on the form.

14. Then click the **Design View** button ▨ again to return to the design view.

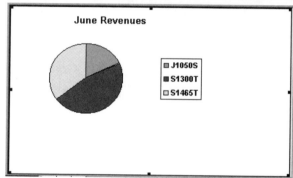

15. Double-click the chart to start Microsoft Graph again. Use the **Chart|Chart ype** menu selection, pick **Column** on the Standard Types tab, and click **OK** to change the graph type.

16. Using the **Chart|Chart Options** selection, pick the **ridlines** tab and click both **a or ridlines** check boxes as shown in the following illustration. Click **OK**.

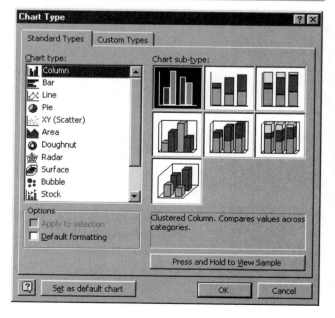

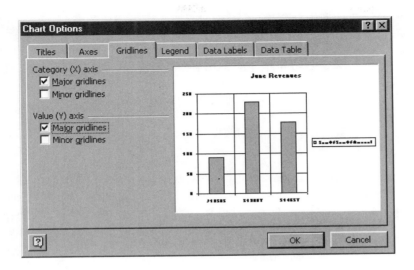

17. Notice how the grid lines are added to your chart.

18. Click the legend box (containing **SumOfSumOfAmount**). Once selected, press **<Del>**.

19. Double-click anywhere outside the chart area and exit back to the Form Design view.

20. Use **File|Save**, type the name **Form With Chart**, and click **OK**. Finally, press **<Ctrl+W>** to close the form.

Summary

This completes the charting activity. As you can see, charting is greatly simplified with the use of Microsoft Graphn and the Microsoft Access wizards. In the next section you continue to develop your Access program skills by creating mailing labels suitable for mailing newsletters and invoices to the membership.

Creating Mailing Labels

Introduction

Microsoft Access provides a report label wizard designed to put names and addresses on a large number of commonly used mailing label formats. Wizards exist for single-column through four-column label stocks. Some label stocks are designed for use with sprocket-fed (or tractor-driven) printers, while other label stocks are designed for use with laser printers. Regardless of the kind of printer you have, there are probably several Access label wizard formats that meet your needs. If there aren't, you can use one that is close and then use the Report Design view to modify the dimensions to fit your needs.

Hands-on Activity

In the following activity you create a mailing label report that produces labels from the Member table. These labels can be affixed to envelopes for mailing such things as monthly statements and newsletters to club members. Begin with the Club: Database window displayed and the Reports tab selected.

1. Click **New** to create a new report.

2. Pick the **Member** table, then pick the **Label Wizard** as shown, and click **OK**.

3. Pick Avery number **5095**, Unit of Measure **English**, and Label Type **Sheet feed** as shown.

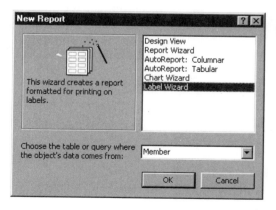

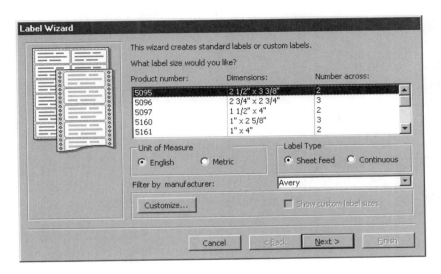

4. Click **Next>**. Set the font name, size, and weight as shown in the following illustration.

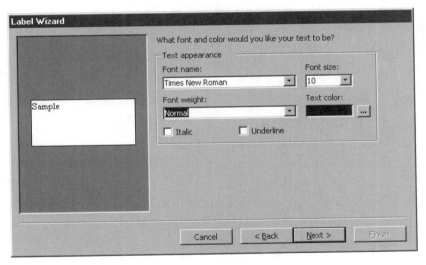

5. Click **Next>**. Transfer the indicated fields from the Available fields box to the Prototype label box as shown. Type spaces between elements and a comma and space between City and State. Use the **Down Arrow** or mouse cursor to move to different lines in the Available fields box and use the **Enter** key or press the > button located between the two boxes to put each item on separate lines in the **Prototype label** box.

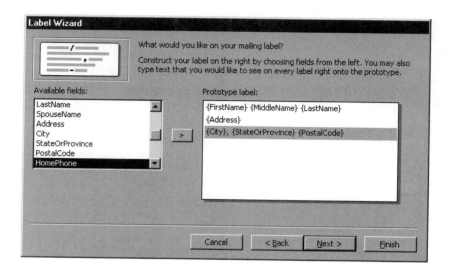

6. Click **Next>** to display the Sort order dialog. Enter **LastName** in the Sort by box as shown. This arranges the labels in last-name order.

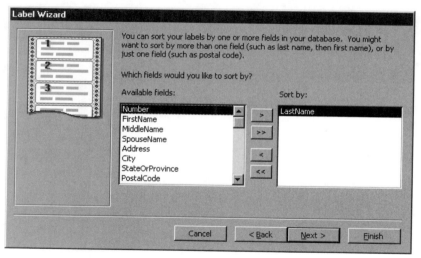

7. Click **Next>**. Notice the following screen. Type **Member Mailing Labels** as the report name. Then click **Finish**.

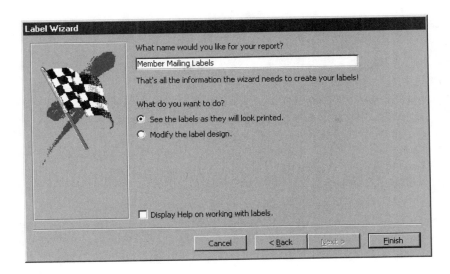

8. Click **Close** to see the Report Design view.

Point of Interest: Notice the =Trim and &" "& format controls. The trim function removes blank spaces following text values. The & symbol
concatenates (or connects) strings. Text within quotes is also concate-
nated to the text field values.

9. Click on **File|Save As** and save the report as **Member Mailing Labels**.

10. Press **<Ctrl+W>** to close the report.

Point of Interest: If you wish to change the layout to a size not listed by the
Report Wizard, you can adjust the height and width to correspond to the
new label dimensions by dragging the edges. Then you can drag the text
boxes for alignment and fit.

Summary

In the last three sections you learned how to create a variety of reports and use
Microsoft Graph. Here, you learned how to create mailing labels. This completes the
report design activities. Printing your reports is also easy. All you have to do is load
paper into your printer and click the Print button. The report printing operation is just
like any other Windows printing task. Now that you know how to create and use
tables, queries, forms, and reports, it's time to learn how to automate frequently used
operations. Therefore, in the next section you learn how to create *macros*. A macro is
a saved series of keystrokes that can be replayed on demand.

Automating Your Work with Macros

Introduction

Macros are created and applied to automate frequently used tasks. Macros are started using the click of a mouse or a simple keypress. This simple action starts a series of underlying commands. Each command is executed in the order encountered just like a simple BASIC program, which executes each program instruction one line at a time. Access macros execute a list of actions typically used to open files, display user prompts, print reports, or perform a variety of other activities limited only by your imagination.

Macros are created one instruction at a time, much like writing a script. Each entry in the script is placed in a tabular Action list. Entries are also created by dragging a table, query, form, or report name from the Database window to the appropriate line in the Macro window. You use both of these approaches to create a few sample macros in the activities contained in this section.

Hands-on Activity: Macro Creation

In the first macro creation activity, you create an Action list that opens a query. Begin with the Club: Database window displayed.

1. Click the **Macros** tab in the Club: Database dialog and then click **New**.

2. Once the Macro window is open, use **Window|Tile Vertically** to see the Club: Database and Macro windows at the same time. Then click the **Queries** tab within the database window. Your screen should resemble the following illustration.

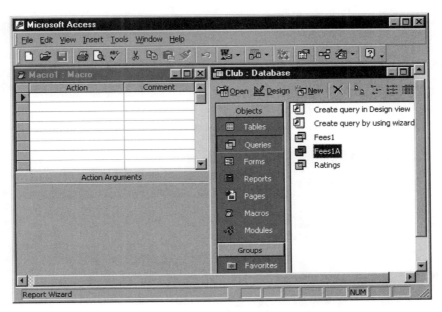

3. Pick the query **Fees1A** and drag it to the first line of the Action column within the Macro window. Check the resulting Action and Action Arguments.

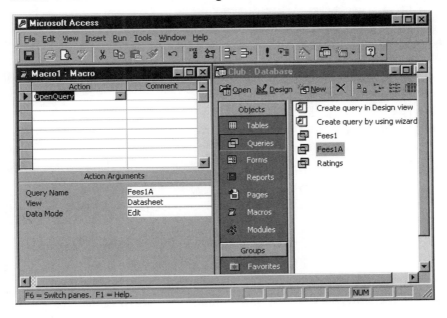

Point of Interest: By dragging a table, form, query, or report to the Action list, the arguments are automatically set for you. If you enter the action manually, you will also have to add the proper arguments. Most argument lines offer a pick list to choose from.

4. Using **File|Save As**, type the name **Member Totals**, and click **OK**.

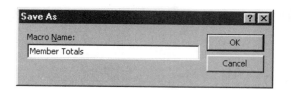

5. Close the Macro window. In the Club: Database window, click on the **Macros** tab. Click the **Run** button ❗ Run on the Macro toolbar to run the macro. Notice that the Fees1A query is displayed.

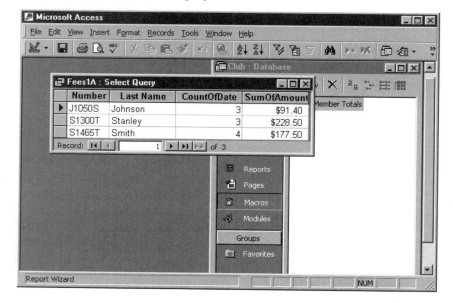

6. Press <**Ctrl+W**> to close the Fees1A query. Highlight **Member Totals**, then click on the **Design View** button ☒ Design in the Club: Database dialog. Now add a few more lines to your new macro to make it more useful.

  a. Put the cursor on the first row of the Macro window (with Open Query), and use **Insert|Rows** to insert a blank row.

  b. On the first row of the Action column, click the down arrow and select **Beep** from the pick list.

  c. On the third row of the Action column, pick **Maximize** from the action pick list.

  d. On the fourth row of the Action column, pick **RunCommand**. Set the Action Arguments to Find by typing **Find** in the Command box.

  e. On the fifth row of the Action column, pick **Restore**. Compare your actions to those shown in the following list. The comments are optional.

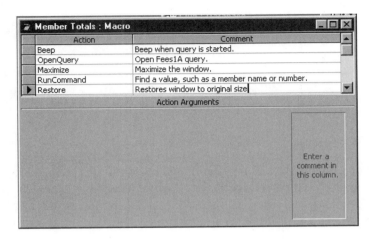

7. Press **<Ctrl+S>** to save your new changes. Close the macro Design View, then click **Run** to see the effect of the added lines.

8. The computer beeps when the macro is started. Once the Fees1A query is displayed, the window is maximized and the Find dialog is displayed, ready for you to enter a member number.

9. Type **S1300T** and click **Find Next**. Notice that Stanley's record is located.

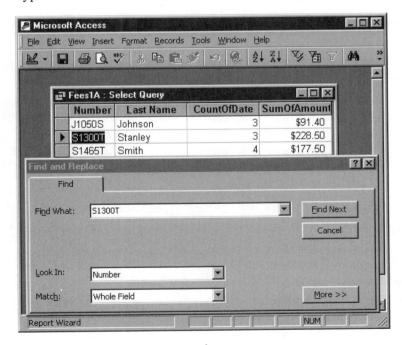

10. Click the **Close** button. Now press **<Ctrl+W>** to close the query and then use **Window|Tile Vertically** to redisplay both the Macro and Database windows.

This simple example only has three items in the query list and therefore a macro to find any item seems kind of pointless—all three items are right there before your eyes. But, have you ever gone down a path only to discover you wished you started on the right foot—instead of the left? Lists grow with time. Or maybe your initial list has hundreds or thousands of items. The ability to quickly find items in long lists is invaluable for saving time.

Macro Command Buttons

You can also create and use a macro command button to run your macros. For example, you may wish to see billing information while looking at the membership roster form. In the following activity, you place a command button on the Roster form. The command button is a control. It does not accept or display data. It performs an action. The command button on the Roster form is used to run the Member Totals macro created and saved above.

Hands-on Activity: Creating a Macro Command Button

1. Press **<Ctrl+W>** to close the Macro window. Then click the **Forms** tab in the Club: Database window and open the **Roster** form in the Form Design view.

2. Use **Window|Tile Vertically** to display the Roster form and Club: Database windows side by side.

3. Drag the line between the Form Header and Detail bars down about one-half inch. Now click the **Macros** tab in the Database window.

4. Select and drag **Member Totals** onto the Form Header work surface. (See the following illustration.)

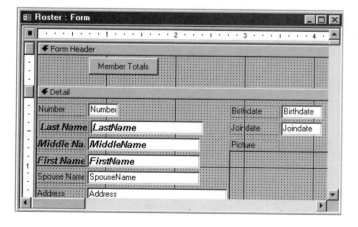

5. With the new Member Totals button selected, click the **Properties** button on the toolbar to view the properties sheet. Scroll down to see the On Click property. The macro name indicates that a click of the button runs the Member Totals macro.

6. Click **Form View** to display the Roster with its new macro button.

7. Click the **Member Totals** button and notice how the macro is automatically executed. Now close the Find and Replace dialog and then press **<Ctrl+S>** and **<Ctrl+W>** to save and close the Fees1A query; this returns you to the Roster form.

Synchronizing Records

If you want the record on the second form to correspond to the selected record on the first, you can edit the Where Condition argument of the Member Totals macro. This argument is available with an OpenForm action but not with an OpenQuery action. Therefore, in the following activity you change the OpenQuery action to OpenForm. The OpenForm action instructs the macro to use the Fees1A form. The Where Condition argument is set so that the records of the two forms match. Knowing how to use an OpenForm action to synchronize your records is an important concept. For example, if you want to look at a customer form and corresponding order or invoice forms at the same time, you can use this approach.

Hands-on Activity: Synchronizing Records

1. Open the Roster form; then use **Window|Tile Vertically** to display the Club: Database window and the Roster form side by side.

2. Click the **Macros** tab on the Club: Database window. With **Member Totals** selected, click **Design** view.

3. Use **Window|Tile Vertically** again to view the Macro, Database, and Roster windows (a total of three windows).

4. Select the entire Maximize line. Use **Edit|Delete** to remove it. Select one line by placing the cursor just to the left of the Action column and adjacent to the word "Maximize" (the cursor changes to a horizontal right-pointing arrow) and then left-clicking.

5. Select the entire Restore line. Use **Edit|Delete** to remove it.

6. Click the **Forms** tab in the Database window. Then drag the **Fees1A** form to the OpenQuery action line on the macro window. Notice that an OpenForm action is inserted above OpenQuery.

7. Maximize the Macro window. Select the OpenQuery action line (the complete line must be selected, not just the OpenQuery text in the Action column) and use **Edit|Delete** to remove it.

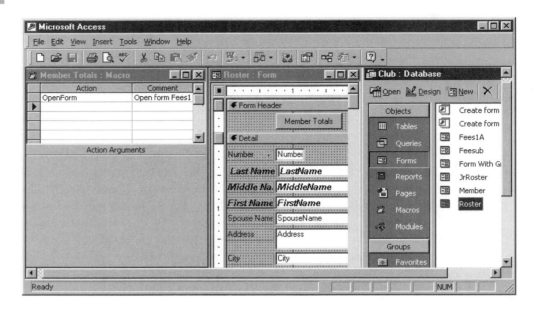

8. Pick the OpenForm action row. Enter the following values in the OpenForm's Action Arguments box (at the bottom of the window):

Form Name:	**Fees1A**
View:	**Form**
Filter Name:	**(Leave blank)**
Where Condition:	**[Number]=[Forms]![Roster]![Number]**
Data Mode:	**Read Only**
Window Mode:	**Normal**

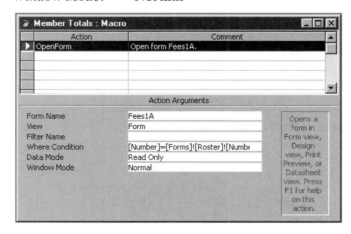

9. Select the RunCommand line. Put the command **TileVertically** in the RunCommand's Action Arguments box.

Your macro Action list should match the screen illustration shown here with the possible exception of your comment lines.

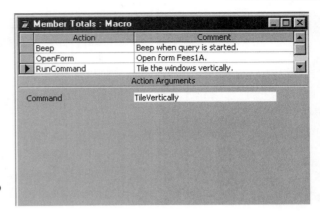

10. Restore the Macro window by clicking on the window's **Restore** button.

11. Press **<Ctrl+S>** and save the changes to your macro and then press **<Ctrl+W>** to close the macro window. Now minimize the Club: Database window. Minimizing the Club: Database window gets it out of the way so that when the macro executes the **Window|Tile Vertically** command, the database window is not tiled with the forms.

12. Click the **View** button to display the form view. Then click the **Member Totals** button on the form. When the macro finishes its work, notice that the displayed records are synchronized—the record displayed in the Fees1A form window is the same as the one in the Member form window. Also, notice that the **Windows|Tile Vertically** selection has positioned the forms side by side for easy viewing.

13. Move to the next record (Lisa Anne Stanley's) and click **Member Totals**. Notice that the Fees1A form now displays Lisa's billing information.

Tip: The third and fourth records are blank, because no billing information was ever entered for these two members. If you wish, you can add billing information to the Fees table now for members A1080T and S1470T. For example, you can add a $50 fee as "Dues for May." Be sure to enter May 31, 1999, as the date.

14. Click on the Member window. Then press **<Ctrl+S>** to save your changes.

15. Press **<Ctrl+W>** twice to close both forms.

16. Maximize the Club: Database window. Then press **<Alt+F4>** to exit Access.

Summary

This completes your macro creation activity. This part of *Learn Office 2000* introduced you to database terminology, database structures, and relational database management. Using the power of Access, you can now manipulate data by creating tables, queries, forms, reports, and macros. At this point, you are ready to use Microsoft Access for your data management tasks. The next section discusses PowerPoint, a powerful presentation application.

Part 5

Microsoft PowerPoint 2000

56 About This Part—Understand the purpose and organization of this part and receive an introduction to PowerPoint and its features.

57 Starting (or "Launching") PowerPoint—Key PowerPoint controls and dialogs.

58 PowerPoint Views—Learn how easy it is to view your presentation information (or "slides") in a variety of ways during the creation and presentation processes.

59 Creating Your First Presentation—Create your first presentation in minutes following the simple procedures in this section.

60 More About Files—Open and save new and existing presentations with ease.

61 Built-in Wizards—Take advantage of PowerPoint's built-in design aids, called *wizards*.

62 Working with Text and Lists—Control the selection, placement, size, and style of your text; learn how to promote and demote elements in lists.

63 Working with Colors and Transitions—Add snap to your slides with color variations, shading, highlighting, and attractive transitions between slides.

64 Adding Headers and Footers—Add logos, thematics, numbers, and more to your slides.

65 Drawing Tools—Add rules, arrows, boxes, and more to your slides.

66 Animation and Sound—Animate elements in your slides and add sound effects for increased impact.

67 Importing Objects from Other Applications—Add clip art, Word tables, Excel worksheets, and graphs to your slides.

68 Automating Your Presentations—Create self-running presentations and product demonstrations.

69 Hyperlinks to External Resources—Making a slide call another slide, a sound, a program, or an object.

70 Printing Your Presentations—Print copies of your presentations and transfer slide notes, action item lists, and meeting notes to Word for editing and printing.

71 Modifying and Integrating Presentations—Use PowerPoint's editing and Slide Sorter features to modify, add, insert, remove, and shuffle the order of your slides.

72 Distributing Presentations with the PowerPoint Viewer—Copy and distribute your presentations on disk to sales representatives, customers, or students.

About This Part

Introduction

Part 5 of this book guides you through the use of Microsoft PowerPoint 2000, which runs under the Windows 95/98 and NT operating systems. From this point forward the common name "PowerPoint" is used. When you complete the sections within this part of the book, you should be able to create, save, and print many kinds of presentations used to communicate your ideas in an impressive, dynamic way. Before moving into the descriptive and tutorial sections of this part, be sure to read the remainder of this section.

What is PowerPoint?

PowerPoint is a full-featured presentation program that is used by millions of people around the world. PowerPoint is used to design presentations for a variety of mediums including computer-based display shows, overhead projection transparencies, and 35 mm slides. You can add sound and animation to your slides to achieve a high level of impact.

PowerPoint gives you the ability to prepare paper-based presentations and handouts for your audience. You can also package and distribute your presentations with a PowerPoint Viewer. You can even package and distribute your presentations in PowerPoint 4.0 (16-bit) format, so those people who are still using Windows 3.x can run your presentations.

As with the other Office 2000 programs, PowerPoint makes use of all of the features available to programs designed specifically to run with a 32-bit operating system such as Windows 95/98 and NT. When acquired as part of Office, PowerPoint uses a number of shared Office resources. This includes fonts, ClipArt, spelling resources, AutoCorrect, Internet Explorer, and more.

Like all other Office 2000 programs, PowerPoint can integrate documents and information created by other Office and Windows programs. For example, you can insert Excel spreadsheets or Word tables directly into a PowerPoint slide. You can also export a slide presentation to a Word document with the click of a button on PowerPoint's Standard toolbar. The ease and flexibility of performing these operations is impressive.

Companion Files

The companion files used with the PowerPoint hands-on activities are supplied on the companion CD-ROM. The Files folder (or your hard drive or the CD) contains the presentations that you develop in this part of the book. You can check these by opening the PowerPoint (*.ppt) files and comparing them to the files that you create and save in the hands-on activities.

When PowerPoint help is started, a dialog is displayed. By clicking on "Finding out what's new in PowerPoint 2000" you will be guided to another dialog that lists many of the new features not found in previous Access versions.

After clicking on "Finding out what's new…" in the dialog that appears, PowerPoint help displays the "What's new…" dialog. Click on any topic of interest for a detailed explanation of the new feature and how it may improve your productivity.

What's Next?

You're ready to begin learning all about PowerPoint. In the next section you examine the PowerPoint screen. Then, in Section 58, you familiarize yourself with PowerPoint *views*. With this background in place, you move to Section 59 where you begin creating a slide presentation. This presentation serves as the basis for many of the hands-on learning activities that follow, as you enhance your presentation by adding many special effects. Of all the Office applications, PowerPoint is one of the most fun to use. So prepare to have a good time as you learn the rich set of features supplied with this program.

Starting (or "Launching") PowerPoint

Introduction

This section introduces you to the main parts of the PowerPoint screen. Descriptions of opening dialog boxes (or simply *dialogs*) and the available menus and toolbars are presented. PowerPoint is rich with toolbars and buttons, having a menu with a large number of selections and 13 toolbars. If you are not sure about where to access a particular feature or its purpose, this section should be helpful.

If you installed the Office toolbar, the easiest way to launch PowerPoint is to click on the PowerPoint button. Otherwise, go to the Programs group (or the group in which you installed PowerPoint); start PowerPoint by clicking the Microsoft PowerPoint line. When PowerPoint starts the PowerPoint dialog loads.

The first time you start PowerPoint you are invited to review "What's New," and the Office Assistant offers help. If you are familiar with previous versions of PowerPoint you may want to close the Office Assistant for now. Go to the menu bar and click on Help,n then click on Hide the Office Assistant. Now the PowerPoint dialog will display. Close the PowerPoint dialog and compare your display to the following illustration, which labels the various parts of the PowerPoint screen.

The above screen illustrates the Normal view. If you wish, you can use the View menu to change the slide view. With a slide open, you can now type your text and use the menus and toolbars to change the page setup, font, text size, and much more. Each

PowerPoint screen control is summarized in the appendices on the accompanying CD. Detailed descriptions are found in the following sections of this book where you are guided through hands-on learning activities.

Microsoft PowerPoint 2000 Controls

The keyed screen illustration shows each of the various controls which are summarized in the list that follows.

Key	Item	Description
1	Menu Bar	Used to access the PowerPoint menus and the Office Assistant (Help)
2	Standard Toolbar	Includes buttons to perform the most frequently used file, editing, web and hyperlink, borders, inserting tables, charts and slides, zoom, and Office Assistant (Help) operations.
3	Formatting Toolbar	Includes buttons to perform the most frequent file formatting operations such as specifying fonts and font size; specifying text characteristics such as bold, italic, underling; text positioning (left margin, center, right margin); bullets and numbering, and formatting indentation operations.
4	View line	Displays the various viewing options.
5	Status line	Displays messages.

Note: The "Tip for new users" area displayed in PowerPoint's opening dialog is designed to give new users information about the application. Once you become familiar with PowerPoint features and tricks, you will probably want to uncheck the Show tips at startup check box to suppress this dialog in the future. The tips may be enabled/disabled by showing the Office Assistant, clicking on the Office Assistant, clicking on Options, and selecting the Options tab from the Office Assistant dialog. Enable/disable the tips as desired by checking/unchecking the box beside Show the Tip of the Day at startup.

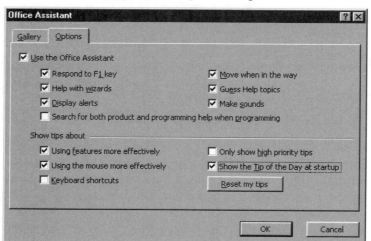

The Main Screen

When you launch PowerPoint, it anticipates that you are going to create a new presentation. The following dialogs are displayed to guide you through some initial design selections.

Create/Open Presentation Dialog

This dialog gives you access to built-in design tools or direct access to a previously prepared presentation. Just click the appropriate button and OK to continue.

Clicking AutoContent Wizard guides you through a list of presentation types and styles from which to choose. The built-in templates include a handsome array of slide styles with varying colors and designs.

If you selected the Blank presentation box you will be presented with the New Presentation dialog.

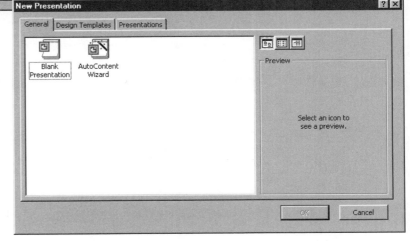

Note: The format of the information in the New Presentation dialog text box is determined by which of the three buttons to the right of the text box is enabled:

- Large Icons
- List
- Details

The New Presentation dialog shown has the Large Icons option enabled. If you select Blank presentation from the New Presentation dialog, you are then given a choice of several layout styles. This dialog presents 24 different slide layouts that include everything from blank layouts to those mixing several elements that designate areas for titles, text, graphics, and charts.

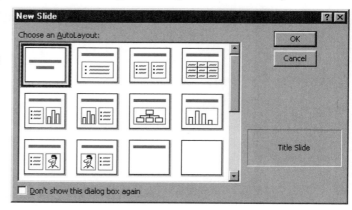

Finally, if you want to open a presentation that you previously created and saved, choose Open an Existing Presentation. This displays a File|Open dialog; using the File menu's Open selection (or File|Open) achieves the same result. Click Cancel to go to the PowerPoint main screen.

The Main Screen

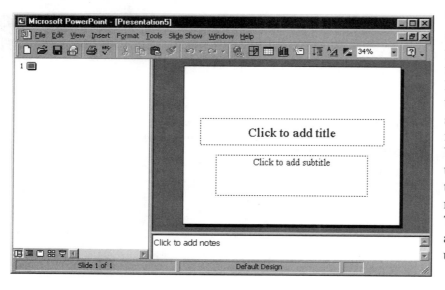

The working area of the main screen remains empty until you open a presentation, click the New button, or select File|New. Once a slide presentation is either opened or started, pick a slide layout from the New Slide screen. Your screen should resemble the following screen illustration which shows the indicated menu bar and toolbar buttons. The illustration uses the autolayout slide, shown at the upper left.

Summary

Now that you know how the PowerPoint screen is organized, you're ready to move to Section 58, where each of the View buttons are described. There, you will open an existing slide presentation and look at the presentation using different views.

PowerPoint Views

Introduction

This section shows you how easy it is to view your presentation information (or "slides") in a variety of ways. All that is necessary is to click one of the View buttons located at the bottom left-hand corner of the working area. You can pick the same views using the selections within the View menu.

The View Buttons

The following illustrations show each of the View buttons. The purpose of each of the buttons follows the illustration, along with an example of the corresponding screen. Notice the Normal, Slide Show, and Slide Sorter view selections are available both from the View menu selection and from the View icons located on the bottom left of the view window.

Normal View—Normal view displays three panes—the outline pane, the slide pane, and the notes pane. The three panes allow you to work on all aspects of the presentation in one place. The sizes of the different panes are adjusted by dragging the pane borders.

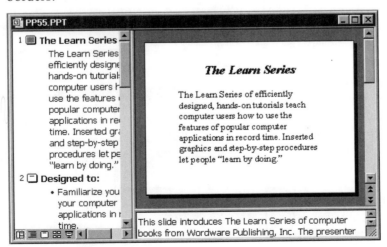

Outline View—The Outline View is used to display an outline format of your slide show. The slide number and text contents are displayed here. In this view you can edit the displayed text, delete slides, and even cut and paste slides from one location to another. Cutting and pasting is possible within the same presentation or between different presentations. Work in Outline View when you wish to organize and develop the content of your file.

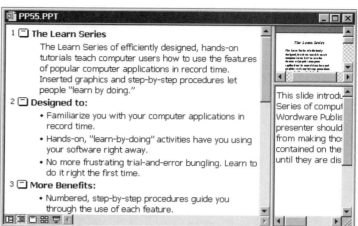

Slide View—The Slide View is used to create and edit your slides. This is the default view when you first open PowerPoint. In this view, all of the menus and toolbars are available for use. Use this view to insert and edit the contents of your slides.

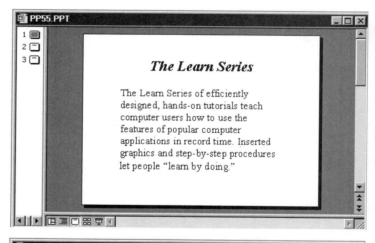

Slide Sorter View—The Slide Sorter View gives you a miniature picture of each slide. You can use this view to select and drag slides from one position to another within your slide show. In this view you can even display two sets of slides simultaneously and then drag and drop slides from one presentation to the other.

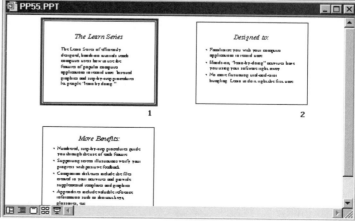

Slide Show—This view displays the slides full screen. It is used to show or simply review your slide presentations. Use this view to check final sizes, colors, animation, transitions between slides, sounds, and other controls. To check the timing of a self-running presentation, use the View|Slide Show menu selection. You can also distribute your presentations with the PowerPoint Viewer program, used to run presentations without the actual PowerPoint program. See Section 72 for more information on packaging and distributing your presentations.

The Learn Series

The Learn Series of efficiently designed, hands-on tutorials teach computer users how to use the features of popular computer applications in record time. Inserted graphics and step-by-step procedures let people "learn by doing."

The following two submenus allow you to adjust the size, orientation, and properties of the various views.

File|Page Setup—File|Page Setup displays the Page Setup dialog. Use it to adjust the size and orientation of your displayed slides, as well as the beginning page number. You can adjust the size of your slides

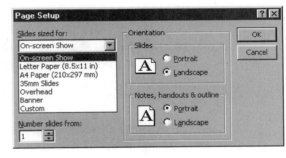

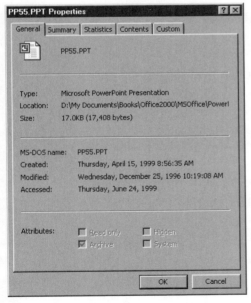

for use as an on-screen show (default), a 35 mm slide show, a paper-based letter- or A4-size presentation, overhead, banner, or custom size slide show. The Height and Width boxes let you set the custom sizes. You can also change the orientation from landscape (horizontal) to portrait (vertical).

File|Properties—Use this menu selection to display general information and detailed statistics about the current slide presentation. Five different tabs are available in this dialog. Each displays a different set of information. The best way to determine the kind of information provided is to open and browse the Properties dialog when a slide presentation is open.

Summary

All of the available views are useful. While working through this part, you should be in the Slide View unless directed otherwise. In the next section, you begin working with PowerPoint by creating a four-slide presentation.

Creating Your First Presentation

Introduction

This section familiarizes you with the most commonly used parts of PowerPoint by guiding you through the actual preparation of a simple slide presentation. In this procedure, you:

- Select a presentation template (or style).
- Use different slide formats.
- Enter both text and graphics.
- Save the slide show.
- Review the slide show and exit PowerPoint.

Hands-on Activity (Putting PowerPoint to Work)

Create your first presentation by following these steps:

1. Launch the PowerPoint program. Click the **OK** button in response to the Tip of the Day dialog.

2. Click the **Cancel** button on the PowerPoint dialog to display a blank screen.

Note: PowerPoint automatically displays the New Presentation dialog at startup. For the time being, you bypass this dialog so you can learn how to develop your presentation using standard menu and toolbar selections. Therefore, canceling the dialogs lets you start your presentation using the conventional PowerPoint tool set. In Section 61, you explore the use of the AutoContent selection, which is designed to guide you through the creation of a new presentation.

3. Once the dialog is closed and a blank screen is displayed, click the **New** button (leftmost button on the Standard toolbar) to begin a new presentation. A New Slide dialog is displayed. At this point, you should be in the Slide View (recall the different views from the previous section).

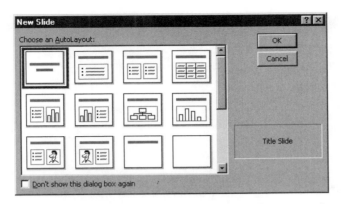

4. With the upper left-hand slide outlined (or *selected*), click **OK**. Your screen should resemble the following illustration.

5. Now create a title slide by typing the information as shown in the following slide illustration.

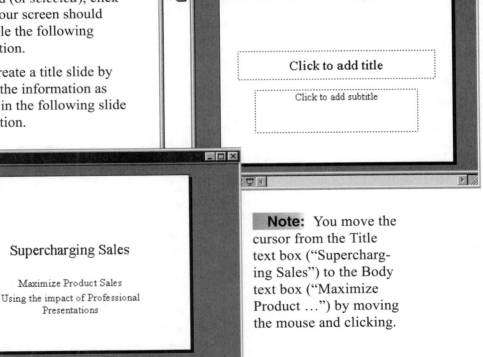

Note: You move the cursor from the Title text box ("Supercharging Sales") to the Body text box ("Maximize Product ...") by moving the mouse and clicking.

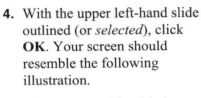

6. Click the **Formatting|Common Tasks|Apply Design Template** button on the Formatting toolbar. Notice the following dialog.

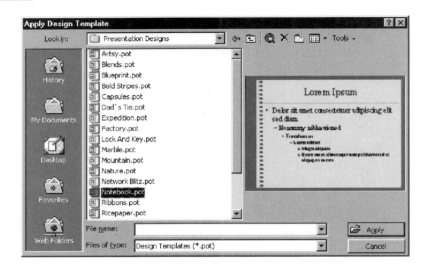

7. Select **Notebook.pot** from the list of design templates. (It's near the bottom of the list.) Then click **Apply** and see how the selected template is applied to the slide.

8. Click on the subtitle text and press **<Ctrl+A>** to select all of the text; then press **<Ctrl+E>** to center the text.

9. Click on the title text and press **<Ctrl+E>** to center the title.

10. Click **<Ctrl+A>** to select all of the title text. Then use the **Font Size** button on the Formatting toolbar to increase the text size to 60 points. Press **<Ctrl+B>** for bold. Compare your slide to the following illustration.

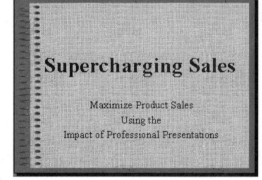

11. Check the status bar at the bottom of the screen. Notice how the slide number (slide 1 of 1) and active design template (Notebook) are displayed. The slide number and active design template are for information. You can use the Common Tasks toolbar selections to choose a different slide layout and apply it to the current slide. The New Slide button displays the New Slide dialog so you can pick the layout for the next slide in your presentation.

12. Click **New Slide** (**Formatting|Common Tasks|New Slide**) and pick the second slide on the top row (Bulleted List). Note that the name of each slide layout is displayed in the box at the right-hand side of the dialog. Click **OK**.

13. Type the information shown on the following illustration for the second slide. Select the title text and change it to bold and italic.

14. Click **Common Tasks|New Slide** menu selection, pick the **Text & Clip Art** layout (the bottom left-hand slide), and click **OK**.

15. Type the title and bulleted text as shown.

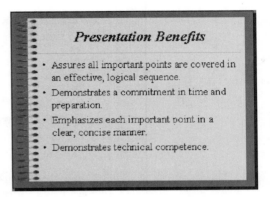

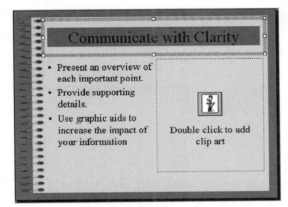

16. Double-click the picture to the right of the text box. If this is your first use of clip art, follow the on-screen instructions to prepare the clip art library for use. Finally, select the Business category, click on the picture in the sixth row and second column from left top, and click **Insert**.

Tip: The ClipArt Gallery displays files from a variety of sources depending on the applications installed on your computer. If you don't have the picture shown here, pick another.

17. Check your progress against the following illustration.

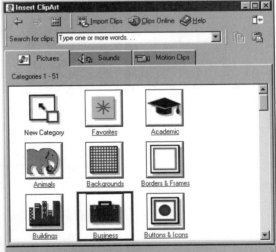

18. Click **Common Tasks|New Slide** and double-click the Bulleted List slide (an alternate way to apply the desired slide).

19. Type the information shown in the following illustration.

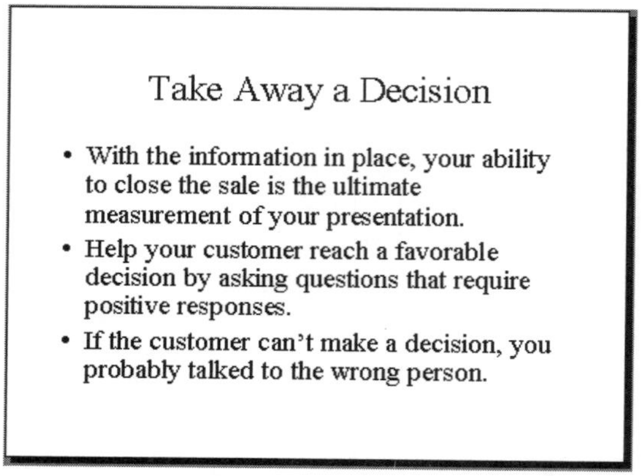

20. Now use **File|Save** to save your presentation. Type the filename **Sales Points** and click **Save**. Notice that it is saved as a "Presentation (*.ppt)" file type.

> ## Take Away a Decision
>
> - With the information in place, your ability to close the sale is the ultimate measurement of your presentation.
> - Help your customer reach a favorable decision by asking questions that require positive responses.
> - If the customer can't make a decision, you probably talked to the wrong person.

21. Press **<Ctrl+Home>** to move back to the first slide. Then click the **View|Slide Show** menu selection.

22. Press **<Page Down>** to view each slide. You can also use **<Page Up>** to view the previous slide.

23. Press **<Alt+F4>** to exit PowerPoint.

Note: The PowerPoint files created and saved in the activities can be found in the \MSOffice\Files folder.

Summary

This concludes the construction of a simple slide presentation. Here, you only used a few rudimentary pieces of PowerPoint's remarkable array of features. In following sections you learn how to use the full set of PowerPoint tools so you can maximize the impact of your presentations.

More About Files

Introduction

The PowerPoint File menu is used to create, open, and save files. If you are familiar with other Microsoft application programs, such as Word or Excel, then you already know how to handle PowerPoint files. However, if you are not a user of these applications, then you can review the following selections found in the File menu. Note that only the first two menu selections are displayed until a presentation is opened. Then the rest of the menu entries are displayed.

File Menu Overview

New—Starts a new slide presentation. You can also click the New button on the Standard toolbar.

Open—Opens an existing slide presentation. Use the Open dialog to locate and select the desired file. You can also click the Open button on the Standard toolbar.

Close—Close the current slide presentation.

Save—Save the active slide presentation.

Save As—Save the active slide presentation with a new name, in a different file path or disk drive, or in a different file format (such as Windows metafile or PowerPoint 95, 4.0, or 3.0 format).

Save as Web Page—Save the current document in Hypertext Markup Language format (compatible with web browsers).

Pack and Go—Prepare one or more presentations for distribution. The Pack and Go Wizard guides you through the preparation process. All necessary presentation and Viewer files are copied to designated destination disks.

Web Page Preview—View the presentation as it will be seen when viewed by Microsoft Explorer. Note that the presentation may be viewed differently by different browsers. While you can use Web Page Preview to get a quick look at the browser view, it is best to actually load the presentation into several browser types to verify the ability of the browser to display the presentation properly.

397

Page Setup—Display or change the size and orientation (portrait or landscape) of the current slide presentation or handouts. Slides can be sized for on-screen, letter or A4 paper, 35 mm, overhead projection, or custom use. Slide numbering is also controlled by this dialog.

Print—Print the current slide presentation. Printing options include printing from one to six slides per page, as well as printing notes and handouts.

Send To—Send the current presentation as e-mail, as a fax through Microsoft Exchange, or to Word. Use the corresponding dialog to make your selections. (This is ideal for computers with a fax/modem or networking card.)

Properties—Display a Properties dialog showing information about the current slide presentation.

Exit—Exit the PowerPoint program.

Available Shortcut Keys

Available file-related shortcut keys include:

File|New   Ctrl+N
File|Open   Ctrl+O
File|Save   Ctrl+S
File|Exit   Alt+F4

Hands-on Activity

You used the New and Save selections in the previous section when you created and saved your first presentation. This hands-on activity guides you through the use of the Open and Save As selections. Begin by starting PowerPoint. Close all dialogs.

1. Use **File|Open**, select the file **Sales Points.ppt**, and click **Open**.

2. Pick **File|Save As**, click the **Save as type** down arrow, and look at the list of available file types.

3. Press **<Esc>** twice to cancel the Save As operation.

4. Use **File|Close** to close the current presentation. Notice that only the File and Help menus are displayed.

5. Use **File|Exit** to close PowerPoint.

Summary

This completes the hands-on activity, which shows you how to use the File menu's Open, Close, and Save As selections. Note that you can also use the Open and Save buttons on the Standard toolbar. The next section introduces you to a number of PowerPoint's built-in wizards. Wizards guide you through the creation of slides including the selection of slide sequences, layouts, colors, and more.

Built-in Wizards

Introduction

Now that you are familiar with some PowerPoint basics, it's time to take a look at PowerPoint's built-in design aids, called *wizards*. You encounter a wizard each time you launch the PowerPoint program. Look at the first dialog.

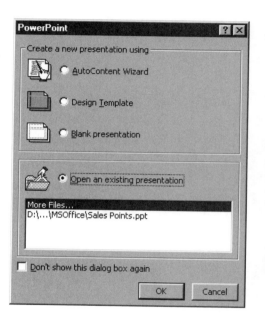

In previous activities you closed this dialog and used File|New or File|Open. However, both of these operations are easily achieved with this dialog. The four choices presented by the dialog are summarized. Then, the AutoContent Wizard selection is explored in more detail:

AutoContent Wizard—This selection launches a series of wizard dialogs that guide you through the creation of a new presentation.

Design Template—This selection allows you to pick a slide design template from a large list of background patterns and colors.

Blank Presentation—This selection opens the New Slide dialog from which you choose the layout of the first slide in a new presentation.

Open an Existing Presentation—This selection uses the File|Open dialog from which you can pick an existing slide presentation file.

Notice the following dialog and the General, Design Templates, and Presentations tabs.

General—Click the Blank Presentation icon to begin the first slide of a new, blank presentation. This selection requires that you design each slide independently, including patterns, colors, and content ideas.

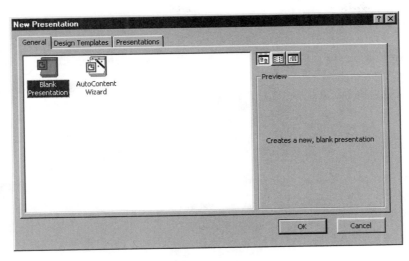

Design Templates—Use this tab to pick a presentation design or background pattern. The Preview area shows the design before you finalize your decision.

Presentations—Use this tab to pick guidelines for the ideas you wish to communicate. There are many outstanding ideas from which to choose.

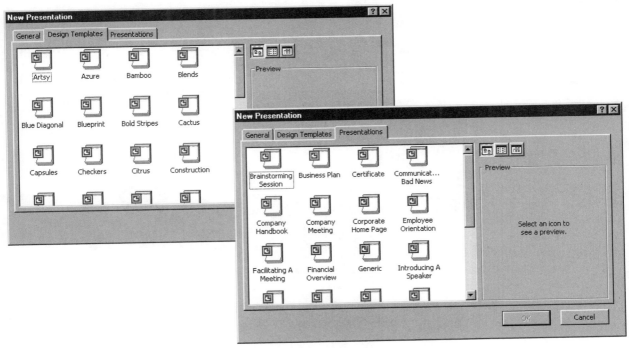

With this background in place, you're ready to proceed to the next section, which introduces you to ways to control the style, placement, and colors of your text elements.

Hands-on Activity: AutoContent Wizard

Use the following procedure to familiarize yourself with the AutoContent Wizard.

1. Start PowerPoint. On the PowerPoint dialog click **AutoContent Wizard**. Then click **OK** to view the opening dialog. Notice that the left part of this dialog outlines the steps used by the AutoContent Wizard.

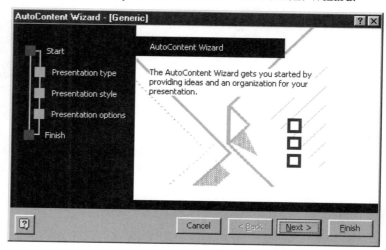

2. Click **Next>** to display the first working dialog.

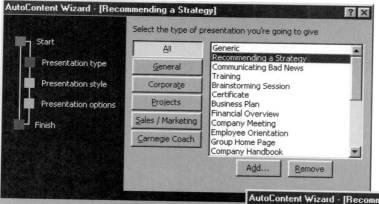

Here, you select the type of presentation you're going to give. The All button displays all types. The other buttons isolate the types that are displayed. Select **All** and **Recommending a Strategy** and then click **Next>**.

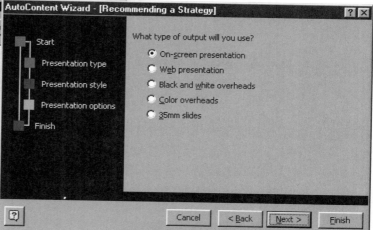

3. Click **On-screen presentation** as the type of output. Then click **Next>**.

4. Type a title for your presentation. You can also put your name and additional descriptive information about the presentation in the footer area of the slide. Click **Next>**.

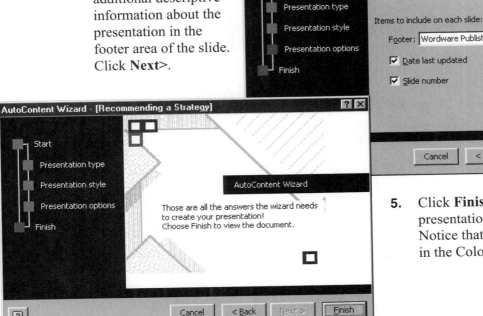

5. Click **Finish** to display your presentation in the Outline view. Notice that a design is preselected in the Color window.

6. Notice that PowerPoint creates an eight-slide presentation for you. The slides already have key points and list suggested information for inclusion in your presentation. At this point you are ready to begin customizing the information to suit your needs.

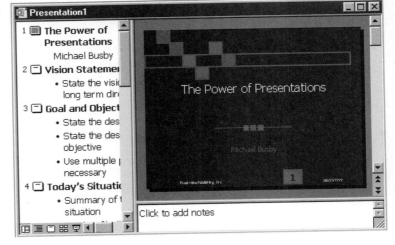

7. Click **Slide View** 📧 to see the first slide of the wizard-produced presentation.

8. Use **File|Exit** (or press **<Alt+F4>**) to exit PowerPoint. Click **No** in response to the Save dialog.

Summary

You can use the AutoContent Wizard to create a rich array of slide presentations. The bulleted lists within each slide of a presentation provide excellent organizational suggestions and key points. Of course you can insert new slides; change the background design, background, and text colors; and add pictures, tables, and more. If you would like to check more presentation types, use File|New and select Blank Presentation.

Working with Text and Lists

Introduction

In this section you learn how to control the look of typed text. This includes placement, font selection, text style, color, and size. Also included is information describing the use and editing of bulleted and numbered lists.

Controlling Text and Lists

Before using PowerPoint's text and list controls, review the Formatting Toolbar and Format Menu items on the companion CD for a review of what you can do with the text and list elements of your slides.

Text Control

The **Format|Fon**t menu selection allows you to change font types, font style, text color, and point size, and add a couple of special effects such as Emboss. Also, you may raise or lower the text above or below surrounding text when faced with special circumstances, such as mathematical formulas.

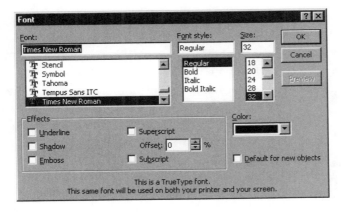

Format|Bullets and Numbering allows you to choose various bulleted and numbered styles, types, colors, and sizes. Using the character button you can even change the characterset bullets and numbers are pulled from. The Color option allows you to set the color of the bullets and numbers. Tired already of the diverse selections available? Then use the Picture button to import your own bullet or numbering image for real diversity.

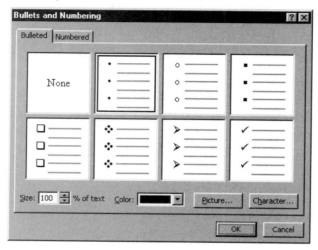

Format|Change Case is useful for making case changes in a standard manner. Sentence case capitalizes each word beginning a sentence. lowercase changes all letters to lowercase. UPPERCASE changes all letters to uppercase. Title Case changes the first letter of each word to uppercase and all other letters to lowercase. tOGGLE cASE inverts the current case of each letter.

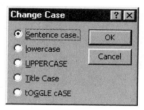

Color Control

You can control the color of text and text object fills and borders using the Formatting and Drawing toolbars and the Menu Bar. The Format menu selection is used to change the color of text by selecting (highlighting) the text and then clicking the Drawing toolbar's Font Color button 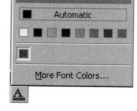. Clicking the More Font Colors button on the Font Color palette accesses many additional colors. A palette of standard colors is available, as is a custom dialog where you can vary standard colors to suit your personal taste.

Hands-on Activity

In this activity you apply a number of the Format controls introduced in this section. Begin by launching PowerPoint. Then open the Sales Points presentation created and saved in Section 59. (A copy of this presentation is supplied on the companion CD.)

1. Select the text area by clicking on the word "Maximize" and pressing **<Ctrl+A>**.

2. Increase the font size to 36 points by clicking the **Increase Font Size** button on the Formatting toolbar.

3. Click the **Bold** button **B** (or press **<Ctrl+B>**) to boldface the selected text.

4. Click the **Format|Colors and Lines** menu selection (click on the double down arrow to see the hidden selections). Pick the **Text Box** tab. Then check **Resize AutoShape to fit text** and uncheck **Word wrap text in AutoShape**.

   This resizes the frame to fit the text.

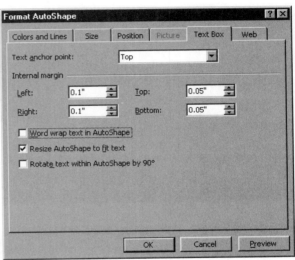

5. Click on **Format|Font** and select **Emboss**. Click on **OK**. Review the text after clicking outside the text area.

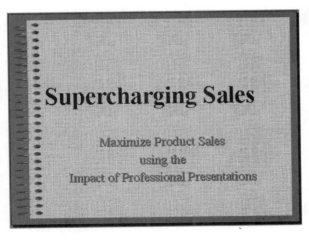

6. Select the text area again by clicking on the word "Maximize" and pressing **<Ctrl+A>**. Select **Format|Alignment** and notice that Center is selected to correspond to the centered text.

7. Use **Format|Change Case**, change the selected text to **UPPERCASE**, and click **OK**. Since the text no longer fits on three lines, change it back to **Sentence case**.

8. Click the Title box. Then use **Format|Colors and Lines** and select the **Colors and Lines** tab. Click the **Fill Color** down arrow, click **Fill Effects**, click the **Texture** tab, select the white marble pattern (second column, second row—notice the texture type name is displayed underneath as you click on each texture type), and click **OK** twice.

9. Click outside the slide. Notice how the title now has a marble texture background (or *fill*).

10. Click the word "Supercharging" and press **<Ctrl+A>** to select all of the text. click **View|Toolbars|Drawing**, then click the **Font Color** button **A** ▾ on the Drawing toolbar. Select **More Font Colors** on the **Standard** tab, pick a dark blue color; and click **OK** to set the text color to dark blue.

Tip: You can use a standard or custom color that is different from those shown on the initial color palette. PowerPoint "remembers" recently used colors and puts them in the opening color palette.

11. Click outside the slide, and see how the text is affected.

12. Click on the next slide button (2 ⬜ Presentation Benefits).

13. Click on the first line of slide 2's body text. Then use **Format|Bullets and Numbering**, pick a different bullet, and click **OK**. Notice how the selected bullet character is used. You may want to put Wingdings in the "Bullets from" box after clicking on Character at the bottom of the **Bullets and Numbering|Bulleted** tab and have some fun selecting off-beat bullets. Try other Wingdings (1,2,3).

14. Click on the title and then click the **Format Painter** button 🖌 on the Standard toolbar.

15. Highlight the first bulleted entry (both lines), then release the mouse button. Notice how the text style of the title is applied to the selected line. Press **<Ctrl+Z>** to undo the last operation.

Tip: The Undo operation, also accessed from the Edit menu, is an important feature to know about. Use this anytime you don't like the result of the previous operation.

16. Click the window **Exit** button (or press **<Alt+F4>**) to exit PowerPoint; do not save the changes.

Summary

As you can see, it is easy to work with the text elements of your slides. You will find that most of PowerPoint's tools are just as easy to use. In the next section you learn how to work with colors and the transitions between slides. When you complete Section 63, you will be well on your way to designing professional-looking presentations.

Working with Colors and Transitions

Introduction

This section shows you how to add snap to your slides with color variations, shading, highlighting, and attractive transitions between slides. The following paragraphs discuss the PowerPoint controls used to modify colors, shading, and transitions.

Background Color Control

In the previous section you learned how to control the color of text and text object fills and borders. You used the Formatting and Drawing toolbars and the Menu Bar. The Format menu selection is also used to color the background of your slides. Recall that the color of text is quickly changed by selecting (highlighting) the text and then clicking the Drawing toolbar's Font Color button 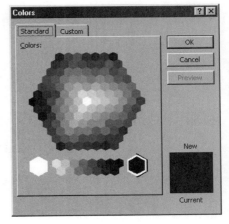. Clicking the More Font Colors option on the Font Color palette accesses many additional colors. A palette of standard colors is available, as is a custom dialog where you can vary standard colors to suit your personal taste.

These two palettes are also available for background coloring. The Format menu selections associated with background color control were listed in the last section. These are the Slide Layout, Slide Color Scheme, and Background selections. Recall that the Slide Layout dialog provides 24 different layouts from which to choose.

Format|Slide Color Scheme—Use this dialog to choose a standard color scheme or to create a custom color scheme of your own. The Standard tab of the Color Scheme dialog offers three choices of schemes. Each scheme shown represents the colors used by that scheme for the particular items displayed. The middle scheme shows black text on a white background and several muted colors used for charting. The three schemes are pretty basic and are useful for getting started, but they are not really eye-catching. But then, eye-catching may not be appropriate for the particular topic and audience. The use of visual stimulation is context sensitive. What may work for

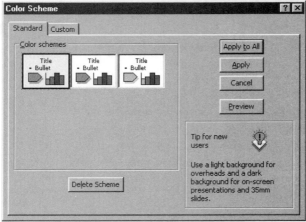

one presentation and audience will not necessarily work for another. Know your audience and your intended purpose.

The Custom tab of the Color Scheme dialog provides an opportunity to enhance your presentations with much more stimulating colors. Here, you can change the colors of any of the items in the Scheme colors list by clicking an item, clicking the Change Color... button, and making a new color selection.

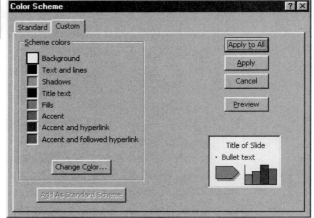

After clicking the Change Color... button a Color dialog appears with a Standard and a Custom tab. The one shown here is the Background Color dialog.

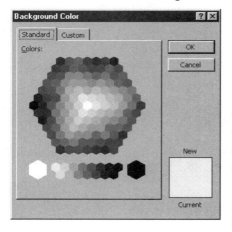

The Standard and Custom tabs are used to change the colors of the feature selected in the Color Scheme dialog. The Standard dialog offers a variety of fixed colors. Just click on the desired color and then click OK.

The Custom dialog lets you adjust the hue, saturation, lumination, and percentage of red, green, and blue of a color. Simply move the cross hair, slide the triangular pointer, or change the numerical values in the spin boxes until you see a color you like.

Once you select your color, use either the Apply or Apply to All button as desired. The Apply button affects the current slide, while Apply to All applies the color scheme to all slides in the current presentation.

Format|Background—Use this dialog to apply a custom background fill to one or all of your slides. Click the down arrow to display more colors or special fill effects.

Format|Apply Design Template—Use this selection to pick a slide design template from a list of 22 different designs.

You can also use the Look In drop-down box to find a presentation or template file. Then, you can apply the format of an existing slide presentation to the current presentation.

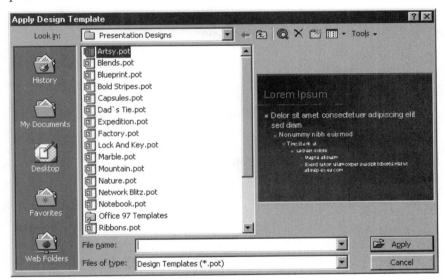

Transition Control

A transition from one slide to the next can be anything from a quick replacement, or *cut*, to an attention-getting dissolve or wipe. For example, a checkerboard dissolve or a horizontal sweep both make for an interesting introduction to the next slide in a series.

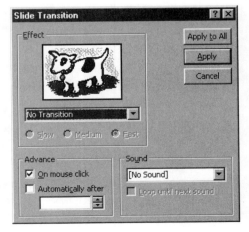

PowerPoint's Slide Transition dialog, which is accessed using the Slide Show|Slide Transition menu selection, offers a list of 41 different transitions. These include wipes, covers, uncovers, strips, checkerboards, dissolves, and more. A Random transition is also included, which randomly picks various effects.

The Sound option allows you to apply sound effects to your presentation when the slide is transitioning. There are 16 included sound effects for emphasizing or entertaining when transitioning to another slide. You may also choose a sound from another source.

You can automatically advance each slide after an allocated period by setting Advance to Automatically after: and specifying the number of seconds to wait. Or, by checking the On Mouse Click option you can control the slide display time by clicking the mouse when you are ready to move on to the next slide.

The amount of time a slide takes to transition to another slide is determined by the Slow, Medium, and Fast radio buttons.

Finally, you can apply the settings to the currently selected slide or you can apply the settings to every slide in the presentation.

Applying a Slide Transition

To apply a slide transition, first display the desired slide in the Slide View. Then click Slide Show|Slide Transition to display the Slide Transition dialog. Click the arrow at the right of the Effect text box to display a list of transitions. Click on the down arrow (or move down with the down arrow) to see the different effects. You can check the effect by watching the preview box. Then set the speed to Slow, Medium, or Fast; again, check the preview box for speed.

If your computer is equipped with a sound card and you want to add sound, pick a sound effect from the Sound pick list. (See Section 66 for more information about adding sound.)

If you are developing a self-running presentation, use the Advance section of the dialog to set the time, in seconds, that the current slide is displayed. When the set time expires, the next slide is displayed. (See Section 68 for more information about self-running presentations.)

Like background colors, slide transitions are also easy to use. The following hands-on activity guides you through the use of both background colors and transitions.

Hands-on Activity

In this activity you use the Sales Points presentation created in Section 59. First you add transitions and change color schemes. Then you run the presentation to see how the changes look. Finally, you save the presentation under a new name. Begin by starting PowerPoint and opening the Sales Points presentation.

1. With the Sales Points presentation displayed in the Normal View, check that slide 1 of 4 is displayed.

2. Use **Slide Show|Slide Transition** and pick the
Box Out effect. Set speed to **Medium**. If you
have a sound card, set Sound to **Drum Roll**.
Leave Advance set to **On mouse click**. Finally,
click **Apply**.

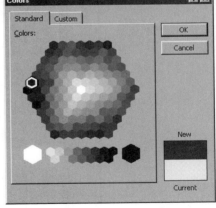

3. Press **<Page Down>** to advance to slide 2.

4. Use **Format|Slide Color Scheme**, pick the
right-hand color scheme, and click **Apply**.

5. Use **Slide Show|Slide Transition**, and pick the
Blinds Horizontal effect, **Medium** speed, and
Whoosh sound. Click **Apply**.

6. Press **<Page Down>** to advance to slide 3.

7. Use **Format|Background**, pick the down arrow, click **Fill Effects**, and then click the
Texture tab. Pick the **Walnut** texture (second column, sixth row) click **OK** then **Apply**.

8. Use **Slide Show|Slide Transition**, and pick the **Checkerboard Down** effect, **Medium**
speed, and **Ricochet** sound. Click **OK**.

9. Press **<Page Down>** to advance to slide 4.

10. Use **Format|Background**, pick the down arrow, and click **More Colors**. Then click the
Standard tab.

11. Pick a dark green swatch (outlined in the adjacent
illustration) and click **OK**.

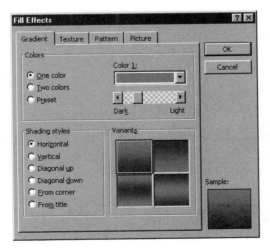

12. Click the down arrow again and then
click **Fill Effect**. Pick the **Gradient**
tab, the **Horizontal** shading style, and
the upper left-hand variant; click **OK**,
then **Apply**.

13. Use **Slide Show|Slide Transition**, and pick the **Cover Right** effect, **Medium** speed, and **Screeching Brakes** sound. Click **OK**.

14. Press **<Ctrl+Home>** to display the first slide. Then click the **Slide Show View** button, and page through the slides by clicking the mouse when you are ready to view the next slide, checking the colors and transitions of each. Then press **<Esc>** to return to the **Slide** view.

15. Use **File|Save As** and save the modified presentation as **Sales Show**.

16. Exit PowerPoint.

Summary

Consider varying the color of each slide to make your presentation more interesting to your audience. You should also vary your transitions for the same reason. With these concepts behind you, you're ready to move to Section 64 where you learn how to add headers and footers to your slides.

Adding Headers and Footers

Introduction

A *header* is one or more text elements contained in the top margin of a document, while a *footer* is one or more text elements contained in the bottom margin. You can add headers and footers to your slides, presentation notes, and audience handouts. Typically, presenters like to include such information as slide numbers, dates, a company name, or a presentation title. In this section you learn how to use the header and footer dialogs.

The Header and Footer Dialogs

The View|Header and Footer menu selection displays the Header and Footer dialogs. There are two dialog tabs: Slide, and Notes and Handouts.

The Slide Dialog

Use the Slide dialog to add a date, slide number, and footer text. The Preview box shows you what's been added. Notice that you can suppress your footer on the title (first) slide by clicking the Don't show on title slide check box.

Click Apply to apply to the current slide; click Apply to All to add to every slide in the current presentation.

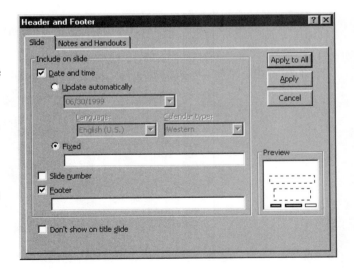

The Notes and Handouts Dialog

Use the Notes and Handouts dialog to add headers and footers to your notes and printed handouts. Notice that this dialog is similar to the Slide dialog, except that it permits you to add a header instead of a footer.

To see the results of this dialog, go to the Notes Pages View, where you can type your presentation notes. Any added headers and footers appear in this view.

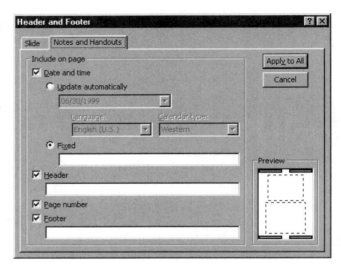

Hands-on Activity

Now that you've learned about the Header and Footer dialogs, it's time to try one out. Begin by launching PowerPoint and opening the Sales Show presentation file saved in the previous section.

1. Use the **View|Headers and Footer** menu selection to open the Header and Footer|Slide dialog.

2. Type the information and check the buttons and check boxes as shown.

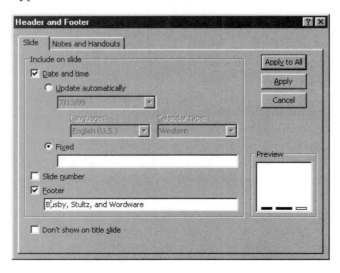

3. Click **Apply to All**. Then use **Format|Apply Design Template**, pick the **Soaring.pot** design, and click **Apply**.

4. Compare your opening slide to the following illustration.

5. Click on each slide's icon in the left margin to display each slide and examine the footer.

6. Press <**Ctrl+Home**> to go to slide 1. Display the Header and Footer|Slide dialog, check the **Don't show on title slide** check box, and click **Apply**.

7. Notice how the footer is removed from the title slide.

8. Use **File|Save As**, type the name **Sales Show B**, and click **Save**.

9. Press <**Alt+F4**> to exit PowerPoint.

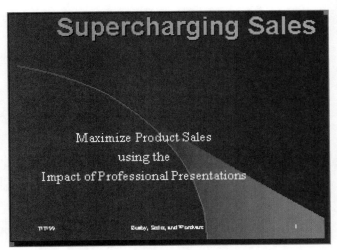

Summary

Now that you know how to add headers and footers and control the colors and shading of your slides, you're ready to begin working with graphics. In the next section you learn how to create and add graphic objects to your slides.

Section 65

Drawing Tools

Introduction

PowerPoint comes with a rich assortment of drawing tools and clip art. When you first open PowerPoint, a Menu Bar and three toolbars are displayed: Standard, Formatting, and Drawing. The Menu Bar, and Standard, Formatting, and Drawing toolbars are shown here. Refer to the companion CD for a concise definition of each menu and toolbar button.

To see the function of each toolbar button, simply slide your cursor over a button and a fly-out label will display descriptive text. Now you can use these buttons to begin adding graphic elements to the displayed slide. Drawing is done in the Slide View, as are all your slide creation and editing tasks. Several of the Drawing toolbar buttons include submenus and dialogs to extend the available features. These buttons include a black down arrow to indicate additional choices. For example, the Draw button Draw ▾ displays many choices if you click on the down arrow. The Draw menu is shown with the Align or Distribute pull-out menu in the illustration here.

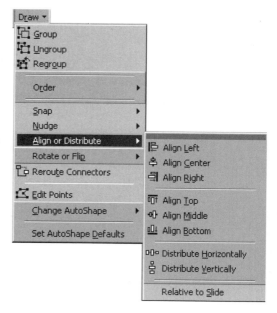

Like many of the Office 2000 menus, individual selections become active when a corresponding object is highlighted. The Draw menu offers many handy choices. Here you can group and ungroup multiple objects, nudge (or move) them, set the snap grid, align, rotate, and flip objects, change the order of how objects are layered (in front or in back), pick autoshapes (special shapes and symbols), and more.

The Snap selection is of particular importance. Objects are positioned (or constrained) by either an invisible grid or by snapping to a vertical or horizontal edge of an adjoining object. You can also use View|Guides to display moveable horizontal and vertical guidelines. These guides are used to align drawing objects in either the horizontal or vertical axis. You can also use the Draw|Align or Distribute feature to align two or more selected objects.

Drawing Tricks and Techniques

Before diving headlong into drawing, there are a few basic drawing techniques that you should know. These are common to the drawing features available in other Office 2000 applications. If you're already an accomplished graphics program user, you can skip to the hands-on activity. If not, take a few minutes to review the following information.

Viewing Guides and Rulers—Use the View|Guides or View|Ruler menu selections to display guidelines or rulers. These can be used as reference tools to align and size objects on a slide.

Drawing Squares and Circles—Squares and circles are created by clicking the corresponding Rectangle or Oval tool. You can constrain a rectangle to a perfect square if you press and hold the Shift key while dragging the square to the desired size. Similarly, you can constrain an oval to a circle by using the Shift key. Additionally, existing rectangles and ovals can be converted to squares and circles by clicking on the object and holding the mouse button down, pressing the Shift key, and then releasing the mouse button. What was previously a rectangle or ellipse becomes a square or circle.

Selecting Objects—Use the Draw|Select Objects tool 🔓 on the Drawing toolbar to select drawing objects. This is accomplished by clicking the Select Objects tool and then clicking the desired object. The object is selected when handles are displayed.

Selecting Multiple Objects—You can select two or more objects by holding down the Shift key as you select individual drawing objects with your mouse. You can also use the Select Objects tool to drag a dashed box around two or more objects. Once selected, they can be moved in unison or grouped as a single item using the Draw|Group selection.

Double click to add clip art

Handles—Handles are squares that are displayed around the perimeter of a selected drawing object at the corners and in the middle. Handles are used to stretch objects. Grab the center top or bottom handle (click on it and hold) and pull it up or down to change the height of an object. Grab a middle side handle (either left or right) to change the width of an object. If you grab a corner handle and pull in or out you will maintain the ratio of width to length, as you change both simultaneously.

If you want to move an object, select it, point to the center or a side (don't grab a handle), and drag the entire object from one location to another.

Text Objects—The Text Box tool ▦ is used to type a text object. Use the Format|Font dialog to control the font, size, and style of the text. These objects can be rotated (see Rotating Objects, below).

Deleting, Cutting, Pasting, and Copying—You can delete an object by selecting it and pressing the Delete key. Cut an object (to the clipboard) by selecting it and pressing Ctrl+X (or use Edit|Cut or the Cut menu button ✂). Copy an object by selecting it and pressing Ctrl+C (or use Edit|Copy or the Copy menu tool ▤). Paste the cut or copied object by pressing Ctrl+V (or use Edit|Paste or the Paste menu tool ▤).

Tip: An alternate way to copy an object is to select it, press Ctrl, and drag and drop the object in a new location. The original object stays in position and a copy is created.

Copying is handy when you create a unique graphic or shape and want to replicate it to another location on the same or another slide. For example, you may create an elongated arrow that designates points of interest or cities on a map. Instead of trying to draw the same size and shape, just copy and paste the original arrow several times and drag each to the desired position.

Grouping and Ungrouping—When you create a drawing item that is made up of two or more elements, you can combine the individual elements using Draw|Group. This lets you select the grouped items as a single object. The group can be dragged, copied, or sent behind other objects. If you wish to change a component part of a grouped item, ungroup it and select and modify the individual element. Then select and group the objects to integrate them back into a single entity.

Sending Backward and Bringing Forward—Use this Draw|Order selection to move drawing objects in front of or behind other drawing objects. For example, if you draw a circle and then surround it with a rectangle, the rectangle, drawn last, covers (and hides) the circle. Just select the rectangle and then click either the Send Backward ▦ or Send to Back ▦ selection. The circle is displayed on top of the rectangle. Send to Back puts the object on the bottom of a stack of objects. Send Backward moves the selected object one layer back.

> Bring to Front
> Send to Back
> Bring Forward
> Send Backward

Rotating Objects—If you want to rotate an object, including a text object created with the Text Box tool, begin by selecting it. Now you can click the Draw|Rotate or Flip selection. Then click one of the Rotate or Flip selections (left, right, vertical, horizontal).

The **Draw|Rotate** or **Flip|Free Rotate** selection is identical to the Free Rotate tool ⟳, which is used for angular rotation. When you click the Free Rotate tool, a filled handle is displayed at each corner of the selected object. Grab and drag the handle up or down until the desired position is achieved. Then release the mouse button and click again to deselect the rotated object.

AutoShapes—Click the AutoShapes tool AutoShapes ▾ to display a variety of shape categories.

Basic Shapes are shown in the adjacent illustration. Click a shape and drag it to the desired size on the current slide. Once it is placed, you can adjust the shape by dragging a handle.

Fill Color—The Fill Color tool 🪣 ▾ operates on solid objects like rectangles, ovals, and autoshapes. This tool operates identically to other color tools, and offers shading, textures, and patterns. Section 63 introduced you to the use of Fill Color, More Fill Colors (Standard and Custom), and Fill Effects.

Lines—The Line Color, Line Style, Dash Line, and Arrow Style tools control the appearance of lines. First, select the desired object. Then use the Line Color tool 🖌 ▾ to change the line color. Use the Line Style tool ≡ to set the thickness. Use the Dash Line ▦ and Arrow Style ⇄ tools to change the selected line into either a dashed, dotted, or arrow line.

Shadow and 3-D Effects—These tools are used to add or remove a shadow or 3-D effect to or from a selected object. Shadow colors, directions, and thicknesses are set using the Shadow Settings dialog. Similarly, 3-D colors, directions, tilts, and other attributes are set using the 3-D Settings dialog. Both of these dialogs are shown here.

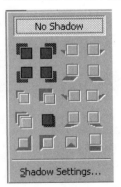

WordArt—WordArt is available to PowerPoint as it is to the other Office 2000 applications. Just click the Insert WordArt tool to launch the WordArt program.

Scaling—You can scale a selected shape object using the Size tab of the Format AutoShape dialog, accessed from the Format menu (Format|Format AutoShape|Size). Under Scale, enter the percentages you want in the Height and Width boxes. You can also check the Lock aspect ratio check box to maintain the exact height-to-width proportions.

The best way to learn to use the drawing tools and techniques described above, as well as some of the common shape tools, is to put them to work. In the hands-on activity that follows, you familiarize yourself with a number of these tools and how they are applied.

Hands-on Activity

In this activity you add several drawing objects to a blank slide. You make use of many of PowerPoint's drawing tools and the Draw menu. Begin by launching PowerPoint.

1. Close the opening dialogs. Then, from a blank PowerPoint screen, click the **New** button on the Standard toolbar.

2. Select **Blank Presentation** from the New Presentation dialog.

3. Select the Blank slide layout (third row, fourth column) from the New Slide dialog and click **OK**.

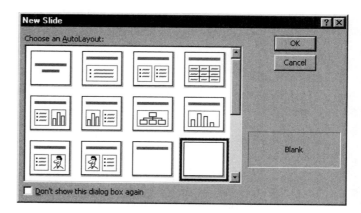

4. Verify that the Drawing toolbar is displayed at the bottom of your screen. If it is not, use **View|Toolbars** and click the **Drawing** selection.

Note: In the remaining steps, illustrations of the drawing progress are included to guide your work. Your drawing objects should resemble the illustrations, although they may not be exact. To display the finished slide created by the author load the Draw.ppt file from the companion disk.

5. Use the **Rectangle** tool ▣ to draw a rectangle. Then select the rectangle object, hold down the **<Ctrl>** key, and drag a second above the first.

6. Now use the **Rectangle** tool to draw a square, pressing <**Shift**> as you drag to constrain the shape to a perfect square. Release the mouse, then the <**Shift**> key when the square is finished.

7. Select all three objects by dragging a selection line around them. Then use the **Fill Color** tool and set the fill to **White**.

8. Use **AutoShapes|Stars and Banners|5-Point Star** to place a star in the center of the square. Drag it to a size and position similar to that shown here.

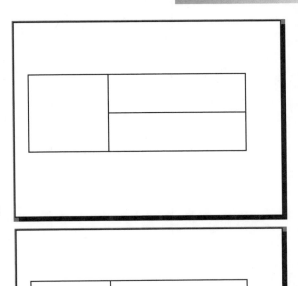

9. Click the square and use the **Fill Color** tool to fill it with blue.

10. Click the bottom rectangle and use the **Fill Color** tool's More Fill Colors dialog to fill it with red.

11. Click the star and use the **Fill Color** tool to fill it with white.

12. Click the star, press <**Shift**> and then click the square so that they are both selected. Use the **Draw|Align or Distribute|Align Middle** tool to center the star in the square.

13. Deselect the objects (click away from them) and then click the star. Use **Draw|Order|Send Backward** to put the star behind the blue field.

14. Deselect the star and then click the square. Use **Draw|Order|Send to Back** to put the star back on top of the square.

15. Use **AutoShapes|Callouts|Rounded Rectangular Callout** (first row, second column) and drag the callout shape as shown.

16. Use the **Fill Color** tool to fill the callout with white.

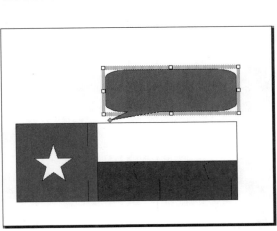

17. Click the **Text Box** tool and insert a text box in the center of the callout as shown. Type **Texas Flag** in the center of the text box.

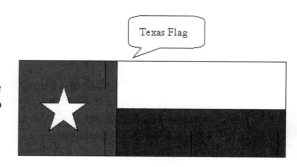

18. With the text box selected, use the **Line Style** tool ≡ and click **More Lines** to display the Format Text Box dialog. Verify that **No Fill** and **No Line** are displayed and click **OK**.

19. Click on the text and press **<Ctrl+A>** to select it. Click the **Bold** button **B** on the Formatting toolbar to change the text to boldface.

20. Compare your completed drawing to the following illustration.

21. Continue experimenting with other drawing tools. For example, draw a line, change the thickness, and add an arrowhead. Draw an oval and a circle. Experiment with the connector AutoShapes. Experiment with Fill Color|Fill Effects|Texture and Pattern. When finished, press **<Alt+F4>** to exit PowerPoint. Do not save the activity. Remember, you can open the Draw.ppt file supplied on the companion CD to see the results of steps 1 through 20.

Summary

Now that you can draw objects, you can add local maps, organizational charts, and similar elements to your slides. In the next section you learn how to use animation features and sound to add even more impact to your presentations.

Animation and Sound

Introduction

You've probably seen overhead transparency presentations in which the presenter guided the audience through key points by covering the slide with a sheet of paper and then revealing each point one at a time. Or, you've seen slides with an arrow next to each point being discussed. You can achieve the same effects using the selections available in PowerPoint's Slide Show menu. Here you'll find a wide range of Animation Settings tools that even include sounds. You can use Insert|Picture and Insert|Movies and Sounds to add clip art and movies that are stored on your CD or the web. Therefore, you can improve immensely on these manual techniques. Instead of uncovering each point, you can add each text element to your slide with the click of a mouse or a keypress, or using preset timing. Instead of just popping up, one at a time, you can use special effects. Each point can slide, wipe, or dissolve onto the slide. Prior points can change color or be hidden.

You can also add a column of arrows to highlight each statement on your slide one at a time, again with a simple mouse click or using preset timing. In addition to interesting visual effects, you can also add sound effects and even "movies." For example, the title might roar across the screen accompanied by the sound of screeching brakes, a ricocheting bullet, or a cash register bell. You can click on an archery target and watch an arrow hit the bull's-eye. These effects, and more, are accomplished using the Slide Show menu in conjunction with the Insert|Movies and Sounds menu selection and the accompanying dialogs.

Preset Animation

The quickest way to animate the paragraphs of a slide is to use Slide Show|Preset Animation. After applying a preset animation effect to one or more entities on a slide, you can use the Custom Animation selection to set timing, sound, and other controls. To make your text build one point at a time, select each text entry and then use Slide Show|Preset Animation to apply an effect to the selected entity. Repeat for the remaining entries on the slide.

Use Custom Animation to display the Custom Animation dialog described next. This dialog lets you apply a number of additional effects. The dialog can also be accessed using the Slide Show|Custom Animation menu selection.

Tip: Animation treats each line of text that ends with a hard carriage return as a separate entity. You should let PowerPoint wrap the text for you. If you must terminate a line, use <Shift+Enter> to end the lines. This inserts a "soft return" and the animation is applied to all lines in the passage in unison.

Custom Animation

The Custom Animation menu selection is also easy to use. Just follow these general steps:

1. Select a text, drawing, picture, or chart object (such as the title or body text or an arrow).

2. Use Slide Show|Custom Animation ![icon] or click the Animation Effects button ![icon] on the Formatting toolbar to display the Custom Animation dialog.

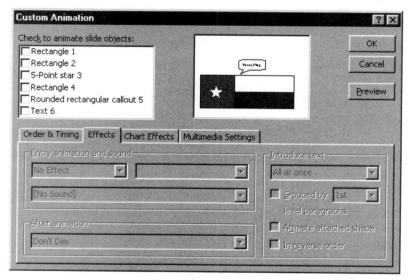

The Animation Effects button ![icon] displays the Animation Effects toolbar. Here you can access the Custom Animation dialog or apply animation effects by clicking.

3. Pick the Slide Show|Custom Animation dialog to add special effects. If you have a sound card, you can accompany your animated text with sound effects. We will look at the Custom Animation dialog tabs.

Order and Timing

The Order & Timing tab is used to select those objects that are animated and those that are not. The animation order is set by selecting an animated object and clicking the up or down arrows. The Start animation section of the Order & Timing dialog gives you two options. First, you can start the animation effect of the selected object upon a mouse click. You can also start animation automatically after a specified number of seconds. Just enter a time value, in seconds, in the spin box. Use the Preview button to see the animation settings in operation. You can make adjustments and then preview the results until you are satisfied with your settings.

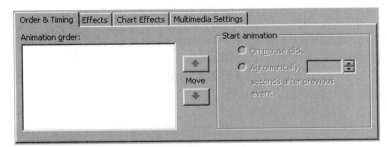

Animation order—this section is used to set the order in which the objects appear on the slide. Just select an object and use the arrows to position it.

Start animation—Use this feature to determine when the animation effects start. Animation may start upon the click of a mouse button or it can be delayed after a mouse click to allow some time for the viewer to contemplate the slide.

Effects

The Effects tab is quite easy to use once you understand what each item does. Following is a description of each of the controls.

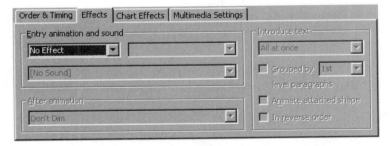

Entry animation and sound—Use the pull-down boxes to select the desired animation effect and sound from the pick lists. Click the Preview button to see the results.

After animation—Here you use a pull-down box to leave the previous object displayed, hide it, or change its color when the next object is displayed.

Introduce text—This section controls the way a text object enters the slide: all at once, by word, or by letter. If you check the In reverse order check box, the text enters the slide backwards, beginning with the last word or character and proceeding in reverse order until the first word or character has entered the slide.

Chart Effects

The Chart Effects tab is used with slides that contain a chart. You can use the Chart and Text slide template to put a chart on a slide or add one with the Insert|Chart menu selection. Descriptions of the features available on this dialog follow.

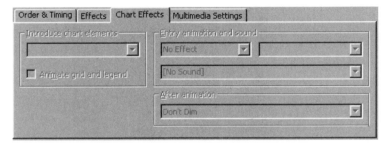

Introduce chart elements—Here you can control how each of the elements of the selected chart are displayed. For example, you may want to introduce each series one by one. You can use the Animate grid and legend check box to add animation to these elements as well.

Entry animation and sound—The two sections of this part of the dialog are used to control the animation effect and the sound effect used by the chart. Just select an item from the drop-down boxes. Then click the Preview button to see the results.

After animation—This section is identical to the After animation section of the Effects dialog. Use the pull-down box to pick an effect, such as dimming, hiding, or changing the color of the previous object as the next one is displayed.

Multimedia Settings

This dialog is used with media clip (or "movie") objects. These objects are inserted using the Insert|Movies and Sounds menu selection. You can also use the Text and Media Clip template of the New Slide dialog.

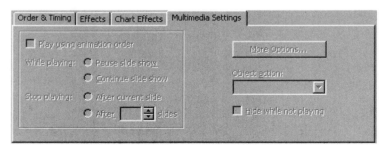

The Multimedia Settings dialog is used to control the operation of the selected video clip object. The parts of this dialog are presented in the list that follows.

Play using animation order—Check here if you want the clip to play in the order set in the Animation order list.

While playing—Use the option buttons to control animation operations of other slide objects while the media clip runs.

Stop playing—Use these option buttons to control the way the media clip stops, i.e., either after the current slide or after a specified number of slides.

More Options—Click this button to display the Play Options dialog. Two sections are available on this dialog. Use the Movie and sound options section with your video and sound clips. You can loop the selected clip continuously until stopped. You can also rewind it when it is done playing. The Play CD audio track section is used to set the start and end points of the CD by track and time within the tracks. The playing time and the filename are also displayed on this dialog.

The Action Buttons dialog is among the available options. Use this dialog to put an action button on your slide. Just click one on the dialog and drag it onto your slide as you would a drawing object. Typical buttons include Forward or Next, Back or Previous, Beginning, End, etc.

Action Settings

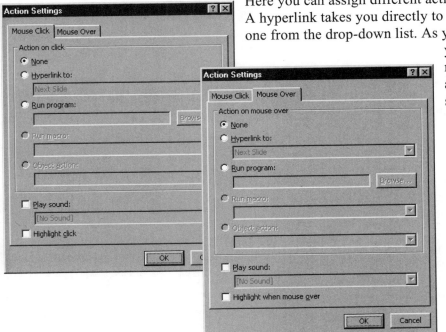

Here you can assign different actions to your action buttons. A hyperlink takes you directly to a selected item. Just pick one from the drop-down list. As you can see by the dialog, you can run a program, run a macro, perform an action on a slide object, or play a sound.

Animation Preview

Use this Slide Show menu selection to preview the animation settings of the current slide. This is a quick way to determine the current settings and serves as a helpful tool during animation development.

Determining What to Animate

Move through each slide to determine what should be animated and what should remain static. Remember, you must click the mouse or press a key to advance each animated element unless you checked Start When Previous Build Ends. However, this effect could display elements faster than you can talk about them. Because PowerPoint lets you animate paragraphs, words, and even letters, it's easy to get carried away. You may find yourself constantly clicking the mouse, which becomes quite distracting during an important presentation. Sounds are also detractors. Therefore, use animation for emphasis, not entertainment. Overdoing animation tends to emphasize everything, causing important points to be overlooked. Just remember that over-animated presentations look amateurish and may result in an unwanted sensory overload on the part of your audience.

Hands-on Activity

In this activity you add animation and sound to the Sales Show B presentation you saved in Section 64. Begin by launching PowerPoint.

1. Open the file Sales Show B last saved in Section 64. (Also on the companion CD.)

2. In the Normal View, move down to slide 2 of 4 by clicking on the slide 2 icon (2 ☐) in the left margin.

3. Click on **Slide Show|Custom Animation**. On the Custom Animation dialog click the **Text 2** option box in the **Check to animate slide objects** text box and ensure the **Start animation - On mouse click** option button is selected.

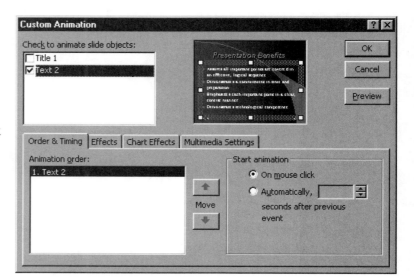

4. Click the **Effects** tab. Put gray in the **After animation** box using the **More Colors** selection. Set up the rest of the dialog as shown in the adjacent illustration.

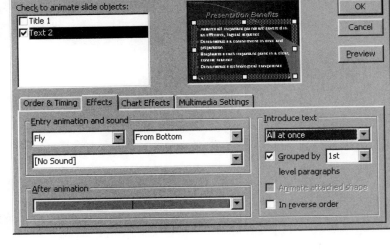

5. Click **Slide Show|Animation Preview** to see the effect. Then close the Preview window.

6. Click the **Slide Show** view. Use mouse clicks to see the animation effects. When the second slide appears, notice how each point dims as a new one is introduced. Remember that you can also hide these points depending on how the Custom Animation dialog is adjusted.

7. Use **File|Save As** and save the file as **Sales Show C**.

8. Press **<Alt+F4>** to exit PowerPoint.

Summary

Now that you've added animation to your slide show knowledge, you're ready to give dazzling presentations. But there's still more. In the next section you learn how to import objects from other application programs, such as Word tables, Excel worksheets, and clip art.

Importing Objects from Other Applications

Introduction

As with other Microsoft Office products, you can import objects from other programs right into your presentation slides. For example, you can insert clip art, media clips, and drawings created by other programs. You can also insert financial data from an Excel worksheet and tables from a Word document. And you can call on Microsoft Graph to create and insert charts into your presentations. Once a presentation is finished, you may want to convert it to a text document. PowerPoint also provides the ability to export the text content of your slides to Microsoft Word. This section shows you how to accomplish all of these powerful capabilities.

The Tool Set

Like many controls, PowerPoint gives you alternative ways to insert objects from external resources. You can use the Insert menu or buttons on the Standard toolbar. Refer to Section 57 for an illustration of the Insert menu and the Standard toolbar. Notice that the bottom group of selections on the Insert menu provides options for inserting a variety of items. You can insert slides from existing presentations using Insert|Slides from Files and Insert|Slides. Selecting Insert|Object displays the Insert Object dialog from which you may select Microsoft Excel data and many other objects for insertion into your presentation.

There are a few buttons used for inserting objects on the toolbar, as well. From left to right, beginning with the Insert|Hyperlink button ![icon], you can insert a Word table ![icon], a chart ![icon], or a new slide ![icon] (from this or another presentation). The following paragraphs guide you through the operation of each of these features.

Clip Art

Office 2000's clip art library is available to PowerPoint as well as the other Office 2000 applications. The Office 2000 CD contains clip art, media clips, and other resources. Also, you may download material from the Internet to give you access to a large collection of clip art, media clips, and other resources over the World Wide Web.

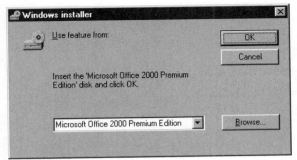

You have a good assortment of resources from which to choose. To insert clip art, display a slide in the Slide View. The first time you use the Insert|Picture|Clip Art menu selection, the following dialog may be displayed if you have not previously installed clip art. Place your Office disk in the CD-ROM drive and click OK.

If clip art was previously installed, you will see the following dialog. There are 16 categories from

which to choose an array of clip art. Also, you can designate a new category by clicking on the New Category image and specifying a name for the category in the subsequent dialog. Then, using the Import Clips feature located at the top of the dialog, you can customize to your heart's content.

Also, choose Insert|Picture|From File and look in the C:\Program Files\Microsoft Office\Clipart directory to find additional clip art. This is an example Insert Picture dialog looking in the Popular subdirectory of the

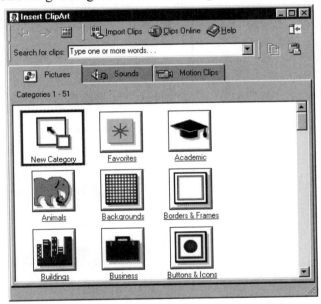

C:\Program Files\Microsoft Office\Clipart directory. Of course, you may have more clip art elsewhere on your computer.

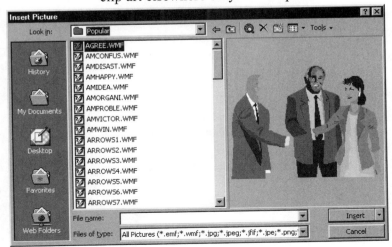

Pick the clip art, picture, sound, or video clip of your choice and click Insert. The selected object is placed on your slide.

Notice that this dialog includes a list of categories and a clip art gallery. Simply select a category, then scroll through the gallery until you find the clip art you want. Click the Preview button to see the image full size. Click the picture and then Insert, or double-click the picture itself to insert it on the current slide. Once it's on the slide, you can drag it, scale it, or even cut and paste it as with other objects.

Excel Worksheets

There are two ways to insert an Excel worksheet onto a slide. Both are described in the following general procedures.

Direct Method:

1. Place your cursor where you want the worksheet to go. Click Insert|Object and select Microsoft Excel Worksheet. Click on OK. Notice you can also insert an Excel chart using this same procedure. An Excel worksheet is now displayed.

2. Enter the information in the cells, including standard Excel formulas. Note that you can drag the borders of the worksheet object to see more cells.

3. Drag the edges of the worksheet object so that only the completed cells are displayed (in other words, hide the unused cells).

4. Click away from the worksheet to display the worksheet data. This also redisplays the PowerPoint toolbars and hides the Excel borders.

5. Now you can drag and scale the worksheet object using the handles. You can edit worksheet values by double-clicking on the worksheet object.

Cut and Paste Method:

1. Launch the Excel program and display a worksheet.

2. Select the cells you want inserted into a slide and press <Ctrl+C> to copy them.

3. Launch PowerPoint (or switch to it if it is already running) and display a blank slide.

4. Place the cursor at the intended location to insert the worksheet. Press <Ctrl+V> to insert the worksheet object.

5. Drag and scale the worksheet object as necessary.

   Use either of the above techniques to insert Excel worksheet data into your presentations.

Tip: You can use Edit|Paste Special if you want the worksheet object linked to the source file. When this is done, changes to the source worksheet automatically update the worksheet object on your PowerPoint slide. This is a good illustration of object linking and embedding, or *OLE*.

Word Tables

Like Excel worksheets, there are also two ways to insert a Word table onto a slide: the direct and cut and paste methods. Although similar, the cut and paste method varies, as you can convert the table to an editable PowerPoint picture object. Examine both methods in the following general procedures.

Direct Method:

1. Click the Insert Microsoft Word Table button ⊞. Set the number of columns and number of rows to the desired number of rows and columns in the Insert Table dialog.

2. Click on OK.

3. Type your tabular information into the cells of the table. You can add more rows and columns to the table by selecting an entire row or column and then copying and pasting it (just like in Word). Another way to add rows is to click on the last row and column and then press <Tab>.

4. When you finish typing your tabular data, display it properly by clicking away from the table. This also redisplays the PowerPoint toolbars and hides the Word table rulers.

5. Now you can drag and scale the table object using the handles. You can edit tabular values by double-clicking on the table object.

Cut and Paste Method:

1. Launch Microsoft Word and display a table document.

2. Select the cells you want inserted into a slide and press <Ctrl+C> to copy them.

3. Launch PowerPoint (or switch to it if it is already running) and display a blank slide.

4. Press <Ctrl+V> to insert the table object.

5. Double-click on the table object. Press and hold <Shift> and drag the handles as necessary to crop out (or remove) the extra space around the table. Release Shift.

6. Drag the handles to resize (scale) the pasted table. Then click off the table to remove the displayed table borders.

7. Drag and scale the table object as necessary. If an exterior rule is missing, use the Drawing toolbar's Line tool to add a new one.

Use either of the above techniques to insert Word tables into your presentations.

Tip: As with worksheets, you can also use Edit|Paste Special if you want the table object linked to the source file. You can insert it as either a Word document or a picture. If inserted as a picture, you may want to group it, as the table may be made up of hundreds of individual line and text objects. For more information, see the tip following the cut and paste method of the Excel worksheets paragraph.

Microsoft Graph

Microsoft Graph 2000 is a companion program that lets you create and insert charts into your slides, as well as into other Office 2000 applications. The general procedure for creating a chart is given in the following steps.

1. Click the Insert Chart button on the Standard toolbar. A data table is displayed, with a graph behind it. Alternately, you can click on Insert|Object|Microsoft Graph 2000 Chart and click on OK.

2. Type the values in the table; check the displayed result by clicking the View Datasheet button on the Standard toolbar (or use View|Datasheet from the menu).

3. Go between the table and the chart using the View Datasheet button (or View|Datasheet) until you've typed all necessary values.

4. Use the Chart toolbars to control the appearance of your charts. Toolbar selections unique to Microsoft Graph are described below:

View—Move between the chart and datasheet views.

Insert—Insert titles, data labels, legends, axes, and gridlines.

Format—Format control for fonts, numbers, object placement, column widths, chart types, and 3-D views.

Tools—Adjust Microsoft Graph default settings using the Options dialog.

Data—Switch between series in rows or series in columns (chart orientation); choose to include or exclude selected cells in the chart.

Chart—Select a different chart type, or use Chart Options to access a variety of chart features including titles, axes, gridlines, and legends.

Window—Open a new window or arrange, fit, or cascade existing windows.

The Standard toolbar buttons unique to Microsoft Graph are described below:

(first row)

Chart Area—Select the chart element you want to change.

Format Chart Area—Formats the selected chart item.

Import File—Imports a selected range of data, an entire data sheet, or a file.

View Database—Displays the datasheet window where data is entered and/or formatted.

(second row)

By Row—Plots chart data series from data across rows.

By Column—Plots chart data series from data down columns.

Data Table—Displays data series values below the chart in a grid.

Chart Type—Changes the chart type for an individual data series, a chart type group, or an entire chart.

Category Axis Gridlines—Hides or shows category gridlines in charts.

Value Axis Gridlines—Hides or shows value axis gridlines in chart.

Legend—Adds a legend to the right of the plot area. Resizes the plot area to accommodate the legend. If a legend is already present, clicking this button will remove the legend.

Drawing—Hides or displays the Drawing toolbar.

5. Use the buttons as shortcuts to the menu items. The purpose of each button is described by a fly-out label.

6. Click away from the chart when it is ready. This displays the chart and redisplays the PowerPoint menus and toolbars.

7. To change the data or appearance of your chart, just double-click the chart object to return to the Microsoft Graph environment.

Inserting Movies and Sound

Media clips, sound, and CD-based audio objects are quickly inserted using the Insert|Movies and Sounds menu.

The Movie from Gallery and Sound from Gallery selections use the same dialog that is used to insert clip art and pictures. Be sure that the Office 2000 CD is inserted in your CD-ROM drive, as a number of media clip and sound resources are available there. The Movie from File and Sound from File selections display dialogs in which you select folder and filenames.

The Play CD Audio Track option displays the dialog shown here.

This dialog operates with a standard audio CD plugged into your CD-ROM drive. It is ideal for background music or other sound effects.

Record Sound is used to make a recording of an audio source such as a tape or CD player or a microphone.

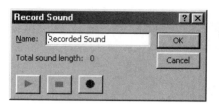

Now that you have some ideas about how PowerPoint works with external objects, it's time to try the hands-on activity so you can actually see how easy it is to embed these objects into your slides.

Hands-on Activities

Creating Slides

In this activity you create four blank slides. As each is created you insert clip art, an Excel worksheet, a Word table, and a Microsoft Graph chart. Begin by launching PowerPoint and starting a blank presentation.

1. Click the Blank slide template (third row, fourth column) in the New Slide dialog and click **OK**.

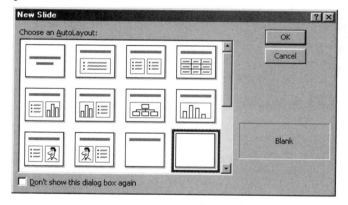

2. Click the **Insert|Picture|Clip Art** button on the Standard toolbar to display the Insert ClipArt dialog.

3. Go to the Map category and click the **World** map picture. (If you don't have this, use another.)

4. Click the **Insert** button and the clip art is inserted onto the slide. Drag and scale the clip art object to a size suitable for viewing on your monitor.

5. Click the **Insert|New Slide** button on the Standard toolbar, pick the **Blank** slide, click **OK**, and notice that slide 2 is added.

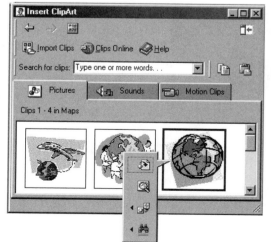

6. Click **Insert|Object** and select **Microsoft Excel Worksheet**; drag a 4 x 4 sheet. Then type the labels, numbers, and formulas as shown.

Category	1998	1999	Total
Sales	125	130	255
Expenses	100	110	210
Net profit	25	20	45

7. Select (or drag across) the labels in column A and row 1 and click the **Bold** button. Select the cells on the Expenses row (row 3, columns A through D) and click the **Borders** button to add an underline. Select row 1, columns A through D and click the **Borders** button again.

8. Click away from the worksheet. Drag and scale the worksheet object into position so that it resembles the following illustration.

Category	**1998**	**1999**	**Total**
Sales	125	130	255
Expenses	100	110	210
Net profit	25	20	45

9. Click the **Insert|New Slide** button on the Standard toolbar, pick the **Blank** slide, click **OK**, and notice that slide 3 is added.

10. Click the **Insert|Table** button ; set the number of rows to **4** and the number of columns to **4**; type the information as shown. Then select the entire table with **<Alt+A, A>** and set the font size to **28**.

Year	High	Low	Average
1997	108	4	76
1998	101	21	73
1999	99	16	75

Tip: In step 11 the column and row labels are set to bold. In step 12 you apply an AutoFormat to the table. This replaces existing format settings with those applied by the new format. Step 11 is simply for practice.

11. Select the column labels and click the **Bold** button **B** , then click the **Italics** button *I* . Then click the row labels and click the **Bold** and **Italics** buttons again.

12. Highlight the data fields, then click on the **Center Text** button .

13. Click away from the table. Drag and scale the table object into position so that it resembles the following illustration.

Year	*High*	*Low*	*Average*
1997	108	4	76
1998	101	21	73
1999	99	16	75

14. Click the **Insert|New Slide** menu selection on the Standard toolbar, pick the **Blank** slide, click **OK**, and notice that slide 4 is added.

15. Click the **Insert|Chart** button; notice that Microsoft Graph is launched and a data sheet is displayed.

16. Change the values as shown in the following illustration.

Section64.ppt - Datasheet		A	B	C	D	E	
		1st Qtr	2nd Qtr	3rd Qtr	4th Qtr		
1 📊	High	82	108	101	87		
2 📊	Low	4	44	49	29		
3 📊	Average	68	78	76	69		
4							

17. Click **Chart|Chart Type** menu selection. In the Standard Types folder of the Chart Type dialog, choose **Line**. Then click away from the data sheet. Drag and scale your chart so that it resembles the following illustration.

Note: To change the chart lines from the light-colored default colors to black, I double-clicked on the chart, then clicked on each line in turn. When a line was selected, I clicked on Fill Color and selected black. Now the lines are black but the color of the circles, rectangles, etc., designating each line remain unchanged. But you will only see black on this page as it is not printed in color.

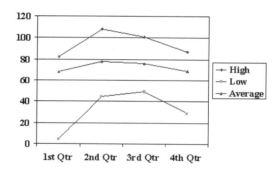

18. Press **<Ctrl+Home>**. Then start the Slide Show view and page through the four slides.

19. Use **File|Save**, give the slide show the name **Objects**, and click **Save**.

Using Cut and Paste to Create Slides

If you want to learn how to cut and paste a Word table or Excel worksheet into a PowerPoint slide, perform the following steps. If not, skip directly to the summary.

1. Leave PowerPoint running; use the Windows Explorer to launch the Monthly Utilities document copied from the CD to the \MSOffice\Files subdirectory.

2. Click inside the table. Then use **Table|Select Table** to select the entire table.

3. Press **<Ctrl+C>** to copy the table. Then use **File|Exit** to exit Word.

4. Click the **PowerPoint** button on the taskbar. Press **<Ctrl+End>** to display the last slide.

5. Click **Insert New Slide** and add new blank slide 5 of 5 to your presentation.

6. Press **<Ctrl+V>** to paste the table on the slide.

7. Use **View|Toolbars** and activate the Picture toolbar. Click the **Crop** tool and drag the right side of the table toward the center to remove the excessive blank space. Then hide the Picture toolbar.

8. Center the table on the slide and click away from the table.

9. Now use the Windows Explorer to launch the Monthly Utilities worksheet copied from the CD to the \MSOffice\Files subdirectory.

10. Drag (select) cells A1 through F14. Press **<Ctrl+C>** to copy the selected range of cells.

11. Click the **PowerPoint** button on the taskbar.

12. Click **New Slide** and add new blank slide 6 of 6 to your presentation.

13. Use **Edit|Paste Special** to display the Paste Special dialog. Click the **Paste** option button. Then select **Microsoft Excel Worksheet Object** and click **OK**.

14. Drag the handles to enlarge and center the worksheet on the slide. Click away from the worksheet to remove the handles.

Tip: The gridlines are displayed if Excel's Gridlines option is selected.

15. Press **<Ctrl+S>** to save the added slides with your presentation.

16. Press **<Alt+F4>** to close PowerPoint.

This concludes the activity. Note that you could have easily added background colors, textures, shading, and transitions using the skills you learned in previous sections. However, these additions would have taken considerably more steps. If you would like to exercise these skills, feel free to reopen the Objects presentation and begin adding title text, backgrounds, and transitions.

Summary

In this section you learned how to integrate objects created by other applications into your slide presentations. This is particularly helpful when presenting financial data and information from databases, where worksheets and document tables make the manipulation and calculation of the involved data easy. In the next section you learn how to create and start self-running presentations.

Automating Your Presentations

Introduction

If you plan to create a self-running presentation or demonstration, it's important to prepare your slide presentation with this in mind. Design each slide to communicate your key points unattended. Add interesting transitions between slides, mix your background colors and shading, insert interesting graphic elements, and consider animating paragraphs and arrows wherever appropriate. Set slide display times so that your audience has ample time to digest the information. However, don't make the times so long that the viewing audience becomes bored and walks away. You can even record and add narration and music if you like.

Setting Times

Recall that the Slide Transition dialog, accessed through Slide Show|Slide Transition, lets you set slide transition effects as well as slide timing. The default setting is to advance only on mouse click. However, if you are preparing a self-running presentation, click Automatically after and enter a value in the seconds box. This value controls the amount of time that the current slide remains on the screen. When the time is up, a new slide is displayed.

Also recall that the Order & Timing tab of the Custom Animation dialog (accessed from the Slide Show|Custom Animation menu) lets you set the timing of individual objects on each slide.

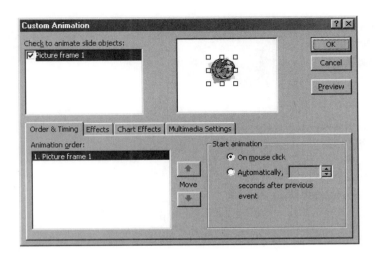

The Effects tab of the Custom Animation dialog, accessed with the Slide Show menu, is used to select different visual and sound effects of each selected slide object.

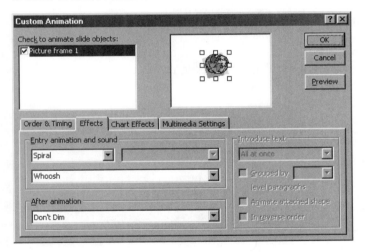

Setting Sounds

The Sound section of the Slide Transition dialog adds a selected sound as the current slide is displayed on your screen.

Here, you can pick No sound, choose a sound from the pick list, or, if you choose Loop until next sound, you may want to pick Stop Previous Sound. You can also load sound from a sound (.wav) file from the Windows\Media directory, the Office 2000 CD, or one that you recorded yourself.

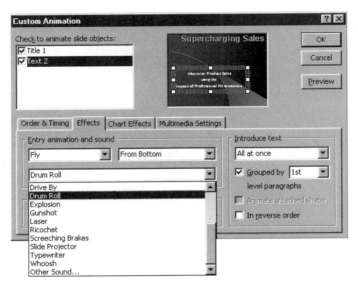

Sounds are applied to individual slide objects using the Custom Animation dialog's Effects tab. As with the slide sound itself, you can use the Entry animation and sound section to pick a sound.

More Slide Show Dialogs

The Slide Show menu features a number of useful selections that access helpful dialogs. These are at the top of the Slide Show menu. The purpose of several of these menu items is summarized in the list that follows.

View Show—Use this selection to run your presentation. Press <Esc> to exit the slide show.

Rehearse Timings—This selection lets you run the show and set the timings by clicking the different buttons on the following dialog.

Here, you can start the timing over by clicking Repeat. Use the Pause or Next buttons as necessary during the rehearsal. Notice that the rehearsal time is displayed. When done, a dialog is displayed that lets you apply the rehearsed times to each slide, and hence the overall show.

This powerful feature takes the guesswork out of your timing and gives you total control of your presentation. If, after all times are set, you want to readjust the timing, simply use Rehearse Timings again and change and save the new settings. You can save your rehearsal timings or choose to cancel them.

Record Narration—This dialog lets you record narration as you rehearse the slide presentation. Think of it as a "dress rehearsal." The Settings button lets you set the recording quality and select a filename for your audio clip.

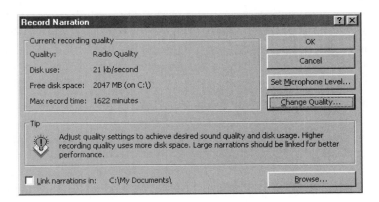

Set Up Show—Here you can set a number of different controls for your slide show. The Show type section is used to set up your presentation for a variety of environments, i.e., either a full screen or in a window. You can also select Loop continuously until 'Esc' to repeat the presentation over and over until the Esc key is pressed. This is ideal for in-store or trade show demonstrations. The Show type section also lets you set the presentation to run with or without narration and/or animation.

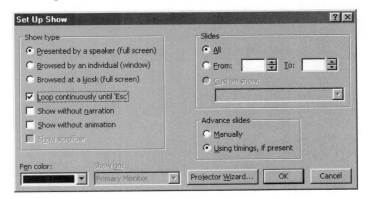

Use the Slides section of the Set Up Show dialog to pick a range of slides, say from two to nine. The Custom show button gives you access to a custom show, which is a variation of a slide show for a particular audience. PowerPoint 2000 permits you to create a presentation within a presentation. Instead of creating multiple, nearly identical presentations for different audiences, you can group together and name the slides that differ and then jump to these slides during your presentation.

For example, you might want to give a presentation to two groups of customers that are interested in different products. The slide show includes slides 1 through 8, which are identical for both groups, and two custom shows, each specific to one of the groups. You can show the first eight slides to both groups and then jump to a custom show named "Group 1" for the first group and to a custom show named "Group 2" for the second group.

You can jump to a custom show with the Action Settings dialog of the Slide Show menu. Then set a hyperlink to the show. Or, during a presentation, you can right-click, point to Go on the shortcut menu, point to Custom Show, and then click on the desired show. After you create a custom show, you can edit it by adding or removing slides from the show.

Use the Advance slides section of the Set Up Show dialog to set the way slides are advanced, using either preset timing or manual advance. Finally, you can set the Pen color using this dialog. A pen is available when slide shows are run. The pen is controlled by your mouse, and is ideal for underlining, checking, and circling important items on the screen. The marks are not a permanent part of the slide, and they disappear as soon as you advance to the next slide. You can change the pen color used to mark your slides. This is important if you are to maintain contrast with the background color scheme of the current slide.

The Projector Wizard, accessed by clicking on the Project Wizard button at the bottom of the Set Up Show dialog, is used to project the slide using a data projector. The wizard guides you effortlessly through the setup procedure.

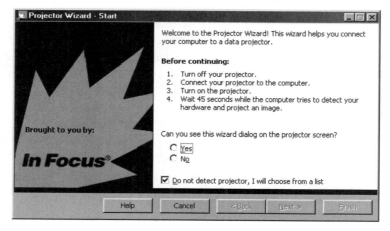

By clicking on Slide Show|Online Broadcast|Setup and Schedule, you can schedule an online broadcast for your audience. Or you can manually start a broadcast immediately by clicking Slide Show|Online Broadcast|Begin Broadcast.

Running the Show

Once you've applied timing, animation effects, and sounds to all the slides in your presentation, use Slide Show|View Show to run the slide show with all of the assigned timing, animation, and sounds.

Now that you are familiar with these powerful features, experience their use with the following hands-on activity.

Hands-on Activity

In this activity you use Sales Show C as a basis for a self-running slide show. First, you add arrows to each of the three points on slide 3. Then you animate the arrows in addition to the three points on slide 4. Begin by launching PowerPoint and opening the Sales Show C presentation in the Slide View. (This presentation was saved in Section 66; a copy is also supplied on the companion CD.)

1. Go to slide 3 of 4. Click **AutoShapes|Block Arrows** on the Drawing toolbar.

2. Select the right pointing arrow ⇨ and drag it so that it covers the first bullet.

3. Press and hold the **<Ctrl>** key and drag two more arrows so that your slide resembles the following illustration. Alternately, just click on the first arrow so it is selected, press **<Ctrl C>**, then **<Ctrl V>**, and move the copied arrow to the correct position.

4. Select each arrow alternately and animate each using the **Animation Effects** button on the Standard toolbar. Apply the Drive In Effect, Flying Effect, and Camera Effect by clicking the corresponding buttons of the Animation Effects dialog.

5. Press **<PgDn>** to advance to slide 4 of 4.

6. Click the text area. Then use the **Slide Show|Preset Animation|Split Vertical Out** menu selection to animate slide 4.

7. Use **Slide Show|Rehearse Timings** and move through the show by clicking the **Next** button on the Rehearsal toolbar (or press **<Enter>** to actuate each event).

Tip: You can reset the timer to zero by clicking the **Repeat** button. Note that you will use your own judgment for the times. To stop the rehearsal, just close the Rehearsal toolbar and you will be asked if you want to save the timings. Click on Yes or No as appropriate. Also, you can pause the timing by clicking the Pause button.

8. After the last event on the last slide, clicking the **Next** button completes the rehearsal. Notice the following dialog.

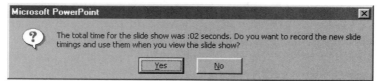

9. Click **Yes** to save the times, or **No** if you want to run through the slides again right away.

10. Now click **Yes** to view the slides in the Slide Sorter View. Here, you can examine the times assigned to each slide in your presentation.

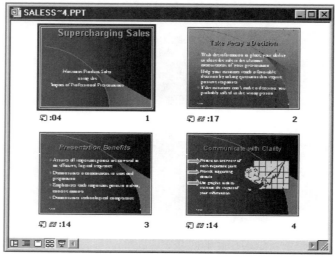

11. Use **Slide Show|Set Up Show**, check the **Loop continuously until 'Esc'** check box, and click **OK**. Now use **Slide Show|View Show** to run the slide show.

12. After watching the resulting slide show for one or two cycles, press **<Esc>** to stop it.

13. Use **File|Save As** and save the animated slide show as **Sales Show D**.

14. Press **<Alt+F4>** to exit PowerPoint.

Summary

Now that you know how to build and run a self-running slide show, you've learned most of the basics. In fact, you now know enough to build impressive presentations for almost any occasion. However, a few more tricks lie in store. In the next section you learn how to make a slide interact with other slides, sounds, programs, and objects by creating hyperlinks to external resources.

Hyperlinks to External Resources

Introduction

You can click an object on a slide and use Slide Show|Action Settings to establish a link between the object and another slide, a program, or another object, such as a picture, Excel worksheet, sound, or media clip. This is ideal for *branching*, which gives you the ability to jump to additional information about a subject in response to requests for more details. For example, you may be announcing a new factory site. If someone asks you about its exact location, just click an object on the slide, such as a small text or graphic object, to pop up a supporting map. The map slide can be at the end of your presentation, so you can move directly to the map slide and then use Action Settings to move back to the slide from which it was called.

The Action Settings Dialog

The Action Settings dialog is available once you select an object on a slide and then select Slide Show|Action Settings. You can also pick the Slide Show|Action Buttons menu selection and pick one of the available button styles from the Action Buttons toolbar.

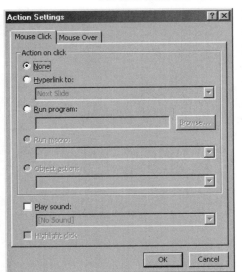

Drag a button outline on the underlying slide and release the mouse button. Upon release, the Action Settings dialog is displayed.

Notice that you can hyperlink directly to another slide or even to a web page (URL), run a macro or program, perform an object action, and play a sound during the selected process.

Go to Another Slide

If you want to branch from the current slide to another, use the Hyperlink to selection:

1. Use Slide Show|Action Buttons to draw a descriptive button or select an existing object on the slide.

2. Use Slide Show|Action Settings to display the Action Settings dialog.

3. Click the Hyperlink to option button.

4. Pick a hyperlink from the pick list, such as Next Slide, Last Slide, Other PowerPoint Presentation, or URL.

5. Click OK to return to the slide.

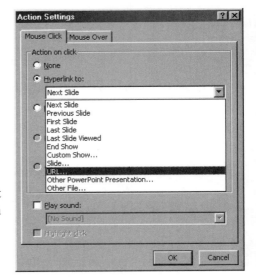

Tips: If you choose an item followed by an ellipses (...), a dialog is displayed from which to select another PowerPoint Presentation file, program name, URL name, etc. This is true for all of the Action Settings choices.

Play a Sound

You can use this dialog to connect a sound to an object on the current slide.

1. Use Slide Show|Action Buttons to draw a descriptive button or select an existing object on the slide.

2. Use Slide Show|Action Settings to display the Action Settings dialog.

3. Check the Play sound check box.

4. Pick a sound from the list.

5. Click OK to complete the job.

Once the Play sound is set, click the corresponding object during a slide show to play the sound.

Run a Program

Running a program, such as Microsoft Excel or Microsoft Outlook, is a simple matter using the Action Settings dialog.

1. Use Slide Show|Action Buttons to draw a descriptive button or select an existing object on the slide.

2. Use Slide Show|Action Settings to display the Action Settings dialog.

3. Click the Run Program option button. Then click Browse and locate the file path and program you want to run; click OK.

4. Click OK once more to complete the link, which closes the Action Settings dialog.

    Once the Run program is set, clicking the object during a slide show launches the selected program. When you are finished using the program, exit it to return to your presentation and the slide from which the program was called.

Run Macro

Just like the other Office 2000 applications, PowerPoint also lets you record and play macros (stored keystrokes and actions). Just use the Tools|Macro menu selection to record and name a series of actions. Once saved, you can use this link to select and run your macro from your presentation.

Hands-on Activity

In this activity you create a three-slide presentation. The first is a title slide. The second includes three action buttons. The first button branches to the last (third) slide, which contains a map. The second launches Microsoft Excel, which can be used to open and edit a worksheet. The third button launches Microsoft Outlook, where you can review a calendar or schedule. Begin by launching PowerPoint.

1. Click **New**, select the Title Slide layout (upper left corner), and click **OK**.

2. Type the text in the following figure in bold in the title and text areas. Increase the size of the title text by selecting it and then clicking the **Increase Font Size** button.

3. Use **Format|Background** to color the background yellow. Shade it as shown. (Use both More Colors and Fill Effects.)

4. Select the title and text and use the Drawing toolbar's Font Color button to color the title red. Use the Shadow button to apply a shadow to the title text.

Tip: Make the shadow black using the Shadow Settings and then the Shadow Color buttons.

5. Select **Slide Show|Slide Transition**, set the Effect to **Cover Right-Down**, and click **Apply**.

6. Click the **Insert New Slide** button, select the Bulleted List layout, and click **OK**.

7. Type the text as shown in the following figure. Use the **Demote** (Indent More) button on the Formatting toolbar to indent (demote) the seven points following the first line, as shown on the following slide illustration.

Factory Site Selected

- Site selected on following basis:
  - Tax concessions made by Madison County.
  - Area includes well educated labor force.
  - Public utilities readily available.
  - Competitive utility rates.
  - Good public and post-secondary schools.
  - Close to major airport.
  - Reasonable land and construction costs.

| Map | Worksheet | Calendar |

8. Use the **Slide Show|Action Buttons** selection to insert and drag the three buttons shown on the slide illustration, i.e., **Map**, **Worksheet**, and **Calendar**. Click on **OK** when the Action Settings dialog appears, then right-click on the selected button. The Properties dialog is now displayed; select **Edit Text** and type the appropriate text.

9. Enter the following Action Settings for each of the action buttons.

   a. Map: Hyperlink to **Last Slide**.

   b. Worksheet: Run program **C:\Program Files\Microsoft Office\Excel.exe** (or the path where the Excel application is located).

   c. Calendar: Run program **C:\Program Fles\Microsoft Office\Outlook.exe** (or the path where the Outlook application is located).

10. Use **Format|Background** to set the slide background color to light green. Then use the Drawing toolbar's **Fill Colors** button to set the button colors to light blue.

11. Use **Slide Show|Slide Transition**, set the Effect to **Blinds Horizontal**, and click **Apply**.

12. Click the **New Slide** button, select the Blank layout, and click **OK**.

13. Draw the map shown using the following Drawing tools:

    Line, **Line Style** for the roads.

    Dash Line, **Arrow Style**, **Line Style** for the dimension line.

    Rectangle, **Fill Color** for the factory.

    AutoShapes|Stars and Banners for the compass rose.

    AutoShapes|Callouts for the Factory Site callout.

    Text Box for the text objects.

    Free Rotate to rotate the highway label and small compass rose star.

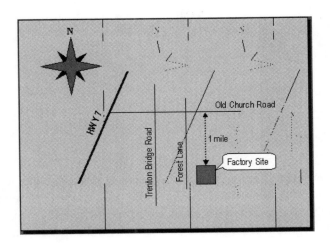

14. Select the Factory rectangle. Then use **Slide Show|Action Settings**, pick **Previous Slide** as the Hyperlink to value, and click **OK**.

15. Use **Slide Show|Slide Transition**, set the Effect to **Box Out**, and click **Apply**.

16. Use **Format|Background** and set the background color to light blue.

17. Press **<Ctrl+Home>** to go to slide 1 of 3.

18. Select **Slide Show|View Show**.

19. Advance through the slide show. Check the use of the pen and other tools at the bottom left-hand corner. Click to the second slide. Test the **Map**, **Worksheet**, and **Calendar** buttons. (Click the Factory to return to Slide 2.)

20. If everything is working properly, use **File|Save** to save the presentation. Type the name **Links** and click **Save**.

21. Press **<Alt+F4>** to exit PowerPoint.

Summary

Now that you understand the concept of branching, you're ready to move on to the next section. There, you learn how to prepare printed materials that accompany almost all good presentations.

Section 70

Printing Your Presentations

Introduction

This section shows you how to create and print speaker notes and other supporting materials that can be used as scripts and handouts. It's a good idea to prepare scripts that guide you through the narrative portion of your presentations. This is true for both live and prerecorded narration. If nothing else, write down the key points you want to make so you can refer to your notes as you go. If you have a sound card, you can use Slide Show|Record Narration to prerecord, save, and play your presentations. However, this is not a dynamic way to make points. Live, expressive narrative is usually superior, unless you are preparing a continuous point-of-sale or exhibit-style demonstration.

Printing Slides

You can print all slides in a presentation, a range of slides, the current slide, or notes or handouts using the Print dialog, accessed through File|Print.

Notice the check boxes at the bottom of the dialog in the following illustration. These control the appearance of your printed slides. Also, you can print multiple slides per page as handouts using the selections in the Print what pick list. Finally, notice that you can print multiple pages using the Number of copies spin box.

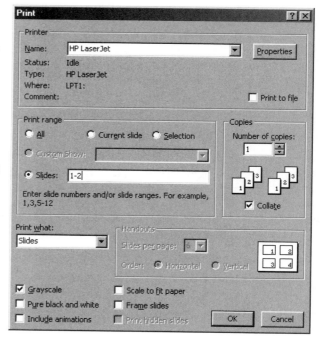

Speaker Notes

Create and edit your notes for each slide as follows:

1. Click in the bottom window of the slide frame to type in your speaker notes. Click in the area where it says "Click to add notes."

2. Use View|Notes Page to see the slide with your notes. Use the Zoom Control as necessary to enlarge the view (75% or larger) so you can see your text. Here, you can modify or enter new text as desired. Create notes that control the content and flow of your presentation.

3. Use <Page Down> and <Page Up> to move between slide notes pages.

4. Print your slide notes by putting Notes pages in the Print what box of the Print dialog.

Meeting Minder

During a meeting, you can use Tools|Meeting Minder to record and view either meeting notes or action item assignments that evolve during your meeting.

Your notes and action items can also be exported to either or both Word and Outlook. The Meeting Minder Export button is active only when meeting minutes or action items exist. Otherwise, it is inactive. Click Export to display the Meeting Minder Export dialog. Use the check boxes to control the destination(s).

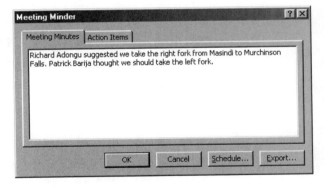

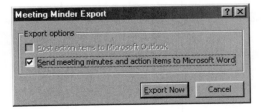

Minutes and action items that are exported to Word take on the following format.

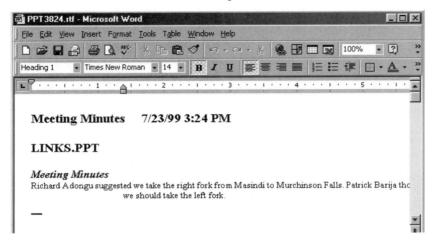

Just save your minutes and action items so you can print and distribute them as required. Now that you are familiar with the procedures used to print slides, notes, minutes, and action items, try the following hands-on activity.

Hands-on Activity

In this activity you open the Links presentation created and saved in the last section. It is also available as a companion file. Display slides 1 and 2 in the Notes Pages view and add a few lines of text to each, as notes. Then use Tools|Meeting Minder to create a Word document. Finally, print and save the document. Begin by launching PowerPoint.

1. Open **Links**. Display the first slide in the **Notes Page** view.

2. Click **Zoom Control** and select **75%**.

3. Click on the text area and type a few notes about the displayed slide.

4. Press **<PgDn>** to advance to slide 2.

5. Click on the text area and type a few notes about this slide.

6. Click **Tools|Meeting Minder**, then click **Action Items**. Type an item similar to the following, and click **Add**.

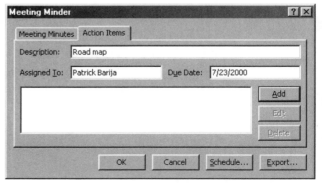

7. Click the **Export** button. In the Export dialog, check **Send meeting minutes and action items to Microsoft Word** and click **Export Now** to launch Microsoft Word; wait for the complete display of your minutes and notes.

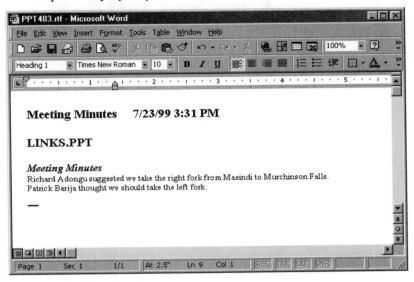

8. From Word, click **Print** to output the document to your printer.

9. Use Word's **File|Save** menu selection and type **Meeting Minutes** as the filename.

10. Exit Word. Use PowerPoint's **File|Save As** menu selection and type **Links B** as the filename.

11. Press **<Alt+F4>** to exit PowerPoint.

Summary

In this section you learned how to create speaker notes, meeting minutes, and action items. You now know how to create, display, and print your presentations with all necessary special effects. In the next section you learn how to create a new presentation by integrating slides from existing presentations.

Modifying and Integrating Presentations

Introduction

There are times when you want to assemble and rearrange existing slides for use in a new presentation. This is a simple operation if you know how to use PowerPoint. This section tells you how to collect slides from existing presentations and mix them with new ones to create a presentation. New slides can be inserted, unwanted ones deleted, and existing ones repositioned in the presentation. You can save a substantial amount of time by using existing slides. Review the following paragraphs to see how these operations are done.

Inserting a New Slide

To insert a new slide in a presentation, first be sure you are in the Slide View. Display the slide preceding the point of insertion. Click New Slide or use Insert|New Slide or press <Ctrl+M>. Pick the slide layout and click OK. The new slide is ready for preparation.

An alternate method is to display a presentation in the Slide Sorter view, and click a slide to copy. Then press <Ctrl+C> to put it on the clipboard. Click the slide that will precede the inserted slide. Press <Ctrl+V> to paste the slide following the selected one.

Tip: This operation can be accomplished between two or more open presentation files by moving between the files using the Window menu. You can also display two presentations simultaneously using Window|Arrange All. Then display both presentations in the Slide Sorter view. Drag and drop between presentations as desired. If you drag a slide out of a presentation you don't want disturbed, be sure to close the source file without saving when you are finished with it.

Deleting a Slide

To delete an existing slide from a presentation, display the slide in the Slide view, and use Edit|Delete Slide to remove the slide.

Alternately, display the slide presentation in the Slide Sorter view. Click on the unwanted slide to select it, and press <Delete>.

Repositioning Slides

To reposition slides, first display your presentation in the Slide Sorter view. Click on a slide to be moved. Then drag and drop the selected slide into its new position.

Tip: Dragging to the top or bottom of the display causes the slides to scroll vertically. This feature allows you to drag a displayed slide in front of one that is hidden from view by simply scrolling to it.

Integrating Slides from Other Presentations

You can copy and paste slides from one presentation to another.

To insert slides from a file, open a new presentation. Use Insert|Slides from Files and select the desired presentation filename. The presentation is inserted following the current slide. Use Edit|Delete Slide to remove all unwanted slides, then use the Slide Sorter view to rearrange the slides as necessary. Check the colors, transitions, and animation, and touch up as necessary.

Hands-on Activity

In this activity you create a new presentation and then insert an existing one from a file. Begin by launching PowerPoint.

1. Click **New**, select a Blank presentation, and click **OK**.

2. Click **Slide Sorter View**.

3. Click **Open**, pick **Links B**, and click **Open**.

4. Click **Slide Sorter View**.

5. Use **Window|Arrange All** to view both presentations at the same time.

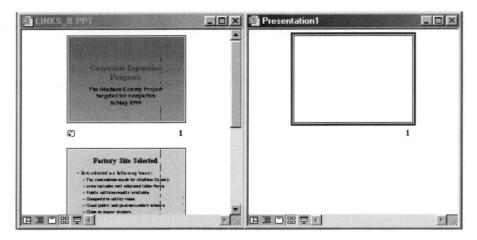

6. Click slide 2, press and hold **Shift**, and click slide 3 of Links B.

7. Press **<Ctrl+C>** to copy the selected slides.

8. Click slide 1 of the new presentation file.

9. Click **<Ctrl+V>** to insert the two copied slides.

10. Maximize the new presentation window, and compare the arrangement of the copied slides to the following illustration.

 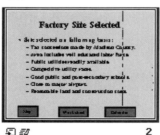 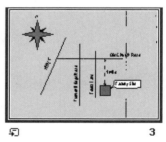

11. Select and drag slide 3 in front of slide 1.

12. Check that your slides are arranged as shown.

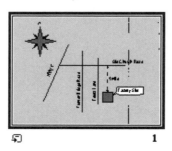  

13. Press **<Alt+F4>** to exit PowerPoint. Do not save the files.

Summary

Now that you know how to use your old slide presentations as resources for new presentations, the time it takes you to create new presentations may be greatly reduced. In the next and final section of this part, you learn how to prepare your presentations for distribution. This includes packaging the necessary presentation files and the PowerPoint Viewer, which is supplied as an integral part of the PowerPoint program.

Distributing Presentations with the PowerPoint Viewer

Introduction

Now that you're a competent presentation designer, it's time to distribute your dazzling creations to others. As a licensed owner of Microsoft PowerPoint, you are authorized to do this by giving a copy of your presentation files and the PowerPoint Viewer to others. The Viewer is a *run-time* program, designed to play presentations without requiring the user to have the PowerPoint program itself.

Packaging a Presentation

Running a presentation with the Viewer offers the features available when you use the Slide Show dialog to run a show. A PowerPoint Pack and Go Wizard guides you through the preparation process. The general steps are:

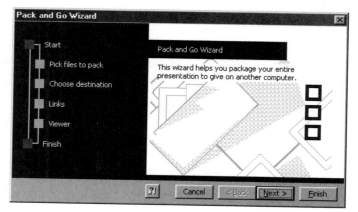

1. Use File|Pack and Go to launch the Pack and Go Wizard dialog.

2. Click Next> to display the following dialog.

3. Notice that you can pick the active presentation or other presentations. When picking other presentations, use the Browse button to find and select one or more presentation files. Press Ctrl to pick two or more files. Once the selections are made, click Next> to advance to the next dialog.

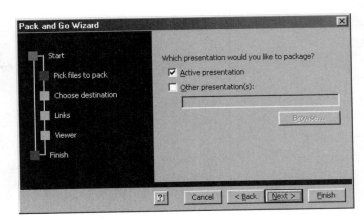

Tip: In the next step you may want to create and use a blank folder from which you can copy your presentation files to several removable diskettes for distribution.

4. Pick a destination. If you plan to put the presentation on a diskette, click either A or B. If you want to put it on your hard drive, click Choose destination and use Browse to select the file folder. Then click Next> to display the following dialog.

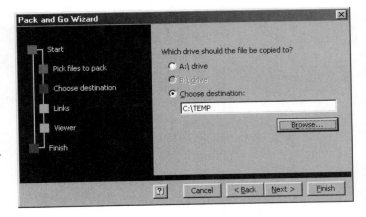

5. If you used an exotic TrueType font that may be unavailable in other computers, check the Embed TrueType Fonts option. If you have embedded objects including sound clips, Word tables, Excel worksheets, and external pictures, leave Include linked files checked. Then click Next>.

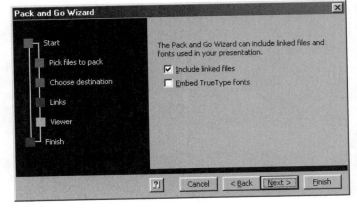

6. This dialog lets you bundle the PowerPoint Viewer with the presentation files. If the recipient of your presentation has PowerPoint, the Viewer is not necessary. If not, include the Viewer with the package. Click Next>.

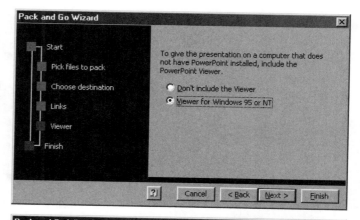

7. This dialog verifies your progress and prompts you to start the packaging process. Notice that the author selected a temporary file path on drive C. Click Finish to complete the process.

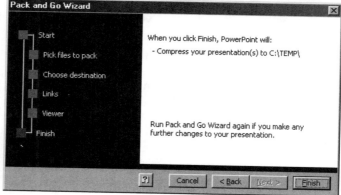

8. The preceding Pack and Go Status box keeps you informed relative to the progress of the packaging task. Once done, the files are ready for distribution. Notice that the files created were put in the C:\Temp folder.

Retrieving the Presentation and PowerPoint Viewer

Notice the Pngsetup application file. This is used to extract the compressed presentation and Viewer files stored in the pres0.ppz file. Proceed as follows, assuming these files are in the folder C:\Temp.

1. Use the Windows Start|Run command, type C:\Temp\Pngsetup, and press <Enter>. Notice the Pack and Go Setup dialog.

2. Type a destination file path, such as C:\Presentations (the author unpacked to the Temp folder), and click OK. Dialogs keep you informed about the progress.

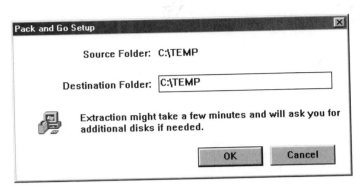

3. When finished, choose to run the show now or launch the PowerPoint Viewer to see it later. The files extracted include the viewer and presentation files.

Running the PowerPoint Viewer

1. You can launch the PowerPoint Viewer by displaying the Ppview32 application file (C:\Temp\Ppview32.exe) and double-clicking it. Pick the presentation file using the following dialog.

2. Click the Show button to run the slide show.

3. Press <Esc> to end the show, or click your mouse (or use <Page Down> to advance and <Page Up> to back up) to advance through the presentation.

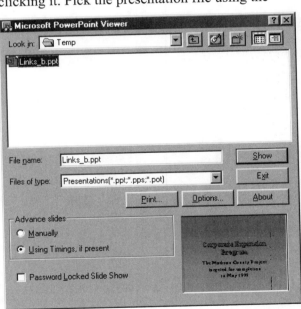

The Pack and Go utility is extremely powerful, as it selects and compresses both presentation and viewer files. It also includes the Viewer setup program so others can install it on their computers. This makes PowerPoint a complete and valuable program.

Hands-on Activities

In this activity you use File|Pack and Go and the Pack and Go Wizard to package the Links B presentation with the PowerPoint Viewer. Format a blank diskette and put it in drive A. Then launch PowerPoint and open your Links B presentation.

Pack and Go

1. Use **File|Pack and Go** to launch the Pack and Go Wizard dialog.

2. Be sure that the Microsoft Office 2000 CD is in your CD-ROM drive. Move through the dialogs one by one by clicking **Next>**. Be sure that you pick the active presentation and select the blank formatted floppy in drive A as the destination.

3. Check the **Include PowerPoint Viewer** check box.

4. Click **Finish** to complete the process. Watch the Pack and Go Status dialog to check the progress.

5. The Pack and Go Status box keeps you informed relative to the progress of the packaging task. Once done, all files are compressed on the diskette in drive A and ready for distribution.

Viewer Setup

To install the PowerPoint Viewer and run the packaged presentation:

1. Use the Windows Explorer or DOS to create the file path **C:\Presentations**.

2. Use the Windows **Start|Run** command, type **A:\Pngsetup**, and press **<Enter>**.

3. Notice the Pack and Go Setup dialog.

4. Type **C:\Presentations** as the destination file path and click **OK**.

5. Click **No** in response to the last dialog.

Using the PowerPoint Viewer

Run the PowerPoint Viewer and Links B presentation:

1. Use the Windows **Start|Run** command, type **C:\Temp\Ppview32**, and press **<Enter>**.

2. Pick **C:\Temp\Links B** and click **Show**; the presentation is launched.

3. Click the mouse to advance the show or let it loop automatically. Press **<Esc>** to end the show.

Summary

You now know how to use PowerPoint's extensive array of powerful features to create multimedia events. And with this section completed, you know how to package and distribute them. All that's left is practice.

We next look at Outlook, Microsoft's premier information management and organizer program designed to keep the busy professional in touch and on top of the heap.

Part 6

Microsoft Outlook 2000

73 About This Part—Introduction to Outlook and its features.

74 Starting (or "Launching") Outlook—Key Outlook controls, summary of Outlook tools, and customizing how Outlook starts.

75 Using Mail—Examine, file, and respond to your messages using this powerful communications tool.

76 Using Calendar—Use the calendar to schedule your activities. Then set reminders for those important events. View a day, week, month, or year at a time.

77 Using Tasks—Use this powerful project scheduling feature to enter major projects, schedule detailed tasks, and display and print valuable reports in a variety of formats.

78 Using Contacts—Maintain your contacts in this full-featured address book. Use the AutoDialer to call your business and personal contacts. Display your address book in a variety of formats. Interface Word to your address book for addressing letters, envelopes, and labels.

79 Using Journal—Want to know what you did last month? Track your work activities using this handy auditing tool. Find out which applications are used most often and when. Launch documents directly from the Journal in any of the Office 2000 applications.

80 **Using Notes**—Write down your ideas, to dos, and reminders using a sticky note metaphor. Just click, write, and save. Then you can view, print, send, and delete your notes from the Outlook interface.

81 **Security**—Protect your data from prying eyes and malicious hackers.

82 **Filters**—Create and apply filters to limit what and who you see.

83 **Miscellaneous Outlook Topics**—Learn interesting and useful ways to get the most out of Outlook's programs.

About This Part

Introduction

This part describes the elements of Microsoft Outlook 2000, hereafter referred to as "Outlook." Included are sections that present the features and operating procedures for each aspect of Outlook.

What is Outlook?

Outlook is a full-featured information management program used to organize information on your desktop and to share information with others. You can use Outlook to manage your messages, appointments, contacts, and tasks, as well as track activities, and view and open files.

Outlook information is organized in folders. When you first start Outlook, the Inbox folder is displayed. Use Mail's Inbox and Outbox to read and send mail messages, meeting requests, and task requests.

To create a message, point to New on the File menu, and then click Mail Message.

You can also use Outlook in place of Windows Explorer to see the files on your hard disk. This is accomplished by clicking Other on the Outlook Bar, and then clicking My Computer, My Documents, or Favorites.

Outlook uses views to sort and organize items in a folder. Click a view in the Current View box on the Standard toolbar to display a different view.

You can use Microsoft Word and Outlook together to produce high-quality e-mail messages. You can turn Word on or off as your editor by closing any displayed message, clicking Options on the Tools menu, and then clicking the Use Microsoft Word as the e-mail editor check box on the E-mail tab of the Options dialog.

When Outlook help is started, a dialog is displayed. By clicking on "Finding out what's new in Outlook 2000" you will be guided to another dialog that lists many of the new features not found in previous Outlook versions.

After clicking on "Finding out what's new…" in the dialog that appears, Outlook help displays the "What's new…" dialog. Click on any topic of interest for a detailed explanation of the new feature and how it may improve your productivity.

With this overview in place, you're ready to examine the component parts of Outlook. Here's a brief description of Outlook's features. Each is described in much more detail in the sections that follow.

Mail

Here you display and read your messages located in the Inbox, Outbox, or Sent Items folder. Just double-click on a message line to see the full text. Your messages can be printed, moved to another folder, archived, or deleted as appropriate.

Calendar

The Calendar is displayed in day, week, or month format by simply clicking the corresponding toolbar button or View menu selection. You can also drag the calendar to see an entire year. The Calendar is used to make appointments, making an excellent daily, weekly, or monthly planner. You can also store notes with your appointments. Appointments are easily entered and viewed. It's also a simple matter to move or delete appointments when the need arises. Reminders can be set to alert you about a pending appointment. You can also set the reminder to give you an audible alarm in advance of a planned event.

Tasks

The Tasks feature lets you add, edit, and print details about planned projects and projects in progress. It ties your project to the calendar, making it easy to plan and update individual events, or tasks, associated with a project. All tasks that comprise a project can be assigned individual attributes, such as the planned and actual time required to complete a task, percent complete, and responsibility. You can group tasks in a number of different ways to provide a large variety of views of your projects and tasks. Once you've organized and entered your projects into Outlook, you can print and distribute your project plans to others in your work group. You can also use the information to guide you and those who work with you relative to which tasks require your attention as well as which ones are most critical or prerequisite to others.

Contacts

The Contacts portion of Outlook adds a full-featured address book and contact manager. You can enter names, addresses, telephone and fax numbers, e-mail addresses, notes, important dates, and more for all of your personal and business acquaintances. A fast find feature is also provided so you can jump directly to the entry you want to see. You can sort the contents of the address book in a variety of ways. It can be viewed in list format or as detailed information. You can enter and display the detailed information by accessing any of five tabs. These tabs are labeled Business, Phone, Address, Personal, and Notes. If you have a modem, you can even use the address book to dial selected telephone numbers.

Journal

The Journal portion of Outlook collects and displays an audit trail of the various documents on which you've worked. It collects the information by application, and displays each time that a document was opened and saved. Just click on an application button and scroll the time line horizontally to see the document names and corresponding dates. Double-click a document to open it via a shortcut.

Notes

The Notes portion of Outlook is like having access to "sticky notes" on your desktop. You can create a new note by clicking the New Note button on the Office 2000 Shortcut Bar. Type your note and save it for later reference. Notes are ideal for writing down ideas, questions, or reminders. Use the Notes portion of Outlook to view, print, and export your notes. You can click the Note button in the upper left-hand corner of the screen to print, delete, or create a new note without having to go through Outlook.

What's Next?

Now that you have some basic information about the features offered by Outlook, it's time to begin exploring it. Turn to Section 74, where you learn to start Outlook.

Starting (or "Launching") Outlook

If you installed the Office toolbar, the easiest way to launch Outlook is to click on the Outlook button. Otherwise, go to the Programs group (or the group in which you installed Outlook); start Outlook by clicking the Microsoft Outlook line. When Outlook starts, the Outlook dialog loads.

The first time you start Outlook you are invited to review "What's New," and the Office Assistant offers help. If you are familiar with previous versions of Outlook you may want to close the Office Assistant for now. Go to the Menu bar and click on Help, then click on Hide the Office Assistant. Now an Outlook dialog will appear. Close the Outlook dialog and compare your display to the following illustration, which labels the various parts of the Outlook screen.

The above screen illustrates the Outlook Today view. If you wish, you can use the View menu to change the view. Each Outlook screen control is summarized in the appendices on the accompanying CD. Detailed descriptions are found in the following sections of this book where you are guided through hands-on learning activities.

Microsoft Outlook 2000 Controls

The keyed screen illustration shows each of the various controls which are summarized in the list that follows. Note that the illustration above is the Outlook Today screen. Changing the view from Today to any other view, such as Inbox, will change the buttons available on the toolbars.

Key	Item	Description
1	Menu Bar	Used to access the Outlook menus and the Office Assistant (Help)
2	Standard Toolbar	Includes buttons to perform the most frequently used operations of that Outlook program.
3	Advanced Toolbar	Includes buttons for performing "advanced" operations in each of the different Outlook programs.

Controlling How Outlook Starts

You can control how Outlook starts. In the folder that Outlook.exe is installed in (typically the C:\Program Files\Microsoft Office\Office folder), right-click the short-cut icon for Microsoft Outlook, drag it to the desktop, then click **Create Shortcuts Here** on the shortcut menu. Right-click on the desktop shortcut just created, and then click on **Properties**. Click on the **Shortcut** tab. In the **Target** box or the **Command Line** box, type a space after the path, and then type one or more of the following command-line options.

Note: Paths with spaces between words, such as C:\Program Files, must be enclosed in quotation marks and are case-sensitive. To specify a path in Outlook, precede the path with "Outlook:\\." As an example, to open the My Documents folder when you start Outlook, the complete entry would be "C:\Program Files\Microsoft Office\Outlook.exe" /select "C:\My Documents."

When Outlook Starts	Type this command-line option
Hide the Outlook Bar	**/folder**
Have the specified folder visible	**/select** *"path/folder name"*
Create an e-mail message	**/c ipm.note**
Create a post	**/c ipm.post**
Create an appointment	**/c ipm.appointment**
Create a task	**/c ipm.task**
Create a contact	**/c ipm.contact**
Create a journal entry	**/c ipm.activity**
Create a note	**/c ipm.stickynote**
Prompt for default manager of e-mail, news, and contacts	**/checkclient**
Create an item with the specified file as an attachment.	**/a** *"path/file name"*

Outlook Tools

The Outlook applications and tools are listed below. A summary of some of the more useful Outlook tools follows:

Attachments Attach files from other programs in Outlook e-mail messages, appointments, contacts, tasks, and journal entries.

Categories Apply a keyword describing the item, such as a task or a contact, to help keep track of the items so you can easily find, sort, filter, or group them. As an example, organize tasks into different categories or projects so you need to maintain only one task list. Also, group activities on a timeline by category so related activities can be viewed together.

Customizable views Create a custom view showing the group, sort, and column settings that is needed.

Outlook Bar Use shortcuts to quickly switch to frequently used folders. Customize the Outlook Bar with favorite shortcuts.

Filter Temporarily show or hide items in the view.

AutoArchive Store or delete out-of-date items, keeping old information out of the way.

Folder List and Folder Banner View all the Outlook folders and file folders in the Folder List. Click on the Folder Banner to quickly view a pop-up Folder List.

AutoCreate Quickly create new items by dragging an item of one type into a folder for items of another type. As an example, drag a contact to Calendar to create a meeting request with information from the contact.

AutoDate Specify times and dates by using descriptions such as "three weeks ago" or "noon." Outlook converts the phrase to actual dates and times.

Find messages, appointments, files, and more Find files, Outlook items, or text in an Outlook item.

Grouping See related items by category together in a table or timeline.

Info Bar Get quick visual cues about the status of a message in the message heading. Messages can be flagged for follow-up, or whether the message is marked private or confidential.

Multilevel sorting and multilevel grouping Sort and group items by fields in a table or timeline.

Microsoft Office Assistant Get assistance when questions about how to use Outlook arise. The Office Assistant also provides Help for wizards and displays tips and messages.

Open modules in separate windows Open other modules, such as Calendar, Contacts, and Tasks, in a separate window without losing the current view.

Outlook and Microsoft Internet Explorer integration Outlook can be started from the **Go** menu in Microsoft Internet Explorer. Also, a Web page can be opened in

Outlook and then you can switch to viewing it in Internet Explorer. View Web pages in the Favorites folder in either program.

Outlook Today View a summary of your Inbox, your appointments for the next few days, and your list of tasks—all in one place.

Rich Text Format and attachments in messages Format text messages, and store files and items directly within an item.

Shortcuts and hyperlinks Open an attached file, Outlook item, or Web page directly from an item. As an example, open a Web page from a shortcut in an e-mail message.

Custom fields Create custom Text, Date/Time, Combination, and Formula fields.

Outlook Forms Easily create unique forms to enter and display any type of information in Outlook.

Voting Request and tally responses to multiple-choice questions sent in e-mail messages.

Autonotify Automatically receive notification when a recipient receives your message.

Synchronize Offline Folders If you use Microsoft Exchange Server, you can work offline and synchronize your Outlook folders so that the folders you use offline match those you use online. Synchronize any or all of your folders, depending on the speed of your connection and how much hard disk space you have.

Access to Applications

Access to the Outlook applications is via the Shortcuts Pane on the left side of the Outlook window. Clicking on the appropriate application's icon will open the application in the application pane on the right side of Outlook's window. Outlook's applications and their associated icons are explained in the following tables.

Outlook Shortcuts

Outlook Today	Displays a summary of the current calendar, tasks, and messages.
Inbox	Displays inbound mail.
Calendar	Displays the calendar in a variety of formats.
Contacts	Displays contact information.
Tasks	Displays tasks to do.
Notes	Displays notes you keep.
Deleted Items	Displays all deleted items.

My Shortcuts

Drafts	Displays messages that have not yet been sent or moved to the Outbox for sending.

Outbox	Displays all messages that are queued for sending and before the message is moved to the Sent Items folder.
Sent Items	Displays all messages that were sent and have not been deleted.
Journal	Displays all items kept in the journal.
Outlook Update	Automatically connects you to the Outlook web page and downloads Outlook updates.

Other Shortcuts

My Computer	Displays the My Computer folder.
My Documents	Displays the My Documents folder.
Favorites	Displays the Favorites folder.

Accessing Outlook's Features

The left pane is used to open the applications and tools in Outlook with the click of your mouse.

As you move through the various applications, notice how some menu selections and Standard toolbar buttons change to correspond with the features offered by the application. Also, the Shortcut menu selections, accessed by right-clicking your mouse, change with the current selection.

Examining Outlook Today

The Outlook Today page, accessed by clicking the Outlook Today icon in the Outlook Shortcuts pane, provides a preview of the day's activities. Outlook Today displays a summary of your appointments, a list of your tasks, and how many new e-mail messages you have. Outlook Today can be the first page that opens when you start Outlook. Additionally, you can easily change the way Outlook Today appears to suit your needs.

Outlook Today opens a window with Calendar, Tasks, and Messages headings. Clicking on any of these headings takes you directly to the respective window. Notice the Customize Outlook Today... button on the right side.

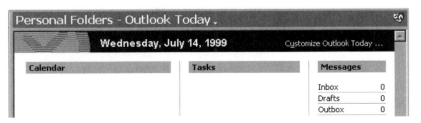

Clicking on this button (Customize Outlook Today) will display a window with various options used to customize the appearance of Outlook. The options are self-explanatory.

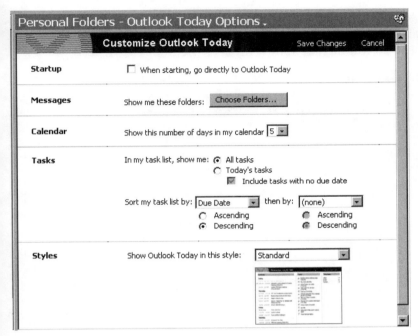

After reviewing the choices and making the appropriate selections, click on either the Save Changes button or the Cancel button located to the right side of the window.

To make Outlook Today the startup page when Outlook is started, click on Outlook Today in the Outlook shortcuts pane. On the Outlook Today page, click on Customize Outlook Today. In the Startup area, select the When starting, go directly to Outlook Today check box. Click on Save Changes.

Examining Mail's Inbox

1. Click on the first message to highlight it.

2. Press <Ctrl+O> and examine the contents.

3. Press <Alt+F4> to close the message window.

4. Click Inbox at the upper left-hand corner of the window. Notice the Outbox, Sent Items, and Deleted Items. These are also accessed by clicking the Mail button in the left pane. Examine the menu and Standard toolbar. Remember that each Outlook application has its own menu and toolbar set.

5. Click the Mail button on the left pane. Notice how you can access the Inbox, Outbox, Sent Items, and Deleted Items from the left pane.

6. Click the Outlook button to redisplay the Outlook application icons.

Tip: Mail requires that Microsoft Mail, Fax, or another mail or messaging service is properly set up prior to its use.

Examining Calendar

Calendar

Use the Calendar to record and display appointments and planned and completed tasks. You can view your planned or past activities in day, week, and month formats. You can enlarge the Month window by dragging it vertically and horizontally to see as many as 15 months at a time on a computer using an 800 x 600 pixel display setting. Look at the Calendar by performing the following steps.

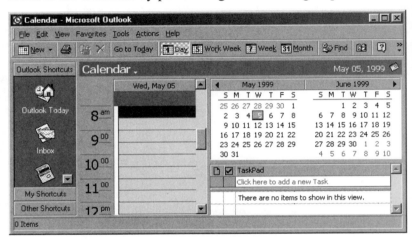

1. Click the Calendar button to display the calendar window

2. Click the Day button ▦Day on the Standard toolbar to display the Day view.

3. Double-click the 9:00 a.m. line to display the following dialog and enter the information shown. The date is not important in this example.

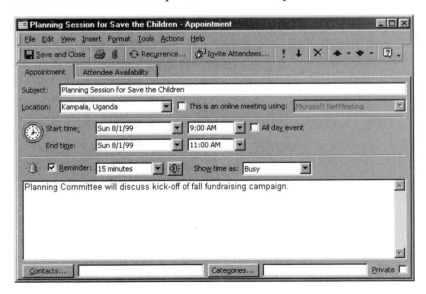

4. Click Save and Close 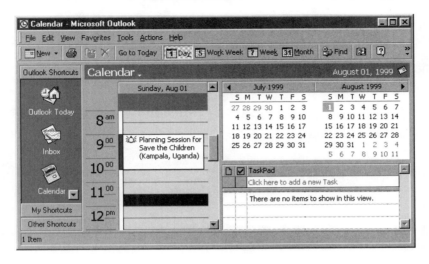 and check the displayed appointment.

5. Now click on the appointment (just click to move the cursor into the colored area outlined in blue alongside the 9:00 a.m. entry). Press <Ctrl+O> to open the appointment dialog again. Click the Meeting Planner tab to see the schedule.

6. Press <Esc> to close the dialog. Now click the Week button and then the Month button to examine each of the corresponding displays.

7. In the Month view, drag the left and bottom edges of the calendar to increase the number of months shown. Then drag the calendar back to its original configuration.

Examining Contacts

Contacts is a full-featured contact manager and address book that contains an extensive repertoire of information about your business and personal acquaintances. You can use the e-mail addresses and phone numbers to automatically send e-mail messages or dial telephone numbers using the AutoDialer. The names and mailing addresses are also useful as a resource for Word mail merge operations. Examine some of the features by performing the following steps.

1. Click the Contacts icon in the left pane.

2. Examine the display.

3. Press <Ctrl+N> to enter a contact. Type the name of a friend or business contact and his or her address, company, and telephone, fax, and e-mail information so that it resembles the following illustration.

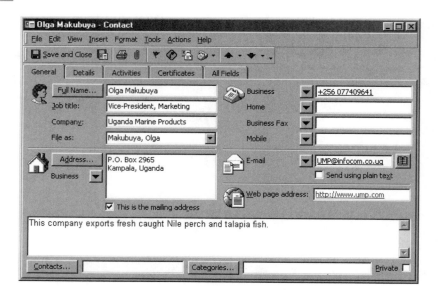

4. Press <Ctrl+S> to save the information. Enter a few additional contacts.

5. Examine the menu and toolbars. In particular, notice the Autodialer  and New Message to Contact buttons.

6. Look at the different views of your information using View|Current View.

Examining Tasks

Tasks is used to schedule to-dos, projects, and other activities that have schedules and/or milestones. Examine some of the features by performing the following steps.

1. Click the Tasks icon in the left pane.

2. Examine the display.

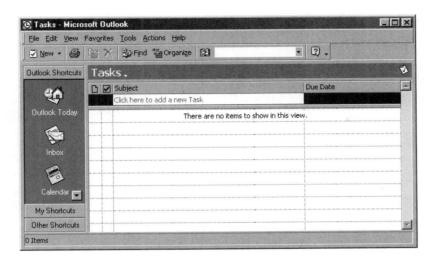

3. Click on the Click here to add a new Task line, then select New Task. Type in the information shown, or something similar:

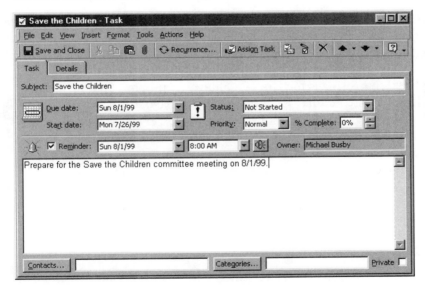

4. Click on Save and Close.

5. Notice how the typed information is now displayed on the first line of the Task list window.

6. Click on the first line and press <Ctrl+O> to open the Tasks dialog. Then examine the controls and fields in each of the Task and Details tabs.

7. Press <Esc> to close the dialog.

Examining Notes

Notes is the equivalent of sticky notes. It is ideal for jotting down ideas, reminders, and questions. Use it exactly as you would a scratch pad. Now examine some of the features by performing the following steps.

1. Click the Notes icon in the left pane. Check your display.

2. Press <Ctrl+N> to display a new, blank note (also accessed with the File|New menu selection). Type a note to yourself similar to the one shown to the right.

3. Press <Esc> to close the note; notice that it now appears in the Notes window.

4. Click on the note and press <Ctrl+D> to delete it.

Examining Deleted Items

Deleted Items displays those items that were previously deleted from the mailbox. By clicking on the Move to Folder button 📂 on the standard toolbar, you may restore an item to the folder of your choice. Or, you may permanently delete the item by clicking the Delete button ✕ on the Standard toolbar. To select more than one item, press and hold the Shift key, then press the up or down arrow.

Examining My Shortcuts

My Shortcuts displays the Drafts, Outbox, Sent Items, Journal, and Outlook Update buttons. Clicking on any of the buttons will transport you to that folder/function. The Drafts folder shows you all the messages that have been created but not yet sent. The Outbox folder shows all the messages you have sent. In the Journal folder, you can view all the activities you have performed and kept a record of. Outlook Update is a function that connects you to Microsoft's web site with the purpose of updating your copy of Outlook.

Examining Drafts

Clicking on Drafts 🗒 opens a window for reviewing any e-mail message drafts that you may have created and are currently storing in the Drafts folder. These messages are static. They stay in the Drafts folder until you either send or delete them.

Click the Drafts icon in the left pane. Check your display.

Examining Outbox

Clicking on Outbox 📤 opens a window for viewing any e-mail messages in the Outbox folder. These are messages that you have created and sent but have not yet departed from your computer. If you suddenly remember that you forgot something, such as an attachment, you can catch the message in the Outbox before it heads on down the road.

Examining Sent Items

Clicking on Sent Items opens a window for viewing any e-mail messages in the Sent Items folder. The e-mail messages here are the messages you have previously sent. They are kept here for review and record-keeping purposes. Be sure to regularly delete or move the sent messages as there is a limit on how many messages can be stored.

Examining Journal

Clicking on Journal opens a window for tracking all manner of desktop activities. The Journal automatically records your activities relating to contacts that you select from the Outlook contact list. In addition to tracking Outlook items such as e-mail, you can keep track of every Office document you create or modify, and also keep a record of any activity you want to remember—even something that is not located on your computer, such as a phone conversation or a handwritten letter you mailed or received.

Each entry in Journal represents one activity. Journal entries are recorded based on when the activity occurs; for example, a Word document is recorded based on when it was created or last modified. You can open a journal entry and review details about the activity, or you can use the journal entry as a shortcut to go directly to the Outlook item or the file that the journal entry refers to.

Journal presents information on a timeline view. You can organize journal entries on the timeline into logical groups—such as e-mail messages, meetings, and phone calls—to quickly locate information, such as all the meetings you attended in the past week or month.

Examining Outlook Update

Outlook Update attempts to connect you to the Microsoft Internet web site. If successful (you must have an Internet account, the computer connected to a phone line, and the Internet account configured correctly), Outlook updates are automatically downloaded.

Examining Other Shortcuts

The Other Shortcuts button is used to display My Computer, My Documents, and Favorites folders.

You can click on a folder to examine the contents. Like using the Windows Explorer, you can then double-click a document to launch it. Create new folders with the File|New|Folder menu selection (or use <Ctrl+Shift+E>).

Summary

As you can see, Outlook has many useful features designed to help you maintain an organized approach to your work. In addition to a powerful message system, calendar, scheduler, task manager, contact manager, work journal, and note taker, it also gives you fast access to your applications and work. If you travel with a notebook computer or conduct business by telephone, Outlook is a full-featured tool. If you want to carry a paper copy of your calendar or project planner, Outlook prints handsome renditions of your itineraries and project tasks. In the following section you look at the Mail section more closely, beginning with the Inbox.

Using Mail

Introduction

Mail is used to send and receive messages. Mail includes an Inbox, Outbox, Deleted Items, and Sent Items folders. The Inbox contains received messages, while the Outbox contains messages that are waiting to be sent. The other folders, as their names imply, contain sent and deleted messages.

Be sure to examine the toolbar buttons and menu selections to appreciate the many features available when composing your messages. Like other Office applications, accessories such as Editing (Cut, Copy, Paste, etc.), Formatting, File Management (Save, Print, etc.), Spelling and Grammar, Thesaurus, and Hyphenation are readily available.

Connecting to a Mail Server

You must be connected to a mail server to send or receive mail. Before using Mail's features, you must select the type of service you intend to use. If you intend to use a dial-up Internet service, use Tools|Accounts and enter the information required for access using the Internet Accounts dialog. If you have set up an Internet account prior to installing Office 2000 using Outlook Express, the Office 2000 installation wizard will recognize the account and configure Outlook accordingly. The following discussion is applicable when you have installed Office 2000 prior to establishing an Internet account.

You will be asked by the Internet Connection Wizard to provide the names of your incoming and outgoing mail servers. Usually the names are the same. You must get these names from your Internet service provider. As an example, my POP3 and my SMTP server names are both *mail@airmail.net*.

The following general procedures show you how to initially set up Outlook for use with an Internet service provider.

1. Click on the Tools|Accounts menu selection.

2. Select the Mail tab of the Internet Accounts dialog, then click on Add. Now select Mail. Enter your name in the text box, then click on Next>.

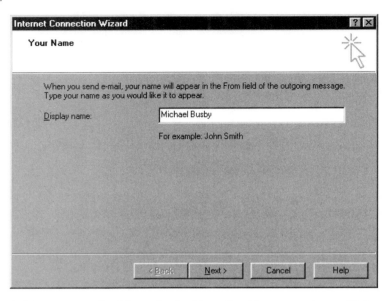

3. Add your e-mail address in the E-mail address text box. Click on Next>.

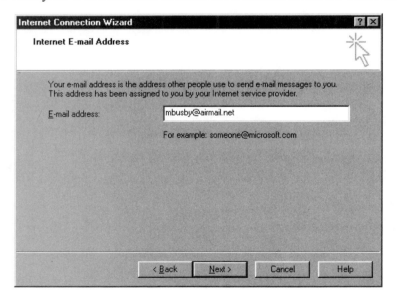

4. Select the type of incoming mail server (POP3 or LDAP) using the server drop-down box. Add the name of the incoming and outgoing mail servers in the appropriate text boxes. Of course, your server names will most likely be different from mail.airmail.net. You must get these names from your Internet service provider (ISP). Click on Next>.

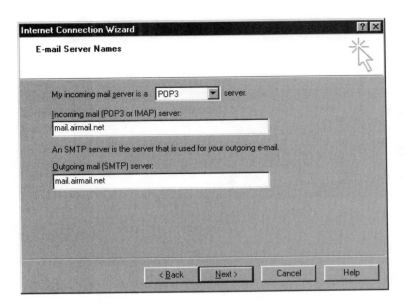

5. Add your logon information in the Account name and Password text boxes. Click on Next>.

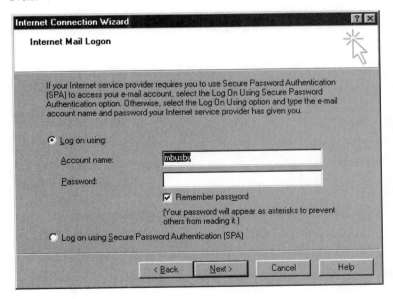

6. Select the appropriate connection method. If you are at home and you connect via a dial-up account, then select the first button—Connect using my phone line. If you are at the office and you are connected to a LAN, then select the second choice—Connect using my local area network (LAN). If you do not know where you are and/or you are adventuresome, select the third choice—I will establish my Internet connection manually. Click on Next>.

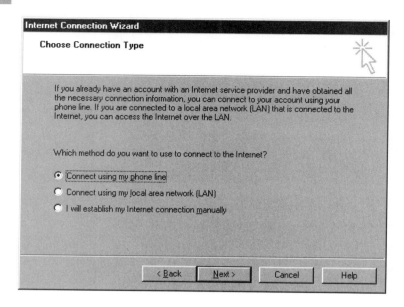

7. If this is the very first Internet account you are setting up (note that the text box will be empty), or you are creating a new dial-up connection, select the Create a new dial-up connection button. If you are setting up a new mail account at an existing Internet account, select the Use an Existing Dial-Up Connection button. Click on Next>.

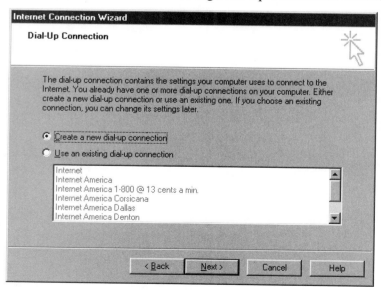

8. Enter the dial-up service telephone number and select the appropriate country name and code. Click on Next>.

Note: If you dial a prefix to access a line, add the prefix to the beginning of the area code. For example, if you dial "9" to get an outside line, such as may occur when staying in a hotel, change the area code to 9-XXX where XXX is the area code. In my case, I must dial the area code even though it is a local number. However, if you do not have to dial the area code, then use the "9" as part of the telephone number and make sure the Dial using the area code and country code box is not checked.

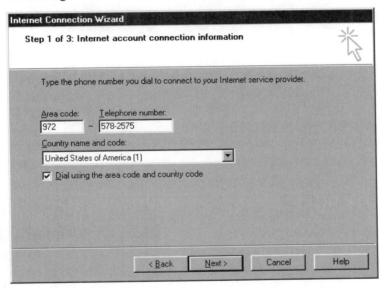

9. Enter your password in the Password text box. Click on Next>.

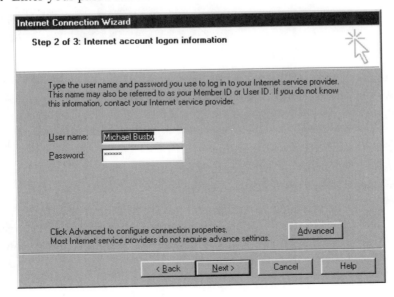

10. Enter a descriptive name for the connection in the Connection Name text box. Click on Next>, then click on Finish.

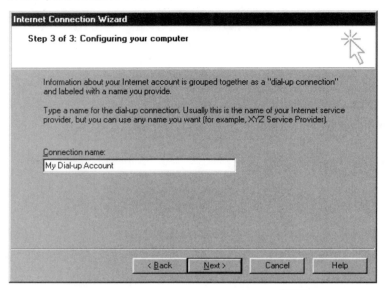

11. You are now ready to send or receive mail! Click on Tools|Send/Receive and select the appropriate mail service (in our case, mail.airmail.net).

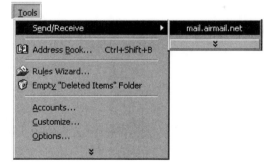

Additional Directory Services

Mail, which is a Microsoft Exchange client, permits you to communicate with numerous electronic mail systems, including Microsoft Mail. You can use the client (your computer) to access your mailbox if it is in a post office created by any of the following:

■ Microsoft Mail version 3.0 or later

■ Microsoft Windows for Workgroups version 3.1 or later

■ Microsoft Windows NT version 3.1 or later

When you start the client (your computer) for the first time, a wizard helps you create your profile. A profile contains default settings that control how messages are delivered to and from your mailbox. Microsoft Mail users can also use the wizard to move the messages in the message file to a folder.

The way you work with mail determines whether you need more than one communications profile. If you use one computer, typically you have one profile that specifies your mailbox located on a Microsoft Exchange Server computer. If you work on more than one computer and you use different information services on each, you may want to create separate profiles listing the information services. If you share a computer with others, each person must have a profile.

Before you can add an information service to a user profile, you must install the service. Use the following general approach to install a service.

Note: You will be asked by the Internet Connection Wizard to provide the name of your LDAP. You must get this name from your Internet service provider. This example uses an LDAP Server used by the author for instructional purposes only.

1. From the Tools menu, select Accounts. The following dialog appears.

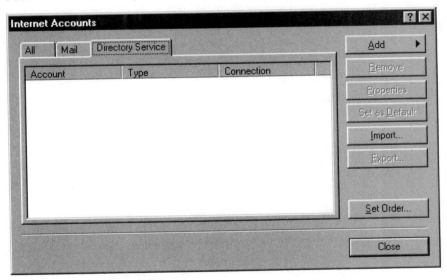

2. Click Add, then click on Directory (LDAP) Service. In the Internet directory server text box, add the name of the directory service you wish to use, then click on Next>.

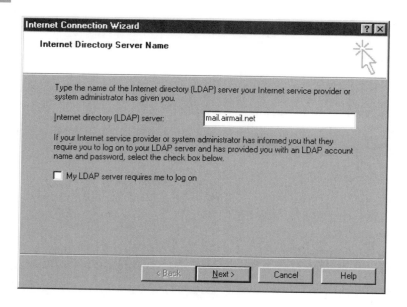

3. Click on the Yes button to use the directory service entered in the last step. Then click on Next> to continue.

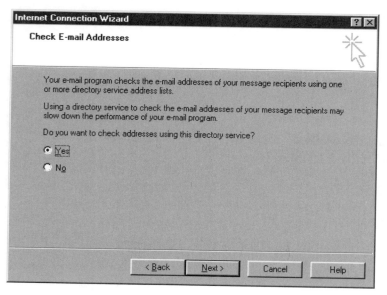

4. Click on Finish to set the directory service and to exit the wizard. Your Internet Accounts dialog should look similar to the following. Note that the directory service account name will most likely be different.

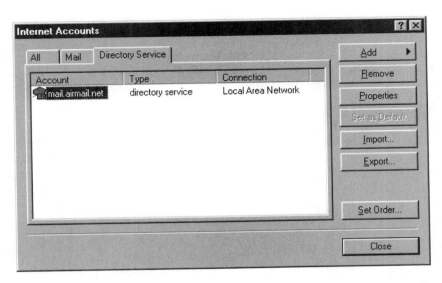

You can temporarily add or remove an Internet directory service to be checked for e-mail names. Click on the Tools|Accounts menu selection. Click the Directory Service tab of the Internet Accounts dialog. In the Directory Services list, click on the directory service to temporarily add, and then click on Properties.

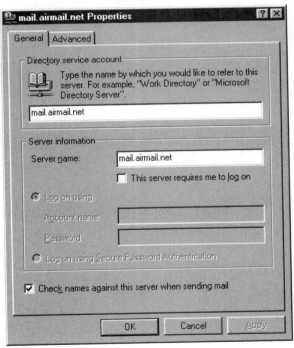

Note that you can permanently remove the directory service by clicking the account name in the Directory Service text box, then clicking on Remove as shown in the illustration above.

To temporarily add or remove a directory service to be checked for names, select or clear the Check names against this server when sending mail check box. Click on OK, then click on Close.

E-mail Editors

In Outlook 2000, you can choose whether you want to use Word as the default e-mail editor or the editor provided by Outlook. Also, you can choose whether you want to send messages as plain text (.txt), HTML (.html), or Rich Text Format (.rtf). You can use any of these message formats whether using Outlook or Word as the e-mail editor.

You can always create a single message in a format or editor other than the default editor selected. Click on Actions|New Mail Message Using, and then click your choice of message format or e-mail editor. You can switch between HTML, RTF, or plain-text editing any time, even in the middle of composing a message.

E-mail Message Formats

Using HTML as the message format offers you the ability to send messages with animated graphics, pictures, multimedia objects, and anything else that a web page can contain. You can also send messages that contain entire web pages. To use HTML as your message format, click on the Tools|Options menu selection, and then click the Mail Format tab. In the Send in this message format list, click HTML.

Create New Message (Outbox)

There are several methods for creating a new message: selecting Outbox and pressing <Ctrl+N>; clicking on the File|New|Mail Message or File|New|Fax Message menu selections; or clicking on the New button 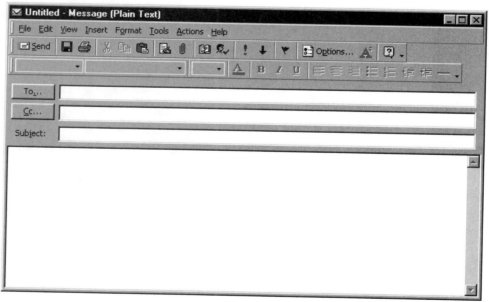 on the Standard toolbar. The Message dialog will be displayed.

Use the To button to pick an addressee from your address book or type an address in the To text box. The Select Names dialog will appear. Highlight the desired name in the left text box, then click the To button to move the name and address over to the Message Recipients text box. Repeat the same procedure to move a name/address over to the Cc (copy to) text box. Note that highlighting a name in the left text box, then clicking Properties allows you to modify and/or add information concerning the contact. Also, you can add new contact information by clicking on New Contact.

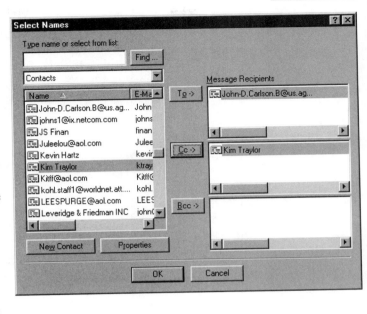

Click OK to return to the message dialog. Then type a subject in the Subject text box. Finally, move the cursor to the message text area and type your message. You move from text box to text box by pressing the tab key or by moving the mouse cursor to the appropriate text box and clicking with the left mouse button. Files can be attached to the message by clicking the Insert|File menu selection or by clicking on the Insert|File button on the (message) Standard toolbar.

Text font, size, and other formatting tools are not available if Format|Plain Text menu selection is selected. If Format|Rich Text menu selection is selected, then the Formatting toolbar is enabled and all the available text formatting tools are at your disposal.

Note that the (message) Standard toolbar also has several buttons not seen elsewhere. By clicking on one of these buttons you may flag your message as having some special significance the recipient may take notice of. The flag will show up in the recipient's Inbox on the left side of the message header in the appropriate column. The flags are High Priority !, Low Priority ↓, and Follow-Up ✶.

When you are finished with the message, click on Send, or click on Close if you decide not to send the message, and either save or discard the message.

Signatures

Use a signature to automatically add text to the messages you send. You can create a signature that includes your name, job title, and phone number or any other text you desire. You may also use a signature to add one or more boilerplate paragraphs about any topic you wish, including information about yourself and/or your company. Also, you can create multiple signatures, then select a specific signature to insert in a message after you have created the message. If you use Microsoft Word as the e-mail editor, you can create a signature in Word.

You add a signature to your outgoing message by typing your signature text, highlighting it, and then using the Tools|AutoSignature menu selection to save the highlighted text as the default signature. An example of a "contact info" signature is:

> Your Name
> Company Name
> Street Address
> City, State, Zip
> E-mail Address
> Voice Phone Number
> Fax Phone Number
> Cell Phone Number

In all new messages, this signature is automatically applied. You can also insert it using the Insert|Signature menu selection.

Tip: To insert a signature into a message when using Microsoft Word as the e-mail editor, click on the Insert|Autotext|E-mail Signature menu selection and then click the name of a signature.

Multiple Signatures

You may create more than one e-mail signature and then select the one that you want to use for each message you send. For example, you might have a signature for messages sent to your business clients, and a different signature for messages to your friends. To create signatures, or to set a default signature to be inserted in all outgoing messages, click on the Tools|Options menu selection, click the Mail Format tab, and then click Signature Picker.

vCards

Michael Busby.vcf

Outlook supports the use of vCards (virtual "business" cards), the Internet standard for creating and sharing virtual business cards. A vCard includes your contact information in a standard format that a recipient can easily retrieve and read. When you receive a vCard, it appears in the Outlook Inbox as an attachment to the message. When you double-click the message to open the Message dialog, it appears as a Rolodex card image at the bottom of the pane.

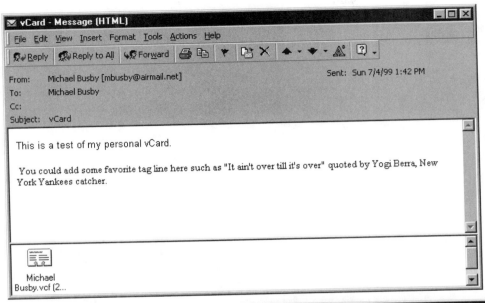

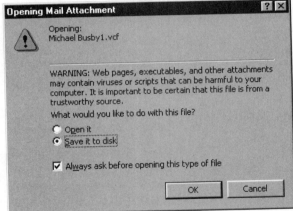

You can double-click the vCard image and see the contact properties of the person who sent it to you.

You can save a contact as a vCard or save vCards sent in other peoples' e-mail messages by clicking the Save It to Disk button on the Opening Mail Attachment dialog.

The following discussion is the general procedure for setting up your own vCard. We recommend you set up at least two vCards—one for business (name it My Business vCard) and another for personal use (name it My Personal vCard). To include your own vCard with your autosignature, click on the Tools|Options menu selection. On the Mail Format tab of the Options dialog, click Signature Picker, then click on New. In the Enter a Name for Your New Signature text box, enter a name for the vCard. A generic My vCard is shown in the example. Now select the "Start with a blank signature" option, then click on Next>.

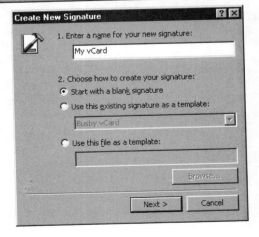

Under vCard Options, click on the New vCard from Contact button.

Note: If you have previously created one or more vCards, you can select a vCard from the Attach This Business Card (vCard) to This Signature drop-down box and then edit it. Click on Finish.

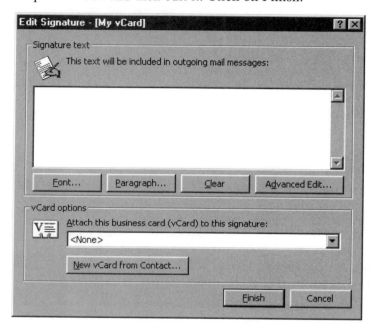

On the Select contacts to export as vCards dialog, click on New Contact.

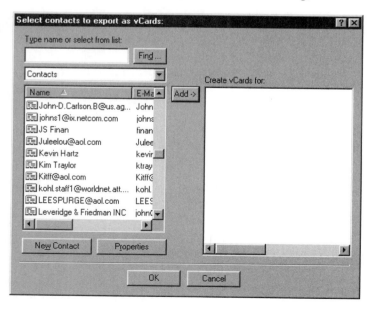

On the Personal tab of the Properties dialog (shown below as the Michael Busby Properties dialog; the dialog changes its name as you type in your name!), type in your name and e-mail address.

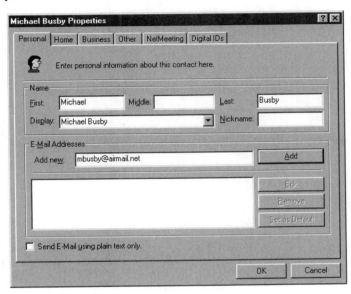

Click on the Home and Business tabs and enter all the information you deem appropriate about yourself. Remember, this vCard will be attached to all outgoing mail, so do not give out your home phone number unless you are prepared to receive calls at home. When you have entered all your information, click on OK. Now highlight your name in the Name column and click the Add button. You should see your name in the

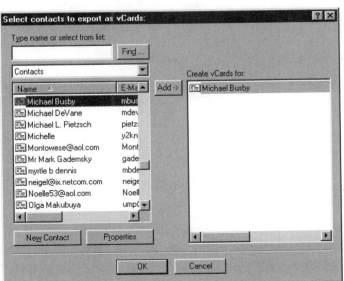

Create vCards for column. Click on OK.

In the Edit Signature - [My vCard] dialog, you can enter a text tag line in the This Text will be included in outgoing mail messages text box. Observe that you must enter the text without the benefit of a cursor. When finished, click on Finish.

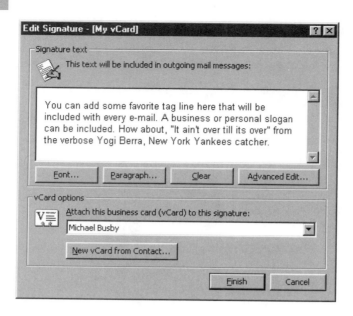

In the Signature Picker dialog, you get the opportunity to preview your tag line. Click on OK. If you decide your tag line is awful or trite, click on Edit to delete or change it.

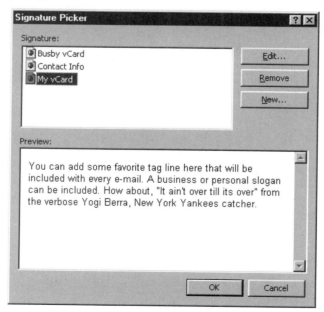

In the Mail Format tab Signature area of the Options dialog, ensure My vCard is selected as the Use this Signature by default choice. Click on Apply. Click on OK.

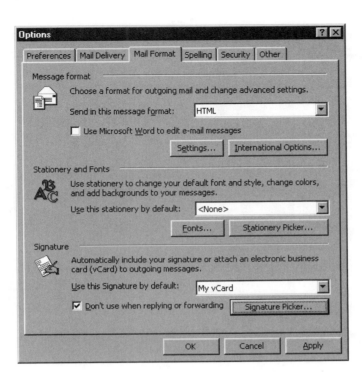

To see your vCard in action, click on the New button on the Standard toolbar.

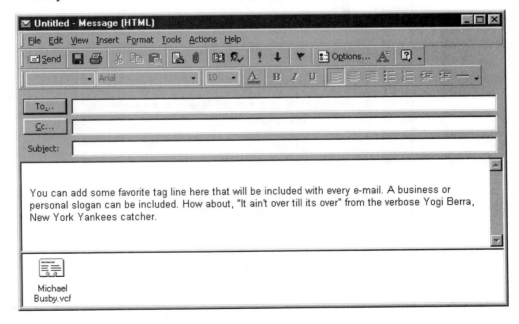

Notice the tag line is present at the bottom of the mail text box and below that is my vCard. Double-click on the vCard to see the Properties dialog.

Select the Open it button on the Opening Mail Attachment dialog.

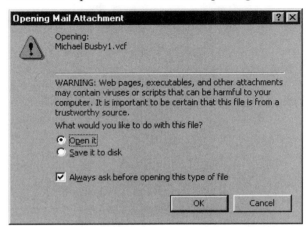

To change any of the properties of your vCard, select Tools|Address Book from the menu. Scroll down to your name and highlight it. Click on the Properties button.

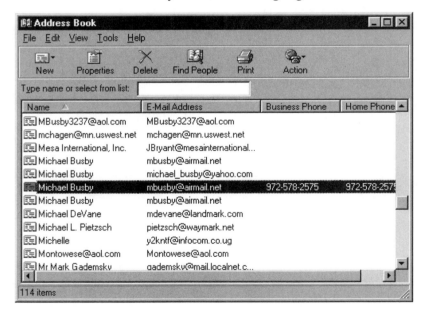

Now you are in the Properties dialog and can change any of the information you desire. When finished, click on OK and close the Address Book dialog.

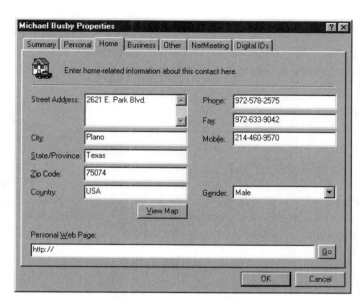

If you want to send a vCard to someone in e-mail, click on Contacts. Click the contact you want to send as a vCard, click on Actions, and then click on Forward as vCard. If the Forward as vCard command is not available, click on Forward.

You can save a contact as a vCard. Click on the Contacts button. Right-click the contact you want to save, and then click Export to vCard file on the shortcut menu.

You can also save a vCard sent to you in an e-mail message. Double-click the attached vCard in the message. Type any additional information you want to include for the contact, then click on the Save and Close button.

You can import a vCard into Outlook. Double-click the vCard, and type any additional information you want to include for the contact. Click on the Save and Close button. You can also drag the vCard onto Contacts on the Outlook bar.

General Signature and vCard Procedures

The following paragraphs explain different basic procedures for using signatures and vCards.

Select the Default Signature

Click on the Tools|Options menu selection, and then click the Mail Format tab of the Options dialog. In the "Send in this message format" box, click the message format you want to use the signature with. Remember, Rich Text Format and HTML format enable graphics and formatting tools. However, if the recipient is not using Outlook or Outlook Express, they may not be able to read your message. In the Use This Signature by Default box, click the signature you want. Select or clear the Don't Use When Replying or Forwarding box, as appropriate.

Insert a Signature in a Message

Create a new message or open an existing message. In the text box, click where you want to insert the signature. Click on Insert|Signature menu selection, and then click the signature you want. If the signature you want is not listed, click More, and in the Signature box, select the one you want to use.

Change a Signature

Click on the Tools|Options menu selection, and then click the Mail Format tab of the Options dialog. In the Send in This Message Format box, click the message format the signature is used with. Click on Signature Picker.

In the Signature box, click the signature you want to change, then click Edit. In the Signature text box, type the text you want to include in the signature. You can also paste text to the Edit Signature dialog box from another document. To change the paragraph or font format, select the text, click Font or Paragraph, and then select the options you want. The text formatting options are not available if you use plain text as your message format.

Note: If you wish to change a signature for a single message only, make your changes directly to the signature in the message.

Stop Using an Automatic Signature or Stationery

Click on the Tools|Options menu selection, then click the Mail Format tab of the Options dialog. To stop using stationery, click <None> in the Use this stationery by default box. To stop using a signature, click <None> in the Use this signature by default box. To turn off a signature for messages you reply to or forward, select the Don't use when replying or forwarding check box.

Note: To remove a signature from a single message only, highlight the signature in the message, and then press the Delete key or click on Cut.

Create a Signature When Using Word as The E-mail Editor

Start a new message in Outlook using Word as the e-mail editor. Click on the Tools|Options menu selection in the new message, then click on the General tab. Click on E-mail Options, then click on the E-mail Signature tab. Type and format the text to use for your signature under Create your e-mail signature. In the Type the title of your e-mail signature or Choose from the list box, type a name for the signature. Click on Add. Under Choose your default e-mail signature, click on the name of a signature in the Signature for new messages list box and the Signature for replies and forwards list box, or click on None if you do not want to use a default signature.

Include a vCard with Your Autosignature

Click on the Tools|Options menu selection. Click on Signature Picker on the Mail Format tab. Click on New. Select the options wanted, then click Next>. In vCard Options, select a vCard from the list or click New vCard from Contact.

Import a vCard into Outlook

Double-click on the vCard. Type any additional information you wish to include for the contact. Click on Save and Close.

Tip: You can also drag the vCard onto Contacts on the Outlook bar.

Send a vCard to Someone in E-mail

Click on the Contacts button in the Outlook Shortcuts pane. Click the contact you want to send as a vCard, then click Actions and Forward as vCard. If the Forward as vCard command is not available, then just click Forward.

File Attachments

If you are sending an e-mail message, you can attach one or more files using the Insert File button 🔘 or the Insert|File menu selection. You must have a New Message dialog box open (by clicking either the New button on the Standard toolbar or the New|Mail Message menu selection) to attach a file to a message. Then you will see the Insert File button on the Standard toolbar. Once your message is composed, click on Send to put it in the Outbox.

Reading Your Messages (Inbox)

Your incoming messages are found in the Inbox. Here, you can select a message in the message list and press <Ctrl+O> or click on the message to open it. The message list appears in the top pane of the Inbox window. The Inbox window resembles the following illustration. The window contains two panes, the Message List pane and the Preview pane. Notice the single message, "Welcome to Microsoft Outlook 2000," highlighted in blue in the message list. Below the Message List pane is the preview pane. Show or hide the Preview pane by clicking on the View|Preview Pane menu selection.

Notice that the Inbox allows you to reply to and forward messages in addition to performing the normal filing, mapping, and other common Office 2000 chores.

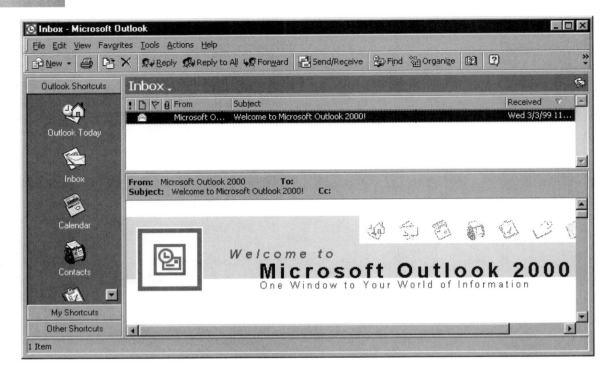

Auto Format Reply

Outlook automatically uses the message format in which the original message was sent when you reply to a message. This ensures that e-mail recipients receive replies they can read easily.

By clicking on the View|Preview Pane menu selection, you can view the entire contents of any selected message at the bottom of the Outlook window, without opening the message. By using the Preview pane, you can quickly decide which messages to read and which to delete. You can adjust the amount of message text you see by dragging the top border of the Preview pane up or down. To set the Preview pane options, click on the Tools|Options menu selection and select the Other tab of the Options dialog. Click on Preview Pane, then select the options desired. To get Help for an option, click the question mark button, and then click the option.

Message Options and Tracking

Use the Tool|Options menu selection and the Options dialog to set the importance, sensitivity, expiration date and time, and tracking options for messages. Click on the E-mail Options button in the E-mail section of the Preferences tab and select the options suitable for you in the following dialogs.

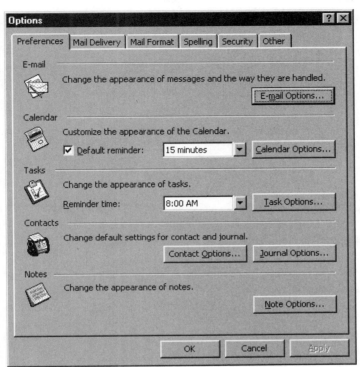

The E-mail Options dialog offers various choices for message handling. If you are an experienced Office user, then set the options to the choices you favor. If you are an inexperienced Office user, it is best to keep the default settings until you have some experience and can make informed choices. Either way, you can always change the options when it suits your needs. Click on the Tracking Options button to view the next dialog.

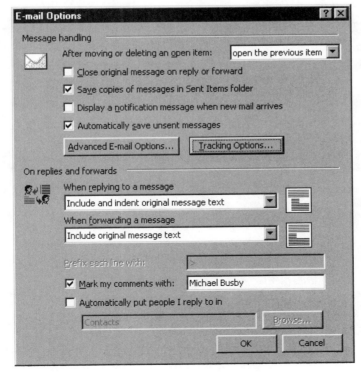

The Tracking Options dialog allows you to set up receipt request and receipt response options. If both the message sender and the message recipient have message tracking enabled, the sender will automatically receive a receipt response from the sender when the sender's machine receives the message. The message sender must have Request a read receipt for all messages I send checked in the Tracking Options dialog and the message recipient must have checked Always send a response for the sender to receive the message receipt. If the recipient has disabled receipt response ("Never send a response" choice in the Tracking Options dialog), no receipt will be sent.

If you click the Advanced E-mail Options button on the E-mail Options dialog, you will open the Advanced E-mail Options dialog. Again, if you are a new Office user, you should probably stick with the default settings. If you are familiar with Office, you may wish to change the settings. Setting message importance and sensitivity are the two selections most often used in this dialog. However,

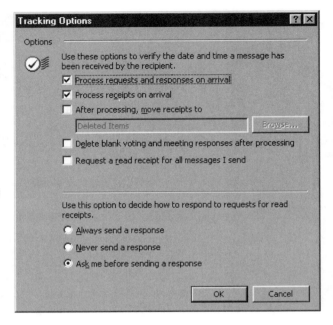

you can set individual message importance from the toolbar using these buttons  and do not need to go to this great length to set the importance or sensitivity of a single message.

Large Messages

Outlook 2000 includes a useful tool for setting the maximum size of messages that Outlook will download. Messages larger than the specified maximum are not downloaded. The option is ignored if you send messages over a local area network (LAN). Click on the Tools|Options menu selection, and click on the Mail Delivery tab of the Options dialog. Now select the Don't download messages larger than check box, and then enter a number representing the maximum message size in the box. If you are not familiar with message sizes, a good default number is 25,000.

Junk E-mail

To automatically color all junk and adult content e-mail messages, click the Inbox button. Click the Organize button on the Standard toolbar, then click Junk E-mail. Select the options you want by clicking the down arrow next to each box, then clicking the Turn on button.

See Section 82 for more information about filtering unwanted e-mail messages.

Sent Items

This selection maintains a list of your sent messages. You can resend these items to either the original addressee or to others upon request. You can save sent messages in a different format, such as a document or text file, so the content can be used for other purposes.

Deleted Items

Deleted Items are copies of all deleted items, including messages, tasks, appointments, and notes. This gives you one last chance to save an item before it is permanently discarded. You may want to copy some important items to a diskette before deleting them from the Delete Items folder; once deleted from the Deleted Items folder, they are gone for good.

Hands-on Activities

In this activity you first create a new message, then add your signature. Begin by starting Outlook and displaying the Outbox.

Start a New Message

1. Press **<Ctrl+N>** to open a New Message dialog. Observe the automatic placement of my signature and vCard in the new message.

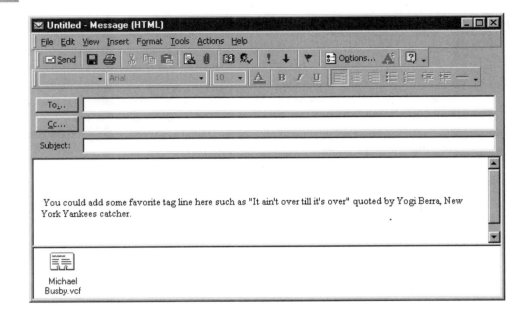

2. Type an e-mail address in the To box. If necessary, use your own e-mail address. Tab to the Subject box and type **My Outlook Message**.

Tip: A valid e-mail address consists of a prefix and a suffix separated by the @ symbol. As an example, my e-mail address is mbusby@airmail.net. "mbusby" is the prefix and "airmail.net" is the suffix.

3. Tab to the text area. Type two lines of text and press **<Enter>** twice.

4. Type your name and e-mail address on separate lines. Then highlight them (drag them with your mouse).

5. Select **Tools|AutoSignature**. Click **Yes** on the dialog that follows to save your name and e-mail address as the default signature.

6. Click **Send** to send the message (or put it in your Outbox).

7. Notice that your message is listed in the Outbox.

8. Select the document and press **<Ctrl+D>** to send it to the Deleted Items folder.

9. Click the **Deleted Items** icon. Look for your e-mail message. You can double-click it to view the contents.

10. Highlight the practice message and press **<Ctrl+D>** to permanently delete it.

11. Click **Yes** to delete the message.

Create a Signature for Messages

1. Click on the **Tools|Options** menu selection, then click the **Mail Format** tab of the Options dialog.

2. In the Send in this message format box, click the message format you want to use the signature with. Remember that plain text does not enable the text formatting tools. If you want to be able to change the font, font size, etc., select the Microsoft Outlook Rich Text Format selection.

3. Click **Signature Picker**, and then click **New**.

4. In the Enter a name for your new signature box, enter a name such as Contact Info (or My Contact Info) for your name, address, e-mail address, and phone numbers.

5. Under Choose how to create your signature, select whether to start from scratch or use an existing signature. If this is the first time, you must start from scratch.

   To select a file to base your signature on, such as one or more boilerplate paragraphs that you created using Microsoft Word, click **Use this file as a template** and type the path and file-name in the box, or click **Browse** to select from a list.

6. Click **Next>**.

7. In the Signature text box, type the text you want to include in the signature.

   You can also paste text to the Signature text box from another document.

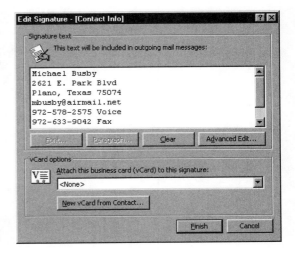

8. To change the paragraph or font format, select the text, click **Font** or **Paragraph**, and then select the options you want. These options are not available if plain text is selected as the message format.

Note: To change the background used in the message, use stationery.

9. Click on **Finish**.

10. Observe the resulting Signature Picker dialog. Your signature preview is shown at the bottom of the dialog. If you wish

to change anything, click on **Edit**, otherwise click on **OK** to accept the signature text as shown.

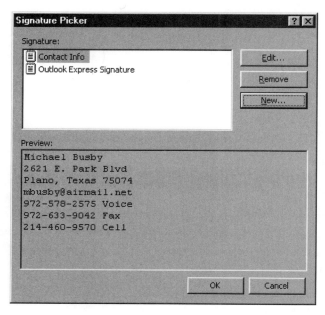

11. Close the remaining dialogs and exit Outlook to complete these activities.

Summary

Outlook's Mail application is a multifaceted messaging system. It is the most complex application within Outlooks repertoire of features, because it is dependent on a number of other applications such as Microsoft Mail, Internet Mail, Microsoft Fax, and others. For Mail to operate properly, it is important for your communications applications to be properly configured. Use the extensive amount of information available in the online help to review the setup of profiles.

Now move on to the next section. There you continue your review of Outlook by taking a closer look at the Calendar application.

Using Calendar

Introduction

Appointment calendars are used to enter and display appointments by day of the month and the starting and ending time of your appointment or meeting. You can select the desired appointment calendar by clicking the Day, Week, or Month buttons on the toolbar. You can also print appointments, which is useful if you are using a desktop computer and wish to carry a paper copy of your itinerary during your travels.

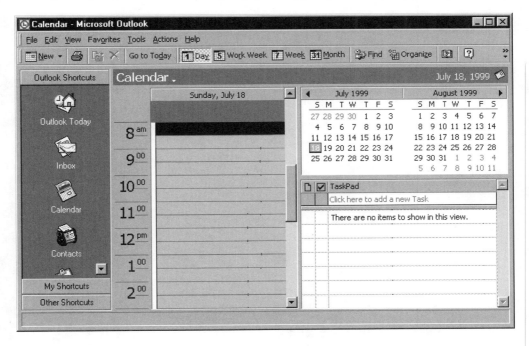

You may schedule appointments, meetings, and events using Outlook. The appointment, meeting, or event may be a single instance or it may be a recurring instance. Outlook views an appointment as a singular type of meeting between you and one other person—say, a dental appointment. A meeting is viewed as a gathering of more than two people at some location that can be specified, such as a specific conference room. An event is viewed as a daylong gathering. Using Calendar, you can easily track all your appointments, meetings, and events, even sending meeting invitations automatically to invitees using the messaging features of Outlook.

Menus and Toolbars

The menu bar and toolbars are the same as previously discussed in other parts of the book with two menu exceptions. The View and Actions menus contain Calendar-specific buttons. These two menus and the functions of their buttons are provided here.

View Menu

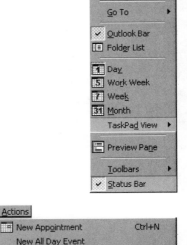

Current View—Changes the view to one of seven views or customize the view.

Go To—Goes to one of 12 destinations including Outlook applications.

Outlook Bar—Displays or hides the Outlook bar.

Folder List—Displays or hides all the Outlook folders.

Day—Displays the day view.

Work Week—Displays the five-day workweek view.

Week—Displays the seven-day week view.

Month—Displays the month view.

TaskPad View—Displays tasks.

Preview Pane—Displays or hides the preview pane.

Toolbars—Displays or hides the toolbars.

Status Bar—Displays or hides the status bar.

Actions Menu

New Appointment—Creates and records a new appointment.

New All Day Event—Create and record a new all-day event.

New Meeting Request—Create and record a meeting request.

Plan a Meeting—Extend invitations to a meeting and display invitees' schedules.

New Recurring Appointment—Create and record a new appointment that repeats at a specified interval.

New Recurring Meeting—Create and record a new meeting that repeats at a specified interval.

Add or Remove Attendees—Add and remove meeting attendees.

Forward as iCalendar—Forward calendar to recipient.

Forward—Forward icalendar to a recipient.

General Calendar Procedures

General calendar procedures include scheduling, editing, deleting, moving, and printing appointments, meetings, and events. The following general procedures describe how to accomplish these.

Entering Appointments

Select the Day view (click the Day button or use the View|Day menu selection). Then pick the month and day from the displayed calendar. (Go to the next or previous month by clicking the right or left arrowhead at the top of the month.) Pick the starting time of the appointment and press <Ctrl+N> for New Appointment. The Appointment dialog is displayed. Type a description and location, adjust the starting and ending times, then prepare the reminder information and click Save and Close.

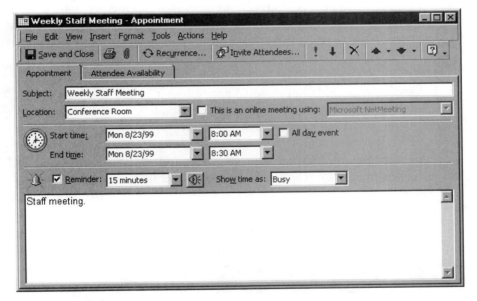

Use the Recurrence button (or the Actions|Recurrence menu selection) if you want to set a recurring daily, weekly, or monthly meeting. Notice that the dialog allows you to set a variety of recurring appointments. You can use the Recur Every Week(s) On box to set quarterly or semiannual meetings. Also notice that you can pick the day of the week using one of the check boxes.

Another way to enter an appointment is to click on the File|New|Appointment menu selection. Type a description in the Subject box. Enter the location of the appointment or meeting in the Location box. Enter appointment or meeting start and end times. Select any other options you want, then click on the Save and Close button.

Editing Appointments

You can change an appointment using the same dialogs shown in the preceding section.

Select the Day or Week view. You can move to the following or previous week by highlighting an entire week on the month calendar. Similarly, you can view two or three weeks by highlighting them on the month calendar. Select the appointment you want to change and press <Ctrl+O> for Open. (Alternately, you can double-click the appointment box.) Change the dates, times, reminders, recurring settings, etc., as necessary. Click Save and Close to save the changes; press Esc to cancel.

Moving Appointments

To move an appointment, first select the Day or Week tab. Select the appointment you want to move and press <Ctrl+O> to open it. Enter the new date and new times, using the displayed dialog. Click Save and Close once your changes are made to move the appointment to the new date and time.

Deleting an Appointment

To delete a canceled or completed appointment, select the Day or Week view. Select the appointment you want to delete and press <Ctrl+D> to delete the appointment. If you are deleting a recurring item, click the appropriate option button to delete one or all of the recurring appointments.

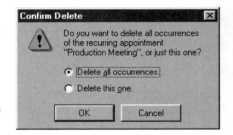

Printing Appointments

Outlook offers a number of printed formats to choose from. The following general procedure is used to print your appointments in the desired format. Select the day, week, or month you want to print. Use the File|Page Setup menu selection. Alternately, click on the Print button 🖨. Pick a view style. The figure on the following page is displayed for the Monthly Style.

Click Print Preview to see the output before it is printed.

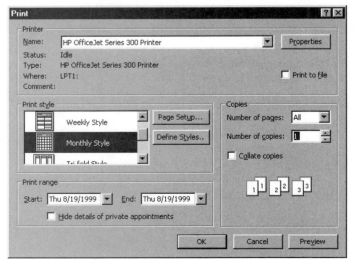

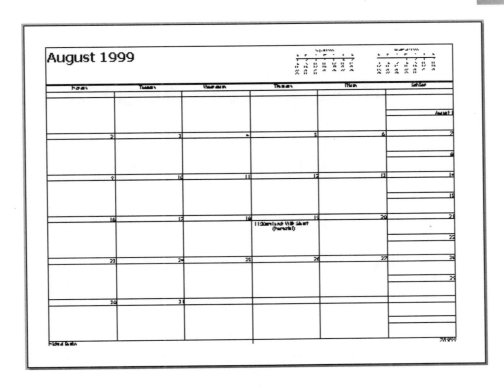

If you are satisfied, click on Print. Click on Close to return to the Calendar view.

Schedule a Recurring Appointment

Click on the Calendar button in the Outlook Shortcuts pane. Click on the Actions|New Recurring Appointment menu selection. Enter the appointment or meeting start and end times.

Click the frequency at which the appointment recurs (Daily, Weekly, Monthly, Yearly) in the Recurrence Pattern area, then select options for the frequency such as day of week. Click on OK. Type a description in the Subject box. Enter the location in the Location box. Select other options you want. Click on the Save and Close button.

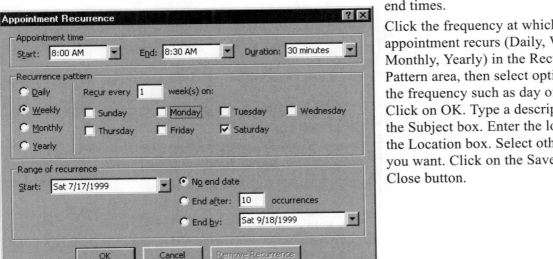

Schedule a Meeting

Click on the Calendar button in the Outlook Shortcuts pane. On the Actions menu, click on Plan a Meeting. Click on Invite Others.

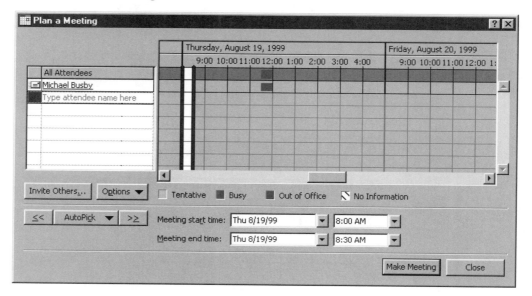

In the Type name or select from list box, enter the name of the person or resource you want to come to the meeting. Alternately, in the All Attendees area, add the names of individuals invited.

For each name entered, click on Required, Optional, or Resources. (The Required and Optional attendees appear in the To box on the Appointment tab, and Resources appear in the Location box.) Click OK, and then use the scroll

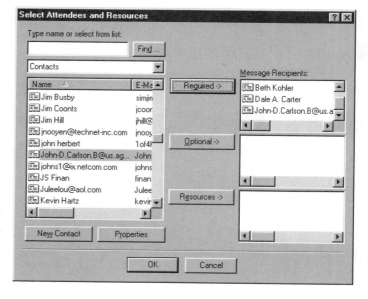

bars to view the free/busy time for invitees. Click a time when all invitees are available. You can use AutoPick to find the next available free time for all invitees. Set the meeting start and end dates and times by clicking on Meeting Start Time and Meeting End Time boxes. Alternately, you may set the day and time by clicking on the day calendar and the appropriate time of day column. Use the slide at the bottom of the day display to change the day of the meeting.

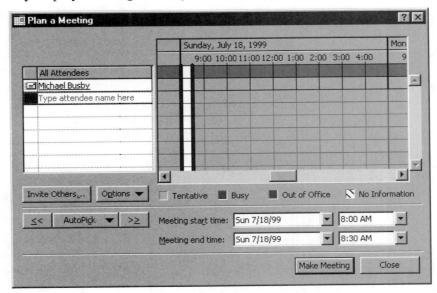

Click AutoPick, and then click an option. Click on Make Meeting.

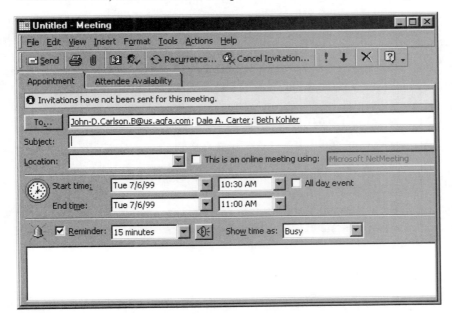

In the Subject box, type a description. Enter the location in the Location box if the meeting will be held in a conference room. Select other options you want. Click on Send.

Tip: To send an agenda or the meeting minutes, attach a file to the meeting request.

Schedule a Recurring Meeting

Click on the Calendar button in the Shortcuts pane. Click on the Actions|Plan a Meeting menu selection. Invite attendees and resources. See Schedule a Meeting above. Click on Make Meeting. In the Subject box, type a description. Enter the location of the meeting in the Location box. Select other desired options. Click on the Actions|Recurrence menu selection. Select the recurrence pattern and range of recurrence options you want. Click on OK, and then click on Send.

Schedule an Online Meeting with NetMeeting

All participants for an online meeting must have Microsoft NetMeeting version 2.1 or later running on their computer. Click on the File|New|Meeting Request menu selection. Select the This is an Online Meeting Using check box. In the To box, enter the names of people you want to schedule an online meeting with. To select names from a list, click the To button. In the Subject box, type a description of the meeting. The description will be used as the NetMeeting conference name. The meeting name can be changed only on this tab. Enter the appropriate times in the Start time and End time boxes. Select any other options desired. Select the "Reminder" check box, and then select the "Automatically start NetMeeting with reminder" check box to set a reminder and have NetMeeting start automatically. Change any default online settings desired for the meeting. Click on Send.

Tip: You can quickly start a meeting immediately with a contact. In Contacts, select a contact. On the Actions menu, click Call Using NetMeeting.

Turn an Appointment into a Meeting

Open the appointment. Click on the Attendee Availability tab and invite attendees and resources. Determine a meeting time. Click on the Appointment tab and enter the location of the meeting in the Location box. Click on Send.

Tip: To quickly change an appointment to a meeting, open the appointment, click the Actions menu, click Invite Attendees, and then enter names in the To box.

Cancel a Meeting

In Calendar, open the meeting you wish to cancel. Click on the Actions|Cancel Meeting menu selection.

Advanced topic

Tip: You may easily delete the meeting by clicking the meeting and then clicking the Delete button or pressing the Delete key.

Change Meeting Information After Extending Invitations

Open the meeting. On the Appointment tab, select the information you wish to change. If you wish to change the meeting to a recurring meeting, click on the Actions|Recurrence menu selection. Enter start and end times. Click the frequency (Daily, Weekly, Monthly, Yearly) at which you want the meeting to recur, and then select options for the frequency. Click on OK, then click on Send.

Tip: You can easily change a meeting time. When viewing days, click the appointment left move/resize handle. When viewing weeks or months, click anywhere on the appointment, then drag the meeting to a new time or to a new day in Date Navigator.

Automatically Decline Recurring Meeting Requests

Click on the Tools|Options menu selection. On the Preferences tab of the Options dialog, click on Calendar Options. Click Resource Scheduling. Select the Automatically Decline Recurring Meeting Requests check box.

Finding Appointments and Meetings with Specific Start Times

Click on the Tools|Advanced Find menu selection. In the Look For box, click on Appointments and meetings. Click on Browse to select from a list if the folder you want to search does not appear in the In box, or you want to search more than one folder. In the Folders box, select the check boxes next to the folders you want to search, and clear the check boxes next to the folders you don't want to search.

Click on OK. In the first Time box, select Starts from the drop-down list. In the second Time box, select a time criteria, such as Next week.

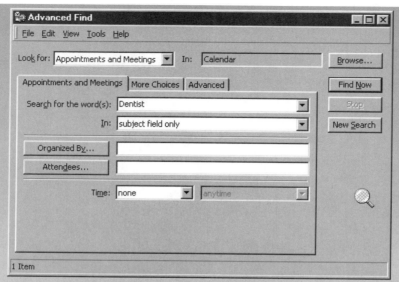

Click on the Find Now button. The Advanced Find dialog will return the search text string and where it is found in a pane at the bottom of the dialog, assuming the text string was found. This example shows a search for the text string "Dentist" and found one occurrence in Calendar.

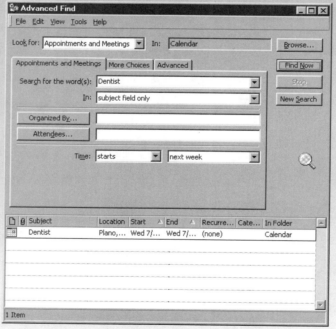

Create a Meeting Request from a Contact

Click the Contacts button in the Outlook Shortcuts pane. Select the contact, click the Actions menu, and then click New Meeting Request to Contact. Type a description in the Subject box. Enter the location in the Location box. Enter start and end times. Select other options desired. Click on the Send button.

Respond to a Meeting Request or Notification

Open the meeting request. Click on Accept, Tentative, or Decline as appropriate.

Tips:
- You can delete a meeting request from the Inbox after you have responded to it.
- Click on the Calendar button to see the meeting in your Calendar before you respond to the request.
- Open the cancellation notification, then click Remove from Calendar to delete a meeting cancellation notification and remove the meeting from the Calendar.

Find a Meeting Attended by a Specific Person

Click on the Tools|Advanced Find menu selection. In the Look For box, click on Appointments and meetings. If the folder you want to search does not appear in the In box, or you want to search more than one folder, click Browse to select from a list. In the Folders box, select the check boxes next to the folders you want to search, and clear the check boxes next to the folders you don't want to search. Click OK. Type the person's name, or click Attendees to select from a list in the Attendees box. Click on Find Now.

Find Meetings Organized by a Specific Person

Click on the Tools|Advanced Find menu selection. In the Look For box, click on Appointments and meetings. If the folder you want to search does not appear in the In box, or you want to search more than one folder, click Browse to select from a list. In the Folders box, select the check boxes next to the folders you want to search, and clear the check boxes next to the folders you don't want to search. Click OK. In the Organized By box, type the person's name, or click on Organized By to select from a list. If you are selecting from a list, point to the person's name, click on the Organized By button, and then click OK. Click on Find Now. The Find Now dialog will return the found information in a pane at the bottom of the dialog.

Copy an Appointment

Click on the Calendar button Selection item, hold down Ctrl, and drag the item to a new time in Calendar.

Tip: Designate the appointment as recurring if appropriate.

Note: You can copy an appointment to any Office 2000 document or application by opening the document or application alongside Outlook and dragging the appointment into the destination window.

Automatically Decline Conflicting Meeting Requests

Click on the Tools|Options menu selection. On the Preferences tab of the Options dialog, click on Calendar Options, then on Resource Scheduling. Click the Automatically Decline Conflicting Meeting Requests check box.

Free/Busy Information

You can access and store another person's free/busy information if they have given you permission. Click on File|New|Contact then click on the Details tab.

Under Internet Free-Busy, in the Address box, type the name of the server where the contact's free/busy information is stored.

Tip: If most of your contacts are storing their free/busy information in the same location, you can specify a default search URL by typing the URL in the Search at this URL box in the Free/Busy Options dialog box.

Update Another Person's Free/Busy Information

In a new or open meeting request, click on the Attendee Availability tab. Click on Show attendee availability. Click on Options and then click Update free/busy.

Viewing a Yearly Calendar

You can drag the month both left and down to increase the number of months displayed.

Create a Single Event

To create a single event, click on the Calendar button in the Shortcuts pane. Click on the Actions|New All Day Event menu selection. Type a description of the event in the Subject box. Enter the location of the event in the Location box. Select any other desired options. To indicate to people viewing your Calendar that you are out of the office instead of free, in the Show Time As list, click on Out of Office. Click on the Save and Close button.

In Day/Week/Month view, you can quickly create an event by double-clicking the date heading of the day of the event.

Create an Annual Event

To create an annual event click on the Calendar button in the Shortcuts pane. Click on the Actions|New All Day Event menu selection. Type a description of the event in the Subject box. Enter the location of the event in the Location box. Select any other desired options. Click on the Actions|Recurrence menu selection. Change the value in the Duration box, as appropriate, if the event lasts longer than a day. Click on Yearly, and then select the date or day of the year. Click on OK, then click on the Save and Close button.

Hands-on Activity

In this activity you enter a series of appointments based on the following list. Use the current calendar year. Begin by starting Outlook and selecting the Calendar application.

Time	Date	Description	Location	Reminder	Recurring
9:00 a.m.-10:00 a.m.	6/5	Production Meeting	Conf. Room B	15 min.	Weekly
1:55 p.m.-2:45 p.m.	6/6	SW 105 Dallas-Houston Hobby	Dallas Love Field	No	No
5:00 p.m.-7:00 p.m.	6/6	Dinner with Dan Lynch	Joe's Barbecue - Alvin	15 min.	No
9:00 a.m.-11:00 a.m.	6/7	Presentation	Houston Conv. Center	No	No
4:00 p.m.-4:50 p.m.	6/7	SW 450 Houston-Dallas	Houston Hobby Airport	No	No
10:15 a.m.-10:45 a.m.	6/8	Dental Appointment	Dr. Bridgeman's Office	15 min	6 mo.

1. Click on **View|Current View|Day/Week/Month** menu selection. Click the **Day** button on the toolbar.

2. Click on the month name to pop up a list of months. Do not click on the arrow to the left of "April" or to the right of "May"—clicking the left or right arrow changes the month one month at a time. Click to the right of the leftmost arrow or click to the left of the rightmost arrow. See the view. Select **June**.

   Note that by moving the cursor, while continuing to press the left mouse button, above or below the list of months, you can quickly scroll to any month/year desired.

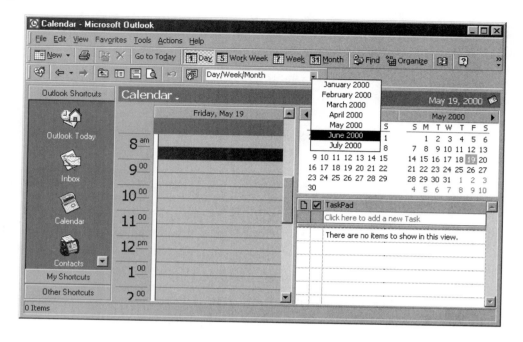

3. Click on the 5th day.

4. Enter the 9:00 A.M. appointment for June 5 as follows:

   a. Click on **9:00 A.M.**

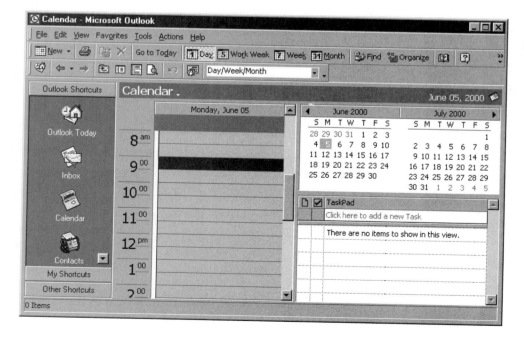

b. Press **<Ctrl+N>** to open a New Appointment dialog and enter the information shown in the dialog. Be sure to click on **End time** and set it for a one-hour meeting.

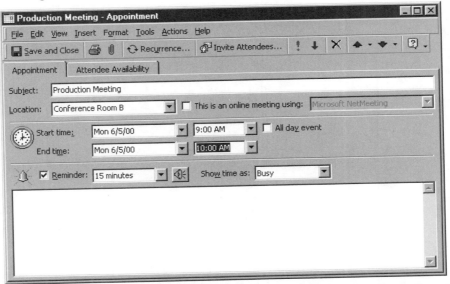

c. Click **Recurrence** and establish a weekly production meeting by setting the Appointment Recurrence dialog as shown.

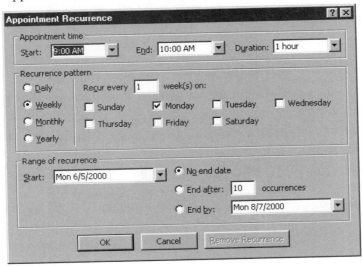

d. Click **OK** on the Recurrence dialog, then click on **Save and Close** on the Appointment dialog; notice the bell and circular arrow symbols on the appointment entry.

e. Memorize the symbols for reminder (bell) and recurring (circular arrows). The symbols reveal additional information about an appointment.

5. Click day **6** on the Month (June) display.

6. Click on the 1:30 P.M. time line and press **<Ctrl+N>**. Enter the information shown in the table for the 1:55 P.M.-2:45 P.M. flight from Dallas to Houston. See tip below for setting the time. Follow the same procedure as the appointment entered for June 5, except this is not a recurring appointment. Click **Save and Close**.

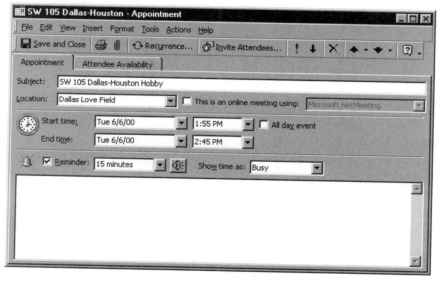

Tips: You can change the hour and minute values by clicking on them and typing new values.

You can extend the beginning and ending times of your appointment planner using the Options dialog. Display the Options dialog using the **Tools|Options** menu selection. Select the **Calendar** options button.

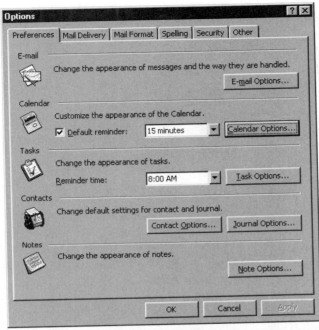

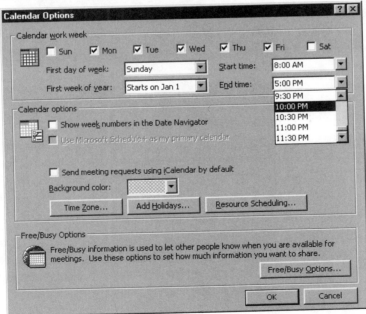

Change the Start or End time as required by either clicking in the text box and typing in a new value or clicking on the down arrow and selecting the appropriate time.

7. Click and drag from 5:00 P.M. to 7:00 P.M.

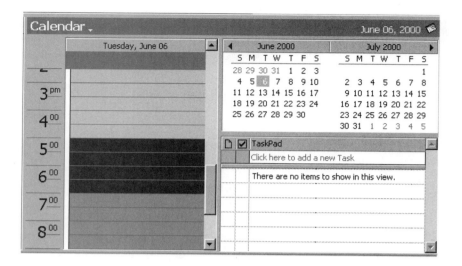

Enter the information shown in the dialog below.

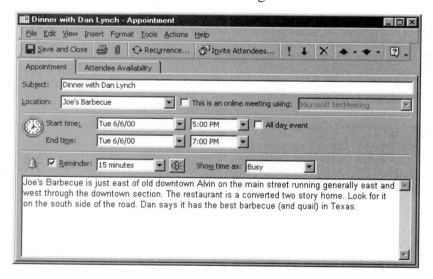

8. Now advance to June 7 and enter the two appointments listed for that day. If you have any difficulty, refer to the above steps and dialogs to review how you entered the settings.

9. Advance to June 8 and enter the dentist appointment.

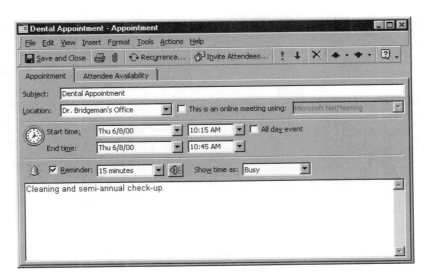

10. Make this appointment recurring using the following dialog. Click on the Monthly option, then click in the months text box and change the value to **6**.

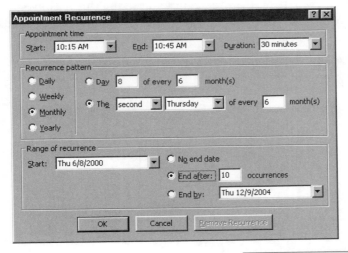

11. Click the Week or Work Week button [5 Work Week] [7 Week] and see all of the appointments for the week. Each one gives you a different view of the schedule. Scroll up or down, as appropriate, using the right scroll bar to view each appointment for the week.

12. Click the Month button [31 Month] and see all of the appointments for the month. Scroll up or down, as appropriate, using the right scroll bar to view each appointment for the week. Notice the recurring production meeting every Monday. Can you find the next dental appointment? (Hint: Use the scroll bar.)

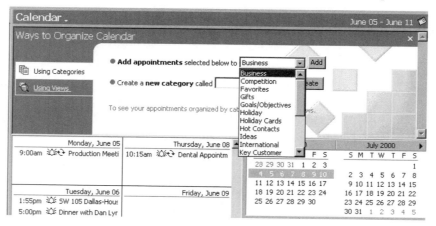

13. Go back to the week view by clicking on the Week button. Highlight or single-click the 5:00 p.m. appointment on June 6. Now double-click on the **Organize** button ▐▓ Organize▐. By clicking on the drop-down arrow of the Add appointments selected below to box, you may add the appointment to any category you wish. This is convenient for looking at your appointment schedule by category types. If you do not see a suitable category, you can add your own using the Create a new category called option.

14. Click on the **Organize** button again.

15. By clicking on the **View|Current View** menu selection, or by clicking on the **Current View** button ▐Day/Week/Month ▼▐ you can view your appointments in a variety of ways. See the choices illustrated to the right.

Day/Week/Month ▼▼
- Day/Week/Month
- Day/Week/Month View With AutoPreview
- Active Appointments
- Events
- Annual Events
- Recurring Appointments
- By Category

16. Press **<Alt+F4>** to exit Outlook. This concludes the hands-on activity for this section.

Summary

In this section you learned how easy it is to enter appointments. You also know how to make recurring appointments. Finally, you learned how to view your appointments in a variety of ways. In the next section you learn more about the use of tasks.

Using Tasks

Introduction

Use Tasks to organize your business and personal to-do lists in one easy-to-manage place. Quickly sort and prioritize tasks, set reminders for when tasks are due, and assign tasks to others. To start Tasks, click on the Tasks button in the Outlook Shortcuts pane. To record a single new task, click on the File|New|Task menu selection when in any Outlook application.

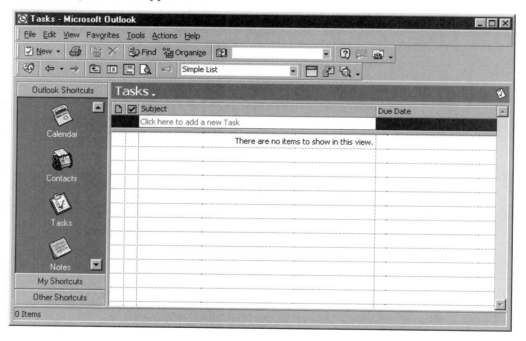

To create a task in the Task application, click in the text box below subject in the Tasks pane (alternately choose File|New|Task), type a description, and press <Enter>. Then click on the task description and press <Ctrl+O> (or double-click it) to open the Task dialog.

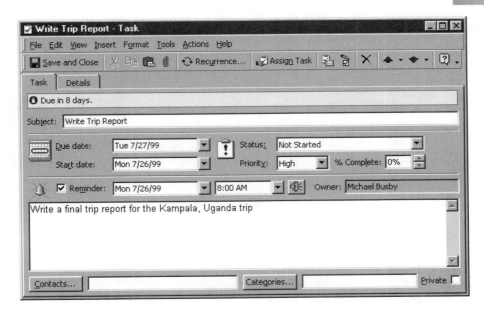

At this point you can enter details about your tasks, including a start date, due date, status, priority, percent complete, and comments about the task. Notice that the due and start dates make use of the calendar. Your tasks are displayed with your calendars as reminders of what needs to be done. The Tasks application also lets you put your to-dos in a number of different categories including Business, Personal, Phone Calls, and Time and Expenses. This is done by clicking the Categories button.

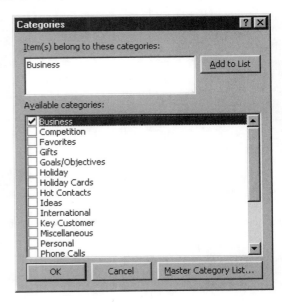

Once your task information is complete, click Save and Close. You can drag your tasks to adjust their position in the list. Dragging them is useful if you want to move only one or two tasks. If you need to move more than a couple, you can sort tasks using the View|Current View|Customize Current View menu selection. See the general procedure for sorting detailed below.

Toolbars and Menus

Below are the toolbars and menus associated with Tasks.

Menu Bar

The Menu bar and Standard toolbars include the usual and by-now-familiar File, Edit, View, Favorites, Tools, and Help buttons and task management tools. However, the toolbar does include one new item, the Actions menu. The Actions menu includes four tools, which are shown in the boxes below.

New Task (Actions menu)

Creates a new task.

Use this tool to create a new task for yourself.

New Task Request (Actions menu)

Creates a new task request.

Use this tool to create a new task for someone else, such as a subordinate.

Save Task Order (Actions menu)

Saves the current order in the task list.

Save the task order after ordering the tasks by some criteria, such as priority.

Forward (Actions menu)

Sends the message or file to the recipient you specify.

Send the task to the person responsible for performing the task or to a higher level of management oversight.

Views

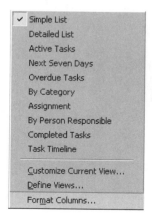

Pay particular attention to the View menu selections. The available view selections are described here.

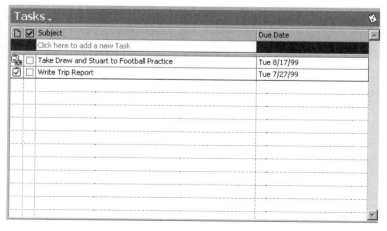

Simple List

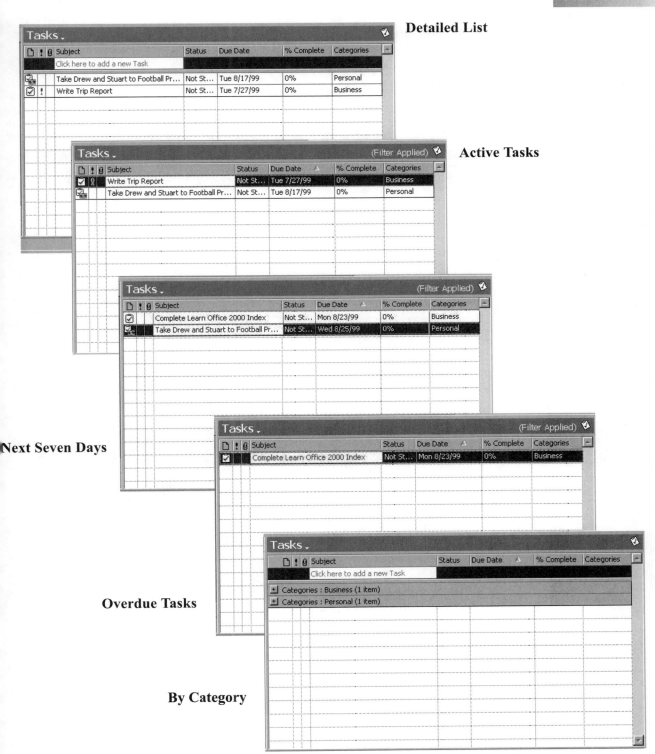

Detailed List

Active Tasks

Next Seven Days

Overdue Tasks

By Category

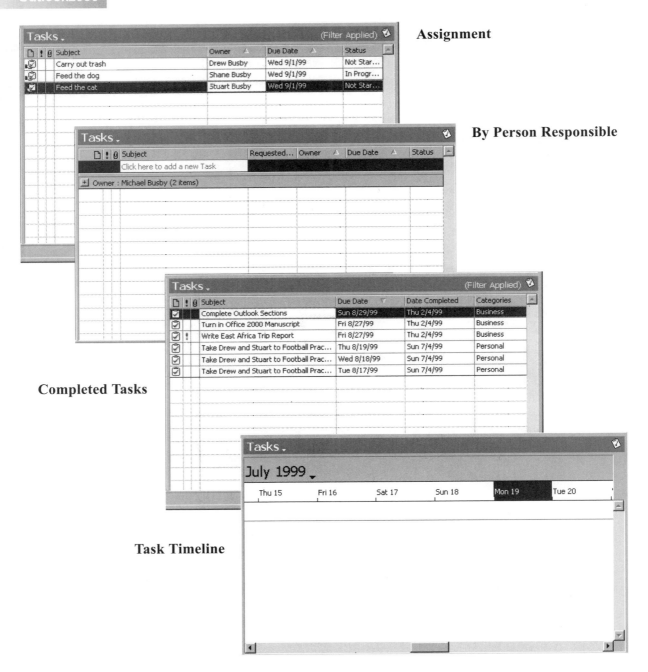

Assignment

By Person Responsible

Completed Tasks

Task Timeline

Advanced Toolbar

The Advanced toolbar includes management tools for organizing and viewing the tasks.

Outlook Today—Change to the Outlook Today window.

Previous Folder—Return to the previous folder viewed if more than one is open.

Next Folder—Go to the next folder viewed if more than one is open.

Up One Level—Go to the next higher folder.

Folders List—Display/hide the list of folders in a pane on the left side.

Preview Pane—Display/hide the message preview pane.

Print Preview—Display a preview of the item as it will look printed.

Undo—Restore the previous configuration.

Current View—Select the task features the Task pane will display.

Group By Box—Group tasks by a selected column header.

Field Chooser—Select the field to sort tasks for display.

AutoPreview—Display/hide the task remarks.

Sorting

The following procedure is the general procedure for sorting tasks.

Click on the View|Current View menu selection, and then click on a view that shows items in a table, card, or an icon view type.

Click on the View|Current View menu selection again, and then click Customize Current View. You will see the following dialog.

Click on Sort.

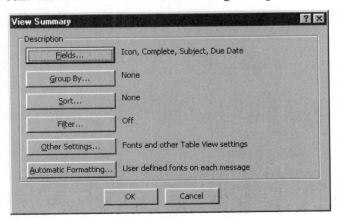

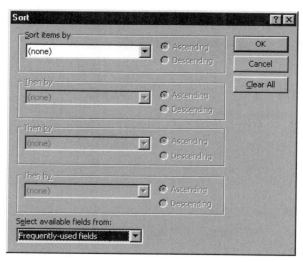

In the Sort items by box, click on a field to sort by.

If the field you want isn't in the Sort items by box, click on a different field type in the Select Available fields from box.

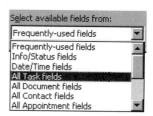

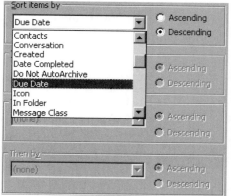

Click Ascending or Descending, as appropriate, for the sort order.

To sort by an additional field, click on a field in the Then by box. The tasks are sorted using the Then by boxes' criteria beginning with the uppermost box shown in the Sort dialog, then proceeding in order to the lowermost box.

Sorting by more than one field sorts all items by the first field selected (the Sort items by selection at the top of the Sort dialog box) and then, within that sort, sorts again by the second field (the uppermost Then by selection in the Sort dialog box).

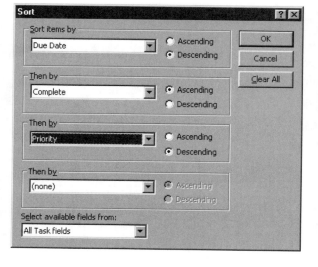

For example, if you choose to sort alphabetically and then by number, the sort structure is A 1 2 3, B 1 2 3. A column created using a custom field or formula field can't be sorted. The abbreviations RE and FW in the Subject box (the Regarding and Forward responses to messages) are ignored when you sort messages alphabetically by subject.

If you are in a table view type, such as Detailed List, you can right-click a column heading to sort or group by the column or change the sort direction of the column. The following pop-up box appears when you right-click a column heading, offering not only sort choices but also formatting options.

The View Summary dialog (accessed through View|Current View|Customize Current View) includes other useful task management tools. A description of the tools follows.

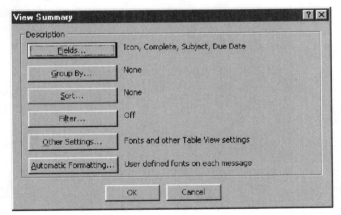

Fields—Use this dialog to select which fields are displayed in the task list. The Show Fields dialog is opened when you select the Fields button.

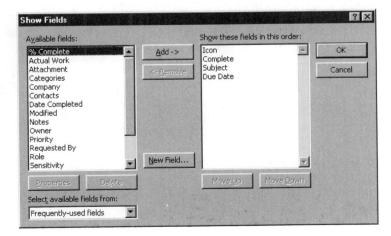

Group By—The Group By dialog lets you pick the way your to-do group is sorted and ultimately displayed. It provides for a four-variable sort. Just pick the first, second, third, and fourth variables and whether you want them sorted in ascending or descending order.

Sort—The Sort dialog lets you choose to sort by tasks within your groups. It also gives you a four-variable sort in either ascending or descending order.

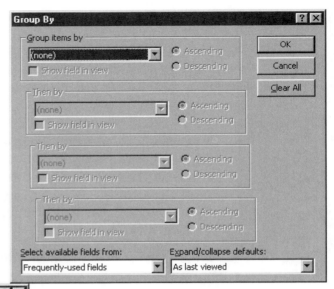

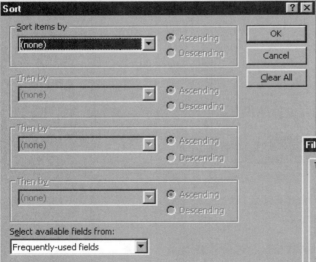

Filter—Use this selection to filter your information so you can limit what is actually displayed in the task list. For example, you can filter out unwanted status information or you can choose to see only those tasks that are from or to a selected individual.

Other Settings—Set font size and types in column headings and row information. Select other cell options such as sizing and grid lines.

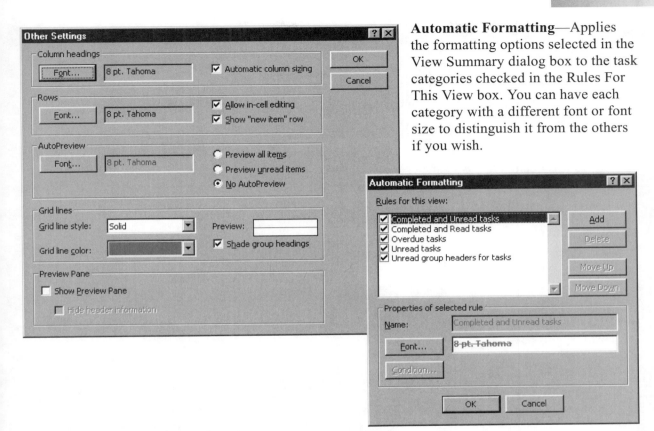

Automatic Formatting—Applies the formatting options selected in the View Summary dialog box to the task categories checked in the Rules For This View box. You can have each category with a different font or font size to distinguish it from the others if you wish.

Displaying Project Information

Project information can be displayed in a number of different ways. Displayed information depends on the Current View setting and the Columns, Group By, Sort, and Filter settings. Remember to use Sort after you make changes to rearrange your entries. Use the View|Filter menu selection to display or print focused reports that only show such categories as completed, not yet complete, overdue, etc.

Printing Your Information

Once a task list displays the content and order you like, you can print it. Use Page Setup to select the Table or Memo style. Use Print Preview to examine the resulting arrangement. If you want more information, use View|Current View menu selection and select the available views until you find one you like. Click the Print Preview button to examine the printed format. If you are satisfied with the appearance of your task list, click Print to send it to the printer.

Hands-on Activity

In this activity you create several task entries, change the way they are displayed, and then view them using Print Preview.

1. Select the **Task** icon to display Outlook's Task application.

2. Set the **View|Current View** menu selection to **Simple List**.

3. Enter the information shown in the following illustration by double-clicking on a blank line in the Task pane or by clicking the **New Task** button ☑ on the Standard toolbar or by clicking the **File|New|Task** menu selection. Use the calendars to pick the month and day shown in the Due Date column.

Tip: If you are reasonably comfortable now using Office 2000, try entering a similar list of your own tasks and to-dos.

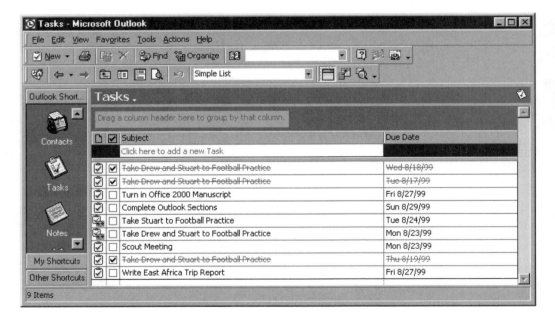

Note: The items with the strikeout through them are those items that are set to 100% complete in the % Complete box on the Task tab of the Task dialog. The user must set the percent complete. Also, the user can set the task as "Not started," "In progress," "Completed," "Waiting on someone else," or "Deferred" in the Status box.

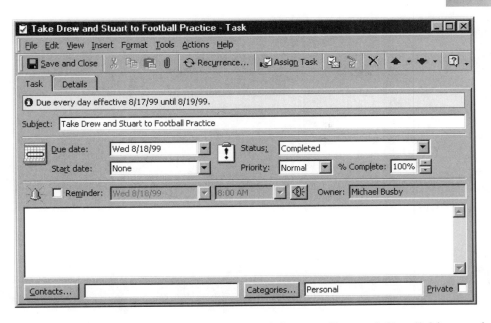

4. Notice the Categories button on the Task tab is set to Personal. By clicking on the **Categories** button, you can set the task category to any one of several different categories, including Business. See the Categories dialog for a list of categories available. If you do not set the category, the task is in the default category defined as None.

Tip: When you click on the **Categories** button you will display the Categories dialog. Clicking on the **Master Category List** button will display the Master Category List dialog.

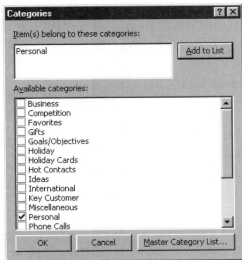

5. In the Master Category List dialog, you can enter a new category type such as **My Category**. Just type the new category name in the New category text box, then click on **Add**. Click on **OK**. If you want to delete a category, highlight it in the category text box, and click the **Delete** button. Then click **OK**.

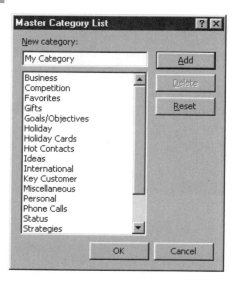

6. Check your screen against the preceding illustration when you finish entering the tasks.

7. Use the **View|Current View** menu selection and the **Print Preview** button to examine different views of your information. The illustration shown is the Detailed List view.

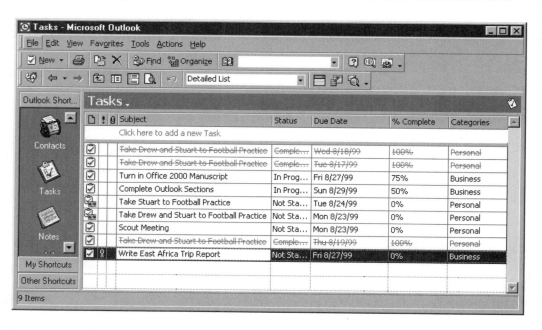

8. Return to the list view; then use the **File|Exit** menu selection to exit Outlook.

Summary

Now that you know how to enter projects into Outlook, you can begin using it to store your tasks, company projects, and action items. You should examine all of the available column categories to determine which ones best suit your needs. For example, you may want to maintain travel expense information in your Task columns. Once you begin using Tasks, your skills will increase with experience. In the next section you learn how to use the Contacts application. If you ever used either the Card File in Windows 3.1 or the Contacts portion of Schedule+, you should like this part of Outlook.

Using Contacts

Introduction

The Contacts application provides you with a comprehensive contact manager and address book. If your computer is equipped with a modem, it can be used as a telephone dialer as well. Hence, in addition to a powerful messaging system, time planner, and project planner, you also have the added feature of a built-in address book with a telephone dialer and notebook. Contacts is used to enter and display the names, addresses, telephone and fax numbers, e-mail addresses, important dates, notes, and more for each of your contacts, whether personal or professional. The following screen illustration shows the opening Contacts display.

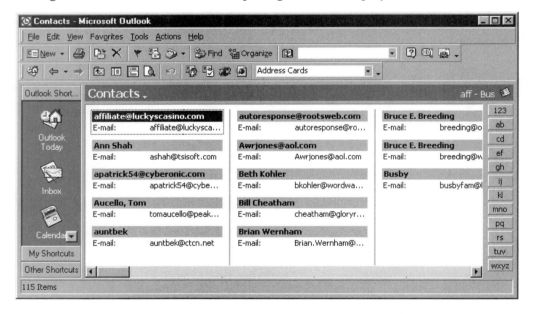

You can use the names and addresses stored here with Word. Word's Address Book button can access and transfer names and addresses from your contact list directly into your Word document. You can also use the Microsoft Office Shortcut Bar to add a new contact by clicking the New|Contact button on the Standard toolbar.

Alternately, you can click on the File|New|Contact menu selection. The Contact dialog appears, ready for a new entry.

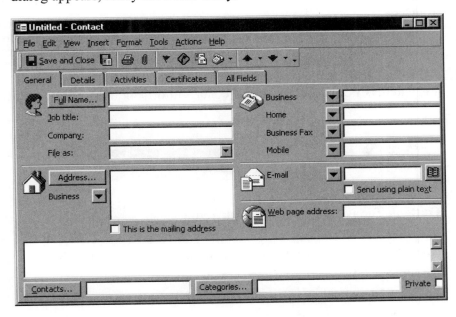

Menus and Toolbars

The menus and toolbars should be very familiar by now. Only those menu selections and toolbar buttons that are unique to Contacts are summarized.

Actions Menu Selections

New Contact—Opens the Contact dialog to create a new contact.

New Contact From Same Company—Opens a new Contact dialog with the same company as the current contact.

New Distribution List—Opens the Distribution List dialog to create a new distribution list.

New Message to Contact—Opens a new Message dialog addressed to the contact.

New Letter to Contact—Opens a new letter in Word addressed to the contact.

New Meeting Request to Contact—Opens a new Meeting Request dialog addressed to the contact.

New Appointment with Contact—Opens a new Appointment dialog addressed to the contact.

New Task For Contact—Opens a new Task dialog addressed to the contact.

New Journal Entry for Contact—Opens a new Journal dialog addressed to the contact.

Link—Link items or files.

Call Contact—Opens the New Call dialog allowing you to place a phone call to the contact.

Call Using NetMeeting—Opens the NetMeeting dialog allowing you to conduct an online meeting.

Flag for Follow Up—Flag the contact.

Forward as vCard—Forward the contact information as a vCard.

Advanced Toolbar

Outlook Today—Open the Outlook Today pane.

Previous Folder—Displays the contents of the previous folder viewed.

Next Folder—Displays the contents of the next folder in the list.

Up One Level—Moves the current view up one folder.

Folder List—Displays the current list of folders.

Preview Pane—Displays contact information in a separate pane of the contact highlighted in the Contacts pane.

Print Preview—Displays the contact information in a print preview pane of the contact highlighted in Contacts pane.

Undo—Removes the last change.

New Meeting Request—Opens the Meeting Request dialog to schedule a meeting with the contact highlighted in the Contacts pane.

New Task for Contact—Opens the New Task dialog to schedule/assign a new task with the contact highlighted in the Contacts pane.

Call Using Net Meeting—Initiate a Net Meeting dialog with the contact highlighted in the Contacts pane.

Explore Web Page—Open the web page of the contact highlighted in the Contacts pane.

Views—Changes the view of the Contacts pane; the views are Address Cards, Detailed Address Cards, Phone List, By Category, By Company, By Location, and By Follow-Up Flag.

Contact Dialog Tabs

New contacts are added by pressing <Ctrl+N> (for File|New|Contact) or clicking the New|Contact button on the Standard toolbar. Then enter the name, address, telephone numbers, and other contact information. Use the Details tab to record additional information. Reopen this dialog by selecting a contact and pressing <Ctrl+O>, using the File|Open|Selected Items menu selection, or double-clicking on the contact entry. Each of the five tabs of the Contact dialog provides a place to view and/or to record additional information about the selected contact.

As the tab label implies, General is where you type general information about the selected contact. You can look at the preceding illustration to see what's contained here.

The Details tab is used to record or view even more information about your contact.

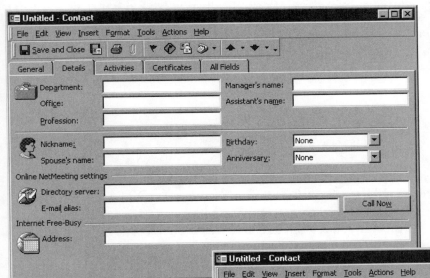

Here, you maintain information about your contact's business position, assistant, birthday, anniversary, nickname, and even the name of the contact's spouse.

The Activities tab is ideal for maintaining records of your last conversation or meeting with the contact. This tab turns your contact application into a *contact manager*, which is ideal for recording all interaction with the contact.

The Certificates tab records the digital certificate belonging to this contact. It is used to authenticate e-mail from the contact.

The All Fields tab displays selected fields. You can change the viewed fields using the Select from pull-down list. Click the New button to define and add your own fields. Once added, you can pick user-defined fields for this item.

Finding a Contact

To find a contact, simply click on a corresponding alphabetical tab at the right-hand side of the display.

Then use the scroll bars as necessary to move to the desired contact. Click on the contact and then press <Ctrl+O> to open the Contact dialog.

Dialing a Telephone Number

If you have a telephone and modem connected to your computer, it's easy to get dialing help from Outlook. Just highlight the contact and then click the AutoDialer button on the Standard toolbar.

Use Dialing Options to set speed dialing and to set up additional dialing properties. Click on Start Call to dial the number.

Printing Your Contacts List

It is easy to prepare a paper copy of the contacts. They can be printed in a variety of formats. Use the File|Page Setup menu selection to pick a format.

For example, if you want to print a phone directory style list of contacts, click "Phone Directory Style" to display the Page Setup dialog. Then click Print Preview to see the result. If you are satisfied with the preview, click Print to commit your directory to paper. Similarly, you can print your contacts in a variety of other formats.

Putting an Address into a Word Document

The programs within Microsoft Office 2000 work together *seamlessly*, as if all programs were part of one big application. Hence, it's no surprise that you can put addresses stored in Outlook directly into an open Word document. Here's the general procedure for using this handy feature.

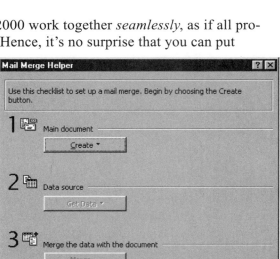

1. Position the cursor at the insertion point within your Word document.

2. Select Tools|Mail Merge.

3. Click Create and pick one of the document types, such as Form Letters or Mailing Labels.

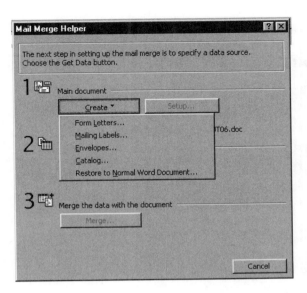

4. Click on Active Window to place the address in the active document. Click on New Main document to open a new document and place the address in it.

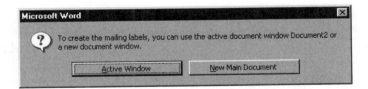

5. Click on Get Data.

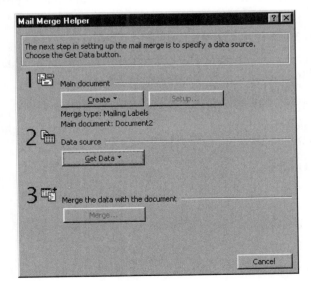

6. Click on Use Address Book.

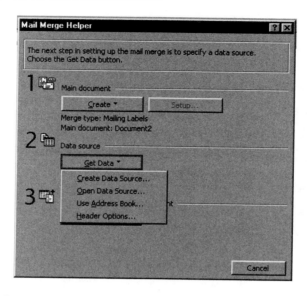

7. Select the Outlook Address Book and click OK. Then click Edit Main Document on the dialog that follows.

8. Use the Insert Merge Field button to insert the name and address information as desired. (See the Mail Merge section of Part 2 for details about the operation of Mail Merge.)

Hands-on Activity

In the following activity you enter personal contacts into the Contact portion of Outlook. Begin with Outlook open and the Contacts application selected.

1. Use the **View|Current View** menu selection and pick **Address Cards**.

2. Press <Ctrl+O> and type a real contact. Be sure to fill in as much information as you can. Click **Save and Close** to save the current contact.

3. Continue adding and saving contacts until you have entered four to six.

4. Use **File|Page Setup** and pick different styles. For each style selection, click the **Page Preview** button on the Page Setup dialog to see the selected style.

5. Use **File|Exit** to leave Outlook.

Summary

Now that you are familiar with Contacts, you should begin using it as a regular tool. If you are using the Card File or a Rolodex application, you can copy your contacts from them into Outlook's address book.

In the next section you continue your examination of Outlook. There, you take a closer look at Journal, which is used to track your work.

Using Journal

Introduction

Outlook's Journal maintains an audit trail of your work with Microsoft Office. Just start Journal and see a display that resembles the following screen illustration. Since you have just started Journal, there are no entries, unless you are a user of Office 97. If you are a previous Office 97 user, your Journal entries will appear in the Office 2000 Journal.

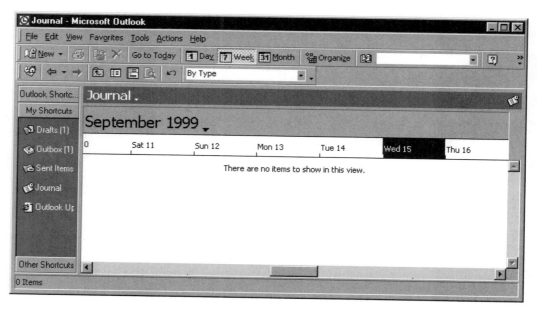

How Journal Works

If you were a previous Office user or you have already entered a few Journal items, you will see a window similar to the following illustration.

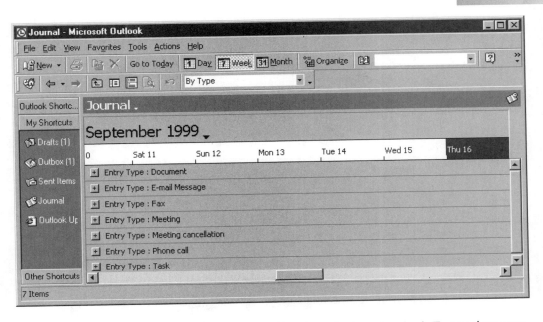

Notice that Journal displays each of the applications that are tracked. Every time you open and save a Microsoft Office document, the event is recorded by Journal. Recorded information includes the application used, author name, date, time, and duration. Just select a document of interest and press <Ctrl+O> for File|Open. In this instance, I highlighted the first entry (Entry Type : Document) to get the following dialog. The dialog is a typical document dialog that shows you what's maintained by Journal.

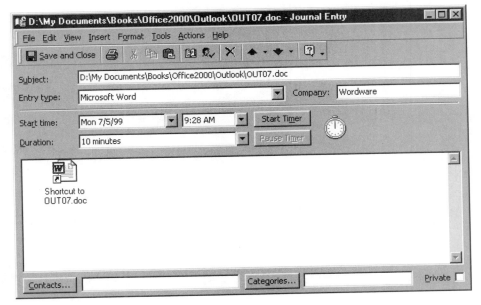

Examine the displayed journal information. If you wish, click the shortcut icon to open the document for a closer look.

You can use the Next Item and Previous Item buttons (the up and down arrows) to see the next or previous document. You can set the items and application files to be recorded using the Tools|Options menu selection. Pick the Journal Options button to see the dialog shown below. Here, simply check the items, applications, and contacts you wish to include in your journal.

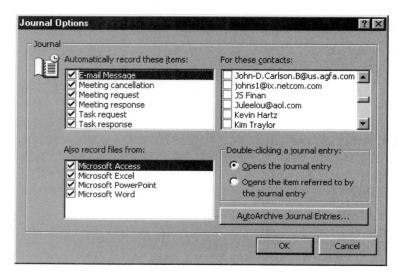

Notice the "Double-clicking a journal entry" area at the lower right-hand corner of the dialog. Here you can choose to open a document directly by double-clicking on the document name. The other option opens the Journal Entry dialog. Use the AutoArchive Journal Entries button to send your journal information to a file named archive.pst. You can also use a name of your own choice, or permanently delete all old items to save the disk space that would otherwise be occupied by the archive file.

Recording Journal Activities

The following general procedures detail how to record various Journal entries.

Automatically Recording Contacts in Journal

Click on the Tools|Options menu selection. Click on Journal Options on the Preferences tab of the Options dialog. In the "Automatically record these items" box, select the check boxes for the items you want automatically recorded in Journal. In the "For these contacts" box, select the check boxes for the contacts you want the items automatically recorded for.

Automatically Recording Documents in Journal

Click on the Tools|Options menu selection. Click on Journal Options on the Preferences tab of the Options dialog. In the "Also record files from" box, select the check boxes next to the programs whose files you want to automatically record in Journal.

Manually Recording an Item or Document in Journal

Locate the item or document you want to record. You can use Outlook, Windows Explorer, or the desktop (use My Computer and go to the folder of the document or select Start|Find|Files or Folders on the desktop toolbar). Drag the item to Journal in My Shortcuts in the left pane; open Journal first and just drag the item onto the Journal pane. Select the options you want for the journal entry.

Manually Recording any Activity in Journal

Click on the File|New|Journal Entry menu selection. In the Subject box, type a description. In the Entry type box, click the type of journal entry you are recording. Select other options you want. Click on the Save and Close button.

Recording in My Journal the Items Published in a Net Folder I Own

Right-click on the shared folder, then click Properties on the shortcut menu. Click on the Sharing tab. Select the Journal events for this folder check box. Journal entries are listed in the Journal folder.

Turning Off Automatic Recording of Journal Entries for a Contact

Click on the Tools|Options menu selection. Click on Journal Options on the Preferences tab of the Options dialog. In the For these contacts box, clear the check box next to the contact you want to stop automatic recording for.

Managing Journal Entries

Open a Journal Entry

Click the Journal button. Go to the date. Right-click the journal entry, and then click Open Journal Entry or Open Item Referred To on the shortcut menu.

Note: To specify whether the journal entry or the item is opened when you double-click journal entries, click on the Tools|Options menu selection, and then click the Preferences tab on the Options dialog. Click on Journal Options, and then click Opens the journal entry or Opens the item referred to by the journal entry.

Modify a Journal Entry

Open the journal entry. Select the options you want to change.

Move a Journal Entry

Open the journal entry. Enter a new start date and time.

Note: Moving a journal entry does not change the start time of the item, document, or contact the journal entry refers to.

View Journal Entries for a Contact

Open the contact you want to view journal entries for by clicking on Contacts in the Shortcuts pane, then clicking on the specific contact. Click on the Activities tab of the Contact dialog. In the Show box, click on Journal.

Delete a Journal Entry

In Journal, select the journal entry. On the Edit menu, click Delete.

Note: Deleting a journal entry does not delete the item, document, or contact that the journal entry refers to. Also, when you delete an item or document that has been recorded in Journal, the journal entry for that item or document is not deleted.

Open the Contact that a Journal Entry Refers To

Click on the Journal button. Open the journal entry that refers to the contact you want to open. To resolve any contact names that are not underlined, click the Tools menu, and then click Check Names. If a name is not underlined after you click Check Names, the name is not in your Contacts folder. In the Contact box, double-click any underlined names.

Archiving Items

Outlook can automatically remove items of a specified age and transfer them to an archive file or delete them. The following general procedures detail how to record various Journal entries.

Turn on AutoArchive

Click on the Tools|Options menu selection. On the Preferences tab of the Options dialog, click on the Journal Entries button, then click on AutoArchive Journal Entries.

To set AutoArchive to turn on when you start Outlook, select the Clean out items older than check box.

To specify how often the AutoArchive process will run, select either Months, Weeks, or Days from the drop-down box, then enter a number in the adjacent box. In the Move old items to box, type a file-name for the archived items to be transferred to, or click the Browse button to select from a list. Now that you have turned on AutoArchive, you must set AutoArchive properties for each folder to activate AutoArchive.

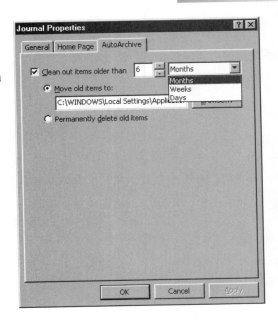

Set AutoArchive Properties for a Particular Folder

Right-click the folder you want to AutoArchive, and then click Properties on the shortcut menu. Click on the AutoArchive tab. To enable automatic archiving of this folder, select the "Clean out items older than" check box. To specify when items should be automatically transferred to the archive file, enter a number in the Months box. To specify a file for the archived items to be transferred to, click on Move old items to. In the Move Old Items To box, type a filename for the archived items, or click Browse to select from a list.

Archive Items Manually

Click on the File|Archive menu selection. To archive all folders, click on Archive All Folders According to Their AutoArchive Settings. To archive only one folder, click Archive This Folder and All Subfolders, and then click the folder that contains the items to archive. In the Archive File box, type a filename for the archived items to be transferred to, or click on Browse to select from a list. In the Archive Items Older Than box, enter a date. Items dated before this date will be archived.

Deleting Items

Delete Old Items Automatically

Right-click the folder that contains the items you want to delete automatically, and then click Properties on the shortcut menu. Click the AutoArchive tab. To enable automatic archiving of this folder, select the Clean Out Items Older Than check box. To specify when items should be deleted, enter a number in the Months box. To have items automatically deleted, click on Permanently Delete Old Items.

Delete Expired E-mail Messages When Archiving

Click on the Tools|Options menu selection, then click the Other tab of the Options dialog. Click on AutoArchive. To delete expired messages, select the Delete Expired Items When AutoArchiving (e-mail folders only) check box.

Hands-on Activity

In the following activity you open a journal document and examine the corresponding dialog. Begin with Outlook open and Journal selected.

1. Click on **Entry Type : Microsoft PowerPoint** (assuming that you've already performed the hands-on activities in Part 5).

2. Press **<Ctrl+O>** to open the Journal dialog. Alternately, you can right-click on the entry, and select **Open**.

3. Examine the dialog entries. In particular, notice the date, time, and duration.

4. Double-click the shortcut to the document to open it. Once open, press **<Alt+F4>** to close it. Next, press **<Alt+F4>** twice to close the Journal dialog and then to close Outlook.

Summary

Now that you are familiar with the Journal application, you're ready to move on to the next section, which familiarizes you with Outlook's Notes application.

Using Notes

Introduction

Notes is a simple but extremely useful Outlook application. As mentioned earlier in this part, Outlook's Notes are just like sticky notes. Use the Outlook Shortcuts pane and click on Notes to open the Notes pane. Double-click on a Notes icon and record a note.

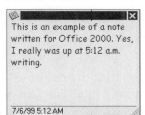

Close the note by clicking the Close button. Review your notes by opening Outlook and selecting the Notes application. Then read and remove your notes or create new ones as desired.

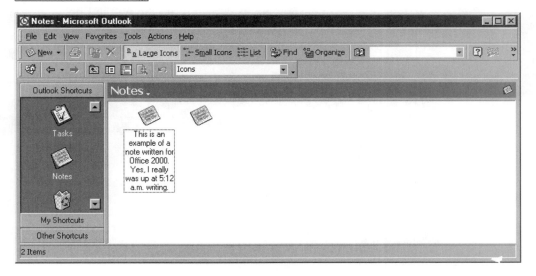

Menus and Toolbars

The Notes menus and toolbars do not have much in the way of new tools or features. The Standard toolbar includes three new buttons that determine the display of the Notes icons. Everything else should be familiar by now.

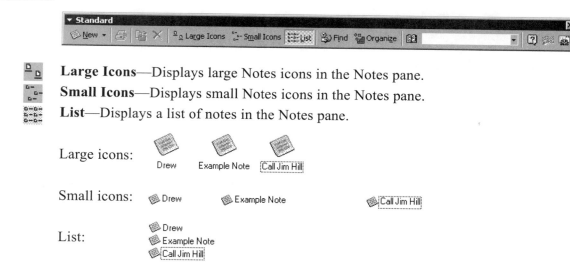

Large Icons—Displays large Notes icons in the Notes pane.

Small Icons—Displays small Notes icons in the Notes pane.

List—Displays a list of notes in the Notes pane.

Reading, Deleting, and Creating Notes

With the Notes application selected, you can examine all of your notes by simply looking at them. Beside creating new notes from the Office 2000 Outlook Shortcuts pane, you can also create a new note by pressing <Ctrl+N> (File|New|Note menu selection) from the Outlook Notes pane or clicking on the File|New|Note menu selection from any Outlook application.

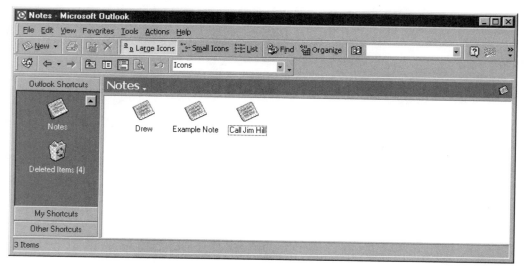

The information at the top of a note is separated by the note's body text with a carriage return. Just type a title and press <Enter>. Then type the text without using <Enter>—the text will automatically word-wrap. For example, the third note in the preceding illustration is shown as it is displayed in the Note application window. The text "Call Jim Hill" was typed on the first line and followed by <Enter>.

Double-click a note or select it and press <Ctrl+O> (for File|Open|Selected Items menu selection) to read the entire contents. In the example, the heading and content text is shown at the right.

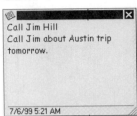

Close a note by pressing <Esc> or clicking on the Close button in the upper right-hand corner of the note. Delete a note by selecting it in the Notes pane and pressing <Ctrl+D> or <Delete>.

Hands-on Activity

In this activity you create, display, and then delete a note. Begin by launching Outlook and choosing the Notes application.

1. Press **<Ctrl+N>** to open a new note.

2. Type **My Note**. Press **<Enter>**. Then type **This is a note to myself.**

3. Press **<Esc>** to close the note. Notice that it is displayed as the first note in the Notes window.

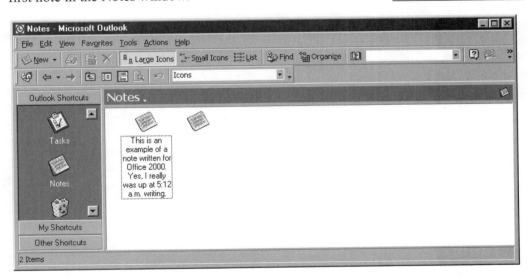

4. Double-click the new My Note note. Notice that it is displayed.

5. Click the **Close** button to close the note.

6. Select the note one final time and press **<Delete>**. The note is deleted.

7. Select **File|Exit** to exit Outlook.

Summary

Notes is a fairly simple Outlook application requiring little in the way of effort to learn or use. Notes is a handy desktop tool that helps you manage your daily tasks. Use Notes for reminders as you would a pen and paper. The next section discusses Outlook's security features.

Security

Inroduction

Security may be a serious issue with some Office 2000 users, while others may not ever give it a single thought. If you send or receive sensitive messages over a shared network (LAN, WAN, Internet, etc.), or create and maintain sensitive information on your computer, then you may be one of those individuals who needs to rely upon security features to keep your information private. Microsoft Outlook provides several security features that allow you to send and receive varying levels of secure e-mail messages and prevent unauthorized access to your computer. The level of security provided by the security features vary from simple to (almost) bullet proof. The simple, or basic, security feature provides a simple encoding scheme that can be decoded by anyone who cares to take a little time and decode the message. The advanced security feature provides for a theoretically (with sufficient resources and time, any code is breakable) unbreakable encoding scheme.

Simple Security

To encode your messages using simple encryption methods, click on the **Tools|Options** menu selection and select the **Mail Format** tab of the Options dialog.

In the Send in this message format box, click on **Plain Text** or **HTML**. Click on the **Settings** button. Select the options wanted in the Encode text using box by selecting either **None**, **Quoted Printable**, or **Base 64** encoding format in the drop-down box. Click on **OK**, then click on **OK** again to close all the dialogs.

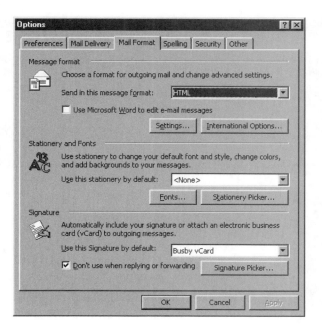

HTML Settings Options

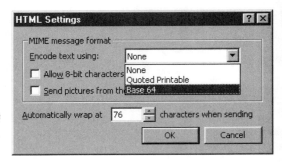

The Quoted Printable encoding format is a bit-based encoding scheme, while the Base 64 encoding format is a binary encoding scheme. Neither format offers bullet-proof security but does prevent the casual observer from reading your messages.

Allow 8-bit characters in heading determines if foreign character sets, high ASCII, or double-byte character sets are allowed in the header without encoding them. If you select this option, the characters are not encoded (i.e., they are allowed).

The Send pictures from the Internet with messages option determines if any images that are part of the message, such as background images, are added to the message. If this option is selected, only a reference, the image name, to the image is included in the message. Including images usually results in a much larger message, which increases the download time.

Plain Text Setting Options

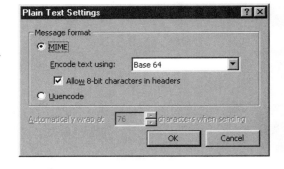

The MIME format is the most common format used to encode messages sent over the Internet. Anyone with a little brain power can decode your message and read it—only the casual observer is prevented from reading your message.

The Uuencode format is typically used to send binary files as attachments in messages posted to newsgroups.

MIME and Uuencode are typically found in the world of UNIX computing.

Advanced Security

An additional layer of security is provided when you encrypt your messages rather than encode them. *Encryption* differs from encoding in the degree to which the message is processed to hide the true nature of the message. "Encode" is used in reference to simple encryption formats (such as replacing a letter with a number) while "encrypt" is used in reference to sophisticated math and formula-based encryption techniques. Encryption techniques are said to be secure in that casual observers may not decode the text of your message. However, if an entity (a foreign government, say) has sufficient time and resources, no encryption format is safe from prying eyes.

To provide the best security currently possible, a digital ID, also called a certificate, is required to send secure messages over the Internet. This is what a digital certificate looks like (for the adventuresome, please note that I have cancelled the certificate so you cannot masquerade as me).

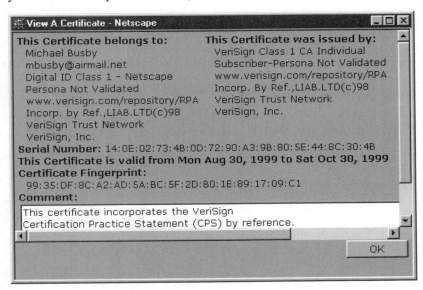

The digital ID provides a means for positively identifying yourself by allowing you to add a digital signature to your messages, proving to the recipient that the message truly came from you and has not been tampered with. If you need this type of security, you may obtain a digital ID from a certifying authority. For additional security when using a digital ID, you can encrypt messages, using a special mathematical formula in an encryption/decryption program, so that only the intended recipient can read your messages and attachments. You may obtain a digital ID from a certifying authority. One such authority is VeriSign, Inc. For more information on the subject, you should consult various in-print books on the topic or check out VeriSign's web site at http://digitalid.verisign.com/. The following Outlook general procedures pertain to using digital IDs and will not work if you have not obtained a valid digital ID. Before sending or receiving a secure message, you and the message recipient must set up the appropriate security options. Then you can use your digital ID to encrypt messages if you have a copy of the recipient's digital ID in your contact list.

Setting Up Security

To set up security for Internet e-mail messages, you need a digital ID and a copy of the digital ID of any recipient to whom you want to send encrypted messages. Acquire a digital ID from a certifying authority by searching the web using "digital ID" as the search string. You will hit a couple of sites that are certifying authorities. Pick one and follow their instructions for getting the ID. Or, you may perform the following procedure.

Click on the **Tools|Options** menu selection, then click the **Security** tab on the Options dialog. Click on **Get a Digital ID**. Outlook opens your web browser, then opens a web page about digital IDs. Follow the instructions on the web page. The certifiying authority will send you additional instructions via e-mail.

After you acquire the digital ID, you must import it into Outlook. Follow this proce-dure for importing the digital ID. Click on the **Tools|Options** menu selection and select the **Security** tab of the Options dialog. Click on the **Import/Export Digital ID** button.

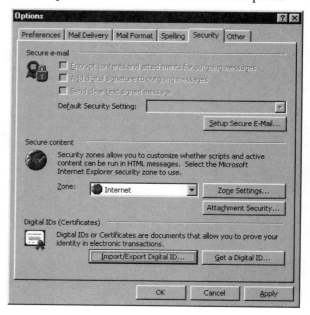

Note: This procedure assumes you have acquired a digital ID from an issu-ing authority. If you have not yet received a digital ID, click on the **Get a Digital ID** button and follow the instructions.

Click on the **Browse** button of the Import/Export Digital ID dialog. Find the digital ID file you saved when you received your digital ID (mine is Digital_ID.p12) and high-light it.

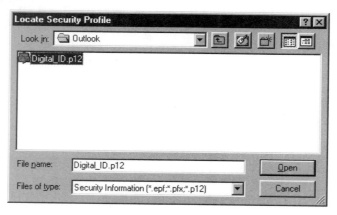

Now click on the **Open** button. Enter your password and your Digital ID Name in the appropriate boxes.

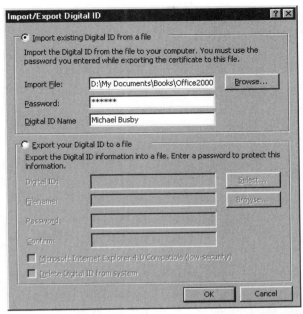

Click on the **OK** button to close the Import/Export Digital ID dialog. Click on **OK** to close the Options dialog.

You must copy all the recipients whom you wish to encrypt/decrypt messages to/from using digital IDs into your contact list. Click on the **Tools|Options** menu selection, and then click the **Security** tab of the Options dialog.

Click on the **Setup Secure E-Mail** button. In the Security Settings Name box, enter a descriptive name such as OpSec or My Secure ID. In the Secure Message Format list, click **S/MIME**.

In the Signing certificate box, click on **Choose**, and then click on your digital ID. In the Encryption certificate box, click **Choose**, and then click on your digital ID. To receive encrypted messages, select the Send these certificates with signed messages check box.

Note: The settings chosen become the default settings whenever you send secure messages. If you do not want these settings to be used by default for all your messages, clear the Default Security Setting for all secure messages check box.

Click on **OK** to close the Change Security Settings dialog. Then click on **Apply** on the Security tab of the Options dialog to apply the new security settings. Finally, click on **OK** to close the Options dialog. You are now ready to send and receive secure messages.

Using Digital Signatures

To send a message with a digital signature to an Internet recipient, first compose a message. In the message window, click on **View|Options**. Select the Add digital signature to outgoing message check box, click on **Close**, then click on **Send** in the Message Properties dialog.

Note: To modify the security options for this message only, click on the File|Properties menu selection and then click the **Security** tab of the Properties dialog.

To send an encrypted message to an Internet recipient, compose a message. In the message window, click on **View|Options**. Choose Add digital signature to outgoing message, click on **Close**, then click on **Send** on the Message Properties dialog.

To back up or copy a digital ID, click on the **Tools|Options** menu selection, then click on the **Security** tab. Click the **Import/Export Digital ID** button. Click on Export your digital ID to a file box. Click on the **Select** button, then click on the digital ID you want to back up. In the **Filename** box, type a name and path for the security file you want to create, or click on **Browse**. In the **Password** box, type your password for this digital ID. Note that the password must be the same as the password you used when you acquired the ID. In the **Confirm** box, type the password again. Outlook will save your digital ID as a .pfx file.

To add a digital ID to your contacts list, simply open a message that has a digital ID attached.

Note: To have the sender attach a digital ID to a message, ask the sender to send you a digitally signed e-mail message. Right-click on the name in the **From** field, and then click on **Add to Contacts** on the shortcut menu. If there is already an entry for this person on your contacts list, click on **Overwrite this address**. The digital ID is now stored with the contact information for this recipient. You can now send encrypted e-mail messages to this person. To view a contact's certificates, double-click the person's name, and then click the **Certificates** tab.

Summary

This section discussed security issues and showed you how to protect your communications with fellow employees, business contacts, etc. from prying eyes. If you use the techniques shown in this section your communications on the Internet and private Networks will remain confidential.

The next section demonstrates the filtering capabilities of Outlook. Using filters, you may exclude all e-mails from annoying mass e-mailers, adult content e-mailers, ex-spouses, or any other individual or group of individuals you choose.

Filters

Introduction

Filters provide a means of specifying conditions where only those items meeting those conditions are displayed. As an example, you can filter all messages with "Dudley Dolittle" in the From box to see only items from Dudley Dolittle. All of the other messages are still in the folder and can be seen again by removing the filter. When a filter is applied to a selected folder, the status bar displays "Filter Applied" in the lower left corner of the screen.

Additionally, unwanted e-mail messages from commercial mailers (for example, messages that contain adult content) can be automatically removed from your Inbox, or you may have them appear in a particular color so you can quickly find them and process them manually. Unwanted e-mail messages may be automatically moved to a specific folder or they may be automatically deleted. Also, a list of the senders of unwanted e-mail messages may be created and all messages from those senders can be removed from your Inbox. This section demonstrate how to use filters.

Filters

To remove a filter, click on the **View|Current View|Customize Current View** menu selection. Click on the **Filter** button in the View Summary dialog. In the lower-right corner, click the **Clear All** button, or delete the appropriate text in the search for the words text box to delete single items.

To show or hide items or files with a filter, click on the folder you want to apply a filter to. Then click on **View|Current View|Customize Current View**. Click on the **Filter** button in the View Summary dialog. Select the filter options desired. To filter using additional filtering criteria such as a category or importance level, click on the **More Choices** tab, then select the options desired. To filter using custom fields, click the **Advanced** tab, then select the options desired.

Note: If more than one option is selected, only the items that meet all of the criteria appear. However, if the same field is used to set multiple criteria, items that meet one criterion within that field are found. If files are not showing in the Filter dialog box, the Integrated File Management component probably wasn't loaded during Outlook Setup and you must load the component.

To show or hide items or files based on time or duration, click the folder you want to apply a filter to, click on the **View|Current View|Customize Current View** menu selection. Click on the **Filter** button in the View Summary dialog. In the first **Time** box, click on a condition. As an example, to see only sent items, click on **Sent**. In the second **Time** box, click on a value for the condition you selected. As an example, to see only items sent in the last week, click on In the last 7 days.

Filtering E-mail

The following procedure initially details how to filter e-mail specifically for junk and adult content messages. However, the latter part of the procedure is a general procedure for filtering e-mail for any variety of reasons. There is a notation in the proper place advising the reader when the more general procedure begins.

To add or remove an e-mail address from the list of unwanted e-mail senders, click on the **Inbox** button in the Outlook Shortcuts pane. Click on the **Organize** button on the Standard toolbar.

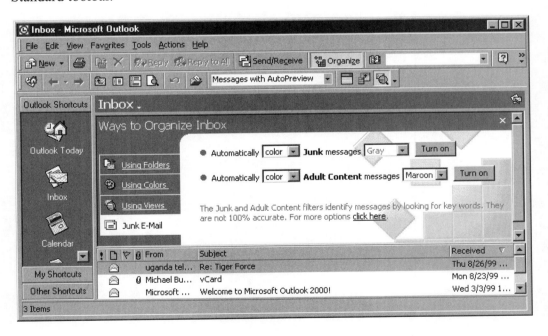

Click on the **Junk E-mail** link and the options link. To change the commercial e-mailers list, click on the **Edit Junk Senders** link. To change the adult content senders list, click on the **Edit Adult Content Senders** link.

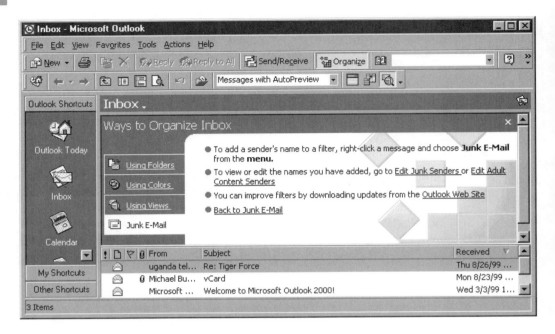

To filter junk senders follow this procedure:

In the Edit Junk Senders dialog, click on the **Add** button.

In the Sender dialog, add the domain name you want to filter.

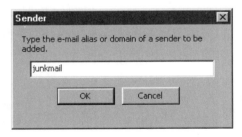

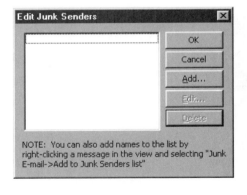

Click on the **OK** button to close the Sender dialog. Observe the domain name is now listed in the Edit Junk Senders dialog.

Add another domain name or click on **OK** to close the Edit Junk Senders dialog.

To filter adult content senders follow this procedure:

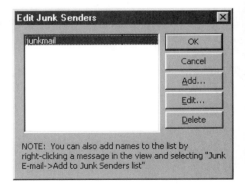

In the Edit Adult Content Senders dialog, click on the **Add** button.

In the Sender dialog, add the domain name you want to filter.

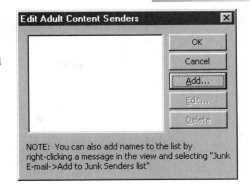

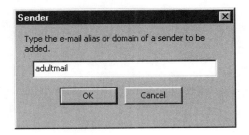

Click on the **OK** button to close the Sender dialog. Observe the domain name is now listed in the Edit Adult Content Senders dialog.

Add another domain name or click on **OK** to close the Edit Junk Senders dialog.

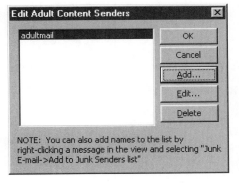

When you are finished adding domain names, click on either • Back to Junk E-Mail button to return to the initial junk e-mail window, or click on the **Organize** button on the Standard toolbar to return to the Inbox view.

Note: The procedure from this point forward is a general procedure for setting up any rules you desire for processing items. The focus of the remaining steps is junk e-mail and adult content e-mail but the steps apply for any processing rules you wish to create.

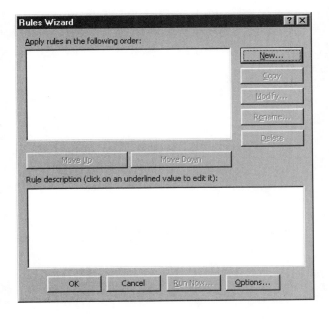

Now click on the **Tools|Rules Wizard** menu selection. Click on the **New** button in the Rules Wizard dialog.

In the Which type of rule do you want to create box, highlight **Check messages when they arrive**. Then click on the **Next>** button.

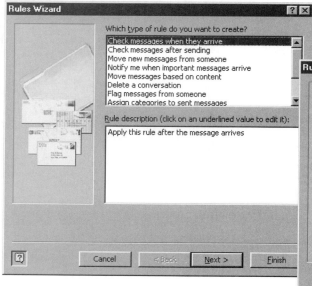

Now check **When received through the spec-ified account** box in the Which condition(s) do you want to check? text box.

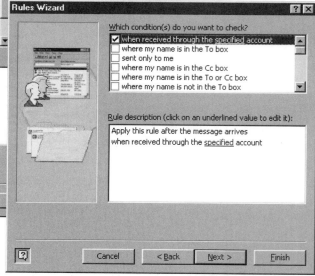

Click on the down arrow of the Which condition(s) do you want to check box and check **suspected to be junk e-mail or from Junk Senders** and **containing adult content or from Adult Content Senders...** boxes.

Note: This procedure applies to setting rules for a variety of purposes. Notice the various conditions for processing items in the Which conditions... box. Just go back to the initial Rules Wizard dialog after finishing this rule, click on **New** again and set up another set of conditions to process items as you wish.

Click on the underlined word **specified** in the rule description text box.

Click on the down arrow to choose from your various accounts, then click on **OK**.

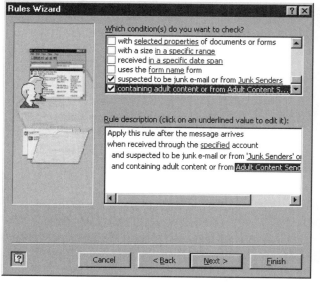

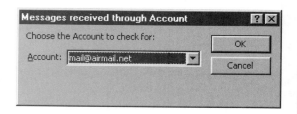

Click on the **Next>** button. In the What do you want to do with this message? box, click on **permanently delete it**.

The following dialog will open asking you if you are sure. Click on **Yes**.

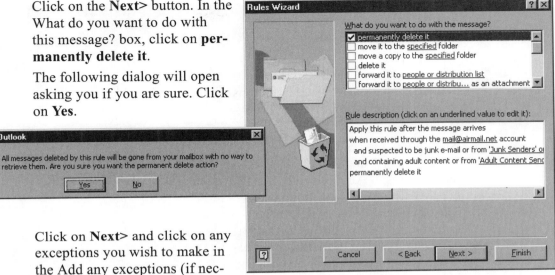

Click on **Next>** and click on any exceptions you wish to make in the Add any exceptions (if necessary) box.

Click on **Next>**. Now specify a descriptive name in the Please specify a name for this rule box for the rule you just made.

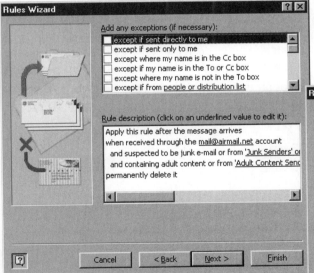

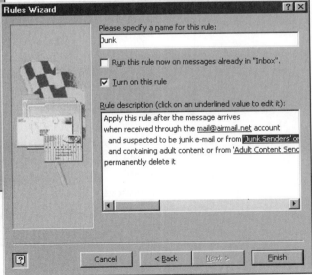

Then click on the **Finish** button.

Click on the **Run Now...** button to begin using the rule. The Options button allows you to import and export rules.

Notice the Copy, Modify, Rename, and Delete buttons. Use these buttons as appropriate in the future to manage your messaging system.

Notice the "Junk Senders or Junk Senders or ..." and the "Adult Content Senders or Adult Content Senders or ..." in the Rule description box. This is normal. Now click on **OK** unless you want to add more rules. If you want to set up more rules for processing your messages or other items, just click on **New** again and go through the same procedure just given.

In the last procedure we chose to permanently delete junk and adult content messages in the example. However, you may have chosen to move them to a folder or to just delete them, which moves them to a special folder. You can change the folder junk or adult content e-mail messages are automatically sent to using the following procedure.

To change the folder where your junk or adult content e-mail is stored, click on **Inbox** in the Outlook Shortcuts pane. Click on **Organize** menu selection. Click on **Junk E-mail**.

To change the folder junk messages are sent to, click on the down arrow adjacent to the Automatically **Color** Junk messages... in the first bulleted item. Select **Move**. To change the folder adult content messages are sent to, click on the down arrow adjacent to the Automatically **Color** Adult Content messages... in the second bulleted item. Select **Move**. Your display should now look similar to the following illustration.

To move junk e-mail to another folder, click on the down arrow adjacent to the Junk E-mail box in the first bulleted line and select the appropriate folder. Note that clicking on **Other folder** will open a dialog where you can create a new folder if desired. Ensure that the button to the right is labeled "Turn on." If it is labeled "Turn off," click on it to change it to "Turn on."

To move adult content e-mail to another folder, click on the down arrow adjacent to the Junk E-mail box in the second bulleted line and select the appropriate folder. Note that clicking on **Other folder** will open a dialog where you can create a new folder if desired. Ensure that the button to the right is labeled "Turn on." If it is labeled "Turn off," then click on it to change it to "Turn on."

Finally, click on the **Organize** button on the Standard toolbar to return to the Inbox pane.

To automatically move or delete all e-mail messages from a particular sender, click on **Inbox** in the Outlook Shortcuts pane. Select a message from the sender whose messages you want to automatically move or delete. Click on the **Actions|Junk E-mail** menu selection, then click on **Add to Junk Senders List** or click on **Add to Adult Content Senders List** as appropriate. Click on the **Organize** button on the Standard toolbar to return to the Inbox pane.

To change the color of junk or adult content e-mail messages in the Inbox, click on **Inbox** in the Outlook Shortcuts pane. Click on the **Organize** menu selection. Click on **Junk E-mail**. For either bulleted item, in the first box click on **Color**, and then click on the color you want in the second box. Click on the rightmost button to display the label **Turn On** (do not click if **Turn On** is already displayed). Click on the **Organize** button on the Standard toolbar to return to the Inbox pane.

Summary

This section covered the procedures for filtering e-mail messages, which is helpful for managing junk e-mail and adult content messages. The next section discusses miscellaneous Outlook topics, including stationery, forms, and the NetMeeting Whiteboard.

Miscellaneous Outlook Topics

Introduction

Outlook includes many other useful tools for assisting the busy person with many day-to-day activities. These tools are applicable to one or more of Outlook's applications and the reader will occasionally have need of them while using Outlook. Such tools include Stationery, Forms, NetMeeting Whiteboard, Categories, Groups, Address Book, and Tables and Cards. This section discusses the general utility of these diverse tools and how to use them.

Stationery

Outlook 2000 includes a stationery feature that allows you to personalize your e-mail messages by adding images and background colors to your outgoing messages. Stationery is only available if the HTML format is used to create your e-mail messages. It is available with either Outlook or Word as the e-mail editor. To experiment with the different stationery designs available, click on the **Tools|Options** menu selection, and then click on the **Mail Format** tab in the Options dialog. In the Send in this message format list, click on **HTML**.

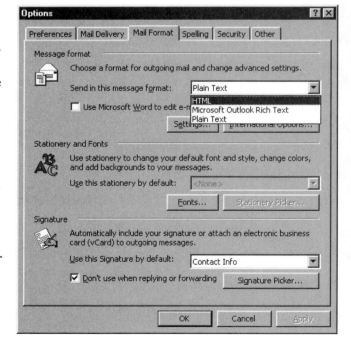

Click on the **Stationery Picker** button and select a stationery image from the Stationery box.

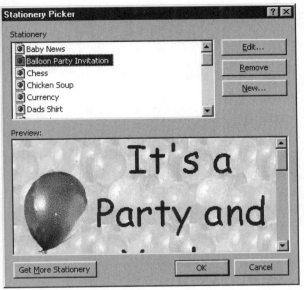

Some stationery images are listed in the box, yet are not yet installed. If you click on such an image, a message will advise you that if you select the image, it will be installed when you create a new message. After selecting an image that is not installed and clicking **OK**, then clicking on the **New|New Mail Message** menu selection, you will see the following dialog.

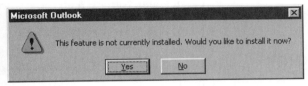

Click on **Yes**. You will be prompted to place the Office 2000 CD in the CD-ROM drive. From this point on, the installer will install the image automatically. When finished, you are presented with a new message window with the image as a background.

Notice on the Stationery Picker dialog the **Edit**, **Remove**, and **New** buttons. Clicking on **Edit** opens the Edit Stationery dialog. You can change, for this message only, the

font size, picture/image, and background color in this dialog. Just click on the appropriate button and select one of the choices available—say a blue background for a boy's party invitation, a pink background for a girl's party invitation, or no background (click on Do not include a background in this stationery).

After clicking on **OK**, you return to the Stationery Picker dialog. Click on **OK** twice to close the dialogs, and you will see a new message window ready for you to compose a new message decorated with the stationery you selected.

You can save changed images by clicking on **New** in the Stationery

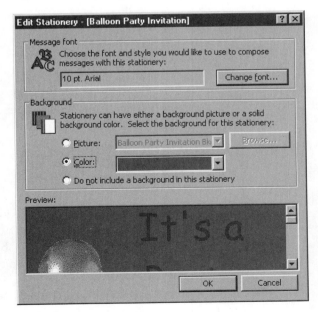

Picker dialog. In the Create New Stationery dialog, enter a name for the new image, select "Use this existing stationery as a template," then click on **Next>**.

Select a blue background color by clicking on the Color button in the Background text area. Click on **OK** to finish. Now you have a new image for use as stationery. Click on **OK** twice and you are ready to compose your new message with the new stationery.

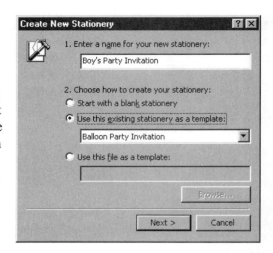

Forms

Outlook contains a Standard Forms Library. Within the library are the forms used with the Outlook applications such as Appointment, Contact, Journal Entry, Message, etc. See the Choose Form dialog, which is accessed by clicking on the **Tools|Forms| Choose a Form** menu selection, to view the choices.

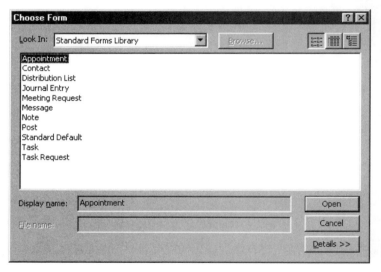

Designing Forms

The ability to design a form gives you some control over the information you keep in Outlook. By modifying the existing forms, you can customize record keeping to suit your particular needs.

Besides the Standard Forms Library, there is a Personal Forms Library. You may access the Personal Forms Library by clicking on the **Tools|Forms|Choose a Form** menu selection and clicking on the **Look In** drop-down arrow. However, the Personal Forms Library is empty unless you have designed one or more personal forms using the **Tools|Forms|Design a Form** menu selection. You can design a new form by basing your new form design on an existing form from the Standard Forms Library.

Click on
**Tools|Forms|Design a
Form** menu selection.
In the Choose Form
dialog, select the Con-
tact form in the Stan-
dards Form Library
(in the Look In text
box of the dialog).

Click on **Open** to
open the Contact
(Design) dialog,
below, and begin the
business of designing
your own contact
form.

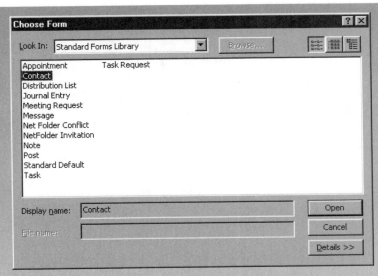

By clicking on the individual fields/text boxes in the General, Details, Activities, etc.,
tabs, the resize/move handles are displayed, allowing you to delete, move, or resize
each field/box. Alternately, you may go to one of the blank tabs (P.x where x = 2 to 6),
where you will find empty space to place fields from the **Field Chooser** list.

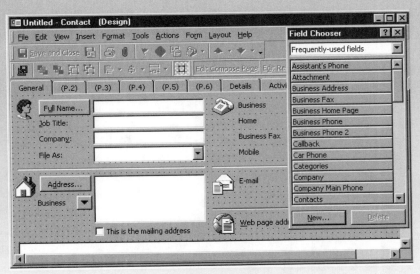

Then you have room to add those fields you desire from the Field Chooser. Add fields
by clicking and dragging the field from Field Chooser to the area on the form you
wish to place the field. Also, you may change to the other tabs and add or delete fields
as you desire. If you do not see a field with the characteristics you are looking for,
click **New** on the Field Chooser dialog, then enter the properties of the new field in

the New Field dialog. Change the type of field by clicking on the Type down arrow and selecting the appropriate type of information that will be placed in the field.

Also, depending upon the type selected, you may need to format the field properly by clicking on the Format down arrow and selecting the appropriate format. Be sure to format number types, or else you may have too many or not enough digits.

You may also right-click on any field or field label and change the Properties/Advanced Properties by clicking on the choices displayed. You are then presented with a Properties dialog that allows you to change such properties as name, size, position, etc.

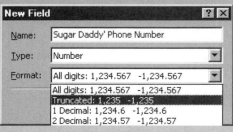

When you are in the Contact (Design) mode the dialog displays the menu bar shown below.

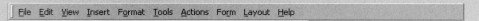

Only two of the menu selections are new: the Form menu and the Layout menu. Both menu selections are shown below without an explanation of the various options.

Click on the **Form|Rename Page** menu selection to rename the currently displayed tab. Of course, you can rename any existing tab.

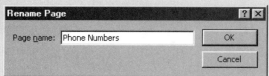

Click **OK** when finished. The following illustration shows a new tab added to the standard Contact form that allows the user to track all of the telecommunication numbers that may be of interest. Note the user-defined field on the bottom right side.

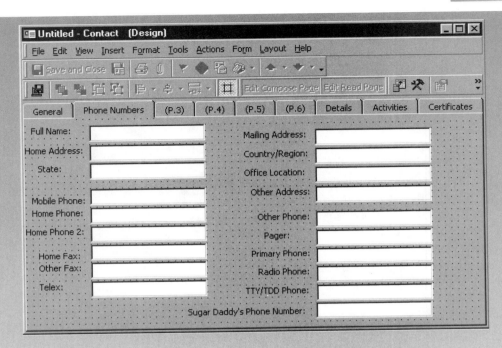

When you are finished designing the form, click on **Close**. You will be asked if you want to save the changes. If you save the changes by clicking on **Yes**, you will be asked for a name for the new form.

NetMeeting Whiteboard

The function of the Whiteboard in Outlook is similar to a dry erase board used in a meeting. Online meeting participants may write to the Whiteboard, which is viewed by every meeting attendee. Note that the Whiteboard is available only if NetMeeting is used for the online meeting.

General Whiteboard Procedures

Click the **Text** tool in the Whiteboard toolbox to write on the Whiteboard. Use **View|Zoom** to zoom in or out on the Whiteboard.

Click on the **Font Options** button at the bottom of the window to change the color, size, or font of the Whiteboard text, then click on **OK**. Click on the Whiteboard at the point where you want the text to begin, then start typing. When you're finished, click the mouse outside of the text area.

Click on the **Highlight** tool in the Whiteboard toolbox to highlight text or graphics. Drag the pointer over the item you want to highlight. If your monitor uses only 16 colors, the highlighting appears behind text or other graphics. You can also use the remote pointer (the hand) to point out text or graphics on the Whiteboard page to other people in the meeting.

Click on the **Draw** or **Line** tool in the Whiteboard toolbox to draw a line. If you want to change the line width or color, click on a line width or color located on the bottom of the toolbox. Drag the pointer across the Whiteboard to draw a line.

If you want to draw a shape on the Whiteboard, click on one of the shape tools: a rectangle or ellipse, either filled or unfilled. If you want to change the line width or color, click on a line width or color located on the bottom of the toolbox. Drag the pointer across the Whiteboard to draw a shape.

If you want to move among the Whiteboard pages, click the forward or back arrow located at the lower right of the Whiteboard. If you want to go to the first or last page, click the page number you want beside either the forward or back arrow. To add another page, click the button on the far right.

If you want to delete a Whiteboard object or text, click on the **Eraser** tool. Then click on a block of text or a drawn object to delete it. If you want to delete individual letters in a text block, click the **Text** tool in the toolbox, and then click on the letters. Then press <Delete> or <Backspace>.

If you want to use a pointer to point out text or objects, click the **Remote Pointer** tool in the Whiteboard toolbox. Drag the hand-shaped remote pointer to the place you want to point to on the Whiteboard. Click on the **Remote Pointer** tool to turn off the pointer.

You must turn off the remote pointer before you can point to another Whiteboard page. Then go to the page where you want to use the pointer, and turn it back on.

Use **Tools|Lock Contents** (when in the Whiteboard) to prevent anyone from making changes to the Whiteboard.

Use **Tools|Synchronize** to remove the check mark to see Whiteboard pages and prevent others from seeing them. Usually everyone in a meeting views the same Whiteboard page at the same time. However, you can specifically look at or work on something out of view of the meeting participants.

Use **Edit|Insert Page Before** to add new pages to the Whiteboard before the current page. Use **Edit|Insert Page After** to insert new pages after the current page. Also, you can add a page after the current page by clicking the button at the lower right of the Whiteboard.

Click on the **Select Area** tool in the Whiteboard toolbox to copy a screen area to the Whiteboard. If the Whiteboard Select Area dialog appears, click on **OK**. Then click a corner of the area you want to capture, and drag the pointer diagonally toward the opposite corner until you have captured the area of interest. Click on the Whiteboard.

Click on the **Select Window** tool in the Whiteboard toolbox to copy a window to the Whiteboard. If the Whiteboard Select Window dialog appears, click **OK**. Click on the window you want to copy. Then click on the Whiteboard.

Timelines

Outlook uses timelines to display everything recorded by Journal and to-do activities and completed activities. You can change the look of timelines and also the information displayed. The following general procedures describe how to manage timelines.

You can change the way time is displayed in a timeline using the following table:

To View:	Click on:
hour increments on the timeline	Day button 1
day increments on the timeline	Week button 7
week increments on the timeline	Month button 31

Every item and document is shown on a timeline at the specific time it was created, saved, sent, received, opened, or modified, according to which of these fields are used to display the item or document. You can change the fields used to display items on a timeline, but the location and the duration of the items may change on the timeline as a result.

To change the fields used to display items on a timeline, select **View|Current View|Customize Current View**. Click on **Fields**. In the Select available fields from box, click the field set desired. In the Available date/time fields box, click on the field that contains the time desired to use for the item start date, and then click on **Start**. In the Available date/time fields box, click the field that contains the time desired to use for the item end date, and then click on **End**.

You can change the length of the item label on a timeline. Open a timeline, then select **View|Current View|Customize Current View**. Click on the **Other Settings** tab. In the Maximum label width box, enter the number of characters in the label you want to display. While in the Other Settings dialog, you can show or hide the item labels in the month view by selecting or clearing the Show label when viewing by month check box. Hiding the labels may become necessary to reduce the clutter if you have many items for a particular month. Also while in the Other Settings dialog, you can show or hide the week numbers by selecting or clearing Show week numbers box.

Categories

Categories are keywords or phrases used to track items so they can be found, sorted, filtered, or grouped. You can use item categories to track different types of related items that are stored in different folders. As an example of the usefulness of categories, you can keep track of all the meetings, contacts, and messages for a particular project by project name. Let's say you are managing a project named My Project. You can create a category named My Project and assign items to it, thereby keeping track of all the work you (and your team) do on that project.

Categories also enable you to keep track of items without putting them in separate folders. As an example, you can keep business and personal tasks in the same task list, then use the Business and Personal categories to view the tasks separately. Outlook provides a Master Category list of categories you can assign items to. You can use this list as it exists and add your own categories to it as needed. An item can be assigned to more than one category. As an example, a task can be assigned to the categories Business, Key Customer, and Strategies.

To quickly view items (except e-mail messages) grouped by category, use **View|Current View|By Category**.

Groups

Outlook defines a group as a set of related items, such as tasks assigned to the same person, e-mail messages from the same source, or by priority. Grouping items is a useful way of grasping the magnitude of tasks and managing your time.

Items can only be grouped if they are in a view based on a table or a timeline view type.

When items are grouped by a field that can contain more than one entry, such as the **Categories** field, items may appear more than once in the table or timeline. As an example, if you group by the field **Categories** and an item has two categories, such as Business and International, the item is listed under both the Business group heading and the International group heading. Though you view the item more than once, it exists as only one item. Any changes made to one instance of the item are stored with all instances of the item. The following are general procedures used to manage groups.

To group items, click on the **View|Current View** menu selection, then click on a view that displays items in a table or timeline.

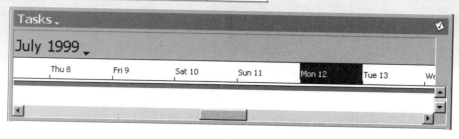

	Dentist	Plano,...	Wed 7/14/...	Wed 7/14/...
	Lunch With St...	Memorial	Thu 8/19/9...	Thu 8/19/9...
	PTA Voluntee...	Schell ...	Tue 8/31/9...	Tue 8/31/9...
	PTA Voluntee...	Schell ...	Thu 9/2/99...	Thu 9/2/99...
	SW 105 Dalla...	Dallas ...	Tue 6/6/00...	Tue 6/6/00...
	Dinner with D...	Joe's ...	Tue 6/6/00...	Tue 6/6/00...
	Presentation	Houst...	Wed 6/7/0...	Wed 6/7/0...
	SW 450 Hous...	Houst...	Wed 6/7/0...	Wed 6/7/0...

Table Example

Tasks Timeline Example

Tasks

July 1999

| Thu 8 | Fri 9 | Sat 10 | Sun 11 | Mon 12 | Tue 13 | We |

Click on the **View|Current View|Customize Current View** menu selection

Click on **Group By**. In the Group items by box, click on a field that you want to group by.

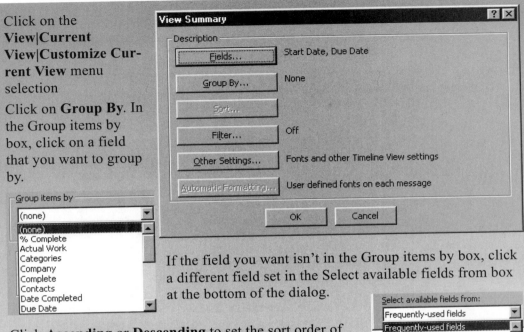

If the field you want isn't in the Group items by box, click a different field set in the Select available fields from box at the bottom of the dialog.

Click **Ascending** or **Descending** to set the sort order of the group headings. If you wish to display the field you're grouping items by, select the Show field in view check box. To group by subgroups, click a field in the Then by box.

To ungroup items click on the **View|Current View|Customize Current View** menu selection. Then click on **Group By**. In the Group items by box, click on **None**.

If you want to reset the Master Category List, select **Edit|Categories**. If **Categories** isn't available, click on any item, then try again. Click on **Master Category List**, then click on **Reset**.

Note: When the Master Category List is reset, only the categories originally supplied with Outlook remain. All added categories are deleted.

To add a group to the Outlook Bar, right-click the background on the Outlook Bar, then click **Add New Group** on the shortcut menu. Type a descriptive name for the group, and then press **<Enter>**.

Address Book

To create a group in Address Book, click on the **Tools|Address Book** menu selection. Click on the **New** button and select **New Group**. Type in a descriptive name for the new group. The example shows **Friends**.

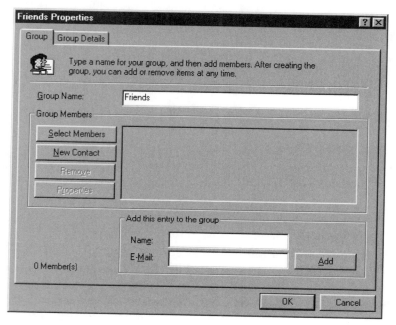

Now click on **Select Members**.

In the left-hand text box, highlight the name of each contact you wish to add to the new group, then click on the **Select** button.

Tip: By holding the left mouse button down and dragging, you can select more than one name at a time. If you accidentally highlight too many names, let go of the mouse button, then left-click in another area.

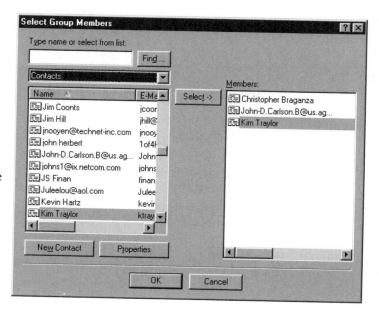

When you are satisfied with the list of members, click on the **OK** button, then click on **OK** button of the Properties dialog.

To add a name to a group in the Address Book, select **Tools|Address Book**. In the Address list, double-click on the group you wish to add a name to. Groups are identified with the Group icon. Click on **Select members**. Click on a name in the list, then click on **Select**.

If you want your personal distribution list to be created in your Personal Address Book, (and not the Contacts folder), click on **Tools|Address Book|New Entry**. Under "Put this entry," click on **Personal Address Book** in the list. In the "Select the entry type" list, click on **Personal Distribution List**.

Tables and Cards

You can add or remove fields of information in a table or card view. Adding or removing one or more fields allows you to customize the view for your particular needs. In a table view, a field is a column that contains information. In a card view, a field is a box with a label that contains information.

	Dentist	Plano,...	Wed 7/14/...	Wed 7/14/...
	Lunch With St...	Memorial	Thu 8/19/9...	Thu 8/19/9...
	PTA Voluntee...	Schell ...	Tue 8/31/9...	Tue 8/31/9...
	PTA Voluntee...	Schell ...	Thu 9/2/99...	Thu 9/2/99...
	SW 105 Dalla...	Dallas ...	Tue 6/6/00...	Tue 6/6/00...
	Dinner with D...	Joe's ...	Tue 6/6/00...	Tue 6/6/00...
	Presentation	Houst...	Wed 6/7/0...	Wed 6/7/0...
	SW 450 Hous...	Houst...	Wed 6/7/0...	Wed 6/7/0...

Table View Example

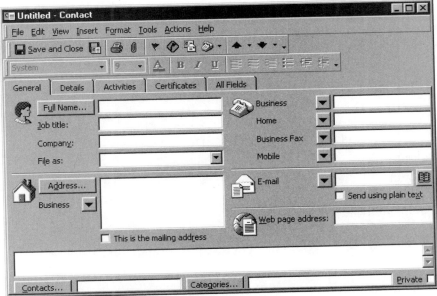

Card View Example

To add a column to a table view, use **View|Current View|Customize Current View**. Click on **Fields** in the View Summary dialog. In the Available fields box, click on the field you want to add. If that field is not in the Available fields box, click on a different field set in the Select available fields from box, and then click a field. Click on **Add**. Click on **OK**, then click on **OK** again to close all the dialogs.

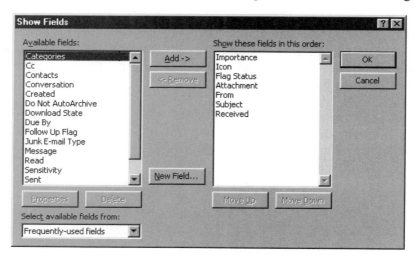

To remove a column from a table, drag the column heading away from the column heading row until an X appears through the column heading, then release the mouse button.

To add a field to a card, click on Contacts in the Outlook shortcuts pane. Click on the **View|Current View|Customize Current View** menu selection. Click on **Fields** in the Summary View dialog. In the Available fields box, click on the field you want to add. If the field you want is not in the Available fields box, click on a different field set in the Select available fields from box. Click on Add. You can change the display order of fields. In the Show these fields in this order box, in the **Show Fields** dialog box, click on a field, and then click **Move Up** or **Move Down**. Click on **OK** twice to close all open dialogs.

To remove a field from a card, click on Contacts in the Outlook shortcuts pane. Click on the **View|Current View|Customize Current View** menu selection. Click on **Fields** in the Summary View dialog. In the Show these fields in this order box, click on the field you want to remove.

Click on **Remove**, then click on **OK** twice to close all open dialogs.

Summary

Outlook is an extensive application. In fact, it would take several hundred more pages to fully cover the capabilities and corresponding operating procedures associated with each application. This part of the book introduced you to the various parts of Outlook. Its goal was to give you a peek at each Outlook application, and, hopefully, to whet your appetite to learn more. Therefore, the author recommends that you review each of the Outlook applications and re-examine the menus and toolbar buttons to help you exploit the full range of features. You should pay particular attention to the Mail section, as there are a host of different settings ranging from network connections to the dialup adapter. To get the most out of Mail, you should be sure that it is configured properly. Mail gives you access to the calendar and tasks of others via your network and/or dialup adapter connections. You must also ensure that those with whom you wish to exchange information are also properly configured and connected.

Part 7

Microsoft Publisher 2000

84 **About This Part**—Introduction to Publisher and its features.

85 **Starting (or "Launching") Publisher**—Key Publisher controls.

86 **Publisher 2000 Fundamentals**—Creating new files, opening existing files, saving files, and importing and exporting files.

About This Part

Introduction

Part 7 of this book guides you through Microsoft Publisher 2000. From this point forward, the name "Publisher" is used.

What is Publisher?

Microsoft Publisher is a full featured desktop publishing application suitable for personal and company use. Publisher comes with many wizards, reducing such publishing tasks as creating newsletters, websites, brochures, catalogs, flyers, greeting cards, invitation cards, business cards, letterheads, business forms, banners, calendars, advertisements, award certificates, labels, menus and programs to a few clicks of a mouse button. If you wish, Publisher makes it very easy to either modify any of the standard document templates or for the really adventuresome, you may start from scratch.

Companion Files

The Microsoft Publisher companion files are located on your *Learn Office 2000* companion CD-ROM in the Files folder.

What's Next?

In the next section you learn how to start Publisher.

Starting (or "Launching") Publisher

If you installed the Office toolbar, the easiest way to launch Publisher is to click on the Publisher button. Otherwise, go to the Programs group (or the group in which you installed Publisher); start Publisher by clicking the Microsoft Publisher line. When Publisher starts the Publisher Catalog dialog loads.

The first time you start Publisher you are invited to review "What's New," and the Office Assistant offers help. If you are familiar with previous versions of Publisher you may want to close the Office Assistant for now. Go to the Menu bar and click on Help, then click on Hide the Office Assistant. Now a Catalog dialog appears. Close the Catalog dialog and compare your display to the following illustration, which labels the various parts of the Publisher screen.

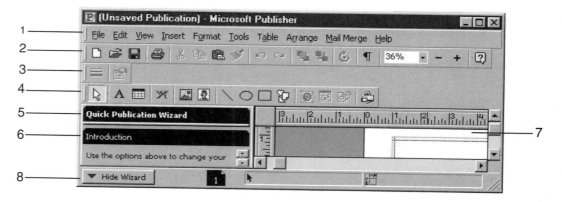

The above screen illustrates the initial start-up view. If you wish, you can use the View menu to change the view. Each Publisher screen control is summarized in the appendices on the accompanying CD. Detailed descriptions are found in the following sections of this book where you are guided through hands-on learning activities.

Microsoft Publisher 2000 Controls

The keyed screen illustration shows each of the various controls which are summarized in the list that follows.

Key	Item	Description
1	Menu Bar	Used to access the Publisher menus and the Office Assistant (Help)
2	Standard Toolbar	Includes buttons to perform the most frequently used file, editing, web and hyperlink, borders, inserting tables, charts and slides, zoom, and Office Assistant (Help) operations.
3	Formatting Toolbar	Includes buttons to perform the most frequent file formatting operations such as specifying fonts and font size; specifying text characteristics such as bold, italic, underling; do/undo, bring to front/back and zoom operations.
4	Objects Toolbar	Includes buttons to set line/border styles and frame properties.
5	Wizard Pane	Displays the Publication wizard.
6	Help Pane	Displays help information related to the selected wizard.
7	Working Pane	Displays the current working window pane.
8	Status Line	Displays messages.

Publisher Fundamentals

Introduction

Publisher 2000 offers a wide array of tools including numerous document templates to create just about any type of business or personal document imaginable. Business cards, invitations, newsletters, menus, programs, business forms, labels, brochures, catalogs, signs, greeting cards, fliers, forms, letterhead, award and gift certificates, postcards, banners, programs, advertisements, envelopes, invitations, and calendars are some of the template categories available for immediate use. If you do not find a suitable template to meet your document needs, you can design your own using Publisher's design wizard.

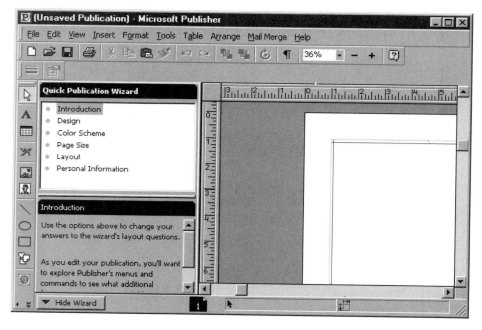

How does Publisher differ from word processing programs? First, Publisher includes a great selection of templates. Second, you have much greater control over placement of document features, including embedded and linked objects, giving you the ability to create virtually any type of document possible. Publisher includes commercial printing tools that allow you to get the polished look of a professionally prepared document if you have a capable printer. Or you can pack the documents and carry them to a professional printer to get that polished, professional look.

Measurements

To demonstrate the versatility of Publisher over typical word processing programs, we will examine the Measurements toolbar a little closer. A significant difference between Publisher and a word processing program is the ability to place objects anywhere you want on a document and in any perspective. Word processing programs cannot accomplish such acrobatics, but they are a breeze for Publisher.

You can follow this discussion by opening the Publisher sample file and making the measurements changes along with the following text. If you make a mistake or do not want to keep the resulting document, just close it without saving it. But, have some fun and experiment along the way. Now, recall the Measurements toolbar:

We will use the following illustration (available in the MyPublisher.pub document in the companion files) to demonstrate how the Measurements toolbar can be used to change the position of a frame within a document. For the sake of brevity, we will not show the complete illustration again, only the applicable portion necessary to portray the changes made. We will begin by selecting the This Is An Example Of frame at the bottom of the illustration and changing the x coordinate in the above Measurements toolbar illustration by clicking the small arrows (up arrow = larger values, down arrow = smaller values) to the right of each specific measurements tool.

You can see that changing the x coordinate to a smaller value moved the text box to the left and lowering the y coordinate moved the box down. So, we can confidently say that the origin of the axis is the lower left-hand corner. Greater x and y numbers move the box to the right and up while smaller numbers move the box to the left and down, respectively.

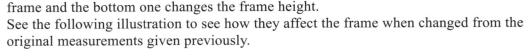

Now we will move the x and y coordinates back to their original positions and change another set of measurements.

These two measurement tools are frame height and frame width. The top one changes the width of the frame and the bottom one changes the frame height. See the following illustration to see how they affect the frame when changed from the original measurements given previously.

This tool controls the angle of the frame with respect to the sides of the document. Using the angle tool, you can rotate text and other objects any amount desired.

The proportional spacing and scaling tools add space between the letters of highlighted text and scale the size of the characters selected. If no text is highlighted, the spacing tool adds the space between the letters of the word at the cursor position. The following illustration shows the effect when a line of text is highlighted. Note that the scaling tool does not have the same effect as the proportional spacing tool. The proportional spacing tool changes the amount of space between selected characters with the amount of change dependent upon the particular characters involved while the scaling tool changes the width of the selected characters.

The expand/condense  tool expands or condenses the selected characters by increasing or decreasing the number of points inserted between the selected characters, respectively. While expand/condense is similar to the previously described proportional spacing tool, they are not exactly the same. The expand/condense tool does not maintain any space proportionality between characters, but the space change between characters is an exact amount. The line spacing tool changes the number of line spaces between selected text. See the following illustration with the expand/condense and line spacing changes.

This concludes the demonstration of Publisher's versatility over word processing programs. Publisher's menus and toolbars are essentially the same as other Office 2000 applications. The significant difference between Publisher tools and Word are the included document templates in Publisher and the Measurements toolbar, giving you a great deal of freedom when placing objects and groups on a document. Since templates are a significant element of Publisher, the following activity will focus on using a template to create a document.

Hands-on Activity

This activity uses a document template from the Publisher catalog to create a single-page document that might be a color advertisement for *Learn Office 2000*. Using the described procedure, you should be able to quickly and easily move on to more complex documents, including multipage documents. Also, at the end of the activity, you are shown how to pack the document for transport to a commercial printer.

1. Select **Accent Box Quick Publication** in the Quick Publications pane, and click the **Start Wizard** button.

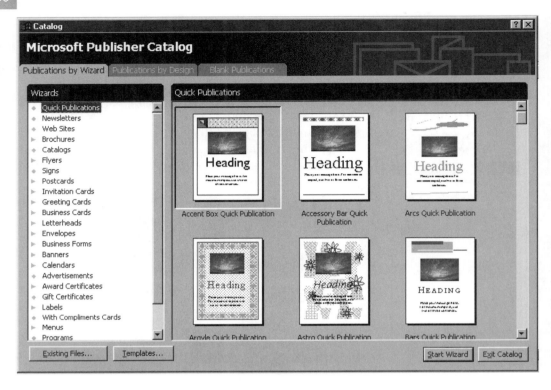

2. If this is the first time you have used Publisher, you will see the following dialog. Click on **OK**.

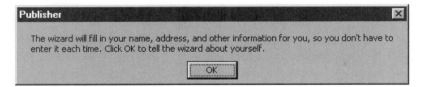

3. In the Choose a Personal Information Set to Edit box, click on the first selection (Primary Business). Now enter appropriate information in all the boxes by clicking in the box, deleting the default text, and keying in your information.

You can set color schemes by clicking the Include Color Scheme in This Set box, then making a selection in the box below.

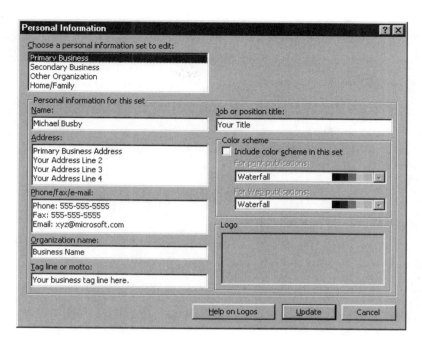

The following illustration shows what the result should look like. You should have something similar. Now click on each of the other Choose a Personal Information Set to Edit selections and make the appropriate changes.

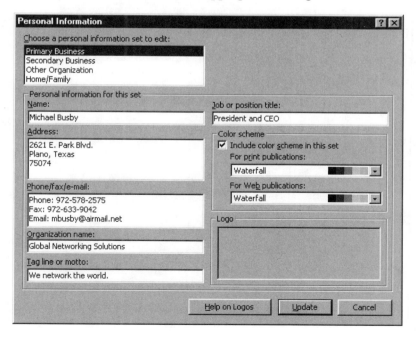

4. Click on **Update** on the Personal Information dialog.

5. Click on **Next**> on the Quick Publication Wizard dialog that appears.

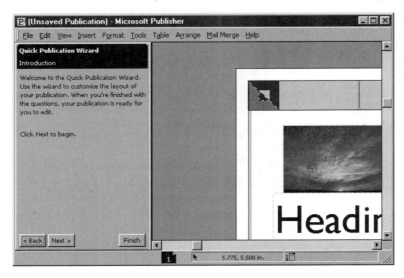

6. Select the Waterfall color scheme to use for your publication, then click on **Next**>.

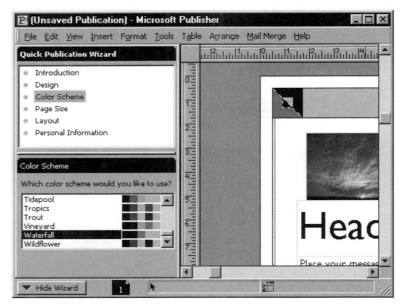

7. Select the Portrait page size, then click on **Next**>.

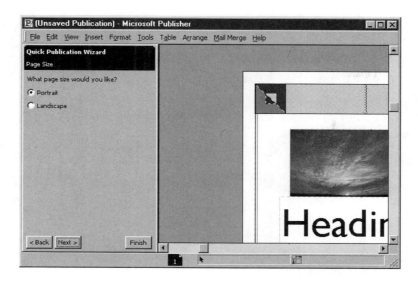

8. Select **Large picture at the top** layout, then click on **Next>**.

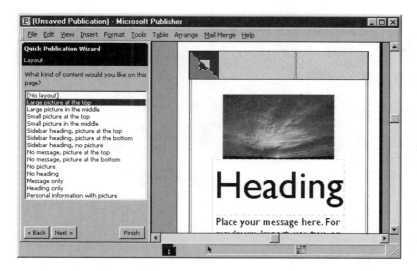

9. Select **Primary Business**, then click on **Finish**.

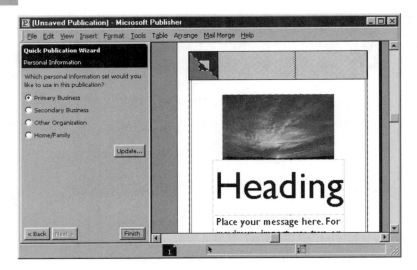

10. You should now see a window similar to the following illustration.

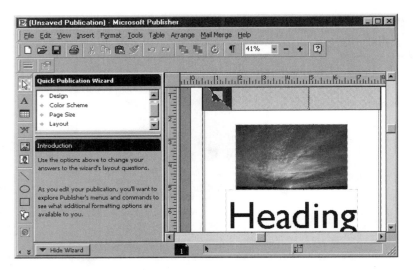

11. Click on the heading in the right pane, highlight the text, then press the **<Delete>** key. Now type in the text shown in the next figure. Repeat the procedure for the text in the box beneath the heading.

Note: Using the same cut and insert procedure used in Word 2000 and other
Office applications, you can delete the picture above the heading and
insert a picture of your own from a scanner, camera, or file.

12. Click **File|Save As** and enter a descriptive name in the **File Save** box for your new
    Publisher document. Click on **Save**.

13. Now click on **File|Pack and Go|Take To a Commercial Printing Service**. Click
    Next> in the Pack and Go Wizard dialog.

14. To send your document to a printer, place a disk in drive A, then click on **Next>**.
    Alternately, you can specify a path in the box to the left of the Browse button and save
    to your desktop.

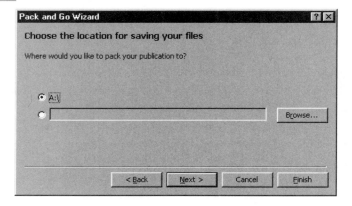

15. You will be asked if you want to include linked graphics and fonts in the publication. For a commercial printer to duplicate your document, graphics and fonts must be included, so ensure each box is checked. Click on **Next>**.

16. Click on **Finish**.

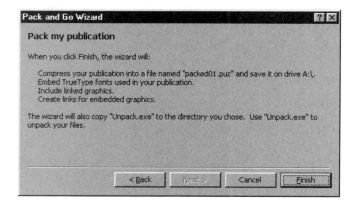

17. If your publication is larger than the space on your disk, you will be prompted to insert another. If this occurs, insert another disk, then click on **OK**.

18. If you want a printed copy of your document, check the **Print a composite** check box. Click on **OK**.

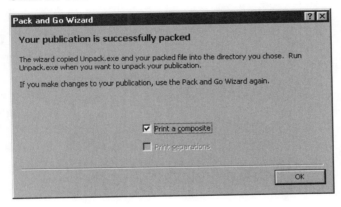

19. Your publication is now ready to take to a commercial printer for publication. Congratulations on a job well done!

Summary

You have created a simple publication using Publisher 2000. Using the available wizards and the skills you now possess, you can add layers of complexity by a little trial and error experimentation. Spend some time looking at the large selection of document templates offered by the catalog. Use the catalog to select from the great number of templates to create whatever particular document type you are interested in. You will soon be creating professional-looking documents for business and personal use with little more effort than the click of a mouse button. Happy publishing.

Our path now takes us to FrontPage, Microsoft's premier web publishing program.

Part 8

Microsoft FrontPage 2000

87 About This Part—Introduction to FrontPage

88 Starting (or "Launching") FrontPage—Key FrontPage controls.

89 FrontPage 2000 Fundamentals—Using FrontPage to create a personal home page with a hyperlink.

About This Part

Introduction

Part 8 of this book guides you through Microsoft FrontPage 2000. From this point forward, the name "FrontPage" is used.

When you complete the sections of this part, you should be able to create, save, and load web pages needed in your work or personal use.

What is FrontPage?

FrontPage is Microsoft's web authoring tool. Using FrontPage, you can create a wide variety of web pages using the by now familiar wizard process. Or, you may elect to create web pages from scratch, using the rich selection of authoring tools. In either case, using a wizard or starting from scratch, you will find everything you need to generate that special personal or company web page.

What's Next?

In the next section you learn how to start FrontPage and familiarize yourself with its key controls.

Starting (or "Launching") FrontPage

If you installed the Office toolbar, the easiest way to launch FrontPage is to click on the Frontage button. Otherwise, go to the Programs group (or the group in which you installed FrontPage) and start FrontPage by clicking the Microsoft FrontPage line. When FrontPage starts, the program begins with a blank page ready for you to begin work.

The first time you start FrontPage you are invited to review "What's New," and the Office Assistant offers help. If you are familiar with previous versions of FrontPage you may want to close the Office Assistant for now. Go to the Menu bar and click on Help, then click on Hide the Office Assistant. Now a FrontPage dialog will appear. Close the FrontPage dialog and compare your display to the following illustration, which labels the various parts of the FrontPage screen.

The above screen illustrates the Page view. If you wish, you can use the View menu to change the view. Each FrontPage screen control is summarized in the appendices on the accompanying CD. Detailed descriptions are found in the following sections of this book where you are guided through hands-on learning activities.

Microsoft FrontPage 2000 Controls

The keyed screen illustration shows each of the various controls which are summarized in the list that follows.

Key	Item	Description
1	Menu Bar	Used to access the FrontPage menus and the Office Assistant (Help).
2	Standard Toolbar	Includes buttons to perform the most frequently used file, editing, web and hyperlink, borders, inserting tables, charts and slides, zoom, and Office Assistant (Help) operations.
3	Formatting Toolbar	Includes buttons to perform the most frequent file formatting operations such as specifying fonts and font size; specifying text characteristics such as bold, italic, underling; text positioning (left margin, center, right margin); bullets and numbering, and formatting indentation operations.
4	Viewing Pane	Window pane displays the current html page you are working on.
5	Viewing Mode	Displays the various viewing modes available.
6	Status line	Displays messages.

FrontPage Fundamentals

Introduction

FrontPage is Microsoft's application program for creating web pages. Using FrontPage, you can create personal or business web pages with no previous experience. FrontPage utilizes the Microsoft wizard approach to help you create many styles and types of web pages with not much more effort than the click of a mouse button. However, to take full advantage of the opportunities offered by the Internet and to polish your pages for that finished professional look, some skill using HTML tags is necessary. This section does not endeavor to present HTML tags, or their format or usage.

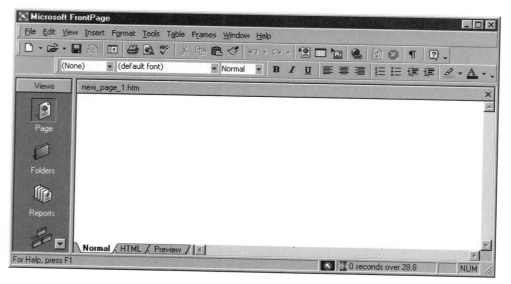

You must have an Internet service provider or other web page-hosting server carry your web page before it can be viewed by other people. Just creating a web page does not automatically get you on the web. You must engage and get instructions from a service provider regarding the procedure for transferring the files, or "web pages," from your computer to the service provider's computer before you can boast of a "web page."

The Web and Web Pages

Historically, "web" means the interconnection of the diverse computing resources around the world that form the Internet. Microsoft attempts to redefine web in the FrontPage application as a set of documents, always known elsewhere as "web pages," that reside on your computer or some other computer. Microsoft's use of the term "web" in FrontPage documentation can therefore be confusing if you are accustomed to the historical and normal usage of "web." To avoid confusion, everywhere you see the term "web" in FrontPage and associated Microsoft documentation, mentally add the word "page" following "web" and there will be no confusion. For clarity, I use the terms "web" and "web page" in the historical sense. The use of the two terms in this section distinguishes between the interconnected computing devices (the web) and what is usually present on them (web pages).

FrontPage Server Extensions

FrontPage has many features that are only available if the server hosting the web page is using Microsoft's FrontPage Server Extensions. Due to security reasons, many service providers do not allow FrontPage server extensions. You must check with your service provider and determine if extensions are enabled. If a web-based server is using the FrontPage Server Extensions, you can increase the functionality of the page by adding FrontPage elements such as hit counters, search forms, and confirmation fields. To ensure compatibility with all servers whether using FrontPage Server Extensions or not, you can enable or disable the commands relying on the presence of the server extensions on the server. If you disable the server extensions for any particular page, the related commands will be unavailable on the FrontPage menus.

To enable or disable FrontPage Server Extensions, click on the Tools|Page Options menu selection, then click on the Compatibility tab of the Options dialog. If you want to enable FrontPage Server Extensions, select the Enabled with Microsoft FrontPage Server Extensions check box.

Note: If your service provider uses the FrontPage Server Extensions and you check the Enabled with Microsoft FrontPage Server Extensions check box, the following commands will be available:

- Hit Counter (Insert|Component menu selection)
- Search Form (Insert|Component menu selection)
- Confirmation Field (Insert|Component menu selection)

However, if you have checked the box and your service provider does not support the extensions, the three extensions will not work even if you have included them on your web page. In this case, clear the check box, and ask your service provider what HTML tags you can include in your web page to provide the same functionality.

Hands-on Activity

The following activity demonstrates the basic features of FrontPage by creating a personal home page with a hyperlink to another personal page.

1. Begin by starting FrontPage. Click on **Start|Programs|Microsoft FrontPage** on the Windows taskbar.

2. Click on **File|New|Page**. In the New dialog, highlight the One-column Body with Contents and Sidebar selection. In the Preview area of the dialog (bottom right side), observe the location of the contents section (left side), the side bar (right side), and the body (in the center).

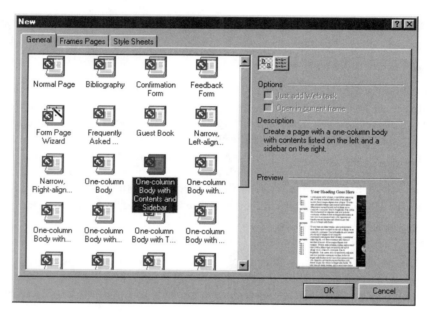

3. Click on **OK**. Your FrontPage display should resemble the following illustration.

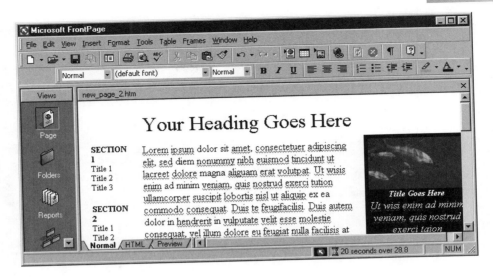

4. Now click in any area where you wish to change the text, delete the text, and type in the text you want. Be careful though. When editing text in an HTML document, you will not necessarily get the results you have come to expect when editing other documents. For example, if the cursor is placed after the line "Title 1" and carriage return is pressed, a carriage return is inserted, but now the line spacing is different. Unless you understand HTML tags and can edit your document in native HTML language, you may be faced with a frustrating experience, as HTML formatting just doesn't work the same as the usual DOC formatting. You can only use trial and error at this stage to get a result that may be close to what you are looking for. Usually, people just get tired of trying and accept things the way they are. Just go slowly, save often, and go back to an earlier version if you accidentally mess it up.

The following illustration shows what you can accomplish with a little patience and careful text editing. I inserted my new text on the same line before deleting the old text. If you adopt this method, you will notice that the text will word-wrap to the next line if at least one space is inserted in the new text. If there are no spaces in the text, word-wrapping does not happen and the body is pushed to the right. If you decide to place a carriage return to force a wrap, then the line spacing gets out of whack. Welcome to the world of HTML tags.

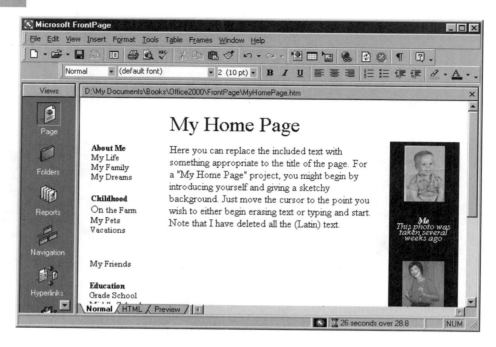

Look at the HTML code for the lines starting with "Childhood" and ending at "Educa-tion." To see the HTML code, click on the **HTML** tab at the bottom of the screen. (To return to the normal view, click on the **Normal** tab at the bottom of the screen.) Scroll down the code until you see the following lines:

```
On </font><font size="2">the Farm<br>
My Pets<br>
Vacations<br>
My Friends</font></p>
<p><strong><font size="2">Education</font></strong><font size="3"><br>
```

Now I will place a carriage return after "Vacations." Observe the change in HTML code after "Vacations."

```
On </font><font size="2">the Farm<br>
My Pets<br>
Vacations</font></p>
<p><font size="2"><br>
My Friends</font></p>
```

Note: An HTML tag refers to the text enclosed by lesser than (<) and greater than (>) signs. This text string is actually an instruction telling a browser program what to do.

The "</font></p> <p><font size="2">" is a result of entering the carriage return. The "<p>" tells HTML to insert a new paragraph, which results in a certain line spacing different from a new line when created from word-wrapping. So, be aware that strange things may happen. Unless you have the desire to learn the complexities of HTML, just chalk them up to the weird stuff computers do. However, if you do have a little patience and desire to learn at least some HTML, then look at your pages in the HTML view from time to time. With a little trial and error you can make changes to your page and observe the resultant HTML code changes by switching between Normal and HTML views, thereby learning which HTML tags perform a particular function.

Note: You can resize your pictures after inserting them by clicking on the picture, then dragging a corner handle toward the center of the picture to reduce the size or dragging it away from the corner to enlarge it. Be aware that the larger the picture the more time it takes to download. A recommended picture size is about 50K bytes maximum. Color pictures require more bytes than a gray scale or a black and white picture of the same size.

After some trial and error and maybe a little hair pulling you should have a home page resembling the previous illustration. Perhaps you used different headings or maybe you deleted some that were not useful for you. But in any case you now have a home page.

5. Save your home page by clicking on **File|Save As**. Enter a descriptive name such as **MyHomePage**, then click on **Save**. We will now extend the functionality of your home page.

6. We wish for the Contents section of the home page to be hyperlinks to documents that provide additional detail regarding the appropriate headings. The "My Life" heading should link to a document that contains material relative to my life.

   Highlight **My Life**, then right-click. Click on **Hyperlink**.

7. We are going to create a new HTML document that includes the "My Life" material and name it MyLife. In the URL box, delete http:// and enter the path to where the "MyLife" document will reside.

Cut	
Copy	
Paste	
Paste Special	
Theme...	
Shared Borders...	
Insert Row	
Insert Column	
Split Cells...	
Page Properties...	
Table Properties...	
Cell Properties...	
Paragraph...	
Font...	Alt+Enter
Hyperlink...	Ctrl+K

Note: My path is file:///D:/My Documents/Books/Office2000/ FrontPage/MyLife.htm. You do not need to add the file:///, as FrontPage adds it automatically. If you do not know your path, click on **File|Save As** in FrontPage, then click on the down arrow of the Save in box and write down the path to the folder that the document will be saved in. Be sure to include the filename at the end of the path. Then click on **Cancel**. However, when you load the files onto a web page server, the path name of the hyperlink must be where the document will be found on the server, not on your computer. You will need to change the path of all the hyperlinks when you are ready to load the pages onto the server. If your web page server is on the Internet, the path will begin with http://. If the server is a LAN, the path will be different. In any case, the service provider will give you the correct pathname. Then you have to reverify all the hyperlinks by using your browser and surfing your pages via the service provider connection. Remember if you need to change anything on a web page after you have loaded it onto a server, you must save the changes, then load the changed documents onto the server again, then refresh your browser's view to be able to see the changes over the Internet.

Click on **OK**. On the "My Home Page" page, deselect "My Life" and observe that the text is now blue, signifying that the text is a hyperlink to another document, which still needs to be created.

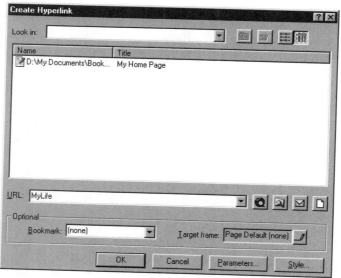

8. Click on **File|New|Page**. In the New dialog click on the **General** tab, then highlight the Wide Body with Headings template. Click on **OK**.

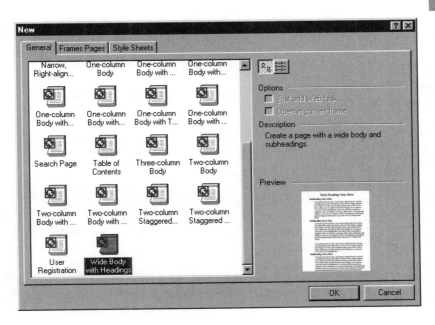

9. Change the headings and text as desired. Again, place the cursor at the point you want to make changes, add the new text, then use the Delete key to delete the unwanted text. Do not use carriage returns. Let the text automatically word-wrap to maintain the line spacing. At any point you place the cursor you can insert pictures. Inserting a picture is the same in FrontPage as it is in Word (click on **Insert|Picture|From File**, then select the picture desired). Your "My Life" page should look something like the following illustration.

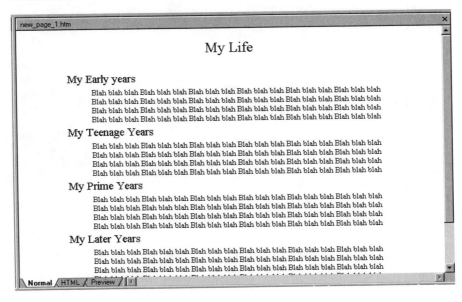

10. Save the document by clicking on **File|Save As** and typing in **MyLife** in the filename box. Click on **Save**.

11. Now we want to go back to "My Home Page" document and check the validity of the "My Life" hyperlink. Click on **Window** in the menu bar and select the "My Home Page" document.

12. Click on **File|Preview in Browser**. You may see the following dialog if you have more than one browser loaded on your machine. Highlight the browser of choice and click on **Preview**.

Note: Using Netscape Navigator will give you a somewhat different view of the page due to formatting nuances between Explorer and Netscape. It is best to switch between the two browsers to achieve a result that is acceptable in both browsers, as both are commonly used.

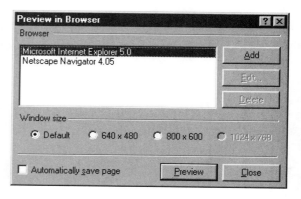

13. Your browser should display your home page. Now click on the blue "My Life" hyperlink.

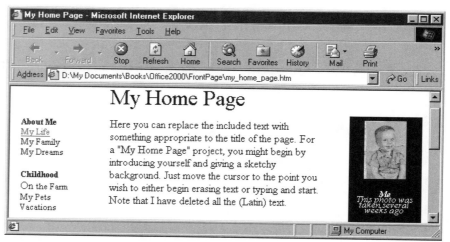

14. If you have entered the correct path to the "MyLife" document in the "My Home Page" document "My Life" hyperlink, you should see your "MyLife" page. Note the path to the document in the Address box of the browser.

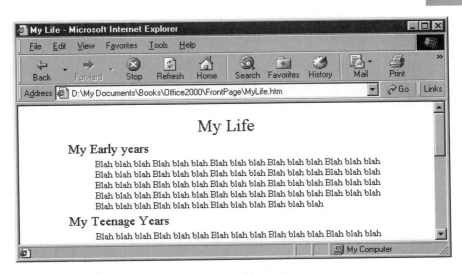

15. Now we will add a way of returning to the home page from "MyLife.htm." On the "MyLife.htm" document (click on **Window** and select the "MyLife.htm" document if it is not the current view in FrontPage) scroll to the bottom of the page and place the cursor at the end of the last line of text. Press **<Enter>** twice. Type the word **Home**. Highlight "Home," then press the right mouse button. Click on **Hyperlink Properties**. Add the path to the "MyHomePage.htm" document in the box.

My path is file:///D:/My Documents/Books/Office2000/FrontPage/MyHomePage.htm. Click on **OK**.

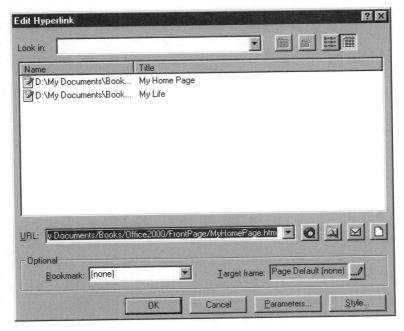

16. Save the change just made to "MyLife.htm" by clicking **File|Save**.

Now in the browser, click on **Refresh** (Explorer) or **Reload** (Netscape). Go to the "Home" hyperlink you just added to "MyLife.htm" document and click on it. Your home page will load into the browser if the pathname to the home page was entered correctly in the "Home" hyperlink URL.

Summary

You have learned how to create a web page and how to add links to navigate from one page to another. Following this general procedure, you can create any number of pages and link them together. Another technique is to add a "Back" link to navigate to the previously viewed page. Simply type the word "Back" somewhere on a document and add the correct path to the document as we did with the "Home" example using the Hyperlink Properties. Of course, you are not limited to just "Home" and "Back" hyperlinks. Experiment with the various templates and tools. If you are adventuresome, you will soon be creating stylish and attractive page designs.

Index

A

Access 2000, 279
    starting, 281
    controls, 281
adjusting displayed elements, 29
animation, 425
    custom, 426
    effects, 427
    order, 427
    preset, 425
    preview, 430
    timing, 427
autocorrect, 120-121
autoformat, 122
automating, 137
autorecovery timer, 35
autotext, 122

B

bookmarks, 90-91
borders, 74

C

Calendar
    appointments,
      changing, 523
      copying, 525
      deleting, 518
      editing, 518
      entering, 517
      finding, 523, 525
      moving, 518
      printing, 518
      scheduling recurring, 519
    cancel meeting, 522
    change meeting, 523
    create meeting request, 524
    decline meeting request, 423, 526

    events
      create, 526
      single/annual, 526
    find meeting, 523
    free/busy information, 526
    respond to meeting request, 525
    schedule meeting, 520
    schedule recurring meeting, 522
    view calendar, 526
chart(s), 110
    effects, 428
    producing, 221
color
    control, 406
    transition, 409
    working with, 409
column(s), 103
    data, 260
    freezing, 303
    hiding, 303
    text, 260
    width, 303
comments, 94-95
companion CD, 4
companion files, 22
Contacts, 550
    dialing, 554
    dialog tabs, 552
    finding, 554
    menu(s), 551
    printing, 554
conventions, 5
customizing shortcut toolbar, 10

D

data
    moving, 341

resizing, 339
    selecting, 339
    validation, 345
database, 242, 283
    creating filters, 349
    finding data, 348
    understanding, 283
dates, 90
dynaset, printing, 318
delimiter, comma separated, 266
dot leaders, 81
drawing techniques, 419

E

edit, 26
editing, 60
ellipsis, 25
encryption, 166
endnotes, 94, 95
Equation 3.0, 129
Excel, 179
    controls, 182
    extracting information, 244
    exiting, 199
    starting, 181
    putting on Web, 268
    using with database programs, 266
    using with dBase, 267
    using with FoxPro, 267
    using with Microsoft Access, 266
exit, 25

F

files, 32, 397
    ASCII, 259
    attachment, 507
    auto conversion, 259
    creating, 32
    default encoding, 35
    exporting, 42, 259
    favorites, 36
    filters, 37
    formats, 37
    inserting, 37, 41
    importing, 37, 41, 259
    opening, 36, 37
    other programs, 258
    query, 259

rich text, 37
    saving, 33, 38, 41
    saving as different type, 36
    versions, 42
filter, 576
filtering,
    ad hoc, 245
    advanced, 247
    e-mail, 577
forms, 115, 285, 323, 337
    design, 49
    putting graph on, 364
fonts, 54, 57
    case, 58
    sizes, 54, 57
footer, 94-95, 155, 225, 415
formatting
    cells, 207
    numbers, 206
    pages, 44
    paragraphs, 44
    sections, 44
    text, 206
    toolbar, 24
frames, 98
FrontPage, 619
    controls, 620
    server extensions, 623
    starting, 620
    web pages, 623
    webs, 623

G

ghosted entry, 25
grammar check, 123
graphs, 110

H

hanging indent, 28, 49
hardware requirements, 4
header, 94-95, 154, 225, 415
headings, 50
    styles, 55
help, 7, 184
horizontal ruler, 28
hyperlinks, 449
hyphenation, 124

I

indents, 48
index, alphabetical, 156
inserting
    movies, 437
    sound, 437

J

Journal, 558
    activities, 560-561
    archive, 562
    autoarchive, 563
    delete, 564
    modify, 562
    move, 562
    open entry, 561

K

keys,
    cancel, 185
    shortcut, 389
    undo, 185

L

labels, 213
    adding, 342
    dates, 215
    editing, 342
    formatting, 340
    moving, 341
    mailing, 368
    selecting, 339
    resizing, 339
list box, 337
lists, 405
    creating, 50
loss prevention, 167

M

macro, 137, 163, 239, 372
    command buttons, 376
    creating, 239
    editing, 138
    running, 240
    storing, 239
macro virus, *see* virus
Mail, 471, 487
    auto reply, 508
    deleted items, 511
    directory services, 492
    editors, 495
    inbox, 479
    junk e-mail, 511
    large messages, 511
    message formats, 496
    message options, 508
    message tracking, 508
    new message, 496
    outbox, 484
    reading, 507
    sent items, 511
    server, 487
    signatures, 497-498, 505
    vcards, 498, 505
margins, 225
master document, 151
memory, 4
menu(s), 25 *see also* CD-ROM
    Data, 242
    Edit, 26
    File, 25
    Format, 27
    Help, 28
    hidden, 25
    Insert, 26
    Options, 29
    shortcut, 61, 309
    Table, 27, 76
    Tabs, 70
    Tools, 27
    View, 26
    Window, 28
menu bar, 24, 25
meeting minder
Microsoft Graph, 360
Microsoft Graph 2000 Chart, 110
mouse, 70
MS-DOS button, adding, 16
multimedia, 428

N

names, 213
    cells, 214
    constants, 214
    formulas, 214
naming procedures, 216

new appointment, 14
new contact, 14
new journal entry, 15
new message, 13
new Office document, 12
new task, 14
Note, 565
    create, 566
    delete, 566
    menu(s), 565
    read, 566
note(s)
    new, 15
    speaker, 455
normal page view, 24

O

objects
    Equation 3.0, 127, 132
    Excel worksheets, 127, 434
    importing, 432
    Microsoft Graph, 436
    Paintbrush, 135
    picture, 332
    Word tables, 435
    WordArt, 127
Office Assistant, 7, 23
open a document, 13
operating system, 5
outdents, 48
Outlook, 471
    address book, 594
    applications, 477
    Calendar, 472, 480, 515, 517
    cards, 595
    categories, 591
    Contacts, 472, 481
    controls, 474
    deleted items, 484
    Drafts, 484
    features, 478
    forms, 586
    groups, 592
    inbox, 479
    Journal, 472, 485
    menu(s), 516
    NetMeeting, 589
    Notes, 472, 484
    outbox, 484
    sent items, 485
    starting, 473
    stationery, 584
    Shortcuts, 484, 485
    tables, 595
    Tasks, 472, 482
    timelines, 590
    tools, 476
    Update, 485
    whiteboard, 589

P

page
    breaks, 90
    new, 154
    numbers, 90
    setup, 225
pages, formatting, 44
paragraphs
    formatting, 44
    indenting, 48
    outdenting, 48
passwords, 166
pictures, 106
pivot table, 2, 48, 270
PowerPoint, 383
    controls, 386
    starting, 385
    viewer, 462
    views, 389
presentation,
    creating, 392
    packaging, 462
    retrieving, 464
    running, 465
print, 141, 225, 227, 454
    area, 226
    envelopes, 143
    mail merge, 144
    multiple documents, 143
    preview, 142, 226
printer, 4
program buttons, 23
properties, 25
protection, 213

Publisher, 601
    controls, 603
    measurements, 605
    starting, 602

Q

query, 286
    changing, 316
    creating, 310
    criteria, 314
    expressions, 315
    operators, 315
    saving, 314
    totaling, 316

R

record,
    adding, 303
    editing, 302
    synchronizing, 377
report(s), 286
    adding graphs, 360
    creating, 353

S

scroll bar, 29
search, 84
    advanced, 86
section, 154
sections, formatting, 45
security, 163, 569
    advanced, 569
    considerations, 166
    HTML, 569-570
    levels, 164
    plain text, 570
    setting up, 571
    simple, 569
settings
    action, 429
    multimedia, 428
sequences, key, 6
shortcut bar, 12
shortcut bar control, 12
Shortcut toolbar, 9
signatures, digital, 65, 574
slide(s), 459
    action settings, 449

inserting, 458
    setting times, 442
    show, 444, 446
software requirements, 4
sound(s), 425
    setting, 443
spell check, 120
Standard toolbar, 24
status bar, 29
styles, 54
    copying, 56
    creating, 55, 56
    deleting, 56
    heading, 55
    modifying, 55
subforms, 334
symbols, 90

T

tab, 28, 73, 69
    dot leaders, 81
    setting, 69
table, 73, 76, 283
    changing contents, 302
    changing design, 302
    changing properties, 304
    column widths, 77
    contents, 155, 302
    convert to text, 76
    creating, 287
    design, 302
    draw tool, 74
    figures, 155
    one-variable, 252
    pivot, 248, 270
    row heights, 77
    two-variable, 255
    types, 252
    using, 252
Tasks, 536
    displaying project information, 545
    menu(s), 538
    printing, 545
    sorting, 541
    views, 538
text, 405
    appearance, 330

boxes, 98
convert text to table, 75
copy, 60
cut, 60
delete, 61
edit, 60
find, 84
insert, 60
overstrike, 60
paste, 60
position, 64
replace, 84
select, 61
special characters, 86
view, 64
thesaurus, 123
toolbar(s), *see* CD-ROM
Drawing, 106
Excel, 185
Equation, 131
Formatting, 209
Mail Merge, 145
Master document, 151
Outlining, 152
tools, 120
drawing, 418
toolset, 7
TrueType fonts, 35

V
vertical ruler, 29
virus, 163

W
web
limitations, 268, 269, 270, 271
preparing pages, 272
publishing, 268, 271
putting Excel data on, 268
saving, 268
window, 228
wizards, 400
Word 2000, 21
controls, 24
enhancements, 31
launching, 23
starting, 23
WordArt, 127
workbooks,
consolidating, 234
creating, 183
linking, 233
opening, 199, 201
saving, 31, 204
worksheets,
creating, 183
Excel, 127, 132
using with word processors, 266

I don't have time for learning curves.

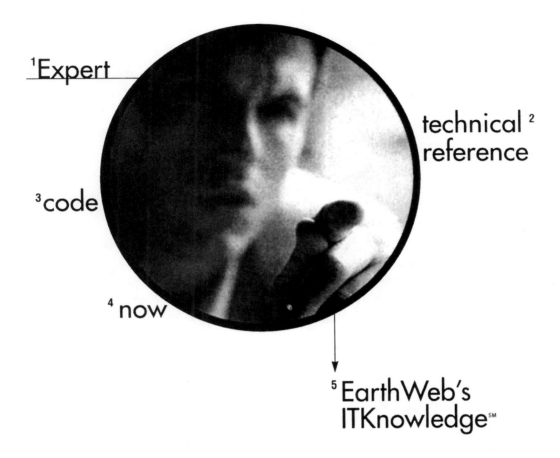

¹Expert

technical ² reference

³code

⁴ now

⁵ EarthWeb's ITKnowledge℠

They rely on you to be the **❶** expert on tough development challenges. There's no time for learning curves, so you go online for **❷** technical references from the experts who wrote the books. Find answers fast simply by clicking on our search engine. Access hundreds of online books, tutorials and even source **❸** code samples **❹** now. Go to **❺** EarthWeb's ITKnowledge, get immediate answers, and get down to it.

Get your FREE ITKnowledge trial subscription today at <u>itkgo.com</u>.
Use code number 026.

EARTHWEB
Go further *faster*

About the CD

The CD-ROM accompanying this book contains the example files used in the hands-on activities; three appendices containing a glossary, Excel shortcut keys, and Access operators and functions; the menus and toolbars for the Office applications; and the text of the book in HTML format.

The structure of the CD is as follows:

Files—Contains files used in the hands-on activities.

Toolbars—Contains illustrations of the menus and toolbars for each Office application, arranged in separate folders for each application.

HTML—Text of the book in HTML format.

Appendices—Glossary, Excel shortcut keys, and Access operators and functions.

It is recommended that you copy the companion files used with the hands-on activities to your hard drive. Additionally, some activities require you to save files in a directory structure you must create. The following instructions create the directory structure required and copy the companion files to hard drive C.

1. Open My Computer by clicking on the icon on the desktop.
2. Click on the drive C icon, then click on **File|New|Folder**.
3. Delete New Folder and rename the folder **MSOffice**.
4. Click on the MSOffice folder, then click on **File|New|Folder** and create a folder named **Files**.
5. Click on the Files folder.
6. Open the CD-ROM and select the Files folder, then select (highlight) and copy all the files to the C:\MSOffice\Files folder.
7. Select all the files you just copied. Right-click with your mouse to display the pop-up menu and click on **Properties**. In the Properties dialog box that appears next, click on the **Read-only** box to deselect it. This turns off the Read-only property attribute.
8. Close all open folders.
9. Remove your companion CD and put it in a safe place when it is not in use.

 Warning: Opening the CD package makes this book **non-returnable**.